SIXTH EDITION

SUBSTANCE ABUSE

INFORMATION FOR SCHOOL COUNSELORS, SOCIAL WORKERS, THERAPISTS, AND COUNSELORS

Gary L. Fisher

University of Nevada, Reno

Thomas C. Harrison

University of Nevada, Reno

330 Hudson Street, NY, NY 10013

Director, Teacher Education & the Helping Professions: Kevin M. Davis
Portfolio Manager: Rebecca Fox-Gieg
Content Producer: Janelle Rogers
Content Project Manager: Pamela D. Bennett
Media Project Manager: Lauren Carlson
Portfolio Management Assistant: Anne McAlpine
Executive Field Marketing Manager: Krista Clark
Executive Product Marketing Manager: Christopher Barry

Procurement Specialist: Deidra Smith
Cover Designer: Melissa Welch
Cover Photo: Shutterstock/Lightspring
Full-Service Project Management: Sudip Sinha, iEnergizer Aptara®, Ltd.
Composition: iEnergizer Aptara®, Ltd.
Printer/Binder: LSC Communications/Crawfordsville
Cover Printer: LSC Communications/Crawfordsville
Text Font: 10/12 Times LT Pro

Library of Congress Cataloging-in-Publication Data
Names: Fisher, Gary L., author. | Harrison, Thomas C., author.
Title: Substance abuse : information for school counselors, social workers, therapists, and counselors / Gary L. Fisher, University of Nevada, Reno, Thomas C. Harrison, University of Nevada, Reno.
Description: Sixth edition. | Boston : Pearson, [2018] | Includes bibliographical references and index.
Identifiers: LCCN 2016035765| ISBN 9780134387642 | ISBN 0134387643
Subjects: LCSH: Social work with drug addicts—United States. | Social work with alcoholics—United States. | Drug addicts—Counseling of—United States. | Alcoholics—Counseling of—United States. | Drug addiction—United States—Prevention. | Alcoholism—United States—Prevention.
Classification: LCC HV5825 .F566 2018 | DDC 362.29—dc23 LC record available at https://lccn.loc.gov/2016035765

2   17

ISBN-10:   0-13-438764-3
ISBN-13: 978-0-13-438764-2

To our beautiful and loving partners,
Daniele and Terianne,
and our children and grandchildren,
Colin, Carola, Brooke, Aaron, Candace,
Cassandra, Celena, Kaya, Miles, Sophia,
and Koa and Iain, Ryan, Becky, and Jordan

ABOUT THE AUTHORS

Gary L. Fisher is Professor in the College of Health Sciences at the University of Nevada, Reno. He was the founder and first director of the Center for the Application of Substance Abuse Technologies, where he developed undergraduate, graduate, and continuing education activities for addiction counselors, prevention specialists, and allied professionals. Dr. Fisher's career has spanned 42 years and includes work as a private practice clinician and a public school psychologist. In addition to this textbook, he is the author of *Rethinking Our War on Drugs: Candid Talk about Controversial Issues* (2006), the senior editor of the *Encyclopedia of Substance Abuse Prevention, Treatment, and Recovery* (2009), and the author of *Understanding Why Addicts Are Not All Alike: Recognizing the Types and How Their Differences Affect Intervention and Treatment* (2011).

Thomas Harrison is the cofounder and first director of the Downing Counseling Clinic at the University of Nevada, Reno. He is also former chair of the Department of Counseling and Educational Psychology, and the former associate dean of the College of Education at the University of Nevada, Reno.

In addition to publishing scholarly articles, Dr. Harrison has also authored six books. His textbooks include *Substance Abuse: Information for School Counselors, Social Workers, and Therapists* (6th edition) and *Consultation for Contemporary Helping Professionals*.

Dr. Harrison received his Ph.D. from the University of Florida in 1983 and developed the University of Florida Athletic Department's Substance Abuse Program and headed that effort for several years. He is a licensed Marriage and Family Therapist and, in addition to his professional duties at the University of Nevada, Reno, he has a private practice in the community.

PREFACE

We teach in a counseling department that offers training in school counseling, marriage and family therapy, and school psychology. Our department requires that all students take a course titled "Models of Prevention, Treatment, and Recovery in Addictions." The goal of the course is to familiarize students with the alcohol and other drug (AOD) field, including basic pharmacology, conceptualizations of AOD, assessment, models of prevention, family issues, and the like.

In teaching this course, we reviewed many textbooks. Many were focused primarily on the pharmacology of alcohol and other drugs. Others were directed toward the person who wanted to work in AOD treatment. Some espoused a narrow orientation to understanding addiction. We never found a book designed for the mental health professional in generalist settings that included all the information we believe to be necessary, and that presented a balanced view of addictions. So we wrote one.

That this book is now in its sixth edition is gratifying, but more importantly: It confirms the need for a generalist text in this area. In Chapter 1, we provide our rationale, explaining why we think mental health professionals (school counselors, social workers, marriage and family therapists, mental health counselors, rehabilitation counselors) need this information. We also offer an overview of the topics covered in this book. Both of us have done most of our clinical work in generalist settings (schools, private practice, community mental health centers, universities), and we have used our experiences to select these topics. Our clients have ranged from those with no alcohol or drug problems to those who have been in numerous treatment programs—and everything in between. We hope that this results in a balanced presentation of some controversial areas.

While writing and revising this book, we have tried to keep in mind the common complaints that students have about textbooks: We have illustrated the application of concepts with many examples from our own clinical experiences; we have tried to personalize the writing and avoid the more stilted language of traditional academia. Let us know if this has worked to make the book more interesting and accessible.

WHAT'S NEW IN THIS EDITION

With each revision, we update the content throughout. This sixth edition includes:

- A new chapter on Co-Occurring Disorders and Other Special Populations (Chapter 9). There was a section on this topic in the treatment chapter in the previous edition; however, the increasing attention to co-occurring disorders warranted an expanded discussion.
- A new section in Chapter 6 on the DSM-V. This replaces the information in the fifth edition on the DSM-IV-TR.
- A new section in Chapter 12 (Chapter 11 in the fifth edition) on recovery and reintegration in the family after treatment.
- The chapter on gambling and other addictions (Chapter 15 in this edition) was revised in light of the DSM-V. This included new information in the DSM-V on behavioral addictions and the diagnosis of eating disorders. In addition, there is new information on treating eating disorders and on Internet addiction.
- The chapter on HIV/AIDS (Chapter 14 in this edition) was revised to reflect new knowledge in this area. This includes new information on testing for HIV, coinfections, treating those with HIV, and disclosure and confidentiality.

- Chapter 4 on culturally and ethnically diverse populations was also revised to reflect new and updated information, including risk factors for diverse populations, immigration and the effects on substance use and abuse, bullying, and cultural competencies.
- As with each edition, we have updated all survey data and included new information on topics that have arisen in the field since the last edition. This includes synthetic cannabinols (Chapter 2), treatment access and effectiveness (Chapter 8), methamphetamine exposure (Chapter 12), women and substance abuse (Chapter 12), phases of codependency (Chapter 13), transmission of HIV (Chapter 14), and assessment and treatment of gambling disorders (Chapter 15).

MYCOUNSELINGLAB®

This title is also available with MyCounselingLab–an online homework, tutorial, and assessment program designed to work with the text to engage students and improve results. Within its structured environment, students see key concepts demonstrated through video clips, practice what they learn, test their understanding, and receive feedback to guide their learning and ensure they master key learning outcomes.

- **Learning Outcomes and Standards measure student results.**
  MyCounselingLab organizes all assignments around essential learning outcomes and national standards for counselors.

- **Video- and Case-Based Exercises develop decision-making skills.**
  Video-and Case-based Exercises introduce students to a broader range of clients, and therefore a broader range of presenting problems, than they will encounter in their own pre-professional clinical experiences. Students watch videos of actual client-therapist sessions or high-quality role-play scenarios featuring expert counselors. They are then guided in their analysis of the videos through a series of short-answer questions. These exercises help students develop the techniques and decision-making skills they need to be effective counselors before they are in a critical situation with a real client.

- **Licensure Quizzes help students prepare for certification.**
  Automatically graded, multiple-choice Licensure Quizzes help students prepare for their certification examinations, master foundational course content, and improve their performance in the course.

- **Video Library offers a wealth of observation opportunities.**
  The Video Library provides more than 400 video clips of actual client-therapist sessions and high-quality role plays in a database organized by topic and searchable by keyword. The Video Library includes every video clip from the MyCounselingLab courses plus additional videos from Pearson's extensive library of footage. Instructors can create additional assignments around the videos or use them for in-class activities. Students can expand their observation experiences to include other course areas and increase the amount of time they spend watching expert counselors in action.

ACKNOWLEDGMENTS

As with any effort such as this, many people have contributed to the final product. We want to thank Gary Pregal, Katie Swanson, Susan Malby-Meade, Frank Tirado, Priscilla Wu, and the late Cheri Dunning for their efforts on the first edition of this text. Julie Hogan, codirector of CSAP's Center for the Application of Prevention Technologies, and Nancy Roget, director of the Center for the Application of Substance Abuse Technologies at the University of Nevada, Reno, provided valuable insights in the development of the second edition. In preparing the third edition, we relied on the work of the Addiction Technology Transfer Centers (funded by the Center for Substance Abuse Treatment) and the Centers for the Application of Prevention Technologies (funded by the Center for Substance Abuse Prevention). These outstanding networks helped us identify relevant issues and concepts. We are also grateful to the late John Chappel, emeritus professor of psychiatry and behavioral sciences at the University of Nevada, Reno, for reviewing Chapter 2 material in earlier editions.

In preparing the fourth edition, we thanked Sabina Mutisya, doctoral student at the University of Nevada, Reno, for her invaluable assistance with research, and the reviewers who provided helpful suggestions for revision: Debra Morrison-Orton, California State University, Bakersfield; Nadine Panter, University of Nebraska, Kearny; and George M. Andrews, Baltimore City College.

In the fifth edition, special thanks were given to Dr. Susan Doctor. She is an expert in fetal alcohol spectrum and shared her incisive knowledge of it in Chapter 12. We also thank Melissa Huelsman, a counseling doctoral student, who did library searches and combined the references.

In this current edition, we want to thank Mona Martinez, a doctoral student, for her assistance with research and references. We also thank the following reviewers for their invaluable suggestions for this revision: Nancy K. Brown, University of South Carolina; Jason Eccker, Washington University; Valerie Gebhardt, University of Illinois, Springfield; and Kevin J. Nutter, University of Arizona and Northern Arizona University.

Gary L. Fisher

Thomas C. Harrison

BRIEF CONTENTS

CONTENTS

Chapter 13   Adult Children and Codependency   219

Chapter 14   HIV/AIDS   238

CHAPTER 1

The Role of the Mental Health Professional in Prevention and Treatment

It has become almost trite to recite the problems related to the use of alcohol and other drugs (AOD)[1] in our society. Various statistics are frequently reported in newspaper articles, surveys, and research studies. The array of graphs, percentages, and dollar amounts in the billions numb the mind. It is not our purpose to contribute to this data avalanche in an effort to convince you that the abuse of AOD causes a variety of serious problems in our country. If you are reading this book, you are probably in a training program to prepare for a career in one of the helping professions and, one hopes, you have some awareness of the severity of this problem. On the other hand, our experience in training mental health professionals has taught us that there is a need for a framework to understand the extent to which AOD issues affect not only the lives of those individuals you will be working with, but also your own lives and the society in which we live. Therefore, allow us to provide this framework with a few facts.

According to annual survey data, in 2013, more than 17 million Americans aged 12 and older needed treatment for an alcohol or illicit drug problem (Substance Abuse and Mental Health Services Administration, 2014). The Substance Abuse and Mental Health Services Administration conducts a yearly survey on the use of all drugs, legal and illegal, in the United States (Substance Abuse and Mental Health Services Administration, 2014). In 2013, 9.4% of all individuals aged 12 and older reported using an illicit drug in the past month. In the 12 to 17 age group, 11.6% had used alcohol in the past month and 6.2% had engaged in binge drinking. In the same age group, 5.6% smoked cigarettes. According to the Centers for Disease Control and Prevention (2014c),

---

[1]As is the case with many areas in the helping professions, terminology can be confusing. In this book, we will use the term *alcohol and other drugs* (AOD) to clearly indicate that alcohol is a drug and to avoid having the reader omit alcohol from any discussion about drugs. If tobacco is relevant to a discussion, we will generally refer to "alcohol, tobacco, and other drugs." The term *illegal drugs* will be used to refer to substances such as marijuana, heroin, cocaine, methamphetamine, and ecstasy, which are illegal under most or all circumstances. *Illicit drugs* are illegal drugs as well as legal drugs used inappropriately, such as prescription pain medications.

The use of terms such as alcoholism, drug addiction, chemical dependency, and substance abuse can also be problematic. In Chapter 2, we will give some definitions of terms used in the field, and, in Chapter 6, we provide the criteria to diagnose AOD conditions. However, because these terms are used in this chapter, you should think of alcoholism as an addiction to the drug alcohol. Drug addiction refers to the addiction to drugs other than alcohol. Chemical dependency includes addiction to AOD. Substance abuse means that there have been individual or societal problems as a result of AOD use. After reading Chapters 2 and 6, you should have a more useful understanding of these terms.

approximately 88,000 annual deaths in the United States are attributable to alcohol, the third leading cause of lifestyle-related deaths in our country. In contrast, almost 40,400 annual deaths are attributable to illicit drugs (Centers for Disease Control and Prevention, 2013b). The Centers for Disease Control and Prevention (2015i) reported 480,000 annual deaths in this country as a result of tobacco use.

The relationship between AOD, crime, and violence has also been clearly established. The National Center on Addiction and Substance Abuse at Columbia University published an extensive study of this relationship. Of the 2.3 million Americans in jails and prisons, 1.5 million met the criteria for a substance use disorder (see Chapter 6) and another 458,000 had a history of AOD problems, were under the influence of AOD at the time crimes were committed, committed crimes to buy AOD, were incarcerated for an AOD violation, or some combination of these factors. AOD were a factor in 78% of violent crimes; 83% of property crimes; and 77% of crimes involving public order, immigration or weapon offenses, and probation/parole violations (National Center on Addiction and Substance Abuse at Columbia University, 2010). In reviewing literature on the relationship between child abuse and substance abuse, Lee, Esaki, and Greene (2009) indicated that between one-half and two-thirds of abuse cases involved caretaker substance abuse, and 80% of cases resulting in foster care were linked to substance abuse. In studying the relationship between substance abuse and domestic violence, Fals-Stewart and Kennedy (2005) found that 50% of partnered men in substance abuse treatment had battered their partner in the past year. Fals-Stewart (2003) reported that these patients were 8 times more likely to batter on a day in which they had been drinking.

The monetary costs of AOD abuse also provide tangible evidence of the significance of these problems. In a study for the Centers for Disease Control and Prevention (2011), the 2006 costs of alcohol abuse were estimated at $223.5 billion. More than 70% of the costs of alcohol abuse were due to lost work productivity, 11% due to health-related issues, 9% attributable to law enforcement and criminal justice involvement, and 6% due to automobile accidents. Other drug abuse costs the United States $193 billion annually (National Institute on Drug Abuse, 2015). Ironically, for every dollar that states spend on substance abuse and addiction, about 96 cents is spent on shoveling up the wreckage caused by AOD use and only about 2 cents is spent on prevention and treatment (the rest is spent on research, regulation, and interdiction; National Center on Addiction and Substance Abuse at Columbia University, 2009).

We risk contributing to the data avalanche to illustrate that the abuse of AOD is like a tree with many branches. The trunk is AOD abuse, but the branches are the multitude of other problems caused by or related to AOD. To avoid totally clogging your mind with statistics and/or completely depressing you before you read the rest of this book, we neglected to describe other branches of the tree such as the decreased work productivity, excessive school truancy and work absenteeism, and detrimental effects on partners, children, and fetuses resulting from AOD abuse. However, these and other branches exist and are the concern of all helping professionals.

THE NEED FOR GENERALIST TRAINING

Some years ago, one of the authors of this text was asked by a local school district to conduct an independent psychological evaluation of a 14-year-old student who was a freshman in high school. The young man's parents were dissatisfied with the school district's evaluation of their son and had asked for another opinion. The youngster was failing most of his classes and was skipping school frequently. The parents were quite sure that their son had a learning disability that would explain his difficulties. The district's school psychologist had tested the student and not found a learning disability. The school counselor had suggested that there may be an emotional problem and recommended family counseling. In addition, a weekly progress check was initiated at school so the parents could be kept informed of assignments and homework that their son needed to complete. They had also hired a tutor. However, none of these interventions seemed to be helping, so the independent evaluation was requested.

In reviewing the test information, no indications of a learning disability were found. An AOD assessment (which will be discussed in Chapter 6) was conducted, and there was evidence that the young man was using AOD on a daily basis. The parents said that they allowed their son and his friends to drink in their home because they believed that this would prevent them from using "drugs" and from drinking and driving. The parents were defensive about their own AOD use and rejected suggestions that the cause of their son's problems could be related to his AOD use. A couple of months later, there was a request for the young man's records from an AOD treatment program. He was referred to the program following an arrest for stealing alcohol from a convenience store.

One of us was supervising a master's student who was in a marriage and family therapy internship. The intern had been seeing a family of four (mom, dad, and two children, aged 3 and 9) who were referred to our university counseling clinic by Children's Protective Services. A child abuse report had been filed at the 9-year-old's elementary school because of bruises on the youngster's face. The father explained that he had slapped his son because of his frustration with the boy's behavior and "back-talking." The parents complained of frequent conflicts related to parenting techniques and family finances. The intern had developed an intervention plan that included referring the parents to a parent education program and working with the family on "communication skills" including "I-messages" and conflict resolution procedures. The intern was frustrated because the parents had failed to follow through on the parent education classes and had not made much progress in improving their communication patterns. It was suggested that the intern assess the AOD use of the parents, and she did so at the next session. The mother and father had a heated argument about the father's drinking. They did not show up for their next appointment and, when the intern called, the mother said that they were discontinuing counseling because the father said it was a waste of time.

We regularly consult with a social worker in private practice. One of the social worker's clients is a woman in her early 30s who sought counseling for "depression." The woman had been married twice and described a series of failed relationships. Her first husband was an alcoholic and the second was a polydrug abuser. For two years, she had been living with a man who was in recovery from cocaine addiction. However, she found out that he had been having numerous affairs during their relationship. The woman, who has a master's degree, could not understand why she continued to become involved with this kind of man. She felt that there must be something wrong with her because the men in her life needed alcohol, other drugs, or other women. Her father was an alcoholic and verbally abusive, and she had also been sexually molested by her paternal grandfather.

In the three situations described, the "helping professionals" (school psychologist, school counselor, marriage and family therapy intern, social worker) were not involved in providing substance abuse treatment, but they needed information and skills in the AOD field to perform their job functions in a competent manner. The authors of this text have worked in schools as a teacher and a school psychologist, in a mental health clinic, in a university athletic department, and in private practice. We currently train school counselors and marriage and family therapists as well as substance abuse counselors. We have found that the frequency of AOD-related problems is so pervasive in the helping field that the lack of training in this area would result in inadequate preparation for mental health professionals. When you read the statistics on the relationship between domestic violence, child abuse, other crime, and AOD, it should be clear that this relationship also applies to criminal justice personnel.

It would be unreasonable to expect all helping professionals to have the same set of skills as substance abuse counselors. We don't expect substance abuse counselors to be able to plan educational interventions or to do family therapy. Similarly, school and mental health counselors, social workers, and marriage and family therapists do not need to be able to monitor detoxification or to develop treatment plans. However, all mental health professionals will encounter individuals who need assessment and treatment for AOD problems and clients who are having problems as a result of relationships with individuals with AOD problems. Included in the related problems that mental health professionals (school counselors, mental health counselors, rehabilitation counselors, psychologists, social workers, and marriage and family therapists) will encounter are children who have been fetally affected by parental AOD use, the psychological impact on children and adults who live or have lived with caretakers who abuse AOD, and the intrapersonal and interpersonal problems of individuals who are in relationships with people who abuse AOD. Many of you have read about fetal alcohol syndrome, adult children of alcoholics, and codependency, which are included in these "related" problems. All of these issues will be discussed in this text.

We hope that you are convinced that mental health professionals need training in the AOD field, not only to identify those clients who need further assessment and treatment, but also for the multitude of related problems that all mental health professionals will encounter on a regular basis. As with many areas in the mental health field, there are differing views on the causes and treatment of alcoholism and drug addiction based on the variety of disciplines concerned with these problems and the philosophical orientation of different individuals.

PHILOSOPHICAL ORIENTATION

Jerome is a 47-year-old African American man who had been arrested for a DUI (driving under the influence). It was his third DUI, and he had previously been in an alcohol treatment program. He had been arrested previously for writing bad checks and spousal abuse. He is unemployed and dropped out of school in the 10th grade. An assessment revealed a long history of AOD use beginning at age 12. Jerome's mother was an alcoholic, and he was raised by his grandmother. He does not know his biological father.

Jerome's problem may be viewed in different ways by different professionals, depending on their training and experiences. A sociologist may focus on the environmental and cultural factors that modeled and encouraged AOD use. Some psychologists might attend to the fact that Jerome experienced rejection by his biological parents that led to feelings of inadequacy. The use of AOD might be seen as a coping mechanism. A physician might be impressed by the family history of alcoholism and hypothesize that Jerome had a genetic predisposition for chemical dependency. A social worker may think that Jerome's unemployment and lack of education resulted in discouragement and consequent AOD use. A criminal justice worker may see his behavior as willful misconduct and believe that punishment is necessary.

These differing views of the causes and treatment of Jerome's problem are not unusual in the mental health field. However, what is unique in the AOD field is that many drug and alcohol counselors, others involved in the treatment of alcoholics and other addicts, and many people who are recovering from AOD problems believe that Jerome has a disease that has affected him mentally, physically, socially, emotionally, and *spiritually*. This spiritual component separates AOD problems from other mental health problems and has had implications for the understanding and treatment of AOD problems. (We will discuss spirituality in AOD recovery in Chapter 10.) One implication is that methods to attend to the spiritual aspect of treatment (e.g., Alcoholics Anonymous) are a common component of treatment. Another implication is that there are many individuals involved in the treatment of AOD problems who do not have formal training as counselors but who are "in recovery" and hold a fervent belief in a particular orientation to treatment. This belief may be based not on scientific evidence, but instead on their own experience and the experience of other recovering individuals. This phenomenon is similar to an individual's religious beliefs that cannot (and should not) be disputed by research since the beliefs are valid for that individual. Clearly, the potential for disagreement and controversy exists when scientific and spiritual viewpoints are applied to the same problem, which has certainly been the case in this field.

In Chapter 3, we will discuss the different models of addiction and will thoroughly discuss the "disease concept" of addiction. Our point here is that we believe that the AOD field requires an openness on the part of the mental health professional to consider a wide variety of possible causes of AOD problems and to employ a multitude of methods by which people recover from these problems. We have worked with people who discontinued their use of AOD without any treatment, individuals who stopped after walking into a church and "finding Jesus," clients and students who swear by Alcoholics Anonymous (AA), and people who have needed a formal treatment program.

If you work in a treatment program, you tend to see people who have experienced many life problems related to AOD use. It is easy to develop a viewpoint about substance abuse based on these clients' experiences. It is important to remember that treatment providers do not see those people who modify or discontinue their AOD use through methods other than formal treatment.

This book is written from the perspective of the mental health professional working in a generalist setting rather than from the perspective of a substance abuse counselor in a treatment setting. Therefore, we will provide the type of information we believe all mental health professionals need in the AOD field to work effectively in schools, community agencies, and private practice, rather than providing all the information needed to work as a substance abuse counselor in a treatment setting. We want to provide a balance in the types of viewpoints that exist in this field so that you can understand these perspectives. We will describe the popular literature in certain areas (e.g., adult children of alcoholics) and contrast this with research in the area so that you can understand that clinical impressions and research do not always match. Finally, we want to communicate our belief that it is not advisable to adopt universal concepts of cause and treatment in this field. In other areas of mental health treatment, we encourage practitioners to assess a client and to develop treatment strategies based on the individual and group characteristics of the client. The same rules should apply in the AOD field.

PROFESSIONAL ORIENTATION

Over the years, this text has been used in undergraduate and graduate courses for students preparing for careers in criminal justice, social work, marriage and family therapy, mental health counseling, rehabilitation counseling, school counseling, school psychology, and substance abuse counseling. As a student, the manner in which you use the information in this book in your career will be dependent on factors such as your personal experiences with the topics, the philosophical orientation of your program, when you take this course in your studies, and your eventual job placement. For example, a social worker who is employed by a hospice may not have as much regular contact with substance abuse issues compared to a social worker involved with investigating child abuse cases. An elementary school counselor will encounter plenty of family issues related to AOD but less abuse by students compared to a high school counselor. The point is that, although you may have a clear vocational goal, it is not possible for you to know in what job setting you will find yourself in 5 or 10 years. Your program of study may have an orientation to understanding human behavior that is not consistent with what you read in some chapters. That is to be expected and is part of the learning process for students preparing for careers in the helping professions. Regardless, we want to encourage you to avoid filtering what you learn through a lens of "I don't need to know that because I won't be dealing with that in my career" or "I don't believe that. It doesn't fit with my view of human behavior." Challenge anything you read here but keep an open mind.

ATTITUDES AND BELIEFS

Close your eyes for a minute and visualize an alcoholic. What did your alcoholic look like? For most people, the alcoholic is a white male, middle-aged, who looks pretty seedy. In other words, the stereotypical skid row bum. Did you visualize somebody who looks like former President Bush? Did you visualize one of your professors? Did you visualize a professional athlete?

Attitudes and beliefs about alcoholics and drug addicts have an effect on the mental health professional's work. Imagine that you are a mental health counselor and a well-dressed, middle-aged woman comes to see you complaining of symptoms of depression. If you hold false beliefs about alcoholics, such as that they must be dirty and drunk all the time, you might fail to diagnose those clients who do not fit your stereotype.

To help students understand their own attitudes about alcoholics and drug addicts, we have our students attend an AA or Narcotics Anonymous meeting as a class assignment. We encourage you to do this as well (if you do go to a meeting, make sure you attend an "open" meeting [see Chapter 11]). In addition to acquiring a cognitive understanding of this type of support for alcoholics and addicts, students report interesting affective reactions that provide information about their attitudes. For example, many students report that they want to tell others at the meeting that they are there for a class assignment and that they are not alcoholics. Our response is that unless you believe that alcoholism or drug addiction is simply a condition that some people develop and has nothing to do with morals or a weak will, you would not care if you were mistakenly identified as alcoholic or drug addicted. If you do care, you must believe that alcoholics and drug addicts have some type of character flaw. This realization helps many potential mental health professionals modify their attitudes and beliefs about alcoholism and drug addiction.

A second type of affective reaction that students report is being surprised with the heterogeneity of the group. At most meetings, they see well-dressed businessmen and women, young people, blue-collar workers, unkempt people, articulate individuals, and people obviously impaired from their years of using AOD. Seeing such a variety of people tends to destroy any stereotypes the students may have.

Although we believe that potential mental health professionals may hold any belief system they want, the belief that alcoholism or drug addiction is due to a moral weakness or a character flaw may have a detrimental effect on providing or finding appropriate help for those with AOD problems. For example, imagine that you are a marriage and family therapist and that you are seeing a couple in which one partner is drinking excessively. You believe that changing heavy drinking to moderate drinking is largely a matter of willpower and desire, and you communicate this to the drinking partner. If this individual is addicted to alcohol, your belief system will be incompatible with this client's reality. Your client may experience shame, because he or she is not strong enough, or anger at your lack of understanding. Resistance and termination are frequent outcomes, and the client fails to get the proper help. Therefore, if you do believe that excessive AOD use is largely due to moral weakness or character flaws, you would be well advised to refer these cases to others.

DENIAL, MINIMIZATION, PROJECTION, AND RATIONALIZATION

Imagine (or maybe you don't have to imagine) that you are in love with someone you believe to be the most wonderful person in the world. You cannot imagine living without this person and firmly believe that you need this person to survive. Your mother sits you down one day and tells you that you must no longer associate with this person. She tells you that this person is destroying your life, that you have changed since becoming involved with this person, and that all of your family and friends believe that you need to break off the relationship before something terrible happens to you.

How would you react? You might tell your mother that she is crazy and that all her complaints about this person are untrue (denial). Perhaps you acknowledge that your person does have some little quirks, but they really don't bother you (minimization). You tell your mother that she and the rest of your family and friends are really jealous because they do not have someone as wonderful as you (projection) and that you may have changed but that these changes are for the better and long overdue (rationalization).

We use this analogy so you can develop an empathic understanding of what many AOD-addicted individuals experience. Obviously, the "love object" in this case is the individual's drug of choice. The addicted individual may be seen as having an intimate and monogamous relationship with alcohol or other drugs and may believe that he or she needs the drug to function and survive. In the same way that people deny that a relationship has become destructive, the addicted individual may deny that alcohol or other drugs have become destructive in spite of objective evidence to the contrary. The defense mechanisms of denial, minimization, projection, and rationalization are used so that the person does not have to face a reality that may be terrifying: a life without alcohol or other drugs.

Although we know that it may be easy for you to intellectually understand, these concepts as applied to alcoholics and other drug-addicted people, we have found it useful for our students to have a more direct experience with their own use of defense mechanisms. At the first session of our substance abuse class, we ask the students to choose a substance or activity and abstain from this substance or activity for the semester, and that the first thing that popped into their heads and was rejected because it would be too hard to give up is the thing they should choose. Students usually choose substances such as alcohol, coffee, chocolate, or sugar, or activities such as gambling (we live in Nevada, where gambling is legal) or watching television. Some choose tobacco and an occasional courageous student will choose an illegal drug. The students record their use of the defense mechanisms through journal entries and write a paper about the experience at the end of the semester.

If you are wondering whether some students "blow off" the assignment and just make up the material in their journals and papers, the answer is "of course." When the assignment is given, this issue is discussed. The students are told that they can do anything they want to; the instructor will never know the difference. However, there is some reason for potential mental health professionals to take a close look at themselves if they are unwilling to abstain from a substance or activity for 15 weeks, particularly when they will be encouraging clients to abstain from alcohol or other drugs for a lifetime.

We encourage you, our reader, to examine your own use of denial, minimization, projection, and rationalization, particularly in regard to your own use of AOD. Mental health professionals are not immune to AOD problems and are just as likely to use these defense mechanisms as anyone else is. As you read the rest of this book, take some time to examine your own substance-using behavior. If there is a problem, this would be the ideal time to get some help. This would certainly be preferable to becoming one of the many impaired professionals who may cause harm to their clients and themselves.

HELPING ATTITUDES AND BEHAVIORS

Although we have encountered many mental health professionals with AOD problems, we have found that a more pervasive problem may be the potential mental health professionals who gravitate to the helping professions because of unresolved issues in their lives. Although there may be a sincere desire to help others, these potential mental health professionals may actually be unhelpful to clients. For example, in our counselor education program, we find that many of our students are adult children of alcoholics. Now, that is no problem in and of itself. In fact, as we will discuss in Chapter 13, many adult children of alcoholics have the same or fewer problems than other adults. However, being raised by one or more alcoholic caretakers may lead to certain characteristic ways of behaving that could have implications for a mental health professional's effectiveness. For example, a graduate student in marriage and family therapy whom we will call Debbie (we are changing all of the names of students and clients we are using in this book to protect anonymity) decided to pursue a career in the helping professions because everyone told her that she was easy to talk to and was a good listener. Debbie said that she was one of those people to whom total strangers immediately told their life stories.

Debbie was raised by her biological parents, both of whom were alcoholics. Within her family, she had developed a method of behaving that would minimize the probability of conflict developing. She did most of the cooking and cleaning at home, took care of her younger siblings, and worked very hard at school. Debbie reported being in a constant state of anxiety because of her worry that she had "missed" something that would send one of her parents into a rage.

In hindsight, it is easy to see that Debbie developed a false belief that she could control her parents' moods and behavior by making sure that everything was perfect at home and by her achievements at school. It is not unusual for children raised by alcoholic caretakers to develop a role designed to divert attention away from the real problem in the family. (Again, this will be discussed in detail in Chapter 13.) However, the development of this childhood role had implications for Debbie's work as a marriage and family therapist. We noticed that she was quite hesitant to confront clients and that she seemed very uncomfortable with conflict. Debbie had more than the usual anxiety for a student when counseling and brooded excessively when her clients did not immediately feel better. Clearly, the characteristic ways Debbie had learned to behave as a child were having a detrimental effect on her development as a marriage and family therapist in spite of the fact that people found her easy to talk to.

Another of our graduate students in counseling, Patricia, was taking our substance abuse counseling course. She failed her midterm examination. Patricia came to see the instructor and explained that the content of the course generated a great deal of emotion for her because her parents were alcoholics and she had been married to a drug addict. Because of these emotions, she said that she had difficulty concentrating on the lectures and the reading material and in following through on class assignments (students were required to attend an AA and an Al-Anon [for family members of alcoholics] meeting). The instructor communicated his understanding that the course could have that impact on people with history and experiences in the substance abuse area and suggested that Patricia drop the course (he offered a passing withdrawal) and pursue counseling for herself. Patricia chose to avoid working on these issues, she stayed in the course, and failed.

Because most of you who are reading this text are graduate students, this may strike you as rather harsh. However, consider the alternative. Let's say that the instructor had offered his understanding and allowed Patricia to remain in the course without dealing with these issues and passed her. Would Patricia be able to work effectively with individuals and families in which there were alcohol or other drug problems, with adult clients who were raised by substance abusing caretakers, or with clients living with alcohol or other drug-abusing partners? In an attempt to avoid these problems, she might do a poor job of assessment, or she might ignore the signs and symptoms of alcohol or other drug problems. Or she might ignore or fail to inquire about substance abuse in the family of origin or in the current family of her clients. In short, we believe that her unwillingness to face these problems would result in her being a less effective counselor.

What about Debbie? Her excessive anxiety and concern with her performance prevented her from objectively looking at her clients and her own counseling behaviors. Debbie's fear of conflict resulted in an unwillingness to confront her clients, which limited her effectiveness. Fortunately, Debbie was receptive to feedback and suggestions. She did some work on her own issues, and she has become a fine marriage and family therapist.

This discussion is not meant to discourage those of you who are adult children of alcoholics, are in recovery from an alcohol or other drug problem, or have lived or are living with an addicted person from pursuing your careers. It is our experience that most people who want to become help-ing professionals have a need or desire to help people that is based on family-of-origin issues that may adversely affect their work. This is certainly the case with both of us. It is not a problem if you enter a training program in one of the helping professions because of your own need to be needed. It is a problem if you avoid examining your own issues and fail to take steps to resolve these issues in order to avoid ineffective (or in some cases, harmful) work with clients.

In this particular field, we find helping professionals who cannot work effectively with clients because of their own AOD use or their experiences with AOD use in their families of origin and/or with partners. In the rest of this book, we will attempt to provide you with information that will enable you to deal effectively with the direct and indirect problems resulting from AOD use that social workers, school counselors, mental health counselors, marriage and family therapists, and other helping profes-sionals will encounter. However, all of this information will be useless if your own use patterns or issues are unresolved and if they impact your work. Because denial is so pervasive, we encourage you to seek objective feedback regarding the necessity to work on your own use of alcohol or other drugs or on other issues and, if necessary, to choose a course of action with professional assistance. But please, for your own benefit and for the benefit of your future clients, don't choose to avoid these issues.

OVERVIEW OF THE BOOK

In our choice of chapter topics and the orientation of each chapter, we have tried to maintain the primary goal of providing useful information in the AOD field to general mental health profession-als. Therefore, Chapter 2 (Classification of Drugs), Chapter 3 (Models of Addiction), Chapter 8 (Treatment of Alcohol and Other Drugs (AOD)), and Chapter 11 (Twelve Step and Other Types of Support Groups) are overviews of these topics. We have attempted to provide enough detail about treatment and Twelve Step groups to reduce any myths about these activities and to allow mental health professionals to make informed referrals. Issues that usually provoke some controversy among generalists (e.g., the disease concept, relative dangers of different drugs) are also discussed.

In several chapters, we have attempted to integrate the role of the mental health professional in working with clients with AOD problems with the specialist in the field. In Chapter 6 (Screening, Assessment, and Diagnosis), Chapter 7 (Motivational Interviewing and Brief Interventions), and Chapter 10 (Relapse Prevention and Recovery), our goal is that you will understand the types of AOD services that mental health professionals in generalist settings provide.

In this latest edition, we have added a chapter (9) titled Co-occurring Disorders and Other Special Populations. Although these topics were covered in earlier editions, there is an increasing trend throughout treatment programs to provide treatment for substance use disorders and other mental disorders simultaneously. Because of this trend, mental health providers are having more direct treatment contact with clients diagnosed with substance use disorders. Therefore, we believe that all helping professionals need to be familiar with co-occurring disorders and the treatment implications of working with these clients.

Chapter 12 (Children and Families), Chapter 13 (Adult Children and Codependency), and Chapter 15 (Gambling and Other Behavioral Addictions) involve issues related to AOD problems. In many instances, mental health professionals may work with clients having these problems. In each of these chapters, we have attempted to provide sufficient depth of coverage so that you will have a conceptual framework to understand the relationship of these topics to AOD and to under-stand the implications for treatment.

Chapter 4 is an in-depth discussion of multicultural issues in the AOD field. As with all mental and other health-related topics, it is essential to understand both individual and group characteristics of clients. The cultural context of AOD use is of crucial importance in both prevention and treatment.

We have chosen to highlight its importance by devoting a chapter to the topic rather than integrating multiculturalism into each chapter. Therefore, we encourage you to maintain an awareness of diversity issues as you read the remaining chapters.

Chapter 5 concerns confidentiality and ethics. In teaching a substance abuse counseling class to mental health generalists, we have found nearly universal ignorance of the fact that almost all mental health professionals are bound by federal confidentiality regulations. Students often perceive this topic as "dry." However, we have seen the consequences of lack of awareness of confidentiality regulations. So, please have the stamina to wade through this chapter.

The relationship between HIV/AIDS and substance abuse is discussed in Chapter 14. Our inclusion of a chapter on this topic reflects the increasing need for awareness among all mental and other health professionals regarding transmission and prevention of this and other communicable diseases.

Having only one chapter on prevention (Chapter 16) does not imply that the subject is unimportant. Indeed, if prevention efforts were more successful, there would be less need for the rest of this book. Clearly, school counselors and school social workers must be well-informed about effective prevention approaches. However, successful prevention involves all aspects of a community, and all helping professionals must be involved. We are particularly interested in increasing your awareness of our public policy regarding the marketing of legal drugs (alcohol and tobacco) and its effect on prevention efforts.

In each chapter after this introductory chapter, there will be case examples at the beginning of the chapter. We have based these case examples on our own clinical experiences, but have obviously changed anything that would personally identify a person. The case examples will be used to illustrate points and concepts.

At the ends of chapters, major points are bulleted in a Summary section. We have added Internet resources for those of you who want more information on subjects in the chapters. Finally, there are some discussion questions designed to provoke your thinking about issues.

We need to mention an aspect of writing style so you understand what we are trying to do in this book. The tone of our writing may be less scholarly than you are accustomed to. We have taught many university courses and have used a lot of textbooks. We also were students for a *long* time. From these experiences, we found that many textbooks were marvelous, nonpharmaceutical methods to induce sleep. Although accurate and scholarly, the stilted style was often a barrier to acquiring information. It has been our intention to make this book accurate and informative but with a lower probability of causing drowsiness. Let us know if it worked.

MyCounselingLab for Addictions/Substance Abuse

Try the Topic 1 Assignments: *Introduction to Substance Abuse Counseling.*

CHAPTER 2

Classification of Drugs

CASE EXAMPLES

1. Casey is a 48-year-old man who visits his primary care physician. He complains of insomnia, anxiety, frequent acid indigestion, and fatigue. On his blood panel, he shows some impairment in his liver functioning. He is borderline diabetic and has hypertension.

2. Matilda is a 33-year-old woman who comes in to an emergency room complaining of severe lower back pain. An x-ray is negative. She is restless and agitated, has a runny nose, and complains of an upset stomach. Her vital signs are normal.

3. Chris and his wife are seeing you for marriage and family therapy. Chris works in the financial industry in a high-paced, stressful environment. His wife says Chris hardly sleeps and does not eat regularly. His moods are erratic. The couple has some financial problems, which Chris attributes to bad investments. The couple was court-ordered to counseling following a domestic violence incident.

As we noted in Chapter 1, this textbook is designed for the mental health professional (e.g., school counselor, mental health counselor, rehabilitation counselor, social worker, marriage and family therapist) who will encounter AOD problems with clientele but who, generally, will not provide treatment for these problems. Therefore, the goal of this chapter is to provide an overview of the drugs (including alcohol and tobacco) that are most often abused and drugs that are used in the treatment of some mental disorders. However, a thorough understanding of the pharmacology of drugs and related issues (e.g., medical management of overdose, use of psychotropic medications in the treatment of mental disorders) would require far more attention than one chapter can offer. Also, information in this area changes rapidly as a result of research. For example, there is no medication that has been found to be effective in significantly reducing cocaine craving. However, there is considerable research in this area. By the time you read this book, there may be pharmacological management of cocaine withdrawal that does not currently exist. We are including an additional reading list at the end of this chapter if you want to acquire more comprehensive information on the topics discussed. In addition, we encourage you to develop contacts with AOD treatment providers who are likely to remain current with regard to research in this area. This will reduce the probability that you will pass along misinformation or outdated information to your clients.

Different methods exist that are used to classify drugs. We will use the method that classifies drugs by their pharmacological similarity. Drugs exist that do not fit nicely into one classification, and these will be noted. For each drug classification, we will mention the common drugs contained in the classification and some common street names, the routes of administration, major acute and chronic effects, signs of intoxication, signs of overdose, tolerance, and withdrawal. First, however, we will present information on the federal schedule of drugs, a discussion of the concept of "dangerousness," some simple definitions of terms that will be helpful in understanding the rest of the chapter, and a brief overview of the neurobiology of drugs.

COMPREHENSIVE DRUG ABUSE PREVENTION AND CONTROL ACT

In 1970, the Comprehensive Drug Abuse Prevention and Control Act (often referred to as the Controlled Substances Act) was passed by the U.S. Congress. As part of this law, drugs are placed in one of five "schedules," with regulatory requirements associated with each schedule. Schedule I drugs have a high potential for abuse, no currently accepted medical use in treatment in the United States, and a lack of a safe level of use under medical supervision. Drugs on Schedule I include heroin, methaqualone (Quaalude), LSD, and marijuana. Schedule II drugs also have a high abuse potential and can lead to psychological or physical dependence. However, these drugs have an accepted medical use in treatment. These drugs include morphine, PCP, cocaine, and methamphetamine. As you can probably surmise, the criteria for the other schedules involve less abuse potential, increased medical uses, and less likelihood of psychological and physical dependence.

As you will see from our discussion of the classification of drugs, the way some drugs are classified is clearly illogical. For example, benzodiazepines such as Valium and Xanax are Schedule IV drugs, with part of the criteria for inclusion being that the drugs have a lower abuse potential than drugs on Schedules I, II, and III. In reality, these drugs have at least the same if not greater abuse potential than marijuana, a Schedule I drug. However, the inclusion of a drug on a certain schedule is related to public policy, which will be discussed in Chapter 16. For example, the reclassification downward of a drug such as marijuana would be politically difficult, and the reclassification of benzodiazepines upward would be resisted by the manufacturers of these drugs.

THE CONCEPT OF DANGEROUSNESS

Related to the preceding discussion of schedules of drugs is the concept of the inherent dangers of certain drugs. Tobacco, alcohol, and other drugs are not safe to use. There are acute and chronic dangers that vary by drug. For example, there is little acute danger from the ingestion of a glass of wine by an adult. The acute danger of injecting cocaine is far greater. Chronic use of any drug (including alcohol) has an increased risk, but the danger of smoking one pack of cigarettes a day for 40 years is greater than the dangers from drinking one beer a day for 40 years. Danger is also related to the method used to administer a drug. Smoking a drug or injecting it produces the most rapid and intense reaction, while ingesting a drug generally produces effects with longer duration, but less intensity. Snorting drugs is in between, but has more similarities to smoking and injecting than ingesting. Although any method of administration may be dangerous both acutely and chronically, smoking or injecting drugs tends to result in the most acute problems because these routes of administration rapidly introduce the drug to the bloodstream and, subsequently, to the brain. Also, smoking drugs causes damage to the respiratory system, and the intravenous use of drugs may cause serious problems including abscesses, blood clots, allergic reactions to the substances used to "cut" the drug, and communicable diseases such as hepatitis and HIV.

It is certainly important that you understand the acute and chronic effects of different drugs and the addictive potential of tobacco, alcohol, and other drugs. However, it is essential that you understand that any of the psychoactive drugs we discuss in this chapter can be used in an addictive manner.

You will learn that hallucinogens are not physically addicting in the sense that body tissues require these drugs for normal functioning. However, this does not imply that people are immune from serious problems resulting from the use of hallucinogens. Alcohol is clearly an extremely dangerous drug in spite of the fact that many people use the drug moderately without problems. Marijuana is not as acutely or chronically dangerous as cocaine, but that does not mean it can be used safely. We have worked with clients who have serious life problems from marijuana use. This is not a sermon to "Just Say No." It is a caution to avoid concluding that you can direct clients away from some drugs to other drugs, and a caution to avoid using your own experience with AOD as a basis for determining which drugs are safe and which are dangerous.

DEFINITIONS

Terminology in the AOD field can be confusing. One author may have a very specific meaning for a particular term, while another may use the same term in a more general sense. An analogy might be the use of the term *neurotic* in the mental health field. Although one professional may use this term when referring to some very specific disorders, another may use it to describe a wide variety of mental health problems. However, there is no universal agreement about how some of these terms should be used. Therefore, the following definitions should assist you in understanding this chapter and the rest of the book, but you may find differences in definitions as you read professional and popular literature in the AOD field.

Addiction: Compulsion to use alcohol or other drugs regardless of negative or adverse consequences. Addiction is characterized by psychological dependence (*see the following section*) and, often (depending on the drug or drugs) physical dependence (*see below*). As we will discuss in Chapter 15, the term *addiction* is sometimes applied to behaviors other than AOD (e.g., eating, gambling).

Alcoholism: Addiction to a specific drug: alcohol.

Chemical dependency: A term used to describe addiction to alcohol and/or other drugs and to differentiate this type of addiction from nonchemical addictions (e.g., gambling).

Dependence: A recurrent or ongoing need to use alcohol or other drugs. Psychological dependence is the need to use alcohol or other drugs to think, feel, or function normally. Physical dependence exists when tissues of the body require the presence of alcohol or other drugs to function normally. All psychoactive drugs can produce psychological dependence and many can produce physical dependence.

Intoxication: State of being under the influence of alcohol or other drugs so that thinking, feeling, and/or behavior are affected.

Psychoactive drugs: Natural or synthetic chemicals that affect thinking, feeling, and behavior.

Psychotropic drugs: Chemicals used to treat mental disorders.

Substance abuse: The continued use of alcohol and/or other drugs in spite of adverse consequences in one or more areas of an individual's life (e.g., family, job, legal, financial).

Tolerance: Requirement for increasing doses or quantities of alcohol or other drugs to create the same effect as was obtained from the original dose. Tolerance results from the physical or psychological adaptations of the individual.

Cross-tolerance: Refers to accompanying tolerance to other drugs from the same pharmacological group. For example, tolerance to alcohol results in tolerance to minor tranquilizers such as Xanax, even when the individual has never used Xanax.

Reverse tolerance: Refers to a condition in which smaller quantities of a drug produce the same effects as did previous larger doses.

Withdrawal: Physical and psychological effects that occur when a drug-dependent individual discontinues alcohol or other drug use.

THE NEUROBIOLOGY OF ADDICTION[1]

Drugs affect the brain by impacting the way nerve cells send, receive, and process information. Drugs such as heroin and marijuana activate neurons by mimicking natural neurotransmitters. Other drugs such as methamphetamine and cocaine cause nerve cells to release extremely large amounts of neurotransmitters or prevent the normal reuptake of neurotransmitters into the nerve cells (see Figure 2.1).

Most drugs of abuse directly or indirectly target the brain's reward system by releasing or blocking the reuptake of the neurotransmitter dopamine. Dopamine is present in regions of the brain that regulate movement, emotion, cognition, motivation, and feelings of pleasure. When dopamine floods the neuron system in the brain's reward center, euphoria results. Natural human behaviors (e.g., eating, sex) also release dopamine and the person experiences pleasure. Because our brains are designed for the survival of the species, we want to repeat these natural, pleasurable activities. However, when drugs stimulate the brain's reward center, our brain is in effect "fooled" into believing that drug taking is also a survival behavior that should be repeated.

Many naturally pleasurable activities are not habitually repeated like drug taking can be. The neurobiological explanation is that 2 to 10 times more dopamine is released by drugs than by natural activities. Furthermore, depending on the method that drugs are administered, this dopamine release is almost immediate and is very intense. Therefore, the euphoric properties of drug taking can be very powerful and highly reinforcing.

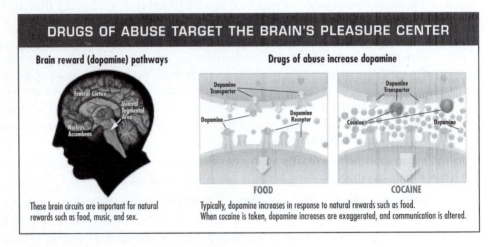

FIGURE 2.1 Effect of drugs on neurotransmitters.

---

[1]This information comes from the National Institute on Drug Abuse (NIDA) *Drugs, Brains, and Behavior—The Science of Addiction* (2010). Available at http://www.nida.nih.gov/scienceofaddiction/index.html. All material, including illustrations, is in the public sector.

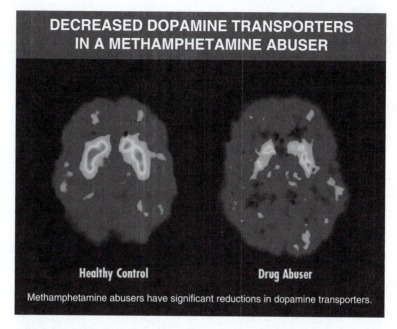

DECREASED DOPAMINE TRANSPORTERS IN A METHAMPHETAMINE ABUSER

Healthy Control   Drug Abuser

Methamphetamine abusers have significant reductions in dopamine transporters.

FIGURE 2.2   Effect of methamphetamine on the brain. *Source: Science Source.*

Unfortunately, the brain adjusts to high levels of dopamine by producing less or reducing the number of dopamine receptors. When this occurs, the drug user has more difficulty experiencing pleasure and must increase the amount of drugs consumed to feel normal. This is referred to as "tolerance." In Figure 2.2, the gray areas in the white oval areas are dopamine transporters from PET scans of a normal brain and the brain of a methamphetamine abuser. You can clearly see the reduction of these gray areas in the methamphetamine abuser. When a drug abuser abstains from drugs for a time, the brain usually returns to normal. However, the length of time it takes depends on the type of drugs abused and the number of years that drugs were abused.

The neurobiology of addiction is a very complex subject, and this brief section is intended to give you only a conceptualized understanding of the topic. (See Table 2.1 for an overview of drug classifications.) There are additional readings at the end of the chapter for those who want to pursue this area in more detail.

CENTRAL NERVOUS SYSTEM DEPRESSANTS

Central nervous system (CNS) depressants (also referred to as *sedative-hypnotics*) depress the overall functioning of the CNS to induce sedation, drowsiness, and coma. The drugs in this classification include the most commonly used and abused psychoactive drug, alcohol; prescription drugs used for anxiety, sleep disturbance, and seizure control; and over-the-counter medications for sleep disturbance, colds and allergies, and coughs. In general, CNS depressants are extremely dangerous. There are approximately 88,000 deaths annually caused by excessive alcohol use

TABLE 2.1 Summary Table of Drug Classifications

	Common Drugs	Main Routes of Administration	Major Acute Effects	Major Chronic Effects	Overdose	Tolerance	Withdrawal
CNS Depressants	Alcohol, barbiturates, benzodiazepines, sleep aids	Drinking, ingesting pills	Relaxation, disinhibition, reduction of anxiety, impaired motor coordination	Alcohol: Damage to every organ system	Common with alcohol, can be dangerous, synergistic effect	Develops rapidly, cross-tolerance occurs	Can be medically dangerous
CNS Stimulants	Cocaine, methamphetamine, caffeine, nicotine	Snorting, smoking, injecting, drinking	Alertness, mood elevation, increased heart rate and blood pressure	Health damage from tobacco products, addiction, depression, suicidal ideation	Tremors, sweating, tachycardia, anxiety, insomnia	Rapid tolerance to pleasurable and stimulating effects	Unpleasant and long-lasting but not medically dangerous
Opioids	Heroin, morphine, methadone, pain pills	Injecting, snorting, swallowing pills	Sedation, pain relief	Addiction, complications from lifestyle and method of administration	Depressed central nervous system functioning, death can occur	Rapid tolerance to pleasurable effects with repeated administration	Very unpleasant but not usually medically dangerous
Hallucinogens	LSD, magic mushrooms, PCP	Ingesting or smoking	Alters perception of sensory stimuli, panic attacks in some users	Flashbacks	Except for PCP, overdose does not occur with hallucinogens, agitation, confusion, aggression	Tolerance to hallucinogenic properties does occur	No physical dependence

Category	Examples	Method of Use	Effects	Adverse Effects	Overdose	Tolerance	Withdrawal
Cannabinols	Marijuana	Smoking or ingestion	Enhanced taste, touch, and smell; relaxation; increased appetite; impaired immediate recall	Adverse effect on lung function, decrease in testosterone, suppression of immune system; impact is controversial	Overdose does not occur; adverse reactions are panic attacks	Tolerance to normal effects occurs but it is probably not physiological	Irritability, insomnia, restlessness
Inhalants and Volatile Hydrocarbons	Solvents, aerosol sprays, amyl nitrate, isobutyl, nitrous oxide	Inhaling (huffing)	Reduced inhibition, dizziness, slurred speech, impaired motor coordination; unconsciousness and death can occur	Damage to liver, kidneys, brain, and lungs	Hallucinations, muscle spasms, coma	Tolerance to nitrous oxide	No known withdrawal syndrome
Anabolic Steroids	Depo-Testosterone, Danocrine, Halotestin	Ingested or injected	Increased muscle strength, body mass, and aggressiveness	Jaundice, liver tumors, mood swings	Increased doses result in chronic problems	No tolerance	Depression, fatigue, restlessness, insomnia

in the United States, one of the leading, preventable causes of death (Centers for Disease Control and Prevention, 2014a). Alcohol alone or in combination with other drugs accounted for nearly 40% of drug abuse-related emergency room episodes in 2011 (Substance Abuse and Mental Health Services Administration, 2013).

Drugs in This Classification

Alcohol is the most well-known CNS depressant because of its widespread use and legality. The alcohol content of common beverages is beer, 3% to 6%; wine, 11% to 20%; liqueurs, 25% to 35%; and liquor (whiskey, gin, vodka, etc.), 40% to 50%. The "proof" on alcohol beverages is computed by doubling the alcohol content. Therefore, a bourbon that is described as "90 proof" is 45% alcohol. It is important to remember that the amount of alcohol in one 12-ounce beer is the same as the amount of alcohol in 6 ounces of wine or in 1.5 ounces of liquor (all standard drinks). The alcohol in beer is simply contained in a larger amount of liquid.

Barbiturates are prescription drugs used to aid sleep for insomniacs and for the control of seizures. These drugs include Seconal (reds, red devils), Nembutal (yellows, yellow jackets), Tuinal (rainbows), Amytal (blues, blue heaven), and phenobarbital. There are also nonbarbiturate sedative-hypnotics with similar effects but with different pharmacological properties. These include Doriden (goofballs), Quaalude (ludes), Miltown, and Equinil. Being a Schedule I drug, Quaalude cannot be legally prescribed in the United States.

The development of benzodiazepines or minor tranquilizers reduced the number of prescriptions for barbiturates written by physicians. These drugs were initially seen as safe and having little abuse potential. Although the minor tranquilizers cannot be easily used in suicide as can barbiturates, the potential for abuse is significant. The benzodiazepines are among the most widely prescribed drugs and include Valium, Librium, Dalmane, Halcion, Xanax, and Ativan. In addition, nonbenzodiazepine hypnotics are being heavily marketed as sleep aids. These include Ambien, Lunesta, and Sonata. These drugs can be abused and do have addictive potential. Rozerem, another widely marketed sleep aid, is not pharmacologically similar to the other nonbenzodiazepine hypnotics and is not addictive. It is like the herbal remedy melatonin.

Finally, certain over-the-counter medications contain depressant drugs. Sleep aids such as Nytol and Sominex, cold and allergy products, and cough medicines may contain scopolamine, antihistamines, or alcohol to produce the desired effects.

Routes of Administration

Obviously, alcohol is administered by drinking. Some over-the-counter medications are also in liquid form. The barbiturates, nonbarbiturate sedative-hypnotics, minor tranquilizers, and nonbenzodiazepine hypnotics come in pill form. As with many psychoactive drugs, liquid forms of the drugs are produced and administered by injection.

Major Acute and Chronic Effects

The effects of CNS depressants are related to the dose, method of administration, and tolerance of the individual, factors that should be kept in mind as the effects are discussed. At low doses, these drugs produce a feeling of relaxation and calmness. They induce muscle relaxation, disinhibition, and a reduction in anxiety. Judgment and motor coordination are impaired, and there is a decrease in reflexes, pulse rate, and blood pressure. At high doses, the person demonstrates slurred speech, staggering, and, eventually, sleep. Phenobarbital and Valium have anticonvulsant properties and are used to control seizures. The benzodiazepines are also used to clinically control the effects from alcohol withdrawal.

In terms of damage to the human body and to society, alcohol is the most dangerous psychoactive drug (tobacco causes far more health damage). Alcohol has a damaging effect on every organ system. Chronic effects include permanent loss of memory, gastritis, esophagitis, ulcers, pancreatitis, cirrhosis of the liver, high blood pressure, weakened heart muscles, and damage to a fetus including fetal alcohol spectrum disorders (see Chapter 12). Other chronic effects include family, social, occupational, and financial problems. Acutely, alcohol is the cause of many traffic and other accidents and is involved in many acts of violence and crime. Certainly, the other CNS depressants can cause the same acute problems that are the result of injury and accident and chronic effects on the individual and family because of addiction.

Overdose

Alcohol overdose is common. We refer to this syndrome as being "drunk." The symptoms include staggering, slurred speech, extreme disinhibition, and blackouts (an inability to recall events that occurred when the individual was intoxicated). Generally, the stomach goes into spasm and the person will vomit, helping to eliminate alcohol from the body. However, the rapid ingestion of alcohol, particularly in a nontolerant individual, may result in coma and death. This happens most frequently with young people who participate in drinking contests.

Because these drugs depress the CNS, overdose is extremely dangerous and can be fatal. Since the fatal dosage is only 10 to 15 times the therapeutic dosage, barbiturates are often used in suicides, which is one reason they are not frequently prescribed. It is far more difficult to overdose on the minor tranquilizers. However, CNS depressants have a synergistic or potentiation effect, meaning that the effect of a drug is enhanced as a result of the presence of another drug. For example, if a person has been drinking and then takes a minor tranquilizer such as Xanax, the effect of the Xanax may be dramatically enhanced. This combination has been the cause of many accidental deaths and emergency room visits.

Tolerance

There is a rapid development of tolerance to all CNS depressant drugs. Cross-tolerance also develops. This is one reason why overdose is such a problem. For example, Bob, a very heavy drinker, is quite anxious and is having difficulty sleeping. He goes to his physician with these symptoms. The physician does not ask about his alcohol use and gives him a prescription of Xanax. Bob follows the directions and takes one pill. However, because he is tolerant to alcohol, he is also cross-tolerant to Xanax and the pill has no effect. He can't sleep so he takes three more pills and has a glass of brandy. The synergistic effect of these drugs results in a coma.

The tolerance that develops to the CNS depressants is also one reason that the use of the minor tranquilizers has become problematic. People are given prescriptions to alleviate symptoms such as anxiety and sleep disturbance that are the result of other problems such as marital discord. The minor tranquilizers temporarily relieve the symptoms, but the real problem is never addressed. The person continues to use the drug to alleviate the symptoms, but tolerance develops, and increasing dosages must be used to achieve the desired effect. This is a classic paradigm for the development of addiction and/or overdose.

Withdrawal

The withdrawal syndrome from CNS depressants can be medically dangerous. These symptoms may include anxiety, irritability, loss of appetite, tremors, insomnia, and seizures. In the severe form of alcohol withdrawal called delirium tremens (DTs), additional symptoms are fever, rapid heartbeat, and hallucinations. People can and do die from the withdrawal from these drugs. Therefore, the detoxification process for CNS depressants should include close supervision and the availability of medical personnel. Chronic, high-dosage users of these drugs should be discouraged from detoxifying without support and supervision. For detoxification in a medical setting, minor tranquilizers can be used, in decreasing dosages, to reduce the severity of the withdrawal symptoms.

The dangerousness of withdrawal from CNS depressants is one reason why supervised detoxification is needed. In addition, supervision and support are usually required because the withdrawal symptoms are unpleasant and rapidly alleviated by using CNS depressants. For example, a 47-year-old man decides that he has been drinking too much and wants to quit. He doesn't tell anyone and is going to "tough it out." Although he doesn't have any medically dangerous symptoms, he is anxious, irritable, and has trouble sleeping. His family, friends, and coworkers remark about how unpleasant he is, and he is quite uncomfortable. He has a few drinks and finds that the symptoms are gone. Very rapidly, he is drinking heavily again.

CENTRAL NERVOUS SYSTEM STIMULANTS

CNS stimulants affect the body in the opposite manner as do the CNS depressants. These drugs increase respiration, heart rate, motor activity, and alertness. This classification includes highly dangerous, illegal substances such as crack cocaine, medically useful stimulants such as Ritalin, drugs with relatively minor psychoactive effects such as caffeine, and the most deadly drug used, nicotine. The drugs in this classification were mentioned in 53% of the drug abuse-related emergency room episodes in 2011 (Substance Abuse and Mental Health Services Administration, 2013).

Drugs in This Classification

Cocaine (coke, blow, toot, snow) and the freebase or smokeable forms of cocaine (crack, rock, base) are the most infamous of the CNS stimulants. Cocaine is found in the leaves of the coca shrub that grows in South America. The leaves are processed and produce coca paste. The paste is, in turn, processed to form the white hydrochloride salt powder most of you know as cocaine. Of course, before it is sold on the street, it is adulterated or "cut" with substances such as powdered sugar, talc, arsenic, lidocaine, strychnine, or methamphetamine. Crack is produced by mixing the cocaine powder with baking soda and water and heating the solution. The paste that forms is hardened and cut into hard pieces, or rocks. The mixing and heating process removes most of the impurities from the cocaine. The vaporization point is lowered so the cocaine can be smoked, reaching the brain in one heartbeat less than if it is injected. Therefore, crack is a more pure form of cocaine than is cocaine hydrochloride salt powder.

Amphetamines are also CNS stimulants, and one form in particular, methamphetamine, is a major drug of addiction. The amphetamines include Benzedrine (crosstops, black beauties), Methedrine or methamphetamine (crank, meth, crystal), and Dexedrine (dexies). There are also nonamphetamine stimulants with similar properties such as Ritalin and Cylert (used in the treatment of attention deficit-hyperactivity [ADHD] disorder) and Preludin (used in the treatment of obesity). These drugs are synthetics (not naturally occurring), and the amphetamines were widely prescribed in the 1950s and 1960s for weight control.

Some forms of CNS stimulants are available without a prescription and are contained in many substances we use on a regular basis. Caffeine is found in coffee, teas, colas, energy drinks, and chocolate as well as in some over-the-counter products designed to help people stay awake (e.g., NoDoz, Alert, Vivarin). Phenylpropanolamine is a stimulant found in diet-control products sold over-the-counter (e.g., Dexatrim). These products are abused by individuals who chronically diet (e.g., anorexics). Pseudoephedrine is a substance in many nasal decongestants. Because it is used in the manufacture of methamphetamine, federal and state laws have been passed to restrict the quantities of these over-the-counter medications that can be purchased.

Although it has mild euphoric properties, nicotine is the highly addictive stimulant drug found in tobacco products. According to the Centers for Disease Control and Prevention (2014b), an estimated 480,000 Americans die each year from smoking-related illnesses. This is more than 5 times as many deaths as result from alcohol. By a wide margin, nicotine is the most deadly drug we will discuss. Ironically, it is not only legal, it is marketed. We will mention this contradiction in public policy in Chapter 16.

Emerging stimulants include "bath salts" a family of drugs containing one or more synthetic chemicals related to cathinone, an amphetamine-like stimulant found naturally in the Khat plant (a plant in Africa whose leaves are chewed as a mild stimulant).

Routes of Administration

With CNS stimulants, every method of administration is possible and used. Caffeine is consumed in beverage form, but it is also eaten (e.g., chocolate) or taken in pill form (e.g., NoDoz). Nicotine is obviously smoked but can be chewed (chewing tobacco, nicotine gum) or administered through a skin patch. Cocaine and amphetamines can be snorted, smoked, injected, and ingested.

Major Acute and Chronic Effects

As with most of the psychoactive drugs, some of the CNS stimulants (cocaine and methamphetamine) have a recreational use. The purpose is to "get high" or to experience a sense of euphoria. Methamphetamine and cocaine users report a feeling of self-confidence and self-assurance. There is a "rush" that is experienced, particularly when cocaine is smoked and when cocaine and methamphetamine are injected. The high from methamphetamine is generally less intense but longer acting than cocaine.

CNS stimulants result in psychomotor stimulation, alertness, and elevation of mood. There is an increase in heart rate and blood pressure. Performance may be enhanced with increased activity level, one reason why athletes use CNS stimulants. These drugs also suppress appetite and combat fatigue. That's why people who want to lose weight and people who want to stay awake for long periods (e.g., truck drivers) will use amphetamines.

The acute effects of CNS stimulants can be dramatic and fatal. These include heart attacks, strokes, seizures, and respiratory depression. However, the results of chronic use cause the most problems. The addictive properties of these drugs are extremely high. Individuals with addictions to cocaine and methamphetamine spend a tremendous amount of money to obtain drugs, and they encounter serious life problems related to their addiction. Also, there is an increased risk of strokes and cardiovascular problems, depression, and suicide in chronic users. Symptoms of paranoid schizophrenia can occur. If cocaine or methamphetamine is snorted, perforation of the nasal septum can occur. Injection of CNS stimulants has the same risks as injecting other drugs (e.g., hepatitis, HIV). Because these drugs suppress appetite, chronic users are frequently malnourished.

Many, if not most, people use caffeine and do so without any major problems. However, caffeine may precipitate panic attacks in individuals predisposed to panic disorders, and the drug may be detrimental to some heart patients. A woman who is considering having a baby should reduce caffeine intake, and pregnant and breastfeeding women are advised to abstain.

Clearly, the chronic effects of nicotine addiction are damaging to health. The number of health-related problems, deaths, and days of work missed because of the chronic use of tobacco products is astounding.

Overdose

CNS stimulants stimulate the reward center of the brain. The most powerful of these drugs result in the body's not experiencing hunger, thirst, or fatigue. There is no built-in satiation point, so humans can continue using cocaine and methamphetamine until there is no more or they die. Therefore, the compulsion to use, the desire to maintain the high, and the unpleasantness of withdrawal make overdose fairly common. There may be tremors, sweating and flushing, rapid heartbeat (tachycardia), anxiety, insomnia, paranoia, convulsions, heart attack, or stroke. Death from overdose has been widely publicized because it has occurred with some famous movie stars and athletes. However, far more people experience chronic problems from CNS stimulant addictions than from overdose reactions.

Tolerance

There is a rapid tolerance to the pleasurable effects of cocaine and methamphetamine and the stimulating effects of tobacco and caffeine. If you drink five or six cups a day of combinations of coffee, tea, energy drinks, and colas, you probably know this with regard to caffeine. You will find that if you stop using caffeine for a couple of weeks and then start again, the initial doses of caffeine produce a minor "buzz," alertness, and/or restlessness.

The rapid tolerance to the euphoric effects of cocaine and methamphetamine leads to major problems with these drugs. The pleasurable effects are so rewarding, particularly when the drugs are smoked or injected, that the user is prone to compulsively use in an effort to recapture the euphoric effects. When injected or smoked, the effects are enhanced, but with a relatively short duration. Continual use to achieve the high leads to rapid tolerance. The user is then unable to feel the pleasure but must continue to use the drug to reduce the pain of withdrawal.

A sensitization or reverse tolerance can occur, particularly with cocaine. In this instance, a chronic user with a high tolerance has an adverse reaction (i.e., seizure) to a low dose.

Withdrawal

Unlike the withdrawal from CNS depressants, the withdrawal from these drugs is not medically dangerous. However, it is extremely unpleasant. If you have an addiction to caffeine and want to get a small taste of the withdrawal from CNS stimulants, discontinue your use of caffeine. The symptoms you can expect include a chronic headache, irritability, restlessness, and anxiety. You may have trouble sleeping and concentrating.

The withdrawal from cocaine and methamphetamine is called "crashing." The severe symptoms usually last 2 to 3 days and include intense drug craving, irritability, depression, anxiety, and lethargy. However, the depression, drug craving, and an inability to experience pleasure may last for several months as the body chemistry returns to normal. Suicidal ideation and attempts are frequent during this time, as are relapses. Recovering cocaine and methamphetamine addicts can become very discouraged with the slow rate of the lifting of depression, and, therefore, support is very important during this time.

If you have been or are addicted to nicotine, you probably have experienced the unpleasant withdrawal symptoms during attempts to quit (we are assuming that nearly everyone addicted to nicotine has tried to quit or has succeeded). Enhance the severity of your experience dramatically, and you may be able to achieve an empathic understanding of the withdrawal syndrome for cocaine and methamphetamine addicts.

OPIOIDS

The opioids[2] are naturally occurring (opium poppy extracts) and synthetic drugs that are commonly used for their analgesic (pain relief) and cough-suppressing properties. Opium was used by early Egyptian, Greek, and Arabic cultures for the treatment of diarrhea because there is a constipating effect to this drug. Greek and Roman writers such as Homer and Virgil wrote of the sleep-inducing properties of opium, and recreational use of the drug in these cultures did occur. Morphine was isolated from opium in the early 1800s and was widely available without prescription until the early 1900s when the nonmedical use of opioids was banned. Heroin was mentioned in 21% of drug abuse-related emergency room episodes for illicit drugs in 2011, whereas other opioids were involved 39% of emergency room visits for nonmedical pharmaceuticals (Substance Abuse and Mental Health Services Administration, 2013). The large number of emergency room visits resulting from nonmedical pharmaceuticals reflects the increasing abuse of prescription pain medications such as oxycodone (i.e., OxyContin) and hydrocodone (i.e., Loratab, Vicodin).

Drugs in This Classification

The opioids include opium, codeine, morphine, heroin (smack, horse), and buprenorphine as well as familiar brand names such as Dilaudid (hydromorphone), OxyContin and Percocet (oxycodone), Loratab and Vicodin (hydrocodone), Dolophine (methadone), and Demerol (meperidine).

Routes of Administration

We are familiar with many of these drugs in the pill or liquid form when used for pain relief or cough suppression. When used illicitly, the opioids are often used intravenously, but this is also a route of administration when these drugs are used medically for pain relief. Heroin, which is used only illicitly in the United States, can be snorted or smoked in addition to the common intravenous method. As the danger of disease from dirty needles has been widely publicized, alternative routes of administration for heroin have become more popular. Opium has been smoked for centuries.

Major Acute and Chronic Effects

Opioids have medically useful effects, including pain and cough suppression and constipation. Obviously, there is also a euphoric effect that accounts for the recreational use of these drugs. They can produce nausea and vomiting and itching. A sedating effect occurs, and the pupils of the eyes become constricted.

Methadone or Dolophine is a synthetic opioid that does not have the dramatic euphoric effects of heroin, has a longer duration of action (12 to 24 hours compared with 3 to 6 hours for heroin), and blocks the symptoms of withdrawal when heroin is discontinued. This is the reason for the use of methadone in the treatment of opioid addiction. In the past few years, methadone in pill form is being frequently prescribed for pain relief. Buprenorphine (usually sold under the brand name Suboxone) is now being prescribed in an office setting to treat opioid dependence.

There is an acute danger of death from overdose from injecting opioids, particularly heroin. Also, the euphoric effects of opioids rapidly decrease as tolerance increases, and, as this tolerance occurs, the opioid use is primarily to ward off the withdrawal symptoms.

---

[2]We will use the term *opioid* to refer to any natural or synthetic drug that has an analgesic (pain relieving) effect similar to that of morphine. The terms *opiate, narcotic,* and *analgesic* are also used to describe this classification of drugs.

Compared with the chronic use of CNS depressants, chronic use of the drugs themselves is less dangerous to the body. However, the route of administration and the lifestyle associated with chronic opioid use clearly has serious consequences. Obviously, there is the risk of communicable disease from the intravenous use of opioids and sharing needles. The lifestyle of heroin addicts often includes criminal activity to secure enough money to purchase heroin. Women may participate in prostitution, which adds the associated risks of diseases and violence. Nutrition is frequently neglected. However, those individuals who have been involved in methadone maintenance programs for long periods do not experience negative health consequences from the use of methadone (which is taken orally).

Overdose

Death from overdose of injectable opioids (usually heroin) can occur from the direct action of the drug on the brain, resulting in respiratory depression. Death can also occur from an allergic reaction to the drug or to substances used to cut it, possibly resulting in cardiac arrest.

Overdose of other drugs in this classification may include symptoms such as slow breathing rate, decreased blood pressure, pulse rate, temperature, and reflexes. The person may become extremely drowsy and lose consciousness. There may be flushing and itching skin, abdominal pain, and nausea and vomiting.

As abuse of prescription pain medications has skyrocketed, so have overdoses from these drugs. Oxycodone is sold in time-release form, which is crushed and snorted to get a more intense effect. This has resulted in unintentional overdose. In addition, methadone in pill form has been increasingly prescribed for pain relief. However, methadone dissipates from the body very slowly. Therefore, an individual may increase the dosage beyond the recommended level or time between doses and overdose because of the residual methadone in the body from prior doses.

Tolerance

Frequency of administration and dosage of opioids is related to the development of tolerance. Tolerance develops rapidly when the drugs are repeatedly administered but does not develop when there are prolonged periods of abstinence. The tolerance that does develop is to the euphoric, sedative, analgesic, and respiratory effects of the drugs. This tolerance results in the individual's using doses that would kill a nontolerant person. The tolerant individual becomes accustomed to using high doses, which accounts for death due to overdose in long-time opioid users who have been detoxified and then go back to using.

Cross-tolerance to natural and synthetic opioids does occur. However, there is no cross-tolerance to CNS depressants. This fact is important because the combination of moderate to high doses of opioids and alcohol or other CNS depressants can (and often does) result in respiratory depression and death.

Withdrawal

When these drugs are used on a continuous basis, there is a rapid development of physical dependence. Withdrawal symptoms are unpleasant and uncomfortable but are rarely dangerous. The symptoms are analogous to a severe case of the flu, with running eyes and nose, restlessness, goose bumps, sweating, muscle cramps or aching, nausea, vomiting, and diarrhea. There is significant drug craving. These symptoms rapidly dissipate when opioids are taken, which accounts for relapse when a person abruptly quits on his or her own ("cold turkey"). When the drugs are not available to the dependent individual, the unpleasant withdrawal symptoms also result in participation in criminal activities to purchase the drugs.

HALLUCINOGENS

Many of the hallucinogens are naturally occurring and have been used for thousands of years. Some have been (and are currently) used as sacraments in religious rites and have been ascribed with mystical and magical properties. Today, many types of hallucinogens are synthetically produced in laboratories. Some of the hallucinogens became very popular in the 1960s and 1970s, with a drop in use in the 1980s. Although there was a resurgence of use from 1992 to 2001 among youth, recent surveys have shown relatively low and stable levels of use (Substance Abuse and Mental Health Services Administration, 2015a).

Drugs in This Classification

This classification comprises a group of heterogeneous compounds. Although there may be some commonality in terms of effect, the chemical structures are quite different. The hallucinogens we will discuss include LSD (acid, fry), psilocybin (magic mushrooms, shrooms), morning glory seeds (heavenly blue), mescaline (mesc, big chief, peyote), STP (serenity, tranquility, peace), and PCP (angel dust, hog). PCP is used as a veterinary anesthetic, primarily for primates.

Routes of Administration

Hallucinogens are usually swallowed. For example, LSD may be put on a sticker, stamp, or sugar cube. Psilocybin is eaten. However, hallucinogens can also be snorted, smoked, or injected. PCP is often sprinkled on a marijuana joint and smoked.

Major Acute and Chronic Effects

These drugs produce an altered state of consciousness, including altered perceptions of visual, auditory, olfactory, and/or tactile senses and an increased awareness of inner thoughts and impulses. Sensory experiences may cross into one another (e.g., "hearing color"). Common sights and sounds may be perceived as exceptionally intricate and astounding. In the case of PCP, there may be increased suggestibility, delusions, and depersonalization and dissociation. Physiologically, hallucinogens produce a rise in pulse and blood pressure.

A fairly common and well-publicized adverse effect of hallucinogens is the experience of flashbacks. Flashbacks are the recurrence of the effects of hallucinogens long after the drug has been taken. Reports of flashbacks more than 5 years after taking a hallucinogen have been reported although abatement after several months is more common.

With regard to LSD, there are acute physical effects including a rise in heart rate and blood pressure, higher body temperature, dizziness, and dilated pupils. Mental effects include sensory distortions, dreaminess, depersonalization, altered mood, and impaired concentration. "Bad trips" involve acute anxiety, paranoia, fear of loss of control, and delusions. Individuals with preexisting mental disorders may experience more severe symptoms. With regard to chronic effects, we have already mentioned the rare but frightening experience of flashbacks.

On the other hand, PCP does result in significant adverse effects. Chronic use may result in psychiatric problems including depression, anxiety, and paranoid psychosis. Accidents, injuries, and violence occur frequently.

Overdose

With the exception of PCP, the concept of "overdose" is not applicable to the hallucinogens. "Bad trips" or panic reactions do occur and may include paranoid ideation, depression, undesirable hallucinations, and/or confusion. These are usually managed by providing a calm and supportive environment. An overdose of PCP may result in acute intoxication, acute psychosis, or coma. In the acute intoxication or psychosis, the person may be agitated, confused, and excited and may exhibit a blank stare and violent behavior. Analgesia (insensibility to pain) occurs that may result in self-inflicted injuries and injuries to others when attempts are made to restrain the individual.

Tolerance

Tolerance to the hallucinogenic properties of these drugs occurs, as well as cross-tolerance between LSD and other hallucinogens. No cross-tolerance to cannabis has been demonstrated. Tolerance to PCP has not been demonstrated in humans.

Withdrawal

There is no physical dependence that occurs from the use of hallucinogens, although psychological dependence, including drug craving, does occur.

CANNABINOLS AND SYNTHETIC CANNABINOLS

Marijuana is the most widely used illegal drug. Nearly 20% of adults in the 18- to 24-year range reported using marijuana in the previous month (Substance Abuse and Mental Health Services Administration, 2015a). The earliest references to the drug date back to 2700 b.c. In the 1700s, the hemp plant (*Cannabis sativa*) was grown in the colonies for its fiber, which was used in rope. Beginning in 1926, states began to outlaw the use of marijuana because it was claimed to cause criminal behavior and violence. Marijuana use became popular with mainstream young people in the 1960s. Some states have basically decriminalized possession of small amounts of marijuana, other states have medical marijuana laws that allow for the use of marijuana for medical purposes, and a few states have legalized recreational marijuana. However, according to the federal government, marijuana remains a Schedule I drug and, therefore, is illegal to possess. Cannabinols were mentioned in 38% of emergency room episodes for illicit drugs in 2011 (Substance Abuse and Mental Health Services Administration, 2013).

Drugs in This Classification

The various cannabinols include marijuana (grass, pot, weed, joint, reefer, dube), hashish, charas, bhang, ganja, and sinsemilla. The active ingredient is delta-9-tetrahydrocannabinol (THC). Hashish and charas have a THC content of 7% to 14%; ganja and sinsemilla, 4% to 7%; and bhang and marijuana, 2% to 5%. For simplicity, we will refer to the various forms of cannabinols as "marijuana."

Synthetic cannabinoids (e.g., spice, K2) are man-made chemicals that are either sprayed on dried, shredded plant material so they can be smoked (herbal incense) or sold as liquids to be vaporized and inhaled in e-cigarettes and other devices (liquid incense).

Routes of Administration

Marijuana is usually smoked in cigarette form or pipes. It can also be ingested, normally by baking it in brownies or cookies.

Major Acute and Chronic Effects

Marijuana users experience euphoria; enhancement of taste, touch, and smell; relaxation; increased appetite; altered time sense; and impaired immediate recall. An enhanced perception of the humor of situations or events may occur. The physiological effects of marijuana include increase in pulse rate and blood pressure, dilation of blood vessels in the cornea (which produces bloodshot eyes), and dry mouth. Motor skills and reaction time are slowed.

As you are all aware, marijuana has been and continues to be controversial. This controversy is related to the facts and myths regarding marijuana's acute and chronic effects. However, the professional community has as many views of the "facts" regarding marijuana as does the general public. Although our interpretation of the research may be different than others, we are confident in saying that this issue is not "black and white." Marijuana should clearly not be a Schedule I drug. However, no psychoactive drug is safe. Marijuana can and does result in significant life problems for many people. However, the growing trend in the United States is the gradual reduction of criminal penalties for marijuana possession and increasing efforts to legalize marijuana at the state level.

Marijuana is certainly not acutely or chronically dangerous when death is the measure of dangerousness. However, the effect on motor skills and reaction time certainly impairs the user's ability to drive a car, boat, plane, or other vehicle.

Chronic use of marijuana does seem to have an adverse effect on lung function, although there is no direct evidence that it causes lung cancer. Although an increase in heart rate occurs, there does not seem to be an adverse effect on the heart. As is the case with CNS depressants, marijuana suppresses the immune system. Chronic marijuana use decreases the male hormone testosterone (as does alcohol) and adversely affects sperm formation. However, no effect on male fertility or sexual potency has been noted. Female hormones are also reduced, and impairment in ovulation has been reported.

Marijuana may be medically useful in reducing nausea and vomiting from chemotherapy, stimulating appetite in AIDS and other wasting-syndrome patients, treating spasticity and nocturnal spasms complicating multiple sclerosis and spinal cord injury, controlling seizures, and managing neuropathic pain. However, further clinical studies are necessary to reach conclusions on the value of marijuana in medical treatment.

For an objective review of the literature on all aspects of marijuana, we recommend *Cannabis Use and Dependence: Public Health and Public Policy* (Hall & Pacula, 2010).

Overdose

Overdose is unusual because the normal effects of marijuana are not enhanced by large doses. Intensification of emotional responses and mild hallucinations can occur, and the user may feel "out of control." As with hallucinogens, many reports of overdose are panic reactions to the normal effects of the drug. In individuals with preexisting mental disorders (e.g., schizophrenia), high doses of marijuana may exacerbate symptoms such as delusions, hallucinations, disorientation, and depersonalization.

Tolerance

Tolerance is a controversial area with regard to marijuana. Tolerance does rapidly occur in animals but only with frequent use of high doses in humans. At the least, chronic users probably become accustomed to the effects of the drug and are experienced in administering the proper dosage to produce the desired effects.

Withdrawal

A withdrawal syndrome can be observed in chronic, high-dosage users who abruptly discontinue their use. The symptoms include irritability, restlessness, decreased appetite, insomnia, tremor, chills, and increased body temperature. The symptoms usually last 3 to 5 days.

INHALANTS AND VOLATILE HYDROCARBONS

Inhalants and volatile hydrocarbons consist largely of chemicals that can be legally purchased and that are normally used for nonrecreational purposes. In addition, this classification includes some drugs that are used legally for medical purposes. As psychoactive drugs, most of these substances are used mainly by young people, particularly in low socioeconomic areas. Because most of these chemicals are accessible in homes and are readily available for purchase, they are easily used as psychoactive drugs by young people who are beginning drug experimentation and by individuals who are unable to purchase other mind-altering substances because of finances or availability.

Drugs in This Classification

The industrial solvents and aerosol sprays that are used for psychoactive purposes include gasoline, kerosene, chloroform, airplane glue, lacquer thinner, acetone, nail polish remover, model cement, lighter fluid, carbon tetrachloride, fluoride-based sprays, and metallic paints. Volatile nitrites are amyl nitrite (poppers), butyl, and isobutyl (locker room, rush, bolt, quick silver, zoom). Amyl nitrite has typically been used in the gay community. In addition, nitrous oxide (laughing gas), a substance used by dentists, is also included in this classification.

Route of Administration

As the name of this classification implies, these drugs are inhaled, a method of administration referred to as "huffing" or sniffing. The industrial solvents and aerosol sprays are often poured or sprayed on a rag and put in a plastic bag. The individual then places his or her head in the plastic bag and inhales rapidly and deeply.

Major Acute and Chronic Effects

The solvents and sprays reduce inhibition and produce euphoria, dizziness, slurred speech, an unsteady gait, and drowsiness. Nystagmus (constant involuntary movements of the eyes) may be noted. The nitrites alter consciousness and enhance sexual pleasure. The user may experience giddiness, headaches, and dizziness. Nitrous oxide produces giddiness, a buzzing or ringing in the ears, and a sense that the user is about to pass out.

The most critical acute effect of inhalants is a result of the method of administration, which can result in loss of consciousness, coma, or death from lack of oxygen. Respiratory arrest, cardiac arrhythmia, or asphyxiation may occur. Many of these substances are highly toxic, and chronic use may cause damage to the liver, kidneys, brain, and lungs.

Overdose

Overdose of these substances may produce hallucinations, muscle spasms, headaches, dizziness, loss of balance, irregular heartbeat, and coma from lack of oxygen.

Tolerance

Tolerance does develop to nitrous oxide, but does not seem to develop to the other inhalants.

Withdrawal

There does not appear to be a withdrawal syndrome associated with these substances.

ANABOLIC STEROIDS

Anabolic steroids are synthetic drugs that are illicitly used to improve athletic performance and increase muscle mass. These drugs resemble the male sex hormone, testosterone. Although some anabolic steroids are approved for use in the United States for medical purposes, the abuse of these drugs led Congress to pass the Anabolic Steroids Act of 1990. This law regulated the distribution and sale of anabolic steroids and added these drugs to Schedule III of the Controlled Substances Act. In 2015, 1.7% of high school seniors reported steroid use in the previous year (Johnston et al., 2016).

Drugs in This Classification

Anabolic steroids approved in the United States include Depo-Testosterone, Durabolin, Danocrine, and Halotestin. Some veterinary anabolic steroids are illicitly sold for human use and include Finiject 30, Equipoise, and Winstrol. Delatestryl, Testex, and Maxibolan are sold legally only outside of the United States.

Routes of Administration

Anabolic steroids are taken orally or injected. "Stacking" refers to combining oral and injectable steroids.

Major Acute and Chronic Effects

Anabolic steroids are used medically for testosterone replacement and treatment of muscle loss, blood anemia, and endometriosis. However, the abuse of these drugs by athletes and by those who wish to improve their physical appearance is prompted by the effects of anabolic steroids on muscle strength, body mass, and personality. These drugs increase muscle strength, reduce body mass, and increase aggressiveness, competitiveness, and combativeness.

For males, atrophy of testicles, impaired production of sperm, infertility, early baldness, acne, and enlargement of the breasts occurs. In females, there are masculinizing effects including increased facial and body hair, lowered voice, and irregularity or cessation of menses. There is an increased risk of coronary artery disease due to reduced "good" cholesterol (HDL) and increased "bad" cholesterol (LDL). An association has also been established between oral anabolic steroids and jaundice and liver tumors. Mood swings, with periods of unreasonable and uncontrolled anger and violence, have been noted.

Overdose

When used illicitly to improve athletic performance or physical appearance, the dosage is well beyond the therapeutic dose. Although there is no immediate danger of death or serious medical problems from high dosage levels of anabolic steroids, there are serious complications from long-term use (see Major Acute and Chronic Effects).

Tolerance

No evidence of tolerance to anabolic steroids exists.

Withdrawal

Physical and psychological dependence on anabolic steroids does occur, and there is a withdrawal syndrome. The symptoms of withdrawal include depression, fatigue, restlessness, insomnia, loss of appetite, and decreased interest in sex.

CLUB DRUGS

Rather than sharing pharmacological similarities, the drugs that will be discussed in this section are grouped together because of the environment in which they are commonly used. The use of these drugs is primarily by youth and young adults associated with dance clubs, bars, and all-night dance parties ("raves").

It would not make sense to discuss the common characteristics of overdose, tolerance, withdrawal, and acute and chronic effects because the drugs are not related pharmacologically. However, we felt that it was important to reference these drugs as a separate class because of the wide media coverage of club drugs. We will refer to the most appropriate pharmacological classification for each drug, and you can refer to the characteristics in the designated section.

Rohypnol (roofies) is a benzodiazepine (CNS depressant) that is illegal in the United States, but widely prescribed in Europe as a sleeping pill. When used in combination with alcohol, Rohypnol produces disinhibition and amnesia. Rohypnol has become known as the "date rape" drug because of reported instances in which women have been unknowingly given the drug while drinking. When women are sexually assaulted after having been given Rohypnol, they cannot easily remember the events surrounding the incident.

MDMA (ecstasy) has the properties of the CNS stimulants and hallucinogens. It is taken in tablet form primarily, but can also be found in powder and liquid forms. It is relatively inexpensive ($10 to $20 per pill) and long lasting. Ecstasy is primarily used by youth and college-age adults. The euphoric effects include rushes of exhilaration and the sensation of understanding and accepting others. Some people experience nausea, and depression may be experienced following use. Deaths have been reported from ecstasy use primarily as a result of severe dehydration from dancing for long periods without drinking water. Ecstasy can be used compulsively and become psychologically addictive.

Ketamine (K or special K) is generally considered to be a hallucinogen. It is used as a veterinary anesthetic and is usually cooked into a white powder from its liquid form and snorted. The euphoric effect of ketamine involves dissociative anesthetics or separating perception from sensation. Users report feeling "floaty" or outside their body. Higher doses expand this experience. They may have some numbness in extremities. Ketamine is very dangerous in combination with depressants because higher doses depress respiration and breathing. Frequent use may lead to mental disorders due to the hallucinogenic properties of the drug. Psychological dependence also occurs in frequent users.

GHB (gamma hydroxybutyrate) is actually a synthetic steroid originally sold over-the-counter in health food stores as a body-building aid. GHB is usually sold as an odorless liquid that has a slight salty taste. The effects are similar to CNS depressants, with low doses resulting in euphoria, relaxation, and happiness. However, higher doses can cause dizziness, drowsiness, vomiting, muscle spasms, and loss of consciousness. Overdoses can result in coma or death, as can mixing GHB with other CNS depressants such as alcohol. Physical dependence can occur.

Other drugs, such as LSD, PCP, mescaline, and marijuana, are sometimes classified as club drugs. However, because these drugs have a wider use, we have discussed them in other drug classifications.

DRUGS USED IN THE TREATMENT OF MENTAL DISORDERS

Mental health professionals will work with clients who are taking a variety of legally prescribed drugs to treat many mental disorders. These drugs generally have little or no euphoric effects and, therefore, are not used for recreational purposes. However, it is certainly important for helping professionals to have some familiarity with the uses and effects of these drugs.

Drugs Used in the Treatment of Psychotic Disorders

Antipsychotic or neuroleptic drugs are used in the treatment of schizophrenia and other psychotic disorders. These major tranquilizers produce psychomotor slowing, emotional quieting, and an indifference to external stimuli. Although these drugs are called "tranquilizers," the effects are not euphoric or pleasant. Therefore, they are not drugs of abuse. The phenothiazines (Thorazine, Stelazine, Prolixin, Mellaril) and nonphenothiazines (Navane, Haldol) control agitation and hallucinations. Disturbed thinking and behavior is reduced. These effects have allowed many schizophrenic individuals to live in noninstitutional settings and to function more effectively. However, if the drugs are discontinued, the psychotic symptoms reappear. The drugs do not produce tolerance or physical or psychological dependence. Acute side effects include dry mouth and Parkinson-like symptoms such as disordered motor movements, slow motor movements, and underactivity. Chronic effects include repetitive, involuntary movements of the mouth and tongue, trunk, and extremities. Massive overdoses are usually not lethal.

A new generation of antipsychotics is now on the market. These drugs include Risperdal, Zyprexa, Clozaril, Seroquel, and Zeldox. They have fewer side effects than the earlier drugs.

Drugs Used in the Treatment of Affective Disorders

Antidepressant drugs elevate mood, increase physical activity, improve appetite, reduce insomnia, and reduce suicidal ideation in most depressed clients. They are used for the treatment of acute and chronic depression. There are three types of antidepressant drugs. The MAO (monoamine oxidase) inhibitors (Nardil, Parnate) are used infrequently today because these drugs can raise blood pressure if foods with tyramine (cheeses, herring, Chianti wine) are consumed. The tricyclics (Tofranil, Elavil, Sinequan) were widely used as antidepressants until the development of the "second-generation" antidepressants (Prozac, Luvox, Paxil, Zoloft). These drugs, although no more effective than the tricyclics, have a more rapid onset of effect and fewer adverse side effects. The tricyclics may take 2 to 3 weeks to produce the desired effects, whereas the newer drugs take about 1 week. This time difference can be critical with depressed clients. The tricyclics can produce cardiac problems and potentiate the effects of alcohol. Lethal overdoses are also possible. The media has widely publicized claims that Prozac has caused homicidal or suicidal behavior, but no cause-and-effect relationship has been scientifically established. However, these drugs have warnings for adolescents as there has been an established relationship between the use of antidepressants and the risk of suicidality in youth (Hammad, Laughren, & Racoosin, 2006). Second-generation antidepressants have also been used in the treatment of obsessive-compulsive disorder and panic disorders.

Lithium is used in the treatment of bipolar disorder. It is an antimanic, rather than an antidepressant, drug. Clients who take lithium must be closely monitored, since high concentrations can cause muscle rigidity, coma, and death.

The treatment of panic attacks has included antianxiety agents (benzodiazepines) that were discussed in the Central Nervous System Depressants section of this chapter (Librium, Valium, Xanax, Ativan). However, these drugs are dependence-producing and are abused. Nonbenzodiazepines that are used to treat panic disorders but are noneuphoric include Atarax, BuSpar, and many antidepressants.

Drugs Used in the Treatment of Attention Deficit Disorder

There has been a great deal of attention directed toward children and adults who have attention deficit disorder. This condition may exist with or without hyperactivity and is characterized by distractibility, inability to concentrate, short attention span, and impulsivity. It has been found that Ritalin, Cylert, and amphetamines (e.g., Adderall) reduce many of these symptoms. Ritalin and amphetamines have a rapid onset of effect and a short duration, although these drugs now can be purchased in time-release form so they can be taken once a day. Cylert is longer acting but also takes longer to work. These drugs are CNS stimulants and can be abused. The use of stimulants to control the symptoms of attention deficit disorder has always seemed paradoxical. However, it may be that this disorder is due to unfocused electrical activity in the brain, and the stimulant drugs may improve the ability of the individual to concentrate and focus. Rather than calming the person down, the affected client is simply better able to focus his or her energy, concentrate, and reduce attention to extraneous stimuli. This may also reduce the anxiety that often accompanies attention deficit disorder.

Because these drugs are CNS stimulants, there are the associated side effects of appetite suppression, sleep disruption, and growth disturbance when these drugs are continuously used by preadolescents. A small number of individuals experience lethargy and emotional blunting. If these symptoms occur, the physician should immediately be contacted to adjust the dose or to prescribe a different drug.

A newer drug to treat attention deficit disorder is atomoxetine, marketed as Strattera. This is a nonstimulant drug that does not seem to have abuse potential. This makes the drug desirable for adolescents who may abuse drugs such as Ritalin, Cylert, or Adderall. Strattera takes longer to work than drugs such as Ritalin, where the effect is very rapid.

It should also be mentioned that these drugs should not be prescribed to control unruly behavior in children. Attention deficit disorder should be diagnosed only after a careful multidisciplinary assessment. The best protocol to evaluate the efficacy of medication is a double-blind procedure in which neither the school nor parent is aware when a placebo or active drug has been taken. Behavior should be observed at school and at home, and the case manager can then determine whether medication will be helpful.

There has been speculation that children with ADHD who are treated with stimulant drugs would be more likely to develop problems with alcohol or other drugs later in life. However, in a meta-analysis of studies, Wilens, Faraone, Biederman, and Gunawardene (2003) found that ADHD children treated with stimulant drugs are *less* likely to develop substance abuse problems later in life than ADHD children who do not take medication.

MyCounselingLab for Addictions/Substance Abuse

Try the Topic 2 Assignments: *The Major Substances of Abuse and the Body.*

Summary

- The federal Controlled Substances Act classifies drugs into five schedules based on the addictive potential and medical uses of the drug.
- Psychoactive drugs mimic natural, pleasurable behaviors by stimulating neurotransmitters in the reward center of the brain.
- The classifications of drugs include CNS depressants (alcohol, minor tranquilizers), CNS stimulants (cocaine, methamphetamine), opioids (heroin, pain pills), hallucinogens (LSD, magic mushrooms), cannabinols (marijuana), inhalants and volatile hydrocarbons, anabolic steroids, and club drugs (ecstasy).
- Drugs are used to treat various mental disorders such as psychotic disorders, affective disorders (depression, anxiety), and ADHD.

Additional Reading

Abadinsky, H. (2011). *Drug abuse: An introduction* (8th ed.). Chicago: Nelson-Hall.

Hanson, G., & Venturelli, P. J. (2014). *Drugs and society* (12th ed.). Boston: Jones and Bartlett.

Inaba, D. S., & Cohen, W. E. (2014). *Uppers, downers, all arounders: Physical and mental effects of psychoactive drugs* (8th ed.). Ashland, OR: Cinemed.

Inciardi, J. A., & McElrath, K. (eds.). (2015). *The American drug scene: Readings in a global context.* (7th ed.). Los Angeles: Roxbury.

Julien, R. M., Advokat, C. D., & Comaty, J. E. (2014). *A primer of drug action: A comprehensive guide to the actions, uses, and side effects of psychoactive drugs* (13th ed.). New York: Worth.

Internet Resources

Comprehensive Drug Abuse Prevention and Control Act
http://www.deadiversion.usdoj.gov/21cfr/21usc/index.html

Facts about specific drugs
nida.nih.gov/drugpages.html

Science of addiction
drugabuse.gov/scienceofaddiction/

Drug use surveys

National Household Survey on Drug Use and Health
http://www.samhsa.gov/data/population-data-nsduh

Monitoring the Future
monitoringthefuture.org/index.html

Further Discussion

1. Review the three case examples at the beginning of the chapter. From the information provided, which drugs or drug classifications do you think each person is struggling with?

2. Do you agree with the classification of marijuana as a Schedule I drug? Why or why not?

3. Compare the monthly rate of use of alcohol for minors to the monthly rate of use of illicit drugs for 8th, 10th, and 12th graders (from the Monitoring the Future website). What conclusions do you reach, and what are the implications?

4. Which classification of drugs is the most dangerous in your opinion? What are the public policy implications of your view?

CHAPTER 3

Models of Addiction

CASE EXAMPLES

1. Bill, a bartender, was diagnosed as alcoholic at the age of 50. He was drinking more than a fifth of whiskey a day. Of his own volition, he went to a treatment program that used aversive conditioning techniques (see Chapter 8). At the time he entered treatment, his liver functioning was at about 20% of normal. In other words, if he had continued to drink much longer, he would have died. After completing the program, Bill returned to his job as a bartender. He never attended an Alcoholics Anonymous (AA) meeting or returned to the treatment program for follow-up. Bill once said, "I'll drink myself to death rather than go back to that (treatment center) place." In 19 years, he never had a slip or relapse. Bill finally died of lung cancer, because he could not quit smoking.

2. Loretta, a 30-year-old woman, was on probation for possession and distribution of methamphetamine. She lived with a man who used drugs and who was physically abusive to her and to her daughter. Another daughter had been removed from her custody. She lost her license to work in her profession because of her felony conviction. After her "boyfriend" was sent to prison, she found a job and a new place to live and was on the road to regaining custody of her other daughter. However, a random urinalysis by her probation officer came up dirty, and she was placed in an inpatient treatment program as an alternative to prison. Loretta lost her job, home, and custody of her children. Before this relapse, she had been sober for six months and was attending Narcotics Anonymous (NA) meetings.

3. Marvin, a 63-year-old man, had been a heavy drinker for 40 years. He was retired and relatively healthy. He developed a respiratory illness that required prolonged use of a medication that affected liver functioning. Marvin was told that he could not drink alcohol while taking the medication and that he was to take the medication for 1 year. His physician suggested that his withdrawal from alcohol be medically supervised because of his prolonged and heavy use. Marvin rejected this suggestion, discontinued his alcohol use, and has been clean and sober with no slips for 10 years. He has never attended an AA meeting or any other form of treatment.

4. Hector, a 30-year-old man, began using alcohol and other drugs at the age of 13. He was in street gangs, involved in crimes, and incarcerated as a juvenile. Hector was placed in a drug treatment program at the age of 16 and attended NA meetings after treatment. He remained sober for about 6 months, at which time he again began to use cocaine, marijuana, and alcohol. At age 23, he married, had a child, and discontinued his heavy use. He continues to use alcohol and marijuana on an irregular basis. Hector is a successful officer in a small company, although he cannot read or write at a functional level.

⑤ Rebecca is currently 43 years old and has been sober for 7 years. She reported that her husband expressed concern about her level of alcohol use before their marriage and that she "just decided to stop." Rebecca did not go through any treatment program, nor has she attended any AA meetings. She says that she has problems doing anything on a moderate basis, and, as a result, she has to monitor her eating behavior and work habits. Rebecca says, "I can't eat just a couple of M&Ms. If I start, I'll keep eating until they are all gone." She likes to drink nonalcoholic beer and wine, saying "It makes me feel like a grown-up."

⑥ Salvador is in his mid-60s. When he was in his 20s, he was addicted to heroin. Salvador was arrested for distribution and possession of drugs and spent some time in federal prison. After being released, he entered a faith-based, residential treatment program and has never used heroin again. Salvador drinks alcohol moderately.

In January 2011, a man named Jared Lee Loughner went to a public event held by Congressional Representative Gabrielle Giffords in Tucson, Arizona. Mr. Loughner opened fire with a semiautomatic gun, seriously wounding Representative Giffords and killing six people, including a federal judge and a 9-year-old girl. In the days and weeks following this horrible event, speculation regarding Mr. Loughner and the reason why he committed this act ran rampant. Mental health professionals thought he was suffering from paranoid schizophrenia. Law enforcement described him as a cold-blooded killer. Others believed that he was driven by political motivations. Some pundits focused on his parents and wondered if they were to blame. There were even some religious leaders who thought he was possessed by the devil. Whatever explanation makes the most sense probably depends on a person's values and beliefs, formal and informal training, and experience. However, it is important to critically examine the explanations of the behavior of someone such as Jared Lee Loughner, because different explanations have different implications for the proper method to deal with him. For example, if you believe that he is possessed by evil spirits, there may be a spiritual method to treat him (i.e., exorcism). If you accept the explanation that he is a cold-blooded killer (i.e., a sociopath), then the appropriate method may be firm punishment for his actions. If his behavior is due to a traumatic childhood, he may deserve our sympathy and be in need of therapeutic interventions. Finally, if Loughner's behavior is due to a serious mental illness caused by a chemical imbalance, then he is not responsible for his behavior and may need medication to manage his condition.

You can see that values and beliefs play a role in whichever explanation you accept. If you believe in evil spirits, this explanation may appeal to you. Formal and informal training will have an effect, becausee you may have taken some courses in sociology or social psychology and been taught that traumatic childhood experiences are related to violent behavior in adulthood. Maybe you work in law enforcement and have directly seen the victims of brutality and, from these experiences, have come to believe that the perpetrators must be lacking in conscience to commit such crimes.

However, all of these explanations for the abnormal behavior of a Jared Lee Loughner may have some validity. He may have a spiritual deficit, lack a conscience in the manner in which most of us understand this concept, be influenced by his childhood experiences, and have some form of physiological abnormality. The "amount" of explanation of his behavior may not be equally divided among these factors (they may not have equal weight in explaining Loughner's behavior), and determining the most appropriate course of action might depend on many different variables. For example, the brutality of the crime, Loughner's lack of remorse, and his potential for future violence may lead to a decision to incarcerate a person such as Loughner, no matter what the "true" explanations are for his behavior.

The alcohol and other drugs (AOD) field has also been characterized by a variety of explanations for the same behavior. This is certainly not unusual in the mental health or medical field. However, the fervor and inflexibility with which some proponents of certain models of addiction adhere to their models has produced controversy in this field. Furthermore, the use of AOD interests and elicits extensive involvement from the legal system, business, government, the religious community as well as from the medical and mental health fields. The differing goals and orientations of these disciplines have resulted in sharp differences regarding the explanation of problematic use of AOD. Consequently, the manner in which those people with AOD problems are dealt has also been a controversial issue. We will discuss some of the various "models" or explanations of addiction, giving particular attention to the popular "disease concept." Also, we will discuss some cases that illustrate that one explanation alone for addictive behavior may be insufficient.

Before we discuss the various models, it is important to understand that these are models of *addiction*, not models that explain AOD use. Most people begin AOD use in adolescence or early adulthood. The reasons why someone starts using AOD are varied and include curiosity, peer pressure, availability, role modeling, and rebelliousness. In this chapter, we are interested in understanding why some of the large number of adolescents/young adults who begin to use AOD progress to addiction, rather than the reasons why someone starts using AOD.

AT A GLANCE

Moral Model: AOD use is a choice; addiction is a symptom of moral deficiency and/or lack of willpower.

Sociocultural Models: Cultural, ethnic, religious, and environmental conditions are causal factors in addiction.

Psychological Models: Addiction is a secondary symptom of underlying psychological disorders; AOD use is learned and reinforced behavior.

Disease Model: Addiction is a primary, chronic, and progressive disease, probably caused by a genetic predisposition.

Biopsychosocial Model: Addiction is the result of multiple, interacting variables, the strength of which vary between individuals.

THE MORAL MODEL

The moral model explains addiction as a consequence of personal choice. Individuals are viewed as making decisions to use AOD in a problematic manner and as being capable of making other choices. This model has been adopted by certain religious groups as well as by the legal system. Drunkenness is viewed as sinful behavior by some religious groups and the use of alcohol is prohibited by certain religions (e.g., the Mormon Church). From this perspective, religious or spiritual intervention would be necessary to change behavior. Years ago, we conducted an AOD workshop for clergy, and the moral model was strongly advocated by many of the members who were present. Many saw acceptance of a particular religious persuasion as the necessary step to overcome AOD problems.

A 1988 Supreme Court decision found that crimes committed by an alcoholic were willful misconduct and not the result of a disease (Miller & Hester, 2003). Certainly, the manner in which states deal with drunk driving violations may relate to the moral model. In states where violators are not assessed for AOD problems and are not diverted to treatment, the moral model guides policy. If excessive alcohol use is the result of personal choice, then violators should be punished.

The moral model is a common way that the general public has of conceptualizing alcoholics and addicts. For example, when you see a homeless person who is obviously affected by alcohol or other drugs, do you experience disgust, laugh at him or her, or express a moral judgment?

Recovery advocates have noted that the moral model of addiction has contributed to creating a stigma about addiction and addicts. This stigma may cause barriers to getting help. For example, if you are having problems with alcohol or other drugs and if those around you believe that alcoholics and addicts are weak-willed and/or immoral, then you are more likely to try to solve the problem yourself or hide it than you would be to seek outside help.

Students frequently express attraction to the Moral Model because, they argue, people make a choice to pick up a drink or a drug. This is an example of using the Moral Model to explain the initiation of AOD use rather than explaining addiction. It would be hard to disagree with the notion that a 17 year old who has a beer at a party has made a choice to use AOD. However, it is a big stretch to suggest that an impulsive decision that most 17 year olds make at some point explains an addictive disorder that occurs many years later.

Any discussion about the Moral Model of addiction generally revolves around the concept of "willpower." The argument would be that a person who is using AOD in a problematic manner should exercise their willpower to modify or stop their AOD use. It is hard to dispute this notion unless you have personal experience with this. That is one of the reasons why we ask our students to abstain from a substance or behavior for the semester. The vast majority of students are not successful abstaining using just "willpower."

SOCIOCULTURAL MODELS OF ADDICTION

Although the moral model explains addiction as a matter of personal choice caused by spiritual or character deficiencies, other explanations of addiction focus on factors that are external to the individual, such as cultural, religious, family, and peer variables or psychological factors. With regard to sociocultural factors, Westermeyer (1999) conducted a thorough meta-analysis of the literature in this area. He defined populations at risk for addiction in special sociocultural settings such as youth in industrial societies, immigrants and refugees, poverty and affluence, and child rearing and culture.

According to Westermeyer (1999), adolescence in the mid-1990s developed as a period of self-doubt and social anxiety as a result of an industrialized society where adolescents had little to contribute. In comparison, adolescence in an agrarian society did not exist as it does today. Children worked when they were physically able. For the adolescent in an industrial society, AOD helped alleviate self-doubt and anxiety while enhancing social interaction. Obviously, not all adolescents in our industrial society became addicts but this could help explain the initiation of heavy AOD use among some members of this group.

Contrary to what might be expected, immigrants and refugees have low rates of substance abuse following relocation, but rates begin to rise after several years (Westermeyer, 1999). In some instances, substances abused in the country of origin are introduced to the United States. For example, opium smoking was virtually nonexistent in this country until it was introduced by Southeast Asian immigrants. In other cases, younger immigrants begin to use and abuse substances that were not common in the country of origin to fit in and because they and their families may not be knowledgeable about the dangers of these unfamiliar substances.

Westermeyer (1999) noted that both poverty and affluence can impact substance use and abuse. It is quite understandable how poverty can lead to substance abuse as a way of coping with the stress of everyday life. In addition, participation in illicit drug dealing may be one of the most readily available methods to make money without education or training. However, rising disposable income is also associated with increasing AOD use. The reasons are not clear, although one would expect that people who are deterred from purchasing AOD when money is tight feel greater freedom to indulge when money is sufficient to cover basic needs.

People who are involved in cultural and religious groups that discourage or prohibit AOD use experience a low rate of addiction as long as they remain in the group. A low rate of addiction is also the case among groups that have culturally sanctioned moderate AOD use that begins in childhood or early adolescence. Obviously, cultures and families who model and support heavy AOD use are much more likely to have children who develop AOD problems.

PSYCHOLOGICAL MODELS OF ADDICTION

Although sociocultural or external factors have been used to explain addiction, psychological explanations of addiction also exist. It is beyond the goals of this text to discuss each of these theories, but we will spend some time on the most widely held psychological explanations of addiction. Perhaps the most accepted view, particularly by those outside the addiction field, is that the problematic use of alcohol and other drugs is secondary to some other psychological problem or condition. The primary psychological problem causes emotional pain, and alcohol and other drugs serve to temporarily relieve this pain. For example, a woman was sexually molested as a child by a relative. She does not tell anyone, or her story is not believed, and she does not receive any assistance. The woman experiences anger, guilt, embarrassment, and anxiety as a result of the experience and gravitates toward alcohol and other drugs to relieve these uncomfortable feelings. Another example is the person who suffers from endogenous depression and self-medicates with stimulants to relieve the constant symptoms of depression.

Related to the view that AOD problems are secondary to other psychological problems is the question about whether an alcoholic or addictive personality exists. Clearly, alcoholics and drug addicts who seem to be free of any identified psychological problems before their problematic use patterns do exist. Proponents of psychological explanations of addiction believe that there may be an "addictive personality" that could be identified and that would explain why individuals with AOD addictions often have problems with nondrug addictive behavior (e.g., gambling, food, work, sex) following successful recovery from their drug of choice. However, this effort to identify the "addictive personality" has largely been unsuccessful. Szalavitz (2015), in describing recent advances in discovering genetic components of addiction, said that this line of research has found that the notion of an addictive personality is a myth.

Social learning theory is another psychological theory that has been used to explain addictive behavior. As a leading proponent of this theory, Alan Marlatt, has described addictive behaviors as a category of bad habits, which include problem drinking, smoking, substance abuse, overeating, and compulsive gambling (Marlatt, 1985). In this conceptualization, drug use is initiated by environmental stressors or modeling by others and is reinforced by the immediate effects of the drug on the feelings generated by the stressor(s) or by acknowledgment or recognition from role models with perceived status. One example would be the case of the sexually molested woman we discussed earlier. From a social learning viewpoint, this woman used alcohol and other drugs to avoid the unpleasant emotions generated by her molestation (environmental stressor). Because alcohol or other drug use provides immediate (although temporary) relief from these negative feelings, its use is reinforced. Another typical example is the individual who uses alcohol to "unwind" after a stressful day at work. Since tolerance to alcohol develops, over time this person must use an increasing amount of alcohol to experience the reinforcing effects of alcohol on tension. A "bad habit" is developed.

The first author has a vivid recollection of his initial experience with alcohol and how modeling contributed to this experience and subsequent alcohol use. A wide variety of alcohol was available in his house, and he saw it used daily with few observed negative consequences. One night when he was 12, he was alone at home and began experimenting with a variety of alcoholic beverages. He became quite ill. Although his parents were upset, they also talked and laughed somewhat about their first experiences with becoming sick from alcohol. He also received a lot of attention from his friends when he told them about the incident. Therefore, in spite of some negative consequences (nausea and parental anger), he received sufficient positive reinforcement to increase the probability of repeated use.

In a social learning model, the sociocultural factors we discussed play a role in determining what type of drug is used, when it is used, and how it is used. For example, social use of alcohol may be acceptable, but drinking alone may be perceived as deviant. Snorting or smoking drugs may be within the behavior parameters of a social group, but intravenous use of drugs may result in ostracism. Furthermore, the psychological state of the person is also important. For example, if a child sees the parents using alcohol excessively in social situations, the child may be more likely to see drug use as acceptable in a social situation as a means of creating social comfort and fun. In contrast, imagine that the father in a family isolates himself and drinks in response to negative emotions. The child may see drug use as the appropriate reaction to negative emotions. The psychological state of the individual would be important because social discomfort might elicit the desire for alcohol or other drugs in the first example, whereas negative emotions would elicit this desire in the second example.

Eventually, as the individual uses more and more, a physiological state of dependence occurs, and, consequently, he or she experiences withdrawal symptoms if the drug is removed. The use of the drug to relieve withdrawal symptoms is highly reinforcing, since an immediate and effective reduction or elimination of symptoms occurs. The social learning model of addiction has been widely used in the development of relapse prevention strategies, a topic that will be discussed in detail in Chapter 10.

Disease Concept of Addiction

This popular and controversial model of addiction is credited to E. M. Jellinek, who presented a comprehensive disease model of alcoholism (Jellinek, 1960; see Figure 3.1 depicting Jellinek's Curve). This model has become an implicit component of the AA and NA programs as well as a guiding model for many treatment programs. The World Health Organization acknowledged alcoholism as a medical problem in 1951, and the American Medical Association declared that alcoholism was a treatable illness in 1956. Following Jellinek's work, the American Psychiatric Association began to use the term *disease* to describe alcoholism in 1965, and the American Medical Association followed in 1966. As with many concepts and theoretical models in the addiction field, the disease concept was originally applied to alcoholism and has been generalized to addiction to other drugs.

The disease of addiction is viewed as a primary disease. That is, it exists in and of itself and is not secondary to some other condition. This is in contrast to the psychological models discussed earlier in which addictive behavior is seen as secondary to some psychological condition. In this very early work, Jellinek recognized that alcoholics gave the impression that there was an "alcoholic personality," but these were secondary behaviors superimposed over many different personality types.

Jellinek (1952) also described the progressive stages of the disease of alcoholism and the symptoms that characterize each stage. The early stage, or prodromal phase, is characterized by an increasing tolerance to alcohol, blackouts, sneaking and gulping drinks, and guilt feelings about

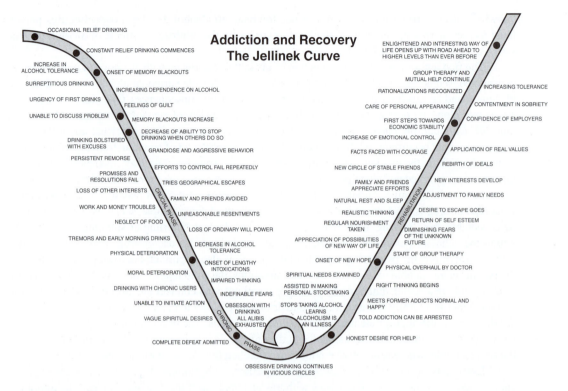

**Addiction and Recovery
The Jellinek Curve**

OCCASIONAL RELIEF DRINKING

CONSTANT RELIEF DRINKING COMMENCES

INCREASE IN ALCOHOL TOLERANCE

ONSET OF MEMORY BLACKOUTS

SURREPTITIOUS DRINKING

INCREASING DEPENDENCE ON ALCOHOL

URGENCY OF FIRST DRINKS

FEELINGS OF GUILT

UNABLE TO DISCUSS PROBLEM

MEMORY BLACKOUTS INCREASE

DECREASE OF ABILITY TO STOP DRINKING WHEN OTHERS DO SO

DRINKING BOLSTERED WITH EXCUSES

GRANDIOSE AND AGGRESSIVE BEHAVIOR

PERSISTENT REMORSE

EFFORTS TO CONTROL FAIL REPEATEDLY

PROMISES AND RESOLUTIONS FAIL

TRIES GEOGRAPHICAL ESCAPES

LOSS OF OTHER INTERESTS

FAMILY AND FRIENDS AVOIDED

WORK AND MONEY TROUBLES

UNREASONABLE RESENTMENTS

NEGLECT OF FOOD

LOSS OF ORDINARY WILL POWER

TREMORS AND EARLY MORNING DRINKS

DECREASE IN ALCOHOL TOLERANCE

PHYSICAL DETERIORATION

ONSET OF LENGTHY INTOXICATIONS

MORAL DETERIORATION

IMPAIRED THINKING

DRINKING WITH CHRONIC USERS

INDEFINABLE FEARS

UNABLE TO INITIATE ACTION

OBSESSION WITH DRINKING

VAGUE SPIRITUAL DESIRES

ALL ALIBIS EXHAUSTED

COMPLETE DEFEAT ADMITTED

CRUCIAL PHASE

CHRONIC PHASE

OBSESSIVE DRINKING CONTINUES IN VICIOUS CIRCLES

STOPS TAKING ALCOHOL

LEARNS ALCOHOLISM IS AN ILLNESS

TOLD ADDICTION CAN BE ARRESTED

HONEST DESIRE FOR HELP

MEETS FORMER ADDICTS NORMAL AND HAPPY

RIGHT THINKING BEGINS

PHYSICAL OVERHAUL BY DOCTOR

START OF GROUP THERAPY

SPIRITUAL NEEDS EXAMINED

ASSISTED IN MAKING PERSONAL STOCKTAKING

APPRECIATION OF POSSIBILITIES OF NEW WAY OF LIFE

ONSET OF NEW HOPE

REGULAR NOURISHMENT TAKEN

DIMINISHING FEARS OF THE UNKNOWN FUTURE

RETURN OF SELF ESTEEM

REALISTIC THINKING

DESIRE TO ESCAPE GOES

NATURAL REST AND SLEEP

ADJUSTMENT TO FAMILY NEEDS

FAMILY AND FRIENDS APPRECIATE EFFORTS

NEW INTERESTS DEVELOP

NEW CIRCLE OF STABLE FRIENDS

REBIRTH OF IDEALS

FACTS FACED WITH COURAGE

APPLICATION OF REAL VALUES

INCREASE OF EMOTIONAL CONTROL

FIRST STEPS TOWARDS ECONOMIC STABILITY

CONFIDENCE OF EMPLOYERS

CARE OF PERSONAL APPEARANCE

CONTENTMENT IN SOBRIETY

RATIONALIZATIONS RECOGNIZED

INCREASING TOLERANCE

GROUP THERAPY AND MUTUAL HELP CONTINUE

ENLIGHTENED AND INTERESTING WAY OF LIFE OPENS UP WITH ROAD AHEAD TO HIGHER LEVELS THAN EVER BEFORE

REHABILITATION

FIGURE 3.1 The Jellinek Curve of addiction and recovery.

drinking and related behaviors. The next stage, the middle or crucial phase, is defined by a loss of control over drinking, personality changes, a loss of friends and jobs, and a preoccupation with protecting the supply of alcohol. The issue of "loss of control" has come to be a central defining characteristic of alcoholism and one of the more controversial aspects of the disease concept. We will examine this issue when discussing criticisms of the disease concept. The late stage, or chronic phase, is characterized by morning drinking, violations of ethical standards, tremors, and hallucinations.

It is important to conceptualize these stages as progressive. In other words, the stages proceed in sequence and, in the disease model of addiction, are not reversible. Therefore, an individual does not go from the middle stage back to the early stage of alcoholism. The rate at which this progression occurs depends upon factors such as age, drug of choice, gender, and physiological predisposition (Royce, 1989). For example, adolescents progress more rapidly than adults, females faster than males, and users of stimulants more quickly than alcohol users (Royce, 1989). Proponents of the disease concept also do not believe that the progression of addiction disease is affected by a period of sobriety, no matter how long the period of sobriety lasts. David Ohlms (1995), a physician, claimed that an alcoholic with many years of sobriety who relapses will quickly return to a stage of a disease that would have existed if he or she had been drinking during sobriety. Although there is only anecdotal evidence for this claim, it is widely believed in the Twelve Step movement and in traditional treatment settings.

Consistent with this concept (that the individual with addictive disease does not reverse the progression of the disease even with a prolonged period of sobriety) is the notion that addictive disease is chronic and incurable. That is, if an individual has this disease, it never goes away, and no drug or other treatment method will allow the alcoholic or addict to use again without the danger of a return to problematic use. One implication of this notion is that the only justifiable goal for the alcoholic or addict is abstinence, which is a critical part of Twelve Step programs such as AA. Furthermore, the idea that addiction is chronic and incurable is the underlying rationale for alcoholics and addicts who are maintaining sobriety for referring to themselves as "recovering" as opposed to "recovered" or "cured" (Royce, 1989).

In addition to the idea that abstinence must be the goal for those with addictive disease, other implications of the disease concept also exist. First, if addictive disease is progressive, chronic, and incurable, then it is logical to assume that a person with this condition who does not enter "recovery" will eventually die. Death occurs as a result of accidents or the physical effects of alcohol and other drugs over time. For example, consider the individual who, after many years of heavy drinking, develops liver disease. Eventually, he or she dies of liver failure. Is the cause of death liver failure or alcoholism? In the disease concept of addiction, these deaths are the result of untreated addiction.

A further implication of the disease concept of addiction is that, if a person has this disease and, for example, the drug of choice of the person is alcohol, the person will continue to exhibit all the symptoms of the disease if he or she discontinues the use of alcohol and begins to use some other drug. This is true no matter what the drug of choice is. Therefore, "drug switching" (an alcoholic stops drinking but starts smoking marijuana) will only lead to problems with the other drug or a return to the primary drug of choice. Complete abstinence from all mind-altering substances is the only solution.

Evidence to Support the Disease Concept

The evidence to support the disease concept is based on the similarity of alcoholism and drug addiction to other chronic diseases and on research on the brain chemistry and brain changes in addicts. McLellan, Lewis, O'Brien, and Kleber (2000) reviewed the literature on chronic illnesses, such as diabetes, asthma, and hypertension, and compared the characteristics of these diseases to addiction. They found that the genetic heritability, established by examining rates of diseases in identical versus fraternal twins, was very similar for alcoholism and drug addiction compared with the other chronic illnesses. In addition, response to treatment is similar. Left untreated, the condition of most alcoholics and drug addicts becomes worse. Remission is unusual. This also occurs with diabetes, asthma, and hypertension. McLellan et al. (2000) also showed that the percentages of clients who comply with treatment and the relapse rates of addiction and other chronic illnesses are the same. Addiction, diabetes, asthma, and hypertension are all conditions in which there is no "cure." However, all these problems can be managed through proper treatment, and this treatment must be followed for life.

McLellan et al. (2000) also discuss the issue of the "voluntary" nature of alcohol and other drug use. Again, they compare the choice to use alcohol and other drugs to other chronic illnesses. For example, diet, physical activity, and stress level are all factors affecting hypertension. These factors are all within voluntary control. However, what is not in voluntary control is the person's physiological response to these factors, and the physiological response is strongly influenced by genetic factors. Therefore, addiction is similar to other chronic diseases in that the management of the condition requires voluntary treatment compliance. However, the development of the disease is not due to choice, but to factors beyond voluntary control.

In addition, the National Institute on Drug Abuse (NIDA) has funded a great deal of research on the neuroscience of addiction. For example, Alan Leshner (2000), former director of NIDA, stated:

> Researchers have already identified some of the changes involved in two of the key phenomena associated with addiction: drug tolerance and drug craving. . . . we now know that drugs significantly increase the availability of dopamine, a neurotransmitter that activates the brain's pleasure circuits.

When cells are exposed to repeated surges of dopamine due to chronic drug abuse, they may eventually become less responsive to dopamine signals. . . . As for drug craving . . . researchers have shown that it is related to widespread alterations in brain activity, especially to changes in the nucleus accumbens area of the forebrain. (p. 1)

Critics of the Disease Concept

As we said earlier, the disease concept is controversial and not without critics. The two most famous critics are Stanton Peele and Herbert Fingarette, both of whom have written books (Fingarette, 1988; Peele, 1988) as well as articles disputing the disease concept of addiction. Some of their arguments will be summarized here.

Because the disease concept is widely attributed to Jellinek, much criticism has been directed at his research, which was the basis for his conclusions about the disease concept. Jellinek's data were gathered from questionnaires distributed to AA members through its newsletter, *The Grapevine*. Of 158 questionnaires returned, 60 were discarded because members had pooled and averaged their responses. Also, the study used no questionnaires from women. Jellinek himself acknowledged that his data were limited. Therefore, one might wonder why Jellinek's concept of the disease of alcoholism received such widespread acceptance. One reason is that the disease concept is consistent with the philosophy of AA, which is by far the largest organized group dedicated to help for alcoholics.

The progressive nature of addiction has also been criticized. George Vaillant (1983), a proponent of the disease concept, has suggested that the stages of alcoholism proposed by Jellinek do not follow an inevitable progression. He suggested that those who drink heavily often stay at this level or return to a lower rate of alcohol use as they mature. Furthermore, those who abuse alcohol also might progress to alcoholism or nonproblematic alcohol use. Royce (1989), another proponent of the disease model, has also acknowledged that the Jellinek steps are not uniformly predictable for each individual with an alcohol problem.

As we have seen, some of those with sympathetic views toward the disease model of addiction have recognized that the concept of a rigid and inevitable progression of stages is not consistent with reality in working with individuals with AOD problems. However, the issue of "loss of control" has been a more contentious one. The first step of the Twelve Steps of AA implies this loss of control: "We admitted that we were powerless over alcohol—that our lives had become unmanageable" (Alcoholics Anonymous World Services, 2009, p. 5).

Several arguments have been advanced to dispute the notion of loss of control. Fingarette (1988) pointed out that if alcoholics lack control only after first consuming alcohol, then they should have no difficulty abstaining. Obviously, however, alcoholics do have difficulty abstaining. If loss of control exists before the first drink (which would explain the difficulty in abstaining), it implies a difficulty in exercising self-control or willpower, which is a much different model of addiction. Furthermore, experimental studies have demonstrated that alcoholics do exert control over their drinking and that variables such as the amount of effort to get alcohol, the environment in which drinking occurs, the belief about what is being consumed, rewards, and the like influence how much is consumed by an alcoholic (Fingarette, 1988; Peele, 1988). In one classic study, Marlatt, Demming, and Reid (1973) divided alcoholics into four groups. One group believed that they were taste-testing three brands of a vodka-tonic beverage when they were actually drinking tonic water only. A second group believed that they were taste-testing tonic water only, when they were actually drinking vodka and tonic. The third group was correctly told they were drinking a vodka-tonic beverage, and the fourth group was correctly told they were drinking tonic water only. The results showed that it was the alcoholic's belief about what they were drinking that determined the amount they drank and not the actual alcohol content of the beverage they consumed. The alcoholics who expected tonic and got alcohol drank an almost identical amount to those alcoholics who expected and got tonic. Both of these groups drank considerably less than the groups who expected alcohol, and the alcoholics who received and expected alcohol drank nearly the same amount as those alcoholics who expected alcohol but got tonic.

Royce (1989) pointed out that an artificial laboratory setting can hardly be extrapolated to the real world and that the experimenters were too literal in interpreting the idea that one drink always leads to getting drunk. Loss of control has been modified to mean that the alcoholic or addict cannot predict the situations in which he or she will exercise control and the situations in which he or she will lose control. As an illustration, an alcoholic is at a bar having a drink. After that one drink, a man pulls a gun and tells the alcoholic he will shoot him if he has one more sip. With his life at risk, the alcoholic stops drinking, thus demonstrating voluntary control over drinking. Of course, the alcoholic will start drinking again as soon as the threat is removed.

The more realistic example involves an alcoholic who is drinking with friends after work. His child is in a school play and he promised to attend. Now, in situations like this, sometimes the alcoholic keeps his promise and shows up albeit a bit intoxicated. However, sometimes he does not show up. His intentions are always good but he doesn't know which times he will stop drinking and which times he won't. His family doesn't know either.

Advantages of the Disease Concept

Perhaps the greatest advantage to the articulation that addiction is a disease has been to remove the moral stigma attached to addiction and to replace it with an emphasis on treatment of an illness. We do not punish a person for having a disease; we provide assistance. In a more functional sense, defining addiction as a disease has also resulted in treatment coverage by insurance companies. Using medical terminology to describe addiction has also led to greater interest in scientific research. Few medical scientists would be interested in investigating the physiological correlates of a lack of willpower or to a moral deficiency. For the individual who has problems with alcohol or other drugs (and for the family as well), the concept of a disease removes much of the stigma and associated embarrassment, blame, and guilt. You would not feel guilty if you were diagnosed with diabetes and, therefore, a person with addictive disease need not feel guilty for having this disease. As we have said, people who believe that addiction is due to a lack of willpower or to a moral deficiency may avoid treatment because the admission of the need for help is an admission that some character flaw exists. Therefore, an acceptance of the disease concept may make it easier for some people to enter treatment. Another advantage of the disease concept is that it is clearly understandable to people and provides an explanatory construct for the differences in their alcohol and other drug-taking behavior compared with others. To reuse the analogy with diabetes, people with diabetes clearly understand that they cannot use certain foods in the same manner as those who do not have diabetes. If they do, there will be certain predictable consequences. Knowledge about the disease allows the alcoholic or addict to understand that he or she is physiologically different from others. In the same way that it may be unwise for the diabetic to eat a hot fudge sundae (in spite of the fact that friends may do so without consequences), the alcoholic learns that it would be unwise to drink (in spite of the fact that friends may do so without consequences). Finally, the disease concept has a logical treatment objective that follows from its precepts: abstinence. If you have a physiological condition that results in severe consequences when alcohol or other drugs are used, you can avoid these consequences by abstaining from alcohol or other drugs. If you attempt to use moderately, you will eventually lose control, progress through predictable stages, and suffer the consequences. Because most individuals who seek treatment for alcohol or other drug problems have experienced some negative consequences already, this argument can be compelling.

Disadvantages of the Disease Concept

As critics of the disease concept have pointed out, the orthodox precepts of the disease concept may not be accurate. The symptoms and stages are not inevitable and completely predictable, nor do they consistently result in loss of control. Therefore, individuals with alcohol or other drug problems who may need some form of intervention or treatment may avoid help because they do not fit the "disease model." For example, we were told by a substance abuse program counselor about an inquiry from a man whose girlfriend thought he had a drinking problem. Although he drank on a daily basis, his use of alcohol had not progressed in the past few years. When asked if he was having any financial, occupational, legal, or family problems, he said that he was not. Now certainly, denial may be at work here, but the point is that the intake counselor did not encourage the man to seek help because he did not fit the classic "disease" characteristics, whereas the program in which the counselor works is based on this model.

The notion that the disease concept removes responsibility from the alcoholic or addict for his or her behavior is frequently cited as a disadvantage of this model. Because the alcoholic or addict is "powerless" over the disease, inappropriate or even criminal behavior may be attributed to the "disease." Relapse may also be blamed on the disease. In other words, if an alcoholic believes the disease concept and the AA slogan "one drink away from a drunk," then a slip (return to use) may result in the alcoholic's giving up responsibility for maintaining sobriety and returning to a previous level of use because the slip is symptomatic of the loss of control. Proponents of the disease concept counter this argument by saying that the addict is not responsible for the disease but is completely responsible for recovery. In addition, court rulings have rarely allowed a defense of addiction for criminal behavior (Miller & Hester, 2003).

BIOPSYCHOSOCIAL MODEL OF ADDICTION

At the beginning of the chapter, we described six people we have known or worked with. Each has a history of heavy alcohol or other drug use.

Although we have changed the names of people, these cases are all real. We are not implying that they are typical or atypical, and we did not include those individuals who completed traditional treatment programs or use AA as a primary method of maintaining sobriety, although we know plenty of people who do so. These cases are meant to illustrate the concept that addiction may best be thought of as a multivariate syndrome. There are multiple forms of problematic AOD use that occur in multiple personality types, with a variety of consequences and differing responses to treatment.

Bill and Loretta had patterns of use that could well fit within the disease model of addiction. Bill's progression was very similar to that described by Jellinek (1952), but he responded to a treatment that was quite unlike the traditional models based on the disease concept. Loretta also continued to use in spite of having every reason to stop, which certainly seems like a loss of control.

In contrast, Marvin's drinking remained at a heavy but nonproblematic stage of use for many years with no apparent progression. In opposition to what might be expected, he had no physical or psychological problems discontinuing his use when faced with a strong motivation to stop. Hector, who seemed to have serious problems with alcohol and other drugs, reverted to moderate use when he matured and acquired responsibilities for others. His behavior could be explained from a social learning perspective. Rebecca seemed to demonstrate an "addictive personality." She constantly had to be aware of her characteristic of going overboard. Her use of nonalcoholic beer and wine is contrary to what is recommended by most treatment programs, but it worked for her. Salvador might be seen as being a disease concept addict whose recovery program was faith-based. However, his moderate use of alcohol would conflict with the disease concept. In Salvador's early social and cultural environment, heroin use was common. Perhaps these social and cultural variables help explain Salvador's heroin use in his early adulthood.

It's quite natural for treatment providers to develop a concept of addiction based on the clients they come in contact with. Helping professionals who work in substance abuse treatment programs see individuals who have had some pretty serious life problems as a result of their alcohol and other drug use. They are not likely to see individuals who have successfully discontinued their use on their own or through a nontraditional method, or to work with clients who interrupt their use patterns before they experience serious life problems. Finally, alcohol and other drug treatment providers do not usually see clients who are heavy users but who do not have life problems as a result of their use. Therefore, it is logical that those professionals who work in the substance abuse treatment field may develop a concept of addiction that is based on a biased sample. This is not to say that the disease concept does not fit many alcoholics and addicts or that traditional treatment approaches and Twelve Step recovery programs are not useful. Certainly, as we illustrated with Bill and Loretta, many alcoholics and addicts fit the characteristics of the disease concept, and many, many people have been helped by traditional treatment programs based on the disease concept and using AA and NA. We are arguing that readers should also consider other explanations for problematic alcohol and other drug use and a variety of treatment options. Interestingly, Jellinek (1960), who is credited with developing the disease concept, identified five different types of problem drinking patterns, only two of which were thought to demonstrate the characteristics of the disease. This seems to be ignored by many disease concept proponents.

People begin AOD use on an experimental basis for lots of different reasons. They continue using because such outcomes as reduction of pain, experience of euphoria, social recognition acceptance, and/or success reinforce their use. Some people progress to abuse and addiction. Why?

It is certainly possible that progression in some people is due to a genetic predisposition and that this genetic predisposition may be understood through physiological differences. It is also plausible that personality characteristics may explain some progression, or that physical or emotional pain may explain some problematic use, or environmental circumstances may provide answers. Any combination of these factors may also be possible. With a certain client, we may find that the reduction of chronic back pain leads to a reduction in alcohol use. Another client (as with Hector) may have a change in environmental factors that leads to a change in use. Through therapy, another client may come to a greater self-awareness with regard to personality characteristics, and thus modify his or her use. With other clients, reduction of pain, change of environment, and self-knowledge does not affect their use at all.

In an effort to reflect the multivariate nature of addiction, many authors now refer to the "biopsychosocial" model of addiction (e.g., Donovan, 2005). In the biopsychosocial model of addiction, the interactions of biological, psychological, cognitive, social, developmental, and environmental variables are considered to "explain" addiction. Therefore, important factors in the treatment of a particular client are not ignored when all variables are considered. For example, the parents of Loretta (our methamphetamine user) were alcoholics. She was sexually and physically abused as a child. Her parents introduced her to alcohol at the age of 9. She consistently became involved with men who abused alcohol and other drugs. As you can imagine, all of these factors would be crucial in understanding Loretta's addiction and in designing a treatment program for her.

The biopsychosocial model is *not* a combination of the other models. It does consider the variables that are a part of other models. For example, psychological variables are certainly part of the biopsychosocial model. In the biopsychosocial model, we are less concerned with the "cause" of addiction and more inclined to view each person as having a combination of factors that may require treatment attention. The relative importance of each variable is different for each person.

We suggest that mental health professionals, whether or not they work with substance abuse problems, thoroughly assess clients (see Chapter 6), develop multiple hypotheses to explain the client's AOD problem based on the assessment, avoid forcing the client to fit a rigid or preconceived notion of addiction, and use a variety of treatment methods and interventions (see Chapter 8) evolving from the assessment, hypotheses, and most important, the needs of the client.

MyCounselingLab for Addictions/Substance Abuse

Try the Topic 3 Assignments: *Etiological Theories of Substance Abuse.*

Summary

- The moral model is not widely accepted among professionals and discourages people from seeking treatment.
- Sociocultural and psychological models explain addiction as a result of environmental or personality factors.
- The disease model is widely accepted because of its medical orientation and because abstinence is logically related to the model.

- The disease model has helped to reduce the stigma of addiction and has enlisted the support of the medical community in treatment.
- A disadvantage of the disease model is that some addicts blame their behavior on the "disease."
- The biopsychosocial model incorporates all the relevant variables in the etiology and treatment of addiction.

Internet Resources

Disease concept of addiction
http://www.addictionpro.com/article/disease-concept-addiction-revisited

Addiction as a brain disease
drugabuse.gov/scienceofaddiction

Criticism of the disease concept
peele.net/index.html

Further Discussion

1. Think about some celebrity you have heard about who has an AOD problem. Given what you know about this person, use different models of addiction to explain the celebrity's condition.

2. Which model of addiction appeals to you the most? Why?
3. Using each of the case examples at the beginning of the chapter, apply a model of addiction to "explain" each case.

CHAPTER 4

Culturally and Ethnically Diverse Populations

CASE EXAMPLES

1. Dawne is a 23-year-old Native American who lives on a reservation 37 miles from the nearest city in the western United States. She lost a brother in a "driving under the influence" (DUI) car accident when she was 12 years old. As a result, Dawne has been diagnosed with depression and anxiety. Although she does her best to refrain, her friends smoke marijuana and engage in binge drinking on the weekends. She was engaged to her boyfriend, John, until he began drinking and physically abusing her. After she broke up with him, her parents sent her to live with her aunt who had three children. When Dawne arrived and began living with her aunt and cousins, her cousins became exposed to Dawne's alcohol use and began drinking themselves.

2. Rumi is an international student from Japan who came to the United States to study for her undergraduate degree in chemistry. Rumi considers her three Euro-Caucasian roommates her best friends. She even spends most holidays with one of her roommate's families. As a result, she has not gone home to visit her parents for 3 years. Her English speaking is nearly flawless, and she says that she really has no deep desire to return home to her families' "old, out-of-date ways." Recently, she began drinking more so that she could decompress from the pressures of school.

3. Rolando is a 64-year-old Hispanic gay man who was adopted at birth. He retired from his job as a computer technician after he fell off a ladder while painting his brother's home and seriously injured his back. His daughter recently found him motionless on the floor of his apartment and called an ambulance. Upon his arrival at the city hospital emergency room, doctors determined that Rolando's condition was due to long-standing addiction to pain medication and alcohol. After stabilizing him, they referred Rolando to a treatment center in the next county, where he was placed on a waiting list.

As mentioned in Chapter 3, it is quite natural for treatment providers to develop a concept of addiction based on the clients with whom they come in contact. An important ingredient in this tentative formulation is the treatment provider's possession of a sound theoretical basis of the general nature of addictions. The same holds true when working with individuals and groups of different cultural and ethnic backgrounds. One needs to be well-grounded in the understanding of the cultural values of that individual or group so that the formation of tentative hypotheses about alcohol and other drug use, abuse, and addiction are more likely to be accurate. As the U.S. population grows, it will become more and more diverse, and this diverse population will also include persons with disabilities (PWDs), who currently number about 50 million (U.S. Census Bureau, 2010).

Without sensitivity to cultural differences and cultural competency, providers will likely be ineffective from the outset because attempts to assess alcohol and other drug involvement will be met with both cultural and therapeutic resistance. This double whammy will undoubtedly preclude an accurate assessment of any type, let alone that of drug involvement.

Room (2005) maintains that ethnic and cultural identity in a diverse society is partly assigned and partly constructed. Ethnic and cultural assignment are particularly amenable for visible minorities who are identifiable by skin color, language differences, age, physical disability, or some other such external sign(s). However, ethnic and cultural assignment is also made for the more invisible minorities as well, such as those with learning disorders/differences and those differing in sexual orientation. Although little is known about adolescents with disabilities and their alcohol and other drug (AOD) use, the few studies published consistently show significantly higher substance use rates for youth with disabilities (Glazier & Kling, 2013; Grafsky, Letcher, Slesnick, & Serovich, 2011).

When assigned (and thus, stereotyped), individuals and groups will often act out or perform the identity. Lurie (1971) believes that the heavy drinking by Native Americans can be likened to the world's oldest ongoing protest demonstration, which serves to demark and maintain the Indian–Euro-American boundary. Some recent research suggests support for this idea. For example, Native Americans and Alaska Natives account for 1% of the U.S. population (U.S. Census Bureau, 2010). Yet, while the rate of alcohol use may be lower than the national average (43.9% versus 55.2%), the rates of binge alcohol use and illicit drug use continue to be high (Denham, 2014). Specifically, Native Americans and Alaskan Natives binge drinking is higher than the national average (30.6% versus 24.5%; 11.2% versus 7.9%, respectively; U.S. Department of Health and Human Services, 2010). In addition, the percentage of Native American or Alaska Native adults who need treatment for AOD use is about twice the national average (18.0% versus 9.6%). Based on the need for cultural awareness, sensitivity, and competency, this chapter will present information on Native Americans and Alaska Natives, Asian and Pacific Islanders, African Americans, and Latino and Hispanic populations. We will also examine persons with disabilities and the elderly (also see Chapter 9). Concerns for helping professionals when working with members of these populations will conclude the chapter.

NATIVE AMERICANS AND ALASKA NATIVES

You need to know at the outset of this section that indigenous peoples around the world have the highest morbidity and mortality rates than nonindigenous people (Freemantle et al., 2015; Jemigan et al., 2015). In the United States, American Indians and Alaska Natives (AI/AN) have the lowest life expectancy of any racial/ethnic group (Landen, Roeber, Naimi, Nielsen, & Sewell, 2014). In general, native populations are not keen on medical research because of the history of medical research portraying them as primitive, dependent, and in need of help (Jemigan et al., 2015). So, there is a very real concern about how to improve the overall health of these peoples. Fortunately, efforts by researchers to partner with tribal communities are increasing.

Native Americans (which include American Indians, Alaska Natives, and Aleuts) have been separated by the U.S. government into three categories: (1) federally recognized tribes and bands, (2) nonfederally recognized tribes and bands, and (3) urban Native Americans. More than 562 tribes/nations who speak 253 different languages are federally recognized. According to the U.S. Census Bureau (2011), there are about 5 million people who identify themselves as American Indian/Alaska Native (AI/AN) alone or in combination with one or more other races, and 27% are younger than 18. As a group, AI/AN make up 1.6% of the total U.S. population. As of 2010, the Native American, Alaskan Native, and Aleut populations residing in the United States tended to live in one of 10 major cultural areas: Northeast, Southeast, Plains, Arctic, Subarctic, Northwest Coast, Plateau, Great Basin, California, and the Southwest (U.S. Census Bureau, 2010). These cultural areas are further subdivided into urban or reservation lifestyles. About 2 million Native Americans/Alaskan Natives live on reservations or trust lands, and 60% live in metropolitan areas—the lowest percentage of any racial group (U.S. Department of Health and Human Services, 2010). If you were to spend a moment reflecting upon the differences between the Euro-Americans living in the northeastern United States and the South, or between the Southwest and the Midwest, or between California and the rest of the United States, you would begin to see that there are now and always have been vast differences in the ways that people speak, eat, dress, and approach life in general. The Native American populations are no different. Alaska Natives, for example, differ along geographic lines that reflect a difference in cultures (Attneave, 1982). Alaskan Eskimos inhabit the coastal areas to the north, whereas the Aleuts occupy settlements along the Aleutian Islands. Fairbanks is the cultural hub for the Athabascan-speaking tribes who reside in the surrounding mountains and valleys. Yet very different are the coastal tribes who reside on the islands close to Juneau and Ketchikan and along the coast of the Alaskan panhandle. An example that underscores the geographic distribution and variety of Native American cultures is that most Native Americans who live outside of the Southwest would consider the silver and turquoise jewelry of the Southwest Pueblo Indians an exotic art form, much as would non–Native Americans, regardless of whether they lived in urban centers, on reservations, or in rural settings (Attneave, 1982).

Background

According to Attneave (1982), no Native American or Alaskan Native person today categorically lives out a traditional lifestyle. All are involved in the non–Native American U.S. culture to some degree. For example, more than half of the Native American and Alaskan Native populations do not use the reservation as their principal residence. Because urban centers offer different opportunities for work, education, and other endeavors, thousands of Native Americans can be found residing in these urban areas for varying lengths of time.

In the late 1700s, trappers, traders, and frontiersmen introduced alcohol as a social beverage to Native Americans on a widespread scale. Before that, little or no use of alcohol existed among Native Americans north of Mexico, with the exception of use for certain ceremonial purposes. Woodland and plains tribes especially used the methods of dancing, fasting, drumming, sleep deprivation, and isolation to obtain altered states of consciousness as a means to communicate with the Great Spirit and the spirits of nature (Westermeyer & Baker, 1986).

As the concept of Manifest Destiny became the accepted orientation fueling the exploration of the lands to the West, so did alcohol become the most important item exchanged for furs (Chittenden, 1935). With little history to guide alcohol consumption, Native Americans as a group were uncertain about how to view it. Many tribes came to believe that alcohol had magical powers associated with curing disease. Other tribes simply viewed drunken people as unaccountable for their behaviors. It has been stated that perhaps Native Americans first learned to drink in a binge pattern at the trade fairs where drinking parties often lasted several days, accompanied by games, acts of bravado, and fighting (Westermeyer & Baker, 1986). Still others saw drinking as more social and economic. Although leaders cautioned them to abstain, alcohol was accepted by many Native Americans as a gesture of friendship from the white-skinned traders. Thus, alcohol took on an economic value. Accepting alcohol, even drinking with the whites, was believed to cement good trade relations.

Many Native American leaders became so disturbed by the spate of drinking among their people that they appealed to government officials for help. Federal intervention finally came in 1832 with the Indian Prohibition Act, which prohibited the selling or providing of liquor to American Indians. However, the act was deemed largely unsuccessful: Alcohol was deeply infused into the trading economy and social practices of many tribes by the 1830s, creating a demand for the drug. As a result, many Native Americans as well as whites turned to smuggling alcohol, and they made good profits. Moreover, by the 1830s, Native Americans had learned to ferment alcohol from their plethora of carbohydrate sources. Although the Indian Prohibition Act was ineffective, the U.S. government did not revoke the law until 1953. In its absence, many Native American leaders remained vigilant about the potentially destructive nature of alcohol, so that currently 69% of all U.S. reservations are under a self-imposed system of prohibition (Young, 1992).

The Native American relationship with alcohol has also been mitigated by the historical events of forced relocation of tribes, the breakup of Native American families, and the constant harassment from settlers and soldiers. In an attempt to assess the influence of these historical events upon Native American drinking behaviors, as many as 42 theories have been promulgated—the most notable of which is the sociocultural explanation (Young, 1992). This theory maintains that, as a culture, Native Americans are continuing to mourn the loss of their heritage and culture and are reacting to the stresses of acculturation and the demands to integrate into the mainstream of Euro-American society. In this theory, alcohol is seen as salubrious, anesthetizing the pain associated with the multiple losses incurred by Native Americans. Aside from whatever biophysiological proclivities that exist among Native Americans (and the jury is still out on this issue), the current state of anomie or normlessness is seen as acting to maintain the abuse of alcohol.

It becomes important, then, to examine the values that are purported to be at the heart of this grieving process. Sadly, it will become apparent that Native American values were functional before the introduction of alcohol, but may have now become seriously compromised in the development of current Indian drinking patterns. The grieving process for the Native Americans and Alaskan Natives thus includes not only mourning the loss of a culture, but mourning the deleterious effects of alcohol on their peoples.

Values

In spite of the enormous diversity among Native American populations, some basic values are thematic for Native Americans and Native Alaskans. These values focus upon orientation to time, the relationship between humans and the natural world, social relationships, and the concept of "noninterference." Many Native American and Euro-American cultures hold these values, but they usually vary in philosophy or in the emphasis placed on them.

TIME   Attneave (1982) and Ivey, D'Andrea, Bradford-Ivey, and Simek-Morgan (2007) explain that Euro-American culture is concerned with present time in terms of minute-by-minute awareness: What time is it? How much time do I have left? How long will it take me to drive to Long Island? Native Americans and Native Alaskan peoples also view time in the present. However, for them, present time is cyclical or universal rather than linear. Native Americans view present time as it relates to personal rhythms (not unlike the popular notion of biorhythms) and seasonal rhythms that encompass days, months, and even years. Native American life is thus organized in broad context around these various rhythms and not organized by traditional calendars and watches—both of which are seen as external.

Attneave (1982) and Ivey et al. (2007) point out that the Native American concept of past time has little or nothing to recommend its revival to the Native American population. The immediate past is measured in one or two generations, and this timeline is filled with a grim and depressing past. The future, no longer anchored to the seasonal variations, remains unknown and unpredictable. In spite of it all, though, it is important to note that today Native Americans will likely have preserved some of their original concept of time and, because of the clash of cultures, some distortions of it as well.

HUMANS, THE NATURAL WORLD, AND SOCIAL RELATIONSHIPS   Since the Industrial Revolution, the prevailing view of nature in Euro-American culture is that it is wild and capricious. Therefore, nature is seen as needing to be controlled, and increasing or improving technology is viewed as increasing control over nature. For Native Americans and Native Alaskans, nature cannot be controlled. They advocate the need to understand and to harmonize with the natural forces of nature rather than to attempt to control or dominate them. Thus, Native American populations aim to surrender control. Surrendering with regard to alcohol means that if one is going to drink, so be it. But surrendering to the forces of nature is not the same as being passive. Moreover, becoming drunk might be met with temporary ostracism.

Native Americans believe that the group takes precedence over the individual, which may go a long way in explaining the rapid spread of alcohol among earlier Native American peoples. In the past, the ability to preserve perishables from season to season was very limited. Sharing of food, clothing, and transportation was the norm as well as the necessity, so it is not unreasonable that in the Native American culture, alcohol would have been passed around until it was gone. For this reason, some consider this idea the underlying explanation for "binge drinking" (Attneave, 1982).

NONINTERFERENCE   Another source of grieving, and a source of explanation for early Native American alcohol use patterns, revolves around a concept called "noninterference." Although the Native American peoples respected the idea of the group, there was an underlying principle explaining the proper place of the individual. Just as there was respect for the natural forces of nature, there was also respect for the natural unfolding of the potential in each person. "Noninterference" is an academic term used to describe this approach to human behavior (Attneave, 1982). This philosophy allows Native American parents to nurture their children while allowing them to learn from their mistakes. In this process, much more emphasis is placed upon having children learn by doing, so they can learn from their own mistakes. Noninterference is also practiced with the elderly. For example, no matter how senile or ill the elders in the tribe may be, they still retain the right to determine their own courses of action. This notion of allowing one to learn from mistakes may have had a significant impact upon the development of alcohol abuse and alcoholism among Native Americans throughout generations.

Risk Factors for Alcohol and Other Drug Abuse

PSYCHOSOCIAL FACTORS   American Indians and Alaska Natives have higher rates of substance abuse disorders compared to non-native populations (Croff, Rieckmann, & Spence, 2014). These populations experience significant alcohol-related health issues. American Indians and Alaska Natives have more alcohol-attributed motor vehicle fatalities, suicides, and falls causing deaths than other racial/ethnic groups (Indian Health Service, 2013; Keyes, Liu, & Cerda, 2012). Westermeyer (1991) believes that the sheer number of miles involved in procuring alcohol significantly increases risks and may contribute significantly to the higher incidence of alcohol-related accidents.

In general, risks are higher for the American Indian and Alaska Native populations than for the White population. For instance, Landen et al. (2014) studied the alcohol-attributable morality among American Indians between 1999 and 2009 and found that there are higher relative risks of alcohol-attributable deaths for American Indians and Alaska Natives than for Whites. In particular, the native population aged 25 to 44 in the Northern Plains had the highest risks.

Psychosocial risk factors are usually divided into personal and social dimensions. Personal risk factors include such things as stress, financial problems, relational victimization, and physical victimization. Social risk factors can involve peer groups, families, and communities. For example, drugs may be easier to obtain in some communities than in others. Some communities may have low neighborhood attachment, a population that is transient, and one that is in poverty. These communities present heightened risk factors. Families can be another source of risk for substance abuse, and this is especially true if persistent family conflict and/or favorable parental attitudes and involvement in the problem behavior occur. It is very important to remember that a risk factor for one person may not be for another. Moreover, risk factors are related to age so that what is a risk factor at one age may or may not be a risk factor at another age or developmental phase. For example, the risk factors for American Indians start early: Stanley, Harness, Swaim, and Beauvais (2014) found that eighth through 10th graders living either on or near to the reservation reported higher rates of alcohol use, drunkenness, and binge drinking than the national average.

Eitle, Johnson-Jennings, and Eitle (2013) state that there is not a great deal of literature that looks at why risks are higher for the American Indian and Alaska Native populations. In particular, there is a dearth of studies examining the association between family structure and alcohol use among American Indian teens. These researchers found that living in a single-parent home provides heightened exposure to stress and alcohol use. However, Eitle et al. found that living in an extended family situation with other under-21-year-old family or nonfamily members was actually both a risk factor and a mediator. Moreover, if the adolescent was not able to be cared for by one's parents, and this teen was then cared for by extended family member, the result was a protective factor against alcohol problems. Yet, those who were living in a home with an extended family member younger than 21 years of age were exposed to a higher risk for alcohol problems. These researchers suggest that when American Indian families open up their homes to include an extended family member, it is wise for them to seek out ways to integrate the adolescent into the family that do not enhance the risks for alcohol use by other adolescents who reside in the home.

Dawne, the Native American female described in Case Example 1 at the beginning of the chapter, reflects a host of risk factors that are present for Native American females. She lost a brother to a DUI accident as he traveled the 37 miles home to the reservation from a party in town. She was diagnosed with anxiety and depression, had friends who misused substances, and was a victim of physical abuse. When her parents could no longer care for her and sent her to live with her aunt's family, who did not have the resources to provide help, her cousins were more at risk for alcohol use. Care would be needed to integrate her into the home.

Paltrow (2004) maintains that another factor that influences the maintenance of AOD problems is the criminal justice system. This includes racial profiling as well as judges who believe in the myth that using drugs is a choice for Native Americans and Alaska Natives rather than seeing female AOD use associated with oppression and socioeconomic injustices. Both Paltrow (2004) and Owen (2004) claim that drug laws along with subsequent incarceration destroy the lives of women. This makes it almost impossible for female Native Americans to recover from such punishing policies. Current laws, Native American views of sexuality, and morality related to homosexuality also influence AOD use and recovery from it for Native Americans. For example, Gilley and Co-Cké (2005) see that Native American gay males often feel alienated from their tribal, ceremonial, and social communities because of homophobia. As with the gay population in general, the gay bar scene makes healthy living difficult for Native American gay males. In addition, Pope (2012) maintains that Native Americans have never really bought into the Euro-American views of sexuality as being dichotomous and categorical. Adding to the structural oppression that a gay lifestyle brings, one can see how complex being Native and gay could be and how it can increase risk factors for developing AOD problems.

BEHAVIORAL RISK FACTORS   Behavioral risk factors relate to such things as school engagement, academic achievement, healthy lifestyle, internalizing/externalizing issues of control, and drug involvement. For Native Americans or Alaska Natives, binge drinking (Ehlers, Stouffer, & Gilder, 2014), methamphetamine use (Forcehimes et al., 2011), and smoking (Centers for Disease Control and Prevention, 2010) are risk factors for multiple adverse outcomes.

Cobb, Espey, and King (2014) found that American Indians and Alaska Natives, with few exceptions, were high in physical inactivity, obesity, and tobacco use while being low in vegetable consumption, cancer screenings, and seatbelt use. Finally, Marlatt and VandenBos (1997) developed 16 substance abuse risk categories for Native American youth that heighten risk factors, and these continue to be risk factors today. These categories are: (1) smoking tobacco; (2) use of smokeless tobacco; (3) family smoking; (4) peer smoking; (5) family smokeless tobacco use; (6) peer smokeless tobacco use; (7) experimentation; (8) intentions to use; (9) peer use of alcohol; (10) inhalants, marijuana, and crack/cocaine; (11) quality of family relationships; (12) school adjustment; (13) orientation; (14) non–substance-related deviant behaviors; (15) perceived deviance in school environment; and (16) cultural identification and religiosity. These are dimensions that mental health providers should pay attention to when assessing this population. The reason for this is because there are individual differences across tribes, reservations, and Native communities. By examining use patterns along Marlatt and VanderBos's (1997) dimensions, mental health professionals can increase the probability that they will have a broader assessment perspective.

AT A GLANCE

Native Americans and Alaska Natives

Population

4.9 million American Indian/Alaska Natives make up 1.6% of U.S. total population.

1.9 million live on reservations in 36 states.

60% live in metropolitan areas.

562 tribes/nations are federally recognized.

253 different languages are spoken.

Education

76% 25 and older have a high school diploma.

14% have a bachelor's degree.

(Continued)

The core of the AA program and the basis of similar groups developed on the AA model are the Twelve Steps. As a statement in the Big Book indicates, "Rarely have we seen a person fail who

AT A GLANCE (Continued)

Income

25% live at poverty level.

$33,627 is the median family income.

Children and Parenting

Practice of noninterference reflects parents allowing children to make mistakes and learn rather than directly controlling children's growth.

Spiritual Beliefs and Practices

Time is viewed as seasonal and chromatic (versus digital), and the immediate past is measured in one or two generations.

People believe that Nature cannot be controlled.

Some Native cultures believe language and thought shape reality and control events.

Family Organization and Communication

Group takes precedence over the individual.

Families are patriarchal and structured with well-defined role expectations.

ASIAN AMERICANS AND PACIFIC ISLANDERS

From your reading of the section on Native Americans, you would accurately anticipate that the Asian population is also diverse. Asians include Asian Indians (India), Pakistanis, Thais, Filipinos, Vietnamese, Laotians, Cambodians, and the Hmong peoples (Highland Laotian). The peoples of East Asia include Chinese, Japanese, and Koreans. Pacific Islanders include Hawaiians, Samoans, and people from Guam. Asian Indians are the fastest growing group of Asian and Pacific Islanders in the United States (Methikalam, Wang, Slaney, & Yeung, 2015).

Typical Western observers tend to view all East Asians as being very similar—if not the same. Nothing could be further from the truth. Asian Americans/Pacific Islanders comprise more than 60 discrete racial/ethnic groups and subgroups, and these groups are heterogeneous with vast variation within. Language is the most apparent difference. Yet, the histories of China, Japan, and Korea reveal vastly differing social and economic development. Moreover, once living in the United States, all Asian groups demonstrate significant within-group differences that will become more pronounced in future years.

Virtually all of the world's great religions are represented in this culturally and ethnically diverse group of Asian and Pacific Islander Americans, including Animism, Hinduism, Buddhism, Judaism, Christianity, and Islam. The culturally and ethnically diverse populations presented in this chapter all have conflict as part of their histories, and Asian Americans are no different. However, the Asian population is distinctive in that its members also have a history of fighting among themselves. This single variable may distinguish Southeast Asians in another significant way: Although Asian Americans (including Southeast Asians) tend to group themselves ethnically,

Southeast Asian Americans, especially those living in urban centers, have demonstrated a lack of pulling together because of their history of internal fighting (Burns & D'Avanzo, 1993). The transitions involving acculturation and accommodation will only exacerbate this cultural tension and can increase the risk factor for alcohol and other drug abuse.

Background

Although Islamic laws eschew alcohol, and most Muslim, Hindu, and Buddhist groups avoid alcohol, many Asian and Pacific cultures do use alcohol in rituals (Shon & Ja, 1982). An example of this is found in the "tribal binge" drinking of Pacific Islanders and in ceremonial and traditional events in Japan. Yet, research consistently shows that the frequency of drinking for Asian Americans is the lowest among minority groups (Centers for Disease Control and Prevention, 2010; Collins & McNair, 2002; Wu & Blazer, 2015).

The Chinese not only allow the use of alcohol at social functions, but virtually push it on guests as a display of hospitality. However, they discourage drunkenness. Traditionally, Hong Kong has few drinking-centered establishments, generally restricts the use of alcohol to males, and values drinking alcohol at meals. In Chinese culture, alcohol is often viewed in a somewhat similar fashion to that of the abolitionist in the temperance movement in America's 19th century (see section on African Americans). That is, alcohol is associated with lack of restraint, but it is not generally feared that drunkenness will lead to violence. In a significant yet early study, Chafetz (1964) noted that Taiwanese have well-defined ways of behaving, have strong social sanctions against excessive drinking, and encourage drinking only at meals or at special events. He also found that the Taiwanese have little official concern about alcohol treatment programs because of the overall lack of psychiatric resources and the low level of alcoholism in the dominant Chinese population.

Polynesians do not use guilt as a means to regulate drinking and drunkenness. However, Tongans and Samoans, many of whom are Christian, do seem to use guilt to control the amount of drinking. Drinking to excess is seen as potentially threatening in the Samoan culture. Studies report that a large number of Samoan wives left their marriages because of the heavy drinking of their physically abusive husbands (Lemert, 1964; Room & Mäkelä, 2000).

Values

When attempting to describe the values held by Asian Americans or Pacific Islanders, the vast within-group differences prohibit any attempt at brevity (Toyokawa & Toyokawa, 2013). What follows are some general descriptions that would more likely apply to recent Asian immigrants and are less likely to describe earlier generations of Asian Americans. Such discrepancies are mostly due to the effects of acculturation. According to Lee and Mock (2005), traditional Asian families see the symbol of the samurai as the epitome of Japanese valor. They view *bushido* as the way of the warrior that combines stoicism, bravery, and self-sacrifice. *Gaman* is the "down-to-earth" version of bushido. This reflects the gritting of one's teeth and getting on with life. It is also associated with the traditional awareness of humankind's powerlessness over an omnipotent nature. If you saw the videos of the great tsunami that hit Japan on March 11, 2011, you saw clearly how the Japanese people responded with all of these values.

Perfectionism is a value in Asian cultures. It is linked with several values held by Asian Americans such as collectivism, filial piety, and conforming to social norms. The role of children within the Asian Indian family is to bring honor through achievements, and Methikalam et al. (2015) see that family obligation and expectation among this ethnic group can be conceptually linked to conditional approval—which is one of the foundations of perfectionism. In addition, the emphasis upon humility can also contribute to perfectionism through the feelings of not being good enough (Wang, Yuen, & Slaney, 2009). Methikalam et al. found that the tendency to continually regard oneself as not ever being good enough may produce poor psychological outcomes.

FAMILY ROLES Most Asian societies are structured with well-defined role expectations. This includes a patriarchal family structure consisting of elders or extended family members and a structure in which children are seen as subordinates. According to Methikalam et al. (2015), Fukuyama and Inoue-Cox (1992), Ivey et al. (2007), and others, a strong sense of "filial piety" and respect for authority reinforces obedience and protection of the family name. The father's decisions are beyond reproach and are categorically accepted. The mother nurtures both her husband and her children. Whereas at one time it was socially desirable for the father to be the disciplinarian, the contemporary Asian father is not home as much, so the discipline is essentially left to the mother.

The male is expected to provide for the economic welfare of his family and in so doing is the one on whose shoulders rests the responsibility for the family's successes or failures. Because the physical appearance of Asians differs significantly from Euro-Americans concomitant with the presence of racial and cultural discrimination toward Asian Americans (Cheng, Lin, & Cha, 2015; Lee & Mock, 2005; Shon & Ja, 1982), Asian men can face extraordinary pressures when attempting to provide financially for their families. Research suggests that it usually takes about 10 or more years for them to find economic security (Burns & D'Avanzo, 1993). This length of time and the pressures to succeed increase their risk for AOD abuse. Risk for substance abuse also seems to increase with the level of educational attainment for these men—especially for Chinese, Korean, and Japanese men. Chi, Lubben, and Kitano (1989) found consumption rates of alcohol increased with educational attainment.

Shame, especially the idea of "saving face," controls behaviors in the Asian family and is learned early in life. The concept of shame and loss of face involves not only the exposing of one's actions for all to see, but also family, community, or social withdrawal of confidence and support (Ivey et al., 2007; Shon & Ja, 1982). Inextricably woven into the value of shame is obligation. Obligation in the Asian/Pacific Islander community contains spoken and unspoken elements of reciprocity, and the greatest obligation is toward one's parents. This is an obligation that cannot ever truly be repaid (Fukuyama & Inoue-Cox, 1992; Lee & Mock, 2005). Regardless of what the parents may do to the child, the child is still obligated to give them respect and be obedient to them. The more Asian children are exposed to Euro-American schools, the more this sense of obligation can come into question and become a source of confusion. The transition will produce a period of anomie for the Asian offspring, and it is during this period of normlessness that they may be at an increased risk for AOD abuse.

COMMUNICATION Roles also play an interesting and important part in communication for the Asian/Pacific Islander population. Communication between individuals is governed by such characteristics as age, gender, education, occupation, social status, family background, marital status, and parenthood (Lee & Mock, 2005; Shon & Ja, 1982). These variables influence behavior in terms of who will bow the lowest, who will initiate and change topics in a conversation, which person will speak more loudly, who will break eye contact first, and who will be most accommodating or tolerant. Most of the newly immigrated Asian Americans/Pacific Islanders are likely to want to avoid confrontation, keeping conversations on a harmonious level, and often maintain self-control over their facial expressions while avoiding direct eye contact. This information is important when assessing for AOD problems because it can work in reverse. If responses from Asian clients appear to upset the professional conducting the assessment, answers may not be given accurately so as to avoid confrontation.

RELIGION   Beliefs about health and responses to offerings of health care are influenced by religious beliefs in the Asian/Pacific Islander population. For example, Buddhism holds that life is suffering, and suffering emanates from desire. Pain or other suffering is seen as punishment for transgressions in this or previous lives. Alcohol and other drug problems may fall into this context. The notion of pain and suffering may so strongly influence one's beliefs that the likelihood of seeking help for AOD problems may be severely diminished (Shon & Ja, 1982). Animism is the idea that evil spirits, demons, or gods have control over one's life. Because of this, the "shaman" may be the primary caregiver or helper in situations involving alcohol or other drug abuse. However, Western helpers may be invited to aid in the process. Confucianism is prevalent among older Vietnamese and is a moral and ethical code that includes the worshipping of ancestors. Because Confucianism stresses a hierarchical order in both family and social systems, it will be the family elder who would have the final say in decisions involving treatment for AOD abuse. As a helping professional, you need to be very careful to demonstrate respect for this individual.

Taoism, which stresses harmony, is also quite prevalent among the Asian population. Harmony also plays a significant role in one's intention to seek help. A passive posture toward treatment may be assumed by an individual of Asian or Pacific Islander descent because anything else would disrupt harmony and perfection.

The Hawaiian term *nā ʻOhana* reflects the family " . . . as a collective that gives life, nourishment, and support for the growth and prosperity of blood relatives as well as extended family, those joined in marriage, adopted children or adults, and ancestors living and deceased" (Kanuha, 2005, p. 66). Children are the foundation of nā ʻOhana and their relationship to elders, their ancestors, and the material, physical, and spiritual surroundings. Clinicians need to understand the key historical events as well as being familiar with the concept of nā ʻOhana and the traditional values of unity, connection, love and affinity, and generosity (Kanuha, 2005).

Risk Factors for Alcohol and Other Drug Abuse

Although at least 32 different national and ethnic groups of Asian Americans and Pacific Islanders exist, research on subgroups has been limited (Park, Anastas, Shibusawa, & Nguyen, 2014). The existing research reflects that subgroups of this population do not always show the same trend. For example, for more acculturated Asian Americans, religiosity is seen as a protective factor because it increases negative beliefs about alcohol thus diminishing the perceived social norms (i.e., lower tolerance for deviation) associated with its use. In addition, religiosity buffers against the effects of life stress and discrimination and emphasizes higher levels of self-control (Luk et al., 2013). Yet, within the Asian American group, religiosity is more of a protective factor for Korean Americans than for Chinese Americans (Luk et al., 2013). They also found differences within the Asian American ethnic population in that Japanese and Filipinos binge drink at higher frequencies than U.S.-born Asian Americans.

Acculturation is an increasingly important topic given that there are 41.3 million immigrants living in the United States as of 2013 (Myers, 2016). The acculturation model has often been used to predict differential effects of cultural exposure to alcohol. The acculturation model reflects immigrant and ethnic minority populations drinking in response to acculturation stresses. Yet, acculturation stress is not often studied, and the populations that are studied are college students and adolescents—not Asian American adults (Park et al., 2014). In their study of young adults, Park et al. found support for acculturation shaping drinking habits among Asian Americans. Pedersen et al. (2013) provide more insight into the issue. These researchers found that those who did not identify strongly with Western culture and also felt less membership in their own ethnic groups were at higher risk for alcohol problems. Further, Asian American young adults may experience marginalization (i.e., a sense of distance and isolation from their original culture as well as from the dominant society) and, if so, young adults may use drinking to cope with the feelings of exclusion.

The sheer number of immigrants concomitant with the age distribution of this group suggests that these families are in a constant state of transition once they arrive. The process of acculturation will impact all family members and will differentially affect their risk for AOD abuse. For example, a newly arrived Asian American homemaker will be confronted with Euro-American values of female independence, assertiveness, achievement, and work. As a result, elder Asian Americans, expecting to be cared for by family members, can experience great shock and loneliness when faced with nursing home care. Such conflicts between newly acquired values and traditional values can place these individuals at risk for AOD abuse.

Although the family hierarchy may provide a stabilizing force to deal with the pressures of financial adjustment, youths who are exposed to the parental pressures for high achievement and financial success may fall victim to feelings of isolation and self-blame. To help brace against fear of long-term insecurity, many Asian Americans also work hard to send their children to schools in hopes that they will become high-paid professionals. This value is reflected in the sheer numbers of Asian American youth attending prestigious universities in the United States. However, attempts to further the education of their children can be met with resistance, in that the younger children are likely to be attending English-speaking schools while their older siblings and parents may still prefer or use their native language. This would suggest that there might be a bicultural splitting within this population in terms of language. Language differences within families can lead to increased levels of stress, thereby increasing individual family members' risk factors for AOD abuse.

AT A GLANCE
Asian Americans and Pacific Islanders

Population
15.5 million live mainly in California, New York, Hawaii, Texas, New Jersey, and Illinois.

Make up 5% of total U.S. population.

1.1 million Native Hawaiians/Other Pacific Islanders (30% younger than age 18) live mainly in Hawaii, California, Washington, Texas, New York, Florida, and Utah.

Asian Americans/Pacific Islanders make up less than 1% of total U.S. population.

Education
86% 25 and older have a high school diploma.

50% have a bachelor's degree.

Income
10% live at poverty level.

Median family income is $15,600 higher than national median for all households.

$50,992 is median family income.

Children and Parenting

Children are seen as subordinates.

Behavior controlled by "saving face" and through shame.

Children's greatest obligation is toward their parents.

Family Organization and Communication

Respect for authority and "filial piety" reinforce obedience and protection of the family name.

Communication is usually governed by age, gender, education, occupation, social status, family background, marital status, and parenthood.

Spiritual Beliefs and Practices

Taoists believe that man is a microcosm for the universe and that the body is tied directly into the five elements of fire, earth, air, water, and ether as well as to the five organs and the seasons.

Traditional Hawaiian religion is polytheistic and animistic, which is based on a belief that spirits are found in nonhuman objects such as animals, the ocean waves, and the sky.

Moreover, language difficulties in school may preclude the Asian Americans/Pacific Islanders' abilities to fulfill their parents' wishes to excel. This would be especially true for first-generation immigrants who came to the United States involuntarily or because of economic hardships faced in their homelands. The sum total of language difficulties and perceived inabilities to meet parental wishes can lead to alienation inside the family (Ivey et al., 2007; Shon & Ja, 1982). For example, the father's insistence upon obedience may be called into question and, when the father's beliefs are called into question, it may significantly contribute to a breakdown of traditional family structure. Thai, Connell, and Tebes (2010) studied the relative influence of acculturation, peer substance use, and academic achievement on adolescent substance use. In their study of 1,248 Asian American youth, they found that peer use is a risk factor and that education was a protective factor. Lo, Cheng, and Howell (2014) used immigration status to explain these findings. In their study of immigration status and drinking, Lo et al. found that those immigrants with less educational attainment consumed less alcohol. Yet, at the same time, they did drink more heavily than their ethnic counterparts who had lived longer in the United States. The researchers also found that recent residents had a higher likelihood of living below the poverty line, thus living with stress. This stress may lead to heavier alcohol consumption—especially among Asian American young males. However, in the final analysis, studies need to be undertaken to examine subgroups of the immigrant population because when the data on Asian Americans and Pacific Islanders are not disaggregated, there are conflicting reports about the impact of acculturation on alcohol use and abuse (see section on Treatment later in this chapter).

AFRICAN AMERICANS

The role of alcohol in the contemporary African American community varies from that of many other groups. African Americans have culturally acceptable means for achieving spontaneity, sociability, and relaxation. Alcohol, then, is not seen as a requisite for a feeling of celebration. In addition, specific drinking patterns of African Americans are found to be somewhat different from those of Euro-Americans. Early ethnographic studies suggest that taverns appear to be social centers for a majority of African Americans who drink (Sterne & Pittman, 1972). As would be true with any group regardless of ethnicity, African Americans who frequent taverns and bars are a group unto themselves and, as you would expect, are regarded as candidates for the underclass in African American culture rather than as responsible participants in community life. The exception would be a man who is a weekend tavern drinker and is otherwise a capable wage earner and family man. Women who frequent taverns and bars, however, would likely be socially compromised in the wider African American community.

In general, alcohol is often perceived to be a "party food" and is associated with being palliative, while the potential harmful effects are often overlooked or not understood. Alcohol consumption at parties or other social gatherings has a minor role in terms of setting the mood of gaiety and spontaneity. Therefore, a person abstaining from alcohol is not perceived as being staid or a "party pooper."

Many African Americans drink almost exclusively on the weekends, traditionally a time of relaxation, visitation, and celebration. Brand names and the quantity of alcohol drunk reflect status in many African American communities. Although earlier studies (e.g., Bourne, 1973; Harper, 1976) reported that African Americans either abstained or drank heavily, began to drink at an earlier age, purchased larger containers of alcohol than their Euro-American counterparts, and concentrated their drinking on the weekends, more recent studies have found that African Americans have later onset drinking problems than their Euro-American counterparts (Chartier, Hesselbrock, & Hesselbrock, 2011).

The history of the relationship between African Americans and alcohol is engaging. Since the institutionalization of slavery in the early 1600s, a broad social and intellectual climate, known as Enlightenment thinking, has prevailed in American thought and has had a significant impact upon views of alcohol and its relationship to African Americans. So, to understand the history of African Americans and alcohol is to trace the institutionalization of slavery up through the prohibition period in the 20th century.

Background

Early stereotyping of Africans (who became "African Americans" after the Emancipation Proclamation) and the institutionalization of slavery in the United States led to subsequent fears of slave insurrection and fueled numerous social measures aimed at controlling this population. In addition to legislation rigidly restricting their ability to trade, Africans were also prohibited from using alcoholic beverages. A West Jersey (New Jersey) law of 1685, for example, stated: "Any person convicted of selling or giving of rum, or any manner of strong liquor, either to a negro or Indian, except the stimulant be given in relief of real physical distress is liable to a penalty of five pounds" (Herd, 1991, p. 355). Similar laws were in effect in many of the states, including Maryland, North Carolina, Georgia, Delaware, Pennsylvania, and those in New England (Larkin, 1965). Rather than being fueled by the fear that drunkenness would lessen their work ethic, the assumptive premise of these laws was based on the fear that intoxicated slaves would foment rebellion. Although the relationship with alcohol and insurrection was presumptive, the manner in which the early African slaves were treated certainly did little to quell the fear of insurrection.

The American Revolution witnessed the abolition of slavery in most of the northern states, but not in the newly formed states of the South. And for southern slaveholders, the discrepancy between the "free north" and the "slave south" exacerbated fears of insurrection. Many new laws were instituted that further restricted the use of alcohol by slaves. However, in spite of laws, the popular views held by slave owners varied on the use of alcohol as a means of controlling Africans. As stated earlier, some believed that prohibiting slaves' use of alcohol would help guard against rebellion. This view was based on the southern planters' widely held view that alcohol was an important cause of every insurrectionary movement in the United States (Freehling, 1968). Another popular view stood in direct opposition. This view was equally concerned with controlling Africans, but held that the sober, thinking slave was the one who was dangerous and needed the constant vigilance of the owner (Douglass, 1855). Herd (1991) summarized these two views:

> One [view of alcohol] inspired images of force and rebellion, whereas the other suggested images of passivity and victimization. From the former perspective liquor was believed to be a powerful agent of disinhibition capable of unleashing violent and irrational behavior in otherwise civilized people. Hence, alcohol was regarded as a cause of crime and violence, a substance that made people commit barbaric and cruel acts. In the latter view alcohol was believed to be a powerfully addicting substance that forced men to drink and left them weak, slothful, and in a thoroughly degraded condition. (p. 357)

What were the views of alcohol held by the Africans themselves? They varied, of course. But interestingly enough, Africans were essentially split on the issue as well. Many regarded drinking as a natural reaction to being held against their will. For example, Stampp (1956) maintains that the consumption of alcohol by slaves was internally motivated as the "only satisfactory escape from the indignities, the frustrations, the emptiness, [and] the oppressive boredom of slavery" (p. 368). According to this view, there was a demand for alcohol by slaves, and Stampp offers a quotation from a former slave to corroborate this assertion: To be sober during the holidays "was disgraceful; and he was esteemed a lazy and improvident man, who could not afford to drink whiskey during Christmas" (p. 370). However, during the same period, black and white abolitionists alike maintained that holidays were perhaps the paragon of travesty. To these abolitionists, when slave owners offered libations to slaves during times of celebration, their intent was anything but to celebrate. They believed that holidays instilled more docile and passive resistance among slaves (Herd, 1991).

The views of alcohol as the enslaver and the disinhibitor, coupled with the Enlightenment philosophy of the time, inspired a spontaneous practice of temperance in the middle 19th century. Temperance ideology was focused on Enlightenment thinking and the role of self-control because it was this ability to control one's irresistible desires that would free humans to be rational and productive. The temperance movement did not stop there, however. Temperance was seen in a broader scope as a vehicle for freeing the will as well as having significant social implications for freeing slaves. Freedom and self-control meant freedom for all and freedom from all. This included freedom from slavery as well as freedom from alcohol. It is not surprising, then, to see that the northern abolitionists embraced a view of alcohol as the enslaver, and therefore, the enemy. Those southern slave owners who believed in temperance adopted the view that alcohol was the disinhibitor and could unleash dangerous impulses in slaves. In describing the abolitionist view, Fredrickson (1971) writes:

> What made slavery such a detestable condition was not simply that it created a bad environment; it was a severely limiting condition that was incompatible with the fundamental abolitionist belief that every man was morally responsible for his actions. (p. 37)

Curiously, the temperance movement among Africans was less a movement toward curtailing high alcohol consumption among their own than it was part of a larger movement of social reform that marked the era. In fact, estimates of the quantity of consumption by Africans during this period conflict. So, it cannot be said that alcohol was the primary motivator for African interest in temperance (Sterne, 1967). Herd (1991) believes the lure of temperance was more a reflection of African abolitionist views on slavery and the lure of Enlightenment thinking that valued the social betterment of all.

At the beginning of the 20th century, stereotyping and the perceived problems with the African American population had become central to the issue of alcohol reform for southern prohibitionists. Influenced by the Victorian Age and the preoccupation with sexual mores, women and children were now seen as needing protection from the disinhibited African Americans who were being portrayed as sexual perpetrators in the sensationalistic periodicals of the time (Sterne, 1967). The hackneyed views of African Americans spilled over into the disenfranchisement campaigns aimed at controlling both the poor white and African American vote (Herd, 1991). "Whiskey-sodden, irresponsible" African American voters "needed" to be controlled. So, many politicians urged restrictive voting rights. The temperance movement, which had advocated freedom, was thus thwarted by restrictions on voting rights, and there was a decline in the movement's popularity among many African American reformists who now saw alcohol regulation as antithetical to the true tenets of the temperance movement (Du Bois, 1928). However, Herd (1991) claims that it was at the popular level where the most profound changes in views of alcohol among African Americans of the time took place. A new fascination with a sensual lifestyle overshadowed the now anachronistic temperance movement.

Accompanying this fascination were significant demographic and socioeconomic changes in the African American population. Escaping intense oppression in the South, thousands migrated to the northern "wet" cities, only to find many northern industrialists, especially those resisting the union movement, offering only low-paying jobs—primarily recruiting African Americans as strikebreakers. Many took these jobs, although many others found bootlegging much more profitable than farm and other unskilled labor. Speakeasies and cabarets, emphasizing excitement and sensual pleasure, became the arenas for this new lifestyle. As a result, the views of alcohol among African Americans shifted 180 degrees: Whereas many African Americans had embraced the temperance movement of 100 years earlier as a means to demonstrate defiance, intemperance in early 20th-century America was the means to demonstrate defiance against an oppressive and restrictive legal system.

Values

Although there is no such thing as "The African American Family," studies on the African American family structure can be used to guide a general understanding of this diverse population. According to Black and Jackson (2005), families of African origin present themselves in diverse ways. They can vary in their geographic origin, level of acculturation, skin color, socioeconomic status, and religious backgrounds. For example, when studying African American families, you might study African immigrants, families of British West Indies descent, Haitians, and African Muslim families.

FAMILY ROLES   As you would expect, the roles of males and females in the African American family vary. Historically, the displacement of African Americans from agriculture into service and industrial employment, with little adjustment in the amount of racism, left this group as the "last hired, first fired." Unemployment was always high outside of southern agriculture, and out of necessity African American women worked outside the home. Perhaps as a result, African American women are seen as the "strength of the family" (Hines & Boyd-Franklin, 2005). Nonetheless, the male/female relationships are influenced by the larger social grand narrative of differential power.

The abilities of African American men to engage in relationships are clearly diminished by incarceration, mental and physical disabilities, death from hazardous jobs, and drug and alcohol abuse. Thus, you can see how Franklin's (2004) term, "invisibility syndrome" influenced views of

African American males as being irresponsible. A more accurate view of the role of fathers reflects the pressures of providing for the family in a society where job ceilings exist and oppression abounds (Hines & Boyd-Franklin, 1982; 2005). These same authors also indicate that the African American father may have to spend an inordinate amount of time and energy trying to provide for the family's basic survival needs, a preoccupation that drains the psychic energy that would otherwise be infused into the family. Faced both with pressures to provide and with barriers thwarting their efforts, underemployed and unemployed African American fathers may be at risk for turning to alcohol and other drugs as a means of relieving the pain.

KINSHIP AND EXTENDED FAMILY BONDS   The flexibility of roles in African American culture is also influenced by an atavistic value emphasizing strong kinship bonds. Although slavery certainly reinforced this value, its origins can be traced to Africa where Africanian thinking had produced the syllogism "We are, therefore I am" (Hines & Boyd-Franklin, 1982). Prevalent among many African American families and tied to the value of kinship is a phenomenon known as "child-keeping." Child-keeping occurs when a child is informally "adopted" or reared by other family members who have more resources than the biological parents. Rather than seeing child-keeping as the disruption of the family system, Hines and Boyd-Franklin (1982; 2005) believe that this occurrence actually elevates the importance of the child. African American children are far more likely to live with extended kin than any other race or ethnic group (Washington, Gleeson, & Rulison, 2013). Yet African American children may be subjected to ridicule and ostracism by a mainstream Euro-American culture that fails to recognize and/or appreciate this value—believing instead that the child who is raised by grandparents reflects a broken home. As a result of these misperceptions and other factors, African American children may experience stress at school and can turn to alcohol and other drugs.

RELIGION   The crucial role of the church in the emancipation of slaves in America is reflected in current views of the importance of a strong religious orientation among many African Americans. In times of slavery, cryptic messages about times and places for escape often came from the pulpit during the church service (Hines & Boyd-Franklin, 1982; 2005). Interestingly, these same authors point out that songs sung today in many African American churches, such as "Steal Away" and "Wade in the Water," often carry the remains of those messages. The power of those messages, hidden in church protocol, and their relationship to emancipation issues should leave no one surprised that some of the most notable contemporary leaders in the African American culture are or were preachers: the Reverend Martin Luther King, Jr., the Reverend Jesse Jackson, Malcolm X, and others. Although these individuals are of international stature, the local church is an important vehicle that allows the emergence of leaders in local African American communities. Free from the oppression that exists in mainstream Euro-American culture, the church allows outlets for creative talents that otherwise might be thwarted. The racism and oppression experienced by low-paying jobs during the week may be offset somewhat by becoming a deacon or trustee on Sunday. Hines and Boyd-Franklin remind us that numerous church activities, such as dinners, trips, singing in the choir, and participation in Sunday school, provide an intricate social life for many African Americans and promote their mental health and a sense of connectedness.

Gutierrez, Goodwin, Kirkinis, and Mattis (2014) assert the importance of religion and spirituality across the life span in the lives of African Americans by stating that 90% of this group rates religion as "very important" in their lives. Mattis and Mattis (2011) show that religion, religious beliefs, and faith-based institutions are significant to the point that these play a major role in almost every aspect of the lives of African Americans. It would not be surprising to note that religiosity is a protective factor against alcohol and substance abuse (Sunshine & Starks, 2010).

Risk Factors for Alcohol and Other Drug Abuse

The results of research on the relationship between African Americans and alcohol and other drugs are complicated and mixed. Yet, some interesting trends indicating use are notable. For example, studies have found that risk for substance abuse problems in the African American population is linked to an interrelationship of individual attributes and characteristics, environmental characteristics, historical experiences, cultural factors, poverty, stress, unemployment, and racism and discrimination (Kingree & Sullivan, 2002; Richardson, Johnson, & St. Vil, 2014).

Zapolski, Pedersen, McCarthy, and Smith (2014) found that although African Americans reported lower initiation of drinking as well as reporting lower rates and levels of use across all age groups, they also report higher levels of alcohol problems for those who do drink. These researchers assert that the highest risk group within the African American population is that of low-income males.

In a number of large urban areas, African American adolescents will not complete high school (Albdour & Krouse, 2014; Richardson et al., 2014). These same authors maintain that black male adolescents are more likely to face harsher discipline in schools and are suspended from school at a rate 3.5 times more than their white counterparts. This translates into one black male adolescent being suspended from school out of every five black students. Although reasons for this are still under exploration, these researcher say that in these cities, African American parents face an inordinate amount of stress that present threats to the healthy development of these youths, and parents often do not have the ability or availability of community and neighborhood resources from which to draw help. A study of African American youth by Burlew, Johnson, Flowers, Peteet, Griffith-Henry, and Buchanan (2009) brings this point home. These authors examined neighborhood risk factors and found that both exposure to negative neighborhood activities and low parental supervision increase the onset of substance use by the eighth grade. To a degree, parental supervision and the value of family obligation can mediate these risk factors and act to protect African American adolescents—especially African American female adolescents (Milan & Wortel, 2015).

Another factor increasing risk is availability, and the history of availability is interesting. For instance, in 1978, Los Angeles had approximately three liquor stores per block in addition to those neighborhood stores offering beer and wine. Gordon (1994) found that, 25 years later (1993), 10 times more liquor stores were in the African American communities than in predominantly Euro-American communities. In 2000, LaVeist and Wallace (2000) researched and found evidence that alcohol continued to be more available in African American communities than in white communities. One factor is that advertising in urban areas entices drinking.

The scope of problems that affects the African American community, especially the younger population, is still poorly understood. Some of the problem comes from the fact that most studies of African American youth come from impoverished urban areas, which are organized differently than other settings, such as rural (Vazsonyi, Trejos-Castillo, & Young, 2008). Yet, it is not only the inner cities that reflect AOD problems. These authors found that levels of drug use and delinquency were higher in rural youth in comparison to nonrural ones. In addition, Boyd, Mackey, Phillips, and Travakoli (2006) found that African American women who live in rural areas experience a disproportionate number of negative health and social consequences as a result of their AOD use when compared with the AOD use of white women.

DEVELOPMENTAL ISSUES Albdour and Krouse (2014) conducted a literature review (1996–2013) on bullying among African American youth. One finding was that urban, lower income African American youth were 3 times more likely to be physically and verbally bullied and were more likely to be involved in bullying activities either as perpetrators or victims than other racial groups. Espelage, Low, Polanin, and Brown (2013) report that regardless of the role as bully/victim, African American adolescents who were involved were at higher risk for violence, alcohol, and other drug use than others. Other issues at school such as failing a class, being held back a grade, being sent to the principal, and having a family conference increase risk factors for African American urban youth. At the same time, there are protective factors at school. Trenz, Dunne, Zur, and Latimer (2015) found that feeling good about school and feeling good about teachers helped decrease the risk. Albdour and Krouse (2014) found that adolescents whose families provided positive and supportive home environments had some level of protection against bullying and violence. These families were seen as understanding of adolescents' problems and were comforting, helpful, and loving.

Studies showing that adolescent substance use is correlated to neighborhood risk and low parental supervision only drive home the risk for Hurricane Katrina survivors (Burlew et al., 2009). A 2010 study by Rowe, La Greca, and Alexandersson (2010) looked at family and individual factors associated with the effects of Hurricane Katrina. They were particularly interested in adolescents and the effects of posttraumatic stress disorder (PTSD) and substance involvement. Adolescents who reported posttraumatic stress and substance involvement were found to have low family cohesion, low parental monitoring, and more adolescent delinquency. A large number of African American families were displaced as a result of Hurricane Katrina, and the effects of this catastrophe will be felt for years to come as these families transition back to a sense of normalcy.

Social networks have an influence on risk. In a study of inner-city African American "drinking buddies," Yang, Davey-Rothwell, and Latkin (2013) found that males who had drinking buddies in their social networks were at greater risk. Specifically, if males had a female drinking buddy, they were more likely to have symptoms of alcohol dependence. On the other hand, females' dependency symptoms were not associated with gender of social network membership: Females who simply had drinking buddies that included sex partner, kin, and nonkin members were more at risk for developing alcohol dependency symptoms. Yang et al. (2013) confirm the idea that alcohol is a social behavior for African Americans.

From the stress that African Americans face, it is not surprising to entertain the idea that African Americans as young as 13 years old report drinking to cope. Furthermore, drinking to cope increases throughout young adulthood (O'Hara et al., 2014). To a degree, this risk is lessened if African American youth live with both biological parents who had at least some higher education and were employed (McDade, King, & Vidourek, 2015).

AT A GLANCE

African Americans

Population

41 million African Americans live mainly in New York, Florida, Texas, Georgia, California, and North Carolina.

African Americans make up 13.2% of the total U.S. population.

(Continued)

AT A GLANCE (Continued)

Education

80% age 25 and older have a high school diploma.

30% have a bachelor's degree.

Income

24.5% live at poverty level.

$33,916 is the median family income.

Children and Parenting

Many childrearing concerns such as caretaking, discipline, financial responsibility, companionship, emotional support, and problem-solving are shared.

Children occupy a central role in the marriage and essentially tie the marriage together.

Family Organization and Communication

Children can be informally "adopted" or reared by other family members who have more resources than the biological parents (child-keeping).

Spiritual Beliefs and Practices

Religion is important, and the church is seen as potentially providing an intricate social life while promoting mental health and a sense of connectedness.

Involvement with the church allows outlets for creative talents that otherwise might be thwarted.

LATINO AND HISPANIC POPULATIONS

The term *Latino American* is used to describe those persons living in the United States who share a common cultural background. The term *Hispanic* refers to Spaniards and Portuguese, whereas *Latino* includes those known as Chicanos, Cubanos, Puerto Ricans, Latin Americans, and Mexican Americans. The Latino population comprises three major groups: Mexican Americans, Puerto Ricans, and Cuban Americans. The following section will present information on these groups as well as some information on Central and South Americans. In general, differences among these three groups of people are influenced largely by educational level, socioeconomic status, immigration status, age/generation, rural versus urban residence, country of origin, and degree of acculturation (Torres, 1993).

Background

The immigration patterns among Cuban Americans, Puerto Rican Americans, Central and South Americans, and Mexican Americans are varied. Joining the 50,000 Cubans already living in the states were large numbers of Cubans who emigrated during the political unrest of the 1950s. The majority of those leaving were the highly educated, professional, and business upper-class people

(Garcia-Preto, 2005). About 3,000 wealthy Cubans left when Fidel Castro came into power in 1959, and they were joined by another wave of middle-class immigrants who came to the United States in 1960. Finally, in 1980, came a wave of working-class Cubans, some 125,000 strong, who were mostly African American Cubans. Puerto Rican Americans have immigrated to the United States mainly for economic reasons in slow but steady rates. Central and South Americans represent the most recent Latino/Hispanic immigrants to the United States. Most of these individuals came because of political upheaval in their respective countries. Exact figures of immigrants are unavailable, mostly because of their being undocumented, but it is known that a majority come from Guatemala, El Salvador, and Nicaragua (Burns & D'Avanzo, 1993; Garcia-Preto, 2005). These same authors note that this group experiences a high incidence of PTSD. The authors attribute the PTSD to the violence experienced by these individuals in their homelands as well as to the trauma, such as beatings and rape, experienced while traveling to the United States through Mexico. With the exception of those living in the southwestern United States, the majority of Mexican families living in the United States are immigrants.

The presence of Latinos/Hispanics in the southwest region of the United States dates back to the early 1500s. The outcome of the Mexican War (1846–1848), caused by conflict over Texas, witnessed the annexation of Arizona, California, Colorado, New Mexico, Texas, and portions of Utah and Nevada. Along with this annexation came more than 75,000 Mexican people who were granted U.S. citizenship (Burns & D'Avanzo, 1993). The Mexican Revolution of 1910 was the cause of another influx of Latino/Hispanic immigrants to the United States. In addition, Burns and D'Avanzo point out that, between World War II and the 1960s, the Braceros Programs allowed for seasonal laborers to enter the country to work in the fields of California, Arizona, Washington, Texas, and the Midwest.

Values

Hispanic and *Latino* are adjectives used to describe people in this country in a way that would not be used in their country of origin (Garcia-Preto, 2005). The term *Hispanic* was initiated in the 1970s and was used by the U.S. Department of Education to track population. It refers to the Spanish culture and language, whereas the term *Latino* refers to Spain's former colonies in South America, Central Mexico, and Mexico. As with the other culturally and ethnically diverse populations discussed in this chapter, values indigenous to the Latino/Hispanic culture come into frequent conflict with the Euro-American value system, which can cause distress for the Latino/Hispanic individual and family. Feelings of guilt, self-doubt, and even betrayal can create disharmony within and among Latino/Hispanic families. Similar disruptions can occur when individual family members take advantage of economic or educational opportunities not taken by other family members. Beutell and Schneer (2014) write about the importance of career success and its relationship to the family. This value is seen as being perhaps more important than the value of family and having children.

FAMILY AND CARING Traditional Latino/Hispanic families value the family above almost everything else except career success (Beutell & Schneer, 2014). Generally speaking, strong family values are seen as a protective factor against Hispanic/Latino substance abuse (Garza & Gasquoine, 2013).

The traditional Latino/Hispanic family is private, and this is especially true with problems such as AOD abuse. The family protects the individual and demands loyalty while stressing the importance of family proximity, cohesiveness, and respect (*respeto*) for parental authority. *Orgullo* (pride), *verguenza* (shame), *confianza* (confidence), *dignidad* (dignity), and *pobre pero honesto* (poor but honest) are typical values in traditional Latino/Hispanic families (Chartier, Negroni, &

Hesselbrock, 2010; Falicov, 2005). However, as Latinos/Hispanics become more acculturated into mainstream Euro-American society, these values become a source of conflict. Joining gangs, where these values operate strongly, becomes one way Latino/Hispanic youths cope with the conflict of values. Similar to, yet different from, many African American families, Latino/Hispanic families usually live in a nuclear arrangement but do have extended families living nearby. The large size of the family, usually consisting of parents and four or five children, influences the family structure in many ways. Depending on the degree of acculturation, Latino/Hispanic families value affiliation and cooperation while placing much less value upon confrontation and competition (Falicov, 2002; 2005). Moreover, many childrearing concerns such as caretaking, discipline, financial responsibility, companionship, emotional support, and problem solving are shared. In traditional Latino/Hispanic families, for example, the role of godparents is very pronounced. The emphasis on intergenerational and lateral interdependence, however, does not diminish the value of *cariño,* or deep caring for the family, nor does it eliminate the need for strong adherence to a high degree of hierarchical organization in which rules are clearly organized around age and gender. Even though, traditionally, older male children are given the greatest authority and power, Latino/Hispanic families place emphasis on equality and on unconditional acceptance of family members. Parents often provide much nurturance and protection for children and do not push them into achievement when it involves unhealthy competition between family members (Falicov, 2002).

Children also occupy a central role in the marriage. Because *el amor de madre* (motherly love) is seen as a much greater love than romantic love, it is the existence of the children that essentially ties the marriage together. Even though children enjoy a central role in the family, their status is lower than that of their parents. It is *respeto* (respect) that maintains the child's status while allowing parents to reinforce a dependence and dutiful posture among their children (Garcia-Preto, 2005).

GENDER ROLES   Almost everyone is familiar with the hackneyed version of Latino/Hispanic *machismo* or *muy hombre.* According to Falicov, this value dictates the need for males to be strong, brave, protective of their women (mothers, sisters, wives), aggressive, sexually experienced, courageous, and authoritarian. The implication is for women to be humble, submissive, virtuous, and devoted to their home and children. This value prevails regardless of whether the woman works outside of the home, and this can cause stress in the home (Beutell & Schneer, 2014). This value for females is known as *hembrismo* or *marianismo* and underscores the importance of the self-sacrificing mother. *Marianismo* and *hembrismo* (discussed later) also serve to counterbalance the male value of *machismo* (Stevens, 1973).

In actuality, many Latino/Hispanic men are dependent and submissive, and it is the women who are dominant and controlling (Falicov, 2002; Garcia-Preto, 2005). In public, the "self-denial" of the mother is reinforced by the father's insistence that the children obey and help her. Often, however, he is much less involved with the children other than to discipline them, and, on more than one occasion, the mother may find herself in covert disagreement with him. When this occurs, she may act as a mediator between the children and the father, thus adding more to her central position in the family (Stevens, 1973).

Hembrismo is the female counterpart to the male machismo and reflects "femaleness" through strength, perseverance, flexibility, and the ability to survive. The conflict of values arising between the male need to demonstrate *machismo* and the female values of *marianismo* and *hembrismo* can create stress for Latino/Hispanic males. Alcohol, the most commonly abused drug among contemporary Latino/Hispanics, at one time helped to build a social structure into their societies. It now appears that drinking alcohol is an accepted way of dealing with stresses of acculturation and the problems related to social, environmental, and political structures (Gallardo & Curry, 2009).

During adolescence, gender differences appear. Hispanic male adolescents are encouraged to increase interactions with peers, increase autonomy, and begin dating. Females, on the other hand, experience a tightening of parental controls (Cervantes, Padilla, Napper, & Goldbach, 2013). These researchers have concerns that this restriction of females may indeed increase their proclivities toward depression and lower feelings of well-being.

Risk Factors for Alcohol and Other Drug Abuse

SOCIOLOGICAL RISK FACTORS   According to Bacio, Mays, and Lau (2013), the majority of immigrants entering the United States are Latino. The acculturation process that ensues is replete with stresses resulting from a clash of cultural norms, including incongruous belief systems, ambiguous legal status, language barriers, discrimination, and beliefs of inferiority. Just in terms of discrimination alone, 70% of Latinos of foreign birth and 49% of Latinos born in the United States see this as a major issue (Lopez, Morin, & Taylor, 2010). As with other culturally and ethnically diverse populations, the resulting tensions involved in acculturation raise the level of risk for alcohol and other drug abuse among the Latino/Hispanic population (Bacio et al., 2013). In terms of risk for substance abuse, it is important to know that being born in the United States is less a risk factor than the amount of time an Hispanic person spends in the country (Blanco et al., 2013).

In general, Latino adolescents drink at the second highest rates—just behind non-Hispanic white teenagers (Vega & Sribney, 2011). Yet, there are differences between immigrant youth and those born in the United States: Latinos born in the United States drink more than their immigrant counterparts. In fact, Vega and Sribney (2011) identify the "immigrant paradox," which means that in spite of (and, perhaps because of), the fact that immigrants face greater health risks than U.S.-born Latinos, the former are less likely to abuse substances (Bacio et al., 2013; Vasquez, 2009; Vega, Canino, Cao, & Alegria, 2009).

It is difficult to determine gender differences in drug use by Hispanics because many studies look more at global differences (Vaughan, Gassman, Jun, & de Martinez, 2015). To address this concern, Vaughan et al. (2015) studied gender and found that Hispanic youth are more likely to be involved with gambling, and this activity puts them at greater risk for substance abuse—regardless of gender. Peer factors are strong predictors of substance use, and as you would expect, the more that a Hispanic person has drinkers in his or her social circle, the greater the likelihood that drinking behavior will ensue. Vaughan, et al. (2015) found that Hispanic male students did perceive their friends and parents approving of substance abuse, gambling, and carrying weapons—all risk factors for substance abuse. Hispanic females who were involved in family activities seem more immune from this risk.

Other sociological risk factors for substance abuse by Latino/Hispanic youth reflect the problems confronted in the schools. Varying degrees of language proficiency are excessive and can pose serious problems both in seeking and maintaining employment or when children attend English-speaking schools. Cleveland, Wiebe, McGuire, and Zheng (2015) studied close to 15,000 ethnic minority American high school students for risk factors related to alcohol use. Similar to findings for other ethnic minorities, these researchers found that when minority high school students associated with white students who drank, it increased the risk factor for drinking behavior. Similar findings were reported in another large-scale study of 54,631 students in grades 7 through 12 (King, Vidourek, & Merianos, 2013). These researchers found that Hispanic youth reported higher incidence of nonmedical prescription drug use, and the risk was higher when Hispanic youth associated with drug-using friends.

As we mentioned at the outset of the chapter, Hispanic is a term that encompasses Mexican, Puerto Rican, Cuban, Central or South American, or other Spanish culture or origin, and studies do not often break down these differences—instead lumping them together. So, it is refreshing and revealing when studies do look at specific populations. This is the case for Chartier, Carmody, Akhtar, Stebbins, Walters, and Warden (2015) who looked at subgroups. These authors found that Puerto Ricans and other Hispanics have the highest rates of using illicit substances during the past month (6.9% and 8.2%, respectively). South Americans had the lowest use rates at 2.1%. Puerto Ricans had the highest use rates for marijuana (5.6%), whereas South Americans and Cubans had the lowest rates (2.1%). Mexicans had the highest rates of alcohol use (7.4%), and this is lowest among Cubans (0.5%).

AT A GLANCE

Latino and Hispanic Populations

Population

46.9 million Hispanics live mainly in California, Texas, New York, Florida, and Illinois.

Latinos and Hispanics make up 15.2% of the total U.S. population.

Education

61% 25 and older have a high school diploma.

12.5% have a bachelor's degree.

Income

21.5% live at poverty level.

55% earn $55,000 or more.

Children and Parenting

Group takes precedence over individual ("We are, therefore I am").

Latinos and Hispanics have strong kinship bonds.

"Family" includes extended family.

Family Organization and Communication

Family protects the individual, demands loyalty, and stresses the importance of family proximity, cohesiveness, and respect (*respeto*) for parental authority.

Family organization is hierarchical.

Traditionally, older male children are given the greatest authority and power, but there is also unconditional acceptance of family members and an emphasis upon equality.

Communication rules are clearly organized around age and gender.

Spiritual Beliefs and Practices

More than two-thirds of Hispanics are Catholic and half of those practice charismatic Catholicism, speaking in tongues, miraculous healings, and prophesying.

THE ELDERLY, DISABLED, AND SEXUAL MINORITY POPULATIONS

Anyone—anytime and anywhere—can become disabled. Some disabilities appear at birth while others can be detected before birth. Other disabilities can be experienced during the course of one's life. The significance of this statement is punctuated by the fact that between 2010 and 2030, the U.S. population of adults aged 65 and older will practically double. This population of "baby boomers" will also live longer. The 65-plus age group will grow from 37 million to more than 70 million, or almost 20% of the U.S. population (Duncan, Nicholson, White, Bradley, & Bonaguro, 2010). Along with growth, this is a group characterized by greater ethnic and racial diversity, higher divorce rates, fewer children, higher levels of education, lower poverty levels, and a greater openness to sexual diversity than previous generations. The swelling baby-boomer population also includes PWDs, who number 49.7 million. Two-thirds of this population have a severe disability (U.S. Department of Labor, Office of Disability Employment Policy, 2011).

People with disabilities have endured a long history of maltreatment, exploitation, and injustice, and this population also experience higher rates of emotional, physical, and sexual abuse than the rest of the population (Bruinius, 2007). Given this, it should come as little surprise that PWDs are at higher risk for substance abuse issues than the rest of the population (Cordova, Parra-Cardona, Blow, Johnson, Prado, & Fitzgerald, 2013; Smedema & Ebener, 2010). In reviewing the literature on trends of substance abuse among PWDs, Glazier and Kling (2013) found that researchers look at three general areas: (1) substance abuse as causing disabilities such as smoking crack, crashing one's car, and becoming disabled; (2) substance abuse as a mediating factor in the rehabilitation and recovery of PWDs such as having rehabilitation thwarted because of an addiction; and (3) substance abuse prevalence studies that consistently show that substance abuse is more common in PWDs than in the rest of the population. These same researchers claim that it is difficult to compare data because different researchers use different methods or define disability differently. Nevertheless, Cordova et al. (2015) studied Latinos with disabilities and found that the higher number of reports of substance abuse among this population was related to ecodevelopmental factors such as poverty, racism, social exclusion, stigma and discrimination, violence, community support and cohesion, and access to services were risk factors. When one generalizes these findings, it can be seen that there are similarities with this population and other minority populations in terms of risk.

Although age-related disabilities are common among the elderly population, it is only one dimension of risk for substance abuse in the elderly population. This larger elderly population of baby boomers will also bring with them drug problems (Choi, DiNitto, & Marti, 2015). For example, the elderly already have a high prevalence of drug-averse reactions. These reactions are simply to legal drugs. Yet, if an older person drinks alcohol, even a moderate amount (one to two drinks), the chances of an adverse reaction jumps 24% than if the person did not drink at all (Immonen, Valvanne, & Pitkälä, 2013; Onder et al., 2002). This is likely because the body is more susceptible to adverse reactions as one ages and clearance mechanisms delay the body's abilities to resolve the interaction.

This aside, this population will also bring with them problems with illicit drugs at higher rates than their predecessors (Rowan & Faul, 2011). Support for this assertion is reflected by Duncan et al. (2010); they say that there has been a significant increase in the number of hospital admissions by the older addicts whose primary substance abuse problem is other than alcohol. Furthermore, the health care system is largely unprepared for the incoming wave of baby boomers and their diverse health needs and especially unprepared for substance abuse treatment; this is significant. The research strongly suggests that elderly persons using drugs will only increase between 2010 and 2030 (Wang & Andrade, 2013).

The rapidly expanding elder population also includes a larger number of lesbian, gay, bisexual, transgender, queer, and questioning individuals (LGBTQQI). The number of LGBTQQI persons living in the United States is difficult to estimate because the earlier versions of individual census forms did not provide space to identify transgender, single, separated, widowed lesbians, gay men, or bisexuals. Nevertheless, Fredriksen-Goldsen et al. (2011) claim that the two million people who identify as a sexual minority will double by 2030.

A rather large study (N = 1,000) provided more information about this group of baby boomer LGBTQQIs (Metlife Mature Market Institute®2 and The Lesbian and Gay Aging Issues Network of the American Society on Aging, 2010). The profile reflected an LGBTQQI as being a well-educated, middle-income employed adult who was living in a committed relationship. One in five was a parent to one or more children. One in 10 of these couples included at least one person aged 65 or older. Eighty-four percent self-identified as white, 3.5% identified as Hispanic, 3.5% as African American, 2.5% as Asian, and 2% as "other." The LGBTQQI population of baby boomers will represent the first cohort to have experienced the visibility that accompanied the modern gay rights movement. This group will bring very different issues than the LGBTQQI that preceded them into retirement. They will also bring both similar and different issues from other minority groups. For instance, within the LGBTQQI community, Social Security benefits are not available to same-sex couples regardless of how long they have been together or structured their financial lives. This holds true regardless of whether they live in a gay marriage, license-granting state. A more subtle and profound issue relates to family bonds. Although the LGBTQQI population lifestyle and values separate it as a group from traditional American values, these differences may also be driving apart LGBTQQI elders from other minority elder groups who value traditional views of the family (Cook-Daniels, 2008).

The potential family implosion further dividing LGBTQQI families is not relegated solely to the elderly population. Asian American/Pacific Islander sexual minority youth struggle to integrate their ethnic identities within the North American culture while also trying to establish an authentic sexual identity. This identity may be incongruent with the norms of both mainstream culture as well as with their parents' culture of origin (Hahm & Adkins, 2009). For South Koreans, that original culture sees homosexuality as a deviant behavior that shames and dishonors the family and brings into question the importance of personal sacrifice for family tranquility (Hahm & Adkins, 2009). African American gay men encounter daily racism and homophobia within multiple contexts within communities. Gresham (2009) maintains that the lived experience of African American gay men reflects marginal disclosure, negative self-referent beliefs, and minimal social engagement. The same author states that scholars have consistently found that the African American community exhibits homophobia because it is seen as a threat to the existence of the African American family structure (Gresham, 2009). Hence, the group of elderly African Americans who are gay or lesbian can face even more stress and isolation. The ensuing isolation from family is among the Asian/Pacific Islander group where sexual minorities were found to be less likely to engage their families for important decisions or emotional support (Rowan & Faul, 2011). The exception is the Native American LGBTQQI individual. Sutton and Broken Nose (2005) say that traditionally, many Native American tribes consider these individuals to be Two Spirits. This is a contemporary name associated with Native American LGBTQQIs that was first adopted in 1990. Two Spirits refer to the male/female spirit, and these individuals are often seen as holding sacred and ceremonial roles.

Adoptees compose another group that is unique. The 2000 census was the first time that data on adoption were collected, and current estimates suggest that more than 6 million adoptees reside in the United States (U.S. Census Bureau, 2011). Although research suggests that adoptees may experience a higher level of psychosocial advantages, they also experience problems in identity development, perceived lack of control, learning disabilities, feelings of shame, loss, guilt, and disruptions in the connections with family (Harrison & Harrison, 2015). They also experience high rates of AOD issues (Westermeyer, Bennett, Thuras, & Yoon, 2007). In their study of 608 adoptee patients, these researchers found that adoptees had substance use disorders 14 times higher than was expected. They conclude that adoptees and their families should remain alert to issues of substance abuse. As we mention later in Chapter 12, this is especially important when one considers that up to 15% of those in residential treatment are adopted and that this population seeks mental health services at a significantly higher rate than the normal nonadopted adult population (Palacios & Brodzinski, 2010).

The *homeless* constitute an ever-growing population with AOD issues. In any given year, 3.5 million people will experience homelessness. A total of 730,000 people are homeless on any given night (National Coalition for the Homeless, 2013). Substance abuse is often a cause of homelessness. Although it is difficult to obtain an accurate number of homeless people who are abusing substances, the National Coalition for the Homeless estimates that 38% of homeless people are dependent on alcohol and 26% abuse other drugs. Some homeless people may view drug and alcohol use as necessary to be accepted among the homeless community (Didenko & Pankratz, 2007).

Risk Factors for Alcohol and Other Drug Abuse

Clearly, sexual minority groups, the elderly, PWDs, adoptees, and the homeless face at least the same risks as other minority groups. In fact, they face greater risks. For example, recall Rolando's case, presented at the outset of this chapter. Rolando is Hispanic. Andrews (2008) found that older Latino men have a history of AOD practices and problems and is convinced that these issues will persist for years to come. This risk of being an older Hispanic male is heightened if he is adopted. In addition, Rolando also has a number of "deviant" labels: baby boomer, gay, and disabled. Li and Moore (2001) believe that deviant labels alone can push individuals into further deviant actions such as AOD abuse. Along the same lines, Taggart, McLaughlin, Quinn, and McFarlane (2007) found reasons that people with disabilities misused alcohol and other drugs centered on "self-medicating against life's negative experiences" (p. 362). Psychological trauma and social distance from the community were cited as specific reasons. It is easy to see that AOD misuse is at least influenced by perceived (and real) trauma that in turn leads to physiological, psychological, financial, and relational problems. This creates more trauma. The vicious cycle that ensues raises the risk of AOD abuse.

More specifically, PWDs face challenges that can include increased likelihood of obtaining a secondary disabling condition, increased likelihood of being a victim of crime, of being unemployed, and of having overall family dysfunction. These risks run 10% to greater than 50% compared with the general U.S. population (West, Graham, & Cifu, 2009). Among the LGBTQQI population, gay males and lesbians are at high risk (Penn, Brooke, Mosher, Gallagher, Brooks, & Richey, 2013; Rowan & Faul, 2011). Even without a disability, elderly individuals are at risk for substance abuse. With advanced technology and medicine, individuals are able to live longer with better quality lives. This is both good news and bad news. According to Lay, King, and Rangel (2008), elderly who have substance abuse issues will be able to enhance their abilities to adapt ways that allow them to continue AOD misuse and abuse as they age. Brucker (2008) is concerned that these same medical advances can also increase the likelihood of prescription drug abuse among the elderly and disabled populations. As with many, if not all, of these special populations, that type of cycle clearly heightens the risks for substance abuse.

HELPING CULTURALLY AND ETHNICALLY DIVERSE POPULATIONS

Issues for the Helping Professionals

Mental health professionals are taught to empathize with their client or clients. Moreover, helping professionals are taught to avoid power struggles and coercive relationships with their clients. Power struggles can come in many forms, and stereotyping is a subtle form of power that can be used to coerce clients of varying cultural and ethnic backgrounds. Another form can be labeling and grouping individuals. By understanding a given group as having certain characteristics and certain drinking or other drug use patterns, a professional can make some gross assumptions about what he or she might be working with. At the same time, we hope you can see that as many differences as commonalities exist among individuals and subgroups.

You, as a mental health professional, should take care to undertake an examination of your own worldview regarding culturally and ethnically diverse groups. You should develop the mindfulness and skills necessary to interact with minority clients in a culturally sensitive and responsive manner.

Chiu, Lonner, Matsumoto, and Ward (2013) maintain that although much research has been undertaken, cross-cultural competencies are still an item of debate. Some researchers focus on the personal characteristics of the counselor (e.g., Matsumoto & Hwang, 2013), some on the neurological mechanisms (e.g., Van der Zee & Van Oudenhoven, 2013), and some on the metacognitive skills of counselors (e.g., Hong, Fang, Yang, & Phua, 2013). It is important to remember that multicultural competency is not solely relegated to race/ethnicity. Diversity also includes differences represented in financial literacy and opportunity, gender, disabilities, social class, religion, immigration status, sexual orientation, age, and the like.

It is critical that multicultural counselors should understand effects of racism, discrimination, and microaggessions as well as the effects of social class, privilege, and acculturation with regard to their diverse client populations. Recall the "immigrant paradox" that was discussed earlier in the chapter. This paradox showed that in many cases those living longer in the United States were at greater risk of AOD use and abuse than their immigrant counterparts, which suggests the long-term deleterious effects of acculturation. Identifying with one's native culture is seen as a protective factor against substance abuse, and it stands to reason that helping clients through the framework of their world views and culture would enhance these protective factors—to say nothing of the respect it would demonstrate.

In their review of several assessments of cultural competence, Matsumoto and Hwang (2013) found that the assessments identified and measured personal traits reflecting tolerance of ambiguity, social initiative, perceptual acuity, flexibility, and empathy on the part of counselors. Both Duan and Brown (2016) and Pedersen, Lonner, Draguns, Trimble, and Scharron-del Rio (2016) would agree that a sense of social justice would also be an important ingredient in cultural competency. Other researchers (e.g., Chiu et al., 2013) suggest that counselor sensitivity to the cultural differences concomitant with an ability to adjust and adapt to varying cultural environments while reflecting on how culture influences one's thoughts and actions are significant factors making up a culturally competent counselor. Finally, in discussing ethical multiculturalism, Harper (2006) sees ethical treatment of a diverse clientele as including moral reasoning, cultural competence, beneficence/nonmaleficence, and respect for persons and communities. Cornish, Schreier, Nadkarni, and Metzger (2010), Cartwright and D'Andrea (2005), Pedersen (2002), and Pedersen et al. (2016) all support the idea that multiculturalism is not a complication as much as it is a complexity. Pedersen favors the term "culture-centered" counseling over the concept of multicultural counseling in order to emphasize the centrality of culture in the counseling process.

Given the stigma associated with alcoholism and being a minority, one can clearly see how important it is to embrace the level of professionalism inherent in cultural competence and culture-centered approaches. Recent research into cultural competency reflects a shift from skills of counselors to the overall management, organizational policy, and processes of care (Guerrero, 2009). An interesting study of processes of care was conducted by Bamatter et al. (2010). Studying the transcripts of 23 counselors, they found that 83% used informal discussions of topics unrelated to treatment with their Hispanic clients, and this was seen as a negative. This was especially true for non-Latino counselors. Results showed that counselors should endeavor to maintain more formal relationships with Hispanic clients in early treatment sessions in order to enhance treatment.

Assessment and Treatment Issues

As an overview, Chartier, Vaeth, and Caetano (2013) studied alcohol consumption across various ethnic groups. They found that ethnicities with higher risks experience higher rates of harmful drinking. Chartier et al. found that factors affecting alcohol use were being socially disadvantaged, one's alcohol metabolism, the level of acculturation, and a person's drinking preferences. These researchers maintain that both Native Americans and Hispanics have higher risks for alcohol-related motor vehicle fatalities, suicides, liver disease, and death by liver disease. African Americans have increased risk for alcohol-related family violence, fetal alcohol syndrome, heart disease, and some cancers.

Remember, this book is written for the generalist in the helping field, rather than for a specialist in the field of addictive behaviors. You will likely assess your client for the extent of involvement with alcohol and other drugs, then refer him or her to a specialist if needed. To make an assessment, mental health professionals must understand how the client's culture views alcohol and other drug use. What may be defined as problematic drug use in a predominantly Euro-American culture may be viewed as normal in a nonwhite culture. For example, an Asian American's frank confrontation with his or her boss when both are drunk is sometimes considered appropriate. Therefore, sharing with clients that you suspect a problem with their use of alcohol or another drug without an understanding of acceptable use in their culture may be incorrect. It may also be inappropriate. Your lack of knowledge may discourage the client from seeking further assistance from you or others in the helping services. If a problem does exist, you may have missed an opportunity to help. If there is a serious problem, it may become more serious.

When assessing for treatment needs of minority populations, Cochran, Peavy, and Cauce (2007) and Cunningham, Foster, and Warner (2010) discuss the issues faced by practitioners. These researchers are in agreement that little is known about the challenges faced by sexual minorities. It is important to identify the psychotherapeutic process that has favorable contributions to client outcomes for these populations, and this is especially important within family-focused, evidence-based treatments for youth.

Treatment does work. Yet, Henderson, Dakof, Greenbaum, and Liddle (2010) say that little is known about why treatments work and which treatments work best for different types of clients. In general, motivation to change or client readiness is considered critical for successful treatment, and enhancing motivation to change substance use is a significant component of many intervention programs. However, Austin, Hospital, Wagner, and Morris (2010) maintain that specific factors predicting the motivation to change are poorly understood, and this is especially true among racial/ethnic minority youth. In their study of 310 substance-abusing minority youth, they found that parental factors may have a strong influence on motivation to change. The involvement of families in treatment is critical (Henderson et al., 2010). The reason for this is because family relationship issues have been found to be significant risk factors for the initiation and maintenance of substance abuse problems, and it stands to reason that involving family members to enhance relationships should be able to counter the risk factors.

WORKING WITH NATIVE AMERICANS When working with Native Americans, remember that "Direct confrontation is limited to making sure the individual is aware of the consequences of behavior. Then, it is left to the innate forces within the individual to operate" (Attneave, 1982, p. 70).

Given that 16% of AI/AN met the criteria for substance abuse disorder in 2010 (Substance Abuse and Mental Health Services Administration, 2012), treatment is a major concern. Yet, access to health services continues to be limited (Campbell et al., 2015). Legha, Raleigh-Cohn, Fickenscher, and Novins (2014) used a qualitative method to study the barriers to treatment, and the results of their study revealed that there are challenges directly associated with providing clinical services, issues with infrastructure of the treatment settings, and issues regarding the greater service delivery system. They recommend that services for the AI/AN population have better integration, be more comprehensive and individualized, and provide longer treatment modalities. Hidden among these challenges is the lack of research. For instance, evidence-based treatment practices for this community are not studied (Gone & Looking, 2011), and clinical trials are hard to come by (Dickerson, Venner, & Duran, 2014).

From studies that have been undertaken, using cultural-based interventions seem to have the most promise. Dialectical-behavioral therapy was found effective in blending cultural norms and traditional practice among AI/AN (Beckstead, Lambert, DuBose, & Linehan, 2015). Drum-Assisted Recovery Therapy for Native Americans (DARTNA) has also found to be effective (Dickerson et al., 2014). DARTNA consists of using the Twelve Steps of AA, Narcotics Anonymous (NA), drumming, talking circles, and the Medicine Wheel (White Bison Inc., 2007). Another treatment program is based upon The Red Road (White Bison Inc., 2002) in which Native Americans in treatment are encouraged to focus on a positive journey of life that embodies the relational world of Native spirituality and values (Chong, Fortier, & Morris, 2009).

Coyhis and Simonelli (2008) identified a similar approach called, the Wellbriety Movement, and the rallying cry of "Our culture is prevention" is good for Native American peoples because it uses their own cultural and ethnic strengths to foster recovery. Wellbriety means achieving sobriety and abstinence from substance abuse while going beyond "clean and sober." It suggests that Native Americans should recover culturally by entering a journey of healing and balance mentally, emotionally, physically, and spiritually. This dimension addresses sociopolitical causes without diminishing the individual's need to do the hard work required for recovery. This also signifies the deep desire for Native Americans to live through the best attributes of traditional Native cultures while living in today's world.

In general, the role of social support is important for mental health professionals to consider when building the clients' social skills. This may be one of the most significant aspects of recovery once formal treatment is terminated (Spear, Crevecoeur-MacPhail, Denering, Dickerson, & Brecht, 2013). Providers can help American Indians and Alaska Natives by facilitating the attendance at self-help meetings during treatment in the hopes that the relationships that are developed there can help sustain sobriety once released from treatment.

WORKING WITH ASIAN AMERICANS/PACIFIC ISLANDERS As with other diverse groups, it is imperative that counseling working with Asian Americans and Pacific Islanders identify cultural variables, themes, and values (Lee & Valencia, 2013). Research suggests that Asian Americans, while exhibiting lower rates of alcohol problems than other minority groups, continue to underuse substance abuse treatment facilities (Yu, Clark, Chandra, Dias, & Lai, 2009). This observation is important because studies have shown that there is a wide variation of drinking habits among this population and show that immigration versus U. S. nativity is a mediating variable (Nishimura, Hishinuma, & Goebert, 2014). It is interesting that Cook et al. found that lower levels of acculturation, indicated by use of their native language, acts as a protective factor for Asian Americans. Although it may be a protective factor against alcohol use, language may paradoxically act as a deterrent for those seeking treatment.

However, once the language and cultural barriers are addressed through culturally sensitive treatment modalities, this group tends to be more committed to achieve their treatment goals (Yu et al., 2009). If, when assessing Asian Americans/Pacific Islanders, you determine that an individual might benefit from treatment, remember that your suggestions for treatment need to be addressed through the father or elder, who will be making the decision for himself or for other family members. An element of cultural sensitivity and bilingualism needs to be intrinsic to whatever intervention is agreed upon. For example, DUI classes are offered for Asian Americans/Pacific Islanders, and Alcoholics Anonymous (AA) groups exist for Japanese-speaking individuals. It is important to remember that when culturally competent services are combined with effective case management and motivational interviewing, Asian clients tend to increase their accomplishment

WORKING WITH AFRICAN AMERICANS Pope, Wallhagen, and Davis (2010) maintain that even though prevalence studies are difficult to obtain for the African American substance abuser population, it is estimated that by 2020, this older group of substance-abusing African American adults will reach almost half a million people. Assessing African Americans for alcohol and other drug abuse varies from that of other culturally and ethnically diverse populations. For instance, African American youth who report substance abuse problems receive less specialty and informal care than Hispanic youth (Alegria, Carson, Goncalves, & Keefe, 2011). For a middle-aged African American male who reports drinking heavily at the local tavern with friends on Saturday, a mental health professional might be well advised to suggest that a friend drive him home rather than refer him for assessment and potential treatment.

In general, African Americans initiate treatment less frequently than whites (Keen, Whitehead, Clifford, Rose, & Latimer, 2014) and wait longer to enter treatment than whites (Andrews, Shin, Marsh, & Cao, 2013). Once in treatment, African American youth are more than twice as likely as other groups to leave treatment prematurely (Andrews et al., 2013; Austin & Wagner, 2010).

Multidimensional family therapy (MDFT; Liddle, 2010) is an effective treatment for substance abusing adolescents. MDFT integrates an assessment and treatment among (1) the adolescent as an individual and as a member of a family and peer network; (2) the parents as individuals and in their respective roles as parents; (3) the family environment and family relationships, focusing on transactional patterns; and (4) extrafamilial sources of influence such as peers, schools, and juvenile justice. Different versions are used for varying age groups so that it is not a "one size fits all" treatment. MDFT has been shown to be effective with African Americans (Greenbaum et al., 2015; Henderson et al., 2010). Specifically, results indicate that it is quite effective with those adolescents who exhibit more severe drug use.

According to Sanders (2002), the 1980s and 1990s reflected attempts to adopt traditional recovery support networks. Networks such as AA and NA were seen as more culturally relevant and attractive to African Americans, and treatment centers that were being developed were aimed at being more culturally sensitive. Currently, taking from Chief Andy Chelsea's proclamation that the Native American community is the treatment center, indigenous addiction treatment for African Americans is also strongly emphasized. The Glide Memorial Methodist Church in San Francisco is an example of such a community-oriented treatment approach. Initiated in 1989, approximately 80% of today's community-based congregation is working on recovery. In this treatment approach, the overt expression of rage and anger is encouraged because the expression of it is seen as an important component of recovery. Another indigenous approach is the Free-N-One recovery program. Sanders (2002) describes this as a Christian-centered recovery program that provides various support groups for addicts and their families. A fourth type of indigenous program is the Nation of Islam program. This program has been in existence since the 1950s and is aimed at helping African American male substance abusers in the criminal justice system. A fifth community-based approach is called the African American Survivors Organization. The purpose of this organization is to provide African American men a safe place to talk about issues. Often, these issues are the very ones that would not be talked about in recovery meetings if a racial mix of members attended. The format of the African American Survivors Organization is somewhat similar to the traditional Twelve Step meetings that we will discuss in Chapter 11.

Myers (2012) studied substance use among rural African American adolescents. She found that risk factors for this group of adolescents were (1) being 15 years or older; (2) spending afternoons after school with friends; (3) having a social network of parents and family members who used drugs; (4) being raised by nonfamily members; and (5) having plans to enter the military after high school. At the same time, if African American adolescents are raised by parents and/or family members who talk to them about the dangers of drugs and disapprove of their use, risk factors go down. Likewise, if the adolescent is involved in church activities, or is involved in after-school or activities, or has plans to attend additional post-high school education, risk factors go down.

There are some barriers to treatment that are important for mental health professionals to know, and these relate to where treatment is offered, individual perceptions of the need for help, and the impact of stigma. Borders, Booth, and Curran (2015) found that rural African Americans abusing cocaine wanted treatment to be outside of their community. In some cases, a barrier to treatment is one's own belief that he or she "can handle it by themselves" (Keen et al., 2014). This is one of the most common barriers to treatment. Stigma and wait lists are also barriers.

WORKING WITH LATINOS AND HISPANICS Traditional values may influence efforts to assess alcohol and other drug use in the Latino/Hispanic population. The traditional value of *machismo* implies that Latina/Hispanic women are not to drink. Yet they do, and younger Latina/Hispanic women are experimenting with alcohol in greater numbers. Many older women may be reluctant to report substance abuse because of the shame associated not only with their loss of control, but also with their violation of tradition. So, when assessing for substance abuse in Latino/Hispanic individuals it is important, if not crucial, to determine the extent of the client's acculturation. Remember that studies consistently show that the longer a person is acculturated in the United States, the higher the risk for substance use.

Because Hispanics and other racial/ethnic populations experience discrimination, and discrimination is associated with higher levels of stress-induced drinking, it is important to design prevention programs that address this issue. Programs that enhance *familismo* and *respeto* and discourage fatalistic beliefs while helping youth deal effectively with discrimination may help reduce the risks of AOD use and abuse in this population (Blanco et al., 2013). These same researchers go on to say that promoting Hispanic traditional culture and values, helping with ethnic identification, and integration of Hispanic social networks can help reduce the risks. Although these are helpful guidelines, a major issue confronting Hispanics are barriers to treatment.

Latinas are more likely to encounter challenges when entering treatment, and the primary issue is problem recognition (Ayón & Carlson, 2014). If she is living in an environment that supports drug use, it is likely that Latinas will not see their drug use as a problem. According to Ayón and Carlson, the problem is most easily recognized if they are dissatisfied with their lives or if child protective services is involved with the possibility of taking children out of the home. Stigma is also a barrier to treatment, and the gender expectations of Latinas reinforce this barrier by increasing the shame associated with using drugs and possibly losing one's children. A third challenge relates to the resources needed to secure a place in treatment. Often, Latinas will need help in filling out paperwork and finding childcare. Once entering treatment, Latinas may find that the system of care is not very compatible with their indigenous culture in that there may be significantly more interactions than they find comfortable. This will naturally lead to more discomfort if the caregiver attempts to hurry the building of trust and/or if the staff are not linguistically or culturally competent (see the section on cultural competence). Finally, earlier studies (e.g., Amaro, Nieves, Johannes, & Cabeza, 1999) have indicated that an overwhelming majority (80%) of a sample of Latina mothers had a history of childhood emotional or sexual abuse and that Latinas with a history of childhood abuse had higher treatment dropout rates than those Latinas with no reported history of abuse.

Ironically, approaching men through the *machismo* value may prove effective in assessing use. While *machismo* allows for heavy drinking, being a strong family provider is also valued and often stands in direct opposition to excessive drinking behavior. By focusing on the man's need to be a strong provider and a good role model for his sons especially, the helping professional may be able to help the Latino/Hispanic father determine whether a problem exists. Nevertheless, *hembrismo*, the female version of *machismo*, reminds us that while approaching Hispanic males through machismo might be helpful, it should not be at the expense of the Hispanic females.

The Latino/Hispanic population generally is a religious one and includes traditional and nontraditional religious practices, with many Cuban Americans and Puerto Ricans following nontraditional practices. Assessment and referrals should include attention paid to services offered by churches and facilities that allow for a variety of religious practices. Helpers also need to keep this in mind because some Mexican families often consult with *curanderos* (folk healers) for help in dealing with stress-related symptoms (Falicov, 2005).

WORKING WITH ELDERLY POPULATIONS   Elderly populations are at risk because of the amount of medications prescribed, potential for adverse effects with psychopharmacology, discrimination, and increasing age-related disabilities. Proehl (2007) believes that we often deny that the elderly population has mental illness and addictions, and when we do acknowledge them, we configure them as anomalies. Substance abuse treatment designed and focused on the elderly is rare in the United States. When one adds elderly homelessness into the equation, the problem only escalates. Proehl believes that the problem escalates because the elderly homeless population is confronted with losses of hearing and vision, which creates hypervigilance and a lack of trust and faith in treatment. Moreover, because the elderly homeless are often targets in homeless shelters, they may prefer to remain on the street rather than face the fear of becoming institutionalized.

WORKING WITH LGBTQQI POPULATIONS   The number of LGBTQQI persons living in the United States is difficult to estimate because the earlier versions of individual census forms did not provide space to identify transgender, single, separated, widowed lesbians, gay men, or bisexuals. As a result of enacted, felt, or internalized stigma, LGBT older adults often avoid using traditional elder services because of a lack of specific LGBT programming (Drazdowski, Perrin, Trujillo, Sutter, Benotsch, & Snipes, 2016). These same researchers claim that this group may also rely upon aging services, home care, and institutionalized care in elevated degrees compared to their heterosexual counterparts due in part to demographic and policy factors. These factors include the lack of transferrable spousal benefits through Social Security and the Veteran's Administration.

In general, treatment for the LGBTQQI has not been well-researched (Cochran, Grella, & Mays, 2012). Yet, there is ample evidence that this population is at increased risk for AOD abuse (Cochran et al., 2012). These same researchers claim that this population also presents with significant levels of mental health issues (i.e., depression, low self-esteem, isolation, and suicide) that result from the stresses of social stigma and marginalization.

Rutherford, McIntyre, Daley, and Ross (2012) maintain that there is a large number of heterosexual substance abuse counselors who have a homophobic attitude towards LGBTQ clients or who do not feel that they have the working expertise to help this population. Penn et al. (2013) conducted interviews with 10 LGBTQ clients and found several themes that emerged: silence about sexual identity, experience of prejudice, negative consequences of coming out, interrelatedness of therapy and life issues, feeling misunderstood, positive experiences relating to others, and treatment recommendation (p. 472). Although some clients reported good experiences with treatment, these researchers found that many therapists did not inquire about sexual orientation, and the clients often did not bring it up because they did not generally discuss their orientations with their families and thus found it awkward to discuss it with a therapist. It was also awkward to discuss the prejudice they experience. Many were silent about their experiences of discrimination. Coming out in therapy was a negative experience for some, and these clients believed providers were resistant to helping and/or tied sexual orientation to deeper psychological problems. This was especially true for the transgender client who felt isolated. She also feared for her safety as a transgender person, and some other clients indicated they generally felt unsafe in treatment settings because they were "different."

Rutherford et al. (2012) recommend that treatment facilities need to construct a LGBTQ-friendly atmosphere such as LGBT-related photos or artwork up at the facility. Having therapists work on their acceptance of this population is also seen as helpful as is having the staff provide more holistic treatment. It may be advantageous to have this clientele talk about their relationships, and specific LGBTQ questions could become a component of the intake procedure. Treatment providers should address sexual identity and orientation within the treatment and weave it together with substance abuse and mental health treatment protocols. When sexual identity is discussed, it tended to increase the clients' perceptions that treatment would be effective. It may actually enhance treatment if the facility provides LGBTQ-specific group counseling as well as having openly LGBTQ personnel on staff. Finally, it is important to acknowledge that when LGBTQ clients present with a co-occurring disorder (see Chapter 9) with substance abuse, this clientele may be even more vulnerable due to the barriers to effective treatment. To counter this vulnerability, LGBTQ clients with co-occurring disorders may actually hide their sexual identity out of fear of being denied mental health services.

SENSITIVITY TO MULTICULTURAL ISSUES   A review of the research suggests that for minority clients, treatment centers should be close to the client's family, residence, and/or social network. Moreover, because the fear of discrimination, stigma, and other forms of oppression is very real in the lives of racial/ethnic minorities, it is critical that this client population be allowed to "be themselves" in treatment. Hence, mental health counselors need to be aware of the extent to which the treatment facility or program promotes the use of the client's language and cultural traditions. It is also important that the facility or program employ people at all levels of staff who reflect the makeup of its clients. With outpatient facilities specifically, the days and hours of operation are important considerations. When referring to a local center, be aware that clients may be working swing-shifts or nights and will need services that are congruent with their work schedules and family-care situations. Subgroups within these larger diverse populations experience risk factors for developing AOD problems, and this includes adolescents, the elderly, persons with disabilities, LGBTQQI, and adoptees. Substance abuse counselors and service providers need to remain culturally responsive and focus on building alliances, using culturally appropriate instruments, becoming aware of sociopolitical issues, and dealing effectively with stigma.

MyCounselingLab for Addictions/Substance Abuse

Start with the Topic 11 Assignments: *Working with Diverse Cultures* and then try the Topic 10 Assignments: *Working with Selected Populations.*

Summary

- Today's minority populations will increase in numbers and make up approximately one-third of the general U.S. population in the next two decades.
- Diverse populations traditionally are at heightened levels of risk for substance abuse.
- These researchers maintain that both Native Americans and Hispanics have higher risks for alcohol-related motor vehicle fatalities, suicides, liver disease, and death by liver disease.
- Factors affecting alcohol use were being socially disadvantaged, one's alcohol metabolism, the level of acculturation, and a person's drinking preferences.

There are within group differences regarding substance abuse.

- Diverse populations generally mistrust the treatment system.
- Puerto Ricans and other Hispanics have the highest rates of using illicit substances during the past month (6.9% and 8.2%, respectively).
- South Americans had the lowest use rates at 2.1%. Puerto Ricans had the highest use rates for marijuana (5.6%), whereas South Americans and Cubans had the lowest rates (2.1%). Mexicans had the highest rates of alcohol use (7.4%) and was lowest among Cubans (0.5%).
- Persons with disabilities are at higher risk for substance abuse issues than the normal population.
- Treatment for adolescence of diverse groups should include family involvement such as multidimensional family therapy because it is viewed as more culturally relevant for many minority groups.
- Cultural competency is critical for counselors working with diverse populations. Research

strongly suggests that there is a lack of sensitivity among mental health workers in general.
- Culture-centered approaches include counselor competencies in knowledge, attitudes, and skills and understanding of social justice, spirituality, political pluralism, and common ground for conflict resolution.
- It is best to use culturally appropriate assessments to enhance the treatment possibilities.
- Treatment centers that are close to the clients' homes should be used as much as possible to preserve the sense of community.
- The "immigrant paradox" suggests that the longer one is exposed to the U.S. culture, the more likely this population will become acculturated which increases the risk for substance abuse.
- This paradox showed that in many cases those living longer in the United States were at greater risk of AOD use and abuse than their immigrant counterparts which suggests the long-term deleterious effects of acculturation.
- The LGBT population is expected to double to 4 million by 2030.
- Recent laws allowing same-sex marriage will put demands on the system because more people will be eligible for health care under the spouse's insurance.
- With the baby boomers growing into the elderly population, there will be increased demands on hospitals to deal with the substance abuse problems of the elderly.
- Up to 15% of those in residential treatment are adopted, and this population seeks mental health services at a significantly higher rate than the normal nonadopted adult population
- If an older person drinks alcohol, even a moderate amount (one to two drinks), the chances of an adverse reaction jumps 24% than if the person did not drink at all.

Internet Resources

Native Americans and AOD
whitebison.org/wellbriety_movement/index.html

African Americans quitting AOD
thehealingministries.net/donaldson.html

Hispanics and AOD
*chestnut.org/li/apss/Common/Multicultural/Hispanic_
Resources.pdf*

Asian Americans and AOD
napafasa.org/

Culture-centered approaches
apa.org/

Further Discussion

1. What role does discrimination play in perpetuating the assessment of AOD problems among diverse populations?
2. How does the issue of social justice influence the treatment of diverse groups with AOD abuse problems?
3. Given the view that Native Americans are engaged in the longest ongoing protest by drinking, what are your thoughts regarding the issue of responsibility?

CHAPTER 5

Confidentiality and Ethical Issues

CASE EXAMPLES

1. A high school counselor has been working with a student with multiple problems. After being caught with marijuana, the student had been referred to an alcohol and other drugs (AOD) treatment center for an assessment. The treatment program specialist determined that the student was not in need of formal treatment but did recommend that the school counselor work with the student on some social skills and minor family issues. During a discussion, the student tells the school counselor that he is selling pot at school. What should the counselor do?

2. A licensed clinical social worker works in a nonprofit mental health agency. The agency does not provide AOD treatment but does provide aftercare services for recovering clients. This social worker has been working with a recovering intravenous drug user on life skills, such as hygiene, appearance, work behaviors, and leisure-time activities. The client tells the social worker that he is HIV-positive and has been having unprotected sex with a number of partners. What should the social worker do?

3. A marriage and family therapist is in private practice. She has been seeing a woman for depression. The woman works in a management position for a large company. The company has a self-funded insurance plan that pays for the woman's treatment. The personnel manager of the company contacts the therapist, reports that evidence has surfaced that the woman is using cocaine, and tells the therapist that the company is considering termination. She asks the therapist for guidance. What should the therapist do?

4. A very large corporation has an employee assistance program counselor on staff. Any employee can see the counselor for three sessions, after which the counselor must develop a plan that, depending on the employee's problem, usually involves a referral to a private therapist or treatment program. This counselor has been contacted by the chief executive officer (CEO) of the corporation and told to see one of the vice presidents who the CEO believes is alcoholic. After talking to the vice president, the counselor believes that a referral to an alcohol treatment program is appropriate. However, the vice president refuses to follow the recommendation and tells the counselor that she will sue the counselor if he reveals any information to the CEO. The vice president claims that the discussions they have had are confidential. What should the counselor do?

5. A middle school counselor has met several times with a 13-year-old student regarding his problems at home. The student has told the counselor that his mother is addicted to prescription pain pills and he admits to taking a few himself. One day, the principal calls the counselor to her office, where the student's mother demands to know what her son has been talking to the counselor about. What should the counselor say?

In these five situations, we have illustrated some confidentiality issues in the AOD area for mental health professionals. In the remainder of the chapter, we will discuss confidentiality laws that can assist mental health professionals in deciding on the appropriate course of action in such situations, provide guidance for helping professionals in documenting their work with clients, and bring up some of the ethical issues for helping professionals related to the AOD field.

CONFIDENTIALITY: 42 CODE OF FEDERAL REGULATIONS, PART 2 (42 CFR)

Confidentiality for mental health professionals is always problematic because many federal and state laws are often complex and confusing, as are the ethical guidelines developed by professional organizations. As a future mental health professional, you may become familiar with confidentiality guidelines in your training program and then, once in the field, be faced with specific situations that do not fit the general guidelines and legal parameters presented in courses and workshops.

In the AOD area, federal regulations exist to govern confidentiality. We will discuss these regulations in some detail because even if mental health professionals are not providing AOD treatment services in their work setting, the regulations usually still apply. However, these regulations can be complex, and an infinite number of situations related to confidentiality can develop. We suggest the following in situations in which you might be unsure of the appropriate action to take:

1. Consult your supervisor and/or legal counsel.
2. Contact your state attorney general's office regarding state laws on privileged communication and mandatory reporting.
3. Contact the Legal Action Center,[1] an organization that specializes in legal and policy issues in the AOD area.

Does 42 CFR Apply to You?

Issued in 1975 and amended in 1987, 42 CFR contains the regulations issued by the Department of Health and Human Services related to the confidentiality of AOD abuse patient records (terminology used in the regulations). These regulations supersede any local or state laws that are less restrictive than the regulations. Federal regulations in this area were seen as necessary because individuals with AOD problems might be hesitant to seek treatment if their confidentiality could not be guaranteed. This was particularly true when treatment for illegal drug abuse was separate from alcohol treatment, and therefore, simply contacting a drug treatment program became an admission of illegal activity.

Before you conclude that these regulations are irrelevant because you will not be providing AOD treatment, please read further. 42 CFR defines a *program* as any person or organization that, in whole or in part, provides alcohol/drug abuse diagnosis, treatment, or referral for treatment and receives federal assistance. Federal assistance is defined as receiving federal funds in *any* form, even if the funds do not directly pay for AOD services. This includes tax-exempt status by the Internal Revenue Service, authorization to conduct business by the federal government (e.g., Medicaid provider), or conducting services for the federal government or for branches of state government that receive federal funds. This means that, if you work in a school district that has a free

---

[1]The Legal Action Center provides direct legal services to individuals, and publications, training, technical assistance, and education to agencies. The Legal Action Center can be reached at 225 Varick Street, New York, NY 10014 (1-800-223-4044), lacinfo@lac.org.

AT A GLANCE

42 CFR requires that patient confidentiality be maintained with regard to AOD assessment, diagnosis, and treatment except:

- With the written consent of the patient
- In internal discussions with program staff who need the information
- To third-party payers
- To a central registry for patients treated with addictive drugs
- If treatment is a condition of criminal proceedings
- In a medical emergency
- In response to a valid court order
- To qualified service organizations
- If there is a commission of a crime on the organization's premises or against program staff
- For research, audit, or evaluation purposes
- In cases of actual or suspected child abuse or neglect

lunch program and also has a program that refers students to treatment, 42 CFR applies. If you work for a mental health agency that accepts Medicaid or TRICARE (Military Healthcare System) and diagnoses substance use disorders, 42 CFR applies. If you are an employee assistance program (EAP) counselor who works for or has a contract with a company that does business with state or federal government, 42 CFR applies. In fact, the only scenario we can imagine in which 42 CFR would not apply to readers of this text would be a counselor or therapist in private practice who does not accept Medicaid or TRICARE or any other state or federal insurance reimbursement and does not refer, diagnose, or treat clients with AOD problems. This scenario is unlikely.

The General Rule

The general rule in 42 CFR regarding disclosure of records or other information on AOD clients (42 CFR uses the term *patients*) is *don't*. Except under the conditions we will describe later, you are prohibited from disclosing *any* identifying information regarding clients who receive any service from a program as defined in the regulations. Clients who never enter treatment but inquire about services or are assessed to determine whether they need services are also included, as is information that would identify someone as a client. Finally, this includes information that a person (other than the patient) may already have or may be able to obtain elsewhere, even if the person is authorized by state law to get the information, has a subpoena, or is a law enforcement official.

Let's make this general rule more concrete. You work in a community mental health center that accepts Medicaid and provides a variety of mental health services, including group counseling for AOD abusers. You do an intake on a self-referred client (Frank) and recommend that he join the group. Frank says, "No thanks" and leaves. A week later, you receive a visit from a detective from another state. He is looking for Frank and has reason to believe that you have seen him. He has a subpoena for any records on Frank. You must say, "Federal confidentiality regulations require that I neither confirm nor deny my contact with clients." You must not provide any records to the detective. If you fail to maintain Frank's confidentiality, you are subject to a fine of up to $500 for the first offense and up to $5,000 for subsequent offenses. Ironically, if you had not met Frank, you could legally tell the detective that Frank had never come to the mental health center, because this would mean that Frank had never been a client (had not applied for, requested, or received services) and, therefore, you are not bound by 42 CFR.

As with any good rule, exceptions to the general rule against disclosure exist, which we will discuss. However, we want to caution you that it is best to seek advice if you are unsure about disclosure, because these exceptions can be complex and difficult to interpret in practical situations.

Written Consent

The first exception to the confidentiality rule is that disclosure can be made if the client gives written consent for the disclosure. 42 CFR specifies that the written consent must include the name of the program making the disclosure; the name of the individual or organization receiving the disclosure; the name of the client; the purpose or need for the disclosure; how much and what kind of information will be disclosed; a statement that the client may revoke the disclosure at any time; the date, event, or condition upon which the disclosure expires; the signature of the client and/or authorized person; and the date the consent is signed. A separate consent form must be signed for each individual or organization receiving information on the client. The consent form must also include a written prohibition against the redisclosure of the information to any other party.

In the case of a minor client, a parent or guardian signature is necessary only if state law requires parental consent for treatment. If parental consent is required, the parent or legal guardian and the minor client must both sign the consent. If a minor contacts a treatment program in a state in which parental consent for treatment is required, the program cannot disclose the contact to the parent(s) unless the program director believes the minor lacks the capacity to make a rational choice or represents a substantial threat to his or her life or well-being. Clearly, these decisions can be subjective.

The regulations regarding written consent for disclosure allow treatment providers to release information to third-party payers (e.g., managed care organizations) and employers. However, the release of this information also provides an opportunity for the misuse of such information. Third-party payers and employers are prohibited from redisclosing this information. Equally important is the stipulation regarding how much and what kind of information will be disclosed. Treatment providers must be careful to limit disclosure to information necessary to accomplish the disclosure's purpose. In the case of a third-party payer, this might be limited to the diagnosis, estimated duration of treatment, and services needed. Employers may need only a general statement regarding participation in treatment and progress.

Clients who enroll in treatment programs that use addictive drugs (e.g., methadone) as part of the treatment program are required to consent to disclosure to a central registry. The purpose of this disclosure is to prevent a client from enrolling in multiple programs that use such drugs. Thus, programs may confer about the client if multiple enrollments are detected. The consent remains in force as long as the client is in a treatment program that uses addictive drugs.

The only situation in which an irrevocable consent is allowed would be in the case of criminal justice referrals. If treatment is a condition of any disposition of criminal proceedings (e.g., dismissal of charges, parole or probation, sentence), the disclosure can be made irrevocable until the client's legal status changes. For example, if a probationary status has been completed, the client may then revoke consent.

It should be noted that written consent does not mandate the program to disclose. There may be situations in which the program staff members believe that disclosure is not in the best interests of the client. This may present an ethical dilemma for the program, which we will discuss later in this chapter. We advise you to seek legal counsel in any situation in which you believe that disclosure in accordance with a valid written consent would be contrary to the client's welfare.

Other Exceptions to the General Rule

In addition to clients' written consent for disclosure, another exception to the prohibition would be communication among staff within an organization, if such communication is necessary to provide services. For example, meetings occur in which clients are discussed among staff members who have either direct or indirect contact with the client. Also, in a multiservice agency (e.g., a hospital), information on clients can be provided to central accounting departments for billing purposes.

This exception can be delicate in public schools. Can or should disclosure of information on a student be made to the student's teachers? The regulations state that the recipient must need the information in connection with duties that are related to providing alcohol or drug abuse diagnosis, treatment, or referral. Let's say that a student assistance program refers a student to a treatment program and the student is admitted for inpatient treatment. The student is in a special education program, and the teacher is asked to provide some assignments for the student during the time he or she is not in school. Does the teacher need to know where the student is to fulfill this responsibility? Probably not. After treatment, the student returns to school, and the teacher is asked to report weekly on the student's behavior and academic performance. Again, the teacher probably does not need to know the reasons for this request. However, the teacher may be better able to help if he or she knows the purpose of monitoring the student. In such cases, the best practice is to request a written consent to disclose to teachers or other school personnel. Having such knowledge will also prevent teachers from innocently asking students where they have been. The problem in schools, as well as other large organizations, is that information is often disclosed to individuals who should not receive it. Therefore, confidentiality education for staff is often needed.

Program staff may discuss clients with people outside of the program as long as the communication does not identify the person as an AOD abuser and does not verify that the client receives AOD treatment services. For example, case histories may be discussed as long as the client cannot be identified from the history. A treatment program may tell a newspaper reporter that 37% of its clients are cocaine users. A hospital that provides a variety of services and has an AOD treatment program can say that John Smith is a patient in the hospital, as long as John is not identified as receiving AOD treatment.

A medical emergency is another exception to the prohibition on disclosure. A medical emergency is defined as a situation that poses an immediate threat to the health of an individual and requires immediate medical intervention. The disclosure must be made only to medical personnel and only to the extent necessary to meet the medical emergency. The name and affiliation of the recipient of the information must be documented, along with the name of the individual making the disclosure, the date and time of the disclosure, and the nature of the emergency. Such an emergency might arise in social detoxification programs, when clients are withdrawing from central nervous system depressants without medication or medical supervision. If a client begins to have a seizure and requires medical attention, emergency medical personnel clearly need to know where the client is and why the seizures are occurring. Other situations considered medical emergencies include drug overdoses and suicide threats or attempts.

Earlier in the chapter, we gave the example of a detective with a subpoena for records on a client of a mental health center. As we discussed, the program must not provide records because a subpoena alone is not sufficient for disclosure according to 42 CFR. However, a subpoena *and* a court order *are* sufficient. Usually, the court notifies the program and client regarding the application for a court order and provides an opportunity for a response from the program and/or client, but this is not the case when a subpoena is issued. Because these issues involve legal proceedings, we suggest you seek legal counsel if you are served with a subpoena or if a court order is issued for client information.

Another exception involves disclosure to an organization with a contract to provide services to programs. These contracts are called Qualified Service Organization Agreements (QSOA). For example, in contracting for drug testing or accounting services, a program must disclose identifying information. This disclosure is allowed as long as the QSOA documents comply with the confidentiality regulations.

Another exception to disclosure includes the commission of a crime by a client on the premises of the program or against program personnel. In such an instance, the crime can be reported to the appropriate law enforcement agency, and identifying information on the client can be provided.

Identifying information regarding clients can also be disclosed for research, audit, or evaluation purposes. Although the research exception does allow programs to disclose confidential client information to individuals with a proper research protocol, the researcher is prohibited from redisclosing the information. Similarly, regulatory agencies, third-party payers, and peer review organizations may have access to client information for audit and/or evaluation of the program, but the information can be used only for these purposes.

Finally, an exception to disclosure occurs in cases of actual or suspected child abuse or neglect. Confidentiality does not apply to initial reports of child abuse or neglect, as when a client is suspected of, or admits to, child abuse or neglect or when a minor client is the victim. After the initial report, any follow-up reports or contacts do require consent. For example, an adolescent female in an inpatient program reports that she has been sexually molested by her stepfather. The program must make an initial report to the appropriate county or state office of children's protective services. However, any follow-up visits by law enforcement officials or child welfare workers require the client's written consent.

One caution regarding the report of child abuse or neglect: A client with children will not be charged with abuse or neglect simply because he or she has abused alcohol or other drugs. A danger to the child must exist before authorities will take action. Child abuse and neglect frequently occur but are not inevitable or always readily apparent when parents abuse AOD.

Other Confidentiality Issues

Mental health professionals often ask about reporting past crimes of clients or clients' threats to commit future crimes. 42 CFR is clear regarding the exception to disclosure when a crime is committed on program premises or against program personnel. If a proper court order is issued, disclosure can also be made without client consent. Crimes may be reported as well if the report can be worded in such a way that the client is not identified as a client in an AOD program (remember the broad definition of program). However, state laws regarding privileged communication vary by state and by profession. Psychologists may have one set of guidelines, social workers another, and licensed professional counselors another. It is essential that you become familiar with the state laws regarding privileged communication in your profession. However, remember that, unless the state laws regarding disclosure of clients in AOD programs are more restrictive, they are superseded by the federal regulations.

Does a mental health professional have the duty to warn a potential victim if an AOD client threatens to harm the person? In *Tarasoff* v. *Regents of the University of California* [17 Cal. 3d 425 (1976)], a case often used as a precedent, the court found a counselor negligent for failing to warn a person whom the client had threatened and did harm. However, this case applies only in California (Brooks, 1992). Because a conflict may occur between the duty to warn and 42 CFR, Brooks suggests that mental health professionals warn potential victims in such a way that the client is not identified as an AOD program client.

Finally, the question of disclosure of communicable diseases, particularly HIV, has become a sticky confidentiality issue. All states mandate health care providers to report cases of communicable diseases to local public health authorities (Lopez, 1994). Lopez suggests several strategies that would allow compliance with such mandates as well as with 42 CFR. Clearly, the simplest strategy is to secure the client's written consent for the mandated report and for follow-up by public health authorities. If the client provides consent, public health officials would have no problem locating the client for examination (that is extremely important in the case of diseases such as tuberculosis [TB] and hepatitis), interviewing to identify partners and contacts, counseling, and monitoring compliance.

If the client does not provide written consent, program personnel could make an anonymous report. However, the client's location could not be provided if this information identified the client as an AOD client, as would be the case in inpatient settings. Also, most states require the person making the report to identify him- or herself, which could also violate 42 CFR. An alternative suggestion (Lopez, 1994) is for the program to enter a QSOA with the local public health authority, who would screen clients for communicable diseases and could then legitimately follow up with clients.

According to Lopez (1994), the "medical emergency" exception to 42 CFR would not apply in cases of sexually transmitted diseases and HIV/AIDS. In both instances, no immediate threat to life is apparent, and, in the case of HIV/AIDS, emergency medical intervention would not impact the condition. However, TB is transmitted by casual contact, is difficult to confirm, and is potentially deadly. Therefore, suspected or confirmed TB may constitute a medical emergency and, therefore, be an exception to disclosure. Although Lopez does not mention hepatitis, the same situation would probably apply.

Program personnel may feel a duty to warn sexual partners of, and those who have shared needles with, an HIV/AIDS client. Again, the best practice is to attempt to convince the client to provide written consent to disclose, but, failing this, anonymous reporting can be considered. The wording in 42 CFR would probably not justify using the medical emergency exception to disclosure.

CONFIDENTIALITY AND SCHOOL COUNSELING

School counselors can face some very tricky confidentiality issues. They are generally working with minors, which may complicate confidentiality. In addition, school districts are covered by the Family Educational Rights and Privacy Act, which gives parents of minor students the right to inspect any educational records kept by the school. Unless you have a state law that provides guidance in this area, school counseling notes may be considered educational records.

The American School Counselor Association has ethical standards that deal with confidentiality (the link to these standards is included in the Internet Resources at the end of the chapter). However, these standards will not provide you much clarity in difficult situations. For example, these are statements from the standards on confidentiality: "Keep information confidential unless legal requirements demand that confidential information be revealed or a breach is required to prevent serious and foreseeable harm to the student" and "Recognize their [school counselors'] primary obligation for confidentiality is to the students but balance that obligation with an understanding of parents'/guardians' legal and inherent rights to be the guiding voices in their children's lives. . . ." You can see that students telling a school counselor about AOD use can be a very difficult area to determine if it fits in these guidelines for confidentiality.

Based on the discussion of 42 CFR, you may think you should keep all information about student drug use confidential. This may be a valid legal argument in a state that does not require parental approval for treatment of a minor child. However, if you are pressured by a parent, principal, and other school administrator, 42 CFR may not be much comfort. We strongly urge school counselors consult with more experienced peers and/or with school administrators whenever they are uncertain about the ethics and legality of maintaining student confidentiality, whether it involves

AOD or another issue. Also, keep in mind that any record about a student that is shared with other personnel is considered an educational record. Therefore, parents can compel the disclosure of notes a school counselor makes if these notes are shared with administrators, teachers, or other school personnel such as a school psychologist. School counselors should keep records about a conversation with a student brief and should not share these records with other school personnel if they are concerned about future disclosure to parents or guardians. School counselor notes that are kept private are not considered to be part of the student's educational record.

HEALTH INSURANCE PORTABILITY AND ACCOUNTABILITY ACT (HIPAA)

HIPAA was passed by Congress in 1996 and requires standardization of electronic patient health, administrative, and financial data; unique health identifiers for individuals, health plans, and health care providers; and security standards to protect the confidentiality and integrity of individually identifiable health information. HIPAA affects health care providers, health plans, employers, public health authorities, life insurers, clearinghouses, billing agencies, information system vendors, service organizations, and universities. All of these organizations were required to comply with the privacy provisions of HIPAA by April 14, 2003.

For most of us, the privacy and confidentiality standards in HIPAA are the most relevant part of the law. Generally, HIPAA and 42 CFR are in agreement on these standards. However, HIPAA involves general health care, whereas 42 CFR is specific to AOD. Therefore, in the areas in which the two laws overlap, providers should follow the *most restrictive* law. HIPAA's privacy and confidentiality standards involve the rights of patients to control the release of their medical information, the use of their medical information, and security of patient records. If you work for any of the applicable agencies or organizations, you should be provided with training on HIPAA. Mental health professionals should ask the agency officials responsible for HIPAA compliance about the integration of 42 CFR with HIPAA.

DRUG TESTING

Drug testing in the workplace and school raises serious privacy issues. The Substance Abuse and Mental Health Services administration has developed guidelines for drug-free workplaces that include drug testing, and the National Institute on Drug Abuse has information on school drug testing (see Internet Resources at the end of the chapter). However, we should note that the current federal stance on drug testing is weighted toward "do it," whereas organizations such as the American Civil Liberties Union oppose many of the ways drug testing is implemented. There have been many court rulings on the topic, but it is beyond the scope of this chapter to review all the complex issues involved. The following general information is based on the court decisions up to this time.

PREEMPLOYMENT TESTING Employers can conduct preemployment drug tests and make offers of employment contingent on a negative drug test. A prospective employee cannot be singled out for preemployment drug testing. In other words, preemployment drug testing must be part of the hiring policy of the organization and applied uniformly.

RANDOM TESTING Employees occupying positions of safety or security sensitivity can be randomly tested without cause. For example, the Nuclear Regulatory Commission, Department of Transportation, and Department of Defense conduct random testing of individuals in designated positions. The issue of who should be considered in a designated position has been the subject of legal actions.

REASONABLE SUSPICION TESTING Clearly, this is a particularly subjective area and has also been the subject of legal actions. However, employers with drug testing policies can require a drug test of an employee if evidence exists such as direct observation of use or possession, physical symptoms of being under the influence, erratic or abnormal behavior, or an arrest for a drug-related offense. Evidence is the critical part of this type of testing and has precipitated many of the legal challenges.

POSTACCIDENT TESTING Employers who intend to do drug testing following job-related accidents must have a clearly stated policy to that effect. In such cases, employees can be required to submit to a drug test directly after an accident. In many cases, insurance carriers require a drug test as part of the claim process.

TREATMENT FOLLOW-UP TESTING This is another ambiguous privacy area. An employer may have a policy of random testing of employees who return to work following drug treatment. However, in the absence of any symptoms of drug use, it is easy to see how this type of testing may be construed as an intrusion of privacy. Furthermore, it is certainly stigmatizing for the individual. Generally, this type of testing has only been upheld for individuals in positions of public safety or high security.

DRUG TESTING IN SCHOOLS In June 2002, the U.S. Supreme Court upheld the use of random drug testing for secondary students participating in competitive extracurricular activities. Schools can conduct random testing for cause (evidence of drug use or possession). It should be noted that a study by Yamaguchi, Johnston, and O'Malley (2003) found that drug testing had no impact on the rate of drug use in schools that conduct such testing compared with schools that do not do drug testing.

DOCUMENTATION

All mental health professionals must be particularly attentive to the issue of written documentation. Not only is written documentation in the best interest of the client (i.e., if a client has to change counselors for whatever reason, a new counselor can see what has been done), but it is also protection for the mental health professional. In a lawsuit, written documentation of services and progress is essential. If there is any question about billable services, written documentation is necessary.

In the AOD treatment field, accrediting bodies and state agencies often have regulations that specify the form and content of treatment plans and progress notes and the frequency with which written documentation must be made. For the mental health professional working in an agency or institutional setting, there may also be a structure to guide written documentation. However, many school counselors and private therapists must depend on their own experiences and judgment. For those mental health professionals who are uncertain about the form and content of their progress notes on clients, the following guidelines should be helpful.

Progress notes should be written with the idea that they could potentially be used in a legal proceeding. Therefore, the entries should be brief and largely factual. Opinion and conclusions should be clearly labeled as such. Terms not commonly recognized in the professional vernacular (e.g., toxic codependency, wounded inner child) should be avoided. Any reports of child abuse and neglect should be clearly documented, including the name and title of the person who received the report. The person making case notes should be especially careful to document any incidents in which the health, safety, or security of the client is an issue. For example, any threat or attempt at suicide should be documented, along with the actions taken by the mental health professional.

ETHICS

Professional organizations, such as the American Psychological Association, American Counseling Association, American Association of School Counselors, National Association of Social Workers, and the American Association of Marriage and Family Therapists, have ethical standards for their members. Many AOD counselors belong to the Association for Addiction Professionals, which also has published ethical standards. You are obligated to become familiar with both the ethical standards of your profession and the state laws relating to ethical practice for licensed or certified professionals in your field. Although most ethical issues are common to all mental health professionals and you will probably receive information about these ethical standards in your training program, we want to mention several areas that present particular problems in the AOD field.

Scope of Practice

Most mental health professionals recognize that their training and expertise is insufficient for an actively psychotic client and would refer such a client to an appropriate treatment setting, which would include medical personnel. The perception that any licensed or certified mental health professional is competent to treat AOD clients is, unfortunately, not uncommon. For example, in our state (Nevada), licensed psychologists can diagnose and treat AOD problems, but the state has no training requirement in this area for licensure. In most cases, it is up to the professional to determine his or her own areas of competence, and an ethical professional will refer clients who fall outside these areas of expertise to the appropriate person and/or agency. We hope that the information in this book will help you make the determination regarding whom to refer. As you will see in Chapter 6, you should have specific training in the diagnosis of Substance Use Disorders before making a diagnosis in this area. Furthermore, it is our belief that a client with a Substance Use Disorder diagnosis (see Chapter 6) should be referred to an AOD treatment program rather than being seen by a mental health generalist.

Scope of practice is also an issue for AOD counselors who do not have other counselor training. Although training in the field is changing, many AOD counselors have minimal formal training, and their training may be specific to AOD treatment. Therefore, the counselor may be unprepared to treat clients with co-occurring disorders (see Chapter 9) or may be unable to differentiate substance use disorders from other disorders. The ethical practice would be to consult with licensed mental health professionals and refer when there is any question regarding the client's diagnosis.

Client Welfare

The mental health professional has a primary responsibility to the welfare of the client. Therefore, if a counselor, social worker, or marriage and family therapist is seeing a client who is not benefiting from treatment, the mental health professional is obligated to terminate treatment and refer the client. This may mean that a client with an escalating pattern of AOD use may need a referral to a treatment program in spite of the rapport you have established, the client's great insurance benefits, or your own conceptualization of AOD problems. For example, if most of the programs in your area operate on the basis of the disease concept (see Chapter 3) and your point of view differs, you are not relieved of your responsibility to refer clients who need treatment. Conversely, you should not refer all clients to the same type of treatment program because you have a professional or personal relationship with a specific treatment program.

Earlier in this chapter, we discussed that written consent for disclosure does not mandate that a program disclose information. Instances may occur in which the client would be harmed by disclosure. Of course, clients can revoke consent at any time (in all instances except criminal justice situations), but they may be reluctant to do so. For example, imagine you are a licensed professional counselor working at a mental health center where you are providing relapse prevention services for a recovering polydrug abuser. The client has provided a written consent to disclose treatment compliance and relapses to the client's company. One day, the client admits to a slip that you believe is an isolated event. In your opinion, the client has actually learned a great deal from the slip. On one hand, the client does not want to revoke consent because it is a condition for continued employment, but on the other hand, you believe that reporting the slip would cause harm to the client, because termination would result. Ethically, you should not disclose the slip even though you have written consent to do so. But, we should add that it would be unethical to lie to the employer. Your best course of action would be to refuse to provide information about slips.

If a client insists that you disclose information that you believe would result in harm to the client, you should seek legal advice. However, instances may occur in which legal advice and ethical practice are in conflict. Remember, your primary responsibility is the welfare of your client.

Managed Care

Many mental health professionals are either employed by managed care companies (e.g., health maintenance organizations) or are under contract with them. Certain ethical issues have arisen as a result of managed care. Although these issues involve scope of practice and client welfare, we want to specifically mention them in this section because they seem to be increasing in frequency as the managed care movement spreads.

Imagine that you are a licensed mental health professional who also has the appropriate certification for addiction counseling. You work for an agency that has contracts with a number of managed care companies. You conduct an assessment on a client and believe that the client has a cocaine and alcohol problem. However, the client's behavioral health care coverage does not include AOD treatment. (Note: Because of laws regarding parity of behavioral health care and other health care, this is not likely to happen anymore.) The only way the client can get any service is if you make another mental disorder diagnosis. Another client is clearly alcohol dependent. You think an inpatient program would be the most appropriate. However, this client is in a managed care program that covers only outpatient treatment. A third client is referred to you after receiving a driving under the influence citation. After a careful assessment, you determine that this was an isolated mistake and the client only needs some education. However, your agency runs an outpatient AOD program and the census has been low. Your client has coverage for outpatient treatment and your agency director is pressuring you to recommend the program to your client. A fourth client clearly needs outpatient treatment. This client's managed care company has a preferred provider arrangement with a local treatment agency. You know that this agency employs "counselors" who are not properly certified to provide AOD treatment services.

In a perfect world, mental health professionals would not be faced with these ethical dilemmas. Your diagnostic decisions and treatment recommendations would be based solely on client welfare, professional judgment, and appropriate practices. However, other issues (i.e., money) have intruded. While you are in a training program, it is very easy for others to tell you how to behave ethically. When you are employed and your boss is pressuring you, when you have clients who need help, or when your livelihood is dependent on paying clients, you may find yourself tempted to cross ethical boundaries. We won't patronize you by lecturing about the need to maintain the ethical standards of any mental health profession. However, we do believe that the frequency of these dilemmas would be reduced if all citizens had access to appropriate AOD treatment services. This might stimulate you to be proactive with policy makers in advocating for this.

APPLICATION OF CONFIDENTIALITY REGULATIONS

Now that you are familiar with the confidentiality regulations, let's see how they apply to the situations presented at the beginning of the chapter. In the first case, a high school counselor is working with a student who was referred through the school's student assistance program, and the student disclosed that he had been selling marijuana on campus. The counselor is covered under 42 CFR because the school district receives federal support and the student assistance program does refer students to treatment. However, this situation would be an exception to confidentiality because it concerns a crime that is committed on the premises. In some states, the discussion between the counselor and the student may be protected as privileged communication, in which case the counselor would not have the option of reporting the crime. In such a state, the state law is actually more restrictive than 42 CFR and therefore takes precedence. If the state has no privileged communication law, the counselor is not obligated to report the crime but could legally report it under the provisions of 42 CFR. In this case, the counselor must decide the course of action that is in the best interests of the client.

In the second case, a social worker is providing aftercare services in a mental health agency. The client is a recovering intravenous drug user who reports being HIV-positive and admits to having unprotected sex with a variety of partners. Again, the social worker must comply with 42 CFR. The social worker is providing treatment services and the agency is nonprofit and, therefore, federally supported. If the client is aware of being HIV-positive, he or she has probably already been reported to public health officials. However, the social worker can probably make a report without violating 42 CFR. Because the agency provides a variety of services and the social worker does not provide AOD services exclusively, the report can be made without identifying the client as an alcohol or other drug treatment client. Of course, the social worker should attempt to get written consent for disclosure from the client. However, if the client lives in a halfway house for recovering addicts, the social worker cannot give the client's address to the public health authority because to do so would identify the client as an alcohol or other drug client.

Because the social worker is able to make a report to the public health authority without violating 42 CFR, the issue of warning sexual partners of the client's condition would best be left to public health officials. If the social worker has the names of sexual partners but the client would not give written consent for disclosure, the social worker can make anonymous reports to the partners. However, the social worker would probably not have names. Of course, we would hope that the social worker would counsel the client regarding his or her sexual behavior.

In the third situation, whether a marriage and family therapist in private practice falls under 42 CFR is questionable. Marriage and family therapists are generally not eligible for Medicaid or TRICARE payments, but the therapist may be a preferred provider for a state-funded insurance plan, and in such an instance would have to comply with 42 CFR. When the personnel manager contacts the therapist to inquire about the employee who is seeing her, the first issue to address is consent. If the client has not given written consent for the therapist to disclose information to the personnel manager, she should neither confirm nor deny that the woman is in therapy. If written consent has been provided, the therapist has several options for handling the suspicion of cocaine use. Because depression has been the focus of treatment, we would hope that AOD use has been assessed and ruled out as a problem. However, the therapist may feel that this issue exceeds her scope of practice, and so she refers the client for a more thorough assessment. Drug testing may also be needed. Clearly, if a therapeutic relationship has been developed, the therapist should discuss the issue of cocaine use with the client.

The EAP counselor for the large corporation will have to comply with 42 CFR if the company does any business with state or federal government. In the situation described, the counselor would have a problem if he or she did not obtain a written consent for disclosure from the vice president *before* providing services. Once the counselor interviews the vice president, the vice president becomes a client, and the information discussed is confidential. The CEO has no right to be informed, regardless of who is paying the bill or that the counselor is an employee of the company. However, if the company does not meet the criteria in 42 CFR for federal support, then the counselor has an ethical dilemma. The EAP counselor first needs to clearly establish the parameters of reporting before providing any services and, ethically, must then ensure that anyone who sees the counselor understands these parameters.

When an employer insists that an employee see the EAP counselor as a condition of avoiding an adverse action, such as suspension or termination, the employee must give written consent to disclose before any services are provided. However, the disclosure is limited to a report of the EAP counselor's recommendation(s) and a report about whether the employee followed the recommendation(s). Clearly, a less restrictive disclosure would inhibit most employees from being open with the counselor. However, EAP counselors should warn clients that, if employees sue employers or file Workers' Compensation claims, all records of contacts with EAP counselors and other mental health professionals may be disclosed during legal proceedings (Schultz, 1994).

In the final situation, the middle school counselor should follow the confidentiality sections in the American Association of School Counselor's ethical standards. As the case is presented, it does not appear that the student's drug use exceeded experimentation. Obviously, the school counselor would want to be very confident that this is the case but, if it was, there would be no reason to violate the student's confidentiality with regard to pill use. Hopefully, the school counselor would have had a discussion with the student regarding what, if any, information the student would be comfortable sharing with the parent. Regardless, the school counselor can keep the conversation general (e.g., "We talk about how he can get along better at school and at home") and use the opportunity to suggest that the parent and student may want to talk to the school counselor together or meet with an outside mental health professional. As we noted in the section on confidentiality and school counselors, the counselor's notes are part of the educational record if they are shared with other school personnel and, therefore, would be available to the parent upon request.

MyCounselingLab for Addictions/Substance Abuse

Try the Topic 13 Assignments: *Ethical and Legal Issues in Substance Abuse Counseling.*

Summary

- 42 CFR ensures that people who seek AOD treatment are in no more legal jeopardy than those who do not seek treatment.
- Almost all mental health professionals will have to comply with 42 CFR.
- The best advice to handle complexity in the law is to keep all identifying information confidential, including confirmation or denial regarding whether someone is a client.

- Any exceptions to confidentiality should be discussed with legal counsel.
- Mental health professionals should conform to ethical standards of professional associations and licensing boards.
- Mental health professionals should be very familiar with ethical standards regarding scope of practice and child welfare issues.

Internet Resources

42 CFR Part 2
*http://lac.org/resources/substance-use-resources/
confidentiality-resources/training-material-patient-
privacy-confidentiality-changing-health-care-
environment-hipaa-42-c-f-r-part-2-health-care-reform/*

Drug testing
http://www.drugabuse.gov/related-topics/drug-testing

HIPAA
hhs.gov/ocr/hipaa

Ethics
http://www.naadac.org/codeofethics_1 (addiction
counselors)

*https://wvde.state.wv.us/institutional/Counselors/
ASCAEthicalStandards.pdf* (school counselors)
*txca.org/Images/tca/Documents/ACA%20Code%20of%
20Ethics.pdf* (counselors)
naswdc.org/pubs/code/default.asp (social workers)
*aamft.org/imis15/content/legal_ethics/code_of_ethics.
aspx* (marriage and family therapists)

Legal Action Center
lac.org

Workplace drug testing
http://www.samhsa.gov/sites/default/files/workplace-kit.pdf

Further Discussion

1. Discuss any laws or administrative regulations in your state regarding confidentiality for AOD counselors, social workers, school counselors, licensed professional counselors, and/ or psychologists.
2. What do you see as the advantages and disadvantages of random drug testing in schools and the workplace?
3. If a housecleaner was seeing you for counseling, what would be the ethical concerns with trading your services for your client's housecleaning service?

CHAPTER 6

Screening, Assessment, and Diagnosis

CASE EXAMPLES

1. Sheldon is a 53-year-old man who is visiting his primary care physician for his annual physical. Sheldon is overweight, has high blood pressure, and is borderline for diabetes. He complains of stress at work and problems at home. Sheldon says he is having difficulty sleeping. The doctor recommends a diet and exercise and prescribes Ativan to help Sheldon sleep.

2. Theresa is a 16-year-old high school sophomore. She is referred to the school counselor by her English teacher after an angry confrontation between the two over Theresa's frequent tardiness. Theresa was a "B/C" student in middle school, but her grades and attendance have deteriorated since the last half of her freshman year.

3. A marriage and family therapist works in a community mental health center. A couple is referred for counseling by the court following an incident of domestic violence (no one was seriously hurt). When the therapist asks the couple why they have come to counseling, they begin to vigorously argue with each other. They accuse each other of being lazy, irresponsible, unreasonable, and poor parents.

A few years ago, we were supervising a marriage and family therapy intern in our clinic at the university. The intern had just seen her first client and was eager to show the videotape of her session during supervision. The client was a middle-aged woman whose presenting problem was management of her seven-year-old son. The intern was excited about working with the woman because the intern had experience with a structured program for parenting skills and, therefore, thought that she knew exactly what to do to help. The intern asked a few questions about the discipline techniques the client used and gathered a little information on the family constellation. She then described the type of parenting strategies that they could work on in counseling. In watching the tape of the session, we noticed how anxious the client appeared to be, and it seemed that she was not really absorbing the information the counselor was presenting. We asked the intern whether she was sure that she had identified the correct problem. The intern seemed surprised because the client had clearly stated that she needed help with the discipline of her child and had given many examples that illustrated her difficulties with parenting. As the third session began, the client immediately began to cry and told the intern that she thought she was alcoholic.

If you know anything about the counseling process, you probably can identify several problems with this description of counseling. You might attribute the intern's actions to inexperience and a desire to demonstrate success. However, imagine yourself working as a school counselor or in a community mental health agency. You have an extremely heavy caseload and see people for a variety of problems, so you feel pressured to make a rapid determination of the problem and to quickly come up with interventions. When a client comes in with a clear statement of the issue and you are familiar with a course of action, it may not occur to you that there is an unstated problem. You are thinking, "Great. I know how to handle this in only a few sessions. Then I can go on to the next person."

Many clients attribute their problems to something other than alcohol or other drugs or, if concerned about their use, the client may be hesitant to discuss these concerns until he or she feels comfortable with the mental health professional. For example, a client comes to a mental health center complaining of depression. A recent relationship has ended, and the therapist works with the client on grief and loss. The therapist never finds out that the client is a frequent cocaine user. Or, a high school student makes an appointment with the school counselor supposedly to discuss his schedule, when in reality he wants to talk about his increasing use of marijuana but wants to "check out" the counselor first.

In any counseling or helping situation, the best methods to identify the "real" problem are to establish a trusting relationship with clients and to conduct a thorough assessment. In your counseling skills classes, you learn about the facilitative conditions that are necessary to build a trusting relationship (i.e., warmth, respect, positive regard, empathic understanding). Hopefully, you have also learned about the assessment process. In this chapter, we will focus on the assessment that any helping professional can (and should) perform, with an emphasis on the signs and symptoms that would indicate the possible existence of an alcohol or other drug problem. In keeping with the goals of this text, the purpose of this discussion of assessment is to ensure that school counselors, social workers, mental health counselors, marriage and family therapists, rehabilitation counselors, and other helping professionals will *always* consider the possibility of alcohol and other drug (AOD) problems in the normal assessment process. We believe that the prevalence of AOD problems in our society necessitates their consideration as a causal or contributing factor with nearly every client. We are not presenting an assessment protocol specific to AOD problems, because this type of assessment would be conducted by those involved in the treatment of AOD problems. However, we will describe some of the instruments that are used in the assessment process so you will be aware of the advantages and disadvantages of these tools.

We also want to discuss the diagnosis of AOD problems. Helping professionals need to be aware of the criteria that are used to determine whether someone does or does not have a substance use disorder. However, awareness does not imply competence in reaching diagnostic decisions. Assessment is the process of gathering information, and diagnosis is the conclusion that is reached on the basis of the assessment. Therefore, we strongly recommend that you refrain from diagnosis unless you have had thorough training specific to assessment and diagnosis of substance use disorders.

DEFINITIONS OF USE, MISUSE, ABUSE, AND DEPENDENCE OR ADDICTION

For most helping professionals who do not have extensive training in the AOD field, it is somewhat difficult to determine whether a client's substance use is or is not problematic. They may rely on personal experience and information (or misinformation) they pick up. For example, a high school counselor gets a call from a parent of one of the students. The young man is 17 years old, came home from a party on Saturday night smelling of alcohol, and admitted to drinking at the party. His parents belong to a religious group that prohibits the use of alcohol, so neither one has any experience with alcohol or other drug use. They want to know whether their son has a problem. The high school counselor did her share of experimentation in adolescence but is a moderate user as an adult. She assures the parents that nearly all adolescents experiment and they have nothing to worry about. Is she right?

A simple conceptualization of the distinction between different levels of use can be helpful to the mental health professional in determining the type of intervention that is appropriate for a client. However, these definitions are not appropriate for diagnosis. They simply are a guide for the mental health professional in recommending the course of action for a client.

Nearly everyone uses alcohol or other drugs (including caffeine and tobacco) at some point in his or her life. We define *use* as the ingestion of alcohol or other drugs without the experience of any negative consequences. If our high school student had drunk a beer at the party and his parents had not found out, we could say that he had used alcohol. Any drug can be *used* according to this definition. However, the type of drug taken and the characteristics of the individual contribute to the probability of experiencing negative consequences. For example, it is illegal for minors to drink alcohol. Therefore, the probability that our high school student will experience negative consequences from drinking alcohol may be far greater than that probability is for an adult. The chances that an adult will experience negative consequences from shooting heroin are greater than experiencing negative consequences from drinking alcohol.

When a person experiences negative consequences from the use of AOD, it is defined as *misuse*. Again, a large percentage of the population misuses alcohol or other drugs at some point. Our high school student misused alcohol because his parents found out he had been drinking at a party and because it is illegal for him to drink. Many people overuse alcohol at some point, become ill, and experience the symptoms of a hangover. This is misuse. However, misuse does not imply that the negative consequences are minor. Let's say that an adult woman uses alcohol on an infrequent basis. It is her 30th birthday, and her friends throw a surprise party. She drinks more than usual and, on the way home, is arrested for driving under the influence (DUI). She really doesn't have any problems with alcohol, but, in this instance, the consequence is not minor.

You may be wondering about the heavy user of alcohol or other drugs who does not *appear* to experience negative consequences. First, remember that these definitions are meant to provide the helping professional with a simple conceptualization as a guide. Second, the probability of experiencing negative consequences is directly related to the frequency and level of use. If a person uses alcohol or other drugs on an occasional basis, the probability of negative consequences is far lower than if one uses on a daily basis. However, because we are talking about probability, it is possible that a person could be a daily, heavy user and not experience negative consequences that are obvious to others. We say "obvious" because a person may be damaging his or her health without anyone being aware of this for a long time.

We define *abuse* as the continued use of alcohol or other drugs in spite of negative consequences. Our high school student is grounded for two weeks by his parents. Right after his grounding is completed, he goes to a party and drinks again. He continues to drink in spite of the consequences he experienced. Now, he might become sneakier and escape detection. However, as we discussed previously, the probability of detection increases the more he uses and, if he does have a problem with alcohol, it is likely that his use will be discovered. As another example, let's go back to the woman who was arrested for a DUI after her birthday party. For people who do not have an AOD problem, getting a DUI would be so disturbing that they would avoid alcohol altogether or drink only at home. If, a month after the DUI, the woman was at another party or a bar drinking when she would be driving, this is considered abuse.

Addiction or dependence is the *compulsive* use of alcohol or other drugs regardless of the consequences. We worked with a man who had received three DUIs in one year. He was on probation and would be sentenced to one year in prison if he were caught using alcohol. But, he continued to drink. The man was clearly addicted to alcohol because the negative consequences did not impact his use.

The relationship between the level of intervention and these definitions can be illustrated with our high school student. If the assessment (which will be described in this chapter) indicates that the student misused alcohol, he may need to suffer a significant consequence to impress upon him that drinking by minors is illegal and unacceptable. He may also need education about the effects and consequences of alcohol use. Furthermore, the student may also need counseling or social skills training if his use is related to peer pressure or to a desire to fit in. If the assessment indicates that he has been abusing alcohol, a referral to a treatment program or helping professional who specializes in alcohol and other drug problems may be the appropriate intervention. Obviously, if he has been using alcohol in a compulsive manner, referral to a treatment program is appropriate.

Although the definitions of use, misuse, abuse, and dependence or addiction provide a rough conceptual framework for the helping professional, it would be erroneous to perceive these categories as discrete. Substance use can more logically be viewed as a continuum. However, as we discussed in Chapter 3, an assumption that there is an inevitable progression along the continuum would be inappropriate. The mental health professional must conduct a thorough assessment to determine a client's placement on the continuum and then decide on the appropriate intervention given the level of use, life problems, and relevant client characteristics.

SCREENING

In today's world of health care (including mental health), screening often precedes a thorough assessment because of time and cost constraints. Screening is usually a brief procedure used to identify individuals with possible problems or who are at risk for developing a problem. Assessment is a more thorough process that should involve multiple procedures and is designed to result in diagnostic, placement, and treatment decisions.

In situations where only a proportion of the population may have an AOD problem, screening can be an effective first step in determining who needs a more thorough assessment for a possible substance use disorder. For example, in primary health care settings, screening through self-report inventories (these inventories are discussed later in the chapter) can be completed by patients before they see health care providers. This is similar to all the other health-related questions patients complete in the waiting room. The patient's responses are used by the health care professionals to focus their limited time on possible areas of concern.

The federal government became convinced that screening in primary health care, emergency rooms, and mental health settings was so effective that initiatives called Screening, Brief Interventions, and Referral to Treatment, or SBIRT, were created. We will focus on the screening and referral part of SBIRT in this chapter and on the brief interventions portion in the following chapter.

Although screening can be very useful in identifying those who may be at risk for substance use disorders, you should be aware of certain cautions. For example, you probably have heard of or participated in some type of cancer screening. If you have a positive result on a cancer screening, you are referred for a thorough evaluation. A proportion of people who are positive on a cancer screening do not have cancer. These are called "false positives." Some people who are negative on a cancer screening actually have cancer. These are called "false negatives." The relative "cost" of false positives and false negatives determines how useful the screening is. In cancer, it is worse to have a false negative, so tolerance for false positives is higher. But, false positives cause a lot of unnecessary anxiety and costly tests.

In AOD screening, we have many more false negatives than false positives. As you will see later in this chapter, screening is normally done through self-report inventories, so you must rely on the honesty of the respondent. If someone self-reports that his or her AOD use is heavy and that he or she has had consequences as a result of use, he or she probably has a problem. However, if some-one does not report honestly, the screening will be negative despite the respondent having an AOD problem. The point is that screening can be a useful process but it is far from infallible.

The potential advantages to screening can be seen in the first case example of Sheldon. All of Sheldon's conditions may be related to heavy alcohol use. If that were the case, the physician's prescription of Ativan would be counterproductive and potentially dangerous. Furthermore, if Sheldon's alcohol use is not addressed, other medical problems (hypertension, obesity, diabetes) will become worse, necessitating more expensive medical treatment. In this case, a very quick alcohol use screening might save time, money, and Sheldon's health.

PSYCHOSOCIAL HISTORY

We assume that you have taken (or will take) a course in assessment as part of your training pro-gram and have learned (or will learn) that a psychosocial history is a critical part of the assessment process, regardless of the client's presenting problem. We want to focus on the information that you would gather on the psychosocial history that may relate to alcohol and other drug use problems. However, a couple of remarks related to assessment in general and the psychosocial history in par-ticular are necessary first.

Assessment is a process that should be ongoing during counseling and that a helping profes-sional should be continually gathering information that will assist the client. The psychosocial his-tory is a structured method of gathering information in areas that may relate to the client's difficulties. This method ensures that a helping professional rules out possible causal factors. However, a psychosocial history is not an interrogation. A helping professional must use the same facilitative skills in a structured interview as would be used in any counseling situation. Certainly, the nature of a psychosocial history necessitates that the interviewer ask questions. However, if the helping professional asks a series of questions without sensitivity to the client, the relationship may be damaged, and the interviewer may elicit resistance from the client that would hinder the assess-ment process. The helping professional should tell a client that the purpose of a psychosocial history is to learn as much about him or her as possible so that the best service can be provided. Often, the analogy of a physician gathering a complete health history before seeing a patient makes sense to clients. Also, it is best to begin a psychosocial history with areas that are the *least likely* to be threat-ening to a client.

Every assessment should consider individual characteristics and group differences of clients and, in Chapter 4, we discussed AOD issues specific to various ethnically diverse groups. Although it would be erroneous to make *a priori* assumptions about clients from ethnically diverse groups, the interviewer must be aware of group differences and must account for these differences during the assessment. The notion of cultural relativism discussed in Chapter 4 may be helpful in this regard.

Finally, we know that taking a complete psychosocial history is not always practical. For example, a school counselor is rarely in a position to gather such a history because of time con-straints, lack of access to the information, or to the restraints of confidentiality. Parents may not be willing to see the school counselor, or a student may ask that the counselor refrain from contacting parents or teachers. In such cases, the helping professional should gather as much information as possible but should exercise caution in reaching conclusions with incomplete information. Although real-world barriers are not excuses for poor practice, these barriers do exist and must be acknowl-edged. However, helping professionals should make every effort to gather a complete psychosocial history to avoid missing the real problem.

With these parameters in mind, we will discuss the areas to be assessed in a psychosocial history and the signs and symptoms of alcohol and other drug use issues related to these areas.

As we stated earlier, the prevalence of AOD problems necessitates consideration of these problems as a causal or contributing factor in most client difficulties. However, believing that all client problems are caused by or related to AOD would certainly be an error. If you want to do a competent job of assessment, you should be open to a variety of possible explanations.

AOD Use History

We suggest beginning the psychosocial history with an area that is least likely to elicit client resistance, and an AOD use history would generally not fit this criterion. Therefore, you probably should not begin the interview with this history. However, it certainly is the most direct manner to assess AOD problems. Clearly, assessment of substance use problems through direct questions about client use requires honesty and accuracy from the client, but this is true with regard to all areas of the psychosocial history. Certainly, some clients minimize their use, particularly if they perceive a problem. However, it is surprising how often clients report heavy use and do not perceive it as a problem, or minimize their actual use when it is still excessive compared with others.

Clients should be asked "How much (alcohol, marijuana, cocaine, etc.) do you use?" rather than "Do you use (alcohol, marijuana, cocaine, etc.)?" Although the latter question elicits a "yes" or "no," the former question is more open-ended. For example, when one client was asked how much alcohol he used, he said, "Not much. About as much as most guys." Follow-up revealed that this was two to three cases of beer a week.

The interviewer should ask about use in each of the psychoactive drug classifications mentioned in Chapter 2. Don't assume—based on gender, ethnicity, appearance, or other characteristics—that a client is involved only with certain drugs. Also, don't forget to ask about tobacco use. Clients should be questioned regarding quantity of use, frequency, setting (alone, at home, with friends), the methods used to procure their supply (e.g., from friends, purchased, stolen, in exchange for sex), and the route of administration (e.g., ingestion, snorting, smoking, intravenously). With adolescents, it is helpful to ask what drugs their friends use, particularly if they deny their own use, since having friends who use is predictive of adolescent drug problems (Hawkins, Catalano, & Miller, 1992).

The alcohol and drug use history of a client is helpful to determine progression (or lack thereof) on the continuum of use and because age of first use (before age 15) is also predictive of later problems (DeWit, Adlaf, Offord, & Ogborne, 2000). With regard to progression, clients who report little or no use should be asked whether there were times when their use was heavy. If so, what occurred to change this pattern—treatment, maturity, life changes, or some other event? If their use is currently heavy, how long has it been at this level? Has there been a gradual or sudden increase in use?

The information in this and other chapters of this book should be helpful to you in determining whether the client's reported use is problematic. However, one simple rule may be helpful. Ask yourself this question: "Does a normal drinker (user) drink (use) as this client does?" To answer this question, you must have some knowledge of "normal" and consider the client's *age, gender, ethnicity,* and other characteristics. For example, you are interviewing a 47-year-old man who suffered a back injury in his construction job and is applying for vocational rehabilitation. He reports drinking a six-pack of beer each night and two cases on the weekend. He has a stable marriage, has never been arrested, and had stable employment until his injury. Does he have a problem? Or, a 20-year-old college junior was found in possession of a quarter-ounce of marijuana in his dorm room. He and his friends smoke on the weekends. He does not drink alcohol, and he began his marijuana use last year. You are a college counselor, and you must determine the type of intervention or discipline required. Does he have a problem? Maybe you are a probation officer. One of your clients is a

27-year-old African American man who lives in an urban area. He was involved in a fight in a bar and was arrested. He drinks alcohol on Friday and Saturday nights and usually drinks to the point of intoxication. His drinking started at age 18 and he does not use other drugs, except tobacco. Does he have a problem?

Does a normal drinker (user) do what these individuals do? Our 47-year-old beer drinker is a heavy drinker with no reported problems. Based on what you have learned about alcohol in Chapter 2, you should know that this level of alcohol use on a daily basis is not normal. If the man has no other problems at this time (which would be surprising but possible), he will probably have physical problems from his alcohol use in the future. The situations with the college student and probation client are less clear. They have both experienced problems related to their use of alcohol and other drugs. However, we also must consider the social and cultural context of their use. The probation client may have an alcohol problem or he may have a problem with his social group, expectations for male behavior in his culture, or the like. The college student may be using marijuana in a manner that is quite consistent with his social group and does not result in any difficulties, with the exception of the illegality of the drug. The rest of their psychosocial histories may help clarify the extent of their problems.

Family History

A psychosocial interview will always have some focus on the client's current family constellation and family of origin. With regard to AOD problems, it is well known that a history of alcoholism or other drug addiction in the family of origin is a risk factor for substance abuse (e.g., Hawkins, Lishner, & Catalano, 1985). However, it is best to ask the client if there were any problems in the family with regard to alcohol or other drugs rather than asking if the parents were (are) alcoholic or drug addicted. The client may be unable to make such a diagnosis and may be hesitant to apply these labels due to the stigma associated with them.

A variety of problems in families may be related to AOD problems (as well as other problems). These include physical and sexual abuse. Because studies have found that a high percentage of women in AOD treatment programs have been sexually abused (e.g., Wiechelt & Straussner, 2015), this is particularly important to assess with women clients. Other types of family problems including financial difficulties, communication problems, and excessive conflict may be caused by or related to alcohol and other drug use, so these issues also should be assessed.

Often clients will report a divorce in the family of origin or current family or the death of a parent or caretaker. The psychosocial interviewer should investigate such events further. For example, a client may say that her parents divorced when she was young because her father was "irresponsible." The interviewer should attempt to determine whether alcohol or other drugs contributed to this "irresponsibility." A parent's death in an automobile accident may have been caused by substance abuse, as well.

The importance of assessing alcohol and other drug use in the family of origin and current family is not restricted to the client's own use. As we will discuss in Chapters 12 and 13, children who live in substance-abusing homes and adult children who were raised by alcoholic or other drug-addicted caretakers may have a variety of problems as a result. The issue of codependency is significant, which will also be discussed in Chapter 13. Although codependency is a controversial issue in the field, it is certainly the case that some individuals are attracted to people with AOD problems and tend to repeatedly choose such people as partners. Therefore, a positive family history of alcohol or other drug abuse may help explain the current problems of some clients, even if the clients have no alcohol or other drug use problems of their own.

Social History

Individuals who have progressed in their alcohol or other drug abuse may go through a gradual change in social activities and relationships. There may be a shift to friends who use in the same manner as the client, while nonusing friends are dropped. Parents of adolescents will frequently notice this, although the reason for the change in social groups may not be identified by the parents. Eventually, more and more isolation may occur if the social group does not "keep up." Clients (or significant others) may report that previously enjoyed activities have been discontinued, which may be attributed to depression in adults and rebellion in adolescents. We worked with an adult who had been an avid snorkeler but had greatly reduced his involvement as his alcohol and tobacco use progressed. An adolescent client had been involved in the school band but had dropped out and was spending his spare time playing his guitar in his room as a result of heavy marijuana use.

It is also important to assess the client's relationship history for involvement with partners who have alcohol or other drug problems. This may provide some evidence for codependency (see Chapter 13). One of our clients was a woman in her mid-30s who was referred by a state agency for depression following a disabling injury that prevented her from working. She was involved in a 10-year relationship with a polydrug abuser and had previously lived with an addict who had been murdered. Her father was alcoholic. In discussing relationships with this client, we found that she had absolutely no idea that it was possible to have a relationship with a man who did not abuse alcohol or other drugs. In treating this client, the social history was important because a good deal of her depression was related to the fact that she could no longer support herself, and she thought that she would be forever dependent on alcoholic and drug-addicted men.

Legal History

A client's report of DUIs or arrests for public intoxication or possession or distribution of drugs is clearly related to AOD. However, as we discussed in Chapter 1, a relationship exists between all types of criminal behavior and AOD use. Therefore, a client's report of a history of shoplifting, assault, robbery, burglary, and other crimes may indicate alcohol or other drug problems. With adolescents, status offenses such as running away, truancy, curfew violations, and incorrigibility may be symptoms of substance abuse problems. Although this area seems very straightforward in a psychosocial assessment, we find it is the most frequently neglected. This may be due to the interviewer's own hesitancy to ask such questions.

The case study at the beginning of the chapter involved a couple referred by the court for counseling following an incident of domestic violence. The relationship between intimate partner violence and AOD problems is very strong (Stuart, O'Farrell, & Temple, 2009). Therefore, given the offense (and the couple's behavior during counseling), the marriage and family therapist should strongly suspect AOD issues. In fact, both of these individuals were heavy methamphetamine users.

Educational History

Educational history is a particularly important area to assess with adolescents. Hawkins et al. (1985) found that academic failure and lack of commitment to school were risk factors for adolescent substance abuse. In addition, Karacostas and Fisher (1993) found that a higher proportion of students identified as learning disabled were classified as chemically dependent compared with non–learning-disabled students. Finally, Archambault (1992) includes the following signs of adolescent substance abuse: truancy, absenteeism, incomplete assignments, sudden drop in grades, verbal abuse toward teachers or classmates, and vandalism.

With adolescents, it is particularly important to determine whether there has been a change in behavior or academic performance over time. In particular, a change that occurs from the elementary grades to middle or high school may suggest alcohol or other drug involvement. Because school counselors may be gathering information in this area from cumulative files, teachers, and parents, they should be particularly attentive to this issue of change. In addition to the signs noted by Archambault (1992), there may be an increase in suspensions or expulsions, fights, or stealing. Teachers may indicate problems with the student's falling asleep in class, belligerence, or increasing withdrawal.

A retrospective report from adults of these kinds of school problems may indicate past or current AOD problems. In addition to inquiring about behavioral and academic issues, the mental health professional should ask whether the client has a history of dropping out of educational programs, including postsecondary institutions.

Educational history can be particularly helpful with a young adult (18 to 25 years of age) who is being seen for presenting problems unrelated to AOD abuse. For example, we assessed a 24-year-old man who had been hit by a car while riding his bike. Some brain damage had resulted, and the man had requested vocational rehabilitation services. The purpose of the assessment was to determine his cognitive and academic capabilities. During the psychosocial history, the man reported increasing academic problems in high school, although he had graduated. Subsequently, he started and dropped out of college three times. He admitted to being under the influence of LSD when the accident occurred (no one had ever asked him if he was using). He had also begun heavy AOD use in his junior year in high school and continued to be a heavy user of alcohol and hallucinogens.

Occupational History

With many adults, work history may indicate more current problems with AOD than an educational history that occurred long ago. However, the same types of issues (poor performance and behavioral and attitudinal problems) that we discussed regarding school may occur in the work setting. For example, frequent job changes, terminations, and reports of unsatisfactory performance may be noted. For a person who maintained a job for an extended period, there may be a report of a gradual progression of deteriorating performance. There may also be frequent absenteeism, moodiness and irritability, uncharacteristic displays of anger, and deteriorating relationships with supervisors and colleagues. A good indication that an employee may have a substance abuse problem is frequent absence from work on Mondays (perhaps the employee has been involved in heavy use on the weekend and is too hungover or too tired to come to work).

Underemployment may be reported by a client whose alcohol or other drug use has progressed to a problematic level. Clients may gradually seek jobs that require less responsibility, skills, or time as their substance use impairs their ability to perform at work, and their AOD use becomes the primary preoccupation.

Military history should also be addressed. Alcohol, marijuana, and heroin were frequently abused in Vietnam, and many veterans from this era returned to the United States with AOD problems. Furthermore, stressful military experiences and the subsequent development of emotional problems may put a veteran at risk for difficulties with AOD. However, the percentage of veterans with substance use disorders is only slightly higher (7.1% versus 6.6%) compared with the general population (Substance Abuse and Mental Health Services Administration, 2014).

Medical History

Not only do alcohol and other drugs cause some specific ailments, but people who abuse substances get sick more often. For example, alcohol abuse results in lowered immunity to infection. Also, substance abusers may not be as attentive to nutrition and exercise as those who abstain or use in a nonabusive manner (refer to the case example of Sheldon). Furthermore, a relationship between substance abuse and injuries caused by accidents that result from impaired judgment, perception, coordination, reaction time, and by violence needs to be recognized. Therefore, a medical history that includes frequent illnesses and/or accidents may indicate substance abuse problems.

In Chapter 2, we discussed some of the medical problems associated with the abuse of different drugs. For example, if a client reports a medical history that includes gastritis, peptic ulcers, or a fatty liver, the mental health professional should certainly suspect alcohol abuse. You should also keep in mind that the long-term use of legal drugs (alcohol and tobacco) may result in medical problems in clients who show no other symptoms of substance abuse.

Psychological and Behavioral Problems

When people see a mental health professional, either of their own volition or through some form of coercion, they may not recognize a causal relationship between their presenting problem and substance abuse. For example, a woman came to see us at the insistence of her husband. She had symptoms of depression, and the husband had threatened to leave her if she did not get help. The woman's physician had prescribed an antidepressant, but this had not helped. During the psychosocial assessment, we learned that the woman used alcohol and Valium on a daily basis.

The common problems cited by people seeking assistance from mental health professionals may be due to or exacerbated by alcohol or other drug use. Depression, anxiety, panic attacks, mood swings, irritability, outbursts of anger, problems in sleeping and eating, sexual dysfunction, and the like may be related to substance abuse. However, we are not implying that all psychological and behavioral problems are due to substance abuse. Certainly, a client could present with any of the problems we have listed and have no substance abuse problem at all. Nor are we saying that the existence of alcohol or other drug abuse is always the cause of the client's problems. A client may be highly anxious for some reason and begin to use alcohol or other drugs to relieve the symptoms of anxiety. Even if the client stopped using, he or she would still be anxious if the cause of the anxiety still existed. However, the client's use can become a *contributing factor* to the anxiety and must, therefore, be a focus of treatment.

You should also be aware that substance use disorders and other mental disorders frequently occur concurrently in clients. In Chapter 9, we will discuss the issue of "co-occurring disorders."

If your reaction to reading this section is, "You seem to be saying that every problem I might see as a mental health professional could be related to AOD use," you get an *A*. That's why we are stressing the assessment of AOD use and are providing information on the signs of substance abuse that you may find on taking a psychosocial history. Ruling out substance abuse as a contributing or causal factor can save you and your clients time, frustration, and (often) money. Furthermore, given the frequency of these problems, we believe it is simply an element of good practice.

SIGNS OF ADOLESCENT SUBSTANCE ABUSE

Although many of the areas of the psychosocial history may be useful with adults and adolescents in determining the probability of an alcohol or other drug problem, additional signs of adolescent substance abuse may be apparent or discernible. Because adolescents may not have experienced the variety or the severity of life problems as adults have, the typical psychosocial history may not assess some of these signs. However, a careful assessment of adolescents who are experiencing school or home problems is important in order to intervene in the adolescent's use pattern before more serious problems occur.

Fisher and Harrison (1992) described a protocol for the assessment of AOD abuse with adolescents who are referred in a school setting. Those of you preparing for careers as school counselors or school social workers might find these procedures useful. As part of this protocol, the authors recommend that assessment procedures involve a careful examination of changes in the adolescent's behavior in a variety of areas. As we discussed in the educational history section of the psychosocial history, these changes may involve a deterioration in academic performance, increased absenteeism and truancy, fighting, verbal abuse, defiance, or withdrawal. This is illustrated in the case example of Theresa. In addition, it is important to look at the adolescent's social relationships. There may be less and less involvement with friends who do not use and more involvement with peers who use. The adolescent may identify with a particular school group that typically uses (e.g., "I'm a stoner"). There may be a decreasing involvement and interest in previously enjoyed activities such as athletics or social groups. Furthermore, adolescents may gravitate toward music and dress that depict AOD use in a positive manner or are associated with substance-using adolescents. Adolescents may need money to support their use and turn to stealing, selling possessions, or dealing drugs. In the latter instance, parents and teachers may become aware that the adolescent has a large amount of cash at various times that cannot be adequately explained. Finally, if an adolescent is in possession or under the influence, a problem exists. It is the severity of the problem that must be assessed.

It is often difficult to differentiate adolescent behavior that may indicate alcohol or other drug problems from normal adolescent behavior. If you tell a group of parents that defiance and changes in friends can be signs of adolescent substance abuse, they may all send their children for drug testing. It is important for a mental health professional who works with adolescents to have a thorough understanding of adolescent development to differentiate "normal" adolescent behavior from unusual behavior and to examine all areas of a psychosocial history as well as the additional signs of adolescent substance abuse. It would be an error to isolate one or two signs and attach undue importance to them. For example, if a lot of kids are wearing T-shirts with the insignias of beer companies and a child buys one, this does not mean that he or she is using or abusing alcohol. (However, we do encourage everyone to express their disapproval of this type of drug advertising.) As with the assessment of any individual, you should consider all the information you gather before making a judgment.

SELF-REPORT INVENTORIES

Many screening and assessment devices and protocols have been developed to help a clinician determine if a client has a substance abuse problem. Many of these devices and protocols have been designed for use in substance abuse treatment programs to determine whether a client is appropriate for treatment and the type of treatment setting and services that would be the most appropriate. Discussing these various devices and protocols goes beyond the objectives of this text, but we will describe the most widely used assessment protocol, the Addiction Severity Index. Generally, we will discuss self-report inventories that are used in both substance abuse treatment and generalist settings. Because these instruments may be used for diagnostic purposes, they should be used only by professionals who have formal training in assessment and diagnosis and who have specific training in the diagnosis of substance use disorders.

Also, we want to caution you about self-report inventories in general. Certainly, as part of a comprehensive assessment, self-report inventories can be useful. However, they are not meant to be used in isolation from other assessment data. Second, all tests have validity issues, and self-report inventories are no exception. Because a self-report inventory is a test in which the client "self-reports," you cannot be sure that the client has responded in a truthful manner. Also, the assumption is often made that the inventory is measuring what it is supposed to be measuring, and this may not always be the case.

Michigan Alcohol Screening Test

The Michigan Alcohol Screening Test (MAST; Selzer, 1971) is a 25-item inventory of drinking habits that is simple to administer and score. It takes about 10 minutes when self-administered, but can also be read to a client. Each item is scored 0 for a nondrinking response or, depending on the item, 1, 2, or 5 for a drinking response. The total possible score is 53. A score of 0 to 4 is considered to be nonalcoholic, 5 to 6 suggests an alcohol problem, 7 to 9 is alcoholism, 10 to 20 is moderate alcoholism, and above 20 is severe alcoholism. Examples of questions on the MAST are "Does your wife, husband, a parent or other near relative ever worry or complain about your drinking?" (No = 0, Yes = 1), "Are you able to stop drinking when you want to?" (Yes = 0, No = 2), and "Have you ever attended a meeting of Alcoholics Anonymous?" (No = 0, Yes = 5).

Based on this sample of questions, you can see that the MAST would be easy to fake. The content of the questions is obvious and this results in many false negatives (client scores in the non-alcoholic category when an alcohol problem does, in fact, exist). Obviously, the test only measures alcohol problems. In addition, the MAST questions do not differentiate between past and current problems so those who have abstained for a period of time may still appear to have a problem. The MAST can be given to other family members (who are asked to respond about their perceptions of the client), and the results can be compared with the client's responses.

A similar instrument to measure other drug use was developed by Skinner (1982). The Drug Abuse Screening Test was derived from the MAST and contains 20 items. It is designed for use with adult clients. Also, Westermeyer, Yargic, and Thuras (2004) adapted the MAST for alcohol and other drugs (MAST-AD).

CAGE

This extremely short and simple screening instrument for alcohol problems was first reported by Ewing (1984). The CAGE consists of four questions, each question associated with a letter in the name of the test: Have you ever felt the need to *C*ut down on your drinking? Have you ever felt *A*nnoyed by someone criticizing your drinking? Have you ever felt bad or *G*uilty about your drinking? Have you ever had a drink first thing in the morning to steady your nerves and get rid of a hangover (*E*ye-opener)? Responding "yes" to two or more questions indicates an alcohol problem.

As might be expected from such a brief test with such obvious content, the CAGE should not be expected to result in precision in identifying those with alcohol use disorders. Many of the criticisms of the MAST occur with the CAGE, too. Therefore, the CAGE should be viewed as a very rough screening and should be followed by further questioning when a respondent gives an affirmative answer to any item (Cooney, Kadden, & Steinberg, 2005).

Alcohol Use Disorders Identification Test

This 10-item questionnaire was designed for use in primary health care settings (Babor, de la Fuente, Saunders, & Grant, 1992). The Alcohol Use Disorders Identification Test (AUDIT) can be used as a self-report survey or as part of a structured interview and then incorporated into a general health interview, lifestyle questionnaire, or medical history. The content of the questions is obvious and involves the consumption of alcohol, symptoms of alcohol dependence, and problems caused by alcohol. The respondent indicates the frequency at which the event or activity in the question occurs. For example, "How often during the past year have you failed to do what was normally expected from you because of drinking?" (never, less than monthly, monthly, weekly, daily, or almost daily). Each frequency has a point value (i.e., 0 for never and 4 for daily or almost daily). A score of 8 in men and 7 in women is considered indicative of a strong likelihood of hazardous or harmful alcohol consumption, and scores of 13 or more suggest alcohol-related harm. As the authors acknowledge, the questions may not be answered accurately because some clients may be hesitant to admit the extent of their alcohol use or the problems it is causing.

The AUDIT has demonstrated excellent detection of alcohol use disorders in a variety of clinical settings and with various populations (e.g., Bradley et al., 2003; Dawson et al., 2012, Johnson et al., 2013). It can be administered and scored via computer and, because it was developed by the World Health Organization, it is available at no cost. Of course, like the other self-report inventories, the AUDIT is vulnerable to false negatives and does not assess drugs other than alcohol.

Problem-Oriented Screening Instrument for Teenagers

The Problem-Oriented Screening Instrument for Teenagers (POSIT) is a 139-item screening instrument developed by a panel of experts for the National Institute on Alcohol Abuse and Alcoholism to identify potential problems in a variety of areas, including substance abuse, mental and physical health, family and peer relations, and vocational functioning. The items are responded to with "yes" or "no," and the test can be administered by school personnel, juvenile and family court workers, medical and mental health care providers, or staff in treatment programs. It is designed for 12- to 19-year-old clients and is available in English and Spanish. The reading level is advertised as being at the fifth-grade level. The POSIT can be scored using templates or through computerized scoring and interpretation services. Two empirically based cutoff scores indicate low, medium, or high risk in each of 10 problem areas. Because the POSIT was developed by a federal agency, it is available at no cost (see Internet Resources at the end of the chapter).

Addiction Severity Index

At the beginning of this section, we said that we wanted to focus on instruments that could be used in generalist and substance abuse treatment settings. The Addiction Severity Index (ASI) is an exception. This instrument should only be used by trained professionals in substance abuse treatment settings. We are mentioning it because it has arguably become the most widely used assessment system in substance abuse treatment programs. Even if you will not be working in substance abuse treatment, you should at least have a basic understanding of the ASI.

The ASI was developed by Tom McLellan and his colleagues (McLellan, Luborsky, O'Brien, & Woody, 1980) and is now in its fifth edition. It is a semistructured interview designed to assess seven potential problem areas for clients referred for substance abuse treatment: medical status, employment and support, drug use, alcohol use, legal status, family and social status, and psychiatric status. It is designed for adults (although an adolescent version has been developed) and takes about an hour to administer. It consists of seven subscales and about 200 items, and it can be scored by hand or through computerized scoring and interpretation. The ASI provides two scores: subjective severity ratings of the client's need for treatment (interviewer generated) and composite scores of problem severity during the prior 30 days (computer generated). The ASI has been normed on a variety of treatment groups and subject groups and has been extensively used as a basis to establish the most appropriate type of treatment setting and the intensity of treatment services needed (see Chapter 8). The ASI is available at no cost (see Internet Resources at the end of the chapter).

REFERRAL

In one of the case examples at the beginning of the chapter, we described Theresa, a high school sophomore who had a confrontation with her English teacher. Imagine you are the school counselor. You interview Theresa, contact her other teachers to find out about her academic performance and behavior, review the cumulative file, and administer a self-report inventory. Based on the assessment, you have some reasons for concern about an AOD issue. You talk to Theresa's parent, who expresses her concern about Theresa's behavior and has seen some evidence of alcohol, marijuana, and pill use. You really didn't know Theresa before you interviewed her, and she was not particularly forthcoming. You have some doubts about Theresa's truthfulness on the self-report inventory. What should you do?

You are unsure about Theresa's placement on the continuum of use, and you do not have the time to work with her individually. So, you want to refer Theresa and her mother to someone or someplace outside the school. Certainly, asking colleagues for referral sources is great. However, we want to discuss a few guidelines in making referrals.

If you are unsure about the results of your assessment and want another opinion, you may refer clients to any AOD treatment program that conducts assessments. Often, these assessments are free of charge. However, you should be aware that assessments are a marketing tool of for-profit treatment programs. There may be a tendency for programs to find problems and refer to themselves. Therefore, you have a professional obligation to make sure that you are referring to a program that conducts objective assessments.

First, be sure that your referral source has the training and experience to work with AOD-related problems because it is erroneous to assume that all credentialed mental health professionals have this capability. In some states, licensure as a psychologist, marriage and family therapist, or other mental health professional does not require training in AOD. Therefore, simply having a license in one of the helping professions does not guarantee expertise in this field.

Each state has an agency (called the "Single State Authority") to coordinate AOD treatment and prevention services. This agency will have a listing of all treatment programs and the services they offer. Generally, the state will have some sort of accrediting process for programs. Most, but not all, states also have a certification or licensing process for AOD treatment providers. There should also be a record of complaints and/or sanctions imposed on credentialed counselors or programs. Not all licensed or certified professionals or accredited programs are competent, and sometimes uncredentialed helpers and programs do a good job. However, you are always safest in referring to an accredited program or certified or licensed individual to ensure that some minimum standards have been met and that there is some method of monitoring competence and ethical practice.

In many work and school settings, programs exist to provide screening, assessment, and referral services for employees and students. Although these programs provide services for a number of life problems, AOD issues are almost always included. In most instances, employees or students can initiate a contact with the program or work supervisors, teachers, or school administrators may refer someone whom they are concerned about. At work, the programs are usually called the *employee assistance program*; in schools, the terms *student assistance program, student intervention team,* or *student identification and referral program* are used. In the workplace, the company or organization may have its own employee assistance program personnel or it may contract with a group that specializes in providing program services. Although the type of services may vary, employee assistance programs normally provide brief (one to three) sessions with a professional to determine a course of action for the employee's problem. In the case of alcohol or other drug problem, the employee would be referred to a treatment program. Schools vary widely in the services provided because of differing school district policies and state laws. In many cases, a team consisting of school personnel (e.g., counselors, teachers, administrators) is trained to recognize the symptoms of many common (but serious) problems of adolescents. When a student is referred, the team may gather information from the student's teachers, and one or more of the team members may meet with the student and/or the parents. After gathering information, the team meets and decides on a course of action. If an alcohol or other drug problem were suspected, the parents would normally be referred to an outside professional or a treatment program for an assessment.

DIAGNOSIS

After all our cautions to avoid diagnosis, it might seem contradictory to include a section on this topic. The cautions involve two issues. First, diagnosing a condition not only implies that you understand the criteria for making that particular diagnosis, but also that you can differentiate that condition from others. For example, if you diagnose a person as alcohol-dependent, were you able to rule out dysthymia, posttraumatic stress disorder, and generalized anxiety disorder? Do any of these conditions exist concurrently? Second, there can be a scope of practice and associated liability issues involved in making a diagnosis. If your training and license or certification does not allow you to diagnose, you are exceeding your scope of practice if you do.

However, many mental health practitioners work in settings that require a diagnosis and either are qualified or are supervised by qualified professionals. Even if you do not diagnose as part of your job, knowing the criteria to diagnose substance use disorders is important in your conceptual framework of what constitutes an alcohol or other drug problem. We will provide such a conceptual framework and then discuss the specific criteria for diagnosing "Substance Use Disorders" as defined in the *Diagnostic and Statistical Manual of Mental Disorders, Fifth Edition (DSM-V)*.

The easiest conceptual framework to diagnose an alcohol or other drug problem is "trouble." Someone who has medical, social, psychological, family, occupational, educational, legal, or financial trouble as a result of alcohol or other drug use usually has a problem. However, the easiest framework is not necessarily the most accurate. In the section on "AOD Use History" on the psychosocial interview, we gave an example of a 47-year-old man who drinks large quantities of beer. No *trouble* was reported, but he does have a problem. We worked with a couple in which the husband drank three or four beers a week. The wife thought he was alcoholic because she was raised in a home in which no alcohol was used and she had no framework to understand moderate use. This man had family trouble related to his alcohol use, but he did not have a substance use disorder. You can see that there can be exceptions, but, usually, *trouble* equals a problem. In some cases, a mental health professional must assist clients in identifying trouble. We recently listened to a woman tell of her family and relationship history. Her grandfather, father, husband, brothers, and so on drank to excess on the weekends, were verbally and physically abusive when intoxicated, and spent a great deal of money on alcohol. She did not know that this behavior was abnormal because it was what she grew up with and observed in her community. Her awareness was stimulated by observations made by a nurse in an emergency room after her husband broke her nose while drunk.

At this point, review the case examples described at the beginning of the chapter. Identify the "trouble" in each case. As you read the diagnostic criteria for substance use disorders in the next section, see how the criteria fit (or do not fit) for the brief descriptions of the cases and what additional information you would need to gather.

The *Diagnostic and Statistical Manual of Mental Disorders, Fifth Edition (DSM-V)*

Members of the American Psychological Association wrote the original *Diagnostic and Statistical Manual* to create a unified way of diagnosing mental health and other physical conditions. Throughout the years, revisions of this manual have occurred. The current version of the manual being used is the *DSM-V* published in 2013. In this manual, criteria (e.g., behaviors, symptoms) are described for diagnosing various mental disorders. An individual cannot be diagnosed with a particular condition if their symptoms do not match the criteria for the condition. For example, there is a condition called Oppositional Defiant Disorder. One criterion for the disorder is: "Deliberately likes to annoy people." While you may know someone who meets this criterion, that person may not meet other criteria for the condition (i.e., under the age of 12). Most helping professionals use the criteria in the *DSM-V* to diagnose individuals with drug and alcohol problems.

According to the *DSM-V*, the conditions of addiction and alcoholism are diagnosed using the term "substance use disorder." When *Diagnostic and Statistical Manual, fourth edition, text revision,* was changed to the *DSM-V*, the two disorders were integrated into a single disorder. The terms *addiction* and *alcoholism* are not used. This is an important distinction to keep in mind. The term *substance use disorder* is used because it more accurately describes the behavior associated with the condition. Plus the words *alcoholic* and *addict* are value-laden. For example, I had a student ask me about getting help for his uncle who is a really bad alcoholic. I wanted to respond to this student by saying "Your uncle is a really bad alcoholic as opposed to a really good alcoholic." Drug and alcohol problems are classified as substance use disorders (think of the acronym SUDS, to help you remember) and substance-induced disorders (substance intoxication, substance withdrawal, and substance-/medication-induced mental disorders). We are only going to worry about substance use disorders. According to the *DSM-V*, a substance use disorder is defined as a cluster of cognitive, behavioral, and physiological symptoms indicating that the individual continues using the substance despite significant problems. A diagnosis is made for a specific substance or classification (alcohol, cannabis, hallucinogens, inhalants, opioids, sedative-hypnotics, stimulants, tobacco, and other or unknown). There are 11 criteria for a substance use disorder, two of which must be met in a 12-month period. The criteria can be classified as impaired control, social impairment, risky use, or pharmacological criteria:

Impaired Control
1. Taking the substance in larger amounts or over a longer period than was originally intended.
2. Expressing a persistent desire to cut down or regulate substance use and/or reporting multiple unsuccessful efforts to decrease or discontinue use.
3. Spending a great deal of time obtaining the substance, using the substance, or recovering from the effects of the substance.
4. Craving, or the intense desire or urge for the drug.

Social Impairment
5. Failing to fulfill major role obligations at work, school, or home.
6. Continuing to use despite having persistent or recurrent social or interpersonal problems caused or exacerbated by the effects of the substance.
7. Giving up or reducing important social, occupational, or recreational activities because of substance use.

Risky Use
8. Recurring substance use in physically hazardous situations.
9. Continuing substance use despite knowledge of having a persistent or recurrent physical or psychological problem that is likely to be caused or exacerbated by the substance.

Pharmacological Criteria
10. Requiring a markedly increased dose of the substance to achieve the desired effect or a markedly reduced effect when the usual amount is consumed (tolerance).
11. Experiencing withdrawal symptoms when the substance is discontinued (symptoms vary according to the substance or drug classification) and using the substance to alleviate the withdrawal symptoms.

Review the criteria for diagnosing an individual with a substance use disorder. Did you see any mention of amounts of drug or alcohol use? Amount of use is not considered when diagnosing. For example, Joe drinks a six pack of beer three times a week. When he drinks, he doesn't get arrested, miss work, or fight with his wife or kids. Jane drinks two glasses of wine per night. When Jane drinks she feels more depressed, withdraws from her family, and falls asleep before 7:30 pm. Falling asleep early prevents her from helping the kids with their homework, and sometimes she picks a fight with her husband so she won't feel so guilty for falling asleep early. Although Jane uses less alcohol than Joe at one time, her use seems to cause more problems. Functional impairment is an important term that relates to the amount of damage the use of alcohol or drugs causes. When assessing an individual to determine the presence of a substance use disorder, helping professionals need to focus on the functional impairment of the use.

Descriptions of substance use disorders for a variety of substances follow the general criteria. Those substances include alcohol; cannabis; phencyclidine (PCP); other hallucinogens; inhalants; opioids; sedative, hypnotic, or anxiolytics; stimulants, tobacco; and other or unknown substances (e.g., anabolic steroids, nitrite inhalants [poppers], nitrous oxide [laughing gas]). Caffeine is included for Caffeine-Related Disorders (e.g., Caffeine Intoxication, Caffeine Withdrawal), but there is no diagnosis for a caffeine use disorder. The section for each substance begins with diagnostic criteria for that particular substance (e.g., Alcohol Use Disorder). There are also specifiers for a diagnosis such as whether the condition is in early or sustained remission (i.e., the individual is abstinent) and/ or the person is in a controlled environment (residential treatment or incarcerated). The diagnosis is referred to as mild (two to three criteria), moderate (four to five criteria) or severe. Following the diagnostic criteria, there are narratives on the specifiers, diagnostic features, associated features supporting diagnosis, prevalence, development and course, risk and prognostic factors, culture-related diagnostic issues, gender-related diagnostic issues, diagnostic markers, functional consequences of the specific disorder, differential diagnosis (i.e., differentiating the disorder from other mental disorders), and comorbidity (i.e., the frequency of other mental disorders). Not all of these narrative sections are included for each of the specific substances because some topics are not relevant.

For each of the specific substances or categories of substances, there can be related disorders. For example, in addition to the alcohol use disorder, this section also includes alcohol intoxication, alcohol withdrawal, other alcohol-induced disorders, and unspecified alcohol-related disorders. Not all of these related disorders are appropriate for each substance or category.

AT A GLANCE

Screening

- Brief, general
- May involve self-report inventories
- Many false negatives

Assessment

- Thorough, leads to diagnosis
- Multiple procedures including psychosocial history, self-report inventories

Diagnosis

- Substance use disorders
- Two or more criteria in the past 12 months
- Impaired control, social impairment, risky use, pharmacological criteria

Summary

- Identification of the signs and symptoms of AOD problems is important for all mental health professionals to avoid misdiagnosing client problems.
- Mental health professionals must be able to differentiate AOD use, misuse, abuse, and dependence.
- Psychosocial histories, with or without self-report inventories, are the best method to identify AOD problems.

- When referring clients for treatment, mental health professionals must be sure providers have the proper license or certification to provide AOD treatment services.
- The criteria in the *DSM-V* should be used in making substance use disorder diagnoses but the proper training, experience, and supervision is needed before mental health professionals make these diagnoses.

Internet Resources

Screening and assessment instruments
lib.adai.washington.edu/instruments

Alcohol Use Disorders Identification Test (AUDIT)
https://www.drugabuse.gov/sites/default/files/files/AUDIT.pdf

Problem-Oriented Screening Instrument for Teenagers (POSIT)
http://www.ncbi.nlm.nih.gov/books/NBK64829/#A46033

Psychosocial history example
ssw.umich.edu/public/currentProjects/icwtp/substanceAbuse/Sub_Abuse_Assess_Form.pdf

Addiction Severity Index (ASI)
http://www.tresearch.org/tools/download-asi-instruments-manuals/

DSM-V (Note: URL provides excerpts only. Full access requires a fee.)
http://www.dsm5.org/Pages/Default.aspx

Further Discussion

1. For each of the case examples at the beginning of the chapter, describe the assessment process you would conduct. What additional information would you need to form a tentative diagnosis?

2. Discuss the importance of using screening instruments in conjunction with clinical interviews when making diagnostic decisions. What potential diagnostic, treatment, and ethical problems can occur if a diagnosis is based solely on the results of screening and assessment instruments?

3. Because the *DSM-V* has specific criteria for diagnosing substance use disorders, what is the problem with having any AOD counselor or mental health professional making diagnoses?

4. Discuss the advantages and disadvantages of computerized psychosocial histories as a way of saving time and money.

CHAPTER 7

Motivational Interviewing and Brief Interventions

CASE EXAMPLES

1. Frank is a 37-year-old man who was arrested for his second driving under the influence (DUI) and court-ordered to outpatient treatment. He has been using cocaine and drinking on a regular basis for over 15 years. Frank is divorced and works sporadically in the construction industry.

2. Angelica is a social worker who works in an employee assistance program with a large corporation. One of the vice presidents comes to her to discuss his concerns about the deteriorating job performance of Drew, one of the managers. Drew's behavior has become unpredictable. He seems to function well one day and the next day is irritable and even explosive. Drew was rude to an important client and yelled at one of the assistants in front of other employees. One of his friends has told the vice president that Drew is a frequent cocaine user. Angelica meets with Drew, who tells her that he has been under a great deal of stress in his job and that the rumors of his drug use were started by jealous colleagues.

3. Sara is a high school counselor. One day, two students come to see her to discuss their concerns about their friend Marlow. The students describe a progression of marijuana and prescription pain pill use. Marlow is frequently under the influence at school and is selling methamphetamine to support his drug use. Sara contacts Marlow's teachers, who describe absenteeism, failure to complete assignments, and sleeping in class. She calls Marlow's home and talks to his mother. The mother is a single parent who says that Marlow's father is an alcoholic who rarely has contact with the family. She tells Sara that she is also concerned about Marlow's drug use but feels completely helpless to do anything about it. In the past, she has tried to get Marlow to go to a treatment program for an assessment but he refuses.

4. Miguel is a marriage and family counselor who works for a community mental health center. He sees a family who was referred by a child protection case worker after an incident of physical abuse of the 10-year-old son was reported by the school. After one session, the father does not return to counseling. The mother describes an increasing pattern of alcohol use and verbal and physical abuse by the father. He has had a DUI in the past month, and she is concerned that he will be fired from his job. When the mother tries to talk to the father about his alcohol use, he becomes angry and leaves the house.

It would be convenient if mental health professionals could learn to identify potential alcohol and other drugs (AOD) problems in their clients, present the client with this information, refer the client to treatment, and move on to something else. Unfortunately, in most cases, this does not reflect reality. To help you understand the reasons for this reality, you must have an empathic understanding of the importance of AOD to the alcoholic or addict. Therefore, we will restate a metaphor from Chapter 1. Think about the most important person in your life. Imagine that one day, a friend comes up to you and says, "(the person you care most about) is no good for you. You need to get rid of him/her right now and never see him/her again." We don't think that your response would be, "You're right. I've been thinking the very same thing. I'll go home right now and tell him/her that it's over." It is much more likely that you would defend this person and your relationship, tell your friend to mind his own business, and leave.

Many alcoholics or addicts have developed a relationship with their drugs of choice that they believe to be critical to their functioning and of primary importance to their lives. Just as you may have difficulty imagining yourself being happy without this most important person, alcoholics or addicts may not be able to imagine functioning without their drugs of choice. Of course, problems do develop in relationships, and there may come a time when the problems outweigh the perceived importance of the relationship. Similarly, alcohol or other drug users may start to have problems as a result of their use and might not experience the euphoria that was once a part of the relationship with their drug(s). In the situations that are described at the beginning of the chapter, you might question the relationship metaphor. After all, the people described in these situations are having significant problems in their lives as a result of their AOD use. Surely, you think, they can see the harm that AOD are having on them and those around them. If this occurs to you, we would ask whether you have ever been in love with someone and, when the relationship ended, you looked back and wondered what you ever saw in the person. If anyone criticized your lover or your relationship while you were in love, you probably responded that no one could possibly understand the depth of your feelings and the intensity of the relationship. Although in hindsight, you may now believe that the relationship was unhealthy, at the time, any objective data to support this perception were ignored. Think about the alcoholic or addict as being "in love" with the drugs of choice.

The reality is that people often do not acknowledge the harm that a relationship is having in their lives, or, if the harm is acknowledged, the person may be reluctant to abandon the relationship. The old saying "Love is blind and lovers cannot see" applies to human relationships as well as the relationship people can have with AOD. Many authorities in the field attribute this "blindness" to the psychological defense mechanism of denial. An alternative explanation is that people are fearful of abandoning a relationship that, although harmful, is familiar. For example, that women who leave abusive relationships frequently return to them generates considerable interest (Griffing et al., 2002). One explanation is that the women have no other concept of relationships, and, although the abuse is unpleasant, they are at least familiar with the "rules" and are afraid of the alternatives. The alcoholic or addict may be aware of the undesirable consequences of addiction but be immobilized by the fear of living without alcohol or drugs.

Whatever the explanation, the mental health professional still faces a problem: a client with alcohol or other drug problems and an unwillingness to change. What can be done? In the rest of this chapter, we will describe a model of motivating an alcohol or other drug-affected person to get help called "motivational interviewing" (Miller & Rollnick, 2013). Finally, we will discuss some strategies to assist clients who have not reached the stage of a substance use disorder (see Chapter 6). These strategies are called *brief interventions*.

CLIENT ENGAGEMENT

Client engagement is a term used to describe the process of motivating a person to actively engage in treatment or less intensive methods of reducing the harm caused by AOD. These "less intensive methods" can range from a school-based educational program for students caught smoking to the brief interventions described later in this chapter. Some methods of client engagement are confrontational and/or coercive, while others use counseling strategies designed to elicit active participation from clients on their own volition.

In the AOD field, the term *intervention* was historically used to describe the process of moving clients from problem identification to treatment. However, intervention implies that something is being done to the client. For example, for many years, the main process to motivate addicts and alcoholics to enter treatment was an "intervention" process described by Johnson (1973). The process involved a planned confrontation of the alcoholic or addict by significant people in his or her life (e.g., spouse, children, friends, employer). This emotionally charged event was designed to break through the denial system of the alcoholic or addict. There are reality television shows today that depict these "Johnson-model interventions." In contrast, client engagement emphasizes the freedom for clients to make a choice to either genuinely participate in treatment or to resist it. For example, the court system can force a person to enter treatment (intervention), but cannot force the person to honestly involve himself or herself in the treatment process. Therefore, we prefer the term *client engagement*.

MOTIVATIONAL INTERVIEWING

An alternative to the Johnson method of client engagement was developed by William Miller and Stephen Rollnick in 1991 and is described in their third-edition book *Motivational Interviewing: Preparing People for Change* (Miller & Rollnick, 2013). Motivational interviewing (MI) is included in the National Registry of Evidence-based Programs and Practices developed by the federal government's Substance Abuse and Mental Health Services Administration. Only programs that have been able to demonstrate significant outcomes through peer-reviewed research can be included in this registry.

Miller and Rollnick (2013) define motivational interviewing as a client-centered but directive method designed to enhance a client's motivation to change by exploring and resolving their ambivalence. By "client-centered," they are referring to the counseling theory of Carl Rogers, which you are probably familiar with from your counseling theory class. MI relies on Rogers's person-centered therapy with its focus on current behavior, thoughts, and feelings (as opposed to the past or the future) and its emphasis on counselor characteristics such as empathy, respect, genuineness, unconditional positive regard, and congruence. However, unlike Rogers's description of the counseling process, MI is consciously directive in that the counselor attempts to resolve client ambivalence (the mixed feelings a client has about changing) and points the client to a particular direction of change.

Miller and Rollnick emphasize that MI is a method of communication rather than a series of strategies or techniques. It does not impose change through extrinsic motivators such as money, fear of punishment, or social pressure but through the internal motivation of the client. The counselor's role is to elicit a client's ambivalence about changing, thoroughly explore this ambivalence, and facilitate the resolution of the ambivalence.

Four General Principles of MI

The four general principles of MI are express empathy, develop discrepancy, roll with resistance, and support self-efficacy. The first principle, express empathy, is a basic concept in person-centered counseling and does not require much explanation. Carl Rogers emphasized that accurate reflective listening was a demonstration of counselor empathy: communicating understanding, comprehension, and validation to the client.

A primary goal of motivational interviewing is to create discrepancy—to make use of it, increase it, and amplify it until the discrepancy overrides the client's need to maintain the status quo. A skilled MI counselor helps clients see the discrepancy between their current behavior and their values and goals without feeling pressured or coerced. This is where MI differs from person-centered counseling by actively directing clients to examine their discrepancies.

When clients examine the discrepancies between their behavior and their values and goals, it is natural for resistance to occur. No one enjoys facing such discrepancies, which is why a client demonstrates resistance. An MI counselor must demonstrate skill by avoiding arguing for change with the client, not directly opposing the resistance, relying on the client for answers and solutions, and recognizing that resistance signals that a different counselor response is needed.

Finally, the first three principles are necessary for the client to believe that he or she can change. Self-efficacy is the belief a person has in his or her own capabilities. The MI counselor strives to communicate that the client is responsible for choosing the type of change and for carrying out this change.

Ambivalence

As Miller and Rollnick (2013) point out, ambivalence is a predictable and normal part of the change process. People who are struggling with substance or other addictions usually have some awareness that their behavior is unhealthy, costly, and risky. However, at the same time, they are frightened to change their behavior. They want to change and are afraid to change. Therefore, they exhibit ambivalence.

Although this ambivalence is normal, a goal of motivational interviewing is to resolve this ambivalence (hopefully, by choosing change). Certainly, the facilitative conditions for counseling (e.g., empathy, respect, warmth, concreteness, immediacy, congruence, genuineness, authenticity) are necessary conditions for change in any counseling situation. In addition, MI counselors are trained to avoid certain traps that may be barriers in resolving client ambivalence.

Perhaps the most common trap that would interfere with client resolution of ambivalence is called the *confrontational trap*. In an earlier section of this chapter, we described the type of confrontational intervention that was commonly used to "motivate" people to get treatment. Interventions of this type are still portrayed in reality shows on television. Treatment providers used to hold a common perception that most addicts were in denial about their condition and that harsh confrontation was necessary to break through this denial system. In MI, where ambivalence is seen as a normal part of the change process, confrontation is counterproductive. If the counselor is arguing for one part of the ambivalence (e.g., "Just admit you are an addict"), the client will take the opposite end of the ambivalence (e.g., "I am not. You are crazy"). If the client is ambivalent and the practitioner argues for the "there is a problem" side of the ambivalence, the client will argue for the "there isn't a problem" side of the ambivalence.

Additional traps are the question-answer trap, in which the client answers a series of closed questions by the mental health professional. Hopefully, you have been taught to avoid this type of interviewing in a basic counseling skills course. Also keep in mind the expert trap, in which a "professional" attempts to fix the problem by exerting expertise. Clients may elicit this from a helping professional to remain passive and thus minimize their responsibility for change. The labeling trap involves the attempt to attach a diagnostic label (e.g., alcoholic) to a client. As Miller and Rollnick point out, no research evidence suggests that the acceptance of such a label predicts favorable treatment outcome, and, clearly, many people resist such labels. Finally, stay alert for the premature focus trap and the blaming trap. In the former, the mental health professional focuses the client on the AOD issue before the client is ready, and, in the latter, the client perceives that blame is being assessed for his or her behavior.

The strategies that Miller and Rollnick suggest for resolving the client's ambivalence use many of the basic counseling interventions of Carl Rogers's person-centered therapy. For example, the use of open-ended questions, reflective listening, affirming and supportive statements, and summarization are all recommended. However, the elicitation of "change talk" is the guiding strategy for resolving ambivalence. The idea is to elicit the arguments in favor of change from the client. It is the counselor's job to facilitate the expression of change talk from the client.

Eliciting Change Talk

Miller and Rollnick categorize change statements as cognitive (problem recognition), affective (statements of concern), and behavioral (intentions to act). Evocative questions can be used to elicit change statements in any of the categories. For example, "In what ways has your marijuana use been a problem for you?" (problem recognition), "What worries you about your cocaine use?" (statement of concern), and "What would be the advantages of changing your drinking habits?" (intention to act) are examples of evocative questions designed to elicit change statements.

Another method to evoke change talk is to have clients rate the importance (e.g., on a 1 to 10 scale) of a behavior and then ask what would it take for her to get to the more favorable rating. For example, the client ranks the severity of his cocaine a "10" (most severe). The counselor says, "What would it take to get you to a 5?" Clients can be asked for both the positive and negative aspects of their AOD use as a method to elicit change statements. Expressions of concern are often elicited when the client lists the negative aspects of use. The client can then be asked to elaborate on these concerns. Related to this technique is asking clients to describe the aspect of their use that concerns them the most, comparing the times that they experienced problems to the present, and imagining what life would be like if they changed their use pattern. The clients can also be asked to examine their goals in life and then to describe how their current use pattern facilitates or hinders their ability to achieve their goals

Client Resistance and Counselor's Behavior

The avoidance of traps and the use of techniques to elicit change statements should be helpful in reducing ambivalence. However, a mental health professional can expect clients to remain ambivalent in spite of these efforts and can also expect that this ambivalence will be demonstrated through client resistance.

A working assumption of MI is persistent resistance is not a client problem, but rather a counselor skill problem. If resistance is increasing during counseling, it is probably because of something the counselor is doing or not doing. In addition, the reduction of client resistance is seen as a favorable outcome of motivational interviewing. The logical extension of this point of view is that helping professionals must change their behavior to reduce client resistance. Miller and Rollnick (2013) describe four categories of resistance: arguing (challenging, discounting, hostility), interrupting (talking over, cutting off), denying (blaming, disagreeing, excusing, claiming impunity, minimizing, pessimism, reluctance, unwillingness to change), and ignoring (inattention, nonanswer, no response, sidetracking). Although it is not important for the helping professional to categorize the type of resistance, it is important to recognize resistance to handle it appropriately.

To illustrate the techniques used to minimize resistance, let's look at a client statement and the helping professional's possible responses. The first case example at the beginning of the chapter will be used for illustration, and we encourage you and your colleagues to role play with the other case examples. To review, the case involves Frank, a 37 year old, and his drugs of choice were cocaine and alcohol. After Frank's second DUI, he was ordered by the court to attend Narcotics Anonymous (NA) and individual counseling. Based on an assessment, Frank was easily diagnosed as having a substance use disorder (see Chapter 6). He recognized that the problems he had were the result of alcohol and cocaine use and was afraid of going to prison, but he resisted the label "alcoholic/addict" and complained about the NA meetings. During the third session with his counselor, Frank said:

> I hate going to those (profanity) NA meetings. Man, you should see those people, bikers with tattoos, old needle pushers, bums. And all that God (profanity). I'm an atheist, man. I'm not like those people. I know I can't drink or do coke any more. If I do, they'll put me away. But I'm no junkie or wino.

Frank's statements are certainly reflective of the denying category of resistance. MI uses reflective responses and other beyond-reflective responses. Reflective responses include simple reflection, a skill that you have probably practiced many times in a basic counseling skills course. A simple reflecting response to Frank would be, "You really feel out of place at NA meetings." This avoids the confrontation trap and provides a sense of empathic understanding to the client that may be helpful in moving the client away from resistance and toward further exploration of the problem.

Amplified and double-sided reflections can also be used to focus on the other side of the client's ambivalence. An amplified reflection exaggerates the client's perception of the situation, which may result in the client's talking about the other side when he or she hears how extreme his or her position sounds. In Frank's case, an amplified reflection might be, "You feel like NA is completely wrong for you. You can't see any similarity between NA members and yourself, and the philosophy is totally wrong for you." The double-sided reflection presents both parts of the client's ambivalence. Such a response to Frank would be, "You don't feel comfortable at NA meetings, but you know you need to stay away from coke and booze."

Responses that go beyond reflections include shifting the focus so that the client does not continue to use the issue as a barrier to movement. In Frank's case, the "God" issue in NA was consistently raised. A "shifting focus" response would be, "You know Frank, I really hear how the 'God' stuff in NA turns you off. You also mentioned that the topic of the meeting last night was gratitude. What did you think about that?" In using "shifting," it is important that the helping professional clearly reflect an understanding of the client's thoughts and feelings before shifting. Again, the helping professional would use this technique when the issue presented is seen as a barrier to the client's moving ahead.

Another approach to working with an issue that causes resistance is to agree with the client but with a twist. In other words, the helping professional concurs with the content of the client's concern but takes the discussion in a slightly different direction. For example, with regard to the "God" issue, Frank's counselor might say, "You are right. There is a heavy emphasis on spirituality in NA, and 'God' is mentioned a lot. In fact, I know some people who go to Alcoholics Anonymous and NA regularly but don't believe in 'God'." The twist in this counselor statement is to motivate Frank to ask about this apparent contradiction, possibly leading to clarification of his resistance to attending NA.

Miller and Rollnick (2013) also suggest that the helping professional emphasize the personal choice and control of the client as a method of reducing resistance. Although Frank may dislike NA because of a genuine philosophical difference, the fear of being labeled, or discomfort, his resistance may also be related to the fact that he was ordered by the court to attend. In this case, you might think that Frank actually does not have personal choice or control. Although, theoretically, he could choose not to attend, the consequence of such a choice would be imprisonment; therefore, it would be not be constructive to point out that he has personal choice. However, the counselor could say, "Well, you are court-ordered to go to NA and maybe that is upsetting to you. But, no one can make you believe what you hear at the meetings, and no one can make you listen. That's up to you."

A helping professional can also reduce resistance by focusing on the content of the client's statements but interpreting them in a different manner. This is called *reframing*. Reframing may result in the client's acknowledging a different point of view, especially if the counselor has developed the client's trust by clearly hearing the client's perspective. In Frank's case, a reframing response might be, "When you say 'junkie' and 'wino,' I know what you mean. But, think about (name some famous athletes or movie stars who are in recovery). They go to Alcoholics Anonymous or NA, and I think you'd agree that they aren't 'junkies' or 'winos.' I wonder if you just focus on the people at the meeting who fit your stereotype and ignore the others. What do you think?"

Finally, MI uses "coming alongside," a special case of amplified reflection. The counselor adopts the same side of the ambivalence argument as the client. Miller and Rollnick (2013) are cautious about calling this a *therapeutic* paradox because of the concern that a paradox is a way to "trick" clients. "Coming alongside" is not used because the counselor has given up or as a last resort. Rather, it may be a helpful way to change client resistance. In Frank's case, the counselor might say, "You know, Frank, maybe you shouldn't go to NA. You aren't finding anything useful there and you don't see any similarity between you and the other members." A statement by the counselor may elicit a more measured response from Frank (e.g., "Well, I didn't mean there isn't anyone like me there"). Notice that this counselor statement is different than the amplified reflection. In "coming alongside," the counselor is taking Frank's position rather than simply reflecting his position.

Transition from Resistance to Change

MI does not end with managing client resistance. When ambivalence is largely resolved and resistance has decreased, the client is ready to take action for change. First, the client's confidence to make change must be enhanced. You may recall that the fourth general principle of MI is to enhance client self-efficacy, and MI includes strategies to elicit and strengthen confidence talk. Even when the client's ambivalence has been resolved, he or she may not feel confident in his or her ability to change. Through the use of evocative questions, reviewing past successes and personal strengths, brainstorming, giving information and advice, reframing, considering hypothetical change, and responding appropriately to confident statements by the client, the MI counselor helps increase client self-efficacy. Finally, the MI counselor works with the client on a change plan that includes setting goals, considering the options to achieve the goals, deciding on a plan, and eliciting commitment to the plan.

If MI sounds appealing to you, we suggest you read Miller and Rollnick's book and take one of the many MI training workshops offered around the country. Like any counseling approach, it is essential that mental health professionals implement the processes and strategies with fidelity. That means that it is important to have supervised practice and feedback.

MI and Stages of Change

The transtheoretical model of intentional behavior change developed by Prochaska and DiClemente (1982) has been closely identified and intertwined with motivational interviewing. The stages of change are (1) precontemplation, (2) contemplation, (3) determination, (4) action, (5) maintenance, and (6) relapse.

AT A GLANCE

- MI is an evidence-based process using person-centered but directive methods to motivate client change.
- The four principles of MI are empathy, develop discrepancies, roll with resistance, and support self-efficacy.
- Ambivalence is normal; the counselor's role is to evoke change talk.
- Client resistance is a counselor skill problem; reflective responses and beyond reflective responses are used to deal with resistance.
- MI can enhance client self-efficacy to transition from resistance to change.

At the precontemplation stage, the individual may not be aware that a problem exists and would generally be surprised to learn that others perceive a problem. A client may need information and feedback at this stage to raise awareness. However, Miller and Rollnick believe that coercion or aggressive confrontation would be counterproductive at this stage. Let's use our case example of Drew, the manager with a possible cocaine problem whom we described at beginning of the chapter. When Drew was 26 and just starting in his career, his social group consisted of people who used cocaine recreationally. He started to date a woman who didn't use drugs and she expresses concern about his cocaine use. Drew is genuinely surprised that his girlfriend perceives a problem. Everyone he works and plays with snorts cocaine, and he has never experienced any negative consequences from his use.

At the contemplation stage, the individual is ambivalent about the problem. He or she has become aware that others perceive a problem and vacillates between considering change and rejecting it. For example, let's say that Drew's girlfriend convinces him to talk to a marriage and family therapist she knows to "get a professional opinion." Drew is interested in pleasing his girlfriend, so he agrees. In the course of the conversation, Drew says things such as, "I know a couple of guys who have gotten pretty strung out on coke and I don't want to end up like that but I know when to stop" and "I guess I should think about not doing so much partying, but everyone would laugh at me." According to Miller and Rollnick, the techniques of motivational interviewing can be helpful at this stage to tip the balance toward change. However, if the therapist moves to the action stage before the client is ready, resistance may develop. At the determination stage, the helping professional is presented with a window of opportunity to facilitate client movement toward action. If the opportunity is missed, the client moves back to contemplation. At this stage, the techniques of motivational interviewing may help the client find a change strategy that is acceptable, accessible, appropriate, and effective. If Drew seems to be at the determination stage and talks about "slowing down," the counselor might suggest a short-term "experiment" in which he limits his cocaine use to once a month and then comes back and discusses the experience.

The action stage is when people intentionally act, with or without assistance, to bring about change. After trying the experiment for a couple of months, Drew goes on a binge with his friends and stays out all night for three nights in a row. His girlfriend finds evidence that he and his friends spent a lot of time in a strip club, and she tells him that she doesn't want to see him anymore. Drew is too embarrassed to go back to the therapist and admit his failure so he "goes on the wagon" on his own.

In the maintenance stage, the person tries to maintain the change that resulted from his or her actions without relapsing. However, people may need specific skills to maintain a behavior change. Drew does well for a while. He doesn't go out at all, and his girlfriend agrees to start seeing him again. They spend their evenings at home watching TV. One Friday, his girlfriend is going to spend the evening with her friends, and Drew feels that he is ready to go out with the guys. The guys want to do a few lines and go out stripping. Drew says "no." His friends start teasing him. At the maintenance stage, Drew needs some skills to deal with this social pressure.

Because Drew does not have these skills, he relapses.[1] (In Chapter 9, we will discuss the strategies of maintaining a behavior change related to AOD use and relapse-prevention techniques.) With regard to motivational interviewing, an important issue in the maintenance and relapse stages is for the mental health professional to create an environment in the counseling relationship so that the client feels safe in discussing difficulties in maintaining the behavior change and to report relapses that often occur during the change process. Because Drew's therapist was not aggressively confrontational and did not impose a label on him, Drew felt comfortable returning after his relapse. He will again go through the stages of change but, hopefully, will begin at the determination stage and avoid the relapse stage. However, the mental health professional that uses motivational interviewing strategies would recognize that clients often cycle through the stages of change several times.

A client in the determination or action stage may be amenable to a confrontational intervention. However, if the confrontation is too aggressive in the determination stage, it may alienate the client, and the client may return to the contemplation stage. We would like to motivate a client to change who is at the contemplation stage, where he or she may not have yet experienced serious consequences of AOD use, and we do not want to alienate clients at the determination stage through aggressive confrontation. Motivational interviewing is designed to accomplish these goals.

MI APPLICATIONS TO CASE EXAMPLES

Review the case examples at the beginning of the chapter. We used the first case of Frank to illustrate some MI counselor responses. In the second case (Drew), we illustrated how he might progress through the stages of change. In the scenario described in the case example, we can assume Drew has resumed his cocaine use and is progressing to the point where other significant people in his life are concerned about him. When Angelica (the social worker) meets with Drew, she may not have any information about his drug use history. Although Drew is very likely at the contemplation stage of change (again), Angelica must be very skilled in her use of MI. Unless Drew is confident that his confidentiality will be maintained (review the material in Chapter 5), he will probably not reveal anything about his cocaine use. Assuming he does believe that whatever he says will be kept confidential, Angelica will spend time ensuring that Drew feels that she understands what he is saying. If you role play this case with your colleagues, focus on the reflective MI statements.

In the case of the school counselor Sara and the student Marlow, Sara must determine Marlow's stage of change. Because his mother has talked to him, and his friends are concerned, it is very likely that he is at least at the contemplation stage and maybe at the determination stage. Assuming that Marlow's drug use is as bad as it is depicted in the case, Sara's goal is to get Marlow to agree to an assessment. Therefore, the goal is not abstinence from drugs but just a step toward determining the extent of the problem. When you role play this example, assume that Marlow's

---

[1] The differences between slips and relapses will be discussed in Chapter 9

ambivalence is about whether he should agree to an assessment. Sara should try to evoke change statements and work to enhance Marlow's self-efficacy.

Miguel (the marriage and family therapist) is going to call the father to encourage him to return to counseling. As with the other examples, he does need to determine the father's stage of change. For this example, we will assume he is in the contemplation stage. Miguel must try to engage the father so he is willing to return. He wants to evoke change statements. In role playing, Miguel should practice both reflective statements and statements that go beyond reflection.

Research Outcome Studies

As we said at the beginning of the section on MI, the fact that it is included in the federal registry of effective, evidence-based practices means that research results support MI. Miller and Arkowitz (2015) review much of this literature to date. In more than 200 randomized treatment studies, MI produced small to medium behavioral changes across many types of issues. The effects seem to be mediated by counselor fidelity to MI. In addition, MI seemed most effective when it was combined with another type of therapy (e.g., cognitive-behavioral therapy). When MI is compared with other evidence-based treatments, the results are similar although MI requires fewer sessions. In clinical studies, MI has been shown to be effective with a wide range of target problems, with a variety of populations, and with various types of trained mental health professionals.

BRIEF INTERVENTIONS

Individuals with moderate or risky levels of AOD use may not be diagnosed with a substance use disorder but still be in need of assistance. This group is responsible for a disproportionate percentage of motor vehicle accidents and other injuries, deaths from AOD, poor workplace performance, medical illnesses, marital problems, and family dysfunction. The techniques to engage these clients to change their AOD behaviors are called *brief interventions*.

Because brief interventions frequently are conducted in general health care settings, schools, or social service agencies, mental health professionals should be familiar with them. The procedures can range from a five-minute explanation of the harm of AOD by a health care provider, to a mental health counselor encouraging a client to see if he or she can stop drinking on his or her own, to more structured programs.

The Center for Substance Abuse Treatment (CSAT) has published a manual titled *Brief Interventions and Brief Therapies for Substance Abuse* (Center for Substance Abuse Treatment, 1999) (see Internet Resources at the end of the chapter). We will summarize the chapter on brief interventions.

The goal for a client is to reduce the risk of harm from AOD. The stages-of-change model and techniques of motivational interviewing are the basis of the brief intervention techniques described in this manual. The type of intervention is generally related to the level of AOD use. Light or moderate users may need education about guidelines for low-risk use and the problems that may occur from increased use. If the light or moderate alcohol user occasionally has five or more drinks (defined as "binge drinking"), he or she can be encouraged to stay within the guidelines of no more than four drinks at any one time and no more than 14 drinks per week. Pregnant women or women contemplating pregnancy can be advised to abstain from AOD. At-risk drinkers are those who frequently exceed recommended guidelines but do not meet criteria for a substance use disorder (see Chapter 6). At-risk drug users are determined by the frequency and level of use and the drug(s) used. For this group, brief interventions are designed to encourage moderation or abstinence. Education about the consequences of continued high-risk use may also be offered.

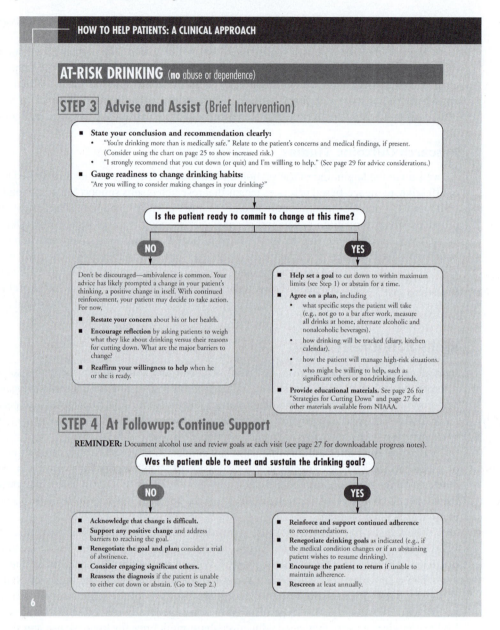

HOW TO HELP PATIENTS: A CLINICAL APPROACH

AT-RISK DRINKING (**no** abuse or dependence)

STEP 3 Advise and Assist (Brief Intervention)

- **State your conclusion and recommendation clearly:**
  - "You're drinking more than is medically safe." Relate to the patient's concerns and medical findings, if present. (Consider using the chart on page 25 to show increased risk.)
  - "I strongly recommend that you cut down (or quit) and I'm willing to help." (See page 29 for advice considerations.)
- **Gauge readiness to change drinking habits:**
  "Are you willing to consider making changes in your drinking?"

Is the patient ready to commit to change at this time?

NO

Don't be discouraged—ambivalence is common. Your advice has likely prompted a change in your patient's thinking, a positive change in itself. With continued reinforcement, your patient may decide to take action. For now,
- **Restate your concern** about his or her health.
- **Encourage reflection** by asking patients to weigh what they like about drinking versus their reasons for cutting down. What are the major barriers to change?
- **Reaffirm your willingness to help** when he or she is ready.

YES

- **Help set a goal** to cut down to within maximum limits (see Step 1) or abstain for a time.
- **Agree on a plan**, including
  - what specific steps the patient will take (e.g., not go to a bar after work, measure all drinks at home, alternate alcoholic and nonalcoholic beverages).
  - how drinking will be tracked (diary, kitchen calendar).
  - how the patient will manage high-risk situations.
  - who might be willing to help, such as significant others or nondrinking friends.
- **Provide educational materials.** See page 26 for "Strategies for Cutting Down" and page 27 for other materials available from NIAAA.

STEP 4 At Followup: Continue Support

REMINDER: Document alcohol use and review goals at each visit (see page 27 for downloadable progress notes).

Was the patient able to meet and sustain the drinking goal?

NO

- **Acknowledge that change is difficult.**
- **Support any positive change** and address barriers to reaching the goal.
- **Renegotiate the goal and plan;** consider a trial of abstinence.
- **Consider engaging significant others.**
- **Reassess the diagnosis** if the patient is unable to either cut down or abstain. (Go to Step 2.)

YES

- **Reinforce and support continued adherence** to recommendations.
- **Renegotiate drinking goals** as indicated (e.g., if the medical condition changes or if an abstaining patient wishes to resume drinking).
- **Encourage the patient to return** if unable to maintain adherence.
- **Rescreen** at least annually.

6

FIGURE 7.1 Brief intervention flow chart.

The flow chart in Figure 7.1 is from a National Institute on Alcohol Abuse and Alcoholism publication called *Helping Patients Who Drink Too Much: A Clinician's Guide* (National Institute on Alcohol Abuse and Alcoholism, 2007). It is designed for use by health care professionals in working with at-risk drinkers. As you can see, it is quite simple and prescriptive.

There are also brief interventions for the client with a substance abuse disorder or substance dependence disorder. However, these clients would normally be seen in a treatment setting, and this will be discussed in Chapter 8.

The CSAT manual (1999) describes six elements for effective brief interventions and five basic steps in the brief intervention process. The six elements use the acronym FRAMES for ease of understanding: 1. **F**eedback (the client[2] is given information about his or her use of AOD and the risks of his or her use pattern), 2. **R**esponsibility (the responsibility for change lies with the client), 3. **A**dvice (the clinician gives the client advice), 4. **M**enu (a variety of options are offered to the client), 5. **E**mpathy (the clinician demonstrates this core condition), and 6. **S**elf-efficacy (the clinician helps the client feel empowered). As you can see, the fifth and sixth elements are consistent with MI principles.

In the first step of the brief intervention process, the clinician introduces the issue in the context of the client's health. This includes building rapport with him or her, defining the purpose of the discussion, obtaining the client's permission to proceed, and helping the client to understand the reason for the brief intervention.

The next step is screening, evaluating, and assessing. You already have an understanding of this step from Chapter 6. This is obviously important to determine whether the person is a light or moderate user or at risk.

Providing feedback follows screening, evaluating, and assessing. Using information from the preceding step, an interactive discussion of the findings is conducted. A specific piece of information should be given, followed by a request for client response. In this step, it is important for the helping professional to assess the client stage of change in order to determine what to do in the next step.

After giving feedback and assessing the client's stage of change, the possibility of changing behavior and setting goals is discussed. You can see how important the stage of change is. For example, you would meet high resistance if you suggested abstinence to an at-risk drinker in the precontemplation stage. The helping professional can suggest a course of action and then negotiate with the client. For example, we worked with a young woman who was an at-risk drinker in the contemplation stage of change. We suggested she limit her drinking to no more than two drinks and no more than two days a week. She resisted this, and we finally agreed to three drinks one day a week and two drinks no more than two days a week.

The final step is summarizing and reaching closure. This is important so that both the helping professional and the client have a clear understanding of the changes that were agreed on. Scheduled follow-up is an important part of this step. Depending on the type of brief intervention and the client's level of use, this follow-up may involve another face-to-face meeting or a telephone call.

The CSAT manual also contains a brief intervention workbook. The workbook is based on the summarized steps and contains useful tools such as substance use contracts.

In a very comprehensive examination of brief interventions (and brief treatments), Madras et al. (2009) analyzed results from nearly 460,000 patients screened in a variety of health care settings across the country for alcohol and illicit drug use. Nearly 16% were recommended for brief interventions with much smaller percentages recommended for brief treatment or referral for treatment. At six-month follow-up, illicit drug use was nearly 68% lower and heavy alcohol use was nearly 39% lower. The results were comparable across sites, gender, race/ethnicity, and age subgroups.

---

[2] The term "client" is used interchangeably with "patient" because brief interventions are often implemented in health care settings.

Summary

- Motivational interviewing is an evidence-based counseling process using person-centered concepts and techniques but is directive in trying to evoke client change.
- Brief interventions are generally used with nondependent clients to reduce the harm that may result from AOD use.

- Most brief interventions are targeted to the stage of change of the client and use motivational interviewing techniques.

Internet Resources

Motivational interviewing
http://www.motivationalinterviewing.org/

Brief interventions
http://pubs.niaaa.nih.gov/publications/Practitioner/ CliniciansGuide2005/clinicians_guide.htm

Further Discussion

1. Given that motivational interviewing is directive and designed to move clients to change, what are the ethical issues involved in this kind of counseling process?
2. In the helping professions, it is often said that for someone to benefit from treatment, they must have the desire to change. In light of this, should clients at the precontemplation stage of change be forced by schools, the legal system, or employers to seek treatment for AOD problems?
3. Discuss the concept of providing screening for AOD problems and brief interventions in all primary health care settings and emergency rooms.

CHAPTER 8

Treatment of Alcohol and Other Drugs (AOD)

CASE EXAMPLES

1. Misty is a 33-year-old single mother. She has been smoking heroin for about 10 years. Her son was removed from her custody. Misty has been through treatment several times but has relapsed following each treatment episode. She wants to regain custody of her child, but her counselor in her last treatment program said she had difficulty "getting it."

2. Ben is a 62-year-old laborer who is seeking treatment for alcohol abuse. Ben also has severe back pain from a work-related injury and has been using opioid pain medication for some time. He has a supportive family.

3. Ralph is 45 years old and was recently paroled after serving time for nonviolent offenses. His crimes were related to his crack cocaine addiction. Ralph did not complete high school and has no marketable job skills. He did attend Alcoholics Anonymous meetings held in prison. A condition of his parole is to get "drug counseling."

In a textbook for helping professionals who are not planning to work in substance abuse treatment, a thorough discussion of treatment may not seem necessary. However, we have found that helping professionals have an almost mystical conception of substance abuse treatment. Once the social worker, school counselor, mental health counselor, rehabilitation counselor, or marriage and family therapist has referred a client for treatment, there seems to be an expectation that the client will return cured. In fact, alcoholics used to say they were going for "the cure" as a euphemism for treatment. This view may be encouraged by the fact that clients often "disappear" (in the case of inpatient treatment) or discontinue other forms of counseling or therapy at the insistence of the substance abuse treatment program. The helping professional may never see the client again, which reinforces the idea that alcoholics and addicts have been cured as a result of treatment.

The questions we are asked most often in teaching helping professionals about the AOD field are "What happens in treatment?" "What are the specific interventions?" and "Does treatment work?" Answers to these questions are important for mental health professionals because clients referred for treatment expect that they are being directed toward an appropriate and helpful program. However, treatment programs differ in their orientation, in the specific strategies used, in the settings in which treatment occurs, and in treatment for special populations. We want to acquaint you with these aspects of treatment to dispel any mystical views you hold and, most important, so that you are familiar with evidence-based treatment strategies. Also, we will discuss the research on the effectiveness of treatment. Finally, we think that it is important for you to understand some of the controversial issues in the treatment of AOD problems.

RECOVERY-ORIENTED SYSTEMS OF CARE

The conceptualization of working with people with substance use disorders has changed in recent years. The material in the remainder of this chapter is concerned with a fairly well-defined period of acute care that has always been referred to as "treatment." In Chapter 10, we discuss relapse prevention and recovery. From this delineation, it would appear that treatment, relapse prevention, and recovery are all separate processes. In fact, if you think of addiction as a chronic condition, treatment, relapse prevention, and recovery (and more) are all part of the same process which is now called recovery-oriented systems of care (ROSC).

The federal government held a number of summits on ROSCs in 2005 and produced a document summarizing the results of these meetings (Substance Abuse and Mental Health Services Administration, 2009). For our purposes at this point in the book, the principles of ROSCs emphasize continuity of care; the inclusion of the family, community, and peers in the process; individualized and comprehensive services across the life span; culturally responsive services; community-anchored services; inclusion of voices and experiences of recovering individuals and their families; and outcomes-driven, research-based services. Although the role of ROSCs is far greater than described here, please keep in mind as you read the rest of this chapter that what we refer to as *treatment* is only one part of ROSCs. ROSCs also include screening and assessment (Chapter 6), client engagement and brief interventions (Chapter 7), and relapse prevention and recovery support (Chapter 10).

HOW MANY ARE IN TREATMENT? HOW MANY NEED TREATMENT?

According to the Substance Abuse and Mental Health Services Administration (2014b), in 2012, more than 1.7 million persons were admitted to treatment programs that report data to state government agencies. Over 21% were in treatment for alcohol problems and nearly 18% for alcohol with a secondary drug involved. Twenty-six percent of the admissions involved opioids (e.g., heroin) as the primary drug problem (almost 50% higher than 10 years ago), nearly 7% cocaine (almost 50% lower than 10 years ago), 17.5% marijuana (down from a high of 18.6% in 2010), and more than 7% stimulants such as methamphetamine (down from a high of 9% in 2005). In 2013, of those clients in treatment for services beyond detoxification, more than 78% were in outpatient treatment and less than 22% were in residential treatment (Substance Abuse and Mental Health Services Administration, 2014c). Treatment settings will be discussed later in the chapter. Of the treatment facilities in this country in 2013, 55% were private, nonprofit; 32% were private for-profit; 10% were federal, state, or local government; and a little more than 2% were tribal government facilities. Forty-three percent of the facilities offered treatment programs for co-occurring disorders, 30% served adolescents, 17% had programs for pregnant or postpartum women, 44% served other adult women groups, 12% had senior citizen programs, 33% had programs for criminal justice populations, and 12% served gay and lesbian groups. Treatment services in sign language for the hearing impaired were available in 28% of all facilities, and 41% used languages other than English (Substance Abuse and Mental Health Services Administration, 2014c).

The Substance Abuse and Mental Health Services Administration (2015b) reported that, in 2014, an estimated 24 million Americans needed treatment for an alcohol or other drug problem (this includes people with both alcohol and drug problems). Of that number, 2.3 million, or about 10%, actually received treatment (the 1.7 million treatment admissions cited in the previous paragraph includes only those admissions reported to state government agencies, whereas treatment agencies or organizations that are not licensed by state government have no reporting requirements, leading to the higher figure). Of the remaining 90% of people who needed treatment, only about 825,000 (4%) *felt* they needed treatment. The vast majority of those who felt they needed treatment made no effort to get help.

WHAT HAPPENS IN TREATMENT?

Approaches to Treatment

As you might expect after reading Chapter 3 on models of addiction, many different approaches to treatment exist that are based on the model of addiction adhered to by the program developer(s). Perhaps the most well-known and widely emulated approach to treatment is the Minnesota Model developed by the Hazelden Foundation in the 1940s and 1950s.

The philosophy of the Minnesota Model can be described by four components (Cook, 1988). The first is the belief that clients can change attitudes, beliefs, and behaviors. Famous persons who have completed the program, such as former First Lady Betty Ford, actress Elizabeth Taylor, comedian Chevy Chase, and actor Robert Downey Jr., are used as models to illustrate this belief. Second, the Minnesota Model adheres to the disease concept of addiction. The term *chemical dependency* is preferred to *addiction* or *alcoholism* and is seen as a physical, psychological, social, and spiritual illness. The major characteristics of the disease concept are taught. That is, the disease model conceptualizes chemical dependency as a primary disease that is chronic, progressive, and potentially fatal. The focus of treatment is on the disease and not on secondary characteristics.

The third philosophical component is illustrated by the long-term treatment goals of the Minnesota Model: abstinence from all mood-altering chemicals and improvement of lifestyle. Clients are not considered cured because the disease is incurable. However, through abstinence and personal growth, a chemically dependent individual can be in the process of recovery, an ongoing, lifelong process. Finally, the Minnesota Model uses the principles of Alcoholics Anonymous (AA) and Narcotics Anonymous (NA) in treatment. While we will devote a large portion of Chapter 11 to AA and NA, at this point it is sufficient to mention that the utilization of AA and NA principles implies a heavy spiritual component to treatment in the Minnesota Model.

Cook (1988) also described the elements and structure of the Minnesota Model program. A continuum of care including assessment and diagnosis, detoxification, inpatient, therapeutic communities, halfway houses, outpatient, and aftercare has been developed using the Minnesota Model. Group therapy is used and is concerned with present and future behavior as opposed to past causal factors. Groups are often confrontational. The family also receives therapy. Didactic experiences including lectures and videotapes are used to educate clients about the disease of chemical dependency and the consequences of the disease. Although the staff is composed of professionals from a number of disciplines (physicians, social workers, psychologists, nurses, and clergy), recovering addicts and alcoholics also function as counselors. Clients have reading and writing assignments, such as reading the AA Twelve Steps and Twelve Traditions (see Chapter 11) and writing their life histories. Attendance at AA/NA meetings is required, and clients are expected to work through the first three to five steps of AA while in treatment. Work assignments and recreational activities may also be expected, depending on the treatment setting. Aftercare includes attendance at AA or NA.

In contrast to the disease model of treatment exemplified by the Minnesota Model, behavioral models of treatment use techniques of classical and operant conditioning in the treatment of AOD problems. Perhaps the best-known behavioral technique applied to alcohol problems is aversion therapy, the goal of which is to produce a conditioned negative response to the sight, smell, taste, and thought of alcohol through classical Pavlovian conditioning (Miller, Wilbourne, & Hettema, 2003). The unpleasant stimuli most widely used are nausea, apnea (paralysis of breathing), electric shock, and various images. Nausea is the oldest and most commonly used of these stimuli, with fairly wide use in the former Soviet Union and in certain hospitals in the United States. The process is to give the client a drug that, when combined with alcohol, produces severe nausea. In a supervised setting, the client is then allowed to drink. In the classical conditioning paradigm, the feeling of severe nausea should quickly become associated with drinking alcohol. Electric shock can also be administered when the client drinks, or a drug can be administered that produces apnea when alcohol is consumed. Because these procedures are painful, stressful, and potentially dangerous, careful screening of clients and medical supervision is necessary. As might be expected, there is also a high dropout rate from programs using these techniques. In Chapter 3, we described Bill, who completed an aversive conditioning program and remained sober for 19 years until his death. Although the treatment was successful, he found the whole experience extremely unpleasant, which was exactly the effect intended. Although electric shock can be used in the treatment of addiction to drugs other than alcohol, most references to aversive conditioning are related to the treatment of alcoholism.

Although aversive conditioning is not widely used in the United States now, other behavioral approaches to treatment have strong research evidence to support their effectiveness. The most widely studied of these is contingency management (CM). According to Stitzer (2006), CM uses tangible incentives to reward abstinence. If you remember your introductory psychology class, CM is based on operant conditioning in contrast to aversive conditioning approaches that are based on classical conditioning. CM has research evidence to support its use with a wide variety of substances and types of addiction. Voucher-based reinforcement therapy, in which vouchers that can be exchanged for goods and services are provided for "clean" urine samples, is one of the many variations of CM (Higgins et al., 1995), as is the "fishbowl" procedure, in which patients with clean urine samples draw a slip of paper from a bowl containing prizes of various value (Petry & Martin, 2002). This is a type of variable reinforcement. Three different meta-analyses of CM (Griffith, Rowan-Szal, Roark, & Simpson, 2000; Lussier, Heil, Mongeon, Badger, & Higgins, 2006; Prendergast, Podus, Finney, Greenwell, & Roll, 2006) have concluded that CM produces clinically significant effects and, therefore, qualifies as an evidence-based practice (Stitzer, 2006).

A comprehensive approach to treatment that incorporates CM is the community reinforcement approach. This multifaceted approach uses voucher-based incentives as well as cognitive-behavioral and pharmacological interventions to promote abstinence. The goal is to change environmental contingencies in all areas of life (i.e., work, leisure time, relationships) to produce a lifestyle that is more rewarding than AOD use (Roozen et al., 2004).

A treatment approach for stimulant (e.g., methamphetamine) abuse was developed by researchers at the University of California, Los Angeles (Rawson et al., 1995). The matrix model includes elements of group and family therapies, education, support groups, and relapse prevention. The relationship between the counselor and the client is emphasized, with the counselor using the relationship to reinforce positive behavior change. The approach is not confrontational and seeks to promote self-esteem, dignity, and self-worth. Detailed manuals have been developed to guide this approach.

Further, the National Institute on Alcohol Abuse and Alcoholism has developed treatment manuals for three very different approaches to alcohol treatment. The manuals were used in a large-scale study to investigate the effects of matching clients to treatment approaches (see "Treatment Effectiveness"). The first manual, "Twelve-Step Facilitation Therapy," is based on the principles of AA. The treatment protocol familiarizes clients with the AA philosophy and encourages participation in AA. This approach is similar to the Minnesota Model. The second manual,

"Cognitive-Behavioral Therapy," is based on a social-learning theory model. Skills to avoid relapse are taught. Many of the specific techniques in this approach will be covered in Chapter 10, when we describe the cognitive-social learning model to relapse prevention. Finally, the third manual, "Motivational Enhancement Therapy," is designed to help clients identify and use personal resources to effect change. This approach is based on motivational psychology and is related to motivational interviewing (see Chapter 7).

Pharmacological procedures are also used in treatment. However, these procedures are rarely the only intervention. Rather, they are usually used in conjunction with other treatment methods. The philosophy of treatment and the treatment setting may also determine whether drugs are used to treat AOD problems. One would expect that treatment programs adhering to the disease concept would be adverse to using drugs in treatment. However, Cook (1988) stated that detoxification at Minnesota Model programs may use medication. Treatment programs in nonhospital settings without medical staff obviously should not use drugs in treatment.

Detoxification, the period in which a client is withdrawing from AOD, is frequently a time when medication is used. In the past, this process occurred in an inpatient, hospital setting. However, outpatient detoxification is now a common practice because of the high costs of hospitalization. In the detoxification process for alcohol and other central nervous system (CNS) depressants, minor tranquilizers such as Valium or Xanax are often used to reduce the danger of seizures and the other uncomfortable and dangerous withdrawal symptoms. Careful medical supervision with a gradually decreasing dosage is necessary, since these minor tranquilizers are in the same drug classification as alcohol (see Chapter 2).

Methadone is widely known for its use in treating opioid addiction. Methadone is a synthetic narcotic with a longer duration of effect than heroin, and ingestion blocks the euphoric effects of opioids. Once a client is stabilized on a particular dose, he or she takes it to reduce or eliminate any withdrawal symptoms from heroin abstinence. The client must visit a methadone clinic to receive the dose. Once a client is stabilized on methadone, he or she can function normally.

A medication that can be administered through outpatient physician offices (as opposed to a specialized clinic) has been approved for use in treating opioid addiction. Buprenorphine is an opioid that has proved to be as effective as methadone. The advantages of buprenorphine are that it is taken in tablet form, daily doses do not appear to be necessary, and it has relatively mild withdrawal symptoms. In the pill form administered to opioid addicts, naloxone is added to buprenorphine. The naloxone decreases the likelihood of abuse because it blocks the "high" that could be achieved by injecting buprenorphine alone. The approval of buprenorphine by the federal government has greatly increased the access to opioid agonist treatment for heroin addicts, particularly for people who would have to travel a great distance to get to a methadone clinic. Buprenorphine is sold under the brand name Suboxone.

Antabuse (disulfiram) has been used in conjunction with other forms of alcohol treatment. When Antabuse is taken and alcohol is ingested during the following 24- to 48- hour period, the client experiences facial flushing, heart palpitations and rapid heart rate, difficulty in breathing, nausea, and vomiting. Because Antabuse takes 30 minutes to work after ingestion, it has been of limited value in aversive conditioning. The client must take Antabuse on a daily basis, and this raises an issue of the need for such medication. If an individual were motivated to take Antabuse daily, it would seem that he or she would probably be motivated to remain abstinent without Antabuse. However, some alcoholics, when tempted to use alcohol, are comforted by the fact that Antabuse will result in an unpleasant reaction if they drink. This awareness often reduces or eliminates the urge to use. Clients who use Antabuse must be warned against using over-the-counter products that contain alcohol because the Antabuse will cause a reaction from the use of these products.

Another drug that is used in alcoholism treatment is naltrexone. Naltrexone is an opioid antagonist (i.e., a drug that blocks the effects of other drugs). However, it has also been found to reduce the craving for alcohol. Therefore, naltrexone is recommended as one strategy in a comprehensive treatment program, but not as the *only* strategy. A panel of experts developed a protocol on the use of naltrexone in alcoholism treatment (Center for Substance Abuse Treatment, 1998) and reported:

> Naltrexone therapy improves treatment outcomes when added to other components of alcoholism treatment. For patients who are motivated to take the medication, naltrexone is an important and valuable tool. In many patients, a short regimen of naltrexone will provide a critical period of sobriety, during which the patient learns to stay sober without it. (p. xx)

In a meta-analysis of studies on naltrexone and acamprosate (another drug used in alcoholism treatment), Maisel et al. (2013) concluded that acamprosate was slightly more effective than naltrexone in promoting abstinence, while naltrexone was slightly more effective in reducing heavy drinking and craving for alcohol. When patients have detoxified before treatment, the effect of both medications is enhanced.

At this point, no effective pharmacological treatments for stimulant (e.g., cocaine, methamphetamine) or marijuana use disorders have been identified.

TREATMENT STRATEGIES AND TECHNIQUES

In describing the major approaches to treatment, we have already mentioned some of the techniques used in the treatment of alcoholics and addicts. For example, the disease or Minnesota Model uses group therapy, education, Twelve Step meetings, and other strategies as well. In this section, we want to describe the most common procedures that are used in treatment. However, understand that not all of these strategies may be used in all treatment programs, or more or less emphasis may be placed on particular interventions depending on the treatment approach and setting. It is a good idea for helping professionals to contact treatment programs in their areas to determine the exact components of the particular program *before* making referrals.

Treatment planning and the treatment plan are the methods by which treatment staff determine what the problems are and what to do about them. Any substance abuse treatment program that is accredited by a state or other accrediting body will have individual treatment plans for all clients. That does not mean that all treatment plans in all treatment programs are comprehensive or useful—just that potential for usefulness exists. Treatment planning involves the assessment and diagnosis of the client (discussed in Chapter 6), the actual written treatment plan, and an aftercare plan. Although the form and content of the treatment plan may vary from program to program and state to state depending on accreditation requirements, every treatment plan should include a statement of the problem(s), long-term goals, short-term objectives that are measurable, strategies to achieve goals and objectives, and review and target dates.

To illustrate a problem statement, long-term goal, and short-term objective, we asked to look at some treatment plans at one of our local treatment programs (with names deleted, of course). This example is representative of the treatment plans we reviewed.

Example of Treatment Plan

Problem Statement: (Client's Name) has used alcohol and cocaine on a daily basis for the past 16 months.

Long-Term Goal: (Client's Name) will remain abstinent from all mind-altering drugs.

Short-Term Objective: (Client's Name) will remain abstinent from all mind-altering drugs for one month.

Strategies:

1. Attend one AA or NA meeting per day.
2. Attend all program lectures.
3. Participate in two individual counseling sessions per week.
4. Participate in three group counseling sessions per week.
5. Participate in one family counseling session per week.

Let's examine these strategies more closely, along with some that are not addressed on this treatment plan.

Individual, Group, and Family Counseling

Because you are preparing for a career as a mental health professional, you have had or will have courses in individual, group, and family counseling. Although it is beyond our scope to thoroughly discuss the processes and theoretical approaches to counseling, we believe that an individual who enters a counseling relationship with any client should be trained and credentialed to perform counseling functions. At the very minimum, mental health professionals should possess the facilitative qualities of counseling, such as empathy, respect, warmth, concreteness, immediacy, congruence, and genuineness. Although you have undoubtedly learned the need for training, credentialing, and facilitative qualities, making this message seem redundant, these issues are of utmost concern in the substance abuse counseling field. In many states, substance abuse counselors need only a high school diploma or GED and little formal training. A master's degree is rarely required for initial certification. Therefore, individual counseling in many treatment programs is less of a psychotherapy model and more like case management and monitoring.

Traditionally, group counseling is often the primary approach of both inpatient and outpatient treatment programs. However, in many treatment programs, group counseling may actually be a confrontation of individuals in the group who are not "working the program" or it may be dissemination of educational information. This is considerably different from the group counseling described by Corey (2016) that is probably part of your training program. It would be more useful for group work to help to develop concrete, usable skills and to rehearse these behaviors in the group. In addition, such group counseling can be used to analyze drinking and drug-taking behaviors and to develop methods of coping, problem solving, and assertiveness, rather than being focused on gaining client compliance to admit to having a disease.

There has been an increasing use of family counseling in treatment programs. As with group counseling, what is sometimes called family counseling is actually education about the disease concept and the family's role in the disease process. However, family counseling is an essential component of treatment since many alcoholics/addicts have relationship, parenting, and family problems. In addition, family dynamics may enable the addict's AOD use and, as recovery begins, the family dynamics may be so dysfunctional that they threaten the patient's recovery (O'Farrell & Fals-Stewart, 2003).

Just as we discussed in individual counseling, real marriage and family therapy (as opposed to educational family lectures) is complex and requires trained and credentialed professionals. There may be dysfunction in the family as a whole and/or in subsystems such as the couple subsystem, sibling subsystems, and parent/child subsystems. Very frequently, there are stepparents, stepchildren, grandparents, and other extended family members to consider.

A treatment approach for adolescents that primarily focuses on the family has been developed by Howard Liddle (Diamond & Liddle, 1996). Multidimensional family therapy is conducted in the treatment setting, in the home, and in community settings. Parents work on their parenting style, learn to distinguish influence from control, and develop a positive and developmentally appropriate influence on their child. Other evidence-based approaches for couples and families include behavioral couples therapy (O'Farrell & Fals-Stewart, 2006), brief strategic family therapy (Szapocznik & Kurtines, 1989), and family behavior therapy (Donohue, Allen, & Lapota, 2009).

Support Groups

We will thoroughly discuss Twelve Step and other forms of support groups in Chapter 11. However, Twelve Step groups are such a central part of most treatment programs that this type of strategy deserves mention here. In fact, many programs throughout the country use an AA or NA Twelve Step approach for both in- and outpatient treatment. Again, we will save a discussion of the components and effectiveness of Twelve Step groups for the following chapter. However, the use of Twelve Step meetings as a treatment strategy and as a philosophy in treatment programs is consistent with the disease model of addiction and, as we have already discussed, with the orientation of the Minnesota Model of treatment.

Although AA and NA are recommended for the alcoholic/addict, family members are encouraged to attend either Al-Anon or Alateen meetings. This is to introduce family members to the potential support available through Al-Anon or Alateen while the client is still in treatment. For those of you unfamiliar with these groups, Al-Anon is a support group for family members of alcoholics/addicts using the Twelve Step model, and Alateen is a similar support group specifically for teenagers who have an alcoholic/addicted parent. Clients and family members may also be referred to ACOA (Twelve Step support for adult children of alcoholics) or CODA (Twelve Step support for codependents).

Many alternative support groups that do not use the Twelve Step model exist. However, the acceptance of these alternatives in disease-model treatment programs may be resisted.

Lifestyle Changes

Irrespective of the orientation of the treatment program, treatment strategies designed to bring about changes in the lifestyle of the client are essential. For example, if clients return to the same friends and activities that were a part of their lives before treatment, relapse is highly probable. The range of lifestyle changes that must be addressed illustrates the complexity of comprehensive treatment and the need for long-term interventions for alcoholic/addicted individuals. We will discuss some of these strategies for lifestyle change in more detail in Chapter 10, "Relapse Prevention and Recovery," because mental health professionals may be involved in the implementation of many of these strategies. The lifestyle areas that should receive attention for a particular client should be determined during the assessment of the client and should then be included in the treatment plan.

The issue of friends, lovers, family members, and acquaintances is a focus of treatment. If a client has close associations with individuals who use AOD, some difficult and painful decisions must be made. These topics may be discussed in individual, group, and family counseling. In addition, clients may need assistance with social skills to enhance their ability to make new friends. Many alcoholic/addicted individuals have relied on the use of AOD to feel comfortable in social situations and/or as a common bond to those with whom they spend time. The difficulty of this particular area can be clearly illustrated with an adolescent who is told during treatment to avoid contact with friends who use. The adolescent returns to school after treatment and perceives his or her options as returning to a previous social group or having no friends at all. If relapse is to be avoided, the adolescent who is treated for an alcohol or other drug problem clearly needs continued support and assistance to help develop a new social group.

Because many individuals with AOD problems have used these substances to avoid negative emotions or to manage stress and pain, alternative methods of dealing with common life problems must also be taught in treatment. Strategies may involve stress management techniques, relaxation procedures, and assertiveness training. The intent of such training is to provide the client with skills to use in situations or in response to situations in which alcohol or other drug use was the only perceived option available. For example, a business executive is treated for alcoholism. He returns to work after treatment and, as happens to everyone, has "one of those days." In the past, he has used alcohol to cope with the stress and tension of work. If the client is not taught alternative methods for managing stress and tension, along with techniques to relax that do not involve drugs, relapse is a predictable response.

Other lifestyle areas that may be a focus of intervention include vocational and educational planning, financial planning, and living environment. To illustrate how these factors can influence recovery, review the third case example of Ralph.

You can easily see all the areas mentioned required attention, any of which could result in a return to use if ignored. Ralph did not complete high school and had never held a job for more than a few months. Because of his criminal records, the only jobs he could get were minimum wage. After leaving prison, he had to move in with some cousins who all were using drugs. These practical issues in treatment go beyond the model used and are critical determinants in whether a client is able to maintain a drug-free lifestyle. So you won't be kept in suspense, this particular situation had a fairly happy ending (as far as we know today). Ralph's parole officer got him involved with a recovery program for ex-offenders (see "Recovery Support Services" in Chapter 10). Through this program, he was able to move into a half-way house for recovering ex-offenders and enroll in a culinary training program. Again, the point of this case is to illustrate how vocational guidance, financial planning, and living arrangements may all be necessary components of treatment.

Education

Many treatment programs, particularly those using a disease-concept model, use lectures and films to provide clients with information on the disease concept, on family issues in AOD use, and on the social, medical, and psychological consequences of AOD use. The rationale for educational interventions is the assumption that lack of knowledge or inaccurate information contributes to AOD. If clients are taught up-to-date, factual material, they will be less likely to use AOD in a hazardous manner.

Although the teaching of educational information is a commonly used strategy in treatment, no evidence exists that providing information to alcoholics/addicts changes their behavior. However, as we discussed in Chapter 7, education can be helpful for light or moderate users and at-risk users. Furthermore, as part of a comprehensive treatment program, it certainly makes sense to provide information to clients and family members. But education and information dissemination should not be expected to produce miraculous changes and, therefore, these activities should not be conducted at the expense of more useful treatment strategies. As an aside, it has always been fascinating to us that didactic methods are used to present information to clients in treatment with little or no regard for the learning capacity or learning style of the client. For example, since research by Karacostas and Fisher (1993) has found a higher-than-expected proportion of learning-disabled adolescents with probable AOD problems, it would be logical to assess clients to determine the most effective method for imparting information. However, we have found that this is rarely a part of the assessment in treatment programs.

Aftercare

For those individuals who enter AOD treatment, recovery can be conceptualized as a three-stage process. The first stage is formal treatment, the second stage is aftercare, and the third stage is ongoing recovery. *Aftercare* refers to the interventions and strategies that will be implemented after formal treatment is completed. However, it more accurately should be called "continuing care" because aftercare programs are usually continuations of many of the strategies from formal treatment. Our focus is on the issues that require attention following discharge from formal treatment.

The multitude of problems that develop during the time that a person has been using AOD cannot possibly be solved in a month-long treatment program. Interventions that were initiated in treatment can be continued during aftercare. Frequently, individual and family therapy will be components of an aftercare program as well as vocational, educational, and financial guidance. Attendance at Twelve Step meetings will usually be mentioned in aftercare plans. Aftercare meetings may be a part of the treatment program, or the client may be referred to a mental health professional for management of the aftercare program. Because the aftercare program is an essential element in relapse prevention, we will discuss this in detail in Chapter 10.

TREATMENT SETTINGS

Choice of Treatment Setting

The strategies and interventions described can be implemented in a variety of treatment settings. Klar (1987) discussed the concept of "least restrictive environment" with regard to the appropriate treatment setting. Those of you with a background in special education are familiar with this concept as it relates to placement of students, and the rationale is similar for AOD treatment. Clients should be placed in the treatment setting that offers the least amount of restriction, with the highest probability of success, while all the factors identified in the assessment are considered. What are some of these factors? Nace (1987) identified criteria for determining whether outpatient alcoholism treatment was appropriate. These criteria included client motivation, ability to discontinue use, social support, employment, medical condition, psychiatric status, and treatment history. Clients who are poorly motivated to discontinue use (i.e., court mandated) or who admit to a failure to abstain if AOD are available may fail in outpatient treatment. Also, we have already discussed the importance of social support. Employment may be a double-edged sword. Although continued employment may strongly motivate a client to succeed in outpatient treatment, the work environment is often a source of stress for people, or coworkers might encourage the client to use (e.g., going out for drinks after work). An individual who is unemployed (and, ironically, is probably the least able to afford more expensive inpatient treatment), may be a poor candidate for an outpatient program because the client is not occupied for a large segment of time by a job. Obviously, individuals with medical and/or psychiatric conditions may need more restrictive treatment environments. A person with liver damage may need medical supervision and an environment that ensures abstinence. Similarly, a client who is receiving pharmaceutical treatment for a psychiatric condition may (but not always) require inpatient treatment. Finally, if someone has already failed in outpatient treatment, more intensive treatment may be needed.

Unfortunately, all of these factors might not be used in determining the treatment setting for a client. In other words, money, insurance, and the availability of publicly funded treatment programs, rather than client factors, may determine where a person is placed for treatment.

As a result of "nonclient" factors being used to determine treatment setting, many states are adopting "uniform patient placement criteria" to determine the appropriate treatment setting. The most widely used patient placement criteria was developed by the American Society of Addiction Medicine (ASAM) and is called ASAM PPC 2R to denote the second edition revision of this system. ASAM PPC 2R uses a multidimensional assessment that includes acute intoxication and/or withdrawal potential, biomedical conditions and complications, emotional/behavioral/cognitive conditions and complications, readiness to change, relapse/continued use/continued problem potential, and recovery environment (i.e., social, family, vocational support) (American Society of Addiction Medicine, 2016). The major levels of care (there are many sublevels) are: Level .5, Early Intervention Services; Level I, Outpatient; Level II, Intensive Outpatient/Partial Hospitalization; Level III, Residential; and Level IV, Inpatient. We will briefly describe these settings as well as therapeutic communities.

Therapeutic Communities

The therapeutic community (TC) is a residential environment usually associated with treatment for drugs other than alcohol. The duration of treatment in TCs is typically longer than other types of treatment, usually one year or more. Synanon (started in 1958), one of the earliest and most famous therapeutic communities, expected permanent involvement by clients. The characteristics of therapeutic communities include a highly structured daily routine, a system of rewards and punishments for behavior, and frequent group confrontation, self-reflection, and confession of past wrongdoing. Because of the isolation and long-term nature of most TCs, the drop-out rates tend to be high. This type of treatment setting is often a treatment of last resort. In other words, most TC residents have failed in one or more other types of treatment setting.

Interestingly, TCs are increasingly popular as a treatment setting in jails and prisons. Obviously, the length of this type of approach is no barrier in these institutions. The needs of institutional clients are often well-suited to this type of program because the primary goal of a TC is "global lifestyle change, including abstinence from (alcohol and other drugs), elimination of antisocial behavior, enhanced education, constructive employment, and development of prosocial attitudes and values" (Center for Substance Abuse Treatment, 1995, p. 51).

Religious-based TCs such as Teen Challenge are also available. This specific program has an evangelical Christian orientation and the TC portion of the program lasts for one year (Teen Challenge, 2016).

Inpatient and Residential Treatment

Although this treatment environment is usually associated with hospitals, this is not always the case. Residential treatment may occur in nonhospital settings. The duration of treatment is shorter than in therapeutic communities, and the social isolation is reduced. Most inpatient and residential programs gradually reintroduce the client to a normal environment through community outings and home passes. These programs generally offer supervised detoxification that may involve medication in a hospital setting or social detoxification (i.e., no medication) in a nonhospital setting. The typical 28-day treatment duration has no research base. It has come about as a result of financial constraints, particularly the reluctance of insurance companies to pay for treatment. Inpatient and residential treatment settings have the advantages of 24-hour supervision, the reduced likelihood of clients using AOD while in treatment, highly structured days, and a total immersion in treatment, with removal from the everyday stressors and pressures that may interfere with treatment. The disadvantages of this setting are the expense (a 28-day program in a hospital setting may be well over $15,000) and the artificiality of the environment. In a supervised, structured, and protective setting, a client may have little difficulty maintaining abstinence. In a well-supervised program, there may be no choice. However, the client may have little or no opportunity to practice new behaviors and may develop a false belief in self-efficacy (competence to deal with the environment). The real world may quickly dispel the client's perception of self-efficacy, resulting in relapse.

Partial Hospitalization and Day Treatment

As you can probably tell from the heading of this section, these types of treatment settings can also occur in hospitals or free-standing treatment centers. The client normally spends all or some of the evenings (and overnight) at home. These programs are less expensive than inpatient or residential programs and allow clients to remain involved with some normal aspects of life while they are in treatment. Because the client's life is less artificial than it would be if he or she were in 24-hour care, the client has greater opportunity to apply the knowledge and skills acquired during treatment. The client also has the opportunity to figure out some of the possible barriers in his or her daily life to a changed lifestyle during the time the client has frequent contact with the treatment program. This allows the client to work on solutions to these barriers before the formal treatment program ends. However, some risks are associated with partial hospitalization and day treatment, the most obvious being opportunities for the client to use AOD. Unless the client admits to using, or if drug testing is conducted, a return to use may not be discovered. Also, if the client's friends and family are using or are not supportive of the client's efforts, living in the "normal" environment for even brief periods may be counterproductive.

Intensive Outpatient and Outpatient

These types of treatment programs are usually associated with free-standing treatment programs or clinics, such as mental health centers. Intensive outpatient programs normally are held for three or four evenings in the week for two to four hours each evening. Outpatient treatment is usually less frequent (one or two evenings a week) and shorter (one to two hours per session). As you might imagine, outpatient clients usually have issues that are less serious than clients in more restrictive settings, although some insurance policies will pay only for outpatient treatment. Outpatient treatment can also be a point in a gradual reduction in treatment intensity (i.e., client starts treatment in a residential setting and transitions to outpatient).

The major advantage (aside from cost) of intensive outpatient and outpatient programs is that clients can continue to work or go to school. It is often the case that a person's only expressed barrier to treatment is the perceived or actual necessity to work or go to school. Whether this barrier is real or used as an excuse, it does not exist in outpatient programs.

AT A GLANCE

Treatment Approaches

- Minnesota Model
- Behavioral Approaches
  - Aversive conditioning
  - CM
  - Community reinforcement approach
- Matrix Model
- Twelve Step Facilitation
- Cognitive-Behavioral Therapy
- Motivational Enhancement Therapy
- Pharmacological Procedures
  - Methadone and buprenorphine
  - Antabuse (disulfiram)
  - Naltrexone
  - Acamprosate

Strategies and Techniques

- Treatment plan
  - Problem statement
  - Long-term goals
  - Short-term objectives
  - Strategies
- Individual, group, family counseling
- Support groups
- Lifestyle changes
- Education
- Aftercare

Treatment Setting

- ASAM PPC 2R for standardized determination
- Therapeutic communities
- Inpatient and residential
- Partial hospitalization and day treatment
- Intensive outpatient and outpatient

PRINCIPLES OF EFFECTIVE TREATMENT

The National Institute on Drug Abuse published a booklet in 2012 called "Principles of Drug Addiction Treatment: A Research-Based Guide," third edition. This short booklet is available online (see Internet Resources at the end of the chapter) and contains evidence-based principles, methods, and programs in treatment. The following 13 principles, which are listed in this booklet, are extremely useful for all mental health professionals.

1. *Addiction is a complex but treatable disease that affects brain function and behavior* Drugs of abuse alter the brain's structure and function, resulting in changes that persist long after drug use has ceased. This may explain why drug abusers are at risk for relapse even after long periods of abstinence and despite the potentially devastating consequences.
2. *No single treatment is appropriate for everyone* Treatment varies depending on the type of drug and the characteristics of the patients. Matching treatment settings, interventions, and services to an individual's particular problems and needs is critical to his or her ultimate success in returning to productive functioning in the family, workplace, and society.
3. *Treatment needs to be readily available* Because drug-addicted individuals may be uncertain about entering treatment, taking advantage of available services the moment people are ready for treatment is critical. Potential patients can be lost if treatment is not immediately available or readily accessible. As with other chronic diseases, the earlier treatment is offered in the disease process, the greater the likelihood of positive outcomes.
4. *Effective treatment attends to multiple needs of the individual, not just his or her drug abuse* To be effective, treatment must address the individual's drug abuse and any associated medical, psychological, social, vocational, and legal problems. It is also important that treatment be appropriate to the individual's age, gender, ethnicity, and culture.
5. *Remaining in treatment for an adequate period of time is critical* The appropriate duration for an individual depends on the type and degree of his or her problems and needs. Research indicates that most addicted individuals need at least three months in treatment to significantly reduce or stop their drug use and that the best outcomes occur with longer durations of treatment. Recovery from drug addiction is a long-term process and frequently requires multiple episodes

of treatment. As with other chronic illnesses, relapses to drug abuse can occur and should signal a need for treatment to be reinstated or adjusted. Because individuals often leave treatment prematurely, programs should include strategies to engage and keep patients in treatment.

6. *Behavioral therapies—including individual, family or group counseling—are the most commonly used forms of drug abuse treatment*   Behavioral therapies vary in their focus and may involve addressing a patient's motivation to change, providing incentives for abstinence, building skills to resist drug use, replacing drug-using activities with constructive and rewarding activities, improving problem-solving skills, and facilitating better interpersonal relationships. Also, participation in group therapy and other peer support programs during and following treatment can help maintain abstinence.

7. *Medications are an important element of treatment for many patients, especially when combined with counseling and other behavioral therapies*   For example, methadone, buprenorphine, and naltrexone (including a new long-acting formulation) are effective in helping individuals addicted to heroin or other opioids stabilize their lives and reduce their illicit drug use. Acamprosate, disulfiram, and naltrexone are medications approved for treating alcohol dependence. For persons addicted to nicotine, a nicotine replacement product (available as patches, gum, lozenges, or nasal spray) or an oral medication (such as bupropion or varenicline) can be an effective component of treatment when part of a comprehensive behavioral treatment program.

8. *An individual's treatment and services plan must be assessed continually and modified as necessary to ensure that it meets his or her changing needs*   A patient may require varying combinations of services and treatment components during the course of treatment and recovery. In addition to counseling or psychotherapy, a patient may require medication, medical services, family therapy, parenting instruction, vocational rehabilitation, and/or social and legal services. For many patients, a continuing care approach provides the best results, with the treatment intensity varying according to a person's changing needs.

9. *Many drug-addicted individuals also have other mental disorders*   Because drug abuse and addiction—both of which are mental disorders—often co-occur with other mental illnesses, patients presenting with one condition should be assessed for the other(s). And when these problems co-occur, treatment should address both (or all), including the use of medications as appropriate.

10. *Medically assisted detoxification is only the first stage of addiction treatment and by itself does little to change long-term drug abuse*   Although medically assisted detoxification can safely manage the acute physical symptoms of withdrawal and can, for some, pave the way for effective long-term addiction treatment, detoxification alone is rarely sufficient to help addicted individuals achieve long-term abstinence. Thus, patients should be encouraged to continue drug treatment following detoxification. Motivational enhancement and incentive strategies, begun at initial patient intake, can improve treatment engagement.

11. *Treatment does not need to be voluntary to be effective*   Sanctions or enticements from family, employment settings, and/or the criminal justice system can significantly increase treatment entry, retention rates, and the ultimate success of drug treatment interventions.

12. *Drug use during treatment must be monitored continuously, as lapses during treatment do occur*   Knowing their drug use is being monitored can be a powerful incentive for patients and can help them withstand urges to use drugs. Monitoring also provides an early indication of a return to drug use, signaling a possible need to adjust an individual's treatment plan to better meet his or her needs.

13. *Treatment programs should assess patients for the presence of HIV/AIDS, hepatitis B and C, tuberculosis, and other infectious diseases as well as provide targeted risk-reduction counseling, linking patients to treatment if necessary*   Typically, drug abuse treatment addresses

some of the drug-related behaviors that put people at risk of infectious diseases. Targeted counseling specifically focused on reducing infectious disease risk can help patients further reduce or avoid substance-related and other high-risk behaviors. Counseling can also help those who are already infected to manage their illness. Moreover, engaging in substance abuse treatment can facilitate adherence to other medical treatments. Substance abuse treatment facilities should provide onsite, rapid HIV testing rather than referrals to offsite testing—research shows that doing so increases the likelihood that patients will be tested and receive their test results. Treatment providers should also inform patients that highly active antiretroviral therapy has proven effective in combating HIV, including among drug-abusing populations, and help link them to HIV treatment if they test positive.

EVIDENCE-BASED TREATMENT

Federal and state government agencies involved in AOD treatment are increasingly requiring that funding provided to agencies must be used for strategies that research has shown to be effective and that have demonstrated consistent results in multiple studies. "Evidence-based" treatment is the term generally used to describe these methods or strategies but "empirically based," "science-based," and "research-based" are also used.

In an effort to standardize the process of designating a strategy, program, or technique as evidence-based, the Substance Abuse and Mental Health Services Administration, a federal agency in the Department of Health and Human Services, developed the National Registry of Evidence-Based Programs and Practices (NREPP). NREPP includes mental health promotion and treatment, substance abuse prevention and treatment, and co-occurring disorders.

At the time this edition is published, 80 AOD treatment interventions in NREPP have been identified. Some are comprehensive manuals for treatment (i.e., "Twelve-Step Facilitation Therapy," "Cognitive-Behavioral Therapy," and "Motivational Enhancement Therapy"); some interventions are for special populations (i.e., "A Woman's Path to Recovery," "Adolescent Community Reinforcement Approach," "Friends Care" [for parole and probationers], "Healthy Living Project for People Living with HIV," "Pathways' Housing First Project" [for co-occurring disorders]); some are for specific substances (e.g., "Cocaine Specific Coping Skills Training," "Brief Marijuana Dependence Counseling," "Broad Spectrum Treatment [BST]," and "Naltrexone for Alcohol Dependence"); and other programs that target discrete parts of the treatment process (e.g., "Computer-Assisted System for Patient Assessment and Referral," "Contracts, Prompts, and Reinforcement of Substance Use Disorder Continuing Care [CPR]").

To be accepted by NREPP, every aspect of the intervention, including outcomes, are evaluated by an independent expert review panel. The intervention is graded on the reliability and validity of the measurement instruments, the fidelity of the intervention (how closely the evaluators make sure that things happen as they are supposed to happen), missing data and attrition, potential confounding variables, and the appropriateness of the data analysis. Because it would not do much good to include an intervention in NREPP that others could not adopt, the program or strategy is also graded on its readiness for dissemination, including the availability of implementation materials, training and support, and quality assurance procedures.

With this rigorous procedure, you can have some faith that the programs and strategies included in NREPP are effective. However, evidence-based interventions may be implemented poorly by clinicians, applied in settings or with populations for which the intervention has not been validated, or employed incompletely, thus negating the effectiveness of the process. So, neither assume that simply because a treatment is described as "evidence-based," its success is inevitable, nor that an approach that has not been labeled "evidence-based" cannot possibly be effective.

CASE EXAMPLE APPLICATIONS

This is an appropriate point in the chapter to take a look at the case examples presented in the beginning. After reading about treatment approaches, treatment strategies and techniques, treatment settings, principles of effective treatment, and evidence-based treatment, you can probably see that designing treatment for each of the cases has to be individualized and is complex. In addition to the treatment issues we have already discussed, we devote the next chapter to special populations, including clients with co-occurring mental disorders. Co-occurring disorders and other special population considerations increase the variables that must be considered in designing treatment to meet the needs of the individual. Although we can't provide you with all of the information you would need to make decisions about each aspect of treatment for each case, consider the following questions. What kind of treatment setting would be most appropriate? Should Misty be in a residential setting? How will she learn to be an effective parent if she doesn't have the opportunity to interact with her child? Does Ben need medical detoxification? Will attending AA meetings and individual counseling be enough to meet Ralph's needs? Should any or all of these persons have specialized treatment? Of all the treatment strategies mentioned, which are the most critical for each case? Which of the treatment approaches and evidence-based practices do you think are most appropriate?

You know that no completely correct answer exists in every case, and we hope you won't be overly frustrated about this. We suggest discussing these questions in your class. The point we want to emphasize is that treatment planning is complicated, and all the questions we have raised have to be addressed based on a comprehensive assessment of the client.

TREATMENT EFFECTIVENESS

Does treatment work? This issue is complex but extremely important, given the time and expense of AOD treatment and the costs to society if people continue abusing AOD following treatment. Although numerous studies have examined treatment effectiveness, making sense of the results is difficult because of several underlying problems. Before discussing some of these studies, let's look at some of these problems.

Treatment programs (for the most part) are not designed to scientifically evaluate the aspects of treatment that are most effective. This makes research immediately problematic because control over the many variables that may affect results is virtually nonexistent. The numerous client variables that may impact treatment effectiveness include age, gender, duration of use, type of substances used, life problems experienced, voluntary or involuntary admission to treatment, prior treatment, client health, psychological problems, criminal activity, level of education, and income. The type of treatment environment (e.g., private, for profit; public, nonprofit; hospital inpatient; free-standing outpatient; therapeutic community) may impact effectiveness. To adequately research the effectiveness of a treatment program or treatment approach, a control group is necessary. Ethical (and practical) issues in the random assignment of clients to treatment must be considered when the researcher hypothesizes that one form of treatment is superior to another.

Equally as important to the issues that create barriers to well-designed research are the types of outcomes in effectiveness studies. Is client success defined by program completion, abstinence, length of sobriety, and/or reduction in life problems? What if a client completes a program, relapses, goes to a different program, and then remains abstinent? Was the first program a failure or did it contribute to the client's sobriety later on?

Fortunately, major long-term studies have been completed to help answer the question "Does treatment work?" The Center for Substance Abuse Treatment sponsored a congressionally mandated study of treatment outcomes for clients in public sector treatment programs. The National Treatment Improvement Evaluation Study (NTIES; Gerstein, 1997) followed 4,411 clients in 78 treatment sites across the country for five years. Clients were from vulnerable and underserved populations such as minorities, pregnant women, youth, public housing residents, welfare recipients, and those involved in the criminal justice system. Many of the persons studied did not complete treatment, which would tend to depress any positive results. In spite of these factors, there were significant reductions in AOD use one year after treatment regardless of the amount of time spent in treatment or the amount of treatment received. In addition, positive outcomes were found in employment income, mental and physical health, criminal activity, homelessness, and high-risk behaviors for HIV infection. This study also demonstrated that the average savings per client in the year after treatment was $9,177. The savings occurred in reduced health care and crime-related costs and increased earnings by clients. Outpatient and long-term residential treatment showed the largest cost savings, but short-term residential treatment and outpatient methadone also were cost-effective.

The National Institute on Drug Abuse followed more than 10,000 clients in nearly 100 treatment programs for two years. The Drug Abuse Treatment Outcome Study (DATOS; Mueller & Wyman, 1997) involved four types of treatment programs: outpatient methadone, outpatient drug-free, long-term residential, and short-term inpatient. In all treatment modalities, significant reductions occurred in the use of heroin, cocaine, marijuana, and alcohol one year following treatment. Positive outcomes were noted in criminal activity, depression, and employment. The outcomes were most pronounced for clients in long-term treatment but were significant for short-term clients as well.

Five-year follow-up data are available on 708 subjects from 45 programs in eight cities who met *Diagnostic and Statistical Manual of Mental Disorders* (*DSM*) criteria for cocaine dependence (Simpson, Joe, & Broome, 2002). Large decreases in cocaine use occurred in the first year after treatment discharge, which were maintained at five years. Similarly, improvements in heavy alcohol use and criminal activity continued. The level of severity of drug use and psychosocial problems at treatment entry were predictive of long-term outcomes. However, outcomes improved in direct relationship to the level of treatment exposure (i.e., those who were in treatment longer did better).

Furthermore, data on 1,167 adolescents from the DATOS sample were also analyzed (Hser et al., 2001). At one year posttreatment, significant reductions in marijuana use, heavy drinking, use of illicit drugs, and criminal involvement were noted. The clients also reported better psychological adjustment and school performance.

The third study was conducted by the National Institute on Alcohol Abuse and Alcoholism and was called "Project MATCH" (Project MATCH Research Group, 1997). This study was designed to determine if different types of alcoholics respond differently to specific treatment approaches. More than 1,700 alcoholics in outpatient treatment or aftercare were studied. The clients were matched with one of three treatment approaches based on client characteristics, including severity of alcohol involvement, cognitive impairment, psychiatric severity, conceptual level, gender, meaning-seeking, motivational readiness to change, social support for drinking versus abstinence, sociopathy, and typology of alcoholism. The three treatment approaches (Twelve Step facilitation, cognitive-behavioral, motivational enhancement) were described earlier in this chapter. Overall, the clients in this study demonstrated significant improvement in increased percentage of abstinent days and decreased number of drinks per drinking days. Few differences among the treatment approaches emerged. In spite of many efforts, researchers have been unable to identify the reasons why one approach was superior to another in the rare instances where differences were noted (Longabaugh, 2001). Positive outcomes were also noted in the use of other drugs, depression, and alcohol-related problems.

Finally, outcome studies on the use of pharmacological approaches to treatment have been conducted. For example, naltrexone has been shown to reduce the percentage of days a client spends drinking, the amount of alcohol consumed on a drinking occasion, and the relapse to excessive and destructive drinking (Center for Substance Abuse Treatment, 1998). Methadone has been shown to be an extremely effective treatment for opioid addiction. For example, Ball, Corty, Petroski, and Bond (1987) found that more than 92% of methadone maintenance clients were abstinent from other opioids after 4½ years on methadone. Improved social functioning, reduced mortality and morbidity, and decreased criminal activity have also been demonstrated (e.g., Ball & Ross, 1991; Hubbard & French, 1991). Methadone treatment is also extremely cost-effective, with $4 in economic benefits for every $1 spent for treatment (Parrino, 2002).

Although it is not possible to comprehensively review all treatment effectiveness research, several conclusions can be reached. Treatment does appear to have a beneficial, long-term effect on a variety of client behaviors, including AOD use. Treatment length may be related to improved outcomes, but even short-term treatment is helpful. A variety of treatment approaches and treatment settings have proven effective, and even the most vulnerable clients benefit from treatment.

SPECIAL PROBLEMS IN TREATMENT

Recovering Individuals as Counselors

Back in 1989, James Royce, in discussing an early treatment program in the mid-1940s, reported that recovering alcoholics had been part of the treatment team even though they did not have professional training. The empathy that recovering alcoholics had from their own experiences was recognized as a valuable contribution to treatment (Royce, 1989). We agree.

The question is not whether recovering individuals should be AOD counselors but whether all counselors receive the appropriate type and amount of training. An assumption has been made in the field that the attribute of being in recovery is sufficient for effectiveness as an AOD counselor. However, we would be hard-pressed to find support for the notion that if one has attempted suicide, he or she would be an effective crisis intervention counselor. We have trained many master's-level counselors who are in recovery, and we believe that the combination of personal experience and professional training can be dynamic. By the same token, an individual who is well trained and has good interpersonal skills can be an effective AOD counselor regardless of whether that person is in recovery. A person with little or no training and poor interpersonal skills will be ineffective, whether he or she is in recovery or not. What about the individual in recovery who has little training and good interpersonal skills? This person might be a natural counselor and can undoubtedly be helpful. Lack of training is simply a factor limiting the type of client issues this counselor should work with. The outstanding natural counselors we have worked with who are in recovery and have returned for formal training have been able to recognize this limitation and have sought assistance to increase their effectiveness.

Confrontation as a Treatment Strategy

The association of confrontation with substance abuse treatment came about from the use of high levels of confrontation in therapeutic communities such as Synanon. Confrontation is seen as the therapeutic technique to break through the alcoholic/addict's denial. However, a hostile, confrontational counseling style has been found to be associated with poor long-term results (Miller, 2003).

The controversy regarding confrontation probably results from the association of this technique with hostility and aggression. In fact, some AOD counselors may use confrontation in this manner because that is what they have seen and heard. However, confrontation is simply a matter of pointing out to a client that a discrepancy exists between what he or she says and he or she means, or between what is said and what is done (Ivey, Bradford-Ivey, & Simek-Morgan, 1996). In this context, confrontation is a valuable technique in AOD treatment just as it is in other counseling situations. The inappropriate use of confrontation by counselors is a result of poor training and/or poor judgment. For the best results, a counselor will determine the proper type of confrontation for a particular client and will not assume that all alcoholics/addicts must be confronted in a hostile and aggressive manner.

The Use of Medication

In the section of this chapter on treatment approaches, we have discussed the use of medications in the management of detoxification and the treatment of AOD addiction. Minor tranquilizers are used to prevent the medically dangerous withdrawal symptoms suffered in the detoxification from CNS depressants. Drugs such as naltrexone and methadone are used to treat alcoholism and opioid addiction, and various nondependence-producing psychoactive drugs are used to treat disorders such as depression and bipolar disorder. The controversy in this area is probably related to a misinterpretation of AA's and NA's position on the use of any mind-altering substances by alcoholics/addicts. It is certainly the case that AA and NA literature cautions about the use of any AOD, even if a particular substance was not the individual's drug of choice. From a disease model perspective, if you are predisposed to addiction, you will develop a problem with any potentially addictive substance. However, Twelve Step groups are made up of people and some may impose a personal belief that is not part of AA/NA positions. We have heard members discourage other members from taking prescribed medications that are not addictive (e.g., antidepressants) or from taking medically necessary drugs that can be addictive (e.g., pain medication following surgery). There is no Twelve Step literature that encourages this kind of advice.

We do believe that recovering individuals should alert their physician to their recovery status as a preventative measure to avoid prescription drug abuse.

Controlled Use

The question of whether alcoholics can learn to use alcohol in a moderate or nonproblematic manner has been a controversial issue in treatment for some time. In the early 1970s, the Sobells (Sobell & Sobell, 1973) were able to demonstrate that chronic alcoholics could successfully be taught controlled drinking in an experimental setting. Also, reports of the Rand study (Armor, Polich, & Stambul, 1978; Polich, Armor, & Braiker, 1981) indicated that many previously treated alcoholics had been drinking in a nonproblematic manner over a four-year period. The Sobell and Sobell study has been criticized because few of the alcoholic subjects maintained controlled drinking over an extended period. The Rand study has been criticized for using too short a time period, taking inadequate care in follow-up, subjective reporting, small number, sampling fallacies, lack of control group, and using artificial settings (Royce, 1989). However, Sobell, Cunningham, and Sobell (1996) reported that large numbers of persons with previous mild to moderate alcohol problems were able to drink in moderation without ongoing problems related to alcohol. Similarly, Hester (2003) provided evidence that behavioral self-control training (a behavioral treatment approach) is effective in maintaining moderate drinking with clients with a shorter duration of problem drinking.

Although the debate about controlled use makes for some fascinating reading in the field, largely because it evokes emotional as well as scholarly arguments and because it pits disease concept proponents against others, the practical issues seem more clear-cut. It makes very little sense to teach a person to use alcohol in a controlled manner when the person has had numerous, serious life problems and has consistently demonstrated an inability to control alcohol use. If an individual can be diagnosed as having a substance use disorder based on the *DSM, Fifth Edition* (see Chapter 6), controlled use is not a reasonable goal. Even proponents of controlled use recognize that this is not a productive goal for everyone (e.g., Hester, 2003). Therefore, treatment programs, particularly if they use a disease model, would oppose controlled use because their clients would usually be classified as alcoholics/addicts.

Who would be a candidate for learning to use in a controlled manner? These types of clients would more often be seen by generalist mental health professionals or AOD counselors in private practice or working in mental health clinics. Generally, the best candidates would be young, healthy drinkers, with few life problems related to alcohol, whose problems with alcohol are of recent duration and who resist abstaining. These drinkers would usually be considered at-risk drinkers and may benefit from brief interventions (see Chapter 7).

If a client can be diagnosed with an alcohol use disorder (see Chapter 6), the decision as to whether or not controlled drinking is a wise option is very difficult. Therefore, we would advise any AOD counselor or mental health professional to be very cautious in working with a client on controlled use. An abstinent client has no risk of problems from use; a client who uses at any level is at risk. However, some clients will resist treatment or drop out of treatment if abstinence is demanded. If such a client fits the criteria previously described, controlled use might be a treatment goal. Also, there are times when working with a resistant client on controlled use demonstrates to the client that he or she is unable to use in a nonproblematic manner. We worked with a young woman in individual counseling who had experienced a few minor problems as a result of her alcohol, marijuana, and cocaine use and would not agree to abstain. We asked her to set goals regarding her intake for two weeks and then to keep track of her actual use. It became very clear to her that her use was out of control since she almost always exceeded her goal. This resulted in her referral to an outpatient program and successful abstinence for at least one year (the last time we saw her).

Again, we suggest that controlled use be a treatment goal only when other alternatives have been explored and when it is probable that the client will experience more serious problems from an insistence on abstinence.

Natural Recovery

The fact that some persons discontinue their problematic use of AOD without treatment has been documented by researchers (e.g., Sobell, Sobell, & Toneatto, 1991; Tuchfield, 1981) and is certainly something we have seen in our own experience. The question that is raised is whether the person who becomes abstinent without treatment is recovering or is a *dry drunk*. A dry drunk is defined as a person who demonstrates the negative thoughts, feelings, and actions of an active alcoholic but is not drinking.

There has been a sense from the treatment community and Twelve Step adherents that persons who try to quit drinking or using on their own end up in the dry drunk syndrome. This sense probably arises from the same dynamics that cause treatment providers to view all alcoholics/addicts as having a disease. In other words, if you are a treatment provider or an AA member, when would you see someone who is trying to abstain on his or her own? You would see this person when he or she was having problems (such as the dry drunk symptoms) and was referred, by self or by others, to a treatment program or to an AA meeting. It would be logical to conclude that discontinuing use without treatment or Twelve Step support is difficult, if not impossible. However, those who discontinue problematic use without experiencing the dry drunk syndrome do not show up in treatment or at meetings. Sobell et al. (1991) suggested that natural recovery is much more frequent than has been suspected. In fact, Cunningham, Sobell, Sobell, and Kapur (1995) and Sobell et al. (1996) have identified significant numbers of people with previous alcohol problems who reported recovering without formal treatment or support groups. These researchers believe that an in-depth investigation of these "natural recovering" individuals may help identify important interventions for treatment providers.

Some research of this type has been conducted. Researchers Granfield and Cloud (2001) interviewed 46 formerly substance-dependent men and women who recovered without treatment. They discovered that the subjects in this research had what they termed *recovery capital.* This was defined as *social capital,* or the presence of a social network or social support of family, friends, or colleagues who were available to provide help and motivation. *Physical capital* included tangible resources that provided flexibility and options for courses of recovery that did not involve formal treatment. Finally, recovery capital included *human capital,* such as knowledge, skills, and personal attributes. The researchers noted that most of their subjects had college degrees or vocational skills and that recovery capital may not be equitably available to everyone.

MyCounselingLab for Addictions/Substance Abuse

Try the Topic 5 Assignments: *Treatment Setting and Treatment Planning.*

Summary

- Recovery-oriented systems of care encompass continuity of care; the inclusion of the family, community, and peers in the process; individualized and comprehensive services across the life span; culturally responsive services; community-anchored services; inclusion of voices and experiences of recovering individuals and their families; and outcomes-driven, research-based services.
- Only about 12% of those with substance use disorders receive formal treatment.
- Approaches to treatment include the Minnesota Model, behavioral models (aversive conditioning, CM), matrix model, and pharmacological procedures.
- Treatment strategies and techniques include individual, group, and family counseling;

- support groups; lifestyle changes; education; and aftercare.
- Treatment occurs in therapeutic communities, inpatient and residential settings, partial hospitalization and day treatment settings, and intensive outpatient and outpatient settings.
- The National Institute on Drug Abuse has established 13 principles of effective treatment.
- Evidence-based practices can be found in the National Registry of Evidence-based Programs and Practices.
- A variety of studies on treatment effectiveness have found all forms of treatment to be effective in reducing alcohol and other drug use, criminal justice involvement, and health care utilization and in improving employment.

Internet Resources

Treatment facility locator
Findtreatment.samhsa.gov

Treatment statistics
drugabuse.gov/infofacts/treatmenttrends.html

Evidence-based treatment
nrepp.samhsa.gov/

Principles of Effective Treatment
https://www.drugabuse.gov/publications/principles-drug-addiction-treatment-research-based-guide-third-edition/

Further Discussion

1. For each of the case examples in the beginning of the chapter, discuss the most appropriate treatment setting, treatment approach, and treatment strategies.

2. How could treatment for AOD problems be improved? Design your ideal treatment program.

3. Why do you think the Principles of Effective Treatment are not used in every treatment program and setting across the country?

CHAPTER 9

Co-occurring Disorders and Other Special Populations

CASE EXAMPLES

1. Celest is a 33-year-old white woman. Her drug of choice is methamphetamine, and she is on probation for possession and court-ordered to treatment. After completing an inpatient, 28-day program, she attends counseling on a weekly basis. Celest regularly attends Narcotics Anonymous (NA) meetings and seems sincerely interested in living a drug-free life. She lives in a small house with 14 people, including her daughter and an abusive, drug-using boyfriend. Celest tells her boyfriend that she wants to leave the relationship and the house. He threatens to kill both her and her daughter. Celest has lost her license to work in her trained profession (slot machine mechanic) because of her felony conviction. She is unemployed, with no child care, and is diabetic. When she does not manage her diet and insulin, she experiences severe mood swings.

2. Juan is a 17-year-old Hispanic male. His mother brings him to a treatment program for an assessment. Juan has been smoking marijuana, drinking beer, and taking prescription pain pills on a regular basis for some time. He dropped out of school in his junior year, and his mother suspects that he is selling marijuana. Juan is reading at the third-grade level, and his primary language is Spanish.

3. Devon is a 47-year-old African American male. Over the past 25 years, Devon has spent 10 years in prison for a variety of offenses including drug possession and distribution, burglary, grand larceny, and assault. He has been a heroin user for many years and is HIV-positive. Devon has just been paroled and is ordered to get some kind of drug counseling.

4. Richard is a 67-year-old retired, white, gay male whose longtime partner recently passed away. Richard's family has convinced him to talk to a counselor about his grief and his increasing alcohol use. Although he has always been a heavy drinker, recently his alcohol use has resulted in increasing confusion, accidents, and medical issues.

In the sixth edition of this text, we have decided to devote an entire chapter to the issues involved in providing assistance to those who have a substance use disorder (SUD) and a co-occurring mental disorder (COMD), as well as those with SUD who have special population needs. Although there has been evidence since the 1970s that individuals with SUDs were more likely to have a COMD, it has been in the past ten years that the federal government has made a concerted effort to address the treatment needs of this population (Substance Abuse and Mental Health Services Administration, 2016a). The Substance Abuse and Mental Health Services Administration (part of the Department of Health and Human Services) has developed publications and Internet resources in the area of COMD on topics such as screening and assessment, building a workforce to treat this population, training for providers, financing treatment for COMD, and integrating SUD and COMD treatment. In each earlier edition, there was a section in Chapter 8 on COMD and other special populations. With the increasing involvement of a variety of mental health professionals in the treatment of COMD, we felt the topic required a separate chapter.

In 1994, the Center for Substance Abuse Treatment produced a series of publications on different issues in the field, one of which was Treatment Improvement Protocol #9, "Assessment and Treatment of Patients with Coexisting Mental Illness and Alcohol and Other Drug Abuse" (Center for Substance Abuse Treatment, 1994). Included in this document are discussions about diagnostic criteria, assessment, psychopharmacology, specific mental disorders, and the need for linkage between the mental health and substance abuse treatment systems. With the expansion of research in this area, Treatment Improvement Protocol #42 was published in 2005 with the title, "Substance Abuse Treatment for Persons with Co-Occurring Disorders" (Center for Substance Abuse Treatment, 2005).

DEFINITIONS

As with other topics in the alcohol and other drugs (AOD) field, there has been an evolution in the precision of terminology in this area. Originally, the term *dual diagnosis* was used. However, that term was also applied to other situations (e.g., mental disorder and intellectual disability), so confusion often occurred. Additionally, "dual diagnosis" implied that there are only two disorders although it is very possible to have a substance use disorder and more than one other mental disorder. Therefore, the current term is *co-occurring disorders*. The term indicates the presence of a substance use disorder and at least one other mental disorder and that these disorders can be diagnosed independent of each other. The mental disorder(s) other than the substance use disorder are in Section II of the *Diagnostic and Statistical Manual of Mental Disorders, Fifth Edition* (*DSM-V*) (see Chapter 6). Many discussions of co-occurring disorders do not include neurodevelopmental disorders such as intellectual disability, autism spectrum disorders, learning disorders, and attention-deficit/hyperactivity disorder. In reviewing literature in the area of co-occurring disorders, it is important to understand how a researcher is defining mental disorders. Obviously, a person can have a substance use disorder and a neurodevelopmental disorder.

PREVALENCE

According to the 2014 National Survey on Drug Use and Health (Center for Behavioral Health Statistics and Quality, 2015), 39% of people with an SUD in the past year had a co-occurring mental disorder. In contrast, 16% of those who did not have an SUD in the past year had a mental disorder. Furthermore, 18% of Americans with any mental illness also had an SUD, while only 6% of adults without any mental disorder had an SUD.

This survey also looked at those with a serious mental illness (SMI), defined as any mental, behavioral, or emotional disorder that substantially interferes with or limits one or more major life activities. A little more than 4% of adults had an SMI in the past year. In contrast, 11% of adults with an SUD also had an SMI. More than 23% of adults with SMI had a co-occurring SUD.

The data presented here represents the prevalence of COMDs among all adults. We can also look at those individuals with an SUD who sought treatment, a much more select group. According to a report of a survey of treatment admissions in 2012, nearly one-third of the patients had a diagnosed co-occurring mental disorder (Substance Abuse and Mental Health Services Administration, 2014b). Furthermore, treatment facility operators estimated that 45% of the patients in these facilities had a COMD (Substance Abuse and Mental Health Services Administration, 2014c).

TYPES OF COMD

Although there are many different types of mental disorders in the *DSM-V*, certain ones occur most frequently among individuals with SUDs. We want to mention some of the most common COMDs. Prior to this discussion, there are some diagnostic issues that must be mentioned.

It can be quite challenging to determine which symptoms are results of an SUD and which are associated with a COMD. For example, Zeke needs medical detoxification for his alcohol use disorder. He reports problems sleeping, poor appetite, agitation, and depression. Are these symptoms of detoxification or a COMD? Well, after detoxification, some of Zeke's symptoms improve but he still reports frequent sadness, melancholy, and lack of energy. Because of his alcohol use, Zeke has lost his family, his job, and most of his friends. He also has some legal problems. So, are Zeke's symptoms of depression understandable but temporary because of the problems he has, or is his depression chronic?

Monica was sexually abused as a child. Because of her feelings of guilt, shame, rejection, lack of trust, and betrayal, she begins to use AOD to mask her feelings. She is arrested for possession and mandated to treatment. Once in treatment, she gets sober and starts to feel better. Is there any reason to worry about a COMD such as posttraumatic stress disorder (PTSD)? As long as she says she is feeling good, should this be explored?

As these situations illustrate, it can be difficult to diagnose a mental disorder when patients are in the detoxification stage or in early recovery. A thorough psychosocial history can help clarify if symptoms of a mental disorder were present before the patient began using AOD. However, there may not be a reliable method to get this history, or the story may be unclear. For example, behavioral issues frequently arise in close proximity to the initiation of AOD use. Therefore, determining if AOD use preceded symptoms of a mental disorder or followed these symptoms is often impossible. Furthermore, there are overlapping symptoms of SUDs and some mental disorders. For example, the criteria for diagnosing antisocial personality disorder include breaking the law, lying, impulsivity, aggressiveness, and irresponsibility. As you have learned, many people with SUDs exhibit these characteristics, but they are the result of AOD use. So, how would a mental health professional determine if a client who had a history of breaking the law, lying, impulsivity, aggressiveness, and irresponsibility just had an SUD or had SUD and antisocial personality disorder? The clinician would have to determine if these symptoms were being exhibited before the age of 15 (part of the diagnosis of antisocial personality disorder) and would have to wait and see how the client behaves once he or she is sober. A sober person with antisocial personality disorder continues to display these undesirable symptoms, while the sober person who does not have antisocial personality disorder behaves more appropriately. Although acknowledging the issues that make it difficult to accurately diagnose SUDs and COMDs, the following mental disorders frequently are diagnosed with SUDs:

Antisocial Personality Disorder.   Although we illustrated the difficulty in differentiating antisocial personality disorder and SUDs, it is true that this disorder often coexists with SUDs. If you are unfamiliar with antisocial personality disorder, it can be thought of as a condition that develops early in life and, to laymen, these are "bad guys" in our society; con men, criminals, those without a conscience. The terms "sociopath" or "psychopath" are frequently used as synonyms. It is quite common that those with antisocial personality disorder are heavy AOD users. Therefore, many people with antisocial personality disorder have co-occurring SUDs. However, as we noted earlier, people with SUDs frequently do "bad" things. Therefore, it is essential to differentiate a person with an SUD who has done many regretful acts but behaves appropriately once he or she has solid recovery from the antisocial personality disorder client who is still causing problems but is sober. This topic is discussed in more detail in Fisher (2011).

Schizophrenia Spectrum and Other Psychotic Disorders.   Although these disorders are rare, those who suffer from them and SUDs are usually found in emergency rooms, homeless situations, and jails and prisons. They exhibit delusions and/or hallucinations. When you see a homeless person talking to himself, yelling at things that aren't there, or talking nonsense, you probably are seeing someone with these disorders. Although medication can control these symptoms, people with psychotic disorders who are not closely monitored may stop taking medication because of unpleasant side effects and use AOD to manage their symptoms. It is also important to understand that paranoid behavior can be the result of chronic use of stimulants such as cocaine and methamphetamine. Therefore, if a client is demonstrating paranoid delusions and is a chronic user of these drugs, the clinician must wait until the client is detoxified to determine if there is this type of COMD.

Depressive Disorders.   It is pretty clear why these disorders co-occur with SUDs. Managing depressive symptoms with AOD is very common. For example, if you are feeling blue, a few drinks may make you feel better, at least temporarily. Additionally, people with SUDs have usually done things and suffered consequences that make them depressed. In many cases, these folks have diagnosable depressive disorders. Antidepressant medication is often prescribed (in situations where there are medical services) even before a client with an SUD is in stable recovery. The thinking is that most people with SUDs are going to have depressive symptoms and antidepressant medication can regulate mood and reduce the probability of relapse due to negative emotions. It should be noted that depression is common in stimulant addicts who are recovering, and these feelings can persist for some time as the body gets back to normal neurotransmitter balance.

Anxiety Disorders.   The discussion about anxiety disorders is similar to that of depressive disorders. Self-medication with AOD is common. We recently worked with a young woman who suffered from panic attacks. She found that marijuana would manage her panic attacks and she continued to use marijuana in spite of legal sanctions. This resulted in incarceration. Fortunately, her involvement with the legal system allowed us to get her the proper psychiatric care. However, you can see how this COMD resulted in serious consequences. Again, experiencing anxiety is very common in the detoxification and early recovery stages.

PTSD.   This specific disorder is classified as one of the Trauma and Stressor-Related Disorders in the *DSM-V*. It is common in military veterans and victims of physical, emotional, or sexual abuse. As with the other mental disorders, those suffering with PTSD self-medicate with AOD to relieve their severe symptoms and an SUD develops. With PTSD, it is very important to closely monitor clients once they have achieved early recovery. Many of these clients have always used AOD to cope with the negative emotions of PTSD. Once they are sober and the negative emotions arise (after all, the PTSD is still there), they may not have the skills and resources to manage these emotions. They are at high risk for relapse during this time. We mentioned Monica earlier in the chapter. With her history of abuse, she is at high risk for PTSD. However, she may not have any symptoms after months of sobriety. Given the probability of PTSD, she should have been prepared for this by making it a focus of treatment.

Although the mental disorders mentioned are the most frequently seen, other mental disorders such as bipolar disorders, Obsessive-Compulsive Disorder, and sexual dysfunctions and others do occur with SUDs.

TREATMENT

According to the most recent report of substance abuse treatment facilities, 43% have programs for clients with COMD (Substance Abuse and Mental Health Services Administration, 2014c). Although that is positive, it is not significantly higher than the 38% that had these programs in 2002 (Center for Substance Abuse Treatment, 2005). Since 2002, the federal government has implemented programs designed to increase the treatment capacity for COMD. There was a co-occurring disorders state incentive grant program that provided funds for infrastructure development and capacity expansion. In 2003, a co-occurring center of excellence was established to disseminate and support the adoption of evidence-based practices in this field. That center no longer exists. Although it is certainly possible that COMD treatment has improved, clearly capacity expansion has increased very slowly. Why?

In many states, the mental health treatment structure and the substance abuse treatment structure have not been integrated. Even when there has been an effort to administer these agencies jointly, there are bureaucratic turf battles and funding issues that have been barriers to integrated treatment. For example, the federal government has separate block grants (funding provided to all states) for mental health and substance abuse treatment. Because this involves money, there are always battles over who gets these funds. A facility that provides substance abuse treatment may feel entitled to mental health funding if they see patients with COMD. A mental health treatment facility may feel entitled to substance abuse treatment funding if they see clients with SUDs. However, because funds are usually tight, no one wants to "share." When states have attempted to integrate their mental health and substance abuse treatment systems, there is usually blowback from existing providers and their allies.

An additional problem with capacity expansion for COMD involves workforce issues. If a substance abuse treatment agency wants to offer COMD services, it must have licensed mental health professionals who are qualified to treat this population. In most states, substance abuse treatment providers are not required to have a master's degree nor are they qualified to treat mental disorders other than substance use disorders. Therefore, they must hire more expensive master's-level licensed mental health counselors, clinical social workers, or marriage and family therapists. In rural areas, it may be very difficult to recruit these types of mental health professionals. Furthermore, an agency must have a psychiatric consultant to prescribe and monitor medications. Again, it can be very challenging to find psychiatrists in many places. So, even if a substance abuse treatment agency wants to offer COMD services, the expense and difficulty recruiting qualified providers may be a barrier.

Although these barriers and challenges have slowed the process of capacity enhancement and expansion for patients with COMD, there is still a need to treat these patients. In 2010, the Center for Substance Abuse Treatment published *Integrated Treatment for Co-occurring Disorders Evidence-Based Practices (EBP) Toolkit*. Integrated treatment services

> . . . are organized in an integrated fashion. For example, assessments screen for both mental illness and substance use. Practitioners in the Integrated Treatment program (called integrated treatment specialists) develop integrated treatment plans and treat both serious mental illnesses and substance use disorders so that consumers do not get lost, excluded, or confused going back and forth between different mental health and substance abuse programs. Consumers receive one consistent integrated message about substance use and mental health treatment. Second, clinical treatment is integrated. Integrated treatment specialists have knowledge of both substance use disorders and serious mental illnesses and understand the complexity of interactions between disorders. They are trained in skills that have been found to be effective in treating consumers with co-occurring disorders. (Center for Substance Abuse Treatment, 2010, p. 9)

There are seven practice principles in the toolkit: (1) Mental health and substance abuse treatment are integrated to meet the needs of people with co-occurring disorders; (2) Integrated treatment specialists are trained to treat both substance use disorders and serious mental illness; (3) Co-occurring disorders are treated in a stage-wise fashion with different services provided at different stages; (4) Motivational interventions are used to treat patients in all stages, but especially in the persuasion stage; (5) Substance abuse counseling, using a cognitive-behavioral approach, is used to treat consumers in the active treatment and relapse prevention stages; (6) Multiple formats for services are available including individual, group, peer support, and family; and (7) Medication services are integrated and coordinated with other services.

Hopefully, you recall the discussions about motivational interviewing and cognitive-behavioral approaches from earlier chapters. We do want to elaborate on principle 3 because it may not be clear. The "stages" in this principle are stages of treatment (engagement, persuasion, active treatment, relapse prevention). Before the focus on co-occurring disorders, the common thinking was that, in treating COMD patients, the substance abuse treatment part of treatment had to be completed before any attention could be paid to other issues. Obviously, that didn't work very well because these patients would frequently relapse due to the untreated co-occurring disorder. However, this principle refers to the services that would be appropriate based on the stage of change (see Chapter 7) of the patient. It does not mean that the treatment of co-occurring disorders is stage of change related.

AT A GLANCE

- COMD usually refers to a *DSM-V* mental disorder that exists along with an SUD
- Between one-third to 45% of clients with an SUD have a COMD
- The most common COMDs include antisocial personality disorder, schizophrenia and other psychotic disorders, depressive disorders, anxiety disorders, and PTSD
- Integrated treatment is recommended for SUDs and COMDs

OTHER SPECIAL POPULATIONS

As with any aspect of the helping professions, the individual and group differences of clients must be considered in designing treatment. We have previously focused on the need to tailor treatment to the unique characteristics of the client rather than forcing a client to fit a particular model of treatment or addiction. Similarly, group characteristics are important to consider in treatment. This is not to imply that clients should be stereotyped simply because they are members of a particular age, gender, or ethnic group. However, demographic information may be relevant in understanding the client and in designing appropriate treatment. A comprehensive discussion of the treatment issues for all special populations would be beyond our goals for this book. However, we do want to acquaint you with some of these issues so you will be informed when directing your clients to treatment.

Ethnically Diverse Populations

The issues with regard to ethnically diverse populations were discussed in detail in Chapter 4, with regard not only to treatment but to other AOD issues as well.

At this point, we want to restate several points specifically with regard to treatment. First, diversity in the treatment population and the staff is clearly beneficial for client comfort and understanding. Second, the attitude of an ethnic group toward AOD problems may present a barrier for the individual seeking treatment. For example, in some African American communities, alcoholism is seen as immoral or sinful behavior, a view that is clearly incompatible with the disease concept of alcoholism. In this view, the person, not alcohol, is responsible for problems, and the use of alcohol could be controlled if the person so desired. This barrier is certainly not unique to African Americans. Any families who hold this view would be less likely to encourage and support family members and friends to seek treatment. This barrier to disease-model programs requires education for the family. Third, the customs, beliefs, and language of the group must be considered in treatment. An obvious example is the barrier presented in treatment for Spanish-speaking clients when the treatment staff are not bilingual. With regard to Native Americans, Coyhis and White (2002) stated:

> The most viable frameworks of addiction recovery for Native Americans tap the deepest roots of tribal cultures. The job of the conscientious addiction counselor is to become a student of these cultures—their histories, their organization, their values, their ceremonies and folkways, and their systems of healing. The addiction counselor can help forge a bridge between the treatment agency and tribal cultures by encouraging the involvement of family elders, tribal elders and traditional medicine people (herbalists, shamanic healers, spiritual advisors) in the design and delivery of treatment services for Native clients. The goal here is to create a menu of words, ideas, rituals and experiences within the counseling milieu that can be selectively used by Native people who bring enormous diversity in terms of their personal histories, personalities, religious and spiritual beliefs, and degree of acculturation. . . . Such an approach recognizes the multiple sources and patterns of Native alcohol problems as well as the multiple pathways and styles of long-term recovery among Native peoples. (p. 3)

Elderly

According to Patterson and Jeste (1999), "baby boomers" (who are now among the elderly) have an increasing risk of substance use disorders because of their relaxed attitudes toward substance use when they were younger. However, diagnosis in this group may be challenging because the *DSM-V* (see Chapter 6) criteria for substance use disorders may not apply to the elderly, or their difficulties can be caused by other problems. Furthermore, health care providers and family members may hesitate to ask about substance use issues because of embarrassment or a belief that symptoms such as falls or cognitive difficulties are due to age-related issues (Drew, Wilkins, & Trevisan, 2010).

With regard to alcohol abuse, the National Institute on Alcohol Abuse and Alcoholism's guidelines recommend that those older than 65 limit their use to no more than three standards drinks in any one day and no more than seven per week (National Institute on Alcohol Abuse and Alcoholism, 2007). Although this is the same for women below the age of 65, it is significantly different than the quantity for men. Therefore, an elderly man may develop problems with alcohol from using the same quantity he was able to drink when he was younger. This is due to the fact that the elderly have slower metabolism and a smaller volume of distribution (Drew et al., 2010).

The problems of the elderly are often different from those of younger clients and may require specific attention in treatment. For example, the elderly client may be experiencing an emotional reaction to retirement, feelings of bereavement from the death of a spouse and/or friends, loneliness, and physical pain from illnesses or age. Drew et al. (2010) cite some evidence that age-specific programs for older alcoholics significantly improve abstinence rates posttreatment. However, as was noted in Chapter 8, only 12% of treatment facilities had specialty programs for the elderly.

The case example of Richard illustrates some of the problems an elderly man can have with alcohol. Although his alcohol intake had not increased, he experienced more consequences from his use. In addition, Richard had the added problems of grief from losing his longtime partner and social isolation.

Adolescents

As was noted in Chapter 8, 30% of treatment facilities have specialized programs for adolescents. Twelve- to 17-year-olds accounted for nearly 7% of treatment admissions in 2012 (Substance Abuse and Mental Health Services Administration, 2014b). Marijuana was the primary drug for this age in group in nearly 76% of the cases, alcohol in 13.5%, and opioids in 3.1% (Substance Abuse and Mental Health Services Administration, 2014b).

We met Juan (one of the case examples at the beginning of the chapter) some time ago. Juan was in an inpatient treatment program, and the senior author conducted a psychological evaluation of him. During the evaluation, Juan reported that he (and others, so he claimed) had learned that if they publicly (defined as being in a group) said that they had a disease and were powerless, they would be released from the program. Juan was quite rebellious (one reason the evaluation had been requested), and he refused to say that he had a disease. In fact, he told everyone that he had every intention to use again when he got out.

Juan's statements are indicative of some of the treatment issues for adolescents. Adolescents have difficulty relating to a concept of a life-long disease. They have rarely experienced the same level of life problems resulting from their AOD use as adults have. When they attend Alcoholics Anonymous (AA) or Narcotics Anonymous meetings, they may hear stories from older adults who have little relationship to the adolescents' lives. If you have worked with adolescents at all, you probably know that they can be skilled at saying what they need to say to get what they want. After working with adolescents with AOD problems for some time, we have little doubt that what Juan said was true. Many of the adolescents told the staff what they wanted to hear. Finally, adolescents may reject the idea that lifestyle change is necessary. Adults who have lost jobs, families, and possessions and have been arrested for driving under the influence (DUI) may have little difficulty accepting the need to change their lives. An adolescent who has been busted at school for smoking pot may not feel the same way. Even when the problems have been more significant, it is very difficult to convince an adolescent that he or she needs to change his or her social group.

In a meta-analysis of treatment outcome studies for adolescents, Waldron and Turner (2008) identified functional family therapy, multidimensional family therapy, and group cognitive-behavioral therapy as efficacious treatments for adolescents.

Persons with Disabilities

Individuals with sensory (hearing or visually impaired), motor, mental, and learning handicaps can and do have AOD problems. For example, Karacostas and Fisher (1993) found evidence that adolescents diagnosed as learning disabled had a higher rate of chemical dependency than did non–learning-disabled peers. Juan, the adolescent case we mentioned earlier, had a reading disability (in addition to his language barriers). Many treatment programs require a great deal of reading and writing "homework," and for clients with learning disabilities, this can represent a barrier. Furthermore, clients identified as defensive, resistant, and rebellious may have unidentified learning or intellectual disabilities. Acting out behavior may be a reaction to these disabilities.

The nature of the disability and the age at which the disability occurred may be factors in the development of a substance use disorder and are certainly factors in treatment. For example, a young person who becomes physically disabled as a result of an accident may have problems handling the grief resulting from the loss of mobility and increased dependence on others. Using substances can be a way of coping with these issues but would be an important focus of treatment if a substance use disorder develops.

Irrespective of the model of addiction, persons with disabilities have treatment needs that require attention. We have already mentioned the grief that a person may experience, particularly if the disability was acquired later in life. Problems communicating are intrinsic to sensory handicaps, so in a program with a heavy educational component, the methods of imparting information must be adapted for the sensory-impaired client. For individuals with learning disabilities, instructional strategies must be modified to accommodate the type of learning disability (Karacostas & Fisher, 1993). Individuals with intellectual handicaps may not be able to grasp abstract concepts and therefore may be unable to understand the disease concept. More behavioral interventions may be necessary.

Designing the treatment of persons with disabilities is clearly consistent with the notion of individualizing treatment based on client needs. Rather than forcing the person to fit a treatment program (which might be impossible with persons with disabilities), the treatment program must meet the client's needs. However, the complexity of treatment for persons with disabilities also indicates the need for greater prevention efforts for this population. Although there are many prevention programs for young people who are not disabled (see Chapter 16), few efforts have been made to design programs for young people with disabilities.

Women

Although it seems ironic to talk about half of the population as a special group, most of the older research and concepts about treatment came from studies with predominantly male subjects. Although about half as many women as men have a substance use disorder (Substance Abuse and Mental Health Services Administration, 2015a), women represented more than 50% of treatment admissions (Substance Abuse and Mental Health Services Administration, 2014b). Greenfield et al. (2007) conducted a review of literature on treatment entry, retention, and outcomes for women. Among the barriers to treatment the researchers identified were pregnancy, lack of services for pregnant women, fear of losing custody of the unborn child, fear of prosecution for drug use while pregnant, and lack of child care outside of treatment or as part of the treatment services. As noted in Chapter 8, only 17% of treatment agencies had specialized services for pregnant or postpartum women, but 44% had special programming for women. Additional barriers for women included lack of employment or other means to pay for treatment, high rates of co-occurring disorders and the associated lack of appropriate treatment, greater social stigma and discrimination than faced by men, and histories of physical and/or sexual abuse making mixed-gender treatment programs undesirable. With regard to this latter barrier, Najavits, Weiss, and Shaw (1997) reported that between 30% and 59% of women in treatment for substance use disorders suffered from posttraumatic stress disorder, mostly as a result of physical and/or sexual abuse.

Greenfield et al. (2007) found that gender was not a significant predictor of treatment retention, completion, or outcome. Although these researchers did not find that women-only treatment was more effective than mixed-gender treatment, treatment that addressed problems more common to women or that was designed for specific subgroups of women did show greater effectiveness.

The case example of Celest contains many of the elements that make treatment and recovery for women challenging. She was economically dependent on an abusive male partner, had a child to consider, and a chronic health condition. Hopefully, you can see how the concept of "recovery-oriented systems of care" (see Chapter 8) makes sense for clients like Celest. Regardless of how successful her episode of acute treatment was, she needed continued support, counseling, and services following treatment.

Lesbian, Gay, Bisexual, and Transgender Individuals

Some research cites evidence to support the fact that lesbian, gay, bisexual, and transgender (LGBT) persons have a greater rate of substance use disorders than strictly heterosexual individuals (e.g., Cochran, Ackerman, Mays, & Ross, 2004; Hughes et al., 2006; Trocki, Drabble, & Midanik, 2009). Senreich (2010) found gay and bisexual men had better outcomes in specialized programs for lesbian, gay, bisexual, and transgender clients, and Rowan and Faul (2011) examined the predictor variables of treatment success within a specialized program for LGBT clients. However, as in Chapter 8, only 12% of treatment facilities have specialized programs for this population.

According to Senreich (2010), lesbian, gay, and bisexual (LGB) clients in nonspecialized treatment often receive heterosexist comments and reactions from other clients. In addition, treatment providers may not have training in the specific issues important to LGB clients. The result for gay and bisexual men (but not women) is that they are less likely to complete treatment and to report that the reason they left treatment early was that their needs were not met (Senreich, 2009).

Additionally, Senreich (2010) pointed out that because LGB clients do not feel safe in the nonspecialized treatment environment, they do not explore two significant issues for this population. The first issue involves the relationship between the use of AOD and being LGB. For gay/bisexual men in particular, the association between sexual behavior and AOD use is important to explore. Because of the central role of AOD in many social environments for the LGB population, social isolation is a great concern in initial recovery. As a result, gay and lesbian AA meetings have developed.

The second issue involves internalized heterosexism and the stress of society's attitudes and actions regarding the LGBT community. As Senreich has indicated, an honest discussion of sexual orientation is essential to resolve these problems and would be hindered by a treatment environment perceived as nonsupportive to LGBT clients. This is another argument for specialized programs for LGBT clients.

Criminal Justice Populations

The interest in treatment issues for individuals involved with the criminal justice system is the result of the large numbers of such people with AOD problems. In Chapter 1, we noted that 65% of adult inmates could be diagnosed with a substance use disorder (see Chapter 6). Nearly a half million of adults in jails and prisons had a history of AOD problems, were under the influence of AOD at the time crimes were committed, committed crimes to buy AOD, were incarcerated for an AOD violation, or some combination of these factors. AOD was a factor in more than three-quarters of all violent crimes and property crimes. In 2004, nearly one-quarter of federal arrests were for drug offenses. Almost 14% of these arrests were for drug possession and nearly 29% for distribution (National Center on Addiction and Substance Abuse, 2010).

Because so many arrests for drug possession and selling are made, many states have implemented "drug courts." Although drug courts vary widely in scope and organization, all have an underlying premise that drug use is not simply a criminal justice problem but a public health problem. Criminal justice agencies collaborate with substance abuse treatment centers and other community resources to design and implement drug court programs. The success of these programs is based on the fact that the postarrest period can provide a good opportunity for interventions designed to break the drug–crime cycle. Drug courts may use a variety of models including supervised or conditional release (offender is released from pretrial custody), diversion from incarceration (offender pleads guilty but goes to treatment instead of to prison), dismissal of charges if the offender successfully completes treatment, and jail-based treatment for those in custody or who fail other forms of treatment.

Treatment options for offenders may take a variety of forms. The least intensive is education, such as in DUI schools. This type of intervention is normally for persons arrested for DUI but who do not have a substance use disorder. However, it should be noted that many areas do not conduct comprehensive evaluations on DUI offenders. DUI school may simply be mandated for first-time offenders. At the other end of the treatment spectrum are therapeutic communities in prison, a type of treatment discussed Chapter 8.

Brown (2010) reviewed the literature on the effectiveness of drug courts. There have been very few randomized effectiveness studies, and many studies have limitations due to methodological issues. The observational and quasi-experimental studies do indicate that drug court participants have fewer incidents of criminal behavior and lower rates of AOD use, at least in the short term, than offenders in traditional criminal justice adjudication.

Although legal involvement is a good motivator and allows for client control (e.g., random urine screening, threat of incarceration), comprehensive services, community links, and aftercare services for these clients are also needed. As you can imagine, the variety of life problems for criminal justice populations is immense.

The third case example at the beginning of the chapter (Devon) illustrates the issues in the treatment of criminal justice clients. Devon did not have the benefit of a drug court diversion program or a treatment program in the prison. Therefore, being ordered to get "some kind of drug counseling" was ineffective. Devon relapsed within three months and his parole was revoked. He died of AIDs while incarcerated. Unfortunately, this sad outcome happens too frequently. Besides the human costs, it is very expensive to have someone like Devon in a revolving door of crime, prison, parole, rearrest, reincarceration. As the National Center on Addiction and Substance Abuse (2010) has shown, treatment of criminal justice populations is very cost-effective.

Summary

- COMDs occur in 33% to 45% of substance use disorder cases.
- The most common COMDs are antisocial personality disorder, schizophrenia and other psychotic disorders, anxiety disorders, depressive disorders, and PTSD.
- Treatment issues for COMD include access, capacity, and a trained workforce.

- The Center for Substance Abuse Treatment has developed a COMD toolkit that stresses integrated treatment.
- Other special populations include the ethnically diverse, the elderly, adolescents, persons with disabilities, women, LGBT, and criminal justice populations.

Internet Resources

OMD toolkit
http://store.samhsa.gov/product/Integrated-Treatment-for-Co-Occurring-Disorders-Evidence-Based-Practices-EBP-KIT/SMA08-4367

Information about COMD
http://www.samhsa.gov/co-occurring

Further Discussion

1. Discuss the issues involved in diagnosing COMD in clients who have recently detoxified?
2. How can mental health professionals contribute to treating COMD?

3. How can mental health professionals contribute to treating other special populations?

CHAPTER 10

Relapse Prevention and Recovery

CASE EXAMPLES

① Anna, a 16-year-old girl, was in an intensive outpatient treatment program for polydrug problems, with her drugs of choice including tobacco, alcohol, marijuana, LSD, and methamphetamine. She was court-ordered to treatment and a psychological assessment following a variety of status offenses and crimes. On the basis of the assessment, Anna was diagnosed with Alcohol Use Disorder, Stimulant Use Disorder (see Chapter 6), and posttraumatic stress disorder (PTSD). The diagnosis of PTSD was related to a history of sexual molestation by Anna's stepfather that began when she was eight and ended when she was 13, when her biological mother discovered the molestation and divorced the perpetrator. The crime had been reported, but Anna had never been in therapy. Shortly after the molestation began, Anna began to demonstrate a series of problems in school, including deteriorating academic performance, fighting, and noncompliance with teachers. These problems continued until she entered treatment. Anna's biological father left the family when Anna was two and was an active alcoholic who had been in two treatment programs. He maintained sporadic contact with his daughter. Anna was slightly obese and had an acne problem. On an IQ test, she scored 88 (low average), and her academic skills were at the sixth- to seventh-grade level (she was a sophomore). Anna's mother was 33 years old, did not complete high school, and worked in a service position at a hotel/casino. She used alcohol and marijuana on an infrequent basis. She and Anna had a volatile relationship with a great deal of conflict. The mother noted a strong similarity between Anna and her biological father. She also expressed guilt over not discovering the sexual molestation sooner. Anna completed her treatment program in three months. She was initially resistant and defiant. However, she bonded with a female counselor in the program and, for the first time, found support and consistency from both adults and peers. She maintained abstinence for the last two months of her program. Her mother participated in the program and began to learn about the disease of addiction (which was the orientation of the program) and about her own enabling. Anna and her mother had four family counseling sessions and made a little progress. There was still a lot to do, so they were referred to a marriage and family therapist. The school counselor was invited to the discharge conference and encouraged to assist Anna in readjusting to school. She had earned just two credits in high school (meaning she had passed only two classes). Anna began attending Alcoholics Anonymous (AA) meetings and was encouraged to go to four to five meetings a week. She was scheduled to attend a weekly two-hour aftercare meeting at the treatment program.

NEED FOR GENERALIST TRAINING IN RELAPSE PREVENTION

Imagine that you are the marriage and family therapist whom Anna and her mother contact, or the school counselor at Anna's high school. We hope that you can identify some of the issues that might lead Anna to return to alcohol and other drugs (AOD) use and would require attention in family therapy or at school. The first issue is the history of sexual molestation, which we have discussed as a frequent issue for women in substance abuse treatment programs. Some of the other issues include academic problems at school, conflict with Mom, contact with an actively drinking father, and physical appearance. (We are not making a judgment here. Just remember what it was like when you were in high school for a kid who was overweight and had acne.) Other problems, although not explicitly stated, might be logically assumed to exist. For example, we would expect that Anna's social group involved kids who use AOD. If she returns to the same school, how will she handle her peer group? She may have some deep-seated emotional issues involving abandonment by her father and anger at her mother for not protecting her from her stepfather. Finally, given her intellectual ability and academic achievement, school may be challenging.

In Chapter 1, we gave examples of how social workers, school counselors, and marriage and family therapists work with clients with AOD problems whether or not these helping professionals work in treatment programs. The area of relapse prevention is a clear illustration of this. In Anna's case, the marriage and family therapist and school counselor would probably have more intensive and a longer duration of contact with Anna than the staff at the treatment program. Therefore, the therapist and counselor are critically important to Anna's success in recovery. She could also have a probation officer and contact with social service professionals (e.g., through vocational training programs). Their work could also impact Anna's abstinence.

Although a formal discharge staffing that included all relevant parties and a formal relapse prevention plan would be nice, our experience is that these are not the norm. The mental health professional usually has sketchy information from the client and/or treatment program and is left to develop his or her own relapse prevention plan. That is why we will spend considerable time in this chapter acquainting you with the specifics of relapse prevention.

DEFINITIONS OF SLIP AND RELAPSE

As we shall see, a need exists to differentiate a *slip* from a *relapse*. A slip is an episode of AOD use following a period of abstinence, whereas relapse is the return to uncontrolled AOD use following a period of abstinence. Usually, a slip or slips precede relapse, and there is some evidence (e.g., Laudet & White, 2004) that slipping is the rule rather than the exception for those clients who receive AOD treatment.

The disease model of addiction and AA slogans (an alcoholic is always "one drink from a drunk") can promote the idea that a slip inevitably leads to relapse. The depiction of addiction as a progressive, chronic disease that can be managed only through abstinence may create a sense that a slip means complete deterioration to pretreatment levels of functioning. The result of clients' adopting this point of view is that, when a slip occurs (as it is likely to), the client may experience guilt, anxiety, or hopelessness. These negative emotions may lead to further, heavier use. The cognitive process of the client may go something like this: "Well, I used again. Since that means I'm back to square one, I might as well do it up right."

Regardless of the model of addiction or orientation to treatment, AOD treatment providers will tell you that a return to some level of use is a frequent occurrence. (Soon, we will examine data on how frequent.) Although we believe that abstinence is the safest and healthiest "level" of use, we also believe that it is foolish to ignore the reality of slips, and it is poor practice to leave clients unprepared to prevent a slip from escalating to a relapse. As we discussed in Chapter 3, there is no evidence that addiction proceeds in an inevitable progression. Therefore, there is no reason to treat a slip as a catastrophe and every reason to view a slip as a signal to the client, treatment providers, and other mental health professionals to reexamine the aftercare plan (see Chapter 8) to prevent slips from occurring in the future and to prevent the current slip from escalating.

FREQUENCY OF SLIPS AND RELAPSES

Regardless of the researcher, drug or drugs of choice, and population studied, a consistent finding from studies is that many people who receive treatment for AOD problems use again after leaving treatment. McLellan, Lewis, O'Brien, and Kleber (2000), in reviewing literature on relapse, noted that 40% to 60% of patients in treatment relapsed within one year and another 15% to 30% had resumed using AOD, but not at dependent levels. Laudet and White (2004) reported that 71% of addicts returned to using AOD and 50% of this group had four or more abstinent periods of at least one month before returning to AOD use. Dennis, Foss, and Scott (2007) found the risk of relapse particularly high in the first three years following treatment.

We are not presenting these data to generate an argument (which is important from a research point of view) regarding the many factors that influence these research results. Certainly, the length of time following treatment, the type of treatment setting and methods, the method of defining *relapse,* the drug or drugs of choice, the client and the environmental characteristics, and other variables influence the data. Our point is that many, if not most, clients return to use at some point following treatment. Therefore, the issue of return to use must be a focus of treatment and aftercare.

IS RELAPSE IN ADDICTION SIMILAR TO OTHER CHRONIC CONDITIONS?

McLellan et al. (2000) wrote a historic paper, "Drug Dependence, a Chronic Medical Illness." Their extensive review of the literature, as noted earlier, revealed that about 40% of patients treated for alcohol, opioid, or cocaine dependence were continually abstinent for one year. An additional 15% returned to a nondependent level of use. In comparison, at least 30% of adult-onset, insulin-dependent diabetic patients and 40% of adult, medication-dependent hypertensive and asthmatic patients annually require restabilization of medication and/or hospitalization because of reoccurrence of symptoms. Furthermore, these researchers found the rates of compliance with prescribed medications (40% to 60%) and with behavioral change regimens (30% to 50%) to be similar between addiction disorders and other chronic illnesses such as diabetes, hypertension, and asthma. Therefore, although the relapse rate of substance disorders is certainly a focus of attention and intervention, it really is no different than the relapse and noncompliance rates for other chronic conditions.

MODELS OF RELAPSE PREVENTION

The Cenaps Model

The Cenaps Model was developed by Terence Gorski (president of the Cenaps Corporation) and articulated in a variety of articles and books (e.g., Gorski, 1988, 1989, 1990, 1992, 1993; Gorski & Miller, 1986). The disease concept is the underlying philosophy of the model, although the methods used are eclectic. The Cenaps Model integrates the principles of AA and the Minnesota Model of treatment and is proposed as a formal program within AOD treatment programs.

With the disease concept as a guiding philosophy, addiction is viewed as a biopsychosocial disease. This means that the disease affects biological, or physical, psychological, and social functioning, although there is a complex interaction among these areas. Because the disease is chronic and affects the brain (causing psychological and social problems), total abstinence is necessary. However, this is not the exclusive goal of the model. Personality, lifestyle, and family functioning are also areas that require change for biopsychosocial health. For example, Gorski acknowledges that being raised in a dysfunctional family can result in personality and other mental disorders. Because he is disease concept adherent, Gorski does not believe that personality and/or mental disorders cause addiction. However, these problems do increase the progression to addiction, and they increase the risk of relapse. Therefore, family of origin issues and mental disorders must be addressed in treatment.

A critical part of the Cenaps Model is to first differentiate clients who have completed the primary goals of treatment from those who have not completed the primary goals of treatment. In this model, the primary goals include recognizing that addiction is a biopsychosocial disease, acknowledging the need for life-long abstinence from AOD, developing a recovery program designed to maintain abstinence, and diagnosing and treating other conditions that may interfere with recovery.

If a client has not completed the primary goals, then, in Gorski's view, a relapse prevention program is inappropriate. The relapse prevention program outlined in the Cenaps Model is for clients who have completed the primary goals of treatment but who are struggling to maintain abstinence. As can be seen from the primary goals of treatment, this would limit the number of clients who would be seen as appropriate for a relapse prevention program.

The Cenaps Model conceptualizes recovery and relapse as related. Recovery follows a sequence of six steps: (1) abstaining from AOD; (2) disengaging from people, places, and things that promote AOD use and establishing a social network that supports recovery; (3) discontinuing self-defeating behaviors that suppress awareness of painful feelings and irrational thoughts; (4) learning how to manage emotions appropriately without AOD or other dysfunctional behaviors; (5) modifying cognitive patterns that create painful feelings and self-defeating behaviors; and (6) changing illogical core beliefs about self, others, and the world that promote the use of irrational thinking.

The relapse process begins at step 6 and proceeds upward. For example, let's take a look at Anna's situation and see how a relapse might occur based on Gorski's model. Remember that she was sexually molested by her stepfather. Anna starts thinking about the molestation and how unfair it is that this happened to her. She believes that she must have encouraged this behavior to get attention and affection from her stepfather and blames herself for the molestation (illogical core belief about herself, step 6). She ponders this and feels guilty, embarrassed, and victimized (painful feelings, step 5). Anna becomes sexually involved with a 22 year old who is initially kind and attentive. When she is with this man, she feels worthwhile and does not experience the feelings of guilt, embarrassment, and victimization (managing feelings in an inappropriate manner, step 4). However, the man becomes verbally abusive and openly sees other women. Anna's painful feelings return, but she tries desperately to hang on to the relationship (self-defeating behavior, step 3). The man uses AOD, as do his friends (people, places, and things that promote AOD use, step 2). In an effort to impress the man and cope with her feelings, she returns to using (step 1).

The Cenaps Model uses a variety of procedures in relapse prevention, including client self-assessment of problems that might result in relapse, education about relapse, identification of the signs of the relapse progression, strategies to manage or modify the signs, and the involvement of others, such as family members. Techniques from cognitive, affective, and behavioral therapies are used (Gorski, 1993). Therefore, although the Cenaps Model is based on the disease concept of addiction, eclectic treatment strategies are used. Furthermore, techniques have been developed for involving the family and the employee-assistance counselor, and procedures have been adapted for adolescents (Bell, 1990).

A Cognitive-Social Learning Model

In contrast to the Cenaps Model, cognitive-social learning approaches to relapse prevention do not have a prerequisite requirement that the client achieve "primary goals" of treatment. Therefore, the strategies of relapse prevention in this model could be used with any client who wants to maintain a behavior change. This change may involve abstinence from AODs or a moderation in use.

The cognitive-social learning model of relapse prevention has been presented by Alan Marlatt (e.g., Marlatt & Gordon, 1985) and Helen Annis (e.g., Annis, 1986, 1990). Marlatt (1985) views addictive behaviors as habits that can be analyzed and modified in the same way as any habit. This model of addiction was discussed in Chapter 3. With regard to relapse prevention, the focus of this model is on the determinants and consequences of addictive behaviors. Determinants include situational and environmental factors, the beliefs and expectations the individual has about AOD use, family history, and prior learning experiences when AOD are used. Consequences involve the reinforcing effects of AOD use and negative experiences that might inhibit AOD use. Social and interpersonal reactions before, during, and after AOD use are also the focus in this relapse prevention model.

Although the language is different from that used by Gorski, the steps of recovery and relapse delineated by Gorski are similar to Marlatt's determinants and consequences of addictive behaviors. Both emphasize the need to attend to behavior, thoughts, and feelings (Marlatt uses the terms "social and interpersonal reactions" for feelings, and "beliefs and expectations" for thoughts). As we will see later in the chapter, the similarities are probably the reason for the overlap in relapse prevention techniques between the two models.

Rather than focus on a model of addiction, Annis argues that the principles that guide the maintenance of a behavior change may be different from the principles that determine the initiation of a change. In other words, a person may enter treatment under coercion, be exposed to and accept the disease concept of addiction, and discontinue his or her use of AOD as a result. However, this same individual may be unable to maintain abstinence. This is the population who Gorski believed was appropriate for the Cenaps Model. However, Annis (and Marlatt) conceptualize this inability to maintain the "habit" change through self-efficacy theory. Self-efficacy refers to a judgment an individual makes regarding their ability to manage a situation. According to Annis and Davis (1989), when a recovering individual (or anyone for that matter) encounters a high-risk situation for AOD use, he or she makes a cognitive appraisal, based on past experiences, regarding the ability to handle the situation. The judgment about the individual's self-efficacy determines whether or not AOD use occurs.

For example, let's say Anna returns to school after treatment. One day after school, she sees a group of students with whom she previously used. They invite her to "party." She says no and the kids make fun of her. In this model, Anna makes a judgment about her ability to cope with the peer pressure. If she decides that she can handle the situation and does so (i.e., asserts herself appropriately and has a social support system), her self-efficacy is enhanced. If she does not believe she can handle the situation or does not have the skills, her self-efficacy is threatened. Annis (1990) reported a high correlation between a client's situation-specific self-efficacy ratings and relapse episodes. Using self-efficacy theory, Marlatt developed a model of relapse that involves the coping strategies that an individual uses in high-risk situations. A high-risk situation is defined as a situation that poses a threat to the individual's sense of control and increases the risk of potential relapse. These high-risk situations may be either unexpected or covertly planned.

Unexpected high-risk situations are similar to the situation in which Anna runs into her former using friends. She did not plan to encounter this situation; it just happened. In Marlatt's conceptualization, if Anna does not possess an appropriate coping response to the high-risk situation, she will experience decreased self-efficacy that may result in a slip. The slip may have associated thoughts and feelings such as conflict, guilt, and blame, which Marlatt termed the "abstinence violation effect (AVE)." The probability of a slip progressing to a relapse is related to the intensity of the AVE, which, in turn, is related to factors such as the length of sobriety, the commitment to abstinence, and the knowledge of the slip by significant others.

Anna does not have an effective coping mechanism to apply. To stop the teasing, she goes with the group and smokes a little pot. Unfortunately, at aftercare the next night, she has a random urinalysis. Anna's counselor calls her to discuss her positive drug test. Anna has an intense AVE. She is disappointed in herself for not resisting her friends and embarrassed that her counselor found out. Due to these painful feelings, Anna begins a relapse.

If Anna did have an effective coping response to the high-risk situation, Marlatt's model predicts that she will experience increased self-efficacy and a resulting decreased probability of slipping. Let's say that Anna asserts herself appropriately with her friends and goes to aftercare that night and reports the incident to her group. She is praised and supported by her peers and her counselor. Anna feels proud of herself and her renewed confidence in her ability to remain abstinent.

High-risk situations can also be encountered because of the covert planning of the individual. This occurs when the person has a "lifestyle imbalance." Marlatt defines this as having "shoulds" that are greater than "wants." Let's use Anna again to illustrate. She is trying to make up lost credits at school, attending four to five AA meetings a week, going to aftercare, trying to get along with her mother, going to counseling, and meeting with her probation officer. She is a busy young woman. Anna is 16 years old and has the same goals as most 16 year olds—have friends and have fun. But her "shoulds" eat up all her time. Anna starts to feel resentful and victimized. When she has felt this way before, she has used AOD because using helps her forget (at least temporarily) her painful feelings. Also, she starts thinking that she deserves a little fun and relaxation. Although she thinks about using, Anna also has pangs of guilt when she imagines herself doing so. So, instead of simply getting AOD and using, she covertly makes decisions that will place her in a high-risk situation. For example, Anna decides to go to Dorothy's house on Friday to get back some video games that she loaned Dorothy before going to treatment. Dorothy is a former using friend, and Anna knows that

AT A GLANCE

Cenaps Model of Relapse Prevention (Gorski)

- Addiction is a biopsychosocial disease.
- Model is appropriate for clients who complete "primary goals" of treatment.
- Recovery and relapse follow a sequence of six steps.

Cognitive-Social Model of Relapse Prevention (Marlatt, Anis)

- Maintaining a behavior and initiating a behavior change may be guided by different principles.
- Belief in self-efficacy determines probability of relapse.
- Ability to cope with high-risk situations is critical.
- An apparently irrelevant decisions (AID) result from lifestyle imbalances and lead to relapse.
- Abstinence violation effect (AVE) results in escalation of slips to relapse.

there are usually kids there on Friday after school getting high. Anna gets there, sees everyone loaded, and joins in. Marlatt calls Anna's decision to go to Dorothy's house an "apparently irrelevant decision (AID)." An AID is covertly planned to result in a high-risk situation. In isolation, it seems unrelated to AOD use.

Annis and Marlatt describe a variety of interventions to prevent slips and also to prevent slips from escalating into relapse. Some of the interventions are designed to teach coping strategies in high-risk situations, and others are directed toward global lifestyle changes. Consistent with the model, the strategies are cognitive and behavioral. Many of these will be described in the following section. For those who are interested in school counseling, Fisher and Harrison (1993a) have applied Marlatt's model and strategies to adolescents in the school setting.

ESSENTIAL COMPONENTS OF RELAPSE PREVENTION

As we have seen from the discussion of models of relapse prevention, differences exist between the two models with regard to the definition of client readiness for relapse prevention programming. In the Cenaps Model, a client must have completed the primary goals of treatment (which involve acceptance of the disease model of addiction) to be appropriate for relapse prevention. Annis and Marlatt do not discuss prerequisite conditions for relapse prevention. However, regardless of whether the Cenaps or a cognitive-social learning model of relapse prevention is the choice, the strategies used to prevent relapse are quite similar. Therefore, we want to describe the strategies of relapse prevention that seem to be necessary in either model. Certainly, some strategies are associated to a larger extent with a particular model, which will be highlighted. However, our goal is to emphasize the techniques that a mental health professional may have to use in helping clients with AOD problems to remain abstinent or avoid relapse. Keep in mind that these strategies often must be developed by generalists in schools, agencies, and private practice settings, since mental health professionals in these settings usually have the most contact with clients after formal AOD treatment has ended.

Assessment of High-Risk Situations

The first step in a relapse prevention program must be to determine the specific situations for each client that may lead to a slip. Calling these situations *high risk* denotes a high probability of use based on experience. The type of situations that are risky varies from client to client, although Cummings, Gordon, and Marlatt (1980) found that 75% of the relapses by alcoholics, smokers, and heroin users were due to negative emotions, interpersonal conflict, and social pressure.

In Gorski's (1990) model, the first step in determining high-risk situations is a client self-assessment that involves the history of AOD use, recovery, and relapse to identify the past causes of relapse. Next, an examination of the client's life history helps identify any lifestyle issues that are associated with relapse. Finally, the client's recovery and relapse history is analyzed, with the goal being to examine each period of abstinence to identify the sequence of warning signs that led back to AOD use.

The cognitive-social learning model incorporates an individualized analysis of a client's AOD use over the previous year to determine the high-risk situations for that particular client. For this purpose, Annis (1982) developed a 100-item self-report questionnaire called the Inventory of Drinking Situations. Obviously, the same type of assessment would occur for clients who use drugs other than alcohol. Anna, our 16 year old with polydrug problems, has a number of high-risk situations. Negative emotions, such as guilt, shame, and embarrassment related to her history of sexual molestation, have resulted in AOD use in the past. She also feels unattractive and unintelligent.

Interpersonal conflicts with her mother and with teachers have also been identified as high-risk situations. Finally, in the past, Anna used when she experienced social pressure from her peers. Anna's current lifestyle involves a lot of time alone because she has not established a nonusing social group. She watches a lot of TV and plays video games, and she has been using food as a substitute for AOD.

Coping with High-Risk Situations

Once the high-risk situations have been identified, it is necessary for the client to have strategies to deal with these situations effectively. Education and information sharing may be useful to clients because recovering individuals who relapse need accurate information about what causes relapse and what can be done to prevent it. This type of education and information sharing occurs in structured relapse education sessions and reading assignments that provide specific information about the recovery and relapse process as well as relapse prevention planning methods.

Daley and Marlatt (2005) recommend that clients be taught that relapse is a process and an event by reviewing the common relapse warning signs identified by recovering clients. Following a relapse, clients should review their experiences in detail to learn the connections among thoughts, feelings, events, or situations, and subsequent relapse.

As we saw in the Chapter 8 discussion on methods of treatment, education is rarely sufficient for long-lasting change. Individualized strategies for high-risk situations are usually needed. Gorski (1990) recommends managing high-risk situations on situational-behavioral, cognitive-affective, and core issue levels. On the situational-behavioral level, the client often must avoid the people, places, and things that are high risk and learn to modify his or her behavioral response if a high-risk situation were to occur. For example, Anna identified peer pressure as a high-risk situation. She should avoid her friends with whom she previously used. She might attend a different school following treatment, but, because this is not always possible, she may not be able to avoid these peers. Anna may need assertiveness skills training to learn how to respond to the peer pressure she encounters.

Because Annis (1990) focuses on self-efficacy as the critical component of relapse prevention, a situational-behavioral intervention from this orientation focuses on having the client complete homework assignments that involve the client demonstrating alternative coping responses in high-risk situations. A hierarchy of progressively riskier situations is developed, and coping behaviors in these situations are planned, imagined, and used when needed. The underlying rationale is that the most powerful way to change thinking about self-efficacy is behavioral performance. For Anna, this hierarchy might begin with a chance meeting with one of her using friends in the hall at school, then progress to having a group of these friends sit down with her at lunch, and finally to encountering the group on Friday afternoon on their way to "party."

On the cognitive-affective level, the irrational thoughts and intense feelings that emerge in high-risk situations may need to be challenged. For those clients in Twelve Step recovery programs, the acronym HALT is used to advise recovering people to avoid getting too hungry, angry, lonely, or tired. The term "stinking thinking" is used to challenge irrational thoughts, and members are told to get off the "pity pot" when they are immobilized by their feelings. Daley and Marlatt (2005) recommend a worksheet that lists the relapse-related thought, a statement or statements that dispute the thought, and a new, rational thought. As an example, Anna forgets to do her homework in math one day. Her teacher points this out in front of the class and tells her that she will fail unless she "gets with the program." Anna becomes angry and tells the teacher to "shut up." She is told to leave class. On the way to the office, Anna is consumed with her anger and has an inner dialog with statements such as "Mr. C. (the teacher) hates me. He's always picking on me." "I should just get loaded. No one cares anyway." Fortunately, Anna goes to see her school counselor, who listens to her, lets her emotions reduce in intensity, and then confronts her about her responsibility in completing her homework and also the fact that she is allowing Mr. C. to control her recovery program. While not condoning the public reproof by a teacher, the counselor points out the irrationality of Anna's thinking: "I should have done my homework. It embarrassed me to have it pointed out in front of the class. I conclude that the teacher hates me, nobody cares about me, and therefore, I have an excuse to use." A more rational sequence of thoughts would be: "I need to remember to do my homework and ask for help if I'm stuck. I don't like to be embarrassed and would prefer that Mr. C. handle the situation differently. None of this has anything to do with people caring about me or using."

The school counselor might also conceptualize that Anna's decision not to complete her homework was part of a covert relapse plan and constitutes the AID we discussed in the cognitive-social learning model. In other words, Anna covertly planned a relapse by deciding not to complete her homework in a class in which the teacher often reacts with a public reprimand. Because interpersonal conflict with teachers is a high-risk situation that Anna has identified, she has an excuse to create a conflict, thus giving her an excuse to use. In this case, it would be useful to determine how much of Anna's thoughts and feelings involve her "shoulds" being greater than her "wants" and, if this is the case, to help her to modify this disparity. In addition, the AID needs to be confronted.

On the core issue level, the psychological issues that lead to high-risk situations need to be identified. Anna has identified guilt, shame, and embarrassment as negative emotions that are high risk for her. Because these feelings originate from her history of sexual molestation, her need for therapeutic attention to this issue is obvious. Low self-esteem, depressive and anxiety disorders, and codependency are examples of other psychological issues that can result in high-risk situations.

An additional issue in coping with high-risk situations involves urges and cravings. Marlatt (1985) defines a craving as the degree of desire for the positive effects a person expects as a result of use and an urge as the intention to engage in use to satisfy the craving. As Anna leaves her math class and is experiencing intense anger, she has an urge to smoke pot to satisfy a craving for the calming effect and the dissipation of her anger. In a high-risk situation, clients often report that the cravings and urges are so powerful that they lose focus on other aspects of relapse prevention. Therefore, strategies specific to coping with urges and cravings are necessary.

Daley and Marlatt (2005) suggest a variety of strategies to cope with urges and cravings. For example, intentional cognitive strategies such as changing thoughts or self-talking through the cravings can be used. Let's say you are mulling over a conflict you had at work and are having trouble falling asleep. You say to yourself, "I'm going to stop thinking about that and think about something more pleasant." Self-talking through the craving might involve an internal dialogue such as,

AT A GLANCE

Coping with High-Risk Situations

- Situational-behavioral: Managing people, places, and things that are high risk (e.g., hierarchy of high-risk situations and strategies to avoid or cope)
- Cognitive-affective: Coping with irrational thoughts and intense feelings (e.g., confront the irrational thought or AID)
- Core issues: Psychological issues that lead to relapse (e.g., counseling)
- Urges and cravings (e.g., self-talk)

"OK, I know what is happening. I'm upset and I'm thinking that a drink will make me feel better. It's happened before and it will probably happen again. I can get through it." It is often helpful for the client to combine this self-talk with an inner dialogue about the negative consequences of use and the positive benefits of not using (e.g., "If I drink, I'll blow nine months of sobriety and feel terrible about myself. If I don't, I'll feel really strong and proud of myself."). For some clients, calling their AA or Narcotics Anonymous sponsor or attending a meeting is helpful, while others find that getting involved in a strenuous or pleasant activity takes their thinking away from the urges and cravings.

Support Systems

As you can see from the discussion up to this point, recovering individuals who are relapse-prone need the help of others to maintain their recovery. "Others" may be Twelve Step sponsors, family members, friends, probation officers, clergy, and helping professionals. In other words, you may be among the "others" in your role as a school counselor, marriage and family therapist, social worker, mental health counselor, or rehabilitation counselor. Many treatment programs do not have a formal, structured relapse-prevention program that coordinates the necessary services and people for successful relapse prevention (one reason we want you to be familiar with relapse-prevention strategies).

In addition, we hope you have concluded that most recovering individuals in early recovery who are relapse-prone should be involved with a mental health professional, preferably one with AOD training and experience. The behavioral, cognitive, and affective strategies we have mentioned require the expertise of trained "helpers." Although Twelve Step meetings are a wonderful form of support in recovery, they are not designed to individually address the needs of recovering individuals. The "core psychological issues" that may lead to relapse require the involvement of mental health professionals. Finally, for adolescents, support involves more than just family members and Twelve Step meetings and sponsors. Imagine that Anna returns to school after treatment. As a 16 year old, her primary goals in life are to have friends and have fun. She also sincerely wants to remain abstinent. If she does not have a school-based support group of nonusing peers and no organized activities are available that are AOD-free, it is highly probable that she will relapse, in spite of her good intentions. We believe school personnel have an obligation and a challenge to help recovering adolescents such as Anna develop school-based support.

The involvement of the family in relapse prevention is certainly critical. Laudet, Savage, and Mahmood (2002) found that family was tied with spirituality/faith as the number one source of support for long-term recovery. Furthermore, as Daley and Marlatt (2005) have noted, the families of addicts are more likely to support rather than sabotage recovery if they are involved in the recovery process and have an opportunity to heal from any emotional pain the family members experienced. This is not as simple a process as it may seem. As we will see in Chapter 12, although family therapy may be necessary in many cases, constellations and dynamics of families are very complex. For example, Anna and her mother are in family therapy. But, what about her actively alcoholic biological father? He's not involved and may have some investment in Anna's returning to use to justify his own use pattern. In a family in which the child with an alcohol or other drug problem plays the "scapegoat" role, the family "hero" may subtly sabotage recovery to maintain the family roles (see Chapter 12).

Lifestyle Changes

At the risk of beleaguering poor Anna, let's look at other aspects of her life that require some attention. We have already mentioned the history of sexual molestation that needs therapeutic attention. In addition to the negative emotions that has generated, implications arise with regard to her sexual behavior, choice of partners in relationships, and more. She is obese and has problems with acne, indicating a need for nutritional and hygiene advice. Her IQ is low average and her academic skills are below grade level, so she needs remediation and vocational guidance. She also needs to work on her social skills, her conflict with her mother, her relationship with her father, developing support systems at school, and more.

Does this seem like a lot of "stuff" to work on? It certainly is, and each area can lead to relapse. Now imagine a 47-year-old man who has been abusing alcohol for 25 years. Because of his use, he has physical, legal, financial, family, and vocational problems, all of which cause stress and conflict—high-risk situations for relapse.

As you can see, successful relapse prevention does not simply involve a client's ability to cope with high-risk situations. Many high-risk situations result from the lifestyle of the client and the client's inability to modify this lifestyle. Many such modifications are difficult and require significant investments of time and resources. Let's examine some of these lifestyle areas and the modifications necessary for relapse prevention.

LEISURE TIME   What do you do in your spare time? (We know. You are a student and you don't have spare time. Just pretend.) Do you read, exercise, have a hobby? Many people with AOD problems have had only one leisure time activity—using. When you remove AOD, these people don't know what to do with themselves. They become bored, but are avoiding their only known method to relieve boredom. We have had clients become intense workaholics after treatment to alleviate the fear of having any free time. We also find clients attending one AA meeting after another because they don't know what else to do. We worked with a middle-aged man who had completed an alcohol treatment program at the Salvation Army. Each day, he would work at the Salvation Army, attend an AA meeting, and then wander around the casinos in town (he lived in Nevada). Not surprisingly, it wasn't long before he started to use again.

SUPPORT SYSTEMS   We have already mentioned the importance of support systems. This is certainly related to leisure time. If a recovering person has a circle of friends, he or she has something to do with his or her free time and will become involved with the interests and activities of friends. However, many recovering people have not had contact for years, if at all, with people who are nonusers. Furthermore, recovering clients are often advised during treatment to discontinue contact with friends who use but, as we will discuss, may not have developed the social and communication skills needed to develop new friendships. If the recovering person does not develop an alternative social support system, the options may be isolation or the resumption of the old relationships that involved AOD use. Certainly, Twelve Step meetings provide a structure to meet nonusing people. However, it is essential to assist in the development of healthy support systems and to not rely solely on Twelve Step meetings, particularly with adolescents.

SOCIAL AND COMMUNICATION SKILLS   If a client does not have appropriate social and communication skills, he or she can attend all the Twelve Step meetings available and still not be able to develop a social network. Many people with AOD problems have not had to rely on social or communication skills to have "friends." Simply having money and alcohol or other drugs probably created a social network. They may have never been in a social situation without being under the influence. Clients might need training in listening skills, asking people questions about themselves, or practice in "small talk." We have found the lack of social skills to be a particular problem with adolescents, who normally feel awkward in new social situations. But many adult clients feel like adolescents too, because their social skill development has been truncated by their AOD use. In addition, assertiveness training and stress and anger management may be needed. Clients may have simply used AOD in situations in which stress was encountered. In the absence of using AOD, these clients may demonstrate passive or aggressive responses to conflict.

SELF-CARE Anna needs advice on nutrition and hygiene in a caring and supportive way. If her self-esteem improves, she might pay more attention to this area, but she simply may not know how to eat, dress, or even wash to make herself look better. She may need an adult's help in making the best of what nature has given her. Self-care is a relapse issue because people tend to tease or reject those who are inattentive to their appearance and hygiene. Teasing and rejection can certainly elicit negative emotional states, which we discussed earlier as a significant cause of relapse. Although self-care is a sensitive area and may be embarrassing to discuss, the following case illustrates the importance of this area in relapse prevention. We worked with a man who was recovering and trying to find employment. He was quite obese, sloppily dressed, and had halitosis and body odor. Needless to say, he was not having much luck in interviews. We would not have been doing a good job if we had not been honest with him about his self-care issues, especially because his discouragement over his lack of a job created a high-risk situation.

Advice on nutrition, dress, and hygiene are not the only self-care issues with which clients may need assistance. Exercise might have been neglected during the time the clients were using, and they may need guidance with the development of an exercise program. Clients may also need assistance with the discontinuation of other unhealthy addictions such as tobacco use. In addition to the health hazards of tobacco use, smoking has an effect on energy level, and the growing intolerance of smoking can have social ramifications.

EDUCATIONAL AND VOCATIONAL GUIDANCE It is common for school and jobs to be affected by AOD problems. Also, these areas can be high-risk situations for many different reasons. As we saw with Anna, her scholastic aptitude and poor academic achievement contributed to making school an unpleasant experience. An unsatisfying or unpleasant job can also elicit negative emotions. Frequently, a client may be reluctant to return to the same school or to the job he or she had before treatment because the people and/or the situation there may be associated with use. With adult clients, community colleges and vocational rehabilitation can be resources for educational and vocational guidance. For school-aged clients, high schools generally have vocational counselors and school psychologists who may be of assistance with low-achieving or low-scholastic-aptitude youngsters.

FINANCIAL PLANNING Clients may need financial guidance for two reasons. The first is that they may have financial problems because of their AOD use. Second, the client may have little experience with budgeting, since the priority for money was to secure the drug(s) of choice. Financial issues may require attention because they can be a source of stress, negative emotions, and interpersonal conflict. For example, a client goes through treatment and is working on remaining abstinent. For the first time in a long time, the client is taking his responsibilities seriously. Whereas creditors were ignored when the client was using, now he is making an attempt to clear up his debts, but he has no idea how to negotiate with creditors and budget his current income. Creditors are making harassing phone calls, he can't get his car fixed, and he has no money for recreation. Does this sound like a setup for relapse?

RELATIONSHIPS A few years ago, we worked with a 37-year-old client named Gene who had been sober for 18 months. Gene had been using AOD since he was 14. The longest relationship he had ever been in had lasted six months. Because of the length of time he had been using, emotional attachment, commitment, and interdependence were all unfamiliar to Gene. He sought therapy when he slipped after the end of a short relationship with a woman he met in AA. After a couple of dates and sex, he had proposed to the woman and she had dumped him. Clearly, Gene needed some help with many aspects of relationship development and management.

Although Gene may seem to be an extreme case, relationship problems are a cause of many relapses. Recovering adults may have virtually no experience in relationships while drug free. They may not be able to make logical decisions in the face of the intense emotions that romantic relationships can generate. They may not have a basis for making decisions about potential partners. In many ways, working with adult recovering clients can be like counseling an infatuated adolescent who is "in lust" for the first time. The emotional roller coaster of relationships can be high risk for many clients.

BALANCE   In reading this section, you may have experienced some sense of being overwhelmed with all the areas that may need attention. Clients can have this experience as well. As a mental health professional, you might contribute to a client's frustrations if you list all the lifestyle changes a client must make to prevent relapse. Presenting a recovering client with all of these lifestyle changes at once would probably result in an immediate relapse. Certainly, these areas must be prioritized and then be worked on in increments. As we discussed in the section on covert relapse planning, if a client perceives a great imbalance between "shoulds" and "wants," this perception alone can lead to relapse. It is usually easy for clients and mental health professionals to develop long lists of "shoulds." But it is also important to help clients achieve a balance in their lives so they can have some fun and pleasure. It takes most people a number of years to mess up their lives with AOD. So in spite of a client's desire to repair everything quickly, it will probably take a number of years to clear up their lives as well.

PREVENTING SLIPS FROM ESCALATING

Earlier in the chapter, we discussed the frequency of slips and relapses. Given that it is more common than not for a client to return to use following treatment, it makes sense to develop strategies to reduce the likelihood of a slip's progressing to a relapse. However, this is a sticky issue in the treatment field. Since most treatment programs are abstinence based, you might feel a hesitancy to introduce such strategies because doing so may provide an excuse to a client to use again. The alternative to withholding these techniques is not attractive either because, if a client does slip, he or she has no "weapons" to use to prevent the slip from escalating. In fact, without the knowledge that slips are common, the client's feeling of failure might contribute to further use. As we stated earlier, the conflict, guilt, and shame a client may experience after a slip has been termed the AVE by Marlatt (1985). In our own experience, we have found it useful to discuss slips, AVE, and strategies to limit slips in the context of an expectation that the client will remain abstinent. We believe that it is important to attempt to limit a client's guilt and blame if a slip occurs, so that the client will be more likely to discuss the slip with a mental health professional.

Marlatt (1985) describes strategies to limit slips. One such strategy is a relapse contract. The purpose of a contract is to establish a working agreement to limit the extent of use should a slip occur. The contract includes an agreement to "time out" if a slip occurs. In other words, the client agrees to leave the situation when this happens. Clients can also carry reminder cards that contain specific steps, including people to call if a slip occurs. The cards also have cognitive and behavioral reminders such as "Remember, you are in control," "This slip is not a catastrophe. You can stop now if you choose," and "Imagine yourself in control." Clients may also carry a decision matrix they have developed with a counselor. The decision matrix contains the immediate and delayed consequences of use and, hopefully, would be reviewed after a slip, reminding the client of the consequences of continuing to use. Clearly, these strategies rely on preplanning that would convince a client to use the techniques immediately following a slip. If the slip continues, the cognitive impairment resulting from use would impact the effectiveness of these strategies.

RECOVERY

Recovery from addiction can be conceptualized as a continuous, life-long process. It begins with an intentional action on the part of a person to discontinue the harmful use of AOD. For many people, this intentional act involves entering a treatment program (voluntarily or involuntarily) and continues with a formal aftercare and relapse-prevention program. For many others, the intentional act involves going to a Twelve Step meeting. For others, it may involve starting a methadone maintenance program. Some people discontinue their harmful AOD use through support from a religious institution. Some people stop on their own with or without various support systems.

In other words, people start the recovery process in many different ways. There is no one right way. For those of us in the helping professions, most of the recovering people we encounter have been through formal treatment programs and/or are involved in Twelve Step groups. These clients are the most likely to define themselves as being "in recovery." However, that does not mean that other methods of beginning the recovery process are less useful. (Although we have never encountered this situation, we might have some disagreement with the person who has moderated his or her use of AOD and defines himself or herself as being "in recovery.")

The concept of a continuous, life-long process may be difficult for you. It may help if we personalize this a bit. As was said in Chapter 1, the first author of this textbook (Gary) is a recovering alcoholic and drug addict. Speaking for myself, I (Gary) see the recovery process as similar to many other therapeutic, religious, or spiritual philosophies. Personal development involves qualities and actions such as introspection, honesty, forgiveness, gratitude, humility, responsibility, and service to others. So, whether I attend Twelve Step groups, participate in a religious program, practice yoga, read self-help books, or attend a therapy group, I will probably be encouraged to do much the same things. In other words, whether you are in recovery or not, you hear a fairly consistent message from a variety of sources about what qualities and actions are likely to produce contentment and serenity. For me, when I am actively engaged in my personal recovery program, I have that sense of contentment and serenity (most of the time). When I get distracted or lazy, I start to feel dissatisfied, restless, angry, and resentful, and I get urges and cravings. Because I don't want to go back to AOD use, I have to keep moving forward for the rest of my life. It doesn't feel like a burden. It is just my reality. I accept it and am grateful that some wise people showed me how to have a great life without AOD.

It's a little weird to write about my personal recovery in a textbook (and I didn't include it in the first two editions). The reasons for this personal disclosure are very well-expressed by William White, a leader of the recovery advocacy movement:

> The stigma of addiction—the price that even those in long-term recovery can pay in disclosing this aspect of their personal history—leads many recovering people to "pass" as a "normal," scrupulously hiding their recovery journey from members of the larger community. Some recovering people live a socially cloistered existence, interacting almost exclusively with others in recovery. Does such isolation constitute a failure at re-entry, a missed opportunity for reconciliation, and an abdication of the responsibility to teach and serve the community?
>
> The answers to these questions are not easy to answer because recovering people and their styles of recovery and the styles of living are extremely diverse. . . .
>
> If recovering people have not fully returned to their communities, it is as much a cultural failure as a personal one. It is the cultural stigma—the very real price that can be exacted for

disclosure of recovery status—that is a primary culprit here. It is time for a new recovery advo-cacy movement that, by removing the cultural stigma that continues to be attached to addiction/recovery, can open the doors for recovering people to return to their communities. It is time recovering people shared the boon of their recovery, not just with others seeking recovery, but with the whole community. (White, 2002, p. 3)

People in recovery are joining together in groups and organizations to advocate for treatment, to combat stigma, and to share the miracle of recovery with those who are still suffering from addic-tion, their family members, policy makers, and the entire community. Faces and Voices of Recovery is a national recovery movement, and you can find information about recovery organizations in your area. In addition, you can find out about National Alcohol and Drug Addiction Recovery Month (held each September) at the Center for Substance Abuse Treatment website listed in the Internet Resources section at the end of the chapter.

Recovery Support Services

In Chapter 8, we discussed recovery-oriented systems of care (ROSC). Recovery support services are an essential part of ROSC. As Kaplan (2008) defined these services in a white paper for the federal government:

Recovery support services (RSSs) are nonclinical services that assist individuals and families to recover from alcohol or drug problems. They include social support, linkage to and coordination among allied service providers, and a full range of human services that facilitate recovery and wellness contributing to an improved quality of life. These services can be flexibly staged and may be provided prior to, during, and after treatment. RRSs [sic] may be provided in conjunction with treatment, and as separate and distinct services, to individuals and families who desire and need them. Professionals, faith-based and community-based groups, and other RSS providers are key components of ROSCs. (pp. 7–8)

RSSs can be provided by recovery community organizations (i.e., nonprofit, community-based organizations created by recovery individuals, their loved ones and allies), treatment agen-cies, and faith-based organizations. The services may include employment services and job training, case management, service coordination, linkages to other services, outreach, housing assistance, child care, transportation, peer recovery services (e.g., mentoring, coaching), support groups, life skills, and parent education. From the previous discussion on relapse prevention, you can see how valuable RSSs can be in this process.

Recovery and Spirituality

In the next chapter, we will discuss Twelve Step groups such as AA. As you probably know, Twelve Step groups involve spirituality. This represents a unique aspect of the AOD field compared to other mental health areas because a very prevalent method of managing addiction involves spirituality. While faith and/or spirituality are certainly a part of many counseling approaches, they are incomparably inte-grated in the addiction field, primarily because of the spirituality component of Twelve Step programs.

The spirituality aspect of recovery can generate uncomfortable feelings and controversy, but our experience is that this occurs most frequently outside of the recovery community. Mental health professionals may believe that spirituality is not an appropriate topic with clients. Religion and spirituality are often confused. Spirituality is not associated with any particular religion or set of beliefs. It does not require a belief in the Judeo/Christian God or any particular notion of deity. All religions use some forms of spiritual methods but spirituality can exist outside of religion.

As we will discuss in the next chapter, secular support groups are available for those clients who are not comfortable with references to God in Twelve Step groups.

MyCounselingLab for Addictions/Substance Abuse

Try the Topic 19 Assignments: *Retaining Sobriety: Relapse Prevention Strategies.*

Summary

- Relapse prevention often involves mental health professionals in addition to AOD treatment providers.
- Relapse prevention strategies common across models or approaches include assessment of high-risk situations, strategies for coping with high-risk situations, lifestyle changes, and strategies for preventing slips from escalating to relapse.
- Mental health professionals must be cautious to avoid overwhelming clients with relapse prevention activities.

- Recovery is a life-long process that can start in many different ways, including support groups, religious or spiritual experiences, and independent efforts.
- Recovering people who choose to do so can help combat stigma, advocate for treatment services, and encourage those still suffering from AOD addiction to seek treatment by sharing their recovery experiences.
- Recovery support services may be offered in the community and include many of the essential elements for relapse prevention.

Internet Resources

Cenaps Model
tgorski.com/gorski_articles/developing_a_relapse_prevention_plan.htm

Faces and Voices of Recovery
facesandvoicesofrecovery.org

National Recovery Month
recoverymonth.gov

Further Discussion

1. You may have been asked to participate in an abstinence experience for the class you are taking. If not, you have probably tried to cut down or stop doing something before (smoking, drinking, caffeine, sugar, shopping, video games). When you have tried to cut down or stop a behavior you felt was nonproductive, what high-risk situations did you encounter? How did you handle these situations?

2. When you read about all the areas that recovering individuals have to attend to in order to avoid relapse, what occurs to you about the nature and duration of posttreatment services and support that recovering people need?

CHAPTER 11

Twelve Step and Other Types of Support Groups

CASE EXAMPLES

1 Meredith is a 43-year-old woman who has just completed a court-mandated, intensive outpatient treatment program for alcohol and polydrug addiction. She has a history of sexual and physical abuse in her family of origin and was working in the sex industry to support her addiction. Meredith was physically and sexually assaulted by her pimp and customers. After completing treatment, she was required to attend Twelve Step support groups three times per week. In a meeting with her probation officer, Meredith says that she cannot tolerate Twelve Step meetings because every time she hears the first step about "powerlessness," she has flashbacks about her sexual and physical abuse. She says she never wants to feel powerless again.

2 Terrance, a 57-year-old man, has been ordered by a judge to attend Twelve Step meetings after receiving a second driving under the influence citation. If he fails to attend meetings twice a week for the next six months, he will be diverted to jail for 30 days. He is employed and will lose his job if he goes to jail. Terrance is gay and was sexually abused by a priest when he was 10. Since that experience and because he believes that religious groups discriminate against gays and lesbians, he completely rejects religion and any concept of God. Terrance is a committed atheist. He is totally opposed to attending Twelve Step groups because they mention God.

If we were to specify one characteristic of the alcohol and other drugs (AOD) field that differentiates it from other areas in mental health, it would be the role of support groups in treatment. One would be hard-pressed to find another area in which the most common method of intervention is through groups that are organized and led by nonprofessionals. The unique contribution of support groups in the recovery of individuals with AOD problems warrants a chapter in this text for several reasons. The first and most obvious reason is that, if you work in the helping professions, you will have clients who have attended, are attending, or have been encouraged to attend some type of support group. Therefore, you need to know about such groups. Second, some inevitable conflict seems to exist between mental health professionals and those who are advocates of support groups, and this conflict requires discussion. Finally, the proliferation of support groups based on the Twelve Steps of Alcoholics Anonymous (AA) has led to considerable confusion with regard to the methods and purposes of these groups.

In Chapter 8, we discussed support groups as a component of AOD treatment programs. As we noted, Twelve Step groups such as AA and Narcotics Anonymous (NA) are an essential part of many, if not most, treatment programs. In particular, treatment programs that are disease model–based will almost always require (or strongly recommend) attendance at AA or NA as part of the treatment program and aftercare plan. Family members may be encouraged to attend Al-Anon and teenagers to attend Alateen. Codependents Anonymous meetings for codependents and Adult Children of Alcoholics meetings are also available. A variety of other Twelve Step groups have developed for group support for other issues: Emotions Anonymous, Overeaters Anonymous, Sexaholics Anonymous, Spenders Anonymous, and Gamblers Anonymous.

Because Twelve Step support groups predominate in the support group area and have generated the most confusion and controversy, we want to thoroughly discuss the origin and elements of this type of group. Because Twelve Step support groups originated with AA, and AA meetings are the most common type of Twelve Step group, we will spend the most time discussing the history, elements, and effectiveness of AA. We will also discuss the advantages and disadvantages of Twelve Step groups. Finally, we want you to be aware of other types of support groups that have developed as alternatives to Twelve Step groups.

The topic of Twelve Step groups can generate emotions in those people who have been or who are still actively involved in these groups. A person who actively attends a group such as AA and maintains sobriety may be a fervent advocate for Twelve Step groups. An individual who had an unfavorable reaction to this type of group may be a vocal critic. Many of you may have had some personal experience with Twelve Step groups and have strong feelings one way or another. Therefore, before discussing AA, we would like you to keep two points in mind. First, Twelve Step groups were not designed as treatment. As you will see from the following discussion, AA groups were developed to support alcoholics who were trying to remain sober. Formal treatment and AA do not conflict. Some people do both, some one or the other, and some neither. The fact that many people remain abstinent with support from AA meetings has resulted in some AA members' preaching a philosophy of "AA is the only way." This point of view is not an official stance of AA and is, in fact, contrary to the AA philosophy.

Second, it is common knowledge that Twelve Step meetings contain references to "God" and "Higher Power." In the previous chapter, we discussed the topic of recovery and spirituality, and we will discuss spirituality in Twelve Step groups later in this chapter as well. In our experience, people tend to have an emotional, as opposed to a logical, reaction to anything that appears to be religious. If you have preconceptions about Twelve Step groups because of the spiritual nature of these groups, we ask that you try to put them aside as you read this chapter. We want you, as a mental health professional, to completely understand a very prevalent type of support group and to know when such groups (or others) may be useful for clients. If you have not attended a Twelve Step meeting before, we strongly encourage you to do so. (Make sure you go to an open meeting.) If Twelve Step meetings have benefited you personally, remember that each client is an individual, and what has worked for you may not work for someone else. The spiritual nature of Twelve Step groups presents some interesting and challenging issues for mental health professionals. However, your primary concern should be to objectively assess the needs of your clients and recommend the interventions that best address those needs. To do so, you must put aside any personal preferences for or against Twelve Step groups and objectively determine whether such groups would benefit your clients.

ALCOHOLICS ANONYMOUS

The oldest and largest Twelve Step support group consists of more than 60,000 groups and nearly 1.4 million members in the United States. More than 115,000 groups and more than 2 million members exist worldwide (Alcoholics Anonymous General Services Office, 2015). According to the most recent survey of members (Alcoholics Anonymous World Services, 2015), the average age of members is 50, 62% are males, and 89% are white.

History of AA

An excellent history of AA is presented in a book by William White (1998), a leading recovery advocate. June 10, 1935, is considered the birth date of AA, because that is the date that Bill Wilson, a stockbroker, and Bob Smith, a surgeon, met, and "Dr. Bob" had his last drink.

The sequence of events that brought Bill W. and Dr. Bob, the cofounders of AA, together began with the famous psychiatrist, Carl Jung, and his treatment of Roland H., an alcoholic and an American businessman. Jung had told Roland H. that he had done all that medicine and psychiatry could do. Jung suggested that he needed a spiritual awakening if he were to recover from his alcoholism. Roland H. joined the Oxford Group, a popular nondenominational religious group that sought to recapture the essence of first-century Christianity. Roland H. was able to abstain from alcohol after associating with the Oxford Group, and he convinced a friend, Ebby T., to do the same. Ebby T. was a friend of Bill W. When Bill offered Ebby a drink, Ebby replied, "I don't need it anymore. I've got religion." Bill W., an agnostic, did not immediately see the implication of Ebby's statement. However, after being admitted to a hospital for detoxification, Bill W. had a spiritual experience. Following his release, he read a book by William James, *The Varieties of Religious Experiences,* which became the foundation of the Twelve Steps. Bill W. was able to stop drinking and his life improved dramatically. During a business trip to Akron, Ohio, Bill W. had a strong desire to drink after a business deal fell through. He wanted to talk to another alcoholic, so he called an Oxford Group minister and was referred to Dr. Bob, an active alcoholic. Dr. Bob reluctantly agreed to talk to Bill W. They ended up talking for hours. Bill W. had made this contact because he needed to talk to another alcoholic to avoid drinking himself. Through this contact, Bill W. avoided relapsing and Dr. Bob stopped drinking. This was the start of the AA method of alcoholics talking to other alcoholics in order to remain sober. Bill W. had no plan or desire to change Dr. Bob. He only wanted to maintain his own sobriety.

What AA Is About

The AA preamble, which is usually read at meetings, is a good description of the purpose of AA:

> Alcoholics Anonymous is a fellowship of men and women who share their experience, strength, and hope with each other that they may solve their common problem and help others to recover from alcoholism.
>
> The only requirement for membership is a desire to stop drinking. There are no dues or fees for AA membership; we are self-supporting through our own contributions. AA is not allied with any sect, denomination, politics, organization, or institution; does not wish to engage in any controversy, neither endorses nor proposes any causes. Our primary purpose is to stay sober and help other alcoholics to achieve sobriety. (*AA Grapevine,* 1985, p. 1)

AA meetings may be closed (for AA members only) or open. Closed meetings are usually "step" meetings in which members can choose which of the Twelve Step to focus on. Open meetings may be "speaker" meetings in which people voluntarily tell their stories (their histories of drinking and recovery) or discussion meetings where a topic is suggested by the meeting chair or a participant. The topics relate to some aspect of recovery or a barrier to recovery, such as "forgiveness," "anger," "humility," or "serenity."

As the AA preamble indicates, the only requirement for membership is a *desire* to stop drinking. Those who relapse are not banned but are offered support in their struggle for sobriety. The bible for AA is the book *Alcoholics Anonymous* (Alcoholics Anonymous World Services, 2001), commonly referred to as "The Big Book." Anonymity, a central concept in AA, protects the identities of members and ensures that no one person or persons become spokespeople for AA. To further the ideal of equality among members, meetings chairs rotate, and there are no elected directors. Special committees and service boards are created as needed from AA members.

At AA meetings, you will hear many slogans that are amusing, catchy, or clever and are easily remembered. For example, the famous "One day at a time" is meant to reinforce the concept that sobriety is a day-to-day (sometimes minute-to-minute) process to keep the alcoholic focused on the present as opposed to the future. Other examples include "Keep it simple" (sobriety is a simple process: don't drink), "Let go and let God," and "Get off the pity pot."

When a person speaks at an AA meeting, he or she usually starts by saying, "Hi. My name is (first name of speaker) and I'm an alcoholic." The rest of the participants respond by saying, "Hi, _____." The statement of the speaker acknowledges his or her alcoholism, and the response of the participants indicates acceptance and support. At some meetings, a person may be called upon to speak. One can always say, "Hi, my name is _____, and I pass."

In the introduction to this book, we told you that we require our students to attend an AA or an NA meeting, and the students generally are impressed with the friendliness and encouragement they encounter at the meetings. However, some of the students are concerned with another aspect of AA meetings, which is the "no cross talk" rule. When someone speaks at an AA meeting, subsequent speakers do not address previous speakers. For example, one of our students was very concerned about a woman at a meeting who was emotionally distraught and disoriented in her speech. The next speaker did not react to the woman at all. As we explained, AA meetings are for support in maintaining sobriety. They are not designed to provide therapy. If cross talk were allowed, there would be a tendency for nonprofessionals to provide therapy. Also, as Bill W. discovered, he was able to avoid drinking simply by talking about himself to another alcoholic. Input and feedback from Dr. Bob was not necessary and, therefore, is not necessary at meetings.

As a helping professional, you might wonder about the advisability of eliminating feedback from members because this can be a valuable method of growth. Although feedback does not occur in meetings members are encouraged to seek a "sponsor" who is an alcoholic with long-term sobriety and has worked all of the Twelve Steps. The sponsor shares his or her experience, strength, and hope with an alcoholic with less sobriety and experience. The sponsor generally does offer advice and guidance to the sponsee outside of the meetings. Sponsors may guide their sponsee through the Twelve Steps. New members are encouraged to get a sponsor as soon as possible, and even members with years of sobriety continue to maintain an ongoing relationship with their sponsor. Although there are no "rules" about sponsorship, AA literature does offer guidance (e.g., Alcoholics Anonymous World Services, 1983). At a minimum, sponsors should have been sober for a year (as a personal opinion, we believe that very few recovering addicts are ready to be sponsors after just one year of sobriety). To avoid dual relationships, sponsors and sponsees should be paired to minimize any possibility of a romantic relationship. In other words, heterosexual members should choose sponsors of the same gender and gay members should choose sponsors who are not gay or are the opposite gender of the gay member. It is common for members to change sponsors along the way. Although there are numerous reasons why a member may want a different sponsor, the bottom line is that AA members are involved in the program to achieve and maintain sobriety. If the relationship with a sponsor is not helping the member to achieve and maintain sobriety, then a change is warranted.

The Twelve Steps and the Twelve Traditions

A.A.'s Twelve Steps are a group of principles, spiritual in their nature, which, if practiced as a way of life, can expel the obsession to drink and enable the sufferer to become happily and usefully whole. A.A.'s Twelve Traditions apply to the life of the Fellowship itself. They outline the means by which A.A. maintains its unity and relates itself to the world about it, the way it lives and grows. (Alcoholics Anonymous World Services, 2009, p. 15)

The core of the AA program and the basis of similar groups developed on the AA model are the Twelve Steps. As a statement in the Big Book indicates, "Rarely have we seen a person fail who has thoroughly followed our path" (p. 58). It is truly astounding that these twelve statements, written more than 80 years ago, have generated so great a number of adherents, groups, and critics. We will present the Twelve Steps and comment briefly on them. If desired, you can find a thorough discussion in *Twelve Steps and Twelve Traditions* by Alcoholics Anonymous World Services.

The Twelve Steps[1]

1. We admitted we were powerless over alcohol—that our lives had become unmanageable.
2. Came to believe that a Power greater than ourselves could restore us to sanity.
3. Made a decision to turn our will and our lives over to the care of God *as we understood Him.*
4. Made a searching and fearless moral inventory of ourselves.
5. Admitted to God, to ourselves, and to another human being the exact nature of our wrongs.
6. Were entirely ready to have God remove all these defects of character.
7. Humbly asked Him to remove our shortcomings.
8. Made a list of all persons we had harmed, and became willing to make amends to them all.
9. Made direct amends to such people wherever possible, except when to do so would injure them or others.
10. Continued to take personal inventory and when we were wrong promptly admitted it.
11. Sought through prayer and meditation to improve our conscious contact with God *as we understood Him,* praying only for knowledge of His will for us and the power to carry that out.
12. Having had a spiritual awakening as the result of these steps, we tried to carry this message to alcoholics, and to practice these principles in all our affairs.

Let us point out a couple of things about the Twelve Steps. First, alcohol is mentioned only in step 1. Steps 2 through 11 are the ways to improve a person's life. You can see how these might be applied to many issues other than alcohol. The focus is on surrender, forgiveness, humility, limitations, and service to others. Rather than thinking about the Twelve Step as a way to stay sober, they can be conceptualized as a way of living that will not only maintain sobriety but will facilitate recovery.

The Twelve Traditions[2]

The Twelve Traditions govern the operation of AA. They are as follows:

1. Our common welfare should come first; personal recovery depends upon AA unity.
2. For our group purpose there is but one ultimate authority—a loving God as He may express himself in our group conscience. Our leaders are but trusted servants; they do not govern.
3. The only requirement for AA membership is a desire to stop drinking.
4. Each group should be autonomous except in matters affecting other groups or AA as a whole.

---

[1]The Twelve Steps and Twelve Traditions are reprinted with permission of Alcoholics Anonymous World Services, Inc. ("AAWS"). Permission to reprint the Twelve Steps and Twelve Traditions does not mean that AAWS has reviewed or approved the contents of this publication, nor that AA necessarily agrees with the views expressed herein. AA is a program of recovery from alcoholism *only*—use of the Twelve Steps and Twelve Traditions in connection with programs and activities that are patterned after AA, but which address other problems, or in any other non-AA context, does not imply

[2]Ibid.

5. Each group has but one primary purpose—to carry its message to the alcoholic who still suffers.

6. An AA group ought never endorse, finance, or lend the AA name to any related facility or outside enterprise, lest problems of money, property, and prestige divert us from our primary purpose.

7. Every AA group ought to be fully self-supporting, declining outside contributions.

8. Alcoholics Anonymous should remain forever nonprofessional, but our service centers may employ special workers.

9. AA, as such, ought never be organized; but we may create service boards or committees directly responsible to those they serve.

10. Alcoholics Anonymous has no opinion on outside issues; hence the AA name ought never be drawn into public controversy.

11. Our public relations policy is based on attraction rather than promotion; we need always maintain personal anonymity at the level of press, radio, and films.

12. Anonymity is the spiritual foundation of all our Traditions, ever reminding us to place principles before personalities.

The emphasis of the Twelve Traditions is on maintaining anonymity and avoiding controversy, thereby reducing the likelihood that AA will be diverted from its mission. You will not find AA endorsing or criticizing any model of addiction or approach to treatment. There is no AA lobbyist to help pass legislation. AA has no "spokesperson" and does not solicit or accept contributions. No matter what your opinion is of AA, you have to be impressed with the singular focus of AA and its ability to maintain this focus for more than 80 years.

Elements of AA Meetings

Although there may be some variability in what you will hear and see at AA meetings, most open meetings have common elements. By describing these, we are not trying to provide a substitute for actual attendance at meetings. However, your experience when you first go to an AA meeting might be similar to attending a religious service of an unfamiliar denomination. You are not quite sure when to do what, and you don't want to call attention to yourself.

Generally, people socialize for a short time before the meeting starts. Coffee and other beverages are usually available. If the meeting is not advertised as nonsmoking, be prepared for cigarette smoke. People who regularly attend the meeting may introduce themselves to those who are obviously new and offer to sit with a newcomer. Remember, last names are not used.

The meeting chair or secretary will introduce the meeting by saying something like, "Welcome to the Gemini meeting of Alcoholics Anonymous. My name is _____ and I am an alcoholic. May we have a moment of silence for those alcoholics who are still suffering." The Serenity Prayer will then be recited: "God grant me the serenity to accept the things I cannot change, the courage to change the things I can, and the wisdom to know the difference." The AA preamble is read, and newcomers (those with fewer than 30 days of sobriety) and out-of-towners are given an opportunity to introduce themselves. Members participate in reading part of Chapter 3 of the Big Book, titled "More about Alcoholism" or Chapter 5, "How It Works," the Twelve Steps, and the Twelve Traditions. The chair then speaks, usually telling his or her story. If the meeting is a discussion meeting, the chair either suggests a topic of discussion, asks for suggestions, or has a member read something from AA literature. The reading selection then becomes the basis for the meeting discussion. If it is a speakers' meeting, the chair asks for volunteers or calls on people to speak. Remember, if you are called upon to speak and do not wish to, you can always say "Pass." It is nice if you say, "Hi, my name is _____ and I pass," but you don't have to. Also, don't be confused by the title "discussion meeting." It really isn't an exchange—rather, a series of speakers talk about the meaning of the topic of discussion in their sobriety. As we stated previously, cross talk is not permitted. After the discussion or speakers, AA-related announcements are made and a basket for contributions is passed around. The chair may sign attendance records for those who are court ordered to attend. "Chips" may be given to those in attendance who have achieved sobriety milestones (i.e., 30, 60, and 90 days; 6 months; 9 months) and those who have "birthdays" (anniversary of sobriety). "A Vision for You" from the Big Book is read, and participants stand in a circle, join hands, and recite the Lord's Prayer. They then say "Keep coming back. It works if you work it, so work it 'cause you're worth it" or simply "Keep coming back" or "Stay" (different meetings have different traditions) and the meeting is over. Participants may socialize for a brief period following the meeting.

Research on AA

A professional work group was formed by the Substance Abuse and Mental Health Services Administration and the Department of Veterans Affairs (2003) to examine self-help organizations. This work group reviewed the literature on the effectiveness of AA and other Twelve Step groups and concluded the following:

1. Longitudinal studies associate 12-step self-help group involvement with reduced substance use and improved psychosocial functioning, (2) Twelve step self-help groups significantly reduce health care utilization and costs, (3) Self-help groups are best viewed as a form of continuing care rather than as a substitute for acute treatment services, (4) Randomized trials with coerced populations suggest that Alcoholic [*sic*] Anonymous (AA) combined with professional treatment is superior to AA alone.

A more recent meta-analysis of studies of AA (Kaskutas, 2009) found that the rates of abstinence are about twice as high for those who attend AA and higher rates of abstinence are associated with the frequency of attendance at meetings. These relationships were similar regardless of the types of samples studied and various follow-up periods.

However, this analysis found mixed results on the specificity of an effect for AA or for Twelve Step Facilitation (a manualized treatment based on the Twelve Steps and described in Chapter 8).

AA and Spirituality

The effectiveness of AA has been related to elements in the group process, ego function development, empathic understanding, disintegration of pathologic narcissism, and so forth (Nace, 2005). However, AA is a spiritual program of thinking and living. Therefore, the well-intentioned efforts to conceptualize the effects of AA in terms of psychological theories or processes and to research AA through traditional scientific methods may be misguided. As we mentioned at the beginning of the chapter, the broad utilization of a spiritual support program is unique in the helping professions. The mental health professional may need to be flexible in order to gain some understanding of the impact of AA on many recovering alcoholics.

Nace (2005) discusses the spiritual themes of AA: release, gratitude, humility, and tolerance. Release is clearly experienced when the alcoholic no longer feels the compulsion to drink. Gratitude results from the release from compulsion. The alcoholic's powerlessness over alcohol elicits humility because it is a humbling experience to acknowledge one's inability to handle this drug. The theme of tolerance of differences among people and of one's own shortcomings helps the recovering individual to achieve serenity. If you now reread the Twelve Steps and Twelve Traditions, you can see the themes of release, gratitude, humility, and tolerance in these basic precepts of AA.

Misconceptions Regarding AA

In the minds of many professionals, AA is associated with a particular model of addiction and specific methods of dealing with alcoholics. For example, AA is often associated with the disease concept of addiction (see Chapter 3) and with the need to confront the denial system of alcoholics (see Chapter 8). Miller and Kurtz (1994) compare different models of addiction with AA through AA literature and the writings of Bill W. They concluded that AA materials do not assert that alcoholism is a hereditary condition, alcoholism is a physical disorder, there is only one form of alcoholism, moderate drinking is not possible for anyone with an alcohol problem, alcoholics must be confronted aggressively because of their denial, there is only one road to recovery, or that alcoholics are not responsible for their actions. Tradition 10 states that AA has no position on outside issues. All of these stereotypes about what AA preaches are considered outside issues. Keep in mind the last line of the preamble of AA that you read earlier in the chapter, "Our primary purpose is to stay sober and to help other alcoholics to achieve sobriety." All of these other issues would divert AA from its primary mission.

However, we should note that many AA members may not be familiar with the original writings of Bill W. and therefore may perpetuate some or all of these misconceptions.

OTHER TWELVE STEP GROUPS

As we mentioned earlier, many other groups have adapted the Twelve Steps to areas other than alcohol. NA was founded in 1953. AA and NA are not officially affiliated. However, NA uses the same Twelve Steps as AA, replacing "alcohol" and "alcoholism" with "drugs" and "addiction." From the first NA group, membership expanded to 1,600 groups in 1982 and to more than 20,000 in 1992 (Fiorentine & Hillhouse, 2000). According to the most recent membership survey, more than 63,000 meetings worldwide now exist (NA World Services, 2014). This increase is understandable considering the tremendous rise in illicit drug use in this country since the formation of NA. Because so many people present polydrug problems, the choice of whether to attend AA or NA has become less clear. It is probably best to let clients with polydrug problems (if one of the drugs is alcohol) attend both AA and NA meetings and decide which is most comfortable. Other organizations exist as well, such as Cocaine Anonymous, and Dual Diagnosis Anonymous and Dual Recovery Anonymous, which are Twelve Step programs for those with co-occurring mental disorders.

When AA was founded, its members were men. The wives of the members would get together and talk about their problems. Lois W., the wife of Bill W., founded Al-Anon Family Groups in 1954. Al-Anon is a recovery program for people who suffer because someone close to them is abusing AOD. Al-Anon stresses that members can recover whether or not their loved one recovers.

The Twelve Steps have been adapted for Al-Anon, with step 1 being an admission that the person is powerless to control the drinking of significant others. Essentially, Al-Anon provides support for family members of alcoholics. Al-Anon does not advocate that family members abandon the alcoholic or coerce the alcoholic into treatment. Rather, it is a spiritual program that encourages detachment and self-improvement. At Al-Anon meetings, you will find family members living with recovering alcoholics, those living with active alcoholics, and those who have separated from alcoholic family members. Alateen is a component of Al-Anon that was started by a teenager in 1957 and is designed for young people who are living with an alcoholic family member. Alateen has its own Big Book, structured along the same lines as that of AA (Al-Anon Family Group, 1973). In our area, Alateen meetings are held at schools, providing these young people with a convenient way to attend and experience the support of others with similar issues. At both Al-Anon and Alateen meetings, you will find participants who are living with or involved with people who have addictions to drugs other than alcohol. We encourage you to attend some Al-Anon meetings so you will have firsthand experience with this type of support group.

As we mentioned previously, numerous other Twelve Step groups have been created that focus on a variety of issues and where the Al-Anon Family Groups are adapted for the particular focus of the group. Twelve Step groups exist for codependency, adult children of alcoholics, eating disorders, sexual behavior, gambling, spending, and other issues.

ADVANTAGES AND DISADVANTAGES OF TWELVE STEP GROUPS

Twelve Step groups have many obvious advantages. First, they are free. In the mental health field, this is certainly unique. Second, meetings such as AA are available at a variety of times and places (of course, this depends on the size of the area and the type of meeting). An AA member who is on either a business or pleasure trip can usually find a meeting. Third, at meetings, Twelve Step participants find a group of people who share similar concerns and problems and who can provide group support. This type of support is helpful to many people and would be difficult for them to achieve on their own. Additionally, a social network is often developed through Twelve Step meetings. For the recovering person, this is a useful way to make nonusing friends. Fourth, the structure and ritual of Twelve Step meetings may be comforting and helpful to people whose lives have been chaotic and unpredictable. Fifth, the spiritual nature of Twelve Step groups, with its themes of release, gratitude, humility, and tolerance, can be a productive focus for self-improvement and general contentment with life. For one who has experienced excessive guilt, blame, and embarrassment, the spiritual themes can refocus the person on more positive emotions. Finally, Twelve Step groups are consistent with the concepts of recovery-oriented systems of care (see Chapter 9) and with the view of addiction as a chronic condition that requires management throughout a person's life. Through regular attendance at Twelve Step meetings, an addict is always focused on recovery.

The disadvantages of Twelve Step meetings are usually focused on the differentiation (or lack thereof) between spirituality and religion and the concept of "powerlessness." Although Twelve Step meetings are supposed to be nondenominational, the recital of the Lord's Prayer implies a Christian orientation. Those who are members of other religious groups may be alienated by this prayer. Atheists can certainly have difficulty with the notion of "Higher Power." Even though steps 3 and 11 refer to "God as we understood Him," the notion of Higher Power in Twelve Step meetings is clearly that of the Judeo-Christian God. However, remember that AA was formed in 1935 when diversity was hardly a predominant concept. In the context of the times, it is a tribute to Bill W.'s openness that "God as we understood Him" was included. Regardless, the rituals of Twelve Step meetings and the references to God and a Higher Power can be problematic for clients who have negative attitudes and/or experiences with organized religion or those who are not Christian.

AA does not promulgate the notion that alcoholics are not responsible for their condition or actions. Although the first of the Twelve Step contains the word "powerlessness" and the third step involves turning "our will and our lives over to the care of God," steps 4 through 8 involve taking responsibility for past wrongs and shortcomings. However, critics of Twelve Step groups and some participants have interpreted steps 1 and 3 to mean that the Twelve Step philosophy supports the notion that addicted individuals are not responsible for their actions. Clearly, such a view would be counterproductive for clients.

Additional disadvantages of Twelve Step groups arise from the individuals involved in such groups rather than from the ideas themselves. As the membership statistics show, AA is predominately composed of white, middle-aged males. This might alienate women, ethnically diverse individuals, and young people. Groups for different demographic groups have developed in response.

Some participants in Twelve Step groups feel so strongly about the benefits of the program that they denigrate other interventions, such as therapy or psychotropic medications. Again, nothing in the AA philosophy opposes other forms of intervention or preaches that AA is the only way to recovery. However, just as some adherents of religious views misinterpret the doctrines based on their personal characteristics and experiences, some twelve-step participants appear dogmatic.

Finally, critics of Twelve Step groups claim that many people simply switch addictions from alcohol and other drugs to going to meetings. Certainly, attendance at Twelve Step meetings can interfere with social, family, and occupational functioning, and, if a person continued with constant participation in spite of these consequences, this would constitute problematic behavior. Personally, we would rather see someone constantly attending meetings than committing armed robbery to get money for drugs. However, we have no doubt that compulsive Twelve Step meeting attendance could be a barrier to mature functioning.

To close this discussion of Twelve Step groups, we want to reemphasize our personal view that Twelve Step meetings should not be confused with treatment. Twelve Step groups, with the support they offer and the emphasis on spiritual development, can be an important part of a comprehensive treatment program. As we said earlier in the chapter, some people maintain sobriety (or whatever behavior change they are focused on) without any other form of intervention or support. Others maintain these changes without ever going to a twelve-step meeting. As we said in Chapter 6, it is the counselor's responsibility to do a thorough assessment on every client and to design treatment strategies designed to meet the client's needs. You will find that many clients can benefit from this type of free, available support group consisting of people with similar problems. Whether the group is a Twelve Step group or one of the other groups we will now discuss depends on the needs, background, and experiences of the client. The recommendation for a support group should not depend on your own preconceptions or stereotypes.

AT A GLANCE

Twelve Step Groups

- AA was started in 1935; NA in 1953; Al-Anon in 1954.
- The Twelve Steps are the basic principles for living; the Twelve Traditions govern the operation of Twelve Step groups.
- Twelve Step support group meetings are associated with abstinence and other positive outcomes but are not a substitute for treatment.
- AA is singularly focused on helping alcoholics to stop drinking; it has no opinion on therapy or other treatment, models of addiction, medications, or any other issue.
- Twelve Step groups are free, readily available, provide an abstinent social group and activities, can provide a structure for improving the quality of life, and help recovering addicts maintain a focus on recovery.
- The spiritual nature of twelve-step groups may present challenges for some addicts.
- The concepts of powerlessness and responsibility for recovery are sometimes misunderstood by addicts and the public.

OTHER TYPES OF SUPPORT GROUPS

Many Roads, One Journey

In her 1992 book (revised in 2002), *Many Roads, One Journey: Moving Beyond the 12 Steps,* Charlotte Davis Kasl argues that issues such as child abuse, sexism, racism, poverty, and homophobia are in opposition to Twelve Step concepts such as conformity, humility, personal failings, and powerlessness.

For example, an adult woman who was sexually molested as a child or has been in an abusive relationship and has a substance abuse problem may find the first of the Twelve Steps unacceptable. To admit powerlessness over anything may rekindle the feelings of powerlessness in the abusive situations.

Kasl has developed 16 steps for discovery and empowerment. For example, the first of these steps is an affirmation that members can take charge of their lives and not be dependent on AOD or other people for their sense of self-esteem. With regard to spirituality, the steps mention God, Goddess, the Universe, Great Spirit, and Higher Power. There is an assertion that members are living in a hierarchal, patriarchal culture and that they must examine their beliefs and behavior in that context. An emphasis is also placed on power*fulness*, choice, and the relationship of behavior to culture.

Kasl also provides guidelines for *Many Roads, One Journey* groups. Rather than suggesting a rigid structure and rituals, the groups are more flexible. Kasl does suggest that the purpose of the group be defined, a moderator chosen, and time constraints adhered to. She also suggests a six-week commitment for new members and two-week notice when a member is leaving. Readings of poems, sayings, or other literature are recommended.

Women for Sobriety

Jean Kirkpatrick found AA meetings to be rigid, dogmatic, and chauvinistic and felt that the meetings increased her desire to drink. She found hypocrisy in AA members' resistance to taking blood pressure medication or using vitamins to control the effects of alcohol withdrawal, and in the heavy use of caffeine and tobacco at meetings. After 28 years of alcoholism, during which Kirkpatrick experienced hospitalization, violence, and depression, she founded Women for Sobriety in 1976. According to Kirkpatrick (1990), Women for Sobriety is a product of the feminist movement. The emphasis is on women taking charge of their alcoholism rather than letting others control their decisions about their health. In this program, women build their self-esteem and sense of competence by discovering and maintaining feelings of self-value and self-worth.

Kirkpatrick believes that women begin to drink because of frustration, loneliness, emotional deprivation, and harassment, while men drink for power. In her opinion, treatment programs have not been responsive to the needs of women, and separate self-help groups are necessary to affirm women's autonomy from men.

Kirkpatrick's program emphasizes a holistic approach to recovery. She emphasizes good nutrition, meditation, and cessation of smoking. Consistent with this philosophy, coffee, sugar, and smoking are not permitted at Women for Sobriety meetings. There are 13 affirmational statements that are consistent with Kirkpatrick's emphasis on competence, power, self-esteem, and self-reliance.

Secular Organizations for Sobriety/Save Our Selves (SOS)

James Christopher had his last drink on April 24, 1978. He attended AA meetings although he was not comfortable with the spiritual emphasis of the program. In 1985, Christopher published an article expressing his frustration with what he perceived as AA's religious orientation and that the needs of free thinkers were not being met. In 1986, the first SOS meeting was held.

Although Christopher (1988) is a firm adherent to the disease concept of addiction, he rejects the notion that spirituality is a necessary component for recovery. The central component of the SOS program is the "sobriety priority." He believes that the antidote for the disease of addiction is the sobriety priority. On a daily basis, the addict must accept and surrender to the disease and must prioritize sobriety. Although the addict has a right to fail in any other area of life, sobriety is the exception.

Christopher suggests five secular guidelines for sobriety. These include an acknowledgment of alcoholism; choosing to remain sober one day at a time; reaching out to those who have been directly or indirectly affected by the person's alcoholism; working toward self-acceptance, change, and growth;

and taking responsibility for providing meaning in life. SOS meetings are one-and-a-half hours long with a different person acting as moderator each week. Often soft, classical music is played and a short selection from secular literature related to alcoholism is read. The group may choose a topic to discuss or have an open discussion. Meetings are closed with a short, humanistic reading. Christopher does suggest an opening for an SOS meeting, which stresses sobriety, personal growth, secularism, and humanism. He also emphasizes that his structure and suggestions may be modified as the group wishes.

Moderation Management

This behavioral change program and support group network was developed in 1994 to assist problem drinkers with modifying their use of alcohol. It was not designed for those who have been diagnosed with an Alcohol Use Disorder (see Chapter 6), but rather for those people who are concerned about their drinking and want to cut back or quit drinking before serious problems develop. The Moderation Management program is based on the premise that alcohol abuse is a learned behavior rather than a disease. Therefore, people can learn to use alcohol in a moderate manner.

Moderate Management advocates a nine-step program that includes attendance at (free) meetings and abstinence from alcohol for 30 days. The rest of the steps are behavioral in nature and involve tracking drinking behavior, setting drinking goals, and making positive lifestyle changes. The program neither encourages nor discourages abstinence as a goal but does acknowledge that moderation may not be a workable goal for all problem drinkers.

Smart Recovery®

Self-Management And Recovery Training (SMART) was started in 1994 and is an alternative support group system that claims to have a scientific rather than a spiritual orientation. According to its website, SMART Recovery differs from Twelve Step recovery because it teaches self-reliance rather than powerlessness. The meetings are discussions and cross talk is encouraged. Labels such as alcoholic and addict are discouraged, and there are no sponsors. Lifetime attendance at meetings is not recommended (SMART Recovery, 2016).

The SMART Recovery program consists of four points: (1) Enhance and maintain motivation to abstain; (2) Cope with urges; (3) Manage thoughts, feelings, and behaviors; and (4) Balance momentary and enduring satisfactions (SMART Recovery, 2016). The strategies involve cognitive–behavioral techniques including a cost-benefit analysis, disputing irrational beliefs about urges and cravings, the ABC analysis from Albert Ellis's rational emotive therapy (i.e., **A**ctivating event or experience; **B**elief about **A**; emotional or behavioral **C**onsequences of **B**). Meetings are free and both online and in person. Meeting facilitators receive training.

CASE EXAMPLE APPLICATIONS

If you go back to the beginning of the chapter and review the case examples, you can see both Meredith and Terrance have alternatives with regard to support groups. Two groups for women that Meredith may find more comfortable are Many Roads, One Journey, or Women for Sobriety. Terrance could participate in SOS or SMART Recovery since neither has a spiritual component.

Unfortunately, the alternatives to Twelve Step support groups are not as readily available as are Twelve Step groups. The alternative groups may be difficult to find where Meredith and Terrance live or at convenient times. As a result, more and more people are choosing to participate in alternative groups online. Online participation is also available for Twelve Step groups.

Another consideration in both Meredith's and Terrance's cases and for other clients who are resistant to attending Twelve Step groups is that both of them felt that they had very good reasons for feeling uncomfortable and out of place at Twelve Step meetings. We could argue about what is meant by "powerlessness" with Meredith and about the meaning of "Higher Power" with Terrance. But, feelings are feelings and both said that they were not willing to attend Twelve Step meetings. As a helping professional, you just want to be sure that resistance to attending Twelve Step meetings is not the client's way of resisting recovery. Both Meredith and Terrance were willing to participate in alternative support groups; therefore, they were motivated to work on their recovery. A client who finds faults with all types of support groups may not be.

MyCounselingLab for Addictions/Substance Abuse

Try the Topic 7 Assignments: *Group Treatment.*

Summary

- Support groups organized around the Twelve Steps of Alcoholics Anonymous have grown to include groups for other drug addicts, family members, and various nondrug problems.
- Twelve Step support groups involve a spiritual approach to recovery and a commitment to the anonymity of members.

- Alternatives to Twelve Step groups are available for those who are uncomfortable with the Twelve Step or a spiritual approach to recovery.
- Mental health professionals should attempt to match clients with the type of support group that matches their needs and values.

Internet Resources

Alcoholics Anonymous
aa.org/

Narcotics Anonymous
na.org

Al-Anon and Alateen
al-anon.alateen.org

Support groups other than twelve-step
womenforsobriety.org http://www.sossobriety.org/ moderation.org smartrecovery.org

Blogs, chatrooms
dryblog.blogspot.com

Further Discussion

1. Should coerced clients (i.e., people mandated to attend treatment by courts, employers, or schools) be required to attend Twelve Step meetings? Why or why not?

2. Do you think that recovering people can become too dependent on support group meetings? Why or why not?

CHAPTER 12

Children and Families

CASE EXAMPLES

1. Mary, the wife of an alcoholic, is sharing in her first recovery meeting:

   "Well . . . Tony is a very successful businessman. We have three children together. They are good kids, you know? They knew their roles and did what they were supposed to do for the most part . . . None of us ever thought that Tony had a problem; or, that he was an alcoholic; or, that our family had a problem until later when our son, Mark, began having problems. It all seemed so normal to us."

2. Mr. Aguilar is Hispanic and had been exposed to drinking at an early age in a culture where heavy drinking was more tolerated than in the United States. As a result, he was caught between his culture of origin and the practices of his current cultural environment. He maintained that his drug use situation was inevitable due to the structural oppression he experienced. He saw his drinking as an appropriate way to cope with stress. His wife was in a paradox: She did not want to be disrespectful of her husband and, at the same time, she had a need to help him manage his problematic drinking.

In Chapter 1, we discussed a conceptualization of addiction in which the alcoholic or drug addict is in an intimate and monogamous relationship with the drug of choice. Clearly, if the primary relationship is with alcohol or other drugs, other relationships will be adversely impacted, and the effect on the family is particularly dramatic. Investigators in the field have identified myriad problems that occur in children in substance-abusing families as well as in the family system itself. Since the early 1980s, studies have consistently shown that children from these families suffer in a variety of ways (Hussong, Huang, Curran, Chassin, & Zucker, 2010; Park & Schepp, 2015; Pienkowski, 2014; Zucker, Donovan, Masten, Mattson, & Moss, 2009). This is not meant to be a comprehensive review of the vast literature related to children and families in which an alcohol or other drug problem exists. Rather, these examples illustrate the obvious fact that, if a family member has an alcohol or other drug problem, the family will be affected. Individuals living in such families did not need researchers to discover this, as evidenced by the development of Al-Anon in 1954 and Alateen in 1975 (see Chapter 11). Furthermore, comprehensive treatment programs include family education and family therapy as a component of treatment (see Chapter 8). They acknowledge that alcoholism and drug addiction affect each member of the family and that successful recovery necessitates the involvement of the entire family.

As we discussed in Chapter 3, different models of addiction and, predictably, differing conceptualizations, occur in families in relation to alcohol and other drugs (AOD) problems. Some may argue that the individual with an AOD problem is reflecting dysfunction in the family. Others see the AOD problem as the primary cause of family dysfunction. As with other controversies in this field, both conceptualizations are probably true. In some families, dysfunction may be acted out through the abuse of AOD. For example, an adolescent female may use drugs to cope with the emotional trauma of sexual abuse. A fairly functional family may become tumultuous as a result of the father's progressive alcoholism. Regardless of the "chicken or the egg" question, we find that the understanding of families and AOD abuse is aided through a family systems conceptualization. You should be aware that even the definition of family varies across cultures. "Family" is a traditional white Anglo-Saxon Protestant definition based on an intact nuclear family, where lineage is of importance when tracing one's ancestry. In contrast, the traditional African American family is focused on a wide, informal network of kin and community that goes beyond blood ties to include close, longtime friends. The traditional Asian American family includes the entire family group and all ancestors and all their descendants. Differences in the life cycle of the family also reflect cultural and ethnic differences. For example, Giordano and McGoldrick (2005) state that the traditional Euro-American family begins with a psychological being, and growth and development is measured by the human capacity for differentiation. In the traditional Asian American family, each member is a social being (as opposed to a psychological being), and growth and development are measured by the capacity for empathy and connection. A great deal of the research into alcoholic families has focused upon the Euro-American population. However, as we pointed out in Chapter 4, culturally and ethnically diverse families are at risk for AOD abuse. While a growing body of literature focuses on diverse family systems, there continues to be a dearth of information focusing on the effects of AOD on these family systems and structures. Notwithstanding, interesting and provocative ideas addressing this issue are appearing in the emerging professional literature. For example, Cornish, Schreier, Nadkarni, and Metzger (2010) and Krestan (2000) write about the issue of addiction as it relates to power and powerlessness in a multicultural society. In her conceptualizations, Krestan maintains the importance of the sociocultural impact of power and powerlessness as they are experienced by various racial/ethnic groups. From this perspective, family theorists and therapists can readily see how racial/ethnic family structures might be affected. For instance, African American males often learn to "play the game" to get ahead in a Euro-American dominated society. When at home, they may and often do behave very differently. Although the strategy of playing the game is successful for many, some individuals may experience distress at having such a marked split between home and work. This split tends to create an additional family structure for some racial/ethnic families. This additional structure and the concomitant stressors can increase risk factors for AOD abuse among this population.

FAMILY STRUCTURE AND DYNAMICS

According to the National Council on Alcohol and Drug Dependence (2015), more than one-half of adults living in the United States have a family history of alcoholism or some type of problem drinking. The National Institute on Alcohol Abuse and Alcoholism (2016) estimates that 76 million adults living in the United States were exposed to alcohol in their families, and 18% have lived with an alcoholic. There are about 27 million children of alcoholics (COAs) in the United States, and approximately 11 million of these individuals are younger than 18 years of age. According to Pienkowski (2014), COAs are four times more likely to develop alcohol or other drug problems and have a significantly higher risk of developing behavioral or emotional problems.

Alcohol affects an average of 4 of 10 people. This means that 92 million people in the United States are directly or indirectly affected by another person's alcoholism, and these numbers translate into one in five (24%) families being affected (Pienkowski, 2014). Because of the alarming statistics, this chapter will focus on families and children who are exposed to alcohol. We will present a brief overview of family structure and then turn our attention to a discussion of children prenatally and interpersonally exposed to alcohol and other drugs and families where alcohol is problematic. We will also provide information on special populations such as stepfamilies, military families, adolescents, and women.

Homeostasis

Regardless of ethnicity, families are dynamic systems and are influenced by changes that occur both within and outside of the family context. The larger social, political, and economic forces exert their influence in the family from the outside, while internal changes such as illness, aging, entering and leaving the family, changes occurring in the workplace, changing geographical locations, and changes in stress levels affect families from within.

Jackson (1957) first used the term *family homeostasis* to describe the natural tendency of families to behave in such a manner as to maintain a sense of balance, structure, and stability in the face of change. Significant to the concept of homeostasis is the notion that, as one family member experiences change in his or her life, the entire family will be affected and will adjust in some fashion. Family members can adjust overtly and covertly in an effort to maintain this balance and will exert much effort during times when the balance is threatened. This natural resistance can be both a blessing and a bane: by facing some changes with resistance, families can avoid losing their structures and becoming chaotic systems. However, there will inevitably be times when change requires the family to adjust (Gladding, 2011).

During these times, the family, to varying degrees, will need to reorganize its roles, rules, boundaries, and values to create a new balance that fits. If families are too resistant to change, they can become rigid and unable to adjust adequately and family dysfunction can follow. In other words, spouses can become involved in rigid behavior patterns where each controls the behavior of the other, and a result is an inability to change.

Wegscheider (1989) believes that, in an alcoholic family, members attempt to maintain balance by compulsively repressing their feelings while developing survival behaviors, as well as emotional walls, to ward off the pain associated with the family member's drinking. If drinking is removed from the family system, the family can be thrown into chaos. For example, an alcoholic father who becomes sober may attempt to reexert his influence as head of the household, thus throwing the marriage out of the balance to which it had become accustomed. The mother is no longer needed as a buffer between the children and their father, so she fades into the background as the children begin to address their father directly. The oldest son is no longer the surrogate father and begins acting out his frustration. The relationship between the mother, who has relied upon this son for support, and her son becomes strained as the father cannot hide his jealousy over this relationship. Unless the family can adjust adequately, drinking may be initiated again to reestablish balance.

Subsystems and Boundaries

All families, regardless of cultural or ethnicity diversity, are made up of subsystems and boundaries. The Euro-American family essentially consists of three family subsystems: marital, parental, and sibling. In Native American, Asian American, African American, and Latino/Hispanic families, the family subsystems would include, to varying degrees, extended family members or other significant individuals. For example, the participation of godparents in the child-rearing practices of many Latino/Hispanic families and its parallel value, known as "child-keeping," is seen in many African American families, might reflect an extended parental subsystem.

The primary subsystem is the marital or couple subsystem made up of the wife and husband. This subsystem is closed in that certain duties and primary functions are performed only by the married partners (e.g., earning money, managing the home). With the birth of a child, the marital subsystem extends to that of a parental subsystem. Interactions continue between the marital partners, which are aimed at the marriage itself (e.g., having a romantic dinner after the child is asleep) or are carried out between the spouses with an aim toward their parenting (e.g., juggling schedules to cover child care). A third main subsystem is the sibling subsystem. The number of children, along with their ages, sexes, and interests, will suggest the number of potential sibling subsystems. In addition, African American and Latino/Hispanic families may have sibling subsystems that include cousins.

Rules or boundaries help define these subsystems. Boundaries are like fences surrounding one's home: They define one's property and regulate the nature and type of interactions between neighbors. In essence, boundaries result from cultural and family values and define who can talk to whom, when one can talk, and what one can talk about. Regardless of cultural or ethnic background, both subsystems and boundaries need to be flexible enough to allow for adjustments to changes brought on either within the family or as a result of outside influences. However, in families where AOD are abused, boundaries are often violated (Kelley et al., 2007).

The issue of disengagement is clearly culturally biased. In traditional Asian American families, the father is expected to be disengaged. Therefore, the construct of disengagement would not always be an appropriate measure of family unity. An African American male who works two jobs and is not home much to help get his family out of poverty may be labeled as disengaged when, in fact, his disengagement is a healthy adaptation to poverty. Likewise, "el amor de madre" (motherly love), a value highly regarded in Latino/Hispanic families, could be described as enmeshment, but this enmeshment is central to Latino/Hispanic culture and is not seen as dysfunctional behavior.

Where AOD abuse exists, all families, regardless of cultural or ethnic background, act as "the fulcrum, the pivot point, the mediator, and the interpreter between its members and their culture" (Reilly, 1992, p. 105). The family thus is seen as having a significant influence upon the socialization of its members. As a social lens, the family screens, filters out, or magnifies social influences from the outside. These influences may be antisocial. Reilly maintains that the disturbed Euro-American family system needs a symptom bearer, and this would be the member who is susceptible to drug abuse. In our example, the symptom bearer was Mark, the eldest son. Reilly also believes that the family will consciously or unconsciously push this individual into antisocial, drug-abusing values as was reflected in our first case example.

THE MARITAL OR COUPLE SUBSYSTEM   Living with an addicted partner is demanding and difficult. Research suggests that partners affect the long-term drinking patterns of their partners most strongly in the initial phase of their relationship (Otten, van der Zwaluw, van der Vorst, & Engels, 2008). Additionally, some research suggests that heavy drinking does have deleterious effects on the drinkers' health.

McKinney, Caetano, Rodriguez, and Okoro (2010) found that the marital relationship where alcoholism exists reflects communication that is hostile, critical, and disapproving. As alcoholism progresses, the communication between spouses tends to increase in hostility, thereby suggesting a growing cycle of hostility and resentment. The cycle of hostility produces couples who are at greater risk for relationship dissolution, unless couples have similar drinking patterns. This means that couples where one drinks and the other spouse does not are more likely to dissolve the relationship than in those relationships where both drink (Ostermann, Sloan, & Taylor, 2005). Dethier, Counerotte, and Blairy (2011) found that the alcoholic's wife experiences quite a bit of stress, including verbal and physical abuse, and this eventually leads to a lowering of her self-esteem. If the relationship lasts into older adulthood, and the drinker stops drinking, research suggests that the nondrinking spouse can regain a sense of efficacy (Moos, Brennan, Schutte, & Moos, 2010).

THE PARENT–CHILD SUBSYSTEM   In a seminal study, Kaufman and Kaufman (1992) identified structural patterns in families affected by AOD abuse, based on the works of Minuchin (1974). Most of their sample was observed for more than six months, and the research design included postgroup discussions of patterns. In addition, verbatim transcripts of all sessions were made and were analyzed to confirm initial clinical impressions. Videotapes were produced and were given to a group of experienced clinicians who rated the structural patterns they observed. The sample consisted of 75 families representing eight different ethnic groups (Latino/Hispanic, 23%; Italian, 19%; Euro-American, 18%; Jewish, 13%; African American, 10%; Irish, 9%; Greek, 1%; and Mixtures, 6%). Kaufman and Kaufman found that of the 75 families, 88% had enmeshed (undifferentiated boundaries) mother–child relationships and 40% had enmeshed father–child relationships. Forty-two percent of the fathers were considered disengaged, whereas only 2% of mothers were seen as such. The mothers of addicts were seen as enmeshed across all ethnic groups. Seven of 13 Italian fathers were described as enmeshed, as were six of 13 Jewish fathers. Puerto Rican, African American, and Euro-American fathers tended to be disengaged. The authors found that, while the sample of African Americans was too small to generalize, "most of the Black families had strong, involved mothers". Categorically, no relationship between the addicted family member and other family members was seen as having clear boundaries. A more recent study of Japanese drinking in relationships found that women's care of their alcoholic husbands was institutionalized and normalized by Japanese views of human relationships that values female dependency (Borovoy, 2009). Hence, a traditional Japanese female spouse would likely be hesitant to confront her drinking husband.

In a study on family dysfunction and alcoholism, Dube, Anda, Felitti, Edwards, and Croft (2002) found interesting results. These researchers agree with the professional literature indicating the relationship between adult alcohol abuse, childhood abuse, and family dysfunction. However, Dube et al. were interested in the impact of multiple adverse childhood experiences (ACEs) with parental alcohol abuse and later alcohol abuse by the child. From their data, they categorized eight adverse childhood experiences associated with parental alcohol abuse. The results indicated a strong association between each of the eight adverse childhood experiences and risk for later alcohol abuse. When multiple ACEs were involved, it did not seem to matter whether parental alcohol abuse was involved or not. Compared with persons with no ACEs, those experiencing multiple ACEs were two to four times more likely to self-report adult alcoholism, marry an alcoholic, and be at risk for heavy drinking.

Although many studies show that dysfunctional family structure imposes a significant influence on the risk for AOD use patterns among family members (e.g., Barrett & Turner, 2006; Ledoux, Miller, Choquet, & Plant, 2002; Meness, 2000), other studies offer hope for families. Results of a systematic review of longitudinal studies on parenting factors associated with adolescent alcohol indicates that families provide strong protective factors against AOD abuse (Ryan, Jorm, & Lubman, 2010). Specifically, these authors identified protective factors that include parental modeling, limiting availability of alcohol to the child, parental monitoring, high-quality parent–child relationship, parental communication, and general parental involvement with their children.

Roles

FAMILY ROLES   We pointed out in Chapter 4 the variety of roles assumed by culturally and ethnically diverse families. Roles are an important part of Euro-American families as well. Role is often defined by the individual's behaviors in performing the rights and obligations associated with a certain position and usually involves a set of complementary expectations concerning one's own actions as well as the actions of others with whom one is involved (Gladding, 2011). Irrespective of the presence of alcohol, one of the basic principles of family homeostasis is predictable family roles. Through these roles, family members can act out the overt and covert family rules in an effort to maintain homeostasis within the family system. According to Satir (1964), because the marital relationship is the "axis around which all other family relationships are formed", it is the interaction of roles in the marital relationship that influences the character of the family homeostasis.

Roles can also be further divided into affective and instrumental areas. Instrumental roles are those aimed at addressing the day-to-day human needs. The latter, affective roles have particular significance in alcoholic or other drug-abusing families. Often in these families, certain individuals will experience and express particular emotions for the family. For example, the alcoholic who becomes angry and sullen when drunk may be carrying the anger for other family members who have difficulty in expressing this emotion. So, when the alcoholic gets angry, things may finally be said (inappropriately or not) to other family members that might not be discussed otherwise because the sober family members do not overtly express their own hostility. In this example, the anger role is carried by the alcoholic, and the emotions of sadness and helplessness may be carried and expressed by other nonalcoholic family members.

CHILDHOOD ROLES   Children in families carry two essential roles. One role is that of child; the other is the role of family member. Roles exist within roles, and the child may assume any of them. For example, many believe that birth order in the Euro-American family affects the child's role in the family and see the oldest child as taking on a dominant role with the second child taking on a more rebellious role. Youngest children are often used to having things done for them and take on a more passive role. Although birth order alone does not determine an individual's perception of relationships, it does have an influence.

These two role structures remain fairly constant across families of varying ethnic and racial origins. However, the manner in which these roles are played out in the family as well as in the larger social contexts, is different. For instance, many Latino families who immigrate to the United States may leave some of their children behind temporarily for practical and financial reasons. In these situations, the mother may tend naturally to overcompensate by showering abundant affection upon those with whom she does have contact. As a result, Latino children may appear infantilized or overprotected to Euro-American teachers and counselors when, in fact, the family's transitions and subsequent reorganization may greatly intensify these behaviors (Garcia-Preto, 2005). In more traditional families, children may also have bonded with their mothers, and the centrality of their position allows them to wield great power when it is used against a disengaged, authoritarian father (Giordano & McGoldrick, 2005). For African American youth, significant family difficulties may be brought on by the compounding effects of poverty, racism, and the general vulnerabilities of adolescence. Families in poverty will vary in structure, coping styles, and levels of resilience (Hines & Boyd-Franklin, 2005). Some families may support themselves by exchanging resources within their family support systems. Ho (1992) and other researchers maintain that in many Asian American families, the roles of family members are highly interdependent. The family structure is arranged so that conflicts in the family are minimized in order not to disrupt family peace and harmony. Even when adult children marry, allegiance to their parents—especially among the adult sons—is to remain paramount. Male offspring have especially revered roles in traditional Asian American families. Native American perceptions of family are universal in that the entire universe is thought of as a family in which every member serves a useful and necessary function. The Native American child may live in several different households at various times (Iron Eye Dudley, 1992). In these traditional Native families, grandparents, aunts, uncles, and community members are all responsible for the raising of the children. One can readily see how the roles of the child in Native American families are both stable and quite varied (Sutton & Broken Nose, 2005).

Little data exist on childhood roles among culturally and ethnically diverse populations in alcoholic or other drug abusing families. Most, although not all, of what we know about childhood roles in AOD-abusing families is the result of early clinical impressions of the Euro-American population and the research that has been reported in the popular literature (Vernig, 2011). It is clear that the roles are very difficult to operationalize, and the researchers' attempts to operationalize roles has not produced consistent results.

Nonetheless, although their clinical utility may not be as significant as previously thought, some understanding of the potential roles and dynamics that can occur in families is important. Black (1981) described the roles adopted by children of alcoholic homes as based upon their perceptions of what they need to do to survive and bring stability to their lives. It was Wegscheider (1989) who first described the dysfunctional family roles of "hero," "scapegoat," "lost child," "mascot," and "enabler." Other researchers have written about these roles since Wegscheider's initial identification.

According to Howard et al. (2010), the hero or heroine child is often a compulsive high achiever who, through accomplishments, defocuses attention from the alcoholism in the family system. Music, sports, and academics are frequent arenas in which the heroes or heroines act out their roles, often at the expense of their own needs. Because they can often excel in one or more undertakings, they create the impression that their family must be quite well-adjusted. In our own practice, we have seen many adolescents who are valedictorians, captains of sports teams, cheerleaders, and/or student government officers who come from homes where alcohol is abused.

The scapegoat child is seen as acting out the family problem by demonstrating defiance and irresponsibility. The unconscious or conscious agenda for these children is to create a need for overt parental attention as they attempt to defocus from the problem of alcohol.

Lost children are believed to be shy, withdrawn, and require very little attention so that the family does not have to worry about them. These children often cope through avoidance that, unfortunately, leaves them isolated from the joys and richness of life, feeling unloved and unworthy of love.

The family mascot is the funny and often mischievous child who defuses the tension inherent in alcoholic families. In the classroom, this child may act out as the class clown.

The enabler is the person who attempts to protect the alcoholic or drug addict from experiencing the natural and logical consequences of his or her behavior. These roles are seen as survival roles in alcoholic families and are deemed as dysfunctional or maladaptive in that they do not allow children to experience the normal, full range of emotions and behaviors.

Family Rules

All culturally and ethnically diverse families as well as Euro-American families have overt and covert contracts between their members that operate as rules governing family interactions (Gladding, 2011). In general, these rules govern (1) what, when, and how family members can communicate their experiences about what they see, hear, feel, and think; (2) who has permission to speak to whom about what; (3) the extent and manner in which a family member can be different; (4) the manner in which sexuality can be expressed; (5) what it means to be a male or female; and (6) how family members acquire self-worth and how much self-worth a member can experience. In all likelihood, culturally and ethnically diverse families are governed by these same rules. The only differences between these families revolve around what happens if the rules are broken. For example, a Euro-American family may punish the child who has talked back to his or her parents. An Asian American family might use shame to correct aberrant behavior.

CHILDREN'S EXPOSURE TO AOD

Essentially two types of AOD exposure occur for children: prenatal and interpersonal. Both types of exposure can have dramatic effects on children. Since the 1970s, concern has increased regarding the passage of drugs through the human placenta and through the mother's breast milk. The resulting research indicates that the use of tobacco, alcohol, and other drugs during pregnancy affects the fetus.

Interpersonal exposure from parental AOD use can affect a child's social and psychological development through adulthood. However, the effects on children will vary. This is due to individual and environmental differences including age of exposure, progression of use, characteristics of the child and of the AOD abuser, family dynamics, and external events. Pienkowski (2014) maintains that more than one-half of children of alcoholics do not become alcoholic. Some children will develop resilience and do not develop significant problems. Therefore, it would be unwise to assume that all children who experience AOD abuse in their families of origin will exhibit similar behaviors.

Prenatal Exposure to Alcohol and Other Drugs

Perhaps you are wondering why we include a section discussing the possible impairment resulting from prenatal substance use and abuse in a textbook providing comprehensive substance abuse information for school counselors, social workers, therapists, and counselors. The answer will probably become apparent to you as you read through the information. In the meantime, to provide a foundation for your understanding of the relationship between what is presented here and your profession(s), let's look at the many facets of prenatal exposure to alcohol and other drugs.

A few of the variables, or "layers," relative to prenatal substance use and abuse are the national attachment to partying; the desire to change how one feels, especially if those feelings are uncomfortable; easy access to and availability of legal and illegal substances regardless of age; the stigma of asking for help with AOD use/abuse, especially for pregnant women; limited long-term residential AOD treatment facilities; few treatment facilities for women; even fewer treatment facilities for women and their children; ignorance regarding this issue and ethnic/cultural considerations; the possible loss of custody of the unborn child at birth as permitted by state law; the possibility of maternal prison time; the possible loss of home and family when in treatment and/or prison; and on and on. . . . When seeking to adequately address the complexities of impairment resulting from prenatal AOD exposure, all of these variables need to be taken into consideration and addressed.

Similar to many issues in the AOD field, prenatal exposure to alcohol and other drugs can generate a great deal of public and media attention. As a result, the topic of the pregnant women's use of AOD has become emotionally charged and widely publicized, enhancing the shame already experienced. The laws governing the ingestion of substances by pregnant women are likely the biggest deterrent to this occurrence. Still, what woman wants to admit that her AOD use has impacted her helpless, unborn child? What woman wants to risk the possibility of having her child removed from her, being forced to go to residential treatment to address her AOD issues, or possibly going to prison? Nonetheless, in spite of laws aimed at protecting the fetus, the prevalence of Fetal Alcohol Spectrum Disorder (FASD) has been estimated at 9 in every 1,000 live births (May et al., 2009). However, qualitative data gathered through interviews in schools suggest that the prevalence rate may be closer to 50 per 1,000 live births (May et al., 2014).

IMPACT OF FETAL EXPOSURE TO AOD   The diagnosis of fetal alcohol syndrome (FAS) was first discovered in 1973 when David Smith and Ken Lyons Jones studied 11 newborns exposed to substantial amounts of alcohol in utero.

FASD is *not* a diagnosis; rather it is an umbrella term under which diagnoses fall. FASD diagnoses include FAS, partial fetal alcohol syndrome, alcohol-related birth defects, and/or alcohol-related neurodevelopmental disorder. You also might hear the term *prenatal alcohol exposure*, although it is not considered an FASD diagnosis; rather, it simply acknowledges in utero alcohol exposure.

We do not want to minimize the problems that can result from prenatal exposure to AOD. At the same time, we also do not want you to conclude that all children prenatally exposed will have serious and permanent learning, behavioral, social, and emotional problems. There is no known amount of alcohol that is safe to drink during a woman's pregnancy, and there is no safe time to drink nor any safe type of alcohol (Substance Abuse and Mental Health Services Administration, 2015a). Even when breastfeeding, a woman who drinks alcohol will expose the newborn to alcohol through the breastmilk. Of particular note is that Native Americans have the highest rates of fetal alcohol syndrome (Substance Abuse and Mental Health Services Administration, 2015b). Using nonqualitative data, prevalence estimates range from 1.5 to 2.5 per 1,000 live births.

Impairments vary from individual to individual and are potentially influenced by many variables. Risk factors such as polysubstance abuse, socioeconomic status, poor nutrition, lack of prenatal care, homelessness, domestic violence, maternal age and health, fetal health, and even placental health may also impact the developing fetus. Sadly, this is far from a complete list. The Affordable Care Act should help in the prevention of FASD by providing affordable insurance to female populations in general and to the poor and near-to-poor women in particular. Still, most children and adolescents with FASD will likely be involved with multiple service providers due to the impairments that can occur.

In addition to alcohol ingestion by pregnant women, children can also be affected by maternal use of methamphetamine (see discussion that follows). Fetal exposure to methamphetamine may cause premature delivery, complications during pregnancy, and low birth weight (Lester, Andreozzi, & Appiah, 2004).

NEONATAL ABSTINENCE SYNDROME   Neonatal abstinence syndrome (NAS); National Institutes of Health and Prevention, 2011b) potentially occurs when a pregnant woman ingests addictive substances, including prescription drugs, during the pregnancy. Drugs pass through the placenta and reach the developing fetus. If the mother becomes chemically dependent on the substance, the fetus does as well. If that mother continues substance use throughout the pregnancy, mother and baby are still chemically dependent on the drug at birth. If the drug dependence is unknown to those caring for mother/baby at delivery, symptoms of withdrawal may be unrecognized and medical treatment delayed.

NAS symptoms depend on the drug used, the quantity of the drug used, the period of time over which the drug was used, whether other substances were used during the pregnancy as well, and the length of time in utero (i.e., premature to full-term birth). NAS symptoms can present within 1 to 3 days after birth, or 5 to 10 days following birth. NAS symptoms are consistent with the symptoms presented by the child's mother. Treatment for the symptoms varies and is determined by medical professionals.

Interpersonal Exposure to Alcohol and Other Drug Abuse

Fraser, McAbee, and the Committee on Medical Liability (2004) maintain that between 11 and 17.5 million children in the United States younger than 18 currently live with a parent with alcoholism. The number of children living in homes where other drugs are abused is relatively unknown. However, multiple studies confirm that many children do experience negative effects as a result of being exposed to the interpersonal and environmental influences of AOD abuse in their homes (e.g., Hussong et al., 2010; Pienkowski, 2014). They also risk being exposed to child maltreatment, violence, crime, and residential disorganization (Kyzer, Conners-Burrow, & McKelvey, 2014). In addition, studies demonstrate that children who grow up in homes where AOD are abused may reflect more externalizing problems such as hyperactivity and aggression, may have low self-esteem, higher levels of depression, negative emotions, difficulties with relationships, and may feel responsible for their parents' substance abuse (Park & Schepp, 2015).

Park and Schepp (2015) did systematic review of the literature on COAs to determine their inherent risks and vulnerabilities. These researchers reviewed 39 articles from 1990 through 2011. Results indicate that although COAs tend to have lower self-esteem, are exposed to chaotic home lives, and have some genetic vulnerability, they do have some protective factors. It is interesting that the results of the literature suggested that ethnicity was not associated with either risk factors or protective factors nor was gender a consistent risk or protective factor. Given the high prevalence of alcohol exposure among the Native American populations, it would be reasonable to assume that this population had more risk factors. The authors did not find this to be validated. Finally, none of the studies examined the relationship between age of exposure to parental alcoholism and its impact on development.

While Park and Schepp's review of the literature had some interesting findings, COAs still have general feelings of alienation, which can lead children into social isolation and reinforce the child's beliefs that they are socially incompetent. A child who comes to school having slept little the night before because of anxiety or because of parental fighting or abuse cannot really be expected to perform well. As a result, the child's self-concept can be diminished by repeated failures at learning. A vicious cycle can be born. The result can be that the child feels hopeless, fearful, and lonely. In some cases, the effects can be fateful. Although the impact on children is not always severe, the possibility exists that parental drug abuse may be a significant factor in adolescent suicide attempts.

Whiteman, Bernard, and McHale (2010) report that siblings influence each other with regard to health risks, smoking, AOD use, violence, and aggressive behaviors. More to the point, though, is that sibling attitudes toward AOD use is positively correlated—meaning that an older sibling's attitude about AOD use does influence younger siblings' attitudes.

METHAMPHETAMINE   One of the more underexamined issues facing children relates to the consequences of living in a home where methamphetamine abuse or production is taking place. The increase in methamphetamine use and production has led to an increase in child abuse and homicides from child abuse (Cunningham & Finlay, 2013; Messina, Jater, Marinelli-Casey, West, & Rawson, 2014). Even though statistics are not usually kept about children in the home when methamphetamine is seized, Messina et al., (2014) reported that 1,000 children were present at the time when authorities seized methamphetamine from the home labs. The children who are present in methamphetamine homes are at a higher risk for poisoning, homicides, and accidental death from the home laboratory blowing up. In addition, these same children often experience neglect, physical or sexual abuse, and family violence as well as other consequences of living where criminal activity takes place. There are other effects, too. For example, children living in homes where there is a methamphetamine lab are also exposed to the highly toxic and psychoactive chemicals used in the production of meth. Among a host of medical and mental problems, this exposure can cause neurological issues and psychotic symptoms. Messina et al. (2014) report that the overall home environment for children living in meth homes can lead to infection and illness. The go on to say that sometimes household pets (as well as children) are neglected, which can lead to a filthy house where there are fleas, rotten food, animal feces, cockroaches, and mice. According to the National Alliance for Drug Endangered Children (2013), there is a dearth of literature evaluating the long-term effects of continuous exposure to the toxic chemicals used in making methamphetamine. Nonetheless, child development researchers assert that the combination of exposure to substances, parental abuse of drugs, child abuse, and neglect, when taken together, pose a greater threat to a child's development than any single risk factor.

FAMILY EXPOSURE TO ALCOHOL AND OTHER DRUGS

So far, we have discussed the effects of AOD misuse only on children. Substance misuse can also negatively impact other family members and disrupt a range of family dynamics and processes including family rules and rituals, routines, communication structures, social life, finances, home-ostasis, and family roles (Arcidiancono, Velleman, Procentese, Berti, Albanesi, Sommantico, & Copello, 2010; Copello, Vellemabn, & Templeton, 2005). Rhodes, Bernays, and Houmoller (2010) reviewed the literature of the impact of drug use on parenting and of the impact of parental drug use on the family functioning. These researchers concluded that drug use is "overwhelm-ingly damaging." No consistent or accurate figures that estimate the number of family members who are affected by substance misuse are available. However, in taking a global perspective, Copello, Templeton, and Powell (2010) estimate that a minimum of 91 million family members are affected across the world.

CASE EXAMPLE

Tony and His Family

In 1981, Black stated three imperatives or rules that govern alcoholic families: Don't talk; Don't trust; Don't feel. In families where alcohol and other drugs are abused, these rules form the basis for family interactions and for the alliances between individual family members and society at large.

Tony, a very successful businessman, was married to Mary, and they had three children (see the case example at the beginning of the chapter): Loretta, Mark, and Donnie, ages 16, 15, and 9. Tony was an alcoholic, but nobody in the family believed his drinking to be problematic. That was rule 1: Do not believe that your father has a drinking problem.

Every night when he arrived home after 12 hours on the job, the children would come down-stairs and greet their father, then allow him to change clothes while their mother would mix their father's usual drink: his favorite Scotch with crushed ice. She would have a glass of red wine. The children would leave their mother and father alone to discuss the day. That was rule 2: Do not dis-turb your father's ritual.

Even when the children had something exciting to talk about that had occurred during the day, they were not to disrupt the ritual until it was time for dinner. Gathered around the table, with Tony nursing his second or third drink or even a beer, the children would then "report" the day to their father. The children were not allowed to leave the table until everyone, including their Dad, was finished. Sometimes, if Tony was drinking a lot, the dinner could last an entire evening. Frustrations about wasting time at dinner were not to be discussed; however, when they were even-tually aired, out of exasperation, Tony would most often respond by becoming argumentative, oppressive, threatening, and upon occasion physically abusive. This was rule 3: Your father is the head of the household and you must do exactly as he wants.

When Tony lost his temper at the table, Mary would jump in to mediate between Tony and the children. Usually, the fighting occurred between Tony and Mark, the oldest son, so Mary usually wound up arbitrating between these two. Although they did not like the situation, Loretta and

Donnie did appreciate Mark's intervening on their behalf because it allowed dinner to be over. The shouting and threatening behavior created so much chaos that Loretta and Donnie could slip away while Mary, Tony, and Mark were fighting it out. This was rule 4: Mark is the scapegoat.

Two or three times during the week, dinners would proceed in a fashion similar to that just described. Hence, rule 5: Even when things are unpleasant and could be changed, do not change the family.

The weekends were just an extension of the weekdays, except that on the weekends Tony would play tennis in the mornings rather than spend time with the family and would begin drinking at lunchtime. Often, he would come home drunk or noticeably high from alcohol. If he had had a good game of tennis, his mood would be pleasant; if he played poorly, he was easily agitated. The children knew enough to be gone all day Saturday to avoid whatever might occur, while Mary would do household chores until Tony came home. Because Tony and Mary would usually go out on Saturday night, the children would most often find something to do until they were sure that their dad and mom were out of the house before coming home to eat the meal their mother had prepared for them. On Saturday nights, whoever was home would sit watching television with the lights out, prepared to run to their rooms and feigning sleep at the first sign of their parents' arrival home.

It was Loretta who first asked her mother about her dad's drinking. This occurred after the school counselor had done a guidance unit on alcohol and other drugs during Loretta's fifth-period social studies class. Her mother readily confessed to having similar concerns but told Loretta that her dad worked very hard and everyone should be understanding because he was under a great deal of stress. She told Loretta not to worry and to keep this information between the two of them. Rule 6: Do not talk about your feelings about your dad's drinking problem to anyone.

As Tony's drinking progressed over the next two years, Mark became the focus of his dad's displaced hostility. Mark felt as if he could do nothing right in his father's eyes, and, during his later teen years, began to express his own hostility toward his dad. However, when Mark confronted his dad about how unreasonable he was when he drank, his father would respond by yelling, pointing his finger in his son's face, and would eventually become more angry than his son. Mark learned to back down, swallowing his pride, his feelings, and his lowered sense of self-respect. Gradually, his grades began to drop. In spite of his being a very talented golfer, Mark lost his eligibility to participate in athletics because of his low grades. Having lost his friends who were busy participating in after-school sports, Mark fell into a crowd who used alcohol and other drugs, and he began drinking alcohol on the weekends and eventually began using marijuana and cocaine. Loretta continued her attempts to soothe her father's nerves by doing whatever he asked but emotionally removed herself from the family and focused her attentions on her boyfriend and her grades. She confided in Mark that she couldn't wait to get out of the house. Donnie was his mother's favorite, and Mary did everything she could to protect Donnie from her husband. Donnie was able to escape the direct wrath of his father by keeping quiet, getting straight As, and devoting himself to helping his mother.

What was most confusing to Loretta, Mark, and to some extent to Donnie was how their father could be seen as so successful at work, yet be so different at home. When their father was away on business trips and the discussion about his drinking would come up during dinner, Mary would consistently respond by saying that the children's father loved them very much so they need not worry. When pressed by Loretta and Mark, their mother would usually start crying, saying that she did not know what to do, yet she would balk at suggestions to see a counselor and/or confront their dad. Loretta and Mark would comfort their mother by telling her that she was a good mother and that she did not need to cry because her children loved her. Rule 7: Believe that your mother is helpless and that you need to take care of her.

This example shows how rules are developed and maintained by family members. Nobody was supposed to confront the alcohol problem because "there was no alcohol problem." That their father loved the children was supposed to be enough. There was to be no anger. If that rule were broken, Tony would become angrier than anyone, thereby overpowering the family's anger and sending it back into a repressed state. Eventually the children, especially Loretta and Mark, learned to control their emotions—especially anger, hurt, and fear. The rigidity of the rule "don't talk, don't trust, don't feel" led to Loretta's desire to leave the family and to never confront her father, so that her father never knew how she really felt. Mark responded to his feelings of help-lessness and frustration by internalizing his shame and coming to believe that he was to blame for his father's drinking because he was usually the one who fought with his dad. As a result of his internalized shame, he began using drugs and acted out his helplessness by becoming irresponsi-ble, thus neglecting his own desires and hopes in life. Donnie eventually became the family "hero" by getting exceptional grades and becoming involved in student government. He posed "no threat and no problem" to the family. Mary worked herself to the bone as a mediator between her chil-dren and their father, all the while attempting to become the apple of her husband's eye. Her whole life was her family, and the centrality of her position provided her with a sense of meaning in an otherwise unhappy marital situation. Because these family rules were rigid, the family sys-tem functioned to maintain itself as best it could, but there were grave consequences. In spite of the severity of the consequences, the family was unable to adjust until Tony's alcohol problem was addressed and the rules changed.

Our example of Tony and Mary reflects a disengaged family in which Tony is rather removed from his spouse and his children. The children are not allowed to talk with their father about his drinking problem and so begin to disengage and live their lives emotionally distant from other fam-ily members. With the onset of Mark's drug use, the disengaged nature of the family makes it very difficult to regroup to address the underlying issue that was Tony's alcohol abuse. Nor is the family able to find ways to deal effectively with Mark's drug use. To avoid interacting with her father, Loretta spends all of her available time with her boyfriend. Donnie, despite his strong feelings for his older brother, remains rather aloof from him because he doesn't understand or like what his brother is doing. Mary, the mother, is emotionally removed from her husband after years of emo-tional neglect by him. She tolerates her husband's drinking patterns so that she can avoid conflict and more hurt and pain in their relationship.

NONTRADITIONAL FAMILIES AND SPECIAL POPULATIONS

STEPFAMILIES   Adults living in the United States are marrying later than at any time, and most of these adults (66%) have cohabitated (Manning, 2013; Manning, Brown, & Payne, 2014). At the same time, Copen, Daniels, Vespa, and Mosher (2012) report that the rate of divorces (per 1,000 total U.S. population) has fallen from 8.2 in 2000 to 6.8 in 2009. Nonetheless, this still confirms that since the 1980s, at least 50% of marriages, many with children, end in divorce (Jay, Freisthler, & Svare, 2004). These statistics coincide with Kreider and Ellis (2011) and Kreider and Lofquist (2014), who report that 8% of all children living in the United States lived with a stepparent in 2009. King, Boyd, and Thorsen (2015) maintain that today's children have an increased likelihood of spending part of their childhood in a stepfamily structure, and Amato (2010) sees these children as having lower well-being—similar to children raised in single-parent households, when compared with children who are raised with two biological parents.

Research has been conducted on the dynamics of other forms of parenting related to AOD. So, when discussing the research on traditionally defined stepfamilies, it is important to consider those observations in a more general way when applying the findings to racial/ethnic groups and gay and lesbian couples (see Chapter 4). Some issues may be the same for these groups as for the Euro-Caucasian population, and some issues may be different or more complex. For instance, think of how different and complex it might be for a stepfamily to learn that one of their new members is gay. This new family would not only be dealing with the adjustments of a new formation, but they would concurrently be dealing with the "coming out" of one (or more) of its members. The stepparent may be drawn into the disciplinarian role if the biological parent has been ineffective in dealing with AOD issues, and this move can result in marital strife if the biological parent steps in to protect the adolescent. Such a situation certainly reinforces the biological parent–child coalition, while continuing to exacerbate the child's feelings of guilt and stress (Jay et al., 2004). This dynamic can also lead to acting out with substance abuse.

Stepfamilies are different in terms of the family developmental tasks. In general, stepfamilies are seen as having psychic and physical boundaries that are more permeable than those in a nuclear family (Anderson, 1992). Emotional bonds or psychic boundaries have to be loose enough to allow for affections to be expressed to both the biological parent as well as to the stepparent. The physical boundaries need to be permeable enough to allow for the revolving door of noncustodial visitation and need to be able to allow for visits of a longer duration, such as coming or leaving for an entire school year. Anderson also identifies the complexities involved in decision making in stepfamilies. Often, a coordinated effort of two households in making plans is required. The stepfamily does not have the history that the nuclear family does, and sometimes children (and their parents) can experience a type of culture shock. Anderson says that this culture shock is "an acute feeling of an unfamiliar, sometimes alien, environment that is very disorienting to their basic sense of what 'my family' is" (p. 174). Because stepfamilies are born out of previous losses resulting from divorce or death, children (and parents) need to be able to grieve the loss adequately. However, grieving the loss is often painful, and many may be reluctant to do so when it appears that the grieving process may impinge upon the happier times of the current relationship.

Although stepfamilies have a host of issues, many factors can produce resilience in these families. For example, Greeff and Du Toit (2009) identified eight factors that can help insulate stepfamilies from problems, including those concerning AOD use and abuse. These factors include, among other things, the strength of supportive family and friend relationships, frequency and nature of supportive communication, the extent to which stepfamilies spend time together and involve themselves in family activities, the presence of spirituality or religious practices, and the ability of stepfamilies to reframe stressful events.

ADOPTIVE FAMILIES The U.S. Census Bureau (2010) reports that 2% to 4% of the American population is adopted. However, for many reasons, this estimation is likely spuriously low because of the manner in which adult adoptees were counted in the census. Each adoption may affect up to 30 individual family members (Sass & Henderson, 2007). Palacios and Brodzinski (2010) maintain that up to 15% of individuals in residential treatment centers or inpatient psychiatric facilities are adopted, and that this population tends to seek mental health services at a significantly higher rate than the nonadoptee population (Weir & Brodzinski, 2013). Weir and Brodzinski (2013) also believe that adopted stepchildren are at risk for having significantly more behavior and emotional issues than children with two biological parents and at higher risk for substance abuse problems—and this is true regardless of the age of the adoptee.

Carlson, Williams, and Shafer (2012) see parental substance abuse as a major factor in children being placed in the child-care system, and the circumstance surrounding the placement into child-care can increase the risk of prenatal exposure or interpersonal exposure to alcohol and other drugs. Given the discussion about methamphetamine and children previously, it is relatively easy to see how children who are in homes where methamphetamine is used and/or produced are at risk of being taken out of their homes and placed in foster care, which then may lead to adoption. The most vulnerable subgroup of this population is that of children who experience extensive stays in foster care before being in a permanent placement. The problem is that parental substance abuse often inhibits placement and decreases the likelihood of reunification (Akin, Brook, & Lloyd, 2015; Courtney & Hook, 2012). A significant issue related to adoptees and their families is that mental health professionals are not trained adequately to deal with adoption. In fact, Weir and Brodzinski (2013) have demonstrated that there is a significant dearth of graduate training in adoption issues. Given the significant body of research showing that adoptees are at high risk for psychopathology—especially conduct disorders—that has a high correlation with substance abuse, the lack of training of mental health professionals is alarming.

SAME-SEX FAMILIES   Because many adoptees often move through the child-care system, you can see how nontraditional family structures like same-sex families can be involved in adoption. In fact, the rates of adoption among the population of gay men and lesbian women who form same-sex families has essentially doubled (Lavner, Waterman, & Peplau, 2014) These researchers claim that that there are roughly 2 million lesbian, gay, and bisexual individuals who are interested in adoption in spite of, and perhaps because of, the legal challenges and lack of support from the child welfare system. These are only some of the challenges faced by tens of thousands of children who are awaiting adoption in the child welfare system. The children who are awaiting adoption in the system will likely have already faced numerous biological and environmental risk factors such as prenatal substance abuse, prematurity, a history of abuse and neglect, and numerous placements, all of which impact their psychological well-being. McKay, Ross, and Goldberg (2010) say that depression among adoptive parents is common.

Although there have been major advances in studying same-sex families, the research on the experiences of adoptive parents as they transition to parenthood is almost nonexistent (McKay et al., 2010). In addition, there is very little research on the impact of AOD use on children from same-sex families. Although, the research does depict studies going beyond white middle-class reflections of lesbian couples to include research on bisexuality, sexual fluidity, and transgender people, new research needs to focus on AOD use among these nontraditional families. As it stands, most of the research involves gay men and lesbians in the GLBTQI population (see Chapter 4) who are at higher risk for substance abuse. However, one study did look at alcohol use among same-sex and different-sex unions (Reczek, Liu, & Spiker, 2014). Using data from National Health Interview Surveys 1997–2011, these researchers found that cohabitation was a factor that distinguished alcohol rates. In other words, same-sex and different-sex married couples reported lower alcohol use than their cohabiting counterparts. Within-group differences were not noted, which means that the individuals within married and cohabiting structures were more similar than different within their own groups regarding alcohol use.

MILITARY FAMILIES   Since 2003, more than 2 million service members have been deployed to Operation Enduring Freedom, Operation Iraqi Freedom, and Operation New Dawn, and close to one-half of these service members have been deployed multiple times (Seigel & Davis, 2013). Approximately 1.9 million children have at least one parent serving active duty in the military, and more than 700,000 children have experienced at least one deployment by a parent since 2001 (Sories, Maier, Beer, & Thomas, 2015). These same authors assert that these numbers actually reflect 2.7 million families who have experienced at least one separation from military family members.

Studies show that child maltreatment and neglect rise during the times of deployment (Sheppard, Malatras, & Israel, 2010), and nearly one-fourth of children aged 11 through 16 have emotional and behavioral symptoms associated with parental deployment. Even though parents may attempt to minimize the disruption for children, the impact of these attempts pales in comparison to the impact that loss and separation have on children and families of military personnel (Hollingsworth, 2011). Additionally, a study by O'Brien, Oster, and Morden (2013) reveals that veterans' substance use, excessive use, misuse, and the resulting associated problems can lead to substance use disorders as well as other mental disorders such as posttraumatic stress disorder (PTSD) and depression. Sheppard et al. (2010) showed that heavy alcohol consumption was very common among personnel regardless of drinking patterns prior to entering the military. This means that even those who did not drink heavily before entering the military could begin to drink heavily once they enlisted.

Returning service members who experience PTSD may find it difficult to reintegrate with the family. Typical household interactions such as children playing and arguing may become relatively intolerable. Ironically, and sadly, the military member who once may have been the rock of the family can return from active duty as the alarming and scary adult for children. For this reason, it is not surprising to entertain the results of studies who say that children of deployed parents face school performance problems and sleep disturbances. If these children happen to be adolescents who are going through their own preadulthood transitions, problems may escalate and involve AOD issues.

ADOLESCENTS   As discussed, the disruptions in family structures caused by separation and divorce, methamphetamine use and production, foster care, adoption, and military deployment can be significant. If one considers the period of adolescence and adolescent development that occurs in these families, it is clear that families who may or may not have alcohol and AOD use would be further stressed. This concern is augmented by reports that of U.S. adolescents 33% report lifetime use of alcohol, 19% report lifetime use of cigarettes, and 16% report lifetime use of cannabis (Waldron et al., 2014a).

The risks of parental separation and divorce to children's early AOD use has not been thoroughly examined (Waldron et al., 2014b). Nonetheless, parental separation or divorce and parental history of alcoholism are among the two highest risk factors. Weichold, Wiesner, and Silbereisen (2014) found that high parental use of alcohol coupled with low educational attainment and adolescent conduct issues at school were common predictors of problematic alcohol use among male and female adolescents. What may surprise you is what Longest and Shanahan (2007) found: Adolescents who work would seem to have employment as a protective factor. The researchers' results showed that high school students who work are actually at risk for higher rates of use of alcohol and marijuana due to the exposure of use by other workers.

Although there is a plethora of research regarding the AOD use of adolescents, there is not a great deal of understanding about AOD use rates for different racial/ethnic groups. (D'Amico, Tucker, Shih, & Miles, 2014). D'Amico et al. raise concerns about why non-whites often have worse health outcomes than their white counterparts. One study aimed at predicting substance use in African American adolescence found weak correlations between parental alcoholism and parental separation as factors that could predict adolescent involvement (Waldron et al., 2014b).

These authors claim that this sample of African American families was "poorly matched" on the risk factors presumed to predate parental separation (see previous discussion) and call for more research with this population. Madara, Rogers, and Zinbarg (2011) studied the relationship between family structure and marijuana use throughout adolescence in an attempt to assess the impact of poverty, quality of neighborhood, and self-control among adolescents' marijuana use. Looking at 1,069 African American adolescents, these researchers found that similar to other research, adolescent women's use was not related to family structure. The same was not found to be true for adolescent males. If an adolescent male's mother never married, divorced early on in the marriage and did not remarry, or divorced and remarried, the adolescent was at higher risk for marijuana use. This risk was also found to be true if the African American male adolescent's father was absent.

Because of the increase in opportunities to gamble, there is concern regarding the co-occurrence of AOD use and gambling among adolescents (Yücel et al., 2015). AOD use among adolescents is also influenced by their gambling practices so that they are at higher risk than the normal population to develop problems (Bray et al., 2014). In a review of the literature of articles related to gambling, tobacco, alcohol, and illicit drug use among U.S. adolescents from 2000 through 2014, Peters et al. (2015) cited a number of methodological problems with the literature on adolescent gambling and associations with AOD use. However, they still maintain that regardless of the problems, the literature does indeed underscore the associations between gambling and AOD use among adolescence (see Gambling).

Siblings do appear to have an influence on adolescent drug use in terms of providing the drug and/or modeling drug behaviors (e.g., Friese et al., 2011; Slomkowski et al., 2009). In a seminal study, Kaufman and Kaufman (1992) studied the impact of siblings upon sibling drug use. In their study, the researchers identified an *environmental reactive mechanism,* which refers to the ways in which brothers are linked through their environment. That is, when the relationship between brothers is characterized by tension, there appears to be an increase in the intrapsychic distress in the younger brother. As a result of that distress, the younger brother may disengage from the relationship and withdraw from responsibility. In the case study example, Donnie's distancing from his brother exemplified the environmental reactive mechanism.

Not much research on the unique experiences of being a sibling of a "user" has been conducted. However, some general themes emerge: efforts aimed at trying to stand out, trying to step back, feelings of anger, hurt, resentment, guilt, compassion, love, frustration, hope, loss, and numerous others (Howard et al., 2010). Sibling violence is often underreported. However, an important finding is that sibling relationships characterized by violence are associated with substance abuse, delinquency, and aggression (Button & Gealt, 2010).

WOMEN AND ALCOHOLISM

Major depression and alcohol abuse are common among women (Gamble et al., 2012). Although alcohol dependency in women is a major problem (Kovač et al., 2014), it has been noted that the gap between men's (57.4% aged 12 or older) and women's (46.5% aged 12 or older) alcohol use is diminishing (Wilsnack, Wilsnack, & Kantor, 2013). Nonetheless, in spite of this news, women who drink heavily have an increased probability of having symptoms associated with depression, PTSD, eating disorders, suicidality, and may have increased risks of being sexually assaulted and/or experience partner violence (Wilsnack et al., 2014). These occur across ethnicities. For example, Conner, LeFauve, and Wallace (2009) reviewed the literature on addictions among diverse women. They found that African American substance abuse was a way to numb painful feelings of loss, racism, prejudice, rejection, physical abuse, incest, and feelings of shame. Another finding was that educated, employed, and/or acculturated Hispanic women faced higher risks for addiction. These authors go on to say that, in general, the psychological fallout from historical trauma, powerlessness, marginalization, gender socialization, violence, and victimizations contribute significantly to addictions in women.

Even though drinking declines in both male and female populations as each ages, there are issues for women across the life span. Kovač et al. (2014) assert that alcohol dependence in women varies by age so that risk factors for younger aged adolescent women are different than those risk factors facing older women. Younger women who have behavioral problems, issues at school, and a family history of alcoholism are at higher risk than the normal population, and older women who face retirement and widowhood have these as risk factors. Other within-group differences are advanced by Krentzman and McClellan (2011), who purport that differences between women gravitate around racial identity and class status, sexual identity and orientation, marital status, as well as pregnancy, maternity, ages, and health issues. Krentzman and McClellan (2011) also report evidence that light-to-moderate drinking may reduce risk of some cardiovascular problems and strokes in women. Yet, low levels of drinking can increase risk for breast cancer, liver problems, hypertension, and bone fractures. In general, Thurang and Tops (2013) found that women who suffer from alcohol dependency have a diurnal existence marked by feelings of alienation and self-degradation and diminished feelings of hopefulness and meaninglessness.

Assessment of Problems in Women

Some global initiatives are aimed at improving the primary care of the 2.5 million women meeting the criteria for alcohol use disorder. Nevertheless, many women with serious problems are not seen, are misunderstood, misdiagnosed, or ignored (McClellan, 2011; Vandermause & Wood, 2009). The complicated presentation of symptoms is only one factor that influences the lower rate of diagnosing alcoholism in women. Women need to seek help before a diagnosis can be rendered, and research suggests that women with alcohol problems have a difficult time coming in for help. This difficulty may be due to the stigma of alcoholism and/or the associated feelings of shame. For example, Corrigan, Miller, and Watson (2006) found that the stigma of "drug dependence" was viewed as more negative than the stigma for "other mental disorders."

Even when women present for help at a physician's office, research indicates many more women than men deny that they have a drinking problem or that they identify problems other than drinking (Chang, 2002). The fact that their situations may be more medically complicated when they do seek help increases the likelihood that other conditions will be identified by the patient as problematic. In many cases, a diagnosis of depression will precede or be concurrent with a diagnosis of substance abuse (Ambrogne, 2007; Gamble et al., 2012). This makes a diagnosis of alcoholism more difficult. A confounding result can be a diagnosis for one disorder and a misdiagnosis for another. Hence, physicians can be prescribing medications for one disorder that obscures the symptoms of the other (van der Walde, Urgensen, Weltz, & Hanna, 2002).

However, a more insidious factor may be the stereotyping of the disease of alcoholism itself. Conner et al. (2009) and Cyr and McGarry (2002) maintain that a major reason for not diagnosing women with alcohol problems is that alcoholism has been seen as a male disease based on male characteristics (McClellan, 2011). In essence, the cultural discourse has not overtly posited a connection between alcoholism and being female, and the myths that have resulted are hard to dispel. Cho and Crittenden (2006) have identified three major streams of research in the professional literature. Some research suggests that women drink more alcohol because of the multiple roles and conflicting expectations they experience when they enter the workforce. In opposition to this perspective is a second line of research holding that performing multiple roles is gratifying to women, which would preclude an increased need for drinking. A third line of inquiry is that working women simply drink more because they have more opportunity. The preceding discussion clearly points to the need for early screening of alcohol problems in women. Both Hughes (2011) and Conner et al. (2009) believe that it is a categorical imperative that counselors understand the values and cultural expectations of diverse women when assessing for addictions. McClellan (2011) believes that counselors must ask themselves such questions as: (1) What are the historical contributions to the shaming and destructive behaviors of diverse women? (2) Does the exploration of family histories (ethnic, cultural, familial) help build resilience or heighten risk among these women? and (3) What are the culturally appropriate guidelines for prevention and treatment of diverse women?

As discussed in Chapter 6, the CAGE is an effective screening instrument that is easy to administer and score. Dhalla and Kopec (2007) maintain that the CAGE is less reliable for white women, prenatal women, and college students. What is important to note is that when used to screen women, the scoring on the CAGE can be adjusted. The CAGE has a cutoff score of 2. This indicates a positive for alcohol disorders in both men and women. In applying this for women, Bradley, Boyd-Wickizer, Powell, and Burman (1998) believe that a cutoff score of 1 point may be indicative of a problem. In addition, Bradley et al. found in their study of brief alcohol screening instruments that the CAGE was relatively insensitive for racial/ethnic minorities. The National Institute on Alcohol Abuse and Alcoholism (2007) recommends that the threshold for a positive Alcohol Use Disorders Identification Test Consumption (AUDIT-C) for women be lowered to 4 (from the standard point of 8). In all cases, these various screening instruments should be used along with other measures because their performance as stand-alone assessments is unclear (Burns, Gray, & Smith, 2010).

Treatment Concerns for Women

Kuhn (2011) asserts that even though men drink more than women at one sitting, they are more likely to drink to excess than women. In addition, men are less likely to be defined as alcoholic. At the same time, though, they are more likely to succeed in treatment.

Clearly, the best treatment for AOD problems is primary prevention. Dethier et al. (2011), Cadiz et al. (2004), and Schuck and Spatz (2003) suggest that efforts to increase women's sense of self-efficacy is also an important protective factors in reducing the risk for alcohol use problems. They assert that this is especially true for women who have been abused or neglected. These same researchers found that high self-efficacy was significantly associated with lower levels of alcohol symptoms among women who were abused or neglected. They suggest that interventions can be aimed at showing the importance of improving educational achievement and increased feelings of self-efficacy. Schuck and Spatz believe that this can potentially be very powerful in enhancing protective factors for these women.

Women are still underrepresented in most substance abuse treatment programs. Multiple research studies have focused on the barriers that women, especially rural women, face (e.g., Greenfield & Grella, 2009; Kim, Xiang, Yang, & Lewis, 2010; Small, Curran, & Booth, 2010; Taylor, 2010). Among the barriers are social stigma, denial, fear of losing children, and a reluctance of primary care physicians to refer. Although researchers maintain that once in treatment, males and females receive similar benefits, many women who abuse alcohol have a history of sexual and physical abuse and are hesitant to come in to work through issues for fear that the environment will not be safe and gender-sensitive. In addition, women are often very concerned about their children and will not present themselves for treatment because of a lack of child care. Once there, these women may drop out of treatment when a problem arises with their children. In addition, economic concerns are seen as potentially significant barriers to treatment (van der Walde et al., 2002). Men will often divorce their alcoholic wives. This can leave a woman with few financial resources. Women who experience divorce are often left with inadequate insurance coverage, and if the alcoholic and divorced woman is unemployed, she is more likely to be uninsured (Blume, 1997). Even though studies show that insurance status is not a consistent predictor for who seeks treatment

(Kim et al., 2010; Mojtabai, 2005), the fear of being left alone and destitute through divorce or legal separation while in treatment can preclude women from wanting to get treatment. Finally, cultural and linguistic gaps in communication, lack of familiarity with the treatment community, and concerns about discrimination and/or stigma can be a significant deterrent for diverse women seeking treatment (Taylor, 2010).

Nonetheless, a growing body of research supports gender-specific treatment for women abusing alcohol in a variety of settings (Greenfield & Grella, 2009; Sideman & Kirschbaum, 2002). In general, helpers who understand, use empathy, invoke good communication skills, and are gender-sensitive and initially less problem-focused are seen as more helpful. Regarding gender-specific treatment, Thurang and Tops (2013) recommend that mental health professionals should work toward well-being by exploring women's inner thoughts and help them adjust to living a life based on women's abilities and wishes. Ullman, Najdowski, and Adams (2012) caution mental health providers about potential gender differences in Alcoholics Anonymous (AA; also see Chapter 11). To date, studies show either no gender differences in AA or that women fare better because they are more involved in the program. These same researchers suggest that more studies should focus on diverse women in AA and include those who are court-ordered, those who have mental health problems, and those who have a history of being sexually abused or have a history of family violence.

Now that there is the Affordable Care Act, more minority women will likely be seeking service for alcohol problems. Hughes (2011) believes that treatment centers and those providing individual treatments to diverse women should be responsible for learning about their client's culture. This is particularly important given that Hughes found no evidence-based practice guidelines for minority status clients to aid alcohol treatment providers. Even though there continues to be a debate about gender-specific treatment, Hughes believes that women can indeed benefit from gender-specific treatment based on differences between them and males on substance use histories, victimization, sexual assault, and gender-role expectations.

HELPING FAMILIES

Underlying Family Themes

Reilly (1992) identifies two underlying themes that serve to fuel the interactive patterns of families experiencing drug abuse: impaired mourning and homeostasis collusion. Impaired mourning refers to the family's preoccupation with "issues of attachment and separation, loss and restoration, and death and rebirth". Because of the strong sense of loss, either through abandonment, death, divorce, rejection, or neglect, concomitant with an inability to transform the experience, children never fully grieve the loss, and the family can become stuck. In the example, Tony's drinking problem precluded his ability to develop a strong attachment to his family. The ensuing abandonment left his children and his wife grieving for a relationship with him. The rules were such that any attempt to work through the grieving process would have been met with severe opposition from Tony. So the children and their mother were left to deal with the problem either indirectly or surreptitiously. As a result, the family was not able to fully grieve the loss of a functional and healthy relationship with their father husband.

Remember how, in Chapter 4, we discussed the issue of Native American mourning and its impact on the risk factors for AOD abuse among this population? Knowing that impaired mourning seems to be characteristic of alcoholic families in general, you can readily see how the issue of impaired mourning may have an additive effect with regard to the Native American family. That is, mourning for their lost culture has been cited as increasing the risk among Native Americans for substance abuse (Young, 1992), and impaired mourning is seen as fueling the dysfunctional interactive patterns among families once AOD are abused in the family. It would seem that mourning, in some form, can be seen as both partly causing alcoholism and helping to maintain the resulting dysfunctional family patterns in the Native American population.

When the whole family becomes stuck or unable to transform itself because of its following the "don't talk, don't trust, don't feel" rule, as it did in this case example, family collusion can occur (Haley, 1973; Noone & Reddig, 1976). Paul (1967) points out that families who have not grieved the losses in the early cycles of their system develop a family style that reflects a lack of empathy, a lack of respect for individuality, and a tenacious and unconscious attempt to hold back the passage of time, with the concomitant need to keep individual family members in a dependent position.

In the example, Mark turned to using AOD as a means to identify with his father. Eventually, Mark's problem became the focus of attention for the family, thereby diminishing the centrality of Tony's drinking. Mark gained much power in the family because he became a rallying point around which the family could address issues of his drug abuse. Without that rallying point, Mary might have chosen to leave the marriage. She stayed to help the family deal with Mark's problems. Also, the family colluded and remained stuck because they covertly reinforced Mark's drug problems. Loretta would occasionally buy marijuana for her brother and often bought him beer until he became of legal age. When she periodically found drug paraphernalia in her son's room, Mary chose to not confront Mark. And Donnie remained distant from his older brother, although he loved him deeply. Although these were all conscious decisions, the family members unconsciously knew that, if Mark's problems were addressed and corrected, Tony's alcohol problems would once again become the focal point of concern as well as reminding each of their shame, grief, and helplessness. To avoid the pain, the family unconsciously colluded to keep Mark the scapegoat and the family member with the problem.

Clearly, the character and extent of family collusion in culturally and ethnically diverse families will be influenced by family values, by values regarding AOD, and by the degree of acculturation among family members. The collusion transpiring in Latino/Hispanic, African American, and Asian American families could include extended family members who likely live nearby and who probably share in child rearing, discipline, and problem solving. Gallardo and Curry (2009) found that "escapist drinking" of alcohol is an accepted way of dealing with the stresses of acculturation for Latino/Hispanic males, and that the value of *machismo* tends to strengthen that notion. In this example, should the alcoholic family member be a less acculturated male, then family collusion might include the male members of the immediate and extended family who share a common value of machismo. The resulting collusion might serve to sharpen the differences between male and female family members as well as exacerbate the generic difficulties found in the process of acculturation.

Fischer, Pidcock, Munsch, and Forthun (2005) believe that the concepts of "hero" or "lost child" are easily recognized by families and are effective to use with some families in treatment. However, in discussing the process of differentiation in families, they caution against limiting the child's roles only to those roles. Interventions should expand the choices for children while honoring the role(s) that they have taken on for the family. They go further to state that when enhancing the positive roles, helpers should not do it by exaggerating the differences between siblings on the negative roles. It is critical that as helpers work through roles they do not substitute one sibling for another. In other words, in the process of helping one work through the scapegoat role, helpers should be cautioned against the possibility of another sibling taking on that role. Finally, these researchers say that in identifying positive forms of differentiation, helpers should work through a perspective of difference rather than labeling one role as better or worse than another.

SPIRITUALITY   The treatment of families is usually aimed at enhancing the cognitive, physical, emotional, social development, and religion/spirituality of individual family members (Haber, Grant, Jacob, Koenig, & Heath, 2011). Pargament (2006) maintains that spirituality involves profound changes across development of individuals and families. Spirituality is different from religiosity in that the former emphasizes a relationship between an individual and a higher power or some other transcendent force, whereas religiosity refers more to religious practices and beliefs. The spiritual development in families reflects individuals attempting to differentiate themselves within families as they attempt to reconcile the dialectical tension of autonomy and connectedness. This means that individual family members are both autonomous individuals and connected members of a family. The process of differentiation increases autonomy and intimacy potential while decreasing emotional reactivity and enmeshment among family members.

Spirituality helps many families cope and be resilient. For instance, the spirituality for African American families is seen as providing buffers against the effects of structural oppression while promoting the values of compassion and service to others (Neff, 2008). In Chapter 4, we discussed the value of the collective or communalism among African Americans. This interpersonal orientation is a core spiritual value, and it is also a key component in treatment of this group for substance abuse disorders. This means that treatment should involve family, friends, church, and others because it is through others that individuals make meaning of their own existence.

In general, families who share common beliefs and who are intrinsically motivated by religious/spiritual orientation report more relationship satisfaction than those whose partners are divided on the issue. Spirituality in families can be especially helpful during times of crisis or dramatic change because it allows families to ground their stress.

To help address the spiritual issues in families, treatment often involves spiritual aspects of recovery. This orientation is clearly embedded in the Twelve Step programs (see Chapter 11). However, various spiritual interventions for substance abuse treatment are available, and these vary across diverse groups. Stoltzfus (2007) found several spiritual interventions that are used in substance abuse treatment. The Native American *sweat lodge ceremonies* use steam and high temperatures in a round, womblike structure. This process is a spiritual one in which people rid themselves of infections and contaminants while helping them contact the sacred substances that include stones, water, and the earth. *Mindfulness meditation* is another spiritual intervention that involves developing an ability to be both focused and detached while being nonjudgmental and self-accepting. *Religious treatment* programs, usually associated with evangelical churches, include such programs as Teen Challenge, Celebrate Recovery, and the Salvation Army Adult Rehabilitation Centers. *Prayer, shamanism, and exorcism* are other spiritual interventions used by diverse groups to treat substance abuse.

Because of the nature of these various spiritual treatments for AOD abuse, it is difficult to study their effectiveness. They do not easily lend themselves to scientific inquiry. A main reason is that spirituality itself is a concept, an awareness, and way of being. It cannot be separated from the rest of an individual's life because it is pervasive and incorporates all aspects of one's being. Nonetheless, its presence and power cannot be disputed, and it is wise for helpers to respect all forms of spiritual perspectives used in treating those with substance abuse issues. For instance, Hodge and Lietz (2014) report that Cognitive Behavioral Therapy (CBT) when infused with a spiritual component may be more effective than CBT without a spiritual component. CBT with spirituality can identify sources of social support, coping mechanisms, and spiritual motivation.

RECOVERY AND REINTEGRATION IN THE FAMILY   In general, the impact of AOD treatment can have a positive effect on participants—especially if the family is participating in some form or another. Families develop rules, roles, and dynamics, and those families where AOD use occurs operate both similarly to and different from non–substance-abusing families. Children and adolescents are vulnerable populations in homes where there is meth, alcohol, or some other type of drug activity. Clearly, substance abuse treatment will have a profound effect upon the dynamics of families and family members, and it is important to acknowledge that the battle is not over once the person leaves treatment. Ewing, Osilla, Pedersen, Hunter, Miles, & D'Amico (2015) believe that treatments involving adolescents should be tailored to include the adolescent's family members and should address the support needed by parents who use AOD. However, for those whose family is not directly involved in treatment, reintegration back into one's family while recovering is another process.

We already noted the host of problems for children living in alcoholic and other substance abusing homes. In reviewing the changes in children's living situations before and after a mother's substance abuse treatment, Kyzer, Conners-Burrow, and McKelvey (2014) found that those women who graduated from treatment programs were 2.5 times more likely to have at least one child living with them and, in general, found that homes and neighborhoods were relatively safe environments for children once the mother returns. Kelly, Bravo, Braitman, Lawless, and Lawrence (2016) studied 61 couples for the risk for child abuse after Behavioral Couples Therapy. Both parents who resided with one or more school-age children completed pretreatment, postintervention, and another follow-up 6 months later. Findings suggest that relationship satisfaction, as opposed to number of sessions attended, was found to lower the risk of child abuse for mothers.

Social support networks are also helpful in recovery and reintegration. Women's social support network is often underutilized when women enter treatment (Tracy et al., 2016), and a social support network is important in the recovery (Mendelson, Dariotis, & Agus, 2013). In the support network, women benefit more if they have included individuals who are not using alcohol or other drugs (Tracy et al., 2016).

Emerging adulthood, the period between ages 18 and 29, is the time when the highest prevalence of substance use occurs (Substance Abuse and Mental Health Services Administration, 2014). Studies have consistently shown this period of emerging adulthood reflects the highest daily use, binge drinking, and drunkenness, fighting and risky behaviors, academic problems, and mortality (Smith, Davis, Ureche, & Dumas, 2016). At the same time, individuals in this age range usually see close peers being more significant to them than do older adults while tending to reduce their interactions with parents. Smith et al. found that a peer-enhanced Community Reinforcement Approach was effective in increasing the number of days abstinent and reducing in binge drinking for clients and peers who were trained to provide social support.

Barón's Integrative Cross-Cultural Model

In discussing addiction treatment for Mexican Americans, Barón (2000) builds on the multidimensional perspectives of several researchers and presents a model aimed at helping therapists integrate the complex individual, family, and culturally related variables that underlie and color the various beliefs, cognitions, and adaptive as well as maladaptive behaviors (p. 227). When used in assessment, this model is thought to constitute a comprehensive assessment of the internal and external influences affecting racial/ethnic minorities. The concepts still guide other culturally sensitive models such as multidimensional family therapy (Liddle, 2010).

The integrative cross-cultural model (ICM) draws from the earlier works of Jones (1985), who conducted research on African Americans. Jones's earlier model identifies four sets of interactive factors that need to be considered with minority clients and their families: (1) personal experiences and endowments, (2) influence of native culture, (3) reactions to racial oppression, and (4) influence of the majority culture (Barón, 2000; Jones, 1985). The more recent ICM enhances the earlier approach by expanding these interactive factors and reorienting them as general *domains of inquiry.* These domains of inquiry include (1) individual and systemic variables and dynamics, (2) cultural and ethnically related variables, (3) dominant group influences, and (4) minority group experiences.

Individual and systemic variables and dynamics incorporate neurobiological conditions, developmental issues, family-of-origin dynamics, childhood experiences, education, and the like. Specific to AOD issues, clients and/or their families might be queried about use, frequency, presence, tolerance and withdrawal symptoms, alcoholic family dynamics, and the centrality of AOD in the client's life. Regarding *culturally and ethnically related variables,* clinicians would likely assess the culturally based beliefs regarding AOD use and the beliefs surrounding being clean and sober. Clinicians would also find it important to assess differences in help-seeking behavior, family organization, family life cycle, hierarchies, gender roles, parenting styles, subsystems, and other related variables. The *dominant group influences* describe the extent to which the individual or family incorporates beliefs, values, attitudes, and patterns of behavior reflecting the dominant discourse. According to Barón, an assessment aimed at AOD abuse would focus on differences and similarities between the client's views of use, misuse, and abuse and those of the dominant culture. Included in this domain of assessment would be the identification and discussion of the client's perspectives on abstinence, sobriety, help-seeking behavior, and the Twelve Step programs. Understanding the degree of congruence or incongruence with the dominant culture's view is also needed. Finally, the client's experience with being a member of a minority group (*minority group experience*) should be examined. This is a type of within-minority group variance in which the assessment would become more specific to the minority person's experience as a unique minority member. According to Barón, differential treatment by members of society's dominant group as well as treatment by other minority groups related to personality development, beliefs, attitudes, and origin and maintenance of the current problem profoundly influence a minority person's experiences. Because of the differential effects on individuals, it is important to examine the prevalence and impact of these particular beliefs on a case-by-case basis.

The four domains are considered effective in the understanding of the significant contextual influences affecting the general experience of racial/ethnic minorities. When working with a racial/ethnic family suspected of having alcohol and other drug problems, a clinician using this ICM approach would first want to construct a profile based on three mediator variables: level of acculturation, stage of ethnic-identity development, and worldview related to locus of control and responsibility. From here, the clinician can advance some hypotheses about the relative contribution of each of the four domains of inquiry (individual and systemic variables, cultural and ethnic variables, dominant group influences, and minority group experiences) that were just described. According to Barón, the ICM can be especially helpful in the early stages of assessment.

CASE EXAMPLE   Imagine a situation in which the ICM was used with a Mexican American couple. As in our case example at the beginning of this chapter, the Mexican American couple was referred to a mental health counselor for help with Mr. Aguilar's (husband's) drinking. The *individual and systemic variables* would reveal valuable information that could help explain why they stated they were experiencing distress over acculturating. It could reflect that the Aguilars are first-generation immigrants without documents. By using the model, the clinician would easily note the Aguilars' preference to speak Spanish to one another while at home and at most places in public. The individual and systemic domain would reflect the fact that Mrs. Aguilar's mother spoke almost exclusively Spanish. As is also common, her mother also lived with her daughter and son-in-law.

The assessment would reveal that the Aguilars' children were bilingual and more acculturated than their parents. The model would allow the interview to guide a discussion of Mr. Aguilar's beliefs about the dominant culture being misguided and that he preferred to mingle with other Mexican Americans. His beliefs were seen as both helpful and hurtful by his children.

Questions guided by interest in the individual and systemic variables could also reveal that Mr. Aguilar had been exposed to drinking at an early age. This exposure came in a culture where heavy drinking was more tolerated. As a result, Mr. Aguilar was seen as being caught between his culture of origin and the practices of his current cultural environment with regard to AOD use. He maintained that his situation was inevitable and blamed his condition on the system. To his way of thinking, drinking was an appropriate way to cope.

An assessment of the second domain, *cultural and ethnic variables,* could reveal the family's proclivity to respond to stress through culturally congruent behaviors, which reflected more toler-ance. Moreover, this assessment domain would show that the family would not ordinarily go about solving problems through the help of a therapist. In assessing the impact of the Aguilars' *dominant group and minority group experiences,* it was clear that he was resentful and bitter over his adapta-tion woes. Perhaps the family's most telling difficulty in seeing the problem from a different per-spective was the fact that they had identified their 15-year-old son, Enrico, who was having academic problems, as the issue.

In the treatment phase of the ICM, initial efforts were aimed at establishing credibility and an effective psychological and therapeutic contract. Motivational interviewing techniques were employed to help to create dissonance for Mr. Aguilar between his perception of what his role as a father and provider needed to be and the impact that his behavior was having on his family—and on Enrico in particular. Barón (2000) suggests the use of psychoeducational approaches as well. In this case, the psychoeducational component was actually a professional's confirmation about the existence of a problem.

It was also pointed out that Enrico was not trying to be disrespectful of his father. Through family therapy, Mr. Aguilar came to see how Enrico's behaviors were a way to signal to his father that something was wrong. The fact that Mrs. Aguilar often wanted to speak to the clinician in pri-vate reflected her own cultural conflicts. She was caught between being seen as disrespectful to her husband and her need to help him to manage his problematic drinking.

In this hypothetical case, the ICM was able to help the clinician formulate the appropriate cultural context for the Aguilars' problems. By understanding the interplay of acculturation, ethnic identity development, and worldviews related to responsibility and locus of control, the clinician was able to be more effective in the planning of treatment.

As previously mentioned in working with racial/ethnic families in Chapter 4, several authors underscore the importance of narrative approaches to individual and family treatment. Harrison and Harrison (2015); Harrison, Gentile, and Harrison (2012); Krestan (2000); Harrison (2004); and oth-ers suggest the relevancy of postmodern narrative principles in working with diverse populations. In writing about the relationship between addiction and power and powerlessness among diverse populations, Krestan (2000) discusses the influence of the dominant social discourse regarding the conceptions of power and powerlessness for racial/ethnic minorities. Krestan notes the particular challenges facing counselors in discussing the culturally powerless client's need to accept the con-cept of powerlessness in recovery.

In general, the narrative approaches underscore the importance of the relationship in the help-ing process. A fundamental principle of the narrative and dialogic approaches is the ability of indi-viduals to create a sense of power through the helping relationship. According to the theory, this power is then re-created over and over in the relationship so that it becomes a dominant reality for helpees (Abney & Harrison, 2003). In relating narrative principles to racial/ethnic families in need of AOD treatment, the approach itself is not so much effective as the adherence to the importance of the helping relationship developed in the process. Because the relationship between the counse-lor and the person being counseled is emphasized to such a great degree, it is imperative that the counselor maintain professional standards in keeping the roles of counselor and counselee distinct.

Application of the narrative approach to counseling can be very effective and can open the doors to a deepened understanding and appreciation of diversity.

Harrison and Harrison (2015), Harrison et al. (2012), and other researchers attempt to describe how the dominant class narrative or discourse related to power, powerlessness, and difference serves to promote the narrative discourse of risk factors for addiction among racial/ethnic families. Researchers such as Coyhis (2000), who writes about Native Americans, and Chang (2000), who writes about Asian/Pacific American addicts, are not asserting that the dominant discourse is causal. They are describing the manner in which this discourse interacts with racial/ethnic populations and the importance of understanding cultural differences in intervening so as to not promote the deleterious components of the dominant discourse.

Kaufman and Kaufman's Family Types

Four types of Euro-American families will likely present themselves for treatment (Kaufman & Kaufman, 1992). In one family type, members might talk openly about drinking or drugging but are more concerned with other important issues. In these families, drinking or drugging may be present but not to the degree that it is a problem, and helping professionals should focus on the presenting problems but should also attempt to emphasize the possible connection between AOD use and other problems in their lives. In the second family type, clues to alcohol and other drug-use problems may be present, but the clues are oblique and difficult to discern. In these families, the symptom bearer will probably be the child who could be involved in drug abuse. Other clues may be found in reports of drinking in the parents' families of origin, in parental role reversals, in children's attempts to protect their parents, in children's fears of talking about the family, or when the parents present themselves as overly concerned about teenage alcohol and drug abuse. The mental health professional should focus on the presenting problem and should attempt to infuse drinking or drugging into the presenting issue. The third family type is the one whose members present themselves for therapy after the alcohol or other drug abuser has completed some type of treatment program and is clean and sober. The issues here will likely be rebalancing the family system to avoid a full-blown relapse. Slips (see Chapter 10) are to be expected, so the work of the mental health professional is to help the family anticipate situations in which a slip might occur and help the family to determine effective ways to keep the slip from becoming a relapse. The fourth family type is the one presenting alcohol or other drug abuse as the major problem. In these families, alcohol or other drug abuse is the focus of the family, and the conflict will be quite open and apparent. Mental health professionals may need to take more control of these sessions if emotional reactivity is running too high.

Regardless of which family type presents itself for counseling, mental health professionals need to attend to the spousal subsystem, the parent–child subsystem, and the sibling subsystem. The reason for this is simple: Families will balance themselves. So, mental health professionals need to take into account how interventions impact these critical subsystems, the individual family members, and the family itself so that the rebalancing that inevitably will take place will be beneficial.

Kaufman and Kaufman (1992) point to situations in which individual counseling may be the preferred mode of treatment for alcoholic families. They see individual work being done in those situations in which family therapy may be misused to deny personal responsibility, psychopathology of one family member can be prevented by individual work, the parents are psychopathological to the point that helping a child cope with the psychopathology is preferred, a family member is deceitful, individual pathology remains after family intervention, and detoxification or getting the client clean and sober is needed prior to family therapy.

Many avenues are open for helping the alcohol or other drug-abusing client or family. The actively drinking or using family member should be directed to a facility where he or she can become clean and sober. Abstinence may be just an ideal for some families. Therefore, if the individual does not want to go into treatment, the family members have a decision to make: They can learn to cope better with the abusing family member, known as maintaining a "wet" system, or they can decide to go further into an intervention (see Chapter 7) and attempt to move their family into a "dry" system. In either case, support groups for family members such as Al-Anon, Alateen, and Codependents Anonymous (see Chapter 11) can be very effective in many, but not all cases.

MyCounselingLab for Addictions/Substance Abuse

Try the Topic 8 Assignments: *Family Treatment.*

Summary

- Children can be exposed to AOD use and abuse while in the uterus as well as interpersonally exposed after birth.
- Prenatal exposure to AOD is a critical health concern because fetal alcohol syndrome is the leading known cause of mental retardation.
- Children living in homes where methamphetamine is used and/or produced face a host of problems including living in filth, being exposed to toxic and potentially fatal chemicals, neglect, and abuse, among other things.
- In general, children interpersonally exposed to AOD abuse can take on survival roles that include hero, mascot, lost child, scapegoat, and/or enabler.
- Research shows that these children experience a host of problems related to loss, denial, distortion, and secrecy as well as attachment and separation, and families suffer also in terms of family functioning, violence, abuse, and living with fear.
- Children from AOD abuse families have difficulty in stating what they need or want in the family.
- Families often invoke rules such as "Don't talk, don't trust, and don't feel."
- One reason that families with AOD problems maintain dysfunction is due to underlying family themes related to impaired mourning, which revolves around separation and loss as well as family collusion.

- Stepfamilies and adoptees are at higher risk for AOD misuse and abuse due to myriad obvious reasons.
- Between 2% and 4% of the U.S. adult population is adopted.
- Adoptees are at higher risk for AOD use and abuse in addition to being at higher risk for a host of other mental illnesses.
- Each adoptee affects 30 individual family members.
- Adoptees comprise 15% of patients in residential treatment centers.
- There are roughly 2 million lesbian, gay, and bisexual individuals who are interested in adoption.
- Approximately 1.9 million children have at least one parent serving active duty in the military, and more than 700,000 children have experienced at least one deployment by a parent since 2001.
- Studies show that child maltreatment and neglect rise during the times of deployment (Sheppard, Malatras, & Israel, 2010), and nearly one-fourth of children aged 11 to 16 have emotional and behavioral symptoms associated with parental deployment.
- Although men drink more than women at one sitting and are more likely to drink to excess than women, they are less likely to be defined as alcoholic.
- Women are more likely to succeed in treatment.

- Researchers suggest that more studies should focus on diverse women in AA.
- Women present much later in the course of alcoholism, by which time other medical issues may obscure a diagnosis; however, once in treatment they benefit about the same as males.
- Although women account for one-third of those abusing AOD, alcoholism is still considered a "male" disease, and women alcoholics often go undiagnosed.
- The CAGE and AUDIT-C are assessment instruments that can be used effectively with the general as well as diverse populations; clinicians can also assess for AOD problems by being aware of Kaufman and Kaufman's four family types.

- Evidence exists that family-based interventions can work.
- Culture plays an important role in determining the type of treatment for alcoholism.
- Spiritual interventions are important for families and individuals.
- Barón's ICM for treating racial/ethnic minority families attends to four domains of inquiry that include individual and systemic variables and dynamics, cultural and ethnically related variables, dominant group influences, and minority group experiences.

Internet Resources

Fetal alcohol syndrome
cdc.gov/ncbddd/fas

Children of alcoholics
coaf.org
aamft.org
adultchildren.org

Stepfamilies
stepfamilies.info
stepfamilies.info/about.php (National Stepfamily Resource Center)
stepfamily.org
myfairystepmother.com/step-family-resources

Adoptees
Adoptionhelp.org/children-of-adoption/resources
Bandbacktogether.com

Women and alcohol
pubs.niaaa.nih.gov/publications/brochurewomen/women.htm
alcohol.gov.au/internet/alcohol/publishing.nsf/Content/wwtk-resources
drugabuse.gov

Military Families
Ausa.org/
Militarychild.org
Militaryfamily.com

Family AOD treatment
treatment-centers.net/women's-recovery.html
supportforfamilies.org
addictionresourceguide.com

Further Discussion

1. What, if any, drugs did your mother engage in while you were in the womb?
2. Because FAS is the leading cause of mental retardation, how is it that this is still a public health crisis?
3. Why would you think that stepfamilies and adoptees are at greater risk for AOD problems?
4. Many issues are related to women and AOD. What role does gender play in the identification and treatment concerns for women?
5. What are the reasons that diverse populations mistrust the treatment system, and what would you recommend be done to counter the problem?

CHAPTER 13

Adult Children and Codependency

CASE EXAMPLES

1. At his wife's urging, Tim attended a weekend workshop on codependence. As a result of his attendance, he began to understand what Becca (his wife) was talking about when she would say that he was "codependent." Tim bought several books related to codependency, Adult Children of Alcoholics (ACOAs), and shame. He began attending Codependents Anonymous (CoDA) meetings during his lunchtime. Although he was the only male in a group of seven women, he found many common themes with what the women were reporting and what he was experiencing.

2. Charlene is the eldest daughter of an alcoholic mother. She has a younger stepsister with whom she has a good relationship. Her younger brother was born after Charlene's mother stopped drinking. She states that she has never had much of a relationship with her mother. Although a loner throughout her freshman and sophomore years at college, Charlene began binge drinking with some friends on the weekends at her sorority during the fall semester of her junior year. She self-identified as an adult child of an alcoholic to her friends and came to find out that her other binge-drinking friends had no history of family alcohol abuse. However, almost every one of them had experienced some type of trauma or neglect by their parents. When her younger sister came to campus for a visit, Charlene was surprised to see that her younger sister did not drink or use other drugs.

In the last chapter, we discussed the impact that alcohol and other drugs (AOD) abuse has on children and families. The topic "Children and Families" could not have been written without some reference to adult children. However, we wanted to look at children as children. Thus, we want to focus the discussion in this chapter on the impact that AOD use has on the lives of adults who grew up in homes where substances were abused. Although we could identify and discuss a variety of populations who could present with AOD issues (such as professionals in recovery, grandparents of addicted individuals, adopted parents and alcoholism), we wanted to spend time on this special population because the labels of ACOAs, "Adult Offspring of Families with Alcohol and Other Drug Problems" (Harkness, Manhire, Blanchard, & Darling, 2011), and "Codependency" revolutionized the field of substance abuse and substance abuse treatment. In many ways, these populations brought issues that were previously only given passing glances to the forefront of the field.

According to Juliana and Goodman (1997), scholarly writing about the effects of alcohol upon children first appeared in the late 19th century with a study on the possible long-term effects of fetal opioid exposure. The more modern movement appears to have been initiated by interest in Cork's (1969) book *The Forgotten Children,* which examined 115 school-aged children of alcoholics and found them to be suffering from varied problems such as difficulty in expressing anger and resentment, low self-confidence, and difficulty in initiating and maintaining friendships. El-Guebaly and Offord (1977, 1979) reviewed the early empirical literature on children of alcoholics and attempted to identify problems that members of this group had across their life spans.

Intense popular interest then ensued with the publication of such books as Wegscheider's (1989) *Another Chance: Hope and Health for the Alcoholic Family,* Black's (1981) *It Will Never Happen to Me,* and Woititz's (1983) *Adult Children of Alcoholics.* As a result of these publications, a Children of Alcoholics (COA) movement began (Sher, 1991). The surging interest in COAs and ACOAs has been prolific enough to have spawned a cottage industry. Essentially, the message promulgated in these books is that one should confront one's chaotic childhood and work through the repressed pain (Blau, 1990).

From time to time, you may have heard people label themselves as being an ACOA or, more simply in support groups and amongst likeminded individuals, as an "adult child." You may also be somewhat familiar with the term *codependency* because some adult children may describe themselves as being "codependent." There is much debate regarding the benefits of such labeling. On the one hand, such a label can act as a shortcut in conversations where others are familiar and/or may subscribe to the same sobriquet. A "shortcut" means that others "know what you mean" when you use that label. However, in professional circles, there is concern that labeling can have its own life. For example, George, La Marr, Barrett, and McKinnon (1999) studied the relationship among alcoholic parentage, self-labeling, and endorsing oneself as an ACOA. They found that parents' drinking did affect whether the subjects labeled themselves as an ACOA–codependent. However, the researchers state that it was unclear if a certain number of subjects were simply responding to the fact that "Since my parents drank, I must be an ACOA–codependent." George et al. (1999) also found that when subjects labeled themselves as codependent, they endorsed more pathological statements. In an earlier study, Sher (1991) found "strong negative stereotypes associated with the COA label, both from peer group and from mental health professionals". These negative consequences are supported by the concept of "secondary deviance." This means that individuals can play into the label and justify deviant behaviors (Li & Moore, 2001). Some of these behaviors can include AOD use and misuse.

Aside from the potentially negative consequences of labeling oneself as a COA during school-aged years, there may be some positive aspects to the labeling process for ACOAs. Burk and Sher (1988) reviewed the literature in an attempt to determine the relevance of labeling theory for research on ACOAs. One of the possible benefits of labeling might be raising one's consciousness about the need for help. In addition, labeling oneself as an ACOA allows access to a variety of self-help support groups such as CoDA and Al-Anon (see Chapter 11). Burk and Sher (1988) take a narrative perspective and suggest that labeling oneself as an ACOA allows for an external attribution to be made that can provide a structure for individuals' insight and understanding into their problems. Kaminer (1990) believes that identifying oneself as an adult child begins a recovery process that can lead to a lifestyle of recovery. In the final analysis, the authors of this text believe that, to the extent to which a label allows an individual to grow, subscribing to a label can be beneficial. However, to label oneself as an ACOA to avoid personal responsibility is not helpful and can serve to maintain one's self-deprecation and self-defeating behaviors.

ACOAS

The labeling controversy aside, Pienkowski (2014) maintains that in the United States there are approximately 15.8 million ACOAs. Thus, regardless of the extent to which one subscribes to the concepts of adult children, this area is a focal point of current research.

Research on ACOAs has focused on three areas. One branch of research, referred to as risk factors for later substance abuse, includes both qualitative and quantitative studies that examine the variables believed to influence ACOAs' own drug or nondrug use in adulthood. The quantitative research is aimed at identifying the characteristics that predispose ACOAs to alcoholism, other drug dependence, or other substance-related problems. The qualitative writings in this area focus upon identifying the personality characteristics and problematic behaviors that increase an ACOA's risk for choosing a partner with an identifiable substance abuse problem. A second branch of research focuses on identifying the clinical characteristics of ACOAs. This area of research is probably the most well-known among the general population of adults. The third branch of research centers on attempts to empirically validate the clinical characteristics. As you will see, the current state of these three research venues generally reveals mixed results.

It is important to remember that many siblings do share a common family environment while growing up, and some parenting will be the same across siblings throughout the family life cycle. Yet, because other aspects of parenting might vary, this could well be the case with alcohol. Just as in the case example of Charlene, a parent might quit drinking between sibling births. This means that an older sibling might be directly affected by a parent's drinking, while the younger sibling is impacted indirectly. So, when discussing ACOAs, it is important to remember that the dynamics can vary between siblings and other family members.

Clinical Characteristics and Empirical Research

Much of the recent research on parental alcoholism and its effects on offspring has focused on COAs (see Chapter 12). Yet, several researchers have identified some of the characteristics distinctive to an adult child of an alcoholic (see Ackerman, 1983, 1987; Beattie, 1987; Black, 1981; Brown, 1988; Cermak, 1986; Goodman, 1987). These characteristics are fundamentally based upon the assumption that children see parental behavior as a reflection of the child's own sense of self-worth (Ackerman, 1983). In general, characteristics of ACOAs are seen as emanating from dysfunctional family systems and include excessive use of denial, all-or-nothing thinking, exaggerated need for control, avoidance of anger and other feelings, avoidance of self-disclosure, lack of trust, difficulty with intimate relationships and/or emotional regulation, and experience more negative life events than non-ACOAs (McCarty, Zimmerman, DiGuiseppe, & Christakis, 2005). These characteristics have been consistently identified across time (Drapkin, Eddie, Buffington, & McCrady, 2015). In addition, after analyzing themes of 504 messages posted over a period of 60 days, Haverfield and Theiss (2014) report that ACOAs experience interference from parents, need to connect to the inner child and reparent themselves, experience low self-esteem, anger, resentment, have relational issues, and have communication problems.

Other research suggests that a central issue for ACOAs relates to boundaries. Recall in the last chapter we discussed boundaries and likened them to a fence between people. Kelley et al. (2007) studied female college students who self-identified as ACOAs. Results reflected a group of participants who reported more *parentification* (a child treated like an adult), instrumental and emotional caregiving, and feelings of past unfairness in their families of origin. It is interesting to note that ACOAs who thought that their mothers had the problem with alcohol reported more parentification and caretaking than did both ACOAs and non-ACOAs who identified their fathers as having the problem. Given the results of this study, ACOAs raised in homes with maternal drinking problems predictably report less positive relationships with their mothers as well as with their peers. At the same time, paternal substance abuse did not predict the quality of parental or peer relationships. In another study, Kelley et al. (2007) also found that those ACOAs who suspected their mothers having alcohol problems reported less support and attachment from their mothers.

In general, empirical studies suggest that ACOAs do often show an increased vulnerability to life stressors and report more symptoms of adjustment difficulties (Hall & Webster, 2002; Hall, Webster, & Powell, 2003). The adjustment difficulties can play out in relationships, where they may regulate their attachments to others by being defensive, self-protective, and mistrusting (e.g., Kearns-Bodkin & Leonard, 2008; Kelley, Cash, Grant, Miles, & Santos, 2004). In a study of college students who identified as ACOAs, Kelley et al. (2014) found that women who had a history of parental alcoholism reported more alcohol-related problems than their partners.

Perhaps the most controversial assertion made about the clinical characteristics of ACOAs is that their relational difficulties can be described as "codependent." Because of the overwhelming popularity of this observation, we will discuss the notion of codependency in detail later in this chapter. It needs to be noted here that codependency is variously described as boundary problems that often result in enmeshed relationships, and codependents engage in dysfunctional relationships in a variety of forms. Although it may be somewhat true that ACOAs have boundary issues in their adult relationships, it cannot be seen as being caused by their families of origin. Family therapists see many couples' boundary problems that may be associated with other variables mitigated by a more generalized anxiety in contemporary couples that translates into power and control issues.

Risk Factors

When considering risk factors for COAs, it is critical to understand that alcoholism is a family disease. One of the strongest predictors of alcohol problems in adulthood is having a parent who was alcoholic (LaBrie, Hummer, Kenney, Lac, & Pedersen, 2011; Kelley et al., 2014; Murphy & Kelley, 2015; Van Damme et al., 2015). Pienkowski (2014) reports that 76 million adult Americans were exposed to alcohol in their family, and about 18% of these adults lived with an alcoholic while growing up.

Research is still inconclusive about whether ACOAs are more different than alike when compared to others who have experienced childhood trauma. At the same time, evidence points to the association between substance abuse in one's childhood home and the risk of developing problems later in life (Braitman et al., 2009).

For instance, ACOAs report initiating substance use earlier than non-ACOAs with respect to alcohol as well as tobacco, cannabis, and other illicit drugs, and this group has greater risk factors in developing adolescent and adult alcohol problems (Waldron et al., 2014).

As illustrated in our case example of Charlene and our previous discussion, some studies suggest that ACOAs do not differ significantly from other adult children who experienced a dysfunctional family home life (Fineran, Laux, Seymour, & Thomas, 2010). Researchers are finding that a number of ACOAs appear stable in spite of their upbringing in alcoholic homes. Moreover, numerous studies on ACOAs and risk factors have been conducted on college students, and research has shown that this population drinks more than the general population (Kendler et al., 2015). The elevated drinking among the college-age population can confound studies using college students to study ACOAs' risk factors. This leads Fineran et al. (2010) to suggest that ACOAs may not be as homogenous a group as it once was perceived to be. Thus, it is imperative that helpers do not assume that because an individual is raised in a family where alcohol was abused that he or she will categorically have problems. To obtain a clearer picture of college student ACOAs, West and Graham (2006) suggest that this population should be examined for risk over time, and measures of risk should be conducted before, during, and after college.

Some studies have concentrated on ACOAs from diverse backgrounds and their risk factors. For instance, Allem, Soto, Baezconde-Garbanati, and Unger (2015) found that the number of adverse experiences, including parental alcoholism, was a risk factor for the substance abuse decisions that emerging adult Hispanics make. De La Rosa et al. (2010) reviewed the clinical literature for adult Latino ACOA substance use and found that Latina adults who had reported low levels of attachment to their substance-abusing mothers were at heightened risk for substance abuse. Hall (2007) found that African Americans raised in alcoholic homes had more depression and lower self-esteem, which was similar to the findings for Caucasian samples.

ASSESSMENT AND TREATMENT CONSIDERATIONS

Assessment of ACOAs

Gąsior (2014) studied differing childhood experiences of ACOAs. Using the Gąsior Family of Origin Dysfunctionality Scale and the CAST (see the subsequent paragraph) to assess childhood experiences, the researcher found that ACOAs appeared to have three types of experiences that indicated that the ACOA was at high, moderate, or low risk. High-risk experiences included family alcoholism and/or violence concomitant with negative impressions of parental dysfunctional practices. Those considered moderate risks had less severe experiences and reported milder dysfunction in the family as well as higher functioning parents. As you can imagine, those with the lowest relative risk reflected more functional family patterns. Both Allem et al. (2015) and Gąsior (2014) found that families can also act as protective factors. In particular, Allen et al. asserted that cohesive and tight Hispanic families can be strong positive factors influencing decisions involving AODs.

A detailed instrument that continues to be used by researchers (e.g., Drapkin, et al., 2015) is the CAST (Jones, 1985), which stands for Children of Alcoholics Screening Test. It is a simple, 30-item, yes/no instrument, and it takes less than 10 minutes to administer. It takes no special training to administer, which makes it both good and bad. The CAST is designed to measure the chaotic and inconsistent behaviors and experiences of the alcoholic home such as emotional instability, inconsistent child care, family conflict, and lack of close, intimate, and trusting relationships between parents and children (Williams & Collins, 1986). The CAST6 is a six-item instrument that is used to assess ACOAs (over 18 years old) as well as COAs. The items measure experiences, attitudes, and perceptions about parental drinking in the same yes/no format as the CAST. Two cutoff scores have been used to identify ACOAs. Three or more "yes" responses are used to determine status from conservative perspective, and scores of 2 are more liberal. Thus, if you were to use a cutoff of 2, you would have more people identified as having problems.

Implications for Intervention

Being associated with AOD abuse either directly, as in the case of the alcoholic, or indirectly, as in the case of many ACOAs, has been shown to be problematic (e.g., Neger & Prinz, 2015). In fact, these researchers state that the rates of substance abuse disorders are tripled between adolescence and early adulthood (7% to 20%, respectively). Neger and Prinz also reviewed 21 studies where both substance abuse and parenting were treated. They found that, in general, treatment outcomes were favorable in terms of diminishing parental substance abuse and the improvement of parenting. There has also been a spate of interest on college campuses to identify and treat students with substance abuse issues because of it being a major public health concern (Laudet et al., 2015). College Recovery Programs are an innovative approach to helping this population. These programs are aimed to serve as a protective factor for recovering students and usually offer onsite sober housing, self-help meetings, and counseling.

In general, mental health professionals may want to provide information regarding AOD use as well as help clients clarify their values about use so that they may make decisions regarding abstention or moderation. Many clients who were raised in homes with alcohol abuse may not identify themselves as ACOAs. So, counselors need to be careful about using jargon that may create client resistance. Mental health professionals who use the label ACOA may leave their clients with the impression that this is a widely accepted clinical syndrome, but such a posture would be misrepresenting the empirical findings about ACOAs.

Adults who were raised in families with substance abuse, physical or sexual abuse, and/or parental death or divorce do seem different from adults with no such history. Moreover, a characteristic of families with AOD abuse is unresolved grief. This grief, coupled with poor communication skills and a lack of role-modeling on how to express feelings, may leave these clients predisposed to difficulty in trusting the counselor. Because ACOAs may control their emotions and attempt to control others as well, it is advisable that mental health professionals focus on developing a strong and deep rapport with the ACOA client.

Although we discuss some concerns with diversity and Twelve Step programs next, it seems that ACOAs may benefit from the same support groups that are identified and discussed in Chapter 11, which include CODA and Al-Anon. Other self-help groups, such as Sex Addicts Anonymous and Emotions Anonymous, could be used as well, depending upon the identified problem.

CODEPENDENCY

The term *codependency* was introduced in the early 1980s. Originally referring to the coalcoholic (Whitfield, 1984), this notion was broadened through the writings of Black (1981), Friel (1984), and others who described a variety of compulsive behaviors. With the possible exception of transactional analysis and the famous phrase, "I'm okay–you're okay" (Harris, 1969), few movements in the mental health field have generated so much popular interest and so much professional controversy as has the codependency movement.

The fields of chemical dependency and mental health were beginning to enjoy a healthy, although somewhat acrid at times, relationship once the notion of the dually diagnosed patient came into vogue in professional circles and more routine. However, it was the phenomenon of the patient with a coexisting disorder that sent shudders down the spine of the community mental health system—administrators and clinicians alike, because this dually diagnosed patient suggested the chicken-or-the-egg idea: What caused what? Which was the primary diagnosis? Did the AOD problem create the mental disorder or was it the other way around? If patients were active in their addictive behaviors during the time of their entry into the mental health system, what was the proper treatment plan? The very real complications resulting from having a coexisting disorder caused the fear that the financial backbone of community mental health centers would be broken. That a professional could be treating the wrong problem was a good possibility.

One direct result of the numbers of such dual diagnoses was a bringing together of chemical treatment providers and mental health providers under one roof. Although it was not an easy operation in terms of administrative logistics, mental health centers made great strides to do exactly that. Staff meetings, which were once held to discuss mental health cases, now included addictions counselors whose training was quite different from that of their mental health colleagues. The friction that resulted was to be expected because often mental health professionals had to move their offices or generate other concessions to make room for their new colleagues. As each group became more familiar with and received direct benefits from the work of the others, issues of turf and prestige gradually gave way to more amiable working relationships. Patients began to receive improved care, and with this came shared respect for each professional group. It appeared that all was well.

Then the chemical dependency field introduced the concept of codependency, and whatever strides had been made in the salubrious relationship between the mental health field and the addiction field turned sour once again. The definition and characteristics of codependency were seen by many mental health professionals as a new name for an old mental health disorder, which once again brought problems of professional boundaries into sharp focus. However, the problem was not only that the chemical dependency field was seen as trespassing onto the field of mental health nor was it only that those in the addictions field were being trained to treat codependency: The problem was more the issue of whether codependency actually existed. And if it did exist, questions about what constituted codependency would become the next cause of battle.

Some of the fiery debate was fueled by differences over the disease concept inherent in various views of codependency. Recall that, in Chapter 3, one's view of alcoholism as being a disease or nondisease was seen to have profound implications for identification and treatment. Moreover, remember how the discriminating variable casting one into a disease or nondisease orientation essentially revolved around one's view of "loss of control" (with the disease model claiming the centrality of a loss of control). Well, the voracity with which mental health professionals have debated the disease concept has been duplicated in the debate over codependency: Are people responsible for the root of their codependency? In other words, are individuals seen as more responsible for how they manage their impulses rather than being responsible for the impulse itself? Another source of debate centered on the traits of a codependent person. Hoenigmann-Lion and Whitehead (2006) studied whether codependency really exists. For these researchers, codependency is another name for a diagnosis already identified in the *Diagnostic and Statistical Manual of Mental Disorders*, fourth edition, text revision (*DSM-IV-TR*), under Borderline Personality Disorder, Dependent Personality Disorder, Posttraumatic Stress Disorder. Is codependency essentially a thematic variation on one of these disorders? Does it simply extend the boundaries of an already established diagnosis so that codependent characteristics lie more along one pole of a continuum in a given disorder?

Furthermore, some feminists argue that the perennial influence of the *codependency* hypothesis suggests that it is a social construct and is heavily influenced by traditional assumptions of gender. For instance, Dear and Roberts (2002) report that many feminists maintain the view of a society that demands that women be nurturing, caring, and sensitive to others' needs. Yet these are the very characteristics deemed dysfunctional when viewed through a *codependency* paradigm. Perhaps this contentious issue surrounds the notion of whether codependency is a progressive disease.

Definitions of Codependency

Definitions of the term *codependency* are influenced by the degree to which one subscribes to the concept. That is, staunch proponents of the concept may see everyone and almost all of our institutions as codependent.

Cermak (1986) noted that efforts to define codependency have included metaphoric and interpersonal approaches as well as those approaches based upon ego psychology, behaviorism, and combinations of behaviorism and intrapsychic dynamics. For example, Anderson (1987) uses a metaphor to state that "being codependent is like being a life guard on a crowded beach, knowing that you cannot swim, and not telling anyone for fear of starting a panic" (p. 16). More formalized definitions of codependency are found in the interpersonal approaches of Black (1981) and Wegscheider (1989). Black talks about rules operating in the family structure that prohibit the honest expression of feelings regarding alcoholism and the alcohol-dependent family member. Wegscheider discusses codependency in terms of it being a preoccupation and dependence upon another person or object. Examples of codependency include individuals who are in a significant relationship with an alcoholic, those having one or more alcoholic parents or grandparents, and those who grew up in a family where there was systematic repression of feelings. Schaef (1987) presents a definition that depicts the belief in the progressive nature of codependency. She sees codependency as a disease emanating from an "addictive process" similar to that of alcoholism. This addictive process, unless confronted in much the same manner as alcoholism, can lead to a type of spiritual death—a life aimed at existing rather than thriving—or physical death (Schaef, 1987).

Friel (1984) extended the interpersonal approaches to include codependency and emphasized the impact of such behaviors upon the ego functioning of individuals. These authors maintain that codependency is an emotional and behavioral pattern of interactive coping resulting from one's protracted exposure to a restrictive environment that does not allow the open or direct expression of feelings about oneself or other family members. For example, children who are consistently told that the mother's or father's drinking binges are not problematic, even in the face of drunken rages and subsequent physical abuse, will grow up confused about their reality. Any attempt to talk about the problem when the parents were sober would likely be met with cognitive resistance: "There is no problem." Any attempt to talk about the problem when the parent(s) were drinking is likewise met with physical abuse. Hence, these children often learn to keep their feelings and thoughts about the parents' drinking to themselves. This fear of talking would be introjected and thus carried into one's adult life and relationships.

Whitfield (1984) believes that codependency is a disease of lost selfhood, and that it is the most common type of addiction that people develop. Whitfield states that codependence develops whenever there is "suffering and/or dysfunction that is associated with or results from focusing on the needs and behavior of others" (p. 9). An intrapsychic approach is reflected in Cermak's (1986) definition in which he sees a codependent person as having a personality disorder based upon an excessive need to control self and others. Other symptoms include neglecting one's own needs, boundary distortions centered on approach and avoidance in intimate relationships, attraction to other individuals demonstrating codependent characteristics, denial, a constricted or restricted emotional expression, low-level and persistent depression, and stress-related physical ailments.

As Irvine (1999, p. 29) and others point out (e.g., Krestan & Bepko, 1990), codependency's "definitional ambiguity should not be taken to be 'so vague as to be meaningless.'" Nonetheless, Irvine maintains that one cannot simply ascribe any and all meanings to it. She goes on to say that the constitution of one person's codependency is really defined by what the person sees as troublesome in his or her own history. According to the same researcher, codependency can stand for different issues in an individual's life. For instance, it might mean a series of loveless and oppressive relationships. In another case, codependency might mean distant, aloof, and isolating interpersonal response patterns to others. In yet another instance, codependency might reflect a sense of chronic low self-esteem and boundary problems in relationships (Watt, 2002).

Characteristics of Codependent Individuals

Because of the lack of clear definitions of codependency, it is somewhat difficult to determine characteristics. As a result, several authors have advanced codependent characteristics, and, like the definitions, these characteristics range from less formal to more pedantic (see Kitchens, 1991; Schaef, 1987; Whitfield, 1984).

Dear and Roberts (2002) identified themes of codependency. These include a tendency to put other people's needs before one's own, the tendency to engage in taking responsibility for another person's actions ("caretaking"), and the fixing of the damage cause by another person ("rescuing"). Potter-Efron and Potter-Efron (1989) identified eight characteristics of codependence: (1) Fear is indicated by a preoccupation with the problems of others, an avoidance of interpersonal risk, a general mistrust of others, persistent anxiety, and manipulative attempts to change another's behavior, especially drinking behavior; (2) Shame and guilt are characterized by a persistence of shame and guilt about another's behavior, self-loathing, isolation, and an appearance of superiority that masks low self-worth; (3) Prolonged despair relates to a generalized pessimism toward the world and feelings of hopelessness about changing one's current situation. One may also demonstrate a low sense of self-worth that stands in direct opposition to one's actual accomplishments; (4) Anger is often present but may be expressed in a passive-aggressive manner. One may also fear that becoming angry will mean a loss of control. Another characteristic of anger is that it is persistent; (5) Denial is usually rather consistent, especially when it involves family pain such as drinking behavior. Denial is also demonstrated by a consistent minimization of problems and the use of justifications or rationalizations aimed at protecting the person from perceived or real consequences; (6) Rigidity is identified by cognitive, behavioral, and moral, spiritual, and emotional inflexibility; (7) Identity development is also impaired. This is usually seen as an inability to take care of one's own emotional needs and as having an excessive need for others to validate one's self-worth. Along with this need is an obsessive concern about how one is perceived by others; and (8) Confusion about what is normal and what is real is another behavioral pattern. Confusion is also indicated by one's gullibility and indecisiveness.

In examining the definitions and characteristics, Doweiko (2011) states that the core aspect of codependency includes four elements: *overinvolvement, obsessive attempts to control, the extreme tendency to use external sources for self-worth, and the tendency to make personal sacrifices.* In codependency, overinvolvement with the abusing family member is coupled with an obsessive attempt to control the abusing member's behaviors. Using external sources for self-worth is similar to Whitaker's (1991) notion of "looking elsewhere." The issue of personal sacrifices comprises those behaviors aimed at "curing" the abusing family member, in which the helper is seen as "saintly."

According to Kitchens (1991), eight indicators can help to determine the severity of codependence: (1) the extent to which the client equates performance with self-value; (2) the extent to which the client equates self-worth with taking care of others' needs; (3) the extent to which the client believes he or she is helpless to control what happens in life; (4) the extent to which the client attempts to feel more powerful or more in control of life than is actually the case; (5) the extent to which the client ruminates about dysfunctional family of origin behavior; (6) the extent to which the client continues to protect or defend against any criticism of his or her parents in the face of contradictory information; (7) the extent to which the client experiences unexplained or overwhelming anger; and (8) the extent to which the client feels stuck in his or her relationships.

Assessing for Codependency

During the period from the mid-1980s to the mid-1990s, assessing codependency in clients was relatively informal, and professionals and nonprofessionals alike used a few notable nonstandardized instruments. However, the subjectivity and informality in the early years of the codependency movement were not categorical and should not be mistaken for a complete lack of validity. In the early years, the differences in the assessment of codependency were probably attributed to variations in the general assessment skills of practitioners, rather than being attributed to differences over the meaning and definition of codependency. Although it is true that clinicians often assessed codependency simply through their subjective clinical impressions of the client, these impressions were partly guided by the professional works of Kitchens (1991), who also cautioned mental health professionals to combine subjective and objective assessment procedures. Interestingly, Harkness and Cotrell (1997) show that the pioneers may have been accurate in their assessments of codependency. These researchers studied more than 2,000 practitioners worldwide and found a remarkable agreement and consistency in the meaning and definition of codependency across practitioner subjects.

Fuller and Warner (2000) reviewed scales that are used to assess codependency. They found the Codependency Assessment Inventory (CAI; Friel, 1985), the Acquaintance Description Form-C3 (Wright & Wright, 1991), Beck Codependence Assessment Scale (Beck, 1991), A Codependence Test (Kitchens, 1991), Recovery Potential Survey (Whitfield, 1991), the Spann–Fischer Codependency Scale (Fischer, Spann & Crawford, 1991), and the Potter–Efron Codependency Assessment (Potter-Efron & Potter-Efron, 1989). According to Fuller and Warner, the CAI is lengthy (60 items), and the validity and reliability have not been thoroughly evaluated. Wright and Wright's Acquaintance Description Form-C3 does not have published statistical information.

Fuller and Warner (2000) used the Spann–Fischer and the Potter–Efron Codependency Assessment (Potter-Efron & Potter-Efron, 1989) to study the relationship of these instruments with self-reported chronic family stress. Results of their study showed that women had higher codependency scores on the Spann–Fischer than did the sample of male subjects. This study raises questions about potential gender bias in the instrument, and this issue will be addressed later in the chapter.

Aside from these efforts to update assessments published in the early years of the codependency movement, a review of the current professional literature reveals continued interest in the introduction of new empirically tested psychometric assessments for codependency. For instance, Harkness, Swenson, Madsen-Hampton, and Hale (2001) studied the reliability and validity of a clinical rating scale for codependency. The researchers developed an example-anchored rating scale, based on how clinicians generally construe the term *codependency* in practice. The researchers administered the instrument to a group of practicing counselors. The design controlled for gender and called for counselors to be randomly assigned to one of four groups. The findings suggest that the rating scale yields reliable and valid clinical evaluations of codependency without appreciable gender bias. The Holyoake Codependency Index (Dear & Roberts, 2000) is a reliable 13-item scale that measures the extent to which a person endorses or rejects codependent sentiments. It comprises three scales: external focus, self-sacrifice, and reactivity. *External focus* is defined as the tendency to rely on other people to obtain approval and a sense of self. *Self-sacrifice* is the tendency to regard others' needs as more important than one's own needs. *Reactivity* is the degree to which one feels overwhelmed by a partner's problematic behavior. According to the authors of the index, these subscales were derived from factor analysis of key themes using a clinical sample of mostly females. As you can see, arguments can be made about the consistency in the validity and reliability of assessment instruments throughout the history of the codependency movement. One current trend in research in assessment is to conduct concurrent validity and reliability studies as ancillary, yet important components, of other research questions. Lindley, Giordano, and Hammer's (1999) study is an example. In this study, the researchers validate the Spann–Fischer scale while primarily looking at the relationship between codependency and age, gender, self-confidence, autonomy, and succorance. These studies, and others like them, provide opportunities for enhancing the clinical assessment of codependency.

Should you, as a mental health professional, choose to administer an instrument, you are advised to use these instruments with extreme caution. Probably the best use of these assessment devices is for the mutual identification of problematic areas occurring in the client's life. Asking the client to share his or her impressions of the assessment results can help focus on areas that might need attention.

PHASES OF CODEPENDENCY   Rusnáková (2014) attempted to define and characterize the phases of codependency. Citing similarities with Beattie (1987), this researcher generally agrees that denial of the reality of the other's drinking is the first phase with anger being the second phase and reconciliation with the reality as the third phase. However, Rusnáková believes that *rescuing* is the third phases and *hatred* and the creation of distancing in the relationship is the fourth phase. Finally, this researcher believes that mental health practitioners should understand that members of an alcoholic family experience the reality differently, and that codependent individuals within families should strive to engage the addict in a uniform manner.

IMPLICATIONS FOR MENTAL HEALTH PROFESSIONALS

As far as the controversy is concerned, the mental health profession has the last word for now: The *DSM*, fifth edition, does not include codependency in its nomenclature on personality disorders. This may or may not dissuade others from adhering to the concept of codependency, but this omission does make a clear statement that may intensify the chasm that exists over the use of the term between mental health practitioners and those practitioners in the chemical dependency field.

A close examination of the concept of codependency and the criticism surrounding the term and its corollaries will likely indicate that much of the argument involves degrees of acceptance.

The very least that can be said about the concept of codependency is that it has helped to describe a variety of interpersonal and intrapersonal dynamics in a language that many can understand. In that AODs are rampant in our society across every economic and social line, the concept of codependency may currently be best operating as a paradigm attempting to make sense out of the confusing, paradoxical, and often deleterious effects of one's extended drug involvement and its impact on others. Whether intuitively understood or empirically proved, it is safe to say that the characteristics identified as codependent operate in almost all of us at one time or another. Differences between individuals exist in incidence, degree, and persistence. Our society is based upon competition and achievement. You, as a reader of this book, might be termed an overachiever, but it is often overachievers who are in positions to help others. The need for belonging to powerful groups, identified as indicative of an antisocial and narcissistic personality disorder (Kitchens, 1991), can be functional, and decisions that affect us all are made by groups of powerful people. We all need humor in our lives, so the histrionic personality identified as maladaptive is necessary for us to have perspective on our lives. Compulsivity is almost a given in undergraduate and graduate school, isn't it? Does that mean you are maladaptive for choosing to go to college or graduate school? The point we are making here is that codependent characteristics, per se, are not inherently good or bad. Sometimes behaving codependently is appropriate, is very adaptive, and can lead to satisfaction with oneself and others. Sometimes these same characteristics can lead to problems. An inflexible adherence to codependency as well as an inflexible avoidance of it may become problematic. The advice given here is for you to remain open to the client and to use an understanding of codependency as it relates to the well-being of that client. Categorically disregarding the presence of codependent behaviors may limit the amount and kind of information being presented by clients and can lead to less than efficacious results in counseling. Moreover, because thousands upon thousands attend CoDA meetings and adhere to the principles of codependency as outlined in *The Coda Book,* a limited or myopic understanding of the larger social, political, and economic implications of codependency for women and racioethnic minorities is questionable practice.

Mental Health Professionals' Own Codependency

Martsolf (2002) sampled 149 males and females whose ages ranged from 23 to 73. The sample included nurses, family physicians, psychologists, and social workers. The results of the study indicate a relatively low incidence of codependency in this sample. This stands in contrast to a preliminary study conducted by Fisher and Harrison (1993b), which assessed codependent characteristics of graduate students in a master's degree counseling program. We found that these prospective mental health professionals reported more codependent characteristics than did students in other graduate programs. Moreover, the graduate students in the mental health profession were more likely to have come from an alcoholic home. This preliminary study suggests that mental health professionals' codependency may be a potential problem in a counseling relationship.

Even though these are only two studies (and both are limited in their own ways), some interesting implications are apparent. Given that the pathological discourse of codependency in this culture has been around long enough to be seen and experienced as oppressive by many in the helping professions, one wonders whether clients now show a tendency to be hesitant in identifying themselves as codependent. Fisher and Harrison's earlier study of graduate students occurred when there was widespread interest in the concept, and helping professionals were thought to be potential codependents because of the nature of the work they performed. During the time in which Fisher and Harrison (1993b) conducted their preliminary study, the stigma of codependency was not as harsh as feminists accused it of being in the 1990s. Thus, in the past, a questionnaire measuring codependency in a population that reflected low incidence may well have been due to a lack of subjects' identification with codependent characteristics. Currently, the stigma of being codependent has many pathological connotations. This has created a situation in which both male and female subjects (mental health practitioners included) who are being assessed for codependency may not want to see themselves or be seen by others as codependent.

PROFESSIONAL ENABLING AND TRANSFERENCE/COUNTERTRANSFERENCE   The dynamics that transpire between client and mental health professional in sessions may also reflect transference and countertransference. Wegscheider (1981) sees attempts to keep an alcoholic from experiencing logical or natural consequences as enabling. Thus, your attempts to keep clients from experiencing the natural consequences of their actions can be framed as professional enabling or countertransference and can reinforce maladaptive client behaviors. You might perceive a client's desire to return to a dysfunctional relationship as reflecting your failure to effect client change. By personalizing the client's progress, you might strongly advise the client to avoid returning to the dysfunctional relationship and become angry with the client if the advice is not heeded. You might also overidentify with the experience of the client, resulting in an enmeshed relationship with the client. The loss of these interpersonal boundaries can diminish the effectiveness of the helping process, or at least confound the process. For example, you might identify with the client's feelings of helplessness in changing an alcoholic partner's behaviors. Rather than recognizing and working with the enabling aspects of the client's behaviors, you might prematurely attempt to steer the client into solutions rather than helping him or her gain insight into how his or her behaviors actually enable or reinforce the partner's alcoholism. In this manner, the client is kept from experiencing the consequences of his or her own behaviors.

We could continue with protracted examples of mental health professionals' potential codependent behaviors. Suffice it to say that codependency in the profession can be problematic. Training programs go a long way in helping mental health professionals understand the parameters of interactions with clients. Yet, if you come from a home where there was alcoholism or other family dysfunction, you may be more prone at times to behaving codependently with clients. Personal work can increase awareness of your codependent behaviors and can help you arrive at some strategies and solutions. It may well be that our profession attracts those who have experienced much of the same pain that clients will have experienced. Your experiences with your own pain and codependency can significantly increase the potential for accurate empathy with your clients and, therefore, can be of potential benefit. The extent of the benefit to clients will likely be related directly to the amount of your own work on codependency issues.

RELATIONSHIP OF ACOA, AA, AL-ANON, AND CODEPENDENCY

In her book *Codependent Forevermore*, Irvine (1999) discusses ACOAs and codependency. She states that "codependency and the support group Codependents Anonymous exist today because of the trail blazed by Adult Children of Alcoholics" (p. 19). Thus, for Irvine, the two movements are related. For her, the debate is essentially focused on the extent that the relationship is complementary and/or supplementary.

However, the relationship between ACOA/codependency and Alcoholics Anonymous (AA)/ Al-Anon is more acrimonious. It goes beyond the fact that AA and Al-Anon were in existence first. According to Irvine, the Adult Child does *not* belong to AA. This is because AA exists for the alcoholic who wishes to become clean and sober and remain so. Second, the ACOA–codependency movement poses a cultural narrative that is in direct opposition to the discourse and tenets of AA and Al-Anon. The ACOA–codependency movement takes the focus off the alcoholic and places the focus on outside factors, specifically on genetic and/or interpersonal factors leading to addictions. In other words, adults who abuse alcohol are seen in the ACOA–codependency movement as doing so because of their childhoods and/or because of some genetic predisposition or proclivity. By locating some, if not all, of the control outside the abuser, a dramatic and deep chasm between ACOA and AA/Al-Anon is drawn.

Another structural difference is even more pronounced at the macro-level, and Irvine (1999) again provides insight. She says that the AA discourse is a conservative narrative. This means that it conforms more closely to the larger social narrative. If "blame" is to be had at all (remember that in AA, blame is seen as a process to be worked through in order to take responsibility), one could feasibly "blame" it on the bottle—not society. From this perspective, the narrative of ACOA–codependency is anti-AA. This is so because, if "blame" is to be had in codependency, the "blame" is placed on the family. It is imperative for you to understand that we are not saying that "blame" is condoned in any of these venues. We are using "blame" as a means of underscoring a difference between these approaches. Although people may enter into these recovery programs blaming, they hopefully learn early on that blaming is a way of avoiding responsibility. In any case, the difference in worldviews, concomitant with the obvious ensuing implications for treatment and recovery, is hard to understate.

On yet another front, the relationship between ACOA and codependency is an interesting one. According to research results (e.g., Dube et al., 2002), it is imperative that mental health therapists not categorically confuse codependency with alcohol use or being an ACOA. As mentioned previously, studies are now showing that the characteristics of ACOAs are not that unique and that these characteristics may also be found in adults who came from homes where there was neglect, abuse, and/or violence.

For instance, Cullen and Carr (1999) studied the differences between young adults on a measure of codependency. Results indicated that those high on codependency scores reported significantly more family-of-origin problems. Yet, the problems were not necessarily alcohol related. The family-of-origin problems included such things as relationships with chemically dependent partners, parental mental health problems, problematic intimate relationships, and personal psychological problems (for example, compulsivity). Moreover, there was no significant difference among those scoring high on codependency levels and the reporting of physical or sexual abuse.

The results of these studies suggest that codependency is one component of a wider multigenerational family systems issue. Thus, it is quite possible that ACOAs may be codependent, yet not all codependents are ACOAs.

Critics of the ACOA–Codependency Movement

POPULAR CRITICISM   The ACOA–codependency movement's narrative was seen (and still is seen by many) as pitting children of any age against parents. The movement is seen as attacking the core structure of family. More significantly, the ACOA–codependency movement has been criticized as blaming *all families and all parents of all children.* Ironically, and to their credit, proponents of the movement adroitly point to the rigidity of the critics' "all or nothing" perspective as demonstrating the very dysfunction of dualistic thinking firsthand. Thus, the separation between AA and Al-Anon is reiterated with the larger social narrative.

Clearly and from a social perspective, any new discourse that runs counter to the larger, prevailing discourse is enough to spawn criticism. It is to be expected, because societies remain stable through the dialectical processes of homeostasis and change. However, at the outset, the ACOA–codependency movement was seen as significantly altering the traditional Euro-Caucasian discourse on families regarding one's position in the family structure. The antifamily nature of the new narrative also had significant structural implications for families themselves.

The movement had its emphasis on confrontation. Rightly or wrongly, it was seen as a movement of "parent bashing." At that time in history, blaming one's (somewhat elderly) parents ran diametrically opposite to the discourse calling for being grateful to one's parents (usually fathers) for fighting in World War II and bringing peace and prosperity to the world. The movement was seen by some women and mothers as a movement that discredited their choices, their sacrifices for their family, and, in some cases, their livelihoods. (As you will see, the feminist researchers had critics of their own.) As such, a core basic orientation of the ACOA–codependency movement was seen as crossing the decades-old narrative of "healthy and loving families" (of the 1940s through the 1980s).

PROFESSIONAL CRITICISM   As the ACOA–codependency movement grew, professional researchers became interested in studying the concept. After all, from a strict research perspective, the ability to identify, isolate, and profile a (albeit reputed) significantly large segment of society (ACOAs) for study was quite appealing. Yet the enthusiasm in being able to identify and isolate this population waned significantly as researchers designed studies and published results. Enormous methodological challenges in studying ACOA–codependency needed to be overcome. Many of the same problems remain today (Jacobs, Windle, Seilhamer, & Bost, 1999).

In the early 1980s, the definitions of *COA* and *ACOA* were precise and clear: COA meant a child of a parent who abuses alcohol, and ACOA meant an adult child of a parent who drank alcohol excessively. However, such a precise definition would eventually narrow the subject pool and create a diminished ability to generalize results. The problems were numerous. For instance, there would be difficulties attributing length of exposure to alcohol and the subsequent effects that it had. Second, because many alcoholics also used other drugs, this condition limited the population of alcohol-only users. Third was the issue of the validity of self-reports. Were the subjects reporting their patterns accurately? Fourth, even if one could argue in favor of self-reports, self-reports were (and are always) about events in the past. The validity of recollection was significant at the time, and debate continues in the courts. Today, the validity of self-reports is challenged under the rubric *recovered memories.* Fifth, assuming that one could validly recall an event and reliably self-report it, Goodman (1987) and then Williams (1990) argue that such things as parental inconsistencies, double-bind messages, the covert expression of feelings, shame, mistrust, and the existence of childhood roles occur in everyone's life. Therefore, because these experiences are ubiquitous, one should not attribute these characteristics solely to COAs and ACOAs.

From the outset of the movement, researchers were not interested in undertaking studies demonstrating the clinical characteristics of COAs, ACOAs, and codependency (Giermyski & Williams, 1986). Thus, if one were to examine the professional journals in the early 1980s, one would find a dearth of systematic and empirically based studies. Today, this has changed. There is moderate professional research interest in the topic of ACOA–codependency per se.

At the same time, it is important to understand the sequence of the growth and development of the ACOA–codependency movement. Alcoholics Anonymous came first, followed in order by

Al-Anon, ACOA, CoDA, and Gamblers Anonymous and other Twelve Step recovery programs. This chronology is interesting because it reflects the importance of the ACOA and CoDA recovery programs. CoDA is the bridge connecting the earlier and more conservative programs of AA and Al-Anon with the other addictions that will be discussed in Chapter 15. As such, the ACOA–codependency narrative has had a significant background effect on the upstream research studies of alcohol, alcoholism, COAs, fetal alcohol syndrome, and other substance abuse. The downstream effects on research affect studies of gambling and other addictions.

CODEPENDENCY AND DIVERSITY

Feminist Critiques of Codependency

As you would expect, codependency has been thoroughly critiqued from researchers in the fields of sociology and women's studies. Criticism is wide-ranging, and most of it relates to white women. The feminist criticisms of codependency can fall into three broad categories: gender bias, the codependency discourse, and victimization and victimhood.

Most of the vociferous objections have come from those who see codependency as perpetuating a state of victimhood. From the manner in which many of these researchers write, it is easy to generalize many of their findings to racial/ethnic women. However, it is critical to note that, although feminists would readily agree about the presence of the oppression of women on an international scale, they would also agree that the West has tended to dominate both the theoretical and practical aspects of the feminist movement. Hence, the grand narrative of feminism is the story of Western endeavor and relegates the experience of non-Western women to the margins of feminist discourse (Kurian, 1999, p. 66).

In the U.S. culture, traditional feminism is not necessarily an appropriate voice for some or many racial/ethnic women. This does not mean that the criticisms advanced by feminists about codependency are irrelevant for the minority populations. It means that some of the criticisms discussed by feminists will be relevant and can be loosely generalized to minority populations. Some criticisms will not be able to be appropriately generalized. Perhaps equally important to note is that the codependent discourse affects both males and females. It just affects them differently. To our way of thinking, the impact of the codependent discourse in general is potentially more harmful to the population of women in general than it is to men. This is due to the social, political, and economic barriers that women face in today's culture.

GENDER BIAS   Researchers are in agreement that, given the multiple meanings of codependency, it is largely a social construct, as much perceiver as perceived (Harkness & Cotrell, 1997). Harkness and Cotrell (p. 473) and Rice (1992) believe that the concepts of codependency and enabling reflect a Twelve Step culture perspective of the world. With this perspective as a backdrop, feminist critiques of gender bias in codependency argue against its many forms. The crux of their argument is that the concept of codependency is prejudicial toward women on social, political, and economic fronts. It also claims that the issue of gender bias and codependency is critical because the consequences for all women are serious (Hurcom, Copello, & Orford, 2000).

A review of the literature on gender bias and codependency reveals that the very notion of gender is a questionable construct and narrative. For instance, Butler (1990) believes that gender is not represented as "real," but as a boundary that is politically regulated. In agreeing with the principles of Butler's work, Phoca (1999) goes on to say that, because there is no essential masculine or feminine subject, both genders can take up masculine and feminine subject positioning. In essence, this perspective blurs the boundaries surrounding gender in the traditional sense.

Although you may not agree with these researchers, the implications of this blurring of boundaries for the AOD field are important to understand. The blurring of gender boundaries directly affects the definitions of codependency, as well as favorably affecting the ability of codependency research results to be generalized to larger populations. For instance, the AOD field has adopted a gender-neutral definition of codependency, such as the use of "adult," "person," "individual," and "family member." In other words, the definitions of codependency do not include or use the gender-driven terms "women" or "men" or any of their derivatives. Thus, the gender lines do not exist and, theoretically, anyone could be codependent.

Yet, in spite of these gender-neutral definitions, earlier studies conducted by Krestan and Bepko (1990) and Parker (1980) showed that the traditional views of addiction and codependency were rather traditional in that they usually reflected male substance abusers connected with helpful females. These helpful females, who were seen as also depending on addicted men, were labeled as codependent. In more current research, Babcock (1995), Babcock and McKay (1995), and Dear and Roberts (2002) reviewed the definitions and various meanings of codependency and enabling and assert that these concepts continue to be framed by traditional views of male and female. These researchers, along with others (e.g., Hurcom et al., 2000; Krestan & Bepko, 1990), argue that the existing structures of codependency nurture the development of caretaking and self-sacrifice in women while keeping men from developing those same qualities. In reality, men (as illustrated in our case example with Tim), can and do develop these traits. In addition, numerous men attend CoDA groups (although figures are kept confidential because of the Twelve Step traditions).

Unfortunately, little empirical research on males and codependency exists. One of the main consequences of this misidentification and gender bias is that the use of such words as "(codependent) person" and/or "(codependent) adult" has failed to successfully assign codependency or codependent traits evenly across males and females. For instance, it is a fact that males receive treatment for alcoholism far more often than do women. It is a tragic irony that this treatment differential occurs in spite of the fact that women, who are significantly underrepresented in studies of AOD abuse, may have higher rates of alcoholism or other substance abuse problems than are reported in the professional literature and databases. Hence, from this gender-bias perspective, not only does the concept of codependency propel women into stereotypic roles, but it also is seen as helping to mask their AOD abuse. At the same time, gender bias is hindering the development of nurturing qualities in the male population.

THE CODEPENDENCY DISCOURSE   Several researchers (e.g., Babcock, 1995; Babcock & McKay, 1995; Krestan, 2000; Krestan & Bepko, 1990; Taleff & Babcock, 1998) write about the nature of discourse in our culture as it relates to codependency. Taleff and Babcock (1998) review the literature in the AOD field and identify five dominant discourses that guided the early AOD treatment culture. Two of these dominant narratives relate directly to the concept of codependency. According to Taleff and Babcock, the dominant discourses "in AOD work" are these:

- Blame the client for treatment failure
- Blame the victim
- Closeness equals pathology
- Too much knowledge is bad (don't think, it will get you in trouble)
- Never trust the client (all addicts are cons and manipulators)

Blaming the victim and closeness equals pathology related directly to the codependency issue. In examining family systems theory and treatment approaches, Babcock and McKay (1995) believe that the notion of codependency has been the most blatant example of blaming the victim. Hurcom et al. (2000) believe that role-specific behaviors that result from a partner being addicted do more than blame. They pathologize the behavior. This followed the research of Taleff and Babcock (1998), who concluded that the AOD field tends to blame family members for the ongoing addiction (p. 37).

This research stream strongly characterizes an essential concern regarding the codependency discourse and feminism. Through this pathological narrative, helping is not perceived as a well-meaning, misguided, and yet unsuccessful attempt to thwart off the addict's self-destruction. Rather, codependency is an insidious strategy used by the addict's significant other(s) aimed at perpetuating the addiction. The discourse of blame and pathology results in the fact that cultural closeness, love, anxiety, and feminine nurturing are ignored. On a core assumptive level, the argument is that the paradigm reflects that people who are engaging in codependent behaviors are insidious and are not to be trusted. Women engaging in these behaviors are posited as untrustworthy as well as antifeminine, because their natural tendency to nurture is now seen as unhealthy and is to blame for the addiction.

These researchers, as well as Krestan and Bepko (1990), see the need to understand the phenomenon of *closeness* as a way of overcoming the problems with this perspective. Clinicians need to be able to distinguish between normal, healthy closeness and pathological closeness or dependency. Moreover, clinicians need to assess families with AOD problems in terms of the amount of healthy *interdependence* that exists. If clinicians have a simplistic understanding of the gender-bias issue and codependency, they will miss what is clearly a complex phenomenon.

VICTIMIZATION AND VICTIMHOOD   A related issue is the social discourse of victimization and victimhood. This broad, social narrative is different from the AOD discourses identified by Taleff and Babcock (1998). Nevertheless, the social discourse of victimization clearly has significant implications for the meanings of codependency.

For example, Irvine (1999) presents a subtle and powerful argument regarding the dominant social discourse and victimization as a response. She maintains that the individuals "left or abandoned" are the ones most often claiming the status of victimhood. Moreover, these "victims" are more likely to be unemployed, have fewer commitments to family, and be less committed to service in CoDA (p. 148). Through this perspective, victimization and victimhood are structurally tied to the person's position with regard to who "left the relationship first". This same researcher maintains that victims usually have fewer social–structural resources available to them. As a result, the narrative of victimization initially responds to and then, ironically, augments these very social–structural losses. Irvine (1999) sees this as a failure of our larger social structure to protect individuals from these social losses and resulting isolation. Given these insightful assertions, it is appropriate for counselors to assess the extent to which victimization is stated and the extent to which it might be more of a trait in individuals with AOD abuse issues (Irvine, 1999, pp. 156–157).

At the core assumptive level, victimization and victimhood place individuals, mostly women and racial/ethnic minorities, underneath the dominant discourse. This is because this discourse, in which these groups are portrayed as always seeking, presupposes an absence of something. Among other things, this seeking behavior is a "less than" position. The result is a vicious cycle that continues to isolate individuals from the mainstream and into a constant search to balance the scale.

Harkness and Cotrell (1997) also advance a thoughtful critique of codependency from feminist perspectives. These researchers agree with the views of Irvine (1999) and Krestan and Bepko (1990) regarding the issues of pathologizing and blame. Citing the works of Asher (1992), Collins (1993), and others, Harkness and Cotrell discuss the notion that codependency is reoppressing women through the recapitulation of patriarchal politics of power in recovery. These same researchers also maintain that, from a certain feminist perspective, the cure for codependency is equally as toxic as the disease itself. They agree with Collins in asserting that the recovery is toxic because it is based on the core basic assumption of subordination.

The argument is similar to the argument about powerlessness and recovery for racial/ethnic minorities discussed in Chapter 12. The argument is based on the idea that recovery is toxic because codependent persons must assume a stance of powerlessness in order to become free from addiction.

This powerlessness is layered by the experience of powerlessness in the sociopolitical realm. Thus, feminist concerns about codependency and recovery reflect the subtle and powerful social realm impacting the identification and treatment of women in need.

RELATIONSHIP BETWEEN SOCIAL OPPRESSION AND CODEPENDENCY Borovoy (2000, 2005, 2009) and Kwon (2001) are both interested in the impact of the larger social narratives on the meanings of codependency for women in Asian cultures. Borovoy states that, because alcoholism in Japan has become more of a social concern, the notion of codependency is becoming a more significant issue. Borovoy agrees with many feminist researchers in believing that the codependency narrative pathologized women in the 1980s. Moreover, Borovoy agrees with Kwon in maintaining that the Western meanings of codependency do not transfer well to the Japanese (Asian) culture.

In Japan, the American version of codependency is seen as normal and not viewed as a compromise of the self. Borovoy goes on to state that the codependency discourse in Japan is reminiscent of its postwar national ideologies. These ideologies reflect the value of a family-like (codependent?) intimacy holding together Japanese society. This dominant discourse also implores its social members to develop a highly cultivated sensitivity to social demands.

Kim (2002) is also interested in the impact of a codependent discourse on women of Korea and other Asian cultures. Kim took an accepted feminist perspective in noting the significant influence that social oppression has on codependency. Kim develops a concept of codependency that is derived from the Korean notion of *jong-sok-euee-jon,* known as "subjugated dependency" (p. 2469). In this context, codependency in Korean women is seen as resulting from the oppressive Confucian patriarchy in marriage and family systems. The hypothesis of this qualitative study was that there would be a strong relationship between the persistence of Confucian patriarchal values and practices in the Korean family structure and females' disposition to codependency in their marriages. Results confirmed the hypothesis for this sample: A positive relationship exists between codependency and the practices of Confucian patriarchal values.

The studies underscore the significance of being sensitive to cultural differences when applying the essential concepts of Western codependency to collective cultures, specifically for women in Korea and Japan. Borovoy (2000, 2005) believes that Japanese women who define themselves as codependent need to distinguish between socially valued interdependence and unhealthy or systematically exploitive forms of asymmetrical ties. Borovoy believes that, in this way, these codependent women can reject the exploitive demands of society while continuing to function in familial and neighboring communities.

MyCounselingLab for Addictions/Substance Abuse

Try the Topic 8 Assignments: *Family Treatment.*

Summary

- The 1980s witnessed a spate of interest in the concept of ACOAs and codependency, concepts that, although different, many associate together.
- The clinical characteristics exhibited by ACOAs include low self-esteem, being overly responsible, having depressive symptoms, exhibiting antisocial behavior, anxiety disorders, parentification, and blurred and enmeshed boundaries in relationships.
- Other traits include difficulty with intimacy, discomfort with emotions, indecisiveness, and excessively giving into the needs of others.

- A great deal of evidence exists that ACOAs are at risk for substance abuse.
- One of the strongest predictors of alcohol problems in adulthood is having a parent who was alcoholic.
- Intervening with ACOAs includes the identification and addressing of early symptoms of problematic drinking and dysfunctional behavior and should also include the development of appropriate coping skills to replace those that may predispose clients to relational issues.
- There are several studies of ACOA among college students, and numerous campuses have or are instituting Campus Recovery Programs to help students who are in recovery.
- There are many definitions of codependency, and these definitions are influenced by the degree to which one subscribes to the concept; many who do not subscribe believe the characteristics have already been identified in various *Diagnostic and Statistical Manual of Mental Disorders (DSM)*, fifth edition, text revision, diagnostic classifications.

- Many see codependency as an addiction that is chronic, progressive, and fatal.
- Some research suggests that codependency has phases similar to grief and loss models.
- Feminists criticize the concept of codependency, asserting that the discourse blames the client for failure, blames the victim, equates closeness with pathology, and advocates for therapists to not totally trust their clients.
- Codependency does not translate well into collective culture narratives because of the emphasis upon "We"; in Asian cultures, many see a positive and unhealthy relationship between codependency and Confucian patriarchal values.
- Regarding treatment concerns, the client's use of the label ACOA and/or the term "codependent" can be helpful in that the terms are easy to understand, and many individuals are familiar with the concepts.
- Mental health professionals should remain aware of their own proclivities toward behaving codependently with their clientele.

Internet Resources

Adult Children of Alcoholics
adultchildren.org/

Codependency
mnwelldir.org/docs/mental_health/codependency.htm
mentalhealthamerican.net

Stepfamilies
stepfamilies.info/stepfamily.org

Further Discussion

1. What are your views of ACOAs? Is there such a concept?
2. Why is there so much controversy about ACOAs?
3. What is beneficial about labeling oneself as an ACOA and/or codependent?

4. Codependency has been criticized for gender bias. To what extent do you agree or disagree with those claims?
5. In what ways does mental health professionals' codependency help or not help this population?

CHAPTER 14

HIV/AIDS

CASE EXAMPLES

1 Ron is HIV-positive and has been on antiretroviral therapy (ART). He has had an undetectable viral load for the past three years. He is applying for a job as a food server and is worried about questions that he may be asked about the lapse of continuous employment that occurred when he first became HIV-infected and depressed. Even though he has been receiving therapy and his risk of transmission is low, he is afraid that if he is truthful about his chronic illness, he will not be able to get the job. He is afraid in spite of the fact that workplace transmission of HIV is rare.

2 Emily and Michael have been married for three years. Both have been aware of Michael's HIV status ever since they began dating. Although Michael is being treated with ART since he first found out and they have been practicing safe sex, Emily is becoming increasingly concerned about getting infected and has stopped wanting to have sex altogether. Michael understands her concerns, yet he feels helpless, angry, and guilty as a result. She does not seem to understand that with treatment, the risk of transmission is very low. He had attended counseling sessions after he first found out that he was infected. However, he stopped going when the counselor pressed him about disclosing his status to potential partners. He did disclose to Emily when they first began to consider sexual relations, but he found himself feeling too vulnerable to want to share more with the counselor whom he perceived as not really understanding.

3 Charneatha is a 13-year-old middle school student who lives in a low-income urban area. She was sexually abused as a child by one of her parent's friends, which her parents became aware of only after it happened. Recently, Charneatha's parents have been arguing over whether or not to provide birth control pills to their daughter, who has been hinting about sexual activity. Charneatha's father is against it, but her mother wants Charneatha to take birth control because she is frightened about her daughter being at high risk. During the course of their conversations, they both realized that neither had really come to closure on their daughter's sexual abuse.

4 Gerardo is a gay male who came out to his friend on his 17th birthday. Neither had been educated about HIV from their families or friends. School policy had precluded any discussion of "safe sex," and both adolescents were raised by heterosexual parents who did not discuss sex at all. He first learned about anal sex from the Internet, where he was watching heterosexual pornography. Still, he did not know about the imperatives of using condoms every time because he did not witness it on the Internet. His first partner was a gay male adolescent of the same age who had only experienced oral sex. Both thought that anal sex was "low risk" if you did not ejaculate. Both also thought that you "make AIDS" rather than contracting it from an infected person.

5   Jenean, 63, began dating again two years after her husband died. Her first date was with a friend she had known for a long time. After a period of dating, she and George (age 57) decided to have sex. Because she was past the childbearing years, she did not believe she needed him to use a condom. And because of their respective ages, she did not ask him about his sexual background. She was shocked when she tested positive for HIV months later.

In May 1981, five cases of *Pneumocystis carinii* pneumonia were reported to the Centers for Disease Control and Prevention (CDC) in Atlanta, Georgia. In December of the same year, more than 100 gay men were diagnosed with Kaposi's sarcoma (a skin cancer). So much interest was generated that, by September 1982, the CDC officially identified and labeled the acquired immunodeficiency syndrome (AIDS) as resulting from HIV infection. To give you some perspective on the disease, consider this: Pretend you were reading this paragraph in 1992, a mere 10 years after the CDC first labeled AIDS. In the time that it would have taken you to read this page in 1992, one American would have been infected with HIV. In the time that it would have taken you to read this chapter in 1992, three more people would have died from AIDS. By the end of one day in 1992, 212 people would have been diagnosed with full-blown AIDS (Primm, 1992). Although a new case of HIV infection occurred about every minute or so in 1992, a new HIV diagnosis occurred about every nine minutes in 2011. HIV/AIDS is now considered a chronic disease for those who have both access to and tolerance for the powerful drugs used in treatment (National Institutes of Health, 2011). There still is no cure. Yet, the fear has subsided. Those who were born in 1992 are now in their mid-20s, and this population and the ensuing ones are much more aware of HIV/AIDS. Other chronic diseases such as hepatitis C virus (HCV), tuberculosis (TB), and pneumonia are now on the forefront.

INCIDENCE AND PREVALENCE

According to the CDC (2014a), there were an estimated 1.2 million people living with HIV infection in the United States, and almost 13% did not know they were infected. In the United States, HIV is seen as an urban disease, with the South having the highest number of those living with HIV. However, the Northeast and Southeast have the highest rates per 100,000 people.

Table 14.1 reflects the estimates of the new HIV diagnosis for the most affected subpopulations in the United States for 2014. From these figures, you can see that black males-seeking-males (MSM; 11,201), white MSMs (9,008), and Hispanic/Latino MSMs (7,552) represent the largest proportion of newly diagnosed HIV individuals. For 2014, the number of new HIV diagnosed MSMs continues to significantly outrank the number new HIV diagnosed heterosexuals.

Although there remains no effective cure for HIV, it can be controlled. In fact, the CDC (2014a) reports that if a person with an HIV diagnosis is treated early, before the disease advances, he or she may live as long as someone who does not have HIV! We have come a long way since the early 1980s when it was first discovered.

TABLE 14.1 Estimated New HIV Diagnosis for Affected Subpopulations, 2014

Race or Ethnicity	Estimated Number of HIV Diagnoses in the United States, 2014
Black MSMs	11,201
White MSMs	9,008
Hispanic/Latino MSMs	7,552
Black women, heterosexual contact	4,654
Black men, heterosexual contact	2,108
Hispanic/Latina women, heterosexual contact	1,159
White women, heterosexual contact	1,115

Source: HIV among African Americans. Published by Centers for Disease Control and Prevention © 2016.

HIV AND AIDS

Because HIV/AIDS has been around for more than 25 years and has received a great deal of attention in terms of prevention and treatment, individuals are now much more aware of what it is and how it is transmitted. The virus attacks a person's immune system—specifically the CD4 cells, and once you get HIV, you have it for life. HIV infection puts individuals at risk for other diseases such as TB and hepatitis. This occurs because of the devastation that HIV causes significantly suppresses one's abilities to fight off other infections.

Stages

Once infected, individuals need to be treated immediately. As mentioned earlier, if treated early with ART, individuals may live as long as those who are not infected. However, this length of life is relegated by the degree to which ART is practiced regularly and the protocol is followed closely. The CDC (2016a) has outlined the stages of HIV.

STAGES OF DEVELOPMENT

Stage One: Acute Infection.   Within two to four weeks of being infected with HIV, an individual may appear with flu-like symptoms, and these symptoms may last several weeks. This is a critical stage because exposure to HIV may not reveal symptoms for a few weeks, often leaving individuals unaware of the association between HIV exposure and infection and symptoms.

Stage Two: Clinical Latency.   This is also known as asymptomatic HIV infection of chronic HIV infection because HIV may not be very active, thus rendering little evidence of the infection. This period can last 10 years or longer if the person is not being treated. For those treated, this stage may last for several decades. At this stage, HIV can still transmit the disease.

Stage Three: AIDS.   This is the most severe phase of HIV infection. At this stage, the individual's immune system is so damaged that co-occurring infections are more likely to take place. These are referred to as "opportunistic illnesses" and often include TB and hepatitis.

Testing for HIV

There are three broad types of tests available (CDC, 2016b), and these include antibody tests, combination or fourth-generation test, and nucleic acid tests (NAT). These tests can be performed on blood, oral fluid, or urine.

Rapid Antibody Screening Tests. It can take from three to 12 weeks for a person with HIV to generate enough antibodies for an antibody test. With these rapid tests, results can be ready in 30 minutes or less. The OraQuick HIV Test is available for purchase online and in retail stores and requires swabbing one's mouth. This test may be performed at home or at a clinic. The Home Access HIV-1 Test System is another home collection kit and involves pricking one's finger. Results are available usually within 24 hours and come back from a licensed laboratory.

Combination or Fourth-Generation Test. This test examines HIV antibodies and antigens. This is a test that is effective in detecting HIV before antibodies are developed. This type of screening is performed in laboratories and is becoming very common in the United States. The CDC (2016b) says that this test is also becoming available as a rapid test.

NAT. This test detects HIV in one's blood and does not detect antibodies themselves. It can determine the actual amount of virus (called viral load) that is present. It can take between seven and 28 days for a NAT test to detect HIV. It is recommended that this test be conducted in conjunction with either an antibody or fourth-generation test to help rule out false negatives.

There are three ways that pregnant women can be tested for HIV: opt-out, opt-in, and mandatory newborn HIV testing (CDC, 2002; 2016d). In the opt-out testing approach, pregnant women are notified that an HIV test will be a component of a standard battery of tests. For the opt-in approach, pregnant women are given pretest counseling and must consent specifically to an HIV test. The third approach, mandatory newborn HIV testing, can occur if the pregnant women's HIV status is unknown at the time of delivery. In this case, newborns are tested with or without the mother's consent.

Transmission of HIV

According to the CDC (2016c), anal sex with someone who has HIV remains the highest risk sexual behavior, and receiving sex (bottoming) is riskier than insertive sex (topping). Vaginal sex is the second riskiest behavior, followed by sharing needles, syringes, rinse water, or other equipment used to prepare drugs for injection. The CDC warns that HIV can live in used needles for up to 42 days. Less common modes of transmission include mother-to-child transmission during pregnancy, birth, or breastfeeding. HIV is not spread through saliva. In rare cases, HIV has been shown to be transmitted from an HIV-infected individual through oral sex, blood transfusions, being bitten or eating already chewed food from an HIV-infected person, open skin wounds or mucous membranes, and from deep kissing or sore/bleeding gums. Transmission from body piercings is also very low and is related to the procedure and equipment.

Figure 14.1 depicts the types of transmission of new HIV infections, and it is clear that male-to-male contact remains the most common way that HIV is transmitted in 2010. Males continue to outnumber females in contracting HIV from injecting drugs. Yet, the number of females who are diagnosed with HIV from heterosexual contact is almost two times more than males. The probable causes for this will be discussed later in the chapter.

Figure 14.2 reflects the stage of care that HIV-infected individuals are engaged in as of 2012. As you can see, 87% of the more than 1.2 million Americans with HIV are aware of their diagnosis. This translates into 1,062,100 individuals. Thirty-nine percent or 476,366 are seeing an HIV physician; 36% (441,422) are receiving some form of treatment; and, 30% (368,338) have a very low viral count in their bodies.

Coinfection: HIV Infection and Other Diseases

Since HIV was first diagnosed, an association between HIV infection, drug use, TB, sexually transmitted diseases (STDs), HCV, hepatitis B virus, fungi, and human cytomegalovirus has been found

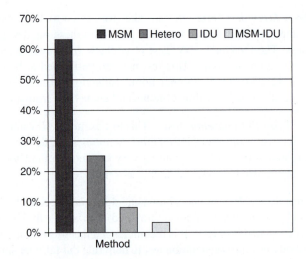

FIGURE 14.1 Estimated New HIV Infections by Route of Transmission, 2010. *Source: CDC fact sheet: HIV testing in the United States.* Published by Centers for Disease Control and Prevention © 2016.

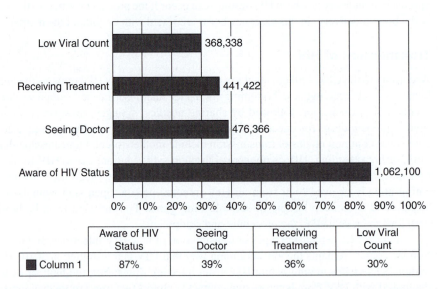

	Aware of HIV Status	Seeing Doctor	Receiving Treatment	Low Viral Count
■ Column 1	87%	39%	36%	30%

FIGURE 14.2 Selected Stages of HIV-Infected Care, 2012. *Source: CDC fact sheet: HIV testing in the United States.* Published by Centers for Disease Control and Prevention © 2016.

(National Institute of Allergy and Infectious Diseases, 2015). Anyone can get TB: people of all races and colors, rich and poor, of any age. Despite a decline in TB nationwide, rates have increased in certain states, and elevated TB rates continue to be reported in certain populations (e.g., foreign-born persons, racial/ethnic minorities). People with HIV are at higher risks for contracting these diseases, and according to the National Institute of Allergy and Infectious Diseases (2015), it is estimated that more than 11.4 million people worldwide have TB and HIV coinfection (National Institute of Allergy and Infectious Diseases, 2009). Although treatable, TB is the leading cause of death for the HIV population.

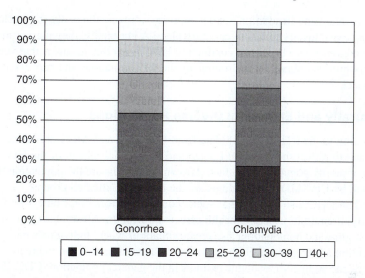

FIGURE 14.3   Reported Cases of Gonorrhea and Chlamydia, 2014. *Source: CDC fact sheet: Reported STDs in the United States, 2014. National data for chlamydia, gonorrhea, and syphilis.* Published by Centers for Disease Control and Prevention © 2015.

STDs remain a major public health challenge in the United States. Although rates of syphilis infections have increased for both males and females, the MSM group has the greatest percentage of cases (83%). The CDC (2014b) estimates that there were 1,441,789 reported cases of chlamydia in the United States, which represents ". . . the highest number of annual cases of any condition ever reported to the CDC" (CDC, 2014b). Figure 14.3 depicts the reported cases of gonorrhea and chlamydia for 2014 by age. As can be seen in this figure, the highest reported number of cases of gonorrhea and chlamydia occurred for the 20 to 24 age group. This information is of critical importance because when compared to those who do not have an sexually transmitted infection (STI), a person contracting an STI is at greater risk of also contracting HIV (CDC, 2015b).

HIGH-RISK GROUPS

Women

Globally, one young woman is infected with HIV every minute (UNAIDS, 2012). According to UNAIDS, between 11% and 45% of adolescent girls report that their first sexual encounter was a forced encounter, and this coincides with the fact women aged 15 to 24 are twice as likely to contract HIV than young men. In the United States in 2013, 37% (1,154) of the 3,096 diagnosed HIV cases were women. Overall in the United States, one in every four who have HIV is a woman. And, chances are that this woman is black/African American (61%) or Hispanic/Latina (17%) (CDC, 2016d).

Although women having sex with women can spread HIV, it is rather rare (womenshealth. gov, 2012). Although health insurance was once an issue that posed a barrier to diagnosis and treatment for this population, the Affordable Healthcare Act has impacted this barrier in a good way to a degree. However, society is still slow in recognizing legal marriage in the gay and lesbian population, and without legal recognition, insurance companies are not obligated to pay for a partner's medical treatment. In addition, sexual minority women will not always disclose their sexual orientation or sexual history to health care providers. Additionally, they may or may not be aware that an STI increases their chances of contracting HIV. What this means is that very often lesbian women will not present themselves for routine medical examinations and may even delay seeking treatment when sick.

Culturally and Ethnically Diverse Populations

According to the CDC (2016b), data from U.S. HIV and AIDS prevalence and incidence surveys continue to reflect the disproportionate and differential impact of the HIV epidemic on racial and ethnic minority populations. In fact, African Americans are the population that is the most severely affected by HIV/AIDS, and Latinos are the next most affected group.

The CDC also reports that socioeconomic factors contribute significantly to the problem. Poverty often limits access to health care, even with the Affordable Care Act. Issues of discrimination, stigma, and homophobia also create situations where individuals may feel discouraged to seek prevention and treatment. Higher rates of incarceration also can indirectly affect HIV infection by limiting the number of available partners in the general population (CDC, 2016e). It is possible that poverty also creates circumstances where individuals may become involved in risky behaviors to deal with the stress.

Adolescents

Figure 14.3 shows the percentage of adolescents (ages 15 to 19) who were diagnosed with certain STIs in the United States in 2014. It may not be surprising to see that roughly one-half of STIs are found among adolescents and young adults. As mentioned, having an STD increases the risk of HIV infection, and this is reflected in the HIV diagnoses for 2014 where there were 1,908 new diagnoses of HIV infection in the 13 to 19 age group. In the United States, African Americans represented approximately 67% of this group, followed by Hispanic/Latino at 18%, and white adolescents at 11%. Overall, 81% of the newly diagnosed HIV-infected adolescents were male and 19% were female. A vast majority of the male adolescents were infected with HIV through male-to-male sexual contact (92.6%). However, 84% of adolescent women contracted the HIV infection through heterosexual contact. Prevalence rates for adolescents show that Louisiana, Florida, Georgia, New York, and Washington, D.C., have some of the highest rates of adolescent HIV diagnoses (CDC, 2016f).

Studies have shown that children and adolescents who were sexually abused were more likely to engage in activities that increased their risk for HIV infection (Capuzzi & Gross, 1996; Jones et al., 2010). Specifically, Capuzzi and Gross found that females who were sexually abused were three times more likely to have injected drugs and five times more likely to have had intercourse before the age of 13. The males who reported sexual abuse were nine times more likely to report injecting drugs and nearly four times as likely to have initiated sexual intercourse before the age of 13. This is the information that Charneatha's mother had in Case Example 3. She felt that her daughter was at risk because of her daughter's sexual abuse. Yet, she was unable to convince her husband that providing birth control was not the same as condoning sex.

Another risk factor for adolescents is their age, upbringing, and exposure to information. As shown in Case Example 4, Gerardo and his companion had very little information about HIV/AIDS and very little information about sex. Instead, they gleaned information off the Internet, where they watched heterosexual pornography. This case study reflects the idea of "folk knowledge" about HIV (Kubicek et al., 2008) as opposed to "professional knowledge." Professional knowledge reflects the idea of a "prevention ethic," which revolves around the notion of "a condom every time" (Race, 2003).

Other High-Risk Groups

THOSE IN THE PENAL SYSTEM   Adolescents, especially male adolescents who cycle through the juvenile justice system, are at high risk for HIV infection (Lauby et al., 2010). The reason for the higher risk is that juveniles in the justice system often have a history of engaging in higher rates of sexual risk behaviors. This can include initiating sexual activity at younger ages, having multiple sex partners, and inconsistent use of condoms.

Little evidence exists to describe the transmission of HIV in prison. However, tattooing, sex, and injection drug use do occur, and if the safety precautions discussed earlier are not followed, infection can occur. It is not just HIV infection that can occur. These behaviors increase the opportunity for HCV to be transmitted, and indeed these behaviors are the most common ways that HCV is contracted (CDC, 2016h). Of the 2.2 million prisoners in the United States, one in three have HCV. Incarcerated individuals are also at greater risk for contracting TB, and this is reflected in the fact that between 4% and 6% of prisoners have TB (CDC, 2015c).

Given the HIV infection prevalence rates for the African American population concomitant with the high rates of incarceration, it is rather clear that these high rates would be reflected in the general prison population. In fact, they are: African American male prisoners are five times more likely than their white or Hispanic counterparts to be diagnosed with HIV, and female African Americans are more than twice as likely to have an HIV diagnosis than either the white or Hispanic/Latina population (CDC, 2016g).

Generally, resources for testing and treatment are often lacking in correctional facilities (CDC, 2016g). In many cases, it is an issue of resource management, and prison officials must weigh the costs against other programs. Rapid turnover among the incarcerated also contributes to the problem. Because nine of 10 inmates are released within 72 hours, there is little or no time to test them and help find treatment. There are also concerns about privacy and stigma among this population.

To address these and other concerns, the CDC has contracted selected state health departments to conduct voluntary rapid testing in jails. This is an attempt to identify undiagnosed cases and refer them for help. In addition to this effort, the CDC has also worked with universities and others to determine effective interventions for the incarcerated population. For example, there is Project START (Success Through Assistive Rehabilitative Technology), which is a prerelease program aimed at lowering the risky behaviors of inmates once they are released. In addition, the CDC published a guide for correctional facilities (CDC, 2009). This guide recommends that inmates be tested upon entering correctional facilities, during incarceration, and again just prior to release. Inmates should be educated about HIV risk and risky behaviors as well as being provided medical treatment.

THE HOMELESS   In any given year, approximately 1% of the general population is homeless (CDC, 2013b). Homeless people may not just live on the street. As a result of the great recession, homelessness is reflected in a variety of ways, including the use of shelters, staying with friends, living in tent cities, and living in cars or rundown motels. It is a lack of mobility and homelessness that contributes to the disconnection from health services. This is significant because even with the Affordable Care Act, homeless people may not enter into the health care system.

As you can imagine, drug abuse, TB, HCV, and HIV statistics for this population are hard to determine. Nonetheless, the population of people who are homeless present another population at high risk for HIV, and they differ from the general population in a number of ways (Friedman et al., 2009; Kerker et al., 2011).

Homeless people may be more likely to abuse substances, engage in survival sex and/or high-risk sex, and less likely to adhere to the demands of complex treatment protocols. Because TB rates are somewhat correlated with HIV rates, it is interesting to note that more than 5% of individuals with TB reported being homeless in the previous year. Factors such as poor hygiene, inadequate nutrition, lack of medical care, crowded shelters, and the unsanitary conditions that prevail among this population all contribute significantly to their high risk.

PEOPLE WITH DISABILITIES AND OLDER ADULTS   In 1998, the U.S. Supreme Court ruled that asymptomatic HIV infection is constituted as disability (Gagnon & Stuart, 2009). Very few studies have been conducted about persons with disabilities (PWDs) and HIV. However, the international literature suggests that this population is at increased risk. One reason is the lack of sex education. Historically, PWDs have been routinely excluded from sex education because PWDs were seen as either asexual or oversexed and not in need of information (Rohleder, 2010). Moreover, adults with learning disabilities have referred to sexual acts as "rude" and said that sex education was "rude" or "bad" (Heyman & Huckle, 1995). In one study of 99 adolescents, of which 56% were males, Maart and Jelsma (2010) found that physically disabled adolescents were engaging in risky sexual behaviors at the same rate as their nondisabled cohorts. Thus, the authors conclude that the population of PWDs should not be overlooked when it comes to being at risk for HIV/AIDS. We are suggesting that you, as mental health professionals, do not fall prey to your own stereotypes about sex and disabilities.

Older Americans often do not know as much about HIV as younger populations (CDC, 2015e). This population is less educated about condoms, not sharing needles, getting tested, and conversing with their health care provider about HIV. At the same time, health care providers do not often talk with their elderly patients about HIV. So, a discussion about an elderly person's sexual history goes by the wayside in many cases. Recall Jenean in Case Example 5 at the outset of this chapter. She assumed that because of her age and the age of her partner, she did not need to be cautious. She was wrong. Yet she was not alone in her assumptions about age and AIDS. She was equating condoms with birth control and not with HIV.

Older adults may be less likely to get tested for HIV. When they do get tested, it may be at a late stage and less likely to respond well to treatment (Kearney, Moore, Donegan, & Lambert, 2010). Older Americans often know less about HIV/AIDS than do younger people. Health care professionals, including doctors, nurses, home health care providers, and educators, assume this population is either unaffected by the virus or is not at risk. This is coupled with the fact that older adults do not easily communicate about sex as much as younger people do. Therefore, the topic often evades discussion between older adults and health care professionals.

ASSESSMENT OF CLIENTS FOR HIV AND AIDS: SIGNS AND SYMPTOMS

As you saw previously in this chapter, early detection and medical treatment can forestall the onset of AIDS and ARC, although to date nothing can eliminate the probability of AIDS once a person has been infected with HIV. Although the diagnosis of HIV can be made only by positive tests for the HIV antibody, several indicators might suggest the presence of the infection in clients who have not undergone medical testing for the virus. Therefore, it is important that you, as mental health professionals, be aware of issues that suggest the presence of HIV in order to urge high-risk clients to be tested and, hopefully, to receive appropriate medical intervention if they show early stages of infection. Referral of the client for assessment of HIV infection is crucial when risk factors are coupled with other signs and symptoms. These other signs and symptoms include physical anomalies and neuropsychiatric disturbances, which are discussed next.

Physical Signs and Symptoms

It is customary for mental health professionals to initially elicit a psychosocial, drug, and brief medical history from their clients. In the course of that interview, clients may mention many symptoms that, to them, may seem unrelated to the risk of HIV infection. Women with HIV symptoms may have extreme fatigue, rapid weight loss, low-grade fevers that occur with frequency, vaginal yeast infections, changes in menstrual cycles, may have sexually transmitted infections, and will often have discolored blotches appearing on the skin or inside the mouth. For others, these signs and symptoms may include complaints of fever, unexplained weight loss or loss of appetite, night sweats, general malaise, coughing and/or shortness of breath, swollen lymph nodes, recurrent or persistent sinusitis, abdominal pain, diarrhea, and visual changes such as visual field defects.

HELPING HIV-INFECTED CLIENTS

A little fewer than one in five (17%) of people living with HIV have private insurance, and 30% do not have coverage at all. Medicaid and Medicare are programs that can provide health care benefits for low-income individuals and those with disabilities. The Affordable Care Act of 2010 has influenced the care of HIV-infected people, and indeed has been one of the most important pieces of legislation in the fight against HIV/AIDS (CDC, 2015d). The law created the Pre-Existing Condition Insurance Plan, which has helped those who were already infected with HIV. This and other legislation allows HIV individuals who fall below the poverty line access to more immediate health care, and this is critical because we have mentioned the importance of early testing and intervention.

Clients with HIV can manage only the disease process and the disease itself, so once a client is diagnosed with HIV or AIDS, your concern as a mental health professional will be to focus on helping the client attempt to manage and cope with the disease. Remember, the only way to know whether a client is infected is to be tested for HIV. Mental health professionals should not rely on symptoms alone because many people who are infected with HIV do not have symptoms for many years. Someone can look and feel healthy but still be infected.

In all cases, it is critical that clients adhere to the medications prescribed for HIV infection. The virus can replicate and mutate readily, especially if doses are missed. In general, non-HIV cases, individuals can adhere to treatment of chronic diseases about 80% of the time and still be successful. However, with HIV, this level does not work. Patients need to adhere almost 100% of the time to keep the virus from replicating. The absence of treatment means that almost all those infected with HIV will eventually get AIDS.

In general, the focus on helping the HIV-infected client is on assisting the client in understanding and accepting the changes that are occurring and will occur in his or her life. Educating the client about the disease and treatment is also important, which includes emphasizing that AIDS is not necessarily fatal. Because practice settings offering HIV care vary according to local resources and needs, mental health professionals need to have some knowledge of the resources that are available for each patient to avoid fragmentation of care. Clearly, a single source, capable of providing comprehensive care for all stages of HIV infection, is preferred. However, this is often not possible. In every case involving HIV-infected clients, mental health professionals should make concerted efforts to avoid long delays between diagnosis of HIV infection and access to additional medical and psychosocial services.

The CDC (2015f) and the World Health Organization (2007) have outlined an approach to helping HIV-infected clients. This approach is called palliative care therapy, and it is indicated for clients who are living with an incurable illness. The aim of this approach is to help provide the best quality of life to clients and to offer support and comfort to loved ones. Palliative care is based on work conducted with hospice cancer patients and addresses emotional, psychological, and spiritual needs. Because HIV patients will probably suffer from severe pain at some point, pain control is a central focus of palliative care. Palliative caregivers affirm life and help clients see that dying is a natural process that can neither be hastened nor postponed.

The CDC treatment guidelines for HIV (2006a) recommend the following for counseling persons with HIV:

- Counseling should include the behavioral, psychosocial, and medical implications of HIV infection.
- Providers should be acutely aware of medical and psychosocial conditions that may be emergent.
- Providers should address other issues such as psychiatric disorders, emotional distress, or substance abuse.
- Providers should follow up on recommendations given to clients.
- Patients should be educated about what to expect from the medical community.

Regarding the medical community, clients need to know that they will be asked for a detailed medical history that will include sexual and AOD history. They will be given a complete physical examination, and blood tests will be conducted. Included will be an assessment for other infectious diseases such as STIs, TB, and HCV. It is also likely that the medical facility will conduct a urinalysis as well as a chest radiograph.

PSYCHOSOCIAL CONCERNS OF HIV-INFECTED CLIENTS Although people infected with HIV and treated early and who follow treatment protocol may now live as long as those who have not been diagnosed, clients with HIV will likely be distressed when they are first informed of a positive HIV test result. According to the CDC (2006b; 2016a), changes will include (1) coping with the stigmatization, (2) the need to develop and adopt new strategies for maintaining physical and emotional health, and (3) initiating changes in behavior to prevent HIV transmission to others. In addition, many persons will require assistance with making reproductive choices, gaining access to health services, confronting possible employment or housing discrimination, and coping with changes in personal relationships.

Vital in the approach to helping drug-abusing clients with HIV is a coordinated effort among the psychological, medical, social services, legal, pastoral and religious, peer support groups, significant family members, and other community-based service networks. The plethora of services required by these clients is due to the myriad tasks needing attention once the individual has AIDS. Another area of concern is the client's sexuality and the risk of HIV transmission. Understanding the sexual aspects of the disease is of paramount importance, and frank communication between you as the mental health professional and your client is essential. Human touch is essential to everyone, and the client should be encouraged to hug his or her loved ones as well as to engage in safe sex. However, if an individual has already been exposed to HIV infection and has unprotected sexual relations with another infected individual, an acceleration of the disease process may be experienced. So it is critical to emphasize the importance of safer sex practices among already infected HIV clients.

EMOTIONAL CONCERNS Although current treatment protocol can now manage a great many emotional concerns through education and treatment, clients who have HIV may present a number of emotional reactions that can include anxiety, stress–distress syndrome, panic reactions, suicidal ideation, rumination, depression, and a plethora of defense mechanisms such as denial, anger, guilt, and isolation (Joseph & Bhatti, 2004; Springer & Lease, 2000).

In Case Example 2, Emily became more and more overwhelmed and scared about Michael's HIV status. Her fears escalated to the point that she did not want him sexually. In this case study, Emily was not as scared of HIV as she was of the communication breakdown that had insidiously crept into their relationship. This situation points out the need for helpers to address more "non–HIV-related" issues than the disease itself. It is critically important to not overlook the "usual" relational issues that can severely impact the mental and emotional health of both.

In general, spiritual themes will be relevant for all individuals. At the same time, the individual's psychosocial development and cultural mores will influence the manner in which these themes are presented and processed. Given the overrepresentation of racioethnic populations with HIV/AIDS, the diverse cultural spiritual beliefs and practices are obviously critical for counselors to consider. For example, mid to late adolescents are already working with issues related to the meaning of life. An aging individual is asking the same questions from the other direction. Although both individuals are experiencing questions about the meaning of life, an adolescent's perspective is different from that of an aging person, and the conversations that occur in counseling with the adolescent will be different from the conversations with an older adult. One difference between the two conversations would relate to the discussion with the older client regarding the client's comorbid health conditions. The multiple losses in physical health experienced by the aging population in general can become overwhelming when HIV/AIDS is present.

MEDICAL CONCERNS   We have already discussed the medical concerns related to helping HIV-infected clients and suggested that the medical questions that clients have should be referred to medical personnel. Medical concerns are greatly diminished the earlier the treatment starts! Adherence to HIV therapy protocol is of critical importance.

There may be some metabolic complications or side effects that occur with ART, which includes but is not limited to lipid abnormalities, hyperglycemia, and decreased bone mineral density. These are monitored by physicians, so mental health professionals should pay attention to any client reported side effects and refer the client to his or her physician or HIV medical provider.

Pain management, a focus of palliative therapy, might also be a potential problem because HIV-infected clients will still frequently require analgesia for the pain syndrome that often accompanies the opportunistic infections (Selwyn, 1992). Because drug-abusing HIV-infected clients probably have access to illegal drugs that can be used to numb the pain, this is one issue counselors need to keep in mind when and if their clients talk about pain. With the drug-abusing HIV-infected client, self-medication with AZT and antibiotics may also be a problem because both can be purchased on the street. Again, clients should be warned of the dangers of self-medicating.

One thing to keep in mind is that insurance often does not pay for alternative treatments for HIV. Hence, alternative methods for treating HIV once the person is on a traditional therapeutic protocol are usually out of pocket. Some alternative approaches, known as complementary and alternative medicine (CAM) do not cost anything but time and dedication. Barnes, Powell-Griner, McFann, and Nahin (2004) identified 10 CAMs: prayer, prayer by others, natural products, deep breathing exercises, participation in a prayer group for one's own illness, meditation, chiropractic care, yoga, massage, and diet-based therapies. Yoga does not cost much and is gaining interest as a treatment for HIV/AIDS (Foster, 1999; Stukin, 2003).

ISSUES IN THE WORKPLACE Hergenrather and Rhodes (2008) and Pereira (2010) estimate that approximately 90% to 97% of people living with HIV are in the economically productive period of their lives, and HIV/AIDS has generated more lawsuits than any disease in the history of the U.S. legal system. These statistics underscore the importance of looking at issues related to HIV/AIDS and the workplace. Workplace transmission of HIV is extremely rare (CDC, 2015g).

According to the Americans with Disabilities Act, private employers with 15 or more employees may not discriminate in any employment practice against qualified individuals with disabilities. This means that, for example, a restaurant may not fire a waitress upon notification that she is HIV-positive, nor can a university fire a physical education instructor because her or his boyfriend has AIDS. Although prospective employees with HIV/AIDS have concerns about accommodations, the Americans with Disabilities Act requires employers to make "reasonable accommodations" to those having a disability. This means that employers are required to modify any aspect of the job so that people living with HIV/AIDS (PLWHA) can perform the essential functions of the job. This would include restructuring the job, modifying work schedules, acquiring or modifying equipment, and reassigning to a vacant position for which the PLWHA is qualified. For example, an HIV-positive individual might be granted longer lunches to keep medical appointments and be required to make up the time in flexible ways.

Obviously, the employer would have to know that the employee is disabled in order to make accommodations. This brings up very complex issues. Conyers and Boomer (2005) maintain that research indicates that the vast majority of PLWHA choose not to disclose their status because of fears of discrimination. Research supports this fear (Hergenrather & Rhodes, 2008). Other reasons for not disclosing include a desire for privacy, concerns about the overall work environment, and fear of other repercussions. At the same time, PLWHA may choose to disclose in order to access social support, assert personal identity, and accommodate a desire to be open.

HIV-RELATED ISSUES SPECIFIC TO THE HELPING PROFESSIONAL

Disclosure Laws and Confidentiality

Although federal law addresses the criminalization of HIV exposure in such isolated areas as blood donation, by and large, the states are free to determine the criminality of other exposure. All states have laws that have been used to prosecute individuals with HIV. These laws include assault and battery, reckless endangerment, and attempted murder (CDC, 2015h). As of 2011, 67 laws in 33 states had been enacted focusing specifically on persons living with HIV (CDC, 2015h). Laws requiring a person to disclose HIV infection to sexual partners are in effect in 24 states, and 14 states require disclosure of HIV to a needle-sharing partners. Yet, most state laws are likely out of date because they were passed before the advent of current ART, which lowers the risk of HIV transmission.

From our discussion here (see also Chapter 5), you can readily see that a PLWHA has a right to keep his or her HIV status confidential. At the same time, certain issues of HIV testing warrant special consideration. The CDC (2015h) maintains that a balance must be struck between individual rights and public's need to know. Both ". . . are vital to enhancing the public's health and maintaining public's trust." The CDC suggests that adherence to consistent policies and standards for data security will indeed help data sharing while addressing confidentiality concerns.

Clearly, health care professionals cannot disclose information without client's approval. At the same time, you as mental health professionals face a quandary regarding duty of care to the sexual partner(s) of your HIV-infected clients. This is essentially an issue of scope and content of the duty. There have been instances of case law where care providers have been found to have breached the law by failing to take steps available to them to protect an HIV-infected individual's partner from becoming HIV-positive (Mair, 2009). Yet, HIV-infected clients do resist disclosure. Stigma and a perceived lack of support are significant barriers (Emlet, 2008). Serovich (2001) discusses two theories of disclosure: *disease progression theory* and *consequences theory*. In the former, disclosure is made only when the progression of the disease makes it almost impossible to receive care and support without clients disclosing information. *Consequences theory* is a process whereby clients assess the potential cost/rewards of disclosing. This scenario contains three options: full disclosure, selective disclosure, or remaining secretive. More often than not, you will be working through the *consequence theory paradigm* because the lack of disclosure through *disease progression theory* becomes next to impossible at the late stage of the disease. In the study about disclosure among HIV-infected clients, Emlet found that some most clients used "protective silence" to avoid fears of rejection and stigmatization. "Anticipatory disclosure" was the next most often process employed. This process reflected a desire to disclose most often to a particular individual while at the same time continuing to assess potential reactions and consequences.

These models of decision making regarding disclosure or nondisclosure can help guide health care providers' discussions with their clients. You may also be confronted with another situation where the information is divulged either unintentionally or intentionally. A client may have told someone about his or her HIV status, and that person told others. In this case, you may need to help clients deal with anger, guilt, remorse, fear, anxiety, and shame at having disclosed and been betrayed. Finally, intentional disclosure is just that: intentional. Health care professionals can help clients process how their disclosure has changed their lives and help clients come to a fuller acceptance of their decision.

Needle Exchange

Another issue that can confront you as a mental health professional relates to the controversial issue of needle exchange in which drug-injecting addicts can receive clean needles so as to diminish the risk of sharing needles that might be carrying HIV.

The more moderate approach advocated by Marlatt is based on a European approach called harm reduction. Taking a middle-of-the-road approach between prohibition and legalization, the harm reduction approach would include methadone programs for heroin addicts and nicotine replacement therapy for tobacco users and would attempt to control such addictive or excessive behaviors as binge drinking and overeating. Harm reduction also includes legalized needle-exchange programs. Harm reduction approach offers the at-risk populations simple behavioral solutions that can dramatically reduce the danger associated with high-risk activities, and these simple behavioral skills can help prevent the spread of AIDS (through needle-exchange programs and safe-sex and condom-use programs). Safe tattooing information and materials, along with bleach and disinfection materials, would also be included in the harm reduction approach.

The North American Syringe Exchange Network currently has 38 member states. Needle exchange programs work. These programs are not in the needle distribution business per se. These programs require injecting drug users to return a used syringe in order to obtain a new, sterile one. After 21 years of debate and failure, the U.S. Congress and President Obama repealed the ban on federal funding for local needle exchange programs by passing a bill in 2009. The legislation did not contain any new monies for needle exchanges; however, it allowed programs to use federal funds to provide clean needles, subject to approval by local authorities, including law enforcement and health officials.

MyCounselingLab for Addictions/Substance Abuse

Try the Topic 10 Assignment: *Working with Selected Populations.*

Summary

- The HIV/AIDS epidemic has come a long way. Now, with proper and early intervention, a person with HIV can live as long as one who is not infected.
- It is still considered a chronic disease.
- Women are approximately twice as likely as men to contract HIV during vaginal intercourse.
- The CDC warns that HIV can live in used needles for up to 42 days.
- Most women with HIV are racial/ethnic minority women living in urban inner cities and are disproportionately affected by poverty, crime, and social disorganization and represent the most disenfranchised sector of our society.
- There is a relationship between STDs and HIV infection.
- By the time older HIV-infected individuals enter treatment, their HIV-related problems may be already beyond the reach of most human service systems because of a lack of screening.
- An individual living with an HIV-infected person is at minimal to no risk if proper precautions are followed.
- Prevalence rates for adolescents show that Louisiana, Florida, Georgia, New York, and Washington, D.C., have some of the highest rates of adolescent HIV diagnoses.
- Persons living with HIV/AIDS are protected under the Americans with Disabilities Act, 1990, and employers are required to make "reasonable accommodations."
- Employers need to know of the disability to make workplace accommodations but the vast majority of PLWHA choose not to disclose their status because of fears of discrimination, stigma, a desire for privacy, concerns about the overall work environment, and the fear of other repercussions.

- In treating the HIV/AIDS client, the CDC Treatment Guidelines for HIV recommend that counseling persons with HIV should include the behavioral, psychosocial, and medical implications of HIV infection.
- Stages of HIV infection include: acute infection, clinical latency, AIDS.
- Testing for HIV includes rapid antibody screening tests, combination or fourth-generation test, and nucleic acid test.
- Generally, resources for testing and treatment are often lacking in correctional facilities.
- African American male prisoners are 5 times more likely than their white or Hispanic counterparts to be diagnosed with HIV.
- Overall, 81% of the newly diagnosed HIV infected adolescents were male, and 19% were female.
- Legislation allows HIV individuals who fall below the poverty line access to more immediate health care; this is critical because, as we have mentioned, early testing and intervention are important.
- Although federal law addresses the criminalization of HIV exposure in such isolated areas as blood donation, by and large the states are free to determine the criminality of other exposure
- Providers should also be acutely aware of medical and psychosocial conditions that may be emergent and should address other issues such as psychiatric disorders, emotional distress, and substance abuse.
- The older adult population is increasing in size and so is the incidence of HIV infection diagnoses.
- The World Health Organization outlines an approach to helping HIV-infected clients called palliative care therapy for clients who are living with an incurable illness to help provide the

best quality of life to clients and to offer support and comfort to loved ones.
- A federal funding ban on needle exchange programs was lifted in 2009.

- More than 5% of individuals with TB reported being homeless in the previous year.
- TB is the leading cause of death for the HIV population.

Internet Resources

General information: HIV/AIDS
aidsinfo.nih.gov cdc.gov
cdc.gov/hiv/resources/factsheets/

HIV/AIDS Data Security Guidelines
http://www.cdc.gov/nchhstp/programintegration/docs/
PCSIDataSecurityGuidelines.pdf

Specific populations: Older adults and GLBTQI
hivoverfifty.org
nia.hin.gov
sageusa.org

HIV/AIDS and disabilities in the workplace
ada.gov/pubs/hivqanda.txt

Women and HIV/AIDS
who.int/gender/hiv_aids/en/

HIV/AIDS State Laws for Healthcare Providers
http://www.cdc.gov/hiv/policies/law/states/index.html

Palliative therapy
cdc.gov/std/treatment/2006/hiv.htm

Needle Exchange State by State Directory
https://nasen.org/directory

Further Discussion

1. What is your experience with HIV/AIDS? Do you know anyone who is infected?
2. Even knowing the success of early ART intervention in the spread of HIV, how comfortable would you be interacting with a PLWHA in a social situation?
3. Would this be different if you were working with a PLWHA?

4. How does the knowledge of older adults and HIV change or not change your perceptions of that population's sexuality?
5. Should we be giving free syringes to addicts?

CHAPTER 15

Gambling and Other Behavioral Addictions

CASE EXAMPLES

1. Samantha, 33, went to seek counseling because she "just didn't feel right" about the amount of time her husband was spending at home on the Internet. She thought he was hiding things from her. When she asked him about it, he maintained that he was just catching up on work. Yet, whenever she would come into the study unannounced, where they kept their computer, it seemed that he would quickly close out the screen he was on. This raised her suspicions. He would continually deny that anything was going on. She thought that it was just her being insecure and let it go. However, she continued to have feelings of worthlessness and saw herself as sexually undesirable because their sexual relationship was almost nonexistent. When asked, her husband agreed to go in for one counseling session, and during that session, neither of them mentioned their sexual problems. Instead, Samantha spent the time crying about being lonely.

2. Melanie, 19, was an only child who lived on a several-acre property in the country with her parents. In her younger years, she would run on the dirt road in front of her house for exercise and found that she liked running. In high school, she made the women's track team as a distance runner and won enough races to be offered a scholarship at a large university that was in another state. Melanie was always thin. However, when she came home for the Thanksgiving break during her freshman year, her mother was shocked to see how much weight Melanie had lost. In response, Melanie told her mother that she was just working out to keep up with the competition and left it at that. When she returned for the December holidays, Melanie had lost even more weight. By pleading, Melanie's mother was able to get Melanie to go to the doctor for a check-up. Because Melanie was 19 years old, the doctor was not able to tell her mother that Melanie was suffering from anorexia nervosa. Instead, Melanie and her doctor had discussed ways that Melanie could tell her mother. When she arrived home from the doctor's appointment, though, Melanie told her mother that everything was okay and that she was losing weight because she did not like the cafeteria food at the university. She assured her mother that "it would be fine."

3. Lynn is a 44-year-old professional woman who has lived in Las Vegas for more than 20 years. Lynn started gambling in her mid-20s. For many years, Lynn's gambling could be described as recreational. She would go to casinos with friends, play video poker, and socialize. She never lost more than she could afford. At 32, Lynn married for the second time. She and her husband started using cocaine and gambling more and more frequently. They ran up debt on their credit cards. Lynn's husband developed an addiction to cocaine and Lynn left him.

He shot himself to death shortly after they separated. After this traumatic event, Lynn stopped using cocaine and curtailed her gambling. However, in her late 30s, she remarried and started gambling with her third husband. Lynn's gambling started to spiral out of control. She applied for numerous credit cards and took out cash advances on them. To hide her activity, Lynn got a post office box so that her husband wouldn't see the mail. She borrowed money from her parents and friends, making up believable stories to justify the loans. Lynn had a job in which she had a lot of independence, and she spent considerable work time in local bars that had video poker machines. When she finally could not hide her debts any longer, she told her husband. Lynn's husband took care of their debts and made Lynn promise to gamble only with him on weekends. Lynn tearfully agreed and was able to moderate her gambling for a short time. However, within a year, Lynn was gambling out of control and had accumulated more than $200,000 in debt. She couldn't sleep and was contemplating suicide.

This case example is a true story, and it does have a happy ending. Lynn has not gambled in many years and regularly attends Gamblers Anonymous (GA). She has cleaned up all her debts, has a demanding professional career, and enjoys an upper-middle-class lifestyle. It's a far cry from the chaos of compulsive gambling, which involved continuous lying, cheating, and stealing. You may be thinking that this kind of problem happens only in places like Las Vegas and Atlantic City. You would be wrong.

PREVALENCE OF GAMBLING AND GAMBLING PROBLEMS

Brand, Laier, and Young (2014, p. 2) list several ways lives are disrupted in proposing diagnostic criteria for gambling that includes: (1) preoccupation, (2) withdrawal symptoms, (3) tolerance development, (4) lessening interest in other activities, (5) continued use in spite of consequences, (6) deception, (7) use for emotional regulation, and (8) relational issues.

The earliest known six-sided pair of dice dates to about 3000 b.c. Some 5,000 years later, in 1997, the U.S. Congress established the National Gambling Impact and Policy Commission. On June 18, 1999, the National Gambling Impact Study Commission's Final Report was released. Before the establishment of the commission, the last federal study of gambling had been conducted in 1976. The growth of gambling in the United States since that time has been astounding.

Some form of legal gambling is now available in 48 states (exceptions are Utah and Hawaii) and the District of Columbia. Before 1990, the only destination casinos in the United States were in Atlantic City and Nevada. Now more than 100 riverboat and dockside casinos are in operation, and more than 260 casinos operate on Native American reservations. Lotteries operate in 43 states, the District of Columbia, Puerto Rico, and the U.S. Virgin Islands (USA.gov, 2011). According to a Gallup Poll taken in December 2007 that included a national sample of 1,027 adults, aged 18 and older, men are two times more likely than women to gamble on professional sports. Younger Americans are much more likely to gamble on sports than older Americans, and college graduates are significantly more likely to gamble on sports than nongraduates. Of the people who gamble on sports, a direct relationship between money and gambling exists: Only 6% of lower income households gamble on sports, whereas 78% of those whose households earn more than $75,000 gamble. Surprisingly, gambling on sports is not the most popular form of gambling. State lotteries are twice as popular. Jones (2008) reports that almost one-half of Americans state that they have purchased at least one lottery ticket in a given year. In addition, social games are inundated with casino types and are the fastest growing segment of the gaming industry (National Council on Problem Gambling, 2015).

The National Council on Problem Gambling (NCPG) is an advocacy organization for services and programs that assist individuals and families with problem gambling. In 2014, the NCPG released Internet Responsibility Gambling Standards, and since that time Nevada, Delaware, and New Jersey instituted online gambling. Several other states (California, Hawaii, Iowa, Illinois, Massachusetts, Mississippi, Pennsylvania, and Texas) are considering legislation that would authorize it. In 2014, the NCPG commissioned a study of online regulations against actual state laws in those states. The study showed that the states are off on the right footing. Yet, there is still a long way to go for best practices. The NCPG also generated consumer protection guidelines aimed at facilitating discussions between such gambling entities as operators, regulators, legislators, consumer advocates, and the public.

We will specify criteria for gambling addiction, as we did for alcohol and other drug problems. However, we will first talk about the scope of the problem as indicated by the number of individuals the commission identified as having gambling problems. Tse, Hong, Wang, and Cunningham-Williams (2012) reviewed 75 empirical studies from 1996 through 2010 and found that gambling has increased dramatically, and for those Americans aged 65 and older, 50% of them had engaged in casino gambling. According to the NCPG (2015, 2009), about 85% of adults in the United States have gambled at least once in their lives and 60% have gambled in the last year (NCPG, 2015). An estimated 2 million adults in the United States meet the criteria for pathological gambling, with another 4 to 6 million adults considered problem gamblers (those not meeting the full diagnostic criteria for pathological gambling). This means that approximately 6 to 9 million adults (3% to 4%) have problems with gambling. Statistics on youth and gambling are equally astounding. For example, the NCPG (2009) says that a vast majority of children in the United States have gambled by the time they are 18, and that children are more likely to develop gambling problems than are adults. According to the NCPG (2015), active-duty military personnel and veterans have higher rates of addiction than the general population. In fact, about 4% of this population is projected to suffer from mild to severe gambling problems. This is in addition to the approximately 36,000 active duty members who meet the criteria for a gambling problem! Interesting is that female veterans are often overlooked, and clinicians are urged to be sure to screen female veterans for gambling issues and all veterans they serve for co-occurring disorders (see Chapter 9). This last recommendation is because mental health disorders can often mask problem gambling. Regardless of the presence of co-occurring disorders, all problem gamblers, including those in the military, have higher rates of suicide, bankruptcies, and family violence.

SOCIAL AND ECONOMIC COSTS   The social cost to families and communities include bankruptcies, divorce, crime, and loss of jobs. Both the NCPG (2009) and Quirk et al. (2010) have estimated the loss of money due to gambling to be about $7 billion each year.

In some geographic areas, casino gambling has resulted in increased employment and income, increased tax revenues, enhanced tourism and recreational opportunities, and rising property values in some economically depressed communities. In other areas, casino gambling has had the opposite effect. For instance, the lack of a broad-based tax structure and almost total reliance on gaming revenues left Nevada with severe economic problems in 2011. Some Native American tribes have used casinos to rebuild infrastructure, diversify holdings, and reduce unemployment. However, most of the major economic benefits of gambling seem to be limited to casino gambling and parimutuel wagering, because these forms of gambling employ the most people and often attract tourists. Other forms of gambling (e.g., lotteries) simply redistribute income among state or local residents. In many cases, lotteries have been shown to be a form of regressive taxation. In other words, those people least able to afford to play lotteries spend proportionately more than those who can afford it.

CRIME   The relationship between crime and gambling has been difficult to establish because of methodological problems in studies designed to examine this relationship. As a result, there are limited studies related to gambling and crime (Lind, Kääriäinen, & Kuoppamäki, 2015). Nonetheless, these same researchers assert that gambling and crime are related in several ways: Gambling can occur illegally, improperly, be penetrated by organized crime syndicates, and can provoke criminal activity. They found that including illegal acts in the diagnostic criteria of pathological gambling was not warranted because it did not influence the internal consistency in the factor structure. It is for this reason that you will not see "illegal acts" included in the *Diagnostic and Statistical Manual of Mental Disorders, Fifth Edition* (*DSM-V*; American Psychiatric Association, 2013) diagnostic criteria for pathological gambling.

In earlier testimony before the commission, anecdotal incidents related pathological gambling and crime. The National Gambling Impact and Policy Study Commission's Final Report (1999) shows that they heard repeated testimony of desperate gamblers committing illegal acts to finance their problem and pathological gambling, including a Detroit man who faked his own son's kidnapping to pay back a $50,000 gambling debt, a 14-year hospital employee who embezzled $151,000 from her employer for gambling, and the wife of a Louisiana police officer who faced 24 counts of felony theft for stealing to fund her pathological gambling. A 2014 study of 184 inmates at a county jail revealed that almost 35% of the inmates surveyed were classified as problem gamblers (Hickey et al., 2014). So, if mental health workers are seeing incarcerated clients, it is important to assess for gambling problems.

FINANCIAL AND OTHER ECONOMIC IMPACT   According to the commission, nearly one-fifth of pathological gamblers have filed for bankruptcy compared to 4.2% of nongamblers. In Iowa, 19% of Chapter 13 bankruptcies involved gambling debt. Three-quarters of the Iowa counties with the highest bankruptcy rates had gambling facilities in or near them. In a study involving Southern Nevada (Las Vegas), the commission estimated the amount of bankruptcy debt losses and civil court costs at $10,000 per pathological gambler. In addition, these researchers estimated the cost of missed work, productivity losses, forced terminations, and unemployment compensation at $6,000 per pathological gambler. With 20,000 to 40,000 pathological gamblers in Southern Nevada, the financial and other economic impact was estimated to be between $320 million and $640 million.

SUICIDE   Pathological gambling is associated with suicidal ideation and attempts (Wong et al., 2010). According to the NCPG (1997), nearly 20% of pathological gamblers have attempted suicide, and Zangeneh and Hason (2006) give similar figures of 18% to 20% of gamblers reporting suicide attempts. This is higher than the suicide rate for any other addictive disorder. The commission heard testimony that a survey of GA members showed that two-thirds had contemplated suicide, 47% had a firm plan, and 77% stated that they have wanted to die. It should also be noted that Nevada regularly has the highest suicide rate in the nation. Although gambling problems cannot be clearly established as a primary cause, they would certainly be suspected.

HOMELESSNESS   The National Gambling Impact and Policy Study Commission (1999) heard testimony associating gambling problems and homelessness. In interviews with 7,000 homeless persons in Las Vegas, 20% reported gambling problems. In a survey of Chicago homeless providers, 33% reported that gambling was a contributing factor to homelessness of people in their program. Finally, the Atlantic City Rescue Mission told the commission that 22% of its residents were homeless because of gambling (National Gambling Impact and Policy Study Commission, 1999).

ABUSE AND NEGLECT   The news stories on the more dramatic cases of abuse and neglect related to gambling are depressing. In 2013, a Las Vegas three-year-old was stabbed to death in her home while her mother and stepfather were gambling. In 2008, a young girl was sexually assaulted and killed in a Southern Nevada casino bathroom in the early morning hours. Her father had left her in the video game section of the casino while he gambled. The commission reviewed two studies that showed that between 25% and 50% of pathological gamblers had abused their spouses. Increases in domestic violence were noted in communities after the advent of casinos. Finally, the commission report stated:

> Children of compulsive gamblers are often prone to suffer abuse, as well as neglect, as a result of parental problems or pathological gambling. The Commission heard testimony of numerous cases in which parents or a caretaker locked children in cars for an extended period of time while they gambled. In at least two cases, the children died.

Intimate partner violence (IPV) has been studied in its relationship to gambling and drinking behavior. However, while the relationship between IPV and alcohol use and the relationship between alcohol and gambling has received some attention, few studies have examined the relationship between IPV, alcohol, and gambling. Brasfield et al. (2012) found that male batterers who were problem gamblers and not court-mandated for treatment were higher (23%) than the general population (1% to 2%).

INTERNET GAMBLING   Ciaccio (2010) asks, "Have you ever wondered whether Internet gambling is legal in the United States?" He answers the question by saying, "The answer seems to depend on the source." This researcher claims that although a federal law was enacted in 2006 and new regulations in 2009 (see discussion on the National Council for Problem Gambling), the laws related to Internet gambling are "frustratingly murky." Laws say nothing about "unlawful Internet gambling" or define what that would be. No federal or state government regulates online sites. It is likely for this reason that FanDuel came into existence and is having great difficulty with the legislative branches of the states in which it is operating.

Ciaccio maintains that the stakes are high because, in 2008, Americans gambled $6 billion online, and the federal government may lose up to $62.7 billion in taxes between 2008 and 2018 by not legalizing and regulating online gaming. McCormack and Griffiths (2013) find that there are structural and situational differences between gambling online and gambling offline. Online gambling is not necessarily public; in fact, most of the time it is done privately. Another characteristic is the speed: Online gambling can have a faster turnaround, and this helps create a strong relationship with the online gambling platform.

In addressing the U.S. House of Representatives in 2006, the executive director of the NCPG, Keith Whyte, stated that between January and March 2006, the National Problem Gambling Helpline received more than 30,000 calls, of which 8% were for problematic Internet gambling. The predominant age range was 18 to 25. He also cited statistics from the Annenberg Foundation reflecting 600,000 youths (aged 14 to 22) gambling online on a weekly basis. In the National Gambling Impact and Policy Study Commission's Final Report (1999), White estimated the social cost of problem gambling from bankruptcy, divorce, job loss, and criminal justice costs at $6.7 billion in 2005. We will discuss Internet addiction later in this chapter. However, suffice it to say here that the Internet makes gambling more available than ever before. The earlier work of Wood, Williams, and Lawton (2007) cites four main reasons why gamblers prefer online to land-based gambling: (1) convenience, (2) an aversion to land-based atmospheres, (3) preference for the pace of online gambling, and (4) the potential for higher wins. However, more current research such as that of Gainsbury et al. (2015) found higher rates of disordered gambling among Internet gamblers.

As mentioned earlier, Internet gambling is regulated to some extent through the Unlawful Internet Gambling Enforcement Act passed into law in October 2006. This law prohibits financial transactions from banks and credit card companies to the Internet casinos, poker rooms, and sports betting sites. Gamblers addicted to the Internet may have more serious gambling problems than other gamblers (British Broadcasting Company [BBC], 2002). According to the BBC report, the reason is that, because Internet addiction can occur in private, these gamblers may go deeper into their addiction and be able to hide their addiction longer. Although Internet gambling addiction has not been widely researched, the data available suggest that those with Internet gambling problems may be more likely to be younger, less educated, have higher household debt, lost more money, and likely used drugs more frequently than those without disordered gambling (Gainsbury et al., 2015).

DEFINITIONS OF GAMBLERS AND PROBLEM GAMBLING

Perhaps the most well-known model for conceptualizing gamblers was developed by Robert Custer (Custer & Milt, 1985). Custer described the following six types of gamblers:

1. *Professional gambler*   This relatively rare type of gambler is not usually considered one who has a gambling problem. However, many people with gambling problems may have a fantasy about becoming, or the illusion of being, a professional gambler. The true professional gambler controls the amount of time spent gambling and the amount of money wagered.
2. *Antisocial gambler*   The antisocial gambler is also relatively rare. This is the individual who is involved with cheating to win at gambling. This may involve the popular shell game that you have most likely seen on television or at the movies, marking cards, or rigging slot machines. This type of gambler may develop a gambling problem but, obviously, has antisocial personality issues as well.
3. *Casual social gambler*   As the label implies, this type of gambler is one who does not experience problems from gambling. Gambling may be a regular activity (e.g., buying a weekly lottery ticket) or part of the person's recreation (e.g., periodic trips to Las Vegas). The casual social gambler would not lose more than intended or find it difficult to stop gambling.
4. *Heavy social gambler*   For this type of gambler, recreation involves gambling. Although the heavy social gambler may rarely lose more money than intended, he or she spends a great deal of time in gambling or gambling-related activities. For example, someone involved with sports betting may spend hours going over point spreads, injury reports, scouting reports, and trades to make "educated" bets. The gambling and associated behavior of this type of gambler can affect vocational functioning and family relationships because of the amount of time spent on preparing for gambling and following bets (i.e., watching games).
5. *Relief-and-escape gambler*   Custer describes this type of gambler as the one who gambles to escape life problems or life situations. Problem gamblers may be lonely, anxious, or depressed and use gambling as a method to numb themselves against negative feelings. This is similar to the way some people use alcohol and other drugs to temporarily dull unpleasant emotions.
6. *Compulsive gambler*   The compulsive gambler is preoccupied with gambling and with getting money to gamble. He or she cannot control the amount of time spent gambling or the amount of money lost gambling. According to Custer, gambling becomes the most important aspect of the person's life. The compulsive gambler may engage in illegal activity to get the money to gamble.

OTHER BEHAVIORAL ADDICTIONS

"Addictive behaviors are among the greatest scourges on humankind" (Gowing et al., 2015, p. 904).

In previous editions of this text, we simply used the term, "Other Addictions" as the heading for this section, in which we described pathological behaviors related to eating, sex and love, the

Internet, and work. For this edition, we changed the heading by adding "Behavioral" because the landscape and level of the debate over other addictions has changed. Behaviors are no longer the only driver of the debate over what should be included in the *DSM*. Data from new studies in cognitive and neurobiological sciences are growing, and researchers are beginning to better understand the neurological similarities of substance abuse and other behaviors. As a result of these advances, classification has become more important, and the field can expect additional changes. The reclassification of gambling disorder in the *DSM-V* is paving the way.

Potenza (2014) says that the debate over delineation of which behaviors constitute addiction is still going on. At the same time, Robbins and Clark (2015) see that behavioral addictions are gradually being recognized as a "valid category of psychiatric disorder." In the *DSM-V*, there is a focus on the compulsivity aspects of drug-taking behavior rather than focusing on the "dependence."

You as a mental health professional are encouraged to familiarize yourself with and formulate an opinion about whether behaviors other than alcohol and other drugs (AOD) use can be classified as addictions. The reason for this is that you will likely encounter clients who believe they are addicted to social media, their smartphones, video gaming, exercise, television, food, work, shopping, the Internet, sex, or relationships. On this front-line level, the professional debate is less important than your real-world understanding of the client's concerns and how to provide effective help.

In this next section, we will further our discussion of nonsubstance use pathological behaviors by outlining the current status of the debate over "other addictions" and provide discussion on pathological eating, sex and love, Internet use, and work behaviors. Following this discussion, we will present information on assessment and treatment issues.

The Debate over Behavioral Addictions

Before the publishing of the *DSM-V*, there were three groups who discounted the notion that behaviors related to such things as eating, excessive work, Internet use, and sexual compulsions could be addictions. One group claimed that classifying compulsive behaviors as *addictions* was inappropriate because these behaviors were already well-defined in the mental health field. The debate was similar to the one regarding codependency that was discussed in Chapter 13. In the previous edition of the *DSM* (*DSM-IV-TR*), it was argued that compulsions involving sex were already identified and no new diagnostic category of sex addiction was necessary. The same argument was made for other interpersonal relationship problems, such as the compulsive need for love and attention that was seen as characteristic of certain personality disorders (e.g., Dependent Personality Disorder, *DSM-IV-TR*).

The second group of critics viewed alcohol and other drug problems as bad habits, willful misconduct, or irresponsible and irrational behavior (Drewnowski & Bellisle, 2007). These conceptualizations have been described in Chapter 3 and may be held by professionals promoting a certain theoretical model of addiction or by lay people who see addictive behaviors from a moral model.

The third group was "purists" who saw addiction from a medical model and restricted this label to those who are dependent on alcohol or other drugs. From this point of view, the demonstration of tolerance and withdrawal (see Chapter 2) in an individual who used alcohol and/or other drugs was indicative of addiction. Purists believed the use of the term *addiction* when applied to behaviors different from alcohol and other drug use actually diminished the disease model of addiction.

At the same time, before the publication of the *DSM-V*, proponents of other addictions were contending that adoption of the "other addictions" concept was useful and resulted in organized efforts to help people with these problems. This group pointed out that popular books and talk shows, the heightening awareness of mental health professionals, and the development of support groups had all helped people label their problems. The open discussion about problems involving eating, gambling, and sex had resulted in many people acknowledging that they had one of these problems, that many people shared their problem, and that they could seek help for these problems. Moreover, proponents of other addictions called attention to the success of Twelve Step support groups (see Chapter 11). Because Twelve Step groups are based on the principles of Alcoholics Anonymous (AA), and because these groups have helped many people with problem behaviors in many areas other than alcohol and other drugs, it was argued that these "other" behaviors should be seen as addictions. To this group of advocates, it was clear that someone could feel powerlessness over eating, gambling, or sex, which was consistent with the first of the Twelve Steps.

Proponents also cited scientific research, and this was their strongest argument for reexamination of inclusion criteria. In general, proponents of other addictions pointed out the similarities between alcoholics and drug addicts and those who engaged in excessive behaviors other than AOD use (Grant, Potenza, Weinstein, & Gorelick, 2010). For example, Yellowlees and Marks (2005) and Young (2004) associated problematic Internet use and Internet addiction. Carnes (2001) and Tripodi (2006) presented research linking compulsive sexual practices with sexual addiction. Sussman, Lisha, and Griffiths (2011) maintained that the range of addictive behaviors is broad, and includes tobacco, alcohol, illicit drugs, eating, gambling, Internet, love, sex, exercise, shopping, and work. Given this range, these researchers suggested that approximately 47% of the U.S. adult population suffers from maladaptive signs of an addictive disorder over a 12-month period. Perhaps it was this type of alarming data that continued to press the mental health community and authors of the *DSM-V* to continue consideration of other addictions.

Currently, there is little disagreement that excessive engagement in compulsive behaviors can result in a variety of problems. For example, Yau, Crowley, Mayes, and Potenza (2012) see potential problematic issues with Internet shopping, viewing pornography, and social-networking, and Sussman and Moran (2013) see potential problematic use with other forms of technology such as non-Internet video-gaming and television viewing. Conditions such as cutting, excessive tanning, and kleptomania lead to problems as well. Still, none of these is recognized as "other addictions" in the *DSM-V*. Gambling disorder is the *only* condition in the subsection of "Non-substance-related disorders" in the category of "Substance-related and Addictive Disorders."

In preparing the new *DSM-V*, the workgroup assigned to this particular section did indeed recognize that there are other Internet-related behaviors such as Internet shopping and viewing pornography that can become problematic (Potenza, 2014). Yet, Potenza and others in that workgroup believed that there was just not enough research on addictive sex, exercise, and shopping for them to be included in the *DSM-V* under "Non-substance or behavioral addictions" (Potenza, 2014). Hence, although the number of studies is increasing, it remains clear that more research is needed before these behaviors are considered addictive—if ever.

Regarding the current state of the debate, one camp is still made up of the scientific community and authors of the *DSM-V*. Residing on the other side are large reaches of the public, practitioners, and some scholars. These lines dividing proponents and antagonists are no longer rigid like they were at the outset of the debate. Instead, the boundaries have become semipermeable. Nonetheless, getting included in the *DSM* remains only one dimension of the controversy. Once included, there is more work to be done, and research in the area of eating disorders (EDs) characterizes the complexities inherent in the *DSM-V* classification. In their analysis of the criteria for EDs, Dazzi and Di Leone (2014) found that the *DSM-V* seems to handle some issues such as making ED less restrictive and thereby handling the high prevalence of EDs Not Otherwise Specified (NOS). Yet, these researchers note that given the complexities of the current approach the *DSM-V* still, ". . . may not prove to be particularly suited to this type of disorder".

THE EATING DISORDERS

Although you are probably familiar with the ED anorexia nervosa (AN), described by Bruch (1986) as the relentless pursuit of thinness, and bulimia nervosa (BN), described as chronic episodes of binge eating followed by purging, you may not know that EDs are not as prevalent as other mental disorders and that it seems to affect mostly women—and, certain populations like athletes and models—are at higher risk. Estimates suggest that clinically diagnosable EDs such as AN and BN affect from 0.5% to 2.8% of the U.S. population (Hudsen, Hiripi, Pope, & Kessler, 2007). These same researchers maintain that EDs are among the most lethal psychiatric illnesses and kill up to 20% of those afflicted.

With all of the attention given to EDs, including binge eating, bulimia, and AN, it is not surprising that there is a subgroup that engages in orthorexia—the preoccupation with nutrition. Although not officially recognized in the *DSM-V*, Koven and Abry (2015) see orthorexia as a desire to achieve optimum health. Although it appears to be a healthy endeavor, preoccupation with nutrition can lead to nutritional disturbances, medical complications, and poor quality of life. Clearly, EDs and associated problems such as body image, defined as one's relationship with one's body, continue to be problematic for adults and adolescents. In an interesting qualitative study of 26 black women, Capodilupo and Kim (2014) found that both gender and race matter when it comes to black women's body image. These researchers found that culture alone is not a protective factor for body dissatisfaction—meaning that even if the black culture says that a large body type is preferable, black women can (and do) still suffer from body image issues.

Body image disturbances can also influence body dysmorphic disorder and clinical depression. Although you are probably somewhat familiar with major depressive states, body dysmorphic disorder may be unfamiliar. Essentially, it is the disorder of *imagined ugliness* at the same time when others look at these individuals and see them as okay or even beautiful or handsome. Researchers have demonstrated the association between disturbances in body image and EDs, including AN, BN, and binge-eating disorder (e.g., Cotter, Kelly, Mitchell, & Mazzeo, 2015; Dakanalis et al., 2015; Zanetti et al., 2013). Although men's body image has not received the attention in the professional literature that women's body image has, Griffiths, Angus, Murray, and Touyz (2014) report that males experience body image dissatisfaction as well. In particular, gay males, as opposed to heterosexual males, may have pronounced concerns with body image and can be at high risk for EDs (Yean et al., 2013). It stands to reason that as we are able to prevent body image disturbance we will also witness a diminishing number of EDs. Current research suggests that in treating body image disturbance it is important to concomitantly create a positive body image (Piran, 2015).

Chronic Obesity

Chronic obesity is a worldwide epidemic (Smith et al., 2014). *Obesity* occurs when one is 20% over the desirable weight for one's height (Burrows, 1992), and *chronic obesity* occurs when individuals are at least 20% overweight for protracted periods. In general, there are mild, moderate, and severe degrees of obesity. Some research suggests that obesity has a genetic component (Lee & Mattson, 2014), and that obesity in childhood has a strong positive correlation with weight status in adulthood (Brownell & Stunkard, 1978; Robinson & Killen, 2001).

In discussing the trends, Ogdon, Carroll, Kit, and Flegal (2014) note that more than one-third (34.9%) of adults in the United States are obese, and approximately 17% of youth are obese. These authors state that there have not been significant changes in the obesity rates in youth and adults between 2003-2004 and 2011-2012. Nevertheless, prevalence remains high. Being overweight increases the risk factors for many diseases and health conditions (Centers for Disease Control and

Prevention, 2007) and obesity in adolescents has now been correlated with school absenteeism (Echeverría, Vélez-Valle, Janevic, & Prystowsky, 2014). Because of this, Jarosz, Dobal, Wilson, and Schram (2007) state that the reduction of obesity is one of the most important public health objectives for the 21st century.

Binge-Eating Disorder

Binge-eating disorder (BED) is a newly recognized entity in the *DSM-V*. Yet, there is no regulatory agency that has approved a drug for treating this disorder (Goracci et al., 2015). Goracci et al. (2015) found two important changes in the new diagnostic criteria: threshold was lowered so that it would also lower the number of EDs NOS. The *DSM-V* reflects lower frequency and duration so that now the diagnosis of BED is defined by binge eating once a week (instead of twice) within a three-month period (instead of six months).

For the general nonveteran population, symptoms include eating an excessive amount of food within a discrete period, usually defined as two days per week for six months, with a sense of lack of control over eating during the episode (Wilson & Sysko, 2009). Generally, the binge-eating episodes include eating much more rapidly than normal; eating until feeling uncomfortably full; eating large amounts of food when not feeling physically hungry; eating alone because of being embarrassed by how much one is eating; and feeling disgusted with oneself, depressed, and/or feeling guilty after overeating. Individuals with BED are distressed about the binge-eating behavior. BED is not associated with regular use of inappropriate compensatory behaviors such as purging or fasting. Although similar to bulimia, the main difference between them is that individuals with BED do not purge their bodies of excess calories. Hence, it would be expected that individuals with this disorder would be overweight for their age and height.

In reviewing empirical studies of binge eating, Leehr et al. (2015) found that negative emotion is also a trigger. Recently, evidence has emerged that stress associated with sexual assault is related to an increase in binge eating (Cameron, Maguire, & McCormack, 2011). Symptoms can include a child eating a lot of food very quickly, feelings of shame and disgust about the amount of food ingested, a pattern of eating in response to emotional stress, eating late at night in secret, and hiding food containers in one's room. Adolescent males and females who display low self-esteem, lack of interoceptive awareness, perfectionism, body dissatisfaction, dietary restraint, weight teasing, and internalization of the "ideal body" are known to be associated with binge eating (Sehm & Warschburger, 2015). Lydecker and Grilo (2016) found that in general binge eating was different across racial groups, and this is the same result reported by Jennings, Kelly-Weeder, and Wolfe (2015), who specifically studied male BED and found it reported by all racial groups. In addition, depression often accompanies BED, and this is especially for Iraq and Afghanistan veterans who also present with posttraumatic stress disorder (Hoerster et al., 2015). A vicious cycle can occur where one becomes depressed and binges, which then creates more depression and more binging.

Bulimia Nervosa and Anorexia Nervosa

AN is often a persistent and severe mental illness that has the highest mortality rate among all psychiatric disorders (Godier & Park, 2014; Hudsen et al., 2007). Research suggests that puberty is the most common period for the onset of EDs, with the onset of binging peaking at age 16 years and the onset of purging peaking at age 18 years (Day et al., 2011). Prepubertal onset of BN is extremely rare, and the highest incidence of BN occurs during adult life. However, given the increase in childhood obesity and the prevalence of dieting among female adolescents, it can be expected that the incidence of BN will increase.

Changes in the *DSM-V* criteria for EDs have had corresponding changes in prevalence. In comparing earlier editions of the *DSM* with the *DSM-V* criteria, these researchers found that among 3,043 adolescents (1,254 males and 1,789 females), the prevalence of EDs increased from 1.8% (*DSM-IV*) to 3.7% (*DSM-V*), and this reflected an increase in BN to 1.6% and the addition of the diagnosis of purging disorder (1.4%). Changes have occurred among adult populations, as well. For instance, Reas and Stedal (2015) found that EDs often occur across the lifespan. Exact figures are difficult to determine in that many older women will not seek treatment. In some cases, these individuals are treated for depression and/or anxiety, while the ED goes undiagnosed. Trends of EDs have changed, too. In a review of the literature, Pike, Hoek, and Dunne (2014) found that trends have changed. EDs are on the increase around the globe. There appears to be lower incidence rates for bulimia in Caucasian North American and Northern European populations and an increase of bulimia and binge eating in North America among Hispanics and African Americans. At the same time, EDs are on the rise in Asian and Arab cultures. Schwitzer and Choate (2015) maintain that ED rates among late adolescents and young college women may be as high as 10% to 15%, and males, especially gay men, represent approximately 5% to 20% of people with EDs (Brown & Keel, 2015).

Research suggests that risk of serious comorbidity is higher with other disorders as well, such as depressive and anxiety disorders, substance abuse, suicide attempts, general psychological distress, impaired social (interpersonal) functioning, and a reduced quality of life (Jappe et al., 2011). Godier and Park (2014) and Humphreys, Clopton, and Reich (2007) maintain that a link exists between EDs and obsessive-compulsive disorder (OCD). They estimate that between 15% and 41% of those with EDs also suffer from OCD. It is clear that serious health consequences result from prolonged BN and AN.

BULIMIA NERVOSA   BN emerged as a new disorder in the 1970s, and incidence rates rose from the 1980s to early 1990s, with concerns being expressed that this disorder might be affecting increasingly larger numbers of adolescents. BN is estimated to occur in about 1% to 4% of the U.S. adult population (Herzog & Eddy, 2009).

In general, BN is characterized by recurrent episodes of binge eating where the person experiences a lack of a sense of control and eats an excessive amount of food within a discrete period. People with bulimia also practice recurrent inappropriate compensatory behavior to prevent weight gain, such as self-induced vomiting or misuse of laxatives, diuretics, enemas, fasting, or excessive exercise. The fact that people with BN usually are within a normal weight range for their age and height is interesting. This is due to the compensatory behaviors that keep weight down. Individuals with this disorder can fear gaining weight and can feel intensely dissatisfied with their bodies to the point of having body image disturbance. Often, compensatory behaviors occur in secrecy. During the episode, individuals report feeling disgusted and ashamed when they binge, yet relieved once they purge. In most cases, bulimia will result after a period of anorexia. Again, it is an "all or nothing" thought process. In other words, these individuals say to themselves, "I won't eat anything today (nothing)." Eventually, the body must receive nourishment, and the bulimic person, after a period of starvation, will gorge with food (all).

ANOREXIA NERVOSA   Garfinkel and Kaplan (1986) state,

> Anorexia is an increasingly common complex order . . . that overrides the patient's physical and psychological well-being. . . . Pursuing a thin body becomes an isolated area of control in a world in which the individual feels ineffective; the dieting provides an artificially dangerous sense of mastery and control. As the weight loss progresses, a starvation state ensues, which eventually develops a life of its own, leading to features of anorexia nervosa. (p. 272)

According to the U.S. Department of Health and Human Services (2007), approximately 0.5% to 3.7% of females suffer from AN in their lifetime. In general, individuals with AN are characterized by intense fear of gaining weight or becoming fat, food restriction and weight loss, body image distortions, amenorrhea, and disturbances in the way in which one's body weight or shape is experienced (Jappe et al., 2011). There may also be negative self-evaluations related to one's body weight as well as a denial of the acute crisis resulting from severe underweight.

The two types of AN are restrictive anorexia and bulimic anorexia. As you would expect, bulimic anorexia is characterized by the use of compensatory measures such as purging. However, the main difference between bulimic anorexia and BN is that the former does not binge before purging. Individuals with the restrictive type of AN can restrict the amount of food intake and/or can engage in excessive exercise.

It is interesting to note that individuals with restrictive anorexia do not suffer from a loss of appetite. Rather, they are "frantically preoccupied with food and eating . . . [they] deliberately, seemingly willfully, restrict their food intake and overexercise. These girls are panicky with the fear that they might lose control over their eating" (Bruch, 1986, p. 331). As a result, the actual process of eating can become obsessive, and unusual eating habits will develop. These habits can include such things as assessing or weighing the portion of food, restricting the foods that one eats to only a few, and/or avoiding food and even missing meals.

The course and outcome of AN vary across individuals. Some will recover after a single episode. Others can have a fluctuating pattern of gaining weight and relapsing. Still others can experience this chronically with a concomitant deterioration of their body. Males can experience anorexia. However, the proportion of females to males with anorexia is approximately 10 to 1 (Lindblad, Lindberg, & Hjern, 2006). Males with anorexia often display perfectionism, obsessions, passive dependencies, and antisocial characteristics (Andersen & Michalide, 1983).

According to the U.S. Department of Health and Human Services (2007), the mortality rate for individuals with anorexia has been estimated at 0.56% per year, or approximately 5.6% per decade. This means that death from anorexia is about 12 times higher than the annual death rate from all causes of death among females ages 15 to 24 in the general population. The most common causes of death among persons who are anorexic are suicide, cardiac arrest, and electrolyte imbalance.

ADDICTION TO SEX AND LOVE

In the 1800s, sexual addiction was referred to as moral insanity, satyriasis, and nymphomania (Levine, 2010). According to Carnes (2001), Levine (2010), and Hall (2014), there are numerous names ascribed to sex addiction. Hall also says that there are several models of sex addiction including biological, moral, and social models. In spite of prevalence rates ranging from 3% to 6% (Weinstein, 2014), there are no models for assessment and treatment that involve attachment, trauma, or a social contexts.

The professional scientific field prefers hypersexuality to sexual addiction, and this perspective is reflected in the fact that *sexual addiction* does not appear in the *DSM-V*. The term, *Hypersexual Disorder* was adapted for inclusion in the *DSM-V*. Repetition and preoccupation with nonparaphilic urges and behaviors that disrupt one's personal and/or private life are central to the diagnosis. There is a co-occurrence of these behaviors with dysphoric mood states and stress reactions (Hook, Reid, Penberthy, Davis, & Jennings, 2014), as well as attention-deficit hyperactivity disorder, posttraumatic stress disorder, and anxiety disorder. It is not surprising to see a list of hypersexual behaviors including excessive masturbation, pornography use, telephone sex, and strip club visiting (Weinstein, 2014).

Sex and love "addiction" is seen by many as comprising three addictions: love passion, love addiction, and sex addiction (Reynaud, Karila, Blecha, & Benyamina, 2010). Griffin-Shelley (1991) writes that our physical and psychological identity is made up in part by sex and love, and "Letting go of sex and love, even for a short amount of time, seems [to addicts] like giving up [their] whole identity" (p. 123). According to Forward (1986) and Norwood (1985), sex addictions are gender-free and cut across all socioeconomic lines, racial/ethnic groupings, and sexual orientations.

Sex and love addiction combines sex and love and can reflect individuals who involve themselves in numerous affairs in spite of promises to the contrary. More often than not, these individuals may use sex in attempting to get the love they feel they need. In many of these cases, sex is only the enticer, or the avenue through which other emotional, intellectual, or spiritual needs are met. But the act of sex does not characterize all individuals addicted to sex and love. Being in a primary relationship and compulsively fantasizing about others is also characteristic of those addicted to sex and love. Constantly fantasizing about someone other than the one to whom a person is making love also reflects a sex and love addiction.

Even without sexualizing the relationship, many sex and love addicts maintain that they compulsively engage in emotional affairs. For example, one of our clients told us of a time when she was paralyzed at a traffic light on a busy street trying to decide whether she should drive by her fantasy lover's office "just to see him, not to talk to him." She remained immobilized for an entire light cycle, with cars honking on both sides of her while she engaged in an internal debate about whether to drive straight ahead or whether to turn and drive by his office. (She drove straight ahead.)

For sex and love addicts, the consequences can be profound. Losses can include serious financial problems, being fired from a job for sexual harassment, overwhelming feelings of shame, personal distress, guilt, and relationship breakups (Garcia & Thibaut, 2010). Kasl (2002) includes other consequences such as issues related to health (e.g., sexually transmitted infections), as well as educational, parental, safety, and spiritual issues. Emotional consequences can revolve around guilt, resentment, suicidal ideation, depression, fear, self-loathing, and a diminished sense of self-worth.

Clearly, the rise of the Internet in the early 1980s completely altered the landscape for sexual and love addiction. MySpace and Facebook are used not only socially for relationships and for sharing information, but also by sexual predators to lure minors into meetings. YouTube gets sexual postings daily. There are disgruntled ex-lovers who post nude pictures of themselves or their former lovers as a way of getting even. A related issue is the use of the Internet for pornography or cybersex and online affairs (cyberaffairs) increasing at an alarming rate (Beard, 2005; Young, 2004).

INTERNET ADDICTION

According to the International Telecommunications Union (2013), only 20% of the populations in North America, the United Kingdom, and Asia lack access to the Internet. Although 80% have access in these countries, that is far from happening elsewhere. For instance, the access rates are lower (45% to 55%) in South America, Africa, and the Middle East. Although low, the rates are rising at astounding speed: 3600% for Africans and 2600% for Middle Easterners in the years 2000 through 2012. Taken together, the total number of Internet users world-wide is approximately 2.5 billion (Internet World Stats, 2013). With such numbers, it is obvious that someone would have had problems with Internet use.

That "first" someone was a 43-year-old female homemaker whom Young (1996) interviewed and deemed her addicted to the Internet. Since the first publication of her work, "Internet Addiction" has been scrutinized in the professional periodicals in ever-increasing numbers (Spada, 2014). From a research standpoint, there are numerous issues regarding Internet Addiction, although there is no single term to describe it. In fact, both Spada (2014) and Van Rooij and Prause (2014) reviewed the literature and found that "Internet Addiction" has been labeled and described in a wide-ranging fashion. For instance, "Internet addiction," "Internet dependence," "pathological Internet use," "excessive Internet use," "impulsive Internet use," "compulsive Internet use," and "abnormal

Internet use" have all been used in the literature. In addition, Van Rooij and Prause (2014) point out that statistically descriptive terms such as "high-frequency use" are conspicuously absent. Nevertheless, the term "problem Internet use" (PIU) is frequently used in the field.

These variations have partially contributed to the confusion about how to categorize it. This confusion is further enhanced by Spada (2014) who agrees with Griffiths (2000) that research has yet to distinguish between "addicted *on* the Internet and addicted *to* the Internet." Essentially, this means that there is debate whether it is the content (shopping) of the Internet or the software (design) behind it that affects the person the most. The confusion over the term, the lack of consistent assessment criteria, and the dearth of large epidemiological research makes estimation of prevalence difficult. These same researchers attribute the difficulty to the fact that no standardized instrument has been used (they cite the use of 27 different ones in their review of the literature) in addition to there being no consistent and clearly defined cutoff scores. Nonetheless, the estimation of PIU in the general population provided by Bakken et al. (2009) of 1% is still cited. Adolescent PIU—especially in Europe and the Far East—has a richer research history. Data from studies reflect European adolescent sample prevalence rates ranging from 1% to 9% (e.g., Villella, Martinotti, & Di Nicola, 2010), Middle Eastern adolescents 1% to 12% (e.g., Canan et al., 2009), and Asian adolescents prevalence rates ranging 2% to 18% (Wang, Wang, & Fu, 2008). Regardless of the debate about how to categorize PIU, these numbers indicate that there is cause for alarm.

It is important for you as a practicing professional to be familiar with the results of scientific inquiry aimed at clarifying the issue, and a persuasive argument for use of the term *Internet addiction* is made by Brand, Young, and Laier (2014). These researchers conducted a structured literature review along the dimensions of Generalized Internet Addiction and Specific Internet Addiction (Davis, 2001), the neuropsychological correlates of Internet Addiction, and the functional neuroimaging of Internet Addiction. After reviewing and summarizing the studies that met the criteria for inclusion (sample size minimum 1,000, for example), these researchers believe that there are strong similarities across all three groupings. Specifically, the loss of control—reduced prefrontal control—is a significant factor. Block (2008) maintains that PIU includes four components: (1) excessive use associated with loss of sense of time or neglect of basic drives; (2) withdrawal that leads to feelings of anger, tension, and/or depression when access is denied; (3) tolerance that lends itself to increased purchasing or accumulation of software or advanced computer equipment; and (4) negative social consequences.

Cyberaffairs

Social media has transformed culture, and the previous discussion about PIU clearly indicates that there are large numbers of users who experience problems. When was the last time you checked your Facebook page? Although there were 750 million users in 2011 (Facebook, 2011), there were 1.18 billion people alone who used Facebook in August 2015 (Facebook, 2015). Or, are you one of the estimated 90.7% (Statistics Brain Research Institute, 2015) of single people in the United States who has used an online dating service at least once? If so, you contributed roughly $1.7 billion to the gross revenue of online dating (Statistics Brain Research Institute, 2015). Women (52.4%) used it about as frequently as men (47.6%). Although Facebook and online dating sites are for social networking, some users become behaviorally addicted to the platform by checking Facebook incessantly or searching websites for sex rather than for dating. An example of this is the Ashley Madison website. You might recall the scandal in 2015 that surrounded the publishing of the list of names who subscribed to this extramarital affair website. Yet, while reflecting a high incidence rate, cybersex still represents only one dimension of compulsive Internet use. Nevertheless, addiction to pornography and/or sex can have deleterious effects on one's life.

A review of the research on Internet sexuality reveals several types of activities (Döring, 2009). *Pornography on the Internet* gives users access to commercial and noncommercial online pornography as well as allows them to produce, distribute, and discuss material. *Sex shops* on the Internet offer a second activity. Here users may purchase sexual aids and toys such as vibrators, condoms, sexy lingerie, and erotic magazines. The sex shops can be commercial and represent offline shops, or they can be independent online sex shops. *Sex work* on the Internet is a third activity in which users can offer services or obtain sexual services. Often these activities are in real time. Broadcasts of sex shows, advertising for brothels, and information about escort services fall under the heading of sex work on the Internet. The fourth type of activity is *sexual education*. This can include traditional sex education material as well as more discrete information related to coming out, sexual awareness, attitudes, and behaviors. *Sex contacts* on the Internet is the fifth type of activity. This is typically referred to as online sex or cybersex. Contacts are initiated exclusively for computer-mediated sexual exchanges that can lead to real-world sexual encounters (offline sex). In this venue, there is no monetary exchange as there might be in the sex work discussed previously. Finally, the sixth activity relates to *sexual subcultures* in which non-mainstream sexual orientations or preferences can be addressed. Usually, these Internet platforms involve the exchange of information such as political activism, social support, and groups that exist offline and online.

There is an increase in research efforts focused on specific symptoms of *cybersex compulsion* (Waskul, 2004). Research reveals 6.5% of male Internet users spend at least six hours per week engaging in cybersex. Orzack (2004) identifies specific psychological and physical symptoms that include the following: (1) euphoria and sense of well-being while online; (2) feeling unable or unwilling to stop; (3) an increasing desire to stay online or to go online; (4) experiencing feelings of emptiness, distress, or irritability when prevented from going online; (5) lying to others about extent of use; (6) carpal tunnel syndrome; (7) dry eyes; (8) neglect of personal hygiene; (9) migraines; (10) sleep disturbances; (11) experiencing more general problems related to work and/or school; and (12) neglecting interpersonal relationships.

Impact of Internet Abuse on Relationships, Students, and Workers

Cyberaffairs are defined as a romantic and/or sexual relationship that are initiated and maintained online (Young, 1999). According to this researcher, online affairs differ dramatically from in vivo affairs in several ways. In cyberaffairs, individuals can be more honest, open, forthright, less inhibited, and can be more culturally diverse (which augments the perceived glamour). The impact of cyberaffairs on existing real-life relationships can be dramatic and can include the following: a change in sleep patterns, a new demand for privacy, ignoring other responsibilities, lying, personality changes, loss of interest in sex, and a declined investment in the real-life relationship. The declined interest in one's real-life relationship is often reflected by no longer valuing rituals, no longer taking vacations together, an avoidance of making long-range plans together, and a general distancing between partners with the concomitant loss of intimacy.

Ceyhan, Ceyhan, and Gürcan (2007) assert that university students were one of the first groups identified as having problems with Internet addiction. Velezmoro, Lacefield, and Roberti (2010) and Young (2010, 2004) see several factors that influence the rise in Internet addiction among college students. These include having free and unlimited use; huge blocks of unstructured time with no or very little monitoring; institutional values that encourage the use of technology for readings, assignments, viewing syllabi online, and taking online courses; higher drinking ages that restrict locations to meet others; and the social intimidation that some students can feel when they arrive on large campuses. Studies have shown that 58% of students who use the Internet excessively suffer from poor study habits or late-night logins (Young, 2004, 1998). Velezmoro et al. 2010 found that perceived stress was predictive of Internet usage for sexual purposes among college students. When college students get bored or perceive hopelessness, they tend to use the Internet for nonsexual purposes.

Employee abuse of the Internet is also of concern to researchers and employers alike, and there is some evidence that the phenomenon is of epidemic proportions. Young (2010) states that nearly 64% of employees use the Internet for personal interest during office hours. Queen's University in Belfast conducted a survey of 350 companies from the United States, Australia, and the United Kingdom and found that 28% of those surveyed admitted downloading sexually explicit content while on the job (Sullivan, 2004). At the same time, employers are allowing employees to spend time working at home while staying in contact through the Internet (O'Neill, Hambley, & Bercovich, 2014).

The impact of Internet abuse on the workplace is multifaceted, and Page (2015) sees "cyberslacking" as on the rise. The loss of productivity is staggering. Stewart (2010) sees the loss to revenues in the billions, and Coffin (2003) puts the figure at $50 billion annually. The losses stem from employees who are slow to respond to customers' needs and, from employees unable to meet deadlines consistently, who often fail to complete tasks because they are preoccupied with surfing the Internet. There is also negative publicity associated with class action suits or individual lawsuits that claim sexual harassment in the workplace as a result of pornography or other content being passed around. Legal liabilities are also involved. This means that as Internet abuse is increasingly being touted as an addiction, it makes those abusing the Internet at work "disabled." With protection under the Americans with Disabilities Act, an employee may in turn sue his or her former employer for wrongful termination.

Because of the increasing demand and availability of computers and the Internet in the workplace, the problems associated with abuse will continue to rise (Nie & Erbing, 2000; Young, 2010). In a study with teachers, Page (2015) found that there was a wide range of Internet use including sending personal emails, banking, and social networking. They studied 222 graduate business students who were employed and found that approximately 90% of them performed nonwork emails, shopping, or visiting new sites while at work. Additionally, 50% of employees booked vacations or visited sports sites, and 40% were job hunting. To combat this, a new industry that focuses on spy software and the development of Internet policies in the workplace has been spawned and is flourishing. It seems as though the Internet has not only changed the landscape of sex and love addiction, it has changed and complicated the construct of workaholism as well. Workaholics, especially those who bring work home, may actually be bringing Internet-based addictive behaviors home instead of the work. Nonetheless, there still remains a discrete issue related to the traditional notions of workaholism.

ADDICTION TO WORK: WORKAHOLISM

Because the Internet provides opportunities for individuals to work more at home, it also provides opportunities for excessive work (Andreassen, 2014). Aziz and Tronzo (2011) maintain that today's workers put in more time than they did in 1990. Robinson (2000, p. 29) sees work as possibly being the "great unexamined therapy issue of our time." This researcher says that, for some, work is the venue in which real life takes place. It can become the secret repository where an individual's life drama and primary emotional experiences take place.

As a student, you probably have engaged in compulsive work behaviors. These behaviors will most often occur around exam time or when assignments are due. Remember the phrase "The early bird catches the worm"? Many of us have subscribed to the tenets of this phrase. However, some believe this phrase and others like "Idle hands are the devil's workshop" to be rules to follow and believe these dictums to be essential to one's very own sense of well-being or survival.

According to Oates (1971), a workaholic is

> a person whose need for work has become so excessive that it creates noticeable disturbance or interference with his [*sic*] bodily health, personal happiness, and interpersonal relations, and with his [*sic*] smooth social functioning. (p. 16)

Since Oates's definition was first published, the term *workaholism* has infused itself into the mainstream U.S. cultural narrative, and it has undergone significant changes (Malinowska & Tokarz, 2014). One would think that because of this infusion, our scientific understanding of the concept would have increased. It really has not. Malinowska and Tokarz (2014) maintain that there is simply no single dominant conceptualization that can explain the causes and maintenance of workaholism. These same researchers believe there are three perspectives. The first is that adopted by Oates (1971) and concentrates on compulsive symptoms and obsessions that reflect, among other things, an inability to regulate work habits and a disruption of relationships with family and friends. The second perspective sees workaholism as a positive behavior or "devotion" to work. This perspective posits workaholism as pleasurable and advantageous for the organization. The third perspective has workaholism as negative or positive—depending upon whether the worker derives pleasure or is compulsively-addicted and driven. You can see that this third perspective essentially differentiates enthusiastic workers from those who are out of control.

Structure of Workaholism

Robinson (2013, 2000) identifies four predominant styles of workaholism. These four styles help therapists organize their thoughts about a given client's symptoms. At the same time, the clients themselves will likely present with a combination of styles or with alternating styles. The *bulimic workaholic style* reflects a perfectionistic orientation toward work. Individuals who use this style often cycle through procrastination, work binges, and exhaustion. It is hard for these individuals to get started. However, once a deadline approaches, they can work excessively to the point of staying up nights to finish before falling into bed from exhaustion.

A second style is the *relentless workaholic style*. This style mirrors the dictum "It has to be finished yesterday" (Robinson, 2000, p. 37). Although the bulimic style reflects procrastination, the relentless style reflects just the opposite. These individuals start early. One reason for this might be the fact that the relentless style of workaholism is also characterized by taking on too much work. Saying no is as difficult as prioritizing. Moreover, these individuals can complete projects long before deadlines without much input from coworkers.

Those who invoke an *attention-deficit workaholic style* are seen as using the adrenaline of overwhelming work pressure as a focusing device (Robinson, 2000, p. 37). Living on the brink of chaos and destruction, persons use this style to get high from the rush of new ideas. Whereas projects are completed early by those using the relentless style, the attention-deficit style reflects a plethora of unfinished projects. Finally, in the *savoring workaholic style* individuals move slowly, methodically, and in an overly scrupulous manner. Projects are savored in and of themselves. When projects are close to completion, additional work is generated because these individuals have difficulty distinguishing when a job is good enough.

If you are a student, the bulimic style probably sounds familiar. This is especially true for those times when you are watching television, playing video games, or otherwise occupied while feeling excessive guilt over not doing what should be done. Remember, this experience does not mean that you are a workaholic. Workaholism and maladaptive styles of workaholics lie on a continuum.

ASSESSMENT AND TREATMENT ISSUES

Gambling

ASSESSMENT AND DIAGNOSIS   With the advent of the *DSM-V* came a significant change in categorizing nonsubstance addictive disorders: The category of "Substance-related Disorders" was supplanted by the new "Substance-related and Addictive Disorder." Potenza (2014) reviewed the decision-making process of the two workgroups assigned to focus on gambling and nonsubstance addictive behaviors. One workgroup focused on substance-related/addictive disorders and the other on obsessive-compulsive spectrum disorders. According to Potenza (year), the goal was to address ". . . how pathological gambling might be considered from a classification perspective" (p. 2). This same author says that a lot of research went into this endeavor since the *DSM-IV* was published in 2000, and based on research showing similarities between substance-use disorders and gambling, the decision was made to group gambling disorder with substance-related disorders in the *DSM-V*.

Much of what you read in Chapter 6 about the screening and assessment of alcohol and other drug problems is applicable to gambling. Most importantly, if a person has experienced problems in school or job, family and other relationships, with finances or the law or in other areas as a result of gambling, then that person has a gambling problem to some degree. Helping professionals should consider gambling as a possible causal factor for the presenting problems of clients and should ask about gambling in the psychosocial history. This is especially true when clients present with depression. The Statistics Canada researchers and others (e.g., Zimmerman, Chelminski, & Young, 2006) conclude that the comorbidities of substance abuse and/or mood/anxiety disorders reflect higher risk for gambling problems.

As with alcohol and other drug problems, screening and assessment instruments have been developed for gambling problems. For a thorough discussion of these instruments, we suggest you read the chapter on this topic in *Best Possible Odds: Contemporary Strategies for Gambling Disorders* by William McCown and Linda Chamberlain (2000).

The best known and most commonly used screening instrument is the South Oaks Gambling Screen (SOGS; Lesieur & Blume, 1987). According to McCown and Chamberlain (2000) and Miller, Meier, and Weatherly (2009), the SOGS is highly correlated to the *DSM-IV-TR* diagnosis of pathological gambling, is easily scored, can be used by helping professionals in generalist settings, and can be used with older adolescents and college students. However, Weibe and Cox (2005) caution against using the SOGS with the older adult population until it can be further refined for this at-risk population. Dixon and Johnson (2007) have developed the Gambling Functional Assessment, which is a 20-item self-report measure that isolates the consequences that may be maintaining the person's gambling behavior.

In our own clinical work, we have found that the Twenty Questions used by GA (Gamblers Anonymous, 2015) are very useful for screening and client self-awareness. As with the SOGS and other self-report inventories, clients can easily lie to either minimize or exaggerate their symptoms in response to these questions. However, for clients and family members with genuine questions or concerns about gambling, we believe that the Twenty Questions are helpful. According to GA, most compulsive gamblers answer yes to at least seven questions.

1. Did you ever lose time from work or school due to gambling?
2. Has gambling ever made your home life unhappy?
3. Did gambling affect your reputation?
4. Have you ever felt remorse after gambling?
5. Did you ever gamble to get money with which to pay debts or otherwise solve financial difficulties?

   6. Did gambling cause a decrease in your ambition or efficiency?
   7. After losing, did you feel you must return as soon as possible and win back your losses?
   8. After a win, did you have a strong urge to return and win more?
   9. Did you often gamble until your last dollar was gone?
  10. Did you ever borrow to finance your gambling?
  11. Have you ever sold anything to finance gambling?
  12. Were you reluctant to use gambling money for normal expenditures?
  13. Did gambling make you careless of the welfare of yourself and your family?
  14. Did you ever gamble longer than you had planned?
  15. Have you ever gambled to escape worry or trouble?
  16. Have you ever committed or considered committing an illegal act to finance gambling?
  17. Did gambling cause you to have difficulty sleeping?
  18. Do arguments, disappointments, or frustrations create within you an urge to gamble?
  19. Did you ever have an urge to celebrate any good fortune by a few hours of gambling?
  20. Have you ever considered self-destruction as a result of your gambling?

Treatment, Resources, and Support

Although similarities exist between treatment for substance use disorders and treatment for pathological or compulsive gambling, so do significant differences. One practical difference is that health insurance rarely covers treatment for gambling problems. Furthermore, federal support is not available for compulsive gambling treatment as it is for alcohol and other drug treatment. Because problem gamblers almost always seek help only when the problem has become severe, they generally have accumulated large debts and cannot afford to pay for treatment. Therefore, unless a family member or friend has the financial resources to pay for treatment (which is usually expensive), the cost of treatment may be prohibitive.

In some states, a portion of the taxes levied on casinos, race tracks, lotteries, or gambling devices is used to provide treatment for compulsive gamblers. For example, Oregon allocates a portion of its lottery proceeds to publicly support compulsive gambling treatment. Nevada, unquestionably the state with the highest proportion of problem gamblers, had also allocated funds for treatment, but economic conditions forced that allocation to be cut in half in order to balance the state budget.

As with treatment for substance use disorders, compulsive gambling treatment can take place in inpatient or outpatient settings and usually includes a component for family members and/or significant others. According to McCown and Chamberlain (2000), inpatient treatment, often in a hospital setting,

> may be medically necessary for a client who has experienced a major life disruption—a vocational, financial, or marital disaster associated with either excessive gambling or suicidal attempts. Inpatient treatment probably is also indicated if the patient is experiencing insomnia, anxiety attacks, depression, mania, tangential thinking, extreme grandiosity, suicidal thinking, or frequent dissociative experiences. (p. 231)

Additionally, McCown and Chamberlain (2000) point out that inpatient treatment may also be necessary for many compulsive gamblers because they tend to be more impulsive and give in to cravings more frequently than alcoholics and drug addicts. Furthermore, a period of isolation may provide relief from the pressure of creditors, loan sharks, and gambling associates.

Outpatient treatment for compulsive gamblers is also available and has the obvious advantages of less expense than inpatient treatment and more convenience for those who continue to work and have families. However, as McCown and Chamberlain (2000) point out, there are no biological tests for gambling equivalent to drug testing for substance abusers. Therefore, the compulsive gambler could, theoretically, continue to gamble undetected while in treatment.

According to de Lisle, Dowling, and Allen (2011), although evaluations of the interventions for gambling problems are still in their infancy, analyses of the problem-gambling treatment literature suggest that gambling is amenable to intervention. For instance, Westphal (2006) studied attrition rates and found attrition rates of 23.5% for short-term pharmacological treatment, 42% for psychosocial interventions, 50.4% for long-term pharmacological treatment, 67.5% for GA, and 75% for community multimodal approaches. Nevertheless, Nower and Blaszczynski (2008) maintain that recovery is a diffuse concept that makes evaluation of interventions complex and difficult. These researchers suggest that future investigations should examine gambling recovery along a continuum. This spectrum should include such dimensions as time spent on gambling, the effects related to financial obligations, symptoms related to feeling out of control, and issues related to negative consequences and quality of life.

Resources

The NCPG (www.ncpgambling.org) is a nonprofit organization whose mission is "to increase public awareness of pathological gambling, ensure the widespread availability of treatment for problem gamblers and their families, and to encourage research and programs for prevention and education." The council administers programs and services, including a 24-hour confidential hotline (800-522-4700), a gambling-specific certification program for treatment professionals, an academic journal (*Journal of Gambling Studies*), literature distribution, and sponsorship of research and conferences. The NCPG has 34 state affiliates. On its website, you can link to a state affiliate. It should be noted that the council maintains a neutral stance on gambling and receives financial support from the gambling industry.

Support

GA is the best known and most widely used source of support for compulsive gamblers. GA was established in 1957 and is based on the Twelve Steps and Twelve Traditions of AA (discussed in Chapter 11). One difference between GA and AA is that more members of AA have been involved in a formal treatment program than those in GA. The reason is simple: There simply aren't as many treatment options for compulsive gamblers. Therefore, for many people with gambling problems, GA may be the *only* form of assistance they receive.

Although some differences in format and language are apparent, open GA and open AA meetings have many similarities. The Twelve Steps and Twelve Traditions are read, people introduce themselves by saying, "Hi, my name is _____ and I am a compulsive gambler," and members share their experience, strength, and hope with each other. Cross talking is not allowed and participants have sponsors. McCown and Chamberlain (2000) argue that GA is less spiritual and more pragmatic than AA and that GA meetings (particularly closed meetings) are more confrontational than AA. We have not found this to be true, but our experience with GA is less extensive than with AA.

A unique part of the GA program is the *pressure relief* group. After about 30 days of continuous abstinence, a member can request a pressure relief group meeting. The meeting usually includes the GA member, the spouse or significant other, the sponsor, and other GA members with long-term recovery. The group helps the new member develop a budget and a plan for repayment of debts. Members of the group may contact creditors and assist in debt negotiation. The spouse or significant other (assuming that he or she doesn't have a gambling problem) is encouraged to take control of the household finances. The new member is given the equivalent of Al-Anon, for the family and significant others.

TREATMENT OF OTHER BEHAVIORAL ADDICTIONS

Assessment and Diagnosis

As we stated in Chapter 6, assessment is crucial in planning for treatment. Individuals with other addictions will probably reflect problems in a variety of areas such as physical health, psychological and social functioning, reproduction and sexuality, cross-addictions, and family relationships. However these same problems may also exist in individuals whose behaviors are not addictive. For example, the client who comes in to work on grieving the intense feelings of a lost relationship may or may not be a sex and love addict. Such a determination will result from exploring thematic patterns in the client's various relationships. Clearly, questions addressing an individual's eating, gambling, sex and love issues, and work habits should be included in your routine psychosocial history. The nature and extent of information gathering in these areas will, of course, depend on the presenting problem. However, as you gather such data, facts disclosed about a client's family of origin or a client's current behavioral patterns may suggest areas for further exploration. For example, in listening to a bright, thin, college-aged woman with a family history of perfectionism and conflict, you might want to ask her about her eating patterns or about her attitudes regarding eating.

EATING DISORDERS   In a 2005 study of EDs in Asians, Cummins, Simmons, and Zane (2005) reviewed the literature and maintained that the multitude of ways to define EDs raises questions about the relevancy of diagnostic criteria for all groups. These researchers asserted that assessments used to measure EDs must be culturally sensitive. As testimony, a number of instruments designed to assess risk and presence of ED assessments have been developed in different countries or translated into different languages. New assessments have been developed in the United Kingdom, Norway, Asia, Sweden, Hungary, and Germany. As mentioned earlier, the *DSM-V* criteria for a diagnosis of ED were changed partly to distinguish differing patterns of EDs as well as in an attempt to minimize the number of NOS, and the result was to increase the number of those with the diagnosis of ED while minimizing the number of those with NOS.

In the United States, there are a number of brief and full-length clinical interviews and traditional paper/pencil instruments used to assess EDs in children, adolescents, and adults. Although there are mild questions as to the reliability of The Children's Eating Disorder Examination (Bryant-Waugh, Cooper, Taylor, & Lask, 1996), this four-dimension (Restraint, Eating Concern, Shape Concern, and Weight Concern) comprehensive clinical interview is still popular. The College Eating Disorders (Pearson et al., 2013) is a brief paper/pencil assessment comprising seven items that use language easily relatable and understandable for adolescents. For example, Item 7 says, "I feel guilty or sad after I eat something fatty." Respondents use a 5-point Likert-type scale. The Eating Disorder Inventory (Garner, 2005) is a popular 91-item standardized test that is easy to administer in order to assess and treat EDs in white women ages 13 to 53. The test consists of three ED-specific scales and nine general psychological scales that are highly relevant to EDs, which yield six composites. One is ED-specific, while the remaining five reflect ineffectiveness, interpersonal problems, affective problems, over-control, and general psychological maladjustment.

Primary care physicians may find it difficult to detect EDs in the early stages of the disorder (Sim et al., 2010). Quite often, seeking professional help comes only after the individual has experienced pressure from family members and cohorts at work or school. In Case Example 2 at the beginning of the chapter, Melanie felt the pressure to go to the doctor only after her mother had pleaded with her. Melanie had downplayed her symptoms for quite some time, and it was only after her weight had dropped so much that she listened to her mother. However, as is often the case, Melanie kept her ED a secret.

Behavioral and attitude changes often accompany AN and BN and include an increased interest in cooking, nutrition, and concomitant increase in exercise. Mental health professionals will want to examine the client's family for evidence of enmeshment, overprotectiveness, rigidity, lack of conflict resolution, and the involvement of the client in unresolved marital and family conflicts. In addition, information about weight loss is critical in assessing the severity of AN and BN. Because of the association with body image disturbance and EDs, clinicians need to be aware of the need to assess body image understanding that gender, sexual orientation, and race are important considerations. Even though the research is mixed regarding protective factors that culture plays for black women (see Bruns & Carter, 2015; Capodilupo & Kim, 2014), the fact that it is mixed demonstrates differences and the need to be sensitive in assessing differences among this and other populations. The same holds true when assessing male body image. In fact, Mellor et al. (2014) studied 401 Western and Asian adolescent males, and their results point to the importance of assessing for dissatisfaction with specific body parts.

ADDICTION TO SEX AND LOVE, THE INTERNET, AND WORK   We stated in Chapter 6 that a simple rule for determining whether a behavior is problematic is to ask yourself the question, "Does a normal drinker drink like this client?" For sex and love addiction, the mental health counselor can assess the normality of the client's relationship with a spouse or companion, the client's past and present extended family environment, other intimate relationships both present and past, and the client's relationships with strangers (Logan, 1992).

Although Rosenberg, Carnes, and O'Connor (2014) maintain that people who are promiscuous, and have multiple affairs or otherwise engage in unusual or aberrant sexual behaviors are not necessarily addicted. Nonetheless, clinicians will also want to examine the client's history of sexual abuse and its relationship to current acting out behaviors. Carnes et al. (2011) developed the PATHOS (see Table 15.1) which is an assessment modeled after the CAGE (see Chapter 6) to measure sexual addiction.

Regarding Internet addiction, Tao et al. (2010) proposed the following criteria for inclusion in the *DSM-V*. Although these criteria do seem to get at the issue, they were not included in the *DSM-V* or in the Appendix. Nevertheless, it is important for you as mental health professionals to have an understanding of the dimensions of the assessment. According to Tao et al., there must be both (1) preoccupation with the Internet and (2) withdrawal if there is no Internet activity. In addition, there needs to be at least one of the following: tolerance, persistent desire and/or unsuccessful attempts to curtail use and continued excessive use of the Internet in the face of problems it creates, loss of interest in other activities, and the use of the Internet to alter moods such as feelings of helplessness, guilt, or anxiety. There must be functional impairments in the areas of relationships, career, and/or education, and the duration of these issues must be at least three months with at least six hours/day of Internet use.

TABLE 15.1 PATHOS Items

1. Do you often find yourself preoccupied with sexual thoughts? (Preoccupied)
2. Do you hide some of your sexual behavior from others? (Ashamed)
3. Have you ever sought help for sexual behavior you did not like? (Treatment)
4. Has anyone been hurt emotionally because of your sexual behavior? (Hurt)
5. Do you feel controlled by your sexual desire? (Out of control)
6. When you have sex, do you feel depressed afterwards? (Sad)

Although there are a few measures used to assess workaholism, the early work of Spence and Robbins (1992) is still considered to be the most recognized and researched. Referred to as the Workaholism Battery (WorkBAT), Spence and Robbins postulate that a workaholic triad consists of work involvement, drive, and work enjoyment. Toward that end, they identify *true workaholics* (high on involvement and drive, low on enjoyment), *work enthusiasts* (high on enjoyment and involvement, low on drive), and *enthusiastic workaholics* (high on enjoyment, involvement, and drive). According to Patel, Bowler, Bowler, and Methe (2012), the WorkBAT has been the assessment of choice for researchers in over 500 studies. These same researchers assert that the Work-Addiction Risk Test (WART; Robinson, 1999) has been used in approximately 120 studies. It is a 25-item, self-administered test that assesses work habits. The higher the score, the more likely one is a workaholic. Both the WorkBAT and WART have been criticized by researchers who say that the Work Enjoyment scale of the WorkBAT is not highly correlated with current definitions of workaholism, and the WART may relate more closely to type A behaviors rather than workaholism. These criticisms aside, these two assessments are still the most popular.

Treatment

EATING DISORDERS   BN appears to have better treatment outcomes than AN (Kass, Kolko, & Wilfley, 2013). Noordenbos and Seubring (2006) maintain that due to the various definitions of "recovery" related to EDs, therapists and other mental health professionals should understand that prioritizing the criteria for recovery may vary among clients. Weight is clearly an issue. However, how much weight needs to be regained in order to be "recovered" is questionable. A pound of weight versus a half-pound of weight is significant for an ED client. In any case, Noordenbos and Seubring state that weight needs to be taken into account with other factors such as age, gender, racioethnicity, height, bone structure, as well as one's physical constitution.

Nevertheless, EDs can be treated and a healthy weight restored in many cases. From your reading, it is clear that EDs require a comprehensive treatment plan that addresses medical and psychological issues. This often includes medical monitoring (including medical management), psychosocial and psychological interventions, and some nutritional counseling. With AN, there are three main phases of treatment: (1) cessation of weight loss and the restoration of weight; (2) addressing the psychological issues related to body image, depression, anxiety, and compulsive behaviors; and (3) achievement of long-term remission and rehabilitation. Medications should be administered after the client has experienced some weight gain.

Forsberg and Lock (2015) report 12-month prevalence rates for AN and BN as being 2.6% for BN and 1% for AN. These researchers maintain that the threshold presentations are occurring at much higher rates and that AN continues to have the highest mortality rates of any psychiatric disorders and has high rates of suicide. Although early studies and narratives blamed the family as being a central culprit in the etiology of EDs, current research suggests that family approaches appear to have the best prognosis. In current family-based treatments, the central principle gravitates around the idea that parents are not to blame and instead are depicted as the cornerstone of recovery. Parents are seen as helping the recovery by managing the distressing behaviors of the afflicted child or adolescent while the therapist acts as a consultant. Generally speaking, family structure is only focused upon if it appears to impede the abilities of the parents to help regulate the family structural interactions.

Treatment modalities for BED and BN include cognitive–behavioral therapy (CBT). Engel et al. (2013) found that CBT and its enhanced version CBT-Enhanced (CBT-E) demonstrate effectiveness with these disorders. Interpersonal psychotherapy is also used, although its efficacy is the same as or somewhat less effective than CBT-E (Spielmans et al., 2013). While in-patient treatment is often recommended for anorexia, BN and BED can be treated through individual psychotherapy. Other treatments include using early memories that focus on the client's current issues (Strauch & Strauch, 2010), group psychotherapy that uses a CBT, and family or marital therapy to improve clients' attitudes about their ED as well as addressing the often co-occurring mood disorder.

New research regarding the treatment of EDs is being conducted related to executive functioning (EF; Juarascio et al., 2015). These researchers claim that this may be a significant omission in the treatment protocols. Although it has not yet been categorically demonstrated, there are concerns that problems with EF may mean that clients are less able to engage in treatments that use traditional CBT. For instance, Juarascio et al. (2015) use the example of clients who have deficits in their working memory may experience greater levels of preoccupation with thoughts related to food, weight, and shape and would experience difficulties processing new information that they glean in therapy. Memory training is suggested as potentially helping as is response inhibition training and cognitive–flexibility training. These last two approaches are directed at impulse control issues that are present with EDs.

As we pointed out in Chapter 8, it is critically important for mental health professionals to determine the client's learning style or learning capacity before initiating psychoeducational approaches. In addition to individual, family, and group psychotherapy, Twelve Step support groups, such as Overeaters Anonymous, may be of some help to clients whose problems include binge eating and overeating. These support groups can be especially helpful with relapse prevention, because clients with full-blown AN and BN will probably have problems in other areas of functioning. Specifically, support groups may help with important issues related to the initiation of pathological eating behaviors. For example, clients with EDs may demonstrate codependent behaviors or complain of other family dysfunction, factors that trigger compulsive eating behavior. Learning how to identify these triggers concomitant with hearing about how others deal with them may help to prevent a relapse.

ADDICTION TO SEX AND LOVE   Treatment for sex and love addiction is varied, and Rosenberg, Carnes, and O'Connor (2014) remind professionals that sex addicts are not very good at sex. Hence, when treating sex addiction the sexual behaviors that are addressed often lead to deeper psychological attachment issues that can alter the relationship. Traditional long-term therapies and multi-model psychotherapy are also used to help clients with insight, awareness of attachment concerns, and understanding of the role that culture plays. Pharmacological treatments with selective serotonin reuptake inhibitors (Weinstein, 2014) concomitant with CBT (Brand, Young, & Laier (2014) has also been found effective.

Carnes (2009) developed a series of workbooks emphasizing self-care, and clients are provided homework and reading assignments aimed at enhancing such things as nutrition, exercise, and introspection. Because sex addicts often have multiple addictions, it may be imperative to address those as well as the dynamic interactions between addicts and their partners which maintain sex addiction. Yet, sex addiction can be difficult to detect in the treatment of couples. Usually, there are other problems that present such as discord, communication issues, infidelity, and/or generic sexual dissatisfaction. Turner (2009) says that couples are often reluctant to talk about sex addiction because the effects of lying, secrets, and emotional distance can create so much distance as to cause suspiciousness or ambivalence about the relationship. This was illustrated in Case Example 1, where Samantha sensed something was wrong in her relationship. Yet, when it came time to discuss the issues in counseling, both were hesitant to do so.

There are other issues that influence the treatment of compulsive behaviors around sex and love. When examined, counselors are likely to see that the sex addiction started in adolescence and reflects some intergenerational family history where children are neglected, mistreated, or exploited. Being vulnerable, these children often inadvertently find addiction as a means to cope with their wounds. Imagine a lesbian woman being treated for sexual addiction, compulsivity, and codependency. While knowledge and interpersonal skills are needed to counsel lesbian women, numerous dynamics need further understanding. According to Manley and Feree (2002), these include understanding patterns of sexual addiction in lesbian relationships and basic knowledge of the issues, such as personal homophobia and feelings of oppression, experienced daily by lesbian women. In addition, awareness of the level of internalized oppression in the lesbian client is essential. From our perspective, the social discourse regarding individuals with gay and lesbian orientations presents a difficult challenge for many. It is important to have dialogue with clients about these issues in order to more fully understand their experience of the coming-out process, along with the subculture dynamics. Manley and Feree also suggest that the need for a broad understanding of the dynamics of oppression can be helpful in facilitating the client's integration.

McCarthy (2002) sees the opportunity to include women in the disclosure, assessment, treatment, recovery, and relapse prevention process for men addicted to sex. Women are viewed as vital in rebuilding couple trust, intimacy, and sexuality. Milrad (1999) believes that couples can benefit in couples therapy for the treatment of codependence and sex addiction. She urges mental health clinicians to understand the beginning recovery stages of codependency, because the stages relate to the dynamics that couples often experience in dealing with a sex-addicted spouse. Feree (2002) believes that more and more women within Christian circles will seek treatment for sexual compulsions. Clinicians need to understand ways to help this special population.

ADDICTION TO THE INTERNET   As mentioned, sex and love addiction have been greatly influenced by the Internet, and Young (2008) sees that our technologically advanced culture makes it very difficult for Internet sex addicts to go "cold turkey". This is because individuals use the Internet, or at least the computer, almost every day. Thus, self-control is usually not effective. As you would expect, discovering that a partner is heavily involved in Internet pornography creates conditions for substantial reappraisal of the relationship. Feelings of worthlessness, of being weak and stupid, sexually undesirable, and of living a lie are common reactions of their partners. Although the nonaddicted partner's focus would likely be on changing the addictive behaviors of the partner, it is more effective if therapists help reframe the situation and provide a clearer understanding of the issue, help the partner become more objective, and help the person be less devastated about it. Young (2008) and Delmonico, Griffin, and Carnes (2002) both see that immediate "first order" interventions should be used to diminish the behavior, and concrete steps include moving the computer to a public area in the house, installing filtering software such as Cyber Patrol, Surfwatch, or Net Nanny, and disclosing the nature of the problem to at least one other individual. "Second order" or more long-term structural changes must also be used. Because adolescents represent the largest groups of Internet addicts, Liu et al. (2015) found that using multifamily group approaches to be effective in changing family structure. The six sessions approach addresses adolescent Internet addiction while enhancing adolescent–parent relations.

These efforts can be supplemented with the development of a concise sexual recovery plan that acts to remind the addict of the issue and challenges. This plan has addicts assessing their current use in order to become clear about the high-risk situations, feelings, and events that trigger the behavior. The plan also identifies target behaviors that increase accountability and responsibility. The treatment of sexual addicts is seen as ". . . an ongoing self-exploration that must separate the behavior from the person, relieve shame about the behavior, correct maladaptive behavior, and promote opportunities to learn from mistakes" (p. 6). Finally, group therapy can be effective because it can help addicts manage their behavior, explore the dynamics of their addictive processes, and help develop bonds with others, thereby diminishing the sense of isolation and loneliness (Hook, Hook, & Hines, 2008).

ADDICTION TO WORK   Workaholism is a major source of marital problems as well as psychological and physical health problems. At the same time, marital strife can influence a person's approach to work, thereby "creating" workaholism. Interestingly, addiction to work and its implications require that treatment include both the organization as well as the individual. This is true because workaholic behaviors are often rewarded by the organizations and because entire organizations can exhibit a workaholic environment.

Malinowska and Tokarz (2014) suggest that organizations themselves need to take some responsibility to study their workforce culture as well as individual workstyles. Human Resources personnel need to disseminate workaholism literature and provide inservice trainings to help curtail excessive work behaviors. Short of treating the organization, specific treatment approaches can be used for individuals. For example, cognitive approaches can be effective. For instance, Robinson (2013, 2000) sees the bulimic workaholic style benefiting from the disputation of irrational beliefs about needing to be perfect. Those with a more relentless work style may benefit by focusing on impulse control, forethought, and attention to detail. Deliberately slowing down, such as slowing one's walking or driving speed, is also an effective treatment approach. Sometimes a medical evaluation might be needed for individuals who work compulsively. This is especially important if the person has trouble focusing on finishing or becomes easily bored with projects at work. It is important to remember that some workaholics make it difficult for other workers in the workplace. So, with the savoring workaholic person, helping him or her to learn the advantages of teamwork, cohesion, and trusting fellow workers will probably be important.

Counselors can also examine the marital relationship of individuals complaining of excessive work patterns. As mentioned, marital discord can pose problems in such a fashion as to help create the conditions of workaholism. Thus, counselors need to assess the extent to which these compulsive patterns are intertwined with marital problems. Obviously, the identification of which comes first is necessary. Because of this, family therapists can use the concept of "equifinality" in their treatment approach. This means that as long as counselors are aware of the possible connections between marital strife and workaholism, counselors can help couples explore their issues from a variety of perspectives and conceptualizations because all of these are connected and lead to the same treatment outcome.

Summary

- Pathological gambling lifetime prevalence rates are between 3% and 4% of the general population.
- Sixty-six percent of underage youth have gambled, and rates of gambling problems are two to four times greater than for adults.
- Eight percent of college students have gambling problems, and college graduates are significantly more likely than nongraduates to gamble on sports.
- Younger Americans are much more likely to gamble on sports than older Americans.

- The cost of problem gambling is approximately $6.7 billion per year.
- From 25% to 50% of pathological gamblers have abused their spouses.
- The rise of Internet use has created a new gambling industry, and Internet gamblers prefer this venue because of convenience, aversion to land-based gambling, the pace of online gambling, and the potential for higher wins.
- There is a significant increase for gambling problems among those with a co-occurring

- psychiatric disorder, and higher rates of suicide are reported for pathological gamblers.
- Types of gamblers include professional, antisocial, casual social, heavy social, relief-and-escape, and compulsive gamblers.
- The South Oaks Gambling Screen is the best-known assessment of pathological gambling.
- Although treatment of gambling problems approximates the approaches for other addictions, most insurance does not cover gambling treatment.
- In treatment, gamblers have very high attrition rates.
- Pathological gamblers can benefit from Twelve Step groups for gamblers, such as Gamblers Anonymous and Gam-Anon (similar to Al-Anon).
- Military personnel, both male and female, have higher rates of gambling problems than the general population.
- "Other Behavioral Addictions" include and are not limited to EDs, compulsive work, Internet and other electronic device abuse, and sex and love addiction. Not all professionals agree that these are addictions, and only some EDs are included in the *DSM-V*.
- Proponents of other behavioral addictions see the benefits as calling attention to a variety of problems associated with work, the Internet, and sex and love.
- EDs include chronic binge eating, AN, BN, chronic overeating, and binge eating.
- BED is a newly recognized entity in the *DSM-V*. Yet, there is no regulatory agency that has approved a drug for treating this disorder.
- EDs are prevalent in women across their life spans, most often diagnosed in younger females; males have lower rates.
- Body Image Disturbance is strongly associated with all of the EDs, including chronic overeating and binge eating.

- Current research suggests that in treating body image disturbance it is important to concomitantly create a positive body image.
- EDs are often medical emergencies, and mental health professionals need to refer clients for medical workups when they suspect these problems.
- EDs are on the rise in Asian and Arab cultures.
- Internet addiction creates problems at the workplace and at home.
- Adolescents represent the largest group of Internet addicts.
- The confusion over the term, the lack of consistent assessment criteria, and the dearth of large epidemiological research make estimation of prevalence of Internet addiction difficult.
- Cybersex and cyberaffairs are results of Internet addiction and are considered double addictions in that there can be an addiction to the Internet without addiction to cybersex or cyberaffairs.
- Sex addicts are not very good at sex.
- There are four types of workaholics: bulimic workaholic (characterized by perfectionistic and work binging), relentless worka-holic (starting early and finishing up late), attention-deficit workaholic (living on the brink of chaos with a lot of adrenaline), and savoring workaholic (loves the work).
- Workaholics may not always be type A personalities.
- Workaholics tend to have strong internal drives that are more related to their behaviors than to the pursuit of accomplishment and praise.
- There is no single dominant conceptualization that can explain the causes and maintenance of workaholism.
- Cognitive–behavioral treatments, the utilization of in-patient treatment facilities, multifamily, family, and group therapies are effective in working with those afflicted with other behavioral addictions.

Internet Resources

Gambling addiction
ncpgambling.org
MyAddiction.com

Assessment for Internet addiction
netaddiction.com

Eating disorders
edap.org

Workaholism
workaholics-anonymous.org

Further Discussion

1. How often have you gambled? Discuss ways in which a person could become addicted to it.
2. What is your experience with disordered eating?
3. Discuss the ways in which the cultural narrative play in the initiation and maintenance of disordered eating and EDs.
4. Do you know anyone who leaves the table immediately after eating? If so, what do you think is going on?
5. When you are on the Internet, what are the alluring features of the interaction between you and the computer? Discuss the ways in which the Internet could become addictive.
6. Discuss the various ways that Internet use should be monitored in the workplace.
7. In what ways have cyberporn and cyberaffairs affected people or couples that you know?
8. Now that you know that type A personalities and workaholism are not necessarily correlated, can you distinguish between the two in your own experience?

CHAPTER 16

Prevention

CASE EXAMPLES

1. Montel is a 12 year old who has just started middle school. He is caught smoking before school with a group of other students.

2. Sarah is a fifth-grader who is doing poorly academically. At a conference with her mother, the school counselor learns that her biological father (who is no longer involved with the family) is an active alcoholic.

3. Manuel is in the fourth grade. He is a good student and is well-behaved in class.

If you have read this text in sequence, you can see that most of the book involves topics related to the abuse of alcohol and other drugs (AOD). This reflects our view regarding the need for mental health professionals to acquire this information, given the frequency of AOD abuse in our society. However, this frequency is related to the effectiveness of efforts to prevent AOD abuse. Therefore, do not conclude that because there is only a single chapter devoted to this topic that prevention is less important than the other topics in this book. On the contrary, we believe that prevention is critically important from both policy and program standpoints. In particular, those of you who are planning to work in public schools as counselors or social workers should go beyond the information in this chapter. Also, a growing number of prevention specialists who work for public and private organizations are involved with substance abuse prevention. These professionals also need a more thorough understanding of this field than is found in this chapter. The section "Prevention Resources" is a good place to start.

WHY ARE PREVENTION EFFORTS NEEDED?

Why are prevention efforts needed? It is not a difficult question to answer. As you have read this text, you have received information on the problems caused by the abuse of AOD. So, if you take some action or actions that decrease the frequency of abuse, logically, the associated problems should also be reduced. For example, if there is a reduction in the number of people who chronically abuse alcohol, there should be a concomitant reduction in the number of people with medical problems resulting from chronic alcohol abuse. Therefore, prevention efforts designed to reduce the number of people who will end up abusing alcohol for many years are important and beneficial.

Most prevention efforts are directed toward young people. Again, this is logical because people generally make decisions about their use of tobacco, alcohol, and other drugs before they reach adulthood. As you know, it is illegal for people younger than 18 to use tobacco, for those younger than 21 to use alcohol, and for any age to use "street" drugs. Therefore, an examination of

TABLE 16.1 30-Day Prevalence and Change-Use Patterns

	Year	8th graders	10th graders	12th graders
Cigarettes	2015	3.6	6.3	11.4
	2014–2015	−0.4	−0.8	−2.2
	2005–2015	−5.7	−8.6	−11.8
Alcohol	2015	9.7	21.5	35.3
	2014–2015	0.7	−2.0	−2.1
	2005–2015	−7.4	−11.7	−11.7
Marijuana	2015	6.5	14.8	21.3
	2014–2015	0.0	−1.8	0.1
	2005–2015	−1.0	−0.4	1.5
Other illicit drugs	2015	3.1	4.9	7.6
	2014–2015	−0.2	−0.7	−0.1
	2005–2015	−1.0	−1.5	−2.7

survey data on the use of tobacco, alcohol, and other drugs by young people can provide information on the need for substance abuse prevention. Although several prominent surveys are conducted annually on the use of tobacco, alcohol, and other drugs by young people, the information in Table 16.1 is from the Monitoring the Future (MTF) study (Johnston et al., 2016). MTF is a survey conducted by the University of Michigan and is funded by the National Institute on Drug Abuse. Approximately 50,000 8th, 10th, and 12th graders are surveyed annually. MTF has been conducted for the past 40 years, which makes trends easy to identify.

Although one may look at the data generated by these surveys in numerous ways, we find it helpful to compare 30-day prevalence rates, which mean that a respondent has said that the substance in question has been used in the past 30 days. Table 16.1 is a report of 30-day prevalence data on 8th, 10th, and 12th graders from 2015, as well as changes since last year and over the past 10 years.

The MTF survey generates much more data than are reported here. However, even this small amount contains interesting information on substance use by young people and has implications for the prevention field. Clearly, tobacco and alcohol use are far more frequent than illicit drug use. Although that is not surprising, it certainly indicates that prevention efforts must involve the legal drugs in our society. The trend over 10 years has been large decreases in tobacco and alcohol use and smaller decreases in marijuana and other illicit drugs. Marijuana use by 12th graders has not decreased in the past decade. Finally, young people frequently believe that "everybody" is using. However, most young people report that they do *not* use tobacco, alcohol, or illicit drugs.

POLICY ISSUES IN PREVENTION

Drug Free?

On a surface level, it might seem that prevention scarcely needs a policy discussion. After all, most people would agree that preventing AOD misuse, especially by young people, is positive and that that's the only policy necessary. Clearly, the issues are more complicated. For example, when federal agencies set "drug-free" goals, *drug-free* does not include tobacco or alcohol. The MTF survey identified that tobacco and alcohol are by far the most widely used drugs by young people. In addition, these legal substances (for adults) cause more harm to society than all illegal drugs combined.

Unfortunately, the illogical dichotomy of legal/illegal drugs persists. So, although *drug-free* may be politically popular, this concept may divert attention and resources from efforts to prevent the use of tobacco and alcohol by young people.

An alternative conceptualization to drug-free is the harm reduction model. This model is based on the premises that drug use (including tobacco and alcohol) cannot be eliminated from our society, that the misuse or abuse of any drug can cause harm, and that strategies can be implemented to reduce the harm caused by misuse or abuse. A widely publicized example of a harm reduction strategy is needle exchange. This example reflects acknowledgment that some people are intravenous drug users who will not discontinue their use. By sharing needles with others, these hardcore drug users spread diseases such as hepatitis and HIV. The distribution of clean needles should reduce needle-sharing as a cause of infection. In fact, these programs have been successful in reducing the spread of AIDS (see literature review in Clark & Fadus, 2010). However, in spite of the evidence supporting needle exchange programs, the federal government, until recently, has fought efforts to fund these programs.

Harm reduction efforts are also directed at the legal drugs in our society. Sobriety checkpoints and designated driver publicity campaigns are intended to reduce the harm caused by alcohol-impaired drivers. Sting operations to identify and penalize retailers who sell tobacco to minors are designed to reduce the access of tobacco to young people. If a minor has trouble purchasing cigarettes, he or she will smoke less or not at all.

Some harm reduction processes involving alcohol use by minors are quite controversial. For example, some parents of teenagers may allow alcohol use at parties to discourage drinking and driving. Parents who allow this are engaging in a dangerous activity because it is a crime to contribute to the delinquency of a minor. In addition, in many cases they are enabling alcohol abuse. On prom and graduation nights, organizations such as Mothers Against Drunk Driving (MADD) may organize volunteers to drive for impaired students. This is certainly a difficult issue because no one wants a situation in which an impaired minor is involved in an accident, and responsible adults do not want minors to drink. Reconciling these issues is a dilemma for parents.

Gateway Drugs

Related to these issues is that federal prevention efforts have not focused on gateway drugs as much as they should. Gateway drugs are those that precede the use of other drugs, and are usually considered to be alcohol, tobacco, and marijuana. In fairness, more recent publications from the Center for Substance Abuse Prevention now refer to "alcohol, tobacco, and other drug problems," and underage drinking initiatives have been developed. But, this has not always been the case. As we will discuss, the reasons for the lack of focus on tobacco and alcohol probably are related to political pressure as opposed to best practice. It makes sense to focus on gateway drugs in prevention programs because drug users rarely begin with drugs such as cocaine or heroin. A young person usually begins drug use with tobacco or alcohol, because these drugs are readily available and their use is perceived as dangerous, exciting, and adult-like. Once a young person "takes the plunge" (begins use), it is much easier to go on to the next class of drugs. Furthermore, Hawkins, Catalano, and Miller (1992) have shown that the age of first use of any drug is related to later drug abuse by adolescents. Finally, alcohol and tobacco cause more health-related problems than other drugs. For example, as we noted in Chapter 1, more than 560,000 deaths annually are associated with tobacco and alcohol, as opposed to 40,000 deaths annually from all of the currently illegal drugs combined (Centers for Disease Control and Prevention, 2013a, 2014c, 2015a).

For all these reasons, it makes sense to focus on preventing the initiation of use of gateway drugs. However, the alcohol and tobacco industries have powerful lobbies that present constant barriers to prevention efforts. To give you one simple example, the tobacco industry is allowed to market a product that has no medically useful purpose, is highly addicting, and kills nearly 500,000 people a year. A product with these characteristics would never be allowed to be introduced today, and the failure to ban the promotion of tobacco is unconscionable. Since the tobacco master settlement agreement in 1998, cigarette advertisements in youth magazines increased by $54 million (Turner-Bowker & Hamilton, 2000). Obviously, alcohol is also marketed widely. In 2007, the alcohol industry spent over $1.6 billion on advertising, including nearly $900 million on television advertising. The beer industry alone spent more than $700 million on television ads (Alcohol Policies Project, Center for Science in the Public Interest, 2008). In comparison, the federal government's National Youth Anti-Drug Media Campaign, designed to convince young people to avoid illicit drugs, was budgeted at $45 million in fiscal year 2010 (Office of National Drug Control Policy, 2010). That is about 3% of what the alcohol industry spent to convince young people to drink. Currently, there is no money budgeted for this effort. According to the Center on Alcohol Marketing and Youth (2007) at the Johns Hopkins Bloomberg School of Public Health, exposure to alcohol advertising and alcohol marketing increases the probability that young people will start drinking and that they will drink more if they are already using alcohol. Of course, the alcohol industry claims that it does not target underage drinkers. However, youth exposure to alcohol advertising on television increased 71% between 2001 and 2009, which was more than the exposure of alcohol to adults older than 21. Furthermore, most of the increase was on cable shows more likely to be watched by minors (Center on Alcohol Marketing and Youth, 2010). The alcohol industry does place "responsibility" advertising on television. However, between 2001 and 2009, the alcohol industry spent 44 times more on advertising their products than on ads regarding responsible alcohol use (Center on Alcohol Marketing and Youth, 2010). Therefore, any efforts designed to prevent young people from initiating alcohol or tobacco use are directly countered by the marketing of these products. Legislators are heavily lobbied and receive campaign contributions from the alcohol and tobacco industries and have little motivation to pass laws that restrict or prohibit advertising. The attempt by the 1998 Congress to pass a comprehensive tobacco bill is an excellent example. The tobacco companies launched a successful effort to defeat this bill. So, research indicates that we need prevention efforts that focus on the gateway drugs, but federal and state government officials do not want to upset the tobacco and alcohol industries. Furthermore, prevention efforts are sabotaged by the sophisticated marketing of tobacco and alcohol. Can you see how policy affects prevention?

Supply versus Demand

The White House Office of National Drug Control Policy (ONDCP) is responsible for the development, management, and implementation of all federal programs involving illicit drugs. These programs are broadly classified as being "supply reduction," including domestic law enforcement, interdiction, and international efforts, or "demand reduction," including treatment and prevention. Our federal public policies regarding illicit drugs are demonstrated by how monetary resources are distributed between supply reduction and demand reduction. Domestic law enforcement includes agencies such as the Drug Enforcement Administration. Interdiction involves efforts by the Coast Guard and Customs and Border Protection to stop illegal drugs from entering the United States. International efforts include the initiatives in Central America to destroy coca plants and in Afghanistan to stop the growing of poppies. Most treatment and prevention dollars are distributed to states by block grants administered by the Center for Substance Abuse Treatment and the Center for Substance Abuse Prevention, both in the Substance Abuse and Mental Health Services Administration in the U.S. Department of Health and Human Services.

In the fiscal year 2015 budget, ONDCP (and ultimately Congress) allocated 57% of the budget to supply reduction and 43% to demand reduction (Office of National Drug Control Policy, 2014). Although this proportional distribution may seem odd to you, it is far better than the one-third demand reduction, two-thirds supply reduction that existed in the early part of the Obama Administration and prior administrations.

With this large proportion of financial resources allocated to law enforcement and military initiatives, it would be expected that the supply of illicit drugs in this country would be significantly disrupted. However, that is not the case. Since 2001, the Department of Justice has issued an annual report called the "National Drug Threat Assessment" on the availability of illicit drugs in this country. According to the 2015 report, the availability of heroin, methamphetamine, and marijuana was widespread and increasing (U.S. Department of Justice, National Intelligence Center, 2015). Cocaine shortages have been seen since 2007 because of reduced production in Colombia, high demand outside of the United States, and increased seizures and efforts to stop smuggling in Mexico. However, availability has stabilized at lower levels.

With all the competing interests for federal funds, reprioritizing the proportion of money allocated to supply reduction and demand reduction would certainly make sense. We now have ample evidence to conclude that the amount of money devoted to supply reduction is not justified. This money would be better spent on prevention and treatment.

Legalization

Legalization is an extremely controversial policy issue and one that generates highly emotional arguments from both sides. Proponents of legalization argue that crime, violence, and diseases would be reduced. If all drugs were legal, the argument goes, the profitability of black-market distribution would be reduced and those who inject drugs could always use clean needles. The quality of currently illegal substances could be controlled to prevent contamination. The number of people incarcerated for possession or for crimes related to the need to buy drugs would be reduced. More money would be available for prevention and treatment due to reduced prison populations and the decreased need to interrupt drug supplies.

Opponents of legalization counter by saying that the use of currently illegal drugs would increase, especially among youth. More social problems would result from drug use because of the increased access. They doubt that black-market distribution would decrease because buying drugs on the street would still be easier than buying them from the government. Therefore, violence and crime would still characterize drug distribution. Both sides use the experience of history (e.g., Prohibition) and policies from European countries to support their arguments.

As with many controversial issues, legalization is not as simple as either side would have you believe. First, drugs are legal. Alcohol and nicotine are drugs. Many other drugs with addictive potential are distributed with a physician's prescription. The legalization issue usually involves marijuana, cocaine, methamphetamine, and heroin. Second, many proponents of legalization are actually supporting *decriminalization*. Decriminalization involves allowing individuals to possess small amounts of currently illegal drugs for personal consumption. Distribution would remain illegal. This would prevent the arrest, prosecution, and incarceration of individuals who use drugs but do not commit other crimes. Third, the concept of legalization can have numerous operational definitions from unlimited and uncontrolled access and distribution to highly controlled access and distribution. Clearly, the consequences of legalization would be dependent on these processes. Finally, discussing the legalization of marijuana, cocaine, methamphetamine, and heroin together makes little sense. As we discussed in Chapter 2, the acute and chronic effects of these drugs are quite diverse, and the concept of dangerousness is vastly different.

We believe that it makes more sense to advocate for a logical and comprehensive discussion of our policies regarding alcohol, tobacco, and illicit drugs than to discuss the legalization of illegal drugs in isolation from other substances. For example, if marijuana were legal and marketed and distributed as alcohol and tobacco are, we have little doubt that use would dramatically increase. We believe that the legalization issue, although fun to discuss, is a diversion from a focus on all the drugs (legal and illegal) we abuse.

PREVENTION CLASSIFICATION SYSTEMS

The Institute of Medicine Classification System

This classification system is based on the target population of prevention activities. Universal prevention strategies are directed toward the entire population of a country, state, community, school, or neighborhood. The goal is to deter the onset of substance abuse by providing all individuals in the population with the information and skills perceived as necessary to prevent substance abuse. Screening to assess the risk of substance abuse is not targeted to subsets of the population because everyone is assumed to be at risk for substance abuse and capable of benefiting from the prevention activities. For example, the national media campaign that used to be part of the federal government's prevention efforts would be an example of a prevention activity directed toward a universal population. The television advertisements created as a part of this campaign were directed at all people who view them. School-based prevention programs that are implemented in the classroom are considered universal prevention.

Selective prevention strategies are targeted at subsets of a population who are considered at risk for substance abuse. For example, children of alcoholics or addicts, students who are failing academically, and abused children are considered "high risk" because research has shown that these children have a higher probability of later substance abuse than other children (Hawkins et al., 1992). The risk factors may be biological, psychological, social, or environmental, and the targeted subgroups may be determined by age, gender, family history, or place of residence (e.g., high-drug-use neighborhoods). The only criterion for inclusion is membership in the selected subgroup. Therefore, some individuals may be at low personal risk for substance abuse, whereas others may already be involved with alcohol or other drug use or abuse. A mentoring program for children from a low-income, high-drug-use neighborhood is an example of a selective prevention strategy. Another example of a selective prevention strategy would be a support group for children of alcoholics and addicts.

Indicated prevention strategies are directed toward individuals who have demonstrated the potential for substance abuse based on their behavior. For example, a minor in possession of tobacco, alcohol, or other drugs would fit this criterion. It is important to determine if the individual has a substance use disorder because that would indicate the need for treatment (see Chapter 6). Other indicated behaviors include involvement with the juvenile justice system for nonalcohol or other drug-related offenses, dropping out of school or excessive truancy, and conduct disorders. Examples of indicated prevention strategies include social skills classes for juvenile offenders, drug education for minors in possession, and family counseling.

Classification by Prevention Strategy

The Center for Substance Abuse Prevention (CSAP), the federal agency that coordinates prevention efforts throughout the country, has used a prevention classification system based on six strategies. This system is not in conflict with the Institute of Medicine system, because a strategy may be targeted to universal, selective, or indicated populations. The six strategies are as follows:

INFORMATION DISSEMINATION   This involves communication of the nature, extent, and effect of substance use, abuse, and addiction on individuals, families, and communities. In addition, these strategies may involve information on prevention programs and services. One-way communication between a source and an audience, with limited or no contact between the two, characterizes information dissemination. Public service announcements, didactic instruction, audiovisual materials, displays of drugs, and publications are examples of information dissemination.

EDUCATION   These activities are designed to build or change life and social skills—such as decision-making, refusal skills, assertiveness, and making friends—that are usually thought to be associated with substance abuse prevention. Education is differentiated from information dissemination in that education encourages interaction between the facilitator or instructor and the participants. Education strategies also imply an expectation that participants will develop skills as a result of the education. Most school-based prevention programs are considered to be education, although they may include an information dissemination component. Programs designed to improve parenting skills are also examples of education strategies.

ALTERNATIVES   These strategies involve the development of activities that are incompatible with substance use. This is based on the assumption that young people may use AOD because of boredom or lack of access to other activities. Therefore, if healthy, productive, and fun activities are available, young people will participate in these activities rather than in AOD use. In addition, this participation may expose high-risk youth to positive role models and provide an expanded view of the possibilities for the future. Midnight basketball is often used as an example of an alternative strategy. Another common alternative strategy is the development of after-school programs, designed to provide a supervised, productive program for young people at a time when much of youth crime is committed (3 to 7 P.M.).

PROBLEM IDENTIFICATION AND REFERRAL   This strategy is generally targeted to indicated populations who have been identified as using tobacco, alcohol, or other drugs or who have engaged in other inappropriate behaviors. Depending on the nature and severity of the problem, referrals may be made to educational programs, family therapy, or other forms of treatment. For young people who are caught in possession of tobacco, alcohol, or other drugs, consequences may be combined with mandatory education.

COMMUNITY-BASED PROCESSES   These strategies involve the mobilization of communities to more effectively provide prevention services. Interagency collaborations, coalition building, and networking are considered community-based strategies. For example, representatives from county government, social services, juvenile justice, education, the faith community, and the business community may join together to develop seamless (i.e., no barriers to access services from different agencies) services for youth.

ENVIRONMENTAL APPROACHES   Within this strategy are the written and unwritten standards, codes, laws, and attitudes that impact substance use and abuse in a community. The clearest examples are laws regarding tobacco and alcohol. States and counties have very different laws relating to the taxation and distribution of tobacco and alcohol.

A social service organization that relies on alcohol-related events (e.g., wine tasting) to raise funds is communicating a value that is counterproductive for prevention. An environmental strategy would be to lobby this organization to change its fund-raising activities. Another example would be efforts to prohibit university campus newspapers from accepting advertisements that promote excessive alcohol use.

Classification by Risk and Protective Factors

David Hawkins and his colleagues at the University of Washington have done a considerable amount of work on the identification of factors that are associated with an increased probability of AOD abuse (risk factors) or with a decreased probability of AOD abuse (protective factors; e.g., Hawkins et al., 1992). This conceptualization has become so popular that many states build their prevention systems by assessing the extent of each risk factor in their communities and then by designing prevention strategies to reduce these risk factors.

Risk factors have been organized by community, family, school, and individual or peer categories. Community risk factors include the availability of tobacco, alcohol, and other drugs; community laws and norms favorable toward substances; community mobility (i.e., frequent movement of people in and out of the community); low neighborhood attachment and community disorganization; and extreme economic deprivation. Family risk factors include a family history of problem behaviors, family management problems, family conflict, and parental attitudes toward and involvement with substance use. In the school area, the risk factors are early and persistent antisocial behavior, academic failure beginning in elementary school, and lack of commitment to school. Finally, individual or peer risk factors include alienation and rebelliousness, association with peers who engage in problem behaviors, favorable attitudes toward problem behaviors, early initiation of problem behaviors, and constitutional factors (i.e., genetic predisposition to addiction or sensation seeking).

In spite of being exposed to multiple risk factors, some young people do not develop problems with AOD. Certain protective factors seem to buffer youngsters by reducing the impact of the risk factors or by changing the way in which the individual responds to the risks. These protective factors have been categorized as individual characteristics, bonding, and healthy beliefs and clear standards. The individual characteristics include gender (females are more protected than males), a resilient temperament, a positive social orientation, and intelligence. Obviously, these individual characteristics are difficult or impossible to change. Bonding involves the attachment to positive families, friends, school, and community. The beneficial aspects of bonding cannot be overemphasized. A child who develops a bond to positive role models or healthy systems can overcome the disadvantages of exposure to risk factors. To facilitate the development of bonding, children need the opportunity to bond, the skills to take advantage of the opportunity, and recognition for making efforts to bond. For those of you who wonder if you can make a difference in a young person's life, this information on bonding should be a strong affirmation that you can have a major impact. Healthy beliefs and clear standards go hand-in-hand with bonding. The people and systems to which young people bond must communicate positive values and hold young people accountable for their behavior. Protection is enhanced when clear standards of behavior are expressed and consequences are applied for violations of these standards.

Although the risk and protective factor model is logical, a caution is necessary. Much of this research is correlational rather than causal. To illustrate, let's look at one family risk factor: family conflict. Family conflict has been identified as a risk factor because of evidence that children from families in which excessive family conflict is present have a higher probability of developing substance abuse problems (and other problems as well) than children who come from families in which minimal family conflict is present. However, this does not mean that family conflict causes substance abuse problems or that reducing family conflict will prevent a child from developing a substance abuse problem. Perhaps the family conflict is due to the substance abuse of one or more of the caretakers in the family. As a result of some type of intervention, perhaps the family learns to resolve its problems in a more reasonable manner. However, the caretaker continues to abuse substances. In this instance, family conflict is just one symptom of dysfunction in the family system as a result of substance abuse. Therefore, treating one symptom is not likely to affect the development of substance abuse (or other problems) in the children.

It should be noted that a causal relationship between risk and protective factors and substance abuse is not proposed in the model developed by Hawkins and his colleagues. However, many intervention programs designed to reduce risk factors and increase protective factors have been based on an assumption that such a causal relationship exists. In our view, these factors interact in a complex fashion. As we will discuss in the next section, the development of prevention strategies and programs should be based on research on what works.

AT A GLANCE

Institute of Medicine Classification System
- Universal (everyone regardless of risk factors)
- Selective (those with some risk factors)
- Indicated (those who have begun to demonstrate high-risk behaviors)

Prevention Strategies
- Information dissemination (no interaction)
- Education (information and skill building with interaction)
- Alternative activities (non-AOD activities for youth)
- Problem identification and referral (usually for indicated populations)
- Community-based processes (mobilization, interagency cooperation, coalition building)
- Environmental approaches (standards, codes, laws, regulations)

Risk and Protective Factors
- Community (availability of AOD, laws and norms, mobility, neighborhood attachment, economic deprivation)
- Family (history of problem behavior, management problems, conflict, involvement with AOD)
- School (antisocial behavior, academic failure, lack of commitment)
- Individual (alienation and rebelliousness, peers who use AOD, favorable attitudes toward AOD, early problem behaviors)
- Protective (bonding and healthy beliefs and clear standards)

WHAT WORKS IN PREVENTION

Evaluation of Prevention Programs

Several issues need to be considered in evaluating prevention programs. Clearly, local, state, and federal government entities are interested in evaluating the success of prevention programs because of the money spent on the programs. As you might imagine, the typical method for evaluating success is the implementation of a prevention program in classrooms or schools and to later see whether the individuals who were involved in the program use AOD to a lesser extent than individuals who were not involved in the program. One problem is that the initiation of use by young people depends on a complex interaction of personal, familial, cultural, and societal variables. To expect a school-based prevention program to singularly impact a behavior influenced by so many variables is unrealistic. Second, we know that attitudes and behavior can be influenced by a consistent, long-term, and comprehensive effort. For example, when many of us were young, cars did not have seat belts. Seat belts were then made optional, but we still never used them. Today, they are standard features in all cars, and many states have legislation requiring their use. So, our children don't even think about it. When they get in the car, they put on their seat belts. We do, too. However, this change in attitude and behavior in adults who grew up with seat-belt-free cars was accomplished through a long-term process involving public policy (legislation) and public awareness. Similarly, school- and community-based prevention programs should be viewed as a part of long-term, consistent, comprehensive prevention efforts and not as isolated "cures" for the problem of tobacco, alcohol, and other drug use by young people.

However, we believe that the effectiveness of prevention efforts would be enhanced if the contradictory messages were less pervasive. Marketing of tobacco and alcohol products, positive depictions of tobacco, alcohol, and drug use in the media, and modeling by adults and peers are powerful influences on young people. It is not currently possible, given financial and practical constraints, for the prevention community to counteract creative and funny beer commercials, cigarette smoking in youth-oriented movies, and mom and dad smoking a joint with their friends in the living room. Society's prevention message is not consistent or comprehensive. Finally, school-based prevention programs are often viewed in a similar manner to other programs in a school. If you want to evaluate a new reading program, you compare the reading performance of children in the new program with the performance of children in another program. However, we would argue that prevention programs are different. For example, imagine that you begin a prevention program that costs $10,000 in materials and training. In the entire school, only one student who would have become dependent on tobacco, alcohol, or other drugs is impacted and avoids use. You will have more than made up for the money invested in the program by preventing the financial and societal impact on health care, work productivity, the legal system, and family members that this person would have caused. We are not arguing that prevention programs should be purchased and implemented without careful evaluation. We are arguing that prevention programs should not be blamed for failing to solve a complex and multifaceted problem.

Because of the importance of the problem and the money spent on prevention, the federal government has become very interested in determining which prevention strategies and programs are the most effective. For example, the National Institute on Drug Abuse has a publication on principles of effective prevention (National Institute on Drug Abuse, 2003). In addition, Paglia and Room (1998) presented an excellent review of the prevention literature, and Tobler (1992) and Tobler and Stratton (1997) conducted meta-analyses of school-based prevention programs. From these sources, conclusions regarding effective (and ineffective) prevention strategies can be reached. We will present these conclusions for each of the six CSAP strategies.

INFORMATION DISSEMINATION   School-based information dissemination methods have been unsuccessful in impacting tobacco, alcohol, and other drug use. Tobler (1992) found that prevention programs that only presented information did increase knowledge of participants but had no effect on attitudes and drug use. This is not surprising when you consider the analogy of the prevention of heart disease. Most Americans know that quitting smoking, regular aerobic exercise, eating fresh fruits and vegetables, and so forth will reduce the risk of heart disease. However, this information alone is usually insufficient to result in a significant behavior change for most people. Similarly, simply learning about the negative consequences of using tobacco, alcohol, and other drugs does not affect the reasons for use by most young people.

Although information dissemination alone is not sufficient, providing accurate information is an important component for school-based prevention programs. Paglia and Room (1998) recommend an emphasis on the short-term adverse effects of use, rather than on the long-term effects. The reasoning is that, from a developmental standpoint, short-term adverse effects have more impact on young people, particularly the effects that involve social attractiveness. Additionally, information on health risks and consequences of use should be based on research and should be delivered in a nonjudgmental manner. Scare tactics and moral lecturing have not been shown to be effective and may actually have a detrimental effect if the information is in conflict with the personal experience of students.

As might be expected, information dissemination via the mass media should be aired at times when young people are likely to be listening or watching. The use of authority figures and exhortations has not been shown to be effective. As with school-based information dissemination, short-term risks involved in substance use should be emphasized (Brounstein, Zweig, & Gardner, 1998).

EDUCATION   In contrast to previously discussed school-based prevention programs that are "information only," Tobler (1992) has categorized some school-based programs as affective. This model is based on the assumption that young people use AOD because of low self-esteem, inadequate social skills, and ambiguous values. Through discussion and activities involving feelings, values, and self-awareness, an attempt is made to improve self-concept and social skills and to clarify the students' values.

The results from Tobler's (1992) meta-analysis show that prevention programs that used only affective education were ineffective in impacting knowledge, attitudes and values, self-reported drug use, or assertive, refusal, and decision-making skills. Furthermore, drug incident reports, school grades and attendance, and achievement test scores also were unaffected. Approaches that combine cognitive (information dissemination) and affective approaches did have a positive effect on knowledge of participants but a negligible effect on the other outcomes. Part of the problem with this approach to prevention may be the consistent finding that very little relationship has been established between self-esteem and drug use (Clayton et al., 1996; Coggans & McKellar, 1994; Schroeder, Laflin, & Weis, 1993).

Another educational approach to prevention is based on the influences on young people that result in the initiation of tobacco, alcohol, and other drug use. Family use patterns (including parents and siblings), peer pressure, and media all may influence young people to use (or not to use). Social resistance skills approaches (also called *social influence* or *refusal skills* approaches) have been developed to counteract environmental influences. A distinctive feature of these prevention models is that they place more emphasis on teaching students specific skills to resist both peer and media pressures to smoke, drink, or use drugs.

According to Botvin and Botvin (1992), social resistance skills approaches generally contain the following components: recognizing situations in which a high probability exists that a young person will experience peer pressure to use, formulating strategies to avoid these high-risk situations, teaching students what to say and how to say it when confronted with peer pressure, and developing awareness of techniques used by the media to encourage use by young people. Peers are frequently used in implementing these programs, because peers, particularly older adolescents with perceived status, may be more influential than teachers or other adults. Information dissemination, with a focus on prevalence of use by young people, is used to counter the argument that "everyone is doing it."

In evaluating social resistance skills approaches, Botvin and Botvin (1992) report that these programs have been associated with reductions in tobacco, alcohol, and marijuana use for up to three years. However, long-term follow-up studies have shown that these reductions are not maintained over time. Tobler (1992) found that programs using peers as implementers had a positive impact on knowledge, attitudes, self-reported drug use, and skills. However, no beneficial effect was noted on drug incident reports or on indirect measures of use such as school grades and attendance.

The age group of the students, number of training sessions, use of booster sessions, instructional materials, and characteristics of the students may all impact evaluation of these programs.

Competency enhancement approaches are more comprehensive than the other approaches and focus on the interaction between the individual and environment in the prevention of substance use by young people. Competency enhancement approaches emphasize the development and use of personal and social skills that are directly related to substance use but that are also applicable to many other adolescent problems. According to Botvin and Botvin (1992), competency enhancement approaches typically teach two or more of the following strategies: problem-solving and decision-making skills, cognitive skills for resisting peer or media influences, skills for increasing self-control and self-esteem; coping strategies for relieving stress and anxiety through the use of cognitive coping skills or behavioral relaxation techniques; and social and assertive skills. These skills are taught using a combination of instruction, demonstration, feedback, reinforcement, practice during class, and extended practice through homework assignments.

Evaluation studies of competency enhancement approaches seem generally positive. In a summary of these studies, Botvin and Botvin (1992) report reductions in initiating use of tobacco, alcohol, and marijuana. Effectiveness has been demonstrated using many types of trainers (e.g., peers, teachers, project staff) as well as with ethnically diverse groups. With booster sessions, the effects have been maintained for up to six years (Botvin et al., 1995). However, this long-term follow-up study has been criticized for failing to report negative results and for issues regarding sample selection (Brown & Kreft, 1998; Gorman, 1998).

In reviewing the literature on school-based prevention, Paglia and Room (1998) and Brounstein et al. (1998) have presented some general guidelines in the structure, content, and delivery of prevention education. The recommendations include prevention programming throughout the grades, with the greatest emphasis on the median ages of first use (late elementary school and middle school). Although long-term programs are superior to short-term programs, periodic booster sessions following the completion of programs are necessary to maintain benefits. Information presented should be factual. If the instructor does not know an answer, this should be admitted to students. Students should have the opportunity to discuss the reasons why people use AOD, alternatives to meeting these needs, and the dangers and benefits to using and not using. Although both short-term and long-term effects should be presented, the short-term effects should be emphasized. Perceptions regarding "everybody does it" should be challenged with data. An interactive style of presentation is most beneficial, including cooperative learning, role-plays, and group exercises. Peer facilitators can be effective if they are trained and are perceived as credible. The instructional atmosphere should be tolerant and free from moralizing and scare tactics. Finally, and most importantly, anything taught in the school must be reinforced in the community by parents, media, and through public policies.

A variety of education programs focused on the family have also been hypothesized to prevent substance use among youth. These programs can involve parent education, parenting skills training, parent support groups, and family therapy. It is particularly useful to combine school-based prevention programs with family-based programs. Most studies of family-based prevention have focused on "high-risk" families. An example of such a program is the Strengthening Families program (Kumpfer, Williams, & Baxley, 1997). Parent, child, and family skills training was targeted to substance abusing families with children in the six- to 10-year range. Improvements were found in the problem behaviors of the children, in intentions to use AOD, in parenting skills, in family communication, and in family conflict.

ALTERNATIVES   The research evidence regarding the effectiveness of alternative activities is mixed. Botvin and Botvin (1992) indicate that entertainment, vocational, and social alternatives programs have been associated with more rather than less substance use, although academic, religious, and sports activities are associated with less use. They report that evaluations of alternatives programs have failed to demonstrate an impact on adolescent use. In contrast, Tobler's (1992) meta-analysis of alternatives programs for high-risk youth showed positive effects on skills and behavior, including school grades, school attendance, and independent reports of observed drug use.

According to the review of literature conducted by Brounstein et al. (1998), alternatives should be part of a comprehensive prevention plan that includes other activities with proven effectiveness. However, when alternative activities are being developed, they must be attractive to the target group or participation will not occur. Therefore, young people must be involved in the planning process. Not surprisingly, the more intensive the activity (in terms of both hours required and length), the more effective it is.

Carmona and Stewart (1996) and Tobler (1986) point out that alternative activities serve a more general purpose than just providing something else to do besides using substances. For some high-risk youth, alternative activities are an opportunity for personal development and positive bonding to adults and the community. The development of these protective factors may be beneficial in a variety of ways. One type of alternative activity that is popular is mentoring. Mentoring programs provide young people, particularly high-risk youth, with structured time with positive adult role models. Mentoring programs have been associated with reductions in substance use; increases in positive attitudes toward others, the future, and school; and increased school attendance. As would be expected, the more highly involved the mentor, the greater the impact. It is particularly important to screen and train potential mentors. Clearly, mentors must be positive role models and must complete their commitment to the young people in the program. Many of the high-risk youth in these programs have been disappointed by adults in the past and should be protected from having similar experiences with mentors.

PROBLEM IDENTIFICATION AND REFERRAL   Certain factors are important to consider in the development of any problem identification and referral system. First, experimental users should be differentiated from problematic users. Although any use of tobacco, alcohol, or other drugs by a minor is a problem, experimentation is not uncommon and does not require intensive intervention. A significant consequence combined with education is usually the appropriate level of intervention for experimental use. In addition, if experimental users are placed in more intensive programs, they will be grouped with problematic users. This could have the unintended consequence of enabling further use. Because of these issues, problem identification and referral programs must have valid procedures and trained personnel to determine where the individual is on the use continuum (see Chapter 6).

Substance use among young people is often associated with other problems, including family dysfunction, school failure, sexual activity, and violence. Therefore, a problem identification and referral program must be prepared to screen for other problems in addition to substance use and must have adequate referral resources to assist the targeted individuals. This may include very concrete issues such as transportation. For example, a 15-year-old female was referred to a guidance team at her high school after she was found in possession of marijuana. She admitted to frequent, unprotected sex with a variety of partners. The young woman was receptive to a referral to the local health department for contraception and testing for sexually transmitted diseases, but she had no way to get there. Fortunately, school personnel were able to arrange public transportation.

COMMUNITY-BASED PROCESSES   Community-based coalitions are formed to improve the nature and delivery of services to the community (comprehensive service coordination), generate community activism to address substance-related problems (community mobilization), or to perform both functions (community linkage). Comprehensive service coordination requires the involvement of the leaders of the organizations in the coalition, whereas community mobilization is dependent on grassroots activists and community citizens. To elicit change at a systems or individual-behavior level, community partnerships must have a clear and shared vision of their objectives, commitments to participate from all partnership members, participation from diverse community groups, and comprehensive prevention activities directed at a large number of individuals.

Appropriate organization, leadership, and evaluation have been shown to be important components in successful community partnerships. Although committees are usually necessary, those with specific purposes sustain higher levels of involvement than those with elaborate structures. A dynamic leader may be effective but this type of individual cannot normally be replaced. Therefore, opportunities for leadership roles from a variety of participants are helpful. Community coalitions are also advised to implement evidenced-based prevention strategies and to incorporate procedures for measuring the effectiveness of their strategies.

ENVIRONMENTAL APPROACHES   The approaches in this category generate a great deal of discussion in the prevention community and in state and federal governments. Environmental approaches have demonstrated a direct impact on the use of tobacco and alcohol and on the problems associated with the use of these substances. However, environmental strategies have not been as effective with regard to illicit drugs, as we saw in the earlier discussion in this chapter on supply reduction efforts.

Increasing the taxes on tobacco and alcohol is one type of environmental strategy. Tax increases have resulted in reductions in the use of both tobacco and alcohol as well as reductions in associated problems, such as alcohol-related traffic accidents. The tobacco legislation considered by the 1998 Congress included a significant tax increase on tobacco and was bitterly fought (and defeated) by the tobacco industry. Moreover, efforts to increase the price of illicit drugs through law enforcement efforts generally have not been successful.

Laws regarding the purchase of tobacco and alcohol by minors have also been effective. When the minimum purchase age for alcohol was raised to 21 in all states, alcohol consumption among minors decreased, as did alcohol-related problems. Sting operations, using underage individuals who attempt to purchase tobacco or alcohol, are effective in increasing retailer compliance with restricting sales to minors. In addition, "use and lose" laws that result in driver's license suspension for minors convicted of an alcohol or drug violation have also been shown to increase compliance with minimum-purchase-age laws.

Deterrence laws and policies have also been shown to be effective in reducing alcohol-related accidents and underage drinking and driving. These include lowering the blood-alcohol level from 0.10 to 0.08 or lower, enforcement of drinking and driving laws, sobriety checkpoints, and zero tolerance for alcohol use by underage drivers. Although sobriety checkpoints do not result in high levels of detection, publicizing that they will occur seems to have a deterrent effect.

Local communities can also implement proven environmental strategies by placing restrictions on the location and number of retail outlets authorized to sell tobacco and/or alcohol. Neighborhoods have been able to disrupt illicit drug sales through citizen surveillance and through pressure on landlords who own property where drug sales occur.

Training for individuals who serve alcohol (i.e., bartenders) and clerks who sell tobacco and alcohol is an effective strategy when it is combined with law enforcement efforts. Training is intended to educate servers and clerks about the laws, as well as teach them to identify intoxication and false identification and to provide skills in refusing to serve or sell.

Although environmental strategies are clearly effective in reducing the use of tobacco and alcohol, the involvement of community coalitions is usually essential to implement these strategies. Because many require action by policy makers and many policy makers receive campaign contributions from the tobacco and alcohol industries, pressure from community groups is often necessary.

CASE EXAMPLE APPLICATIONS

Our three cases at the beginning of the chapter illustrate the three possibilities in the Institute of Medicine classification system. Montel would be included in an indicated population. He has already begun to demonstrate the problem behavior by smoking cigarettes at a very young age. It would be important to assess how frequently Montel smokes and whether he has begun to experiment with AOD. This assessment would determine what type of intervention would be the most appropriate. In this case, Montel was not smoking regularly and had not really begun to use AOD. It was determined that he was smoking to "fit in" with a peer group in middle school. Therefore, for breaking a school rule, Montel received a consequence that included staying after school for an educational group on AOD (including tobacco) and cleaning up the school grounds. In addition, he was provided a peer mentor (a ninth grader) and had some visits with the school counselor.

Sarah would be part of a selective population because she has risk factors for substance abuse. Her poor academic performance and family history of alcoholism are both risk factors. Sarah was placed in a tutoring program to improve her academic skills and a support group at the school for children from substance abusing homes.

Manuel is in the universal population. No risk factors are present and he has not engaged in any high-risk behaviors. Manuel participates in an evidence-based school prevention program for his grade level.

EVIDENCE-BASED PREVENTION

In Chapter 8, we discussed evidence-based treatment and the National Registry of Evidence-Based Programs and Practices (NREPP). Although this registry currently contains prevention, intervention, and treatment programs, it was initially started as a process to determine which prevention programs could be called "model programs" and, as of 2016, contains 131 programs in substance abuse prevention. Because so many evidence-based programs are available, states can ensure that the prevention programs they fund have evidence to support their effectiveness. In Chapter 8, we reviewed the process that NREPP follows to determine if a program should be included as evidence-based.

So you can get a sense of the variety of prevention programs on NREPP, the following are some of the programs and a brief description: (1) Across Ages, a school- and community-based substance abuse prevention program for youth aged nine to 13. The unique feature of Across Ages is the pairing of older adult mentors (55 years and older) with young adolescents, specifically those making the transition to middle school. (2) The Border Binge-Drinking Reduction Program provides a process for changing the social and community norms associated with underage and binge drinking that has proven effective at reducing alcohol-related trauma caused by young Americans' binge drinking across the U.S.–Mexican border. (3) Building Assets—Reducing Risks is a multifaceted school-based prevention program designed to decrease the incidence of substance abuse (tobacco, alcohol, and other drugs), academic failure, truancy, and disciplinary incidents among ninth-grade youth. (4) Celebrating Families! is a parenting skills training program designed for families in which one or both parents are in early stages of recovery from substance addiction and in which a high risk for domestic violence and/or child abuse exists. (5) Familias Unidas is a family-based intervention for Hispanic families with children ages 12 through 17. The program is designed to prevent conduct disorders; use of illicit drugs, alcohol, and cigarettes; and risky sexual behaviors by improving family functioning. (6) LifeSkills Training is a school-based program that aims to prevent alcohol, tobacco, and marijuana use and violence by targeting the major social and psychological factors that promote the initiation of substance use and other risky behaviors. (7) Start Taking Alcohol Risks Seriously for Families is a health promotion program that aims to prevent or reduce alcohol use among middle school youth ages 11 to 14. The program is founded on the Multi-Component Motivational Stages prevention model, which is based on the stages of behavioral change found within the Transtheoretical Model of Change (Substance Abuse and Mental Health Services Administration, 2016b).

PREVENTION RESOURCES

The federal Substance Abuse and Mental Health Services Administration (SAMHSA) has federal prevention (and treatment) publications available, generally at no cost. The website is included in "Internet Resources."

In addition, the federal Center for Substance Abuse Prevention (in SAMHSA) has a program called the Center for the Application of Prevention Technologies (CAPT). The purpose of the CAPT is to help states and community-based organizations apply evidence-based prevention strategies. The CAPT includes regionally based staff members and consultants to cover different areas of the country. The website is included in Internet Resources. In addition, each state has a single state agency for treatment and prevention coordination. Some staff in this agency will be involved with prevention efforts.

Finally, for those of you who are interested in exploring the prevention field in more depth, we recommend a textbook by Hogan, Reed-Gabrielsen, Luna, and Grothaus (2003), *Substance Abuse Prevention: The Intersection of Science and Practice.*

PREVENTION SPECIALISTS

Many institutions of higher education, community-based organizations, and school districts hire professional staff members to coordinate prevention programs. In many cases, the prevention specialist has responsibility for the prevention of suicide, violence, teen pregnancy, and other public health issues in addition to substance abuse. Prevention specialists are involved in developing and implementing programs, providing training and technical assistance, writing grants, evaluating programs, and preparing policies and procedures.

Because of an increase in the number of prevention specialists, many states have adopted certification standards and have recognized prevention specialists as a distinct professional group. Although you must consult your particular state for requirements, many states have adopted the certification standards and examination process developed by the International Certification and Reciprocity Consortium (IC&RC). We have included the certification standards for the IC&RC prevention specialist in Internet Resources.

MyCounselingLab for Addictions/Substance Abuse

Try the Topic 12 Assignments: *Prevention.*

Summary

- Public policies regarding tobacco, alcohol, and other drugs have an impact on prevention efforts.
- Prevention activities are classified by the target audience (universal, selective, indicated) or the type of prevention strategy (information dissemination, education, alternative activities, problem identification and referral, community-based processes, environmental).
- The Risk and Protective Factor theory is widely used to identify variables associated with the increased or decreased probability of AOD abuse.
- Evidence-based prevention programs have been identified through a federal review process.

Internet Resources

National Registry of Evidence-Based Programs and
Practices
nrepp.samhsa.gov

Center for the Application of Prevention Technologies
captus.samhsa.gov

Prevention principles
https://www.drugabuse.gov/publications/preventing-drug-abuse-among-children-adolescents-in-brief/prevention-principles

Substance Abuse and Mental Health Service
Administration Publications
store.samhsa.gov/home

Prevention specialist certification
http://internationalcredentialing.org/creds/ps

Further Discussion

1. What would be the advantages and disadvantages of parents teaching their children to drink responsibly?

2. After reading the risk factors for adolescent substance abuse, do you think it is possible to significantly reduce these risk factors? How would you design a prevention program to accomplish this?

3. Is the goal of "drug-free" schools realistic? If so, how would you go about accomplishing this? If not, how would you minimize the harm from adolescent drug use? Do you include tobacco and alcohol in your definition of "drug-free"? Why or why not?

REFERENCES

AA Grapevine. (1985). New York: Alcoholics Anonymous Grapevine.

Abney, P. C., & Harrison, T. C. (June 19, 2003). *RESOURCERY counseling: A model for the 21st century.* Paper presented at the annual convention of the International Association of Phenomenology, Constructivism, and Psychotherapy. Bari, Italy.

Ackerman, R. J. (1983). *Children of alcoholics. A guidebook for educators, therapists, and parents.* New York: Simon & Schuster.

Akin, B. A., Brook, J., & Lloyd, M. H. (2015). Examining the role of methamphetamine in permanency: A competing risks analysis of reunification, guardianship, and adoption. *American Journal of Orthopsychiatry*, 85(2), 119–130. doi:10.1037/ort0000052

Al-Anon Family Group. (1973). *Alateen: Hope for children of alcoholics.* New York: Al-Anon Family Group Headquarters.

Albdour, M., & Krouse, H. J. (2014). Bullying and victimization among African American adolescents: A literature review. *Journal of Child and Adolescent Psychiatric Nursing*, 27(2), 68–82. doi:10.1111/jcap.12066

Alcohol Policies Project, Center for Science in the Public Interest. (2008). *Alcoholic-beverage advertising expenditures. Fact sheet.* Retrieved February 16, 2016, from http://www.cspinet.org/booze/FactSheets/AlcAdExp.pdf

Alcoholics Anonymous General Services Office. (2015). Estimates of A.A. groups and members as of January 1, 2015. Retrieved February 11, 2016, from http://www.aa.org/en_pdfs/smf-53_en.pdf

Alcoholics Anonymous World Services (1983). *Questions and answers about sponsorship.* Retrieved February 11, 2016, from http://www.aa.org/assets/en_US/p-15_Q&AonSpon.pdf.

Alcoholics Anonymous World Services. (2001). *Alcoholics Anonymous* (4th ed.). New York: Alcoholics Anonymous World Services.

Alcoholics Anonymous World Services. (2009). *Alcoholics Anonymous: Twelve steps and twelve traditions.* New York: Alcoholics Anonymous World Services.

Alcoholics Anonymous World Services. (2015). Alcoholics Anonymous 2014 membership survey. Retrieved February 11, 2016, from http://www.aa.org/assets/en_US/p-48_membershipsurvey.pdf

Alegria, M., Carson, N. J., Goncalves, M., & Keefe, K. (2011). Disparities in treatment of substance use disorders and co-occurring disorders for ethnic/racial minority youth. *Journal of the American Academy of Child and Adolescent Psychiatry, 50*(1), 22–31.

Allem, J., Soto, D. W., Baezconde-Garbanati, L., & Unger, J. B. (2015). Adverse childhood experiences and substance use among Hispanic emerging adults in Southern California. *Addictive Behaviors, 50*, 199–204. doi: 10.1016/j.addbeh.2015.06.038

Amaro, H., Nieves, R., Johannes, S. W., & Cabeza, N. M. L. (1999). Substance abuse treatment: Critical issues and challenges in the treatment of Latina women. *Hispanic Journal of Behavioral Sciences, 21*(3), 266–282. doi:10.1177/0739986399213005

Amato, P. R. (2010). Research on divorce: Continuing trends and new developments. *Journal of Marriage and Family, 72*, 650–666. doi:10.1111/j.1741-3737.2010.00723.x

Ambrogne, J. A. (2007). Managing depressive symptoms in the context of abstinence: Findings from a qualitative study of women. *Perspectives in Psychiatric Care, 43*(2), 84–92.

American Psychiatric Association. (2013). *Diagnostic and statistical manual of mental disorders* (5th ed.). Washington, DC: American Psychiatric Association.

American Society of Addiction Medicine (ASAM) (2016). The ASAM criteria. Retrieved February 4, 2016, from http://www.asam.org/publications/the-asam-criteria/about/

Andersen, A. E., & Michalide, A. D. (1983). Anorexia nervosa in the male: An underdiagnosed disorder. *Psychosomatics, 24*, 1066–1069, 1072–1075.

Anderson, G. L. (1987). *When chemicals come to school.* Greenfield, WI: Community Recovery Press.

Anderson, J. Z. (1992). Stepfamilies and substance abuse: Unique treatment considerations. In E. Kaufman & P. Kaufman (Eds.), *Family therapy of drug and alcohol abuse* (2nd ed., pp. 172–189). Boston: Allyn & Bacon.

Andreassen, C. S. (2014). Workaholism: An overview and current status of the research. *Journal of Behavioral Addictions, 3*(1), 1–11. doi:10.1556/JBA.2.2013.017

Andrews, C. (2008). An exploratory study of substance abuse among Latino older adults. *Journal of Gerontological Social Work, 51*(1), 87–108.

Andrews, C. M., Shin, H., Marsh, J. C., & Cao, D. (2013). Client and program characteristics associated with wait time to substance abuse treatment entry. *The American Journal of Drug and Alcohol Abuse, 39*(1), 61–68. doi:10.3109/00952990.2012.694515

Annis, H. M. (1986). A relapse prevention model for treatment of alcoholics. In W. R. Miller & W. Heather (Eds.), *Treating addictive behaviors: Process of change* (pp. 407–433). New York: Plenum.

Annis, H. M. (1990). Relapse to substance abuse: Empirical findings within a cognitive-social learning approach. *Journal of Psychoactive Drugs, 22*, 117–124.

Annis, H. M., & Davis, C. S. (1989). Relapse prevention. In R. K. Hester & W. R. Miller (Eds.), *Handbook of alcoholism treatment approaches: Effective alternatives* (pp. 171–182). New York: Pergamon.

Archambault, D. L. (1992). Adolescence: A physiological, cultural, and psychological no man's land. In G. W. Lawson & A. W. Lawson (Eds.). *Adolescent substance abuse: Etiology, treatment, and prevention* (pp. 11–28). Gaithersburg, MD: Aspen Publications.

Arcidiancono, C., Velleman, R., Procentese, F., Berti, P., Albanesi, C., Sommantico, M., & Copello, A. (2010). Italian families living with relatives with alcohol or drug problems. *Drugs: Education, Prevention, and Policy, 17*(6), 659–680.

Armor, D. J., Polich, J. M., & Stambul, H. B. (1978). *Alcoholism and treatment.* New York: Wiley.

Asher, R. (1992). *Women with alcoholic husbands: Ambivalence and the trap of codependency.* Chapel Hill: University of North Carolina Press.

Attneave, C. (1982). American Indians and Alaska Natives families: Emigrants in their own homeland. In M. McGoldrick, J. K. Pierce, & J. Giordano (Eds.), *Ethnicity and family therapy* (pp. 55–83). New York: Guilford Press.

Austin, A., Hospital, M., Wagner, E. F., & Morris, S. L. (2010). Motivation for reducing substance use among minority adolescents: Targets for intervention. *Journal of Substance Abuse Treatment, 39*(4), 399–407.

Austin, A., & Wagner, E. F. (2010). Treatment attrition among racial and ethnic minority youth. *Journal of Social Work Practice in the Addictions, 10*(1), 63–80.

Ayón, C., & Carlson, B. E. (2014). A family affair: Latinas' narratives of substance use and recovery. *Journal of Ethnic & Cultural Diversity in Social Work: Innovation in Theory, Research & Practice, 23*(1), 55–77. doi:10.1080/15313204.2014.872008

Aziz, S., & Tronzo, C. L. (2011). Exploring the relationship between workaholism facets and personality traits: A replication in American workers. *Psychological Record, 61*(2), 269–285.

Babcock, M. (1995). Critiques of codependency: History and background issues. In M. Babcock & C. McKay (Eds.), *Challenging codependency: Feminist critiques* (pp. 3–27). Toronto: University of Toronto Press.

Babcock, M., & McKay, C. (1995). *Challenging codependency: Feminist critiques.* Toronto: University of Toronto Press.

Babor, T. F., de la Fuente, J. R., Saunders, J., & Grant, M. (1992). *AUDIT: The alcohol use disorders identification test: Guidelines for use in primary health care.* Geneva, Switzerland: World Health Organization.

Bacio, G. A., Mays, V. M., & Lau, A. S. (2013). Drinking initiation and problematic drinking among Latino adolescents: Explanations of the immigrant paradox. *Psychology of Addictive Behaviors, 27*(1), 14–22. doi:10.1037/a0029996

Bakken, I. J., Wenzel, H. G., Götestam, K. G., Johansson, A., & Øren, A. (2009). Internet addiction among Norwegian adults: A stratified probability sample study. *Scandinavian Journal of Psychology, 50*(2), 121–127.

Ball, J. C., Corty, E., Petroski, S. P., & Bond, H. (1987). Treatment effectiveness: Medical staff and services provided to 2,394 patients at methadone programs in three states. *National Institute on Drug Abuse: Research Monograph Series #76,* 175–181.

Ball, J. C., & Ross, A. R. (1991). *The effectiveness of methadone maintenance treatment: Patients, programs, services and outcomes.* New York: Springer-Verlag.

Bamatter, W., Carroll, K. M., Añez, M. P., Ball, S. A., Charla, N., Franforter, T. L., . . . Martino, S. (2010). Informal discussions in substance abuse treatment sessions with Spanish-speaking clients. *Journal of Substance Abuse Treatment, 39*(4), 353–363.

Barnes, P. M., Powell-Griner, E., McFann, K., and Nahin, R. L. (2004). Complementary and alternative medicine use among adults, 2002. *Centers for Disease Control and Prevention: Vital and Health Statistics: Advance data, (343),* 1–2. Retrieved on March 14, 2016 from http://www.cdc.gov/nchs/data/ad/ad343.pdf

Barón, M. (2000). Addiction treatment for Mexican-American families. In J. Krestan (Ed.), *Bridges to recovery. Addiction, family therapy, and multicultural treatment* (pp. 219–252). New York: Free Press.

Barrett, A. E., & Turner, R. J. (2006). Family structure and substance use problems in adolescence and early adulthood: Examining explanations for the relationship. *Addiction, 101,* 109–120.

Beard, K. W. (2005). Internet addiction: A review of current assessment techniques and potential assessment questions. *CyberPsychology & Behavior, 8*(1), 7–14.

Beattie, M. (1987). *Codependent no more: How to stop controlling others and start caring for yourself.* Center City, MN: Hazelden.

Beck, W. H. (1991). *Codependence assessment manual.* Chicago: Administrative Services.

Beckstead, D. J., Lambert, M. J., DuBose, A. P., & Linehan, M. (2015). Dialectical behavior therapy with American Indian/Alaska Native adolescents diagnosed with substance use disorders: Combining an evidence based treatment with cultural, traditional, and spiritual beliefs. *Addictive Behaviors, 51,* 84–87. doi:10.1016/j.addbeh.2015.07.018

Bell, T. L. (1990). *Preventing adolescent relapse: A guide for parents, teachers, and counselors.* Independence, MO: Independence Press.

Beutell, N. J., & Schneer, J. A. (2014). Work-family conflict and synergy among Hispanics. *Journal of Managerial Psychology, 29*(6), 705–735. doi:10.1108/JMP-11-2012-0342

Black, C. (1981). *It will never happen to me.* Denver: MAC.

Black, L., & Jackson, V. (2005). Families of African origin: An overview. In M. McGoldrick, J. Giordano, & N. Garcie-Preto (Eds.), *Ethnicity and family therapy* (3rd ed., pp. 77–86). New York: Guilford Press.

Blanco, C., Morcillo, C., Alegría, M., Dedios, M. C., Fernández-Navarro, P., Regincos, R., & Wang, S. (2013). Acculturation and drug use disorders among hispanics in the U.S. *Journal of Psychiatric Research, 47*(2), 226–232. doi:10.1016/j.jpsychires.2012.09.019

Blau, M. (1990). Adult children: Tied to the past. *American Health, 9*, 56–65.

Block, J. J. (2008). Issues for DSM-V: Internet addiction. *American Journal of Psychiatry, 165*, 360–370.

Blume, S. A. (1997). Women and alcohol: Issues in social policy. In S. Wilsnack & R. Wilsnack (Eds.), *Gender and alcohol* (pp. 462–477). New Brunswick, NJ: Rutgers Center for Alcohol Studies.

Borders, T. F., Booth, B. M., & Curran, G. M. (2015). African American cocaine users' preferred treatment site: Variations by rural/urban residence, stigma, and treatment effectiveness. *Journal of Substance Abuse Treatment, 50*, 26–31. doi:10.1016/j.jsat.2014.10.004

Borovoy, A. (2000). Recovering from codependence in Japan. *American Ethnologist, 28*(1), 94–118.

Borovoy, A. (2005). *"The too-good wife": Alcohol, codependency, and the politics of nurturance in postwar Japan.* Berkeley: University of California Press.

Borovoy, A. B. (2009). "The too-good wife": Alcohol, codependency, and the politics of nurturance in postwar Japan. *The Journal of Japanese Studies, 35*(2), 460–464.

Botvin, G. J., Baker, E., Dusenbury, L., Botvin, E. M., & Diaz, T. (1995). Long-term follow-up results of a randomized drug abuse prevention trial in a White middle-class population. *Journal of the American Medical Association, 273*, 1106–1112.

Botvin, G. J., & Botvin, E. M. (1992). School-based and community-based prevention approaches. In J. H Lowinson, P. Ruiz, R. B. Millman, & J. G. Langrod (Eds.), *Substance abuse: A comprehensive textbook* (2nd ed., pp. 910–927). Baltimore: Williams & Wilkins.

Bourne, P. G. (1973). Alcoholism in the urban Negro population. In P. G. Bourne & R. Fox (Eds.), *Alcoholism: Progress in research and treatment* (pp. 211–226). New York: Academic Press.

Boyd, M. B., Mackey, M. C., Phillips, K. D., & Travakoli, A. (2006). Alcohol and other drug disorders, comorbidity and violence in rural African American women. *Issues in Mental Health Nursing, 27*, 1017–1036.

Bradley, K. A., Boyd-Wickizer, J., Powell, S. H., & Burman, B. L. (1998). Alcohol screening questionnaires for women: A critical review. *Journal of the American Medical Association, 280*, 166–171.

Bradley, K. A., Bush, K. R., Epler, A. J., Dobie, D. J., Davis, T. M., Sporleder, J. L., . . . Kivlahan, D. R. (2003). Two brief alcohol screening tests from the Alcohol Use Disorders Identification Test (AUDIT): Validation in a female Veterans Affairs patient population. *Archives of Internal Medicine, 163*, 821–829.

Braitman, A. L., Kelley, M. L., Ladage, J., Schroeder, V., Gumienny, L. A., Morrow, J. A., & Klostermann, K. (2009). Alcohol and drug use among college student adult children of alcoholics. *Journal of Alcohol and Drug Education, 53*(1), 69–88.

Brand, M., Laier, C., & Young, K. S. (2014). Internet addiction: Coping styles, expectancies, and treatment implications. *Frontiers In Psychology, 5*, 1–14.

Brand, M., Young, K. S., & Laier, C. (2014). Prefrontal control and Internet addiction: A theoretical model and review of neuropsychological and neuroimaging findings. *Frontiers in Human Neuroscience, 8*, 1–13.

Brasfield, H., Febres, J., Shorey, R., Strong, D., Ninnemann, A., Elmquist, J., & Stuart, G. L. (2012). Male batterers' alcohol use and gambling behavior. *Journal of Gambling Studies, 28*(1), 77–88. doi:10.1007/s10899-011-9246-0

Bray, B. C., Lee, G. P., Liu, W., Storr, C. L., Ialongo, N. S., & Martins, S. S. (2014). Transitions in gambling participation during late adolescence and young adulthood. *Journal of Adolescent Health, 55*(2), 188–194. doi:10.1016/j.jadohealth.2014.02.001

British Broadcasting Company. (2002, March 17). *Internet gambling TA breeds addiction.* Retrieved August 2, 2003, from http://news.bbc.co.uk/1/hi/health/1872731.stm

Brooks, M. K. (1992). Ethical and legal issues of confidentiality. In J. H. Lowinson, P. Ruiz, R. B. Millman, & J. G. Langrod (Eds.), *Substance abuse: A comprehensive textbook* (pp. 1049–1066). Baltimore: Williams & Wilkins.

Brounstein, P. J., Zweig, J. M., & Gardner, S. E. (1998). *Science-based practices in substance abuse prevention: A guide.* Rockville, MD: Center for Substance Abuse Prevention.

Brown, J. H., & Kreft, I. G. (1998). Zero effects of drug prevention programs: Issues and solutions. *Evaluation Review, 22*, 3–14.

Brown, R. (2010). Systematic review of the impact of adult day-treatment courts. *Translational Research, 155*, 263–274.

Brown, S. (1988). *Treating children of alcoholics: A developmental perspective.* New York: Wiley.

Brown, T. A., & Keel, P. K. (2015). A randomized controlled trial of a peer co-led dissonance-based eating disorder prevention program for gay men. *Behaviour Research and Therapy, 74*, 1–10. doi:10.1016/j.brat.2015.08.008

Brownell, K. D., & Stunkard, A. J. (1978). Behavioral treatment of obesity in children. *American Journal of Diseases in Children, 132*, 403–412.

Bruch, H. (1986). Anorexia nervosa: The therapeutic task. In K. D. Brownell & J. P. Foreyt (Eds.), *Handbook of eating disorders* (pp. 328–332). New York: Basic Books.

Brucker, D. L. (2008). Prescription drug abuse among persons with disabilities. *Journal of Vocational Rehabilitation 29*, 105–115.

Bruinius, H. (2007). *Better for the world. The secret history of forced sterilization and America's quest for racial purity.* New York: Vintage Books.

Bruns, G. L., & Carter, M. M. (2015). Ethnic differences in the effects of media on body image: The effects of priming with ethnically different or similar models. *Eating Behaviors, 17*, 33–36. doi:10.1016/j.eatbeh.2014.12.006

Bryant-Waugh, R. J., Cooper, P. J., Taylor, C. L., & Lask, B. D. (1996). The use of the eating disorder examination with children: A pilot study. *International Journal of Eating Disorders, 19*, 391–397. doi:10.1002/ (SICI)1098-108X(199605)19:4391::AID-EAT63.0.CO;2-G

Burk, J. P., & Sher, K. J. (1988). The "forgotten children" revisited: Neglected areas of COA research. *Clinical Psychology Review, 8*, 285–302.

Burlew, A., Johnson, C., Flowers, A., Peteet, B., Griffith-Henry, K., & Buchanan, N. (2009). Neighborhood risk, parental supervision and the onset of substance use among African American adolescents. *Journal of Child and Family Studies, 18*(6), 680–689.

Burns, C. M., & D'Avanzo, C. E. (1993). Alcohol and other drug abuse in culturally diverse populations: Hispanics and Southeast Asians. Faculty resource. Washington, DC: Cosmos Corporation.

Burns, E., Gray, R., & Smith, L. A. (2010). Brief screening questionnaires to identify problem drinking during pregnancy: A systematic review. *Addiction, 105*(4), 601–614.

Burrows, B. A. (1992). Research on the etiology and maintenance of eating disorders. In E. M. Freeman (Ed.), *The addiction process: Effective social work approaches* (pp. 149–160). White Plains, NY: Longman.

Butler, J. (1990). *Gender trouble: Feminism and the subversion of identity.* London: Routledge.

Button, D. M., & Gealt, R. (2010). High risk behaviors among victims of sibling violence. *Journal of Family Violence, 25*(2), 131–140.

Cadiz, S., Savage, A., Bonavota, D., Hollywood, J., Butters, E., Neary, M., & Quiros, L. (2004). *The portal project: A layered approach to integrating trauma into alcohol and other drug treatment for women.* Retrieved August 3, 2007, from www.haworthpress.com/web/ATQ

Cameron, M. J., Maguire, R. W., & McCormack, J. (2011). Stress-induced binge eating: A behavior analytic approach to assessment and intervention. *Journal of Adult Development, 18*, 81–84.

Campbell, A. C., Turrigiano, E., Moore, M., Miele, G. M., Rieckmann, T., Hu, M., & Nunes, E. V. (2015). Acceptability of a web-based community reinforcement approach for substance use disorders with treatment-seeking American Indians/Alaska Natives. *Community Mental Health Journal, 51*(4), 393–403. doi:10.1007/s10597-014-9764-1

Canan, F., Ataoglu, A., Nichols, L. A., Yildirim, T., & Ozturk, O. (2009). Evaluation of psychometric properties of the Internet addiction scale in a sample of Turkish high school students. *Cyberpsychology & Behavior, 13*, 317–320.

Capodilupo, C. M., & Kim, S. (2014). Gender and race matter: The importance of considering intersections in black women's body image. *Journal of Counseling Psychology, 61*(1), 37–49. doi:10.1037/a0034597

Capuzzi, D., & Gross, D. R. (Eds.). (1996). *Youth at risk.* Alexandria, VA: American Counseling Association.

Carlson, B. E., Williams, L. R., & Shafer, M. S. (2012). Methamphetamine-involved parents in the child welfare system: Are they more challenging than other substance-involved parents? *Journal of Public Child Welfare, 6*, 280–295. doi:10.1080/15548732.2012.6833

Carmona, M., & Stewart, K. (1996). A review of alternative activities and alternatives programs in youth-oriented prevention. (CSAP Technical Report No. 13). Rockville, MD: Center for Substance Abuse Prevention.

Carnes, P. J. (2001). Cybersex, courtship, and escalating arousal: Factors in addictive sexual desire. *Sexual Addiction and Compulsivity, 8*, 45–78.

Carnes, P. J. (2009). *Recovery zone, volume 1: Making changes that last-The internal tasks.* Carefree, AZ: Gentle Path Press.

Carnes, P. J., Green, B.A., Merlo, L. J., Polles, A., Carnes, S., & Gold, M. S. (2011). PATHOS: A brief screening application for assessing sexual addiction. *Journal of Addiction Medicine, 6*, 29–34. doi:10.1097/ADM.0b013e3182251a28.

Cartwright, B. Y., & D'Andrea, M. (2005). A personal journey toward culture-centered counseling. *Journal of Counseling and Development, 83*, 214–221.

Center for Behavioral Health Statistics and Quality. (2015). Behavioral health trends in the United States: Results from the 2014 National Survey on Drug Use and Health (HHS Publication No. SMA 15-4927, NSDUH Series H-50). Retrieved March 1, 2016, from http://www.samhsa.gov/data/

Center for Substance Abuse Treatment. (1994). *Assessment and treatment of patients with coexisting mental illness and alcohol and other drug abuse* (Treatment Improvement Protocol #9). Rockville, MD: Center for Substance Abuse Treatment.

Center for Substance Abuse Treatment. (1995). *Planning for alcohol and other drug abuse treatment for adults in the Criminal Justice System* (Treatment Improvement Protocol #17). Rockville, MD: Center for Substance Abuse Treatment.

Center for Substance Abuse Treatment. (1998). *Naltrexone and alcoholism treatment* (Treatment Improvement

Protocol #28). Rockville, MD: Center for Substance Abuse Treatment.

Center for Substance Abuse Treatment. (1999). *Brief interventions and brief therapies for substance abuse* (Treatment Improvement Protocol #34). Rockville, MD: Center for Substance Abuse Treatment.

Center for Substance Abuse Treatment. (2005). *Substance abuse treatment for persons with co-occurring disorders.* Treatment Improvement Protocol (TIP) #42. DHHS Publication No. (SMA) 05-3922. Rockville, MD: Substance Abuse and Mental Health Services Administration. Retrieved February 29, 2016, from http://www.ncbi.nlm.nih.gov/books/NBK64201/

Center for Substance Abuse Treatment. (2010). Integrated treatment for co-occurring disorders evidence-based practices (EBP) toolkit. Retrieved on March 16, 2015, from http://store_SAMHSA.gov/product/sma08-4367.

Center on Alcohol Marketing and Youth. (2007). Alcohol advertising and youth. Retrieved February 16, 2016, from http://www.camy.org/resources/fact-sheets/alcohol-advertising-and-youth/

Center on Alcohol Marketing and Youth. (2010). Youth exposure to all alcohol advertising on television, 2001–2009. Retrieved May 23, 2011, from http://www.camy.org/bin/u/r/CAMYReport2001_2009.pdf

Centers for Disease Control and Prevention. (2002). HIV testing among pregnant women—United States and Canada, 1998–2001. *Morbidity and Mortality Report, 51*(45), 1013-1016. Retrieved on March 18, 2016, from http://www.cdc.gov/mmwr/preview/mmwrhtml/mm5145a1.htm

Centers for Disease Control and Prevention. (2006a). *Sexually transmitted diseases treatment guidelines 2006.* Retrieved August 8, 2007, from www.cdc.gov/std/treatment/2006/hiv.htm#hiv1 #hiv1

Centers for Disease Control and Prevention. (2006b). *Trends in reportable sexually transmitted diseases in the United States, 2005: National surveillance data for chlamydia, gonorrhea, and syphilis.* Retrieved August 7, 2007, from www.cdc.gov/std/hiv/STDFact-STD#HIV.htm #WhatIs

Centers for Disease Control and Prevention. (2007). *Preventing obesity and chronic diseases.* Retrieved August 1, 2007, from www.cdc.gov/search.do?queryText=chronic+obesity&action=search&searchButtonx=22&searchButtony=8

Centers for Disease Control and Prevention. (2009). *HIV testing implementation: Guidance for correctional settings.* Retrieved on March 14, 2016, from http://www.cdc.gov/hiv/pdf/risk_Correctional_Settings_Guidelines.pdf

Centers for Disease Control and Prevention. (2010). *Alcohol & public health.* Retrieved December 16, 2010, from http://www.cdc.gov/alcohol/

Centers for Disease Control and Prevention. (2011). *CDC reports excessive alcohol consumption cost the U.S. $224 billion in 2006.* Retrieved July 22, 2015, from http://www.cdc.gov/media/releases/2011/p1017_alcohol_consumption.html

Centers for Disease Control and Prevention. (2013a). *Drug-induced deaths-United States, 1999–2010.* Retrieved July 22, 2015, from http://www.cdc.gov/mmwr/preview/mmwrhtml/su6203a27.htm

Centers for Disease Control and Prevention. (2013b). *TB in the homeless population.* Retrieved on March 14, 2016, from http://www.cdc.gov/tb/topic/populations/Homelessness/default.htm

Centers for Disease Control and Prevention. (2014a). *Alcohol deaths.* Retrieved July 21, 2015, from http://www.cdc.gov/features/alcohol-deaths/index.html

Centers for Disease Control and Prevention. (2014c). *Diagnosis of HIV infection in the United States and dependent areas.* Retrieved on March 2, 2016, from http://www.cdc.gov/hiv/group/racialethnic/africanamericans/index.html

Centers for Disease Control and Prevention. (2014d). *CDC fact sheet: Reported STDs in the United States, 2014 National data for chlamydia, gonorrhea, and syphilis.* Retrieved on March 12, 2016, from http://www.cdc.gov/std/stats14/std-trends-508.pdf

Centers for Disease Control and Prevention. (2015b). *Health effects infographics.* Retrieved July 21, 2015, from http://www.cdc.gov/tobacco/data_statistics/tables/health/infographics/index.htm

Centers for Disease Control and Prevention. (2015d). *The Affordable Care Act helps people living with HIV/AIDS.* Retrieved on March 14, 2016, from http://www.cdc.gov/hiv/policies/aca.html

Centers for Disease Control and Prevention. (2015e). *STDs and HIV—CDC fact sheet.* Retrieved on March 12, 2016, from http://www.cdc.gov/std/hiv/STDFact-STD-HIV.htm

Centers for Disease Control and Prevention. (2015g). *CDC Fact Sheet: HIV testing in the United States.* Retrieved on March, 5, 2016, from http://www.cdc.gov/nchhstp/newsroom/docs/factsheets/hiv-testing-us-508.pdf

Centers for Disease Control and Prevention. (2015h). *TB in correctional facilities in the United States.* Retrieved on March 14, 2016, from http://www.cdc.gov/tb/topic/populations/correctional/default.htm

Centers for Disease Control and Prevention. (2015i). *Health effects infographics.* Retrieved July 21, 2015, from http://www.cdc.gov/tobacco/data_statistics/tables/health/infographics/index.htm

Centers for Disease Control and Prevention. (2015j). *Health and aging: HIV, AIDS, and older people.* Retrieved on March 14, 2016, from https://www.nia.nih.gov/health/publication/hiv-aids-and-older-people#more

Centers for Disease Control and Prevention. (2015k). *HIV/AIDS: Guidelines and recommendations.* Retrieved on March 14, 2016, from http://www.cdc.gov/hiv/guidelines/index.html

Centers for Disease Control and Prevention. (2015l). *Occupational HIV transmission and prevention among health care workers.* Retrieved on March 14, 2016, from http://www.cdc.gov/hiv/workplace/occupational.html

Centers for Disease Control and Prevention. (2015m). *HIV specific criminal laws.* Retrieved on March 18, 2016, from http://www.cdc.gov/hiv/policies/law/states/exposure.html

Centers for Disease Control and Prevention. (2016a). *About HIV/AIDS.* Retrieved on March 5, 2016, from http://www.cdc.gov/hiv/basics/whatishiv.html

Centers for Disease Control and Prevention. (2016b). *HIV/AIDS: Testing.* Retrieved on March 5, 2016, from http://www.cdc.gov/hiv/basics/testing.html

Centers for Disease Control and Prevention. (2016c). *Today's HIV/AIDS epidemic: Care and prevention for people living with HIV.* Retrieved on March 5, 2016, from http://www.cdc.gov/nchhstp/newsroom/docs/factsheets/today-sepidemic-508.pdf

Centers for Disease Control and Prevention. (2016d). *Fast facts: HIV among women.* Retrieved on March 12, 2016, from http://www.cdc.gov/hiv/group/gender/women/index.html

Centers for Disease Control and Prevention. (2016e). *HIV prevention in the United States: Socioeconomic factors affecting HIV risk.* Retrieved on March 14, 2016, from http://www.cdc.gov/nchhstp/ux-test-2015/newsroom/hiv-factsheets/epidemic/factors.htm

Centers for Disease Control and Prevention. (2016f). *HIV surveillance adolescents and young adults.* Retrieved on March 14, 2016, from http://www.cdc.gov/hiv/pdf/statistics_surveillance_Adolescents.pdf

Centers for Disease Control and Prevention. (2016g). *HIV among incarcerated populations.* Retrieved on March 14, 2016, from http://www.cdc.gov/hiv/group/correctional.html

Centers for Disease Control and Prevention. (2016h). *Hepatitis C and incarceration.* Retrieved on March 14, 2016, from http://www.cdc.gov/hepatitis/HCV/PDFs/HepCIncarcerationFactSheet-BW.pdf

Cermak, T. L. (1986). *Diagnosing and treating codependence: A guide for professionals who work with chemical dependents, their spouses, and children.* Minneapolis, MN: Johnson Institute.

Cervantes, R. C., Padilla, A. M., Napper, L. E., & Goldbach, J. T. (2013). Acculturation-related stress and mental health outcomes among three generations of Hispanic adolescents. *Hispanic Journal of Behavioral Sciences,* September 8, 0739986313500924.

Ceyhan, E., Ceyhan, A. A., & Gürcan, A. (2007). The validity and reliability of the Problematic Internet Usage Scale. *Educational Sciences: Theory and Practice, 7*(1), 411–416.

Chafetz, M. E. (1964). Consumption of alcohol in the Far and Middle East. *New England Journal of Medicine, 271,* 297–301.

Chang, G. (2002). Brief interventions for problem drinking and women. *Journal of Substance Abuse Treatment, 23,* 1–7.

Chang, P. (2000). Treating Asian/Pacific American addicts and their families. In J. Krestan (Ed.), *Bridges to recovery. Addiction, family therapy, and multicultural treatment* (pp. 192–219). New York: Free Press.

Chartier, K. G., Carmody, T., Akhtar, M., Stebbins, M. B., Walters, S. T., & Warden, D. (2015). Hispanic subgroups, acculturation, and substance abuse treatment outcomes. *Journal of Substance Abuse Treatment, 59,* 74–82. doi:10.1016/j.jsat.2015.07.008

Chartier, K. G., Hesselbrock, M. N., & Hesselbrock, V. M. (2011). Alcohol problems in young adults transitioning from adolescence to adulthood: The association with race and gender. *Addictive Behaviors, 36,* 167–174.

Chartier, K. G., Negroni, L. K., & Hesselbrock, M. N. (2010). Strengthening family practices for Latino families. *Journal of Ethnic & Cultural Diversity in Social Work: Innovation in Theory, Research & Practice, 19*(1), 1–17. doi:10.1080/15313200903531982

Chartier, K. G., Vaeth, P. A., & Caetano, R. (2013). Focus on: Ethnicity and the social and health harms from drinking. *Alcohol Research: Current Reviews, 35*(2), 229–237. Retrieved from http://unr.idm.oclc.org/login?url=http://search.proquest.com/docview/1512625243?accountid=452

Cheng, H., Lin, S., & Cha, C. H. (2015). Perceived discrimination, intergenerational family conflicts, and depressive symptoms in foreign-born and U.S.-born Asian American emerging adults. *Asian American Journal of Psychology, 6*(2), 107–116. doi:10.1037/a0038710

Chi, I., Lubben, J. E., & Kitano, H. H. (1989). Differences in drinking behavior among three Asian-American groups. *Journal of Studies on Alcohol, 50,* 15–23.

Chittenden, H. (1935). *American fur trade of the Far West: A history of pioneer trading posts and early fur companies of the Missouri Valley and Rocky Mountains and of the overland commerce with Santa Fe* (Vol. 1). New York: Barnes & Noble.

Chiu, C., Lonner, W. J., Matsumoto, D., & Ward, C. (2013). Cross-cultural competence: Theory, research, and application. *Journal of Cross-Cultural Psychology, 44,* 843–848. doi:10.1177/0022022113493716

Cho, Y. I., & Crittenden, K. S. (2006). The impact of adult roles on drinking among women in the United States. *Substance Use and Misuse, 41,* 17–34.

Choi, N. G., DiNitto, D. M., & Marti, C. N. (2015). Alcohol and other substance use, mental health treatment use, and perceived unmet treatment need: Comparison between baby boomers and older adults. *American Journal on Addictions, 24*(4), 299–307. doi:10.1111/ajad.12225

Chong, J., Fortier, Y., & Morris, T. L. (2009). Cultural practices and spiritual development for women in a Native American alcohol and drug treatment program. *Journal of Ethnicity in Substance Abuse, 8*(3), 261–182.

Christopher, J. (1988). *How to stay sober: Recovery without religion.* Buffalo, NY: Prometheus Books.

Ciaccio, C. P. (2010). IV. Cyber Law: A. Notes: Internet gambling: Recent developments and state of the law. *Berkeley Technology Law Journal Annual Review.* Berkeley: Regents of the University of California.

Clark, P. A. & Fadus, M. (2010). Federal funding for needle exchange programs. *Medical Science Monitor, 16,* PH1-13.

Clayton, R. R., Leukefeld, C. G., Grant-Harrington, N., & Cattarello, A. (1996). DARE (Drug Abuse Resistance Education): Very popular but not very effective. In C. B. McCoy, L. R. Metsch, & J. A. Inciardi (Eds.), *Intervening with drug-involved youth* (pp. 101–109). Thousand Oaks, CA: Sage.

Cleveland, H. H., Wiebe, R. P., McGuire, J., & Zheng, Y. (2015). Predicting high school minority adolescents' drinking from their exposure to white schoolmates: Differences and similarities among Hispanic, black, and Asian U.S. adolescents. *Journal of Ethnicity in Substance Abuse, 14*(2), 166–186. doi:10.1080/15332640.2014.973626

Cobb, N., Espey, D., & King, J. (2014). Health behaviors and risk factors among American Indians and Alaska Natives, 2000–2010. *American Journal of Public Health, 104*(S3), S481–S489. doi:10.2105/AJPH.2014.301879

Cochran, B. N., Peavy, K., M., & Cauce, A. M. (2007). Substance abuse treatment providers' explicit and implicit attitudes regarding sexual minorities. *Journal of Homosexuality, 53*(3), 187–207.

Cochran, S. D., Ackerman, D., Mays, V. M., & Ross, M. W. (2004). Prevalence of non-medical drug use and dependence among homosexually active men and women in the US population. *Addiction, 99,* 989–998.

Cochran, S. D., Grella, C. E., & Mays, V. M. (2012). Do substance use norms and perceived drug availability mediate sexual orientation differences in patterns of substance use? Results from the California Quality of Life Survey II. *Journal of Studies on Alcohol & Drugs, 73*(4), 675–685. doi:10.15288/jsad.2012.73.675

Coffin, B. (2003). Breaking the silence on white collar crime. *Risk Management, 50*(9), 8.

Coggans, N., & McKellar, S. (1994). Drug use amongst peers: Peer pressure or peer preference. *Drugs: Education, Prevention, and Policy, 1,* 15–24.

Collins, B. (1993). Reconstructing codependency using self-in-relation theory: A feminist perspective. *Social Work, 38,* 470–476.

Collins, R. L., & McNair, L. D. (2002). Minority women and alcohol use. *Alcohol Research and Health, 26*(4), 251.

Conner, L. C., LeFauve, C. E., & Wallace, B. C. (2009). Ethnic and cultural correlates of addiction among diverse women. In K. T. Brady, S. E. Back, & S. F. Greenfield (Eds.), *Women and addiction* (Chapter 27, pp. 453–470). New York: Guilford Press.

Conyers, L., & Boomer, K. B. (2005). Factors associated with disclosure of HIV/AIDS to employers among individuals who use job accommodations and those who do not. *Journal of Vocational Rehabilitation, 22,* 189–198.

Cook, C. C. (1988). The Minnesota model in the management of drug and alcohol dependency: Miracle, method, or myth? (Part I: The philosophy of the programme). *British Journal of Addiction, 83,* 625–634.

Cook-Daniels, L. (2008). Transforming mental health services for older people: Gay, lesbian, bisexual, and transgender (GLBT) challenges and opportunities, *Journal of GLBT Family Studies, 4*(4), 469–483.

Cooney, N. L., Kadden, R. M., & Steinberg, H. R. (2005). Assessment of alcohol problems. In D. M. Donovan & G. A. Marlatt (Eds.), *Assessment of addictive behaviors* (2nd ed.). New York: Guilford Press.

Copello, A. G., Templeton, L., & Powell, J. (2010). The impact of addiction on the family: Estimates of prevalence and costs. *Drugs: Education, Prevention, and Policy, 17*(1), 63–74.

Copello, A. G., Velleman, R. D. B., & Templeton, L. J. (2005). Family interventions in the treatment of alcohol and drug problems. *Drug and Alcohol Review, 24,* 369–385.

Copen, C. E., Daniels, K., Vespa, J., & Mosher, W. D. (2012). *First marriages in the United States: Data from the 2006–2010 national survey of family growth.* (National health statistics reports, 49). Retrieved on March 22, 2016, from Centers for Disease Control and Prevention website: http://www.cdc.gov/nchs/data/nhsr/nhsr049.pdf#x2013;2010 National Survey of Family Growth [PDF - 419 KB

Cordova, D., Parra-Cardona, R., Blow, A., Johnson, D. J., Prado, G., & Fitzgerald, H. E. (2013). The role of intrapersonal factors on alcohol and drug use among Latinos with physical disabilities. *Journal of Social Work Practice in the Addictions, 13*(3), 244–268. doi:10.1080/15332 56X.2013.812007

Cordova, D., Parra-Cardona, J. R., Blow, A., Johnson, D. J., Prado, G., & Fitzgerald, H. E. (2015). 'They don't look at what affects us': The role of ecodevelopmental factors on alcohol and drug use among Latinos with physical disabilities. *Ethnicity & Health, 20*(1), 66–86. doi:10.1080/1355 7858.2014.890173

Corey, G. (2016). *Theory and practice of group counseling* (9th ed.). Belmont, CA: Brooks/Cole.

Cork, M. (1969). *The forgotten children: A study of children with alcoholic parents.* Toronto: Addiction Research Foundation.

Cornish, E., Schreier, B. A., Nadkarni, L. I., & Metzger, L. H. (2010). *Handbook of multicultural counseling competencies.* Hoboken, NJ: Wiley.

Corrigan, P. W., & Miller, F. E., & Watson, P. J. (2006). Blame, shame, and contamination: The impact of mental illness and drug dependence stigma on family members. *Journal of Family Psychology, 20*(2), 239–246.

Cotter, E. W., Kelly, N. R., Mitchell, K. S., & Mazzeo, S. E. (2015). An investigation of body appreciation, ethnic identity, and eating disorder symptoms in black women. *Journal of Black Psychology, 41*(1), 3–25. doi: 10.1177/0095798413502671

Courtney, M. E., & Hook, J. L. (2012). Timing of exits to legal permanency from out-of-home care: The importance of systems and implications for assessing institutional accountability. *Children and Youth Services Review, 34*, 2263–2272. doi:10.1016/j.childyouth.2012.08.004

Coyhis, D. (2000). Culturally specific addiction recovery for Native Americans. In J. Krestan (Ed.), *Bridges to recovery: Addiction, family therapy, and multicultural treatment* (pp. 77–114). New York: Free Press.

Coyhis, D., & Simonelli, R. (2008). The Native American healing experience. *Substance Use and Misuse, 43*(12/13), 1927–1949.

Coyhis, D., & White, W. (2002). *Addiction and recovery in Native America: Lost history, enduring lessons.* Retrieved May 12, 2011, from http://www.quantumunitsed.com/materials/1540_addictionrecoveryinnativeamericans.pdf

Croff, R. L., Rieckmann, T. R., & Spence, J. D. (2014). Provider and state perspectives on implementing cultural-based models of care for American Indian and Alaska Native patients with substance use disorders. *The Journal of Behavioral Health Services & Research, 41*(1), 64–79. doi:10.1007/s11414-013-9322-6

Cullen, J., & Carr, A. (1999). Codependency: An empirical study from a systemic perspective. *Contemporary Family Therapy, 21*, 505–526.

Cummings, C., Gordon, J. R., & Marlatt, G. A. (1980). Relapse: Strategies of prevention and prediction. In W. R. Miller (Ed.), *The addictive behaviors: Treatment of alcoholism, drug abuse, smoking and obesity* (pp. 291–321). New York: Pergamon Press.

Cummins, L. H., Simmons, A. M., & Zane, N. (2005). Eating disorders in Asian populations: A critique of current approaches to the study of culture, ethnicity, and eating disorders. *American Journal of Orthopsychiatry, 75*(4), 443–453.

Cunningham, J. A., Sobell, L. C., Sobell, M. B., & Kapur, G. (1995). Resolution from alcohol problems with and without treatment: Reasons for change. *Journal of Substance Abuse, 7*, 365–372.

Cunningham, P. B., Foster, S. L., & Warner, S. E. (2010). Culturally relevant family-based treatment for adolescents' delinquency and substance abuse: Understanding within-session processes. *Journal of Clinical Psychology, 66*(8), 830–846.

Cunningham, S., & Finlay, K. (2013). Parental substance use and foster care: Evidence from two methamphetamine supply shocks. *Economic Inquiry, 51*(1), 764–782. doi:10.1111/j.14657295.2012.00481.x

Custer, R., & Milt, H. (1985). *When luck runs out: Help for compulsive gamblers and their families.* New York: Facts on File.

Cyr, M. G., & McGarry, K. A. (2002). Alcohol use disorder among women. *Postgraduate Medicine, 112*, 31–40.

Dakanalis, A., Favagrossa, L., Clerici, M., Prunas, A., Colmegna, F., Zanetti, M. A., & Riva, G. (2015). Body dissatisfaction and eating disorder symptomatology: A latent structural equation modeling analysis of moderating variables in 18- to 28-year-old males. *The Journal of Psychology: Interdisciplinary and Applied, 149*(1), 85–112. doi:10.1080/00223980.2013.842141

Daley, D. C., & Marlatt, G. A. (2005). Relapse prevention. In J. H. Lowinson, P. Ruiz, & R. B. Millman (Eds.), *Substance abuse: A comprehensive textbook* (4th ed., pp. 772–785). Baltimore: Williams & Wilkins.

D'Amico, E. J., Tucker, J. S., Shih, R. A., & Miles, J. V. (2014). Does diversity matter? The need for longitudinal research on adolescent alcohol and drug use trajectories. *Substance Use & Misuse, 49*(8), 1069–1073. doi:10.3109/10826084.2014.862027

Davis, R. A. (2001). A cognitive-behavioral model of pathological internet use. *Computers in Human Behavior, 17*, 187–195. doi 10.1016/S0747-5632(00)000041-8

Dawson, D. A., Smith, S. M., Saha, T. D., Rubinsky, A. D., & Grant, B. F. (2012). Comparative performance of the AUDIT-C in screening for DSM-IV and DSM-V alcohol use disorders. *Drug and Alcohol Dependence, 126*, 384–388.

Day, J., Schmidt, U., Collier, D., Perkins, S., Van den Eynde, F., Treasure, J., & Eisler, I. (2011). Risk factors, correlates, and markers in early-onset bulimia nervosa and EDNOS. *International Journal of Eating Disorders, 44*(4), 287–294.

Dazzi, F., & Di Leone, F. G. (2014). The diagnostic classification of eating disorders: Current situation, possible alternatives and future perspectives. *Eating and Weight Disorders, 19*(1), 11–19. doi:10.1007/s40519-013-0076-1

Dear, G. E., & Roberts, C. M. (2002). The relationship between codependency and femininity and masculinity. *Sex Roles, 46*, 159–165.

De La Rosa, M., Dillon, F. R., Ganapati, E., Rojas, P., Pinto, E., & Prado, G. (2010). Mother-daughter attachment and drug abuse among Latinas in the United States. *Journal of Drug Issues, 40*, 379–404.

de Lisle, S. M., Dowling, N. A., & Allen, J. S. (2011). Mindfulness-based cognitive therapy for problem gambling. *Journal of Clinical Case Studies, 10*(3), 210–228.

Delmonico, D. L., Griffin, E., & Carnes, P. J. (2002). Treating online compulsive sexual behavior: When cybersex is the drug of choice. In A. Cooper (Ed.), *Sex and the Internet: A guidebook for clinicians* (pp. 147–167). New York: Routledge.

Denham, B. E. (2014). Adolescent perceptions of alcohol risk: Variation by sex, race, student activity levels and parental communication. *Journal of Ethnicity in Substance Abuse, 13*(4), 385–404. doi:10.1080/15332640.2014.958638

Dennis, M. L., Foss, M. A., & Scott, C. K. (2007). An eight-year perspective on the relationship between the duration of abstinence and other aspects of recovery. *Evaluation Review, 31,* 585–612.

Dethier, M., Counerotte, C., & Blairy, S. (2011). Marital satisfaction in couples with an alcoholic husband. *Journal of Family Violence, 26,* 151–162.

DeWit, D. J., Adlaf, E. M., Offord, D. R., & Ogborne, A. C. (2000). Age at first alcohol use: A risk factor for the development of alcohol disorders. *American Journal of Psychiatry, 157*(5), 745–750.

Dhalla, S., & Kopec, J. A. (2007). The CAGE Questionnaire for alcohol misuse: A review of reliability and validity studies. *Clinical & Investigative Medicine, 30*(1), 33–41.

Diamond, G. S., & Liddle, H. A. (1996). Resolving a therapeutic impasse between parents and adolescents in Multidimensional Family Therapy. *Journal of Consulting and Clinical Psychology, 64,* 481–488.

Dickerson, D. L., Venner, K. L., & Duran, B. (2014). Clinical trials and American Indians/Alaska Natives with substance use disorders: Identifying potential strategies for a new cultural-based intervention. *Journal of Public Mental Health, 13*(4), 175–178. doi:10.1108/JPMH-01-2014-0003

Dickerson, D. L., Venner, K. L., Duran, B., Annon, J. J., Hale, B., & Funmaker, G. (2014). Drum-Assisted Recovery Therapy for Native Americans (DARTNA): Results from a pretest and focus groups. *American Indian and Alaska Native Mental Health Research, 21*(1), 35–58. Retrieved from http://search.proquest.com.unr.idm.oclc.org/docview/1521936350?pq-origsite=summon

Didenko, E., & Pankratz, N. (2007). Substance Use: Pathways to homelessness? Or a way of adapting to street life? *Visions: BC's Mental Health and Addictions Journal, 4*(1), 9–10. Retrieved April 25, 2011, from http://www.heretohelp.bc.ca/

Dixon, M. R., & Johnson, T. E. (2007). The gambling functional assessment (GFA): An assessment device for identification of the maintaining variables of pathological gambling. *Analysis of Gambling Behavior, 1,* 44–49.

Donohue, B., Allen, D. A., & Lapota, H. (2009). Family Behavior Therapy. In D. Springer & A. Rubin (Eds.), *Substance abuse treatment for youth and adults* (pp. 205–255). New York: Wiley.

Donovan, D. M. (2005). Assessment of addictive behaviors for relapse prevention. In D. M. Donovan & G. A. Marlatt (Eds.), *Assessment of addictive behaviors* (2nd. ed.). New York: Guilford Press.

Döring, N. M. (2009). The Internet's impact on sexuality: A critical review of 15 years of research. *Computers in Human Behavior, 25*(5), 1089–1101.

Douglass, F. (1855). *My bondage, my freedom.* New York: Ortin and Mulligan.

Doweiko, H. E. (2011). *Concepts of chemical dependency* (5th ed.). Pacific Grove, CA: Brooks/Cole.

Drapkin, M. L., Eddie, D., Buffington, A. J., & McCrady, B. S. (2015). Alcohol-specific coping styles of adult children of individuals with alcohol use disorders and associations with psychosocial functioning. *Alcohol and Alcoholism, 50*(4), 463–469. doi:10.1093/alcalc/agv023

Drazdowski, T. K., Perrin, P. B., Trujillo, M., Sutter, M., Benotsch, E. G., & Snipes, D. J. (2016). Structural equation modeling of the effects of racism, LGBTQ discrimination, and internalized oppression on illicit drug use in LGBTQ people of color. *Drug and Alcohol Dependence, 159,* 255–262. doi:10.1016/j.drugalcdep.2015.12.029

Drew, S. M., Wilkins, K. M., & Trevisan, L. A. (2010). Managing medication and alcohol misuse by your older patients. *Current Psychiatry, 9,* 21–24, 27–28, 41.

Drewnowski, A., & Bellisle, F. (2007). Is sweetness addictive? *Nutrition Bulletin, 32* (Suppl. 1), 52–60.

Duan, C., & Brown, C. (2016). *Becoming a multiculturally competent counselor.* Los Angeles, CA: Sage.

Dube, S. R., Anda, R. F., Felitti, V. J., Edwards, V. J., & Croft, J. B. (2002). Adverse childhood experiences and personal alcohol abuse as an adult. *Addictive Behaviors, 27,* 713–725.

Du Bois, W. E. B. (1928). Drunkenness. *The Crisis, 35,* 348.

Duncan, D. F., Nicholson, T., White, J. B., Bradley, D. B., & Bonaguro, J. (2010). The baby boomer effect: Changing patterns of substance abuse among adults ages 55 and older. *Journal of Aging & Social Policy, 22*(3), 237–248.

Echeverría, S. E., Vélez-Valle, E., Janevic, T., & Prystowsky, A. (2014). The role of poverty status and obesity on school attendance in the United States. *Journal of Adolescent Health, 55*(3), 402–407. doi:10.1016/j.jadohealth.2014.03.012

Ehlers, C. L., Stouffer, G. M., & Gilder, D. A. (2014). Associations between a history of binge drinking during adolescence and self-reported responses to alcohol in young adult Native and Mexican Americans. *Alcoholism: Clinical and Experimental Research, 38*(7), 2039–2047. doi:10.1111/acer.12466

Eitle, T. M., Johnson-Jennings, M., & Eitle, D. J. (2013). Family structure and adolescent alcohol use problems: Extending popular explanations to American Indians. *Social Science Research, 42*(6), 1467–1479. doi:10.1016/j.ssresearch.2013.06.007

El-Guebaly, N., & Offord, D. R. (1977). The offspring of alcoholics: A critical review. *American Journal of Psychiatry, 134*(4), 357–365.

El-Guebaly, N., & Offord, D. R. (1979). On being the offspring of an alcoholic: An update. *Alcoholism: Clinical & Experimental Research, 3*(2), 148–157.

Emlet, C. A. (2008). Truth and consequences: A qualitative exploration of HIV disclosures in older adults. *AIDS Care, 20*(6), 710–717.

Engel, S. G., Wonderlich, S. A., Crosby, R. D., Mitchell, J. E., Crow, S., Peterson, C. B., . . . & Gordon, K. H. (2013). The role of affect in the maintenance of anorexia nervosa: Evidence from a naturalistic assessment of momentary behaviors and emotion. *Journal of Abnormal Psychology, 122*(3), 709.

Espelage, D. L., Low, S., Polanin, J. R., & Brown, E. C. (2013). The impact of a middle school program to reduce aggression, victimization, and sexual violence. *Journal of Adolescent Health, 53*(2), 180–186.

Ewing, B. A., Osilla, K. C., Pedersen, E. R., Hunter, S. B., Miles, J. V., & D'Amico, E. J. (2015). Longitudinal family effects on substance use among an at-risk adolescent sample. *Addictive Behaviors, 41*, 185–191. doi:10.1016/j.addbeh.2014.10.017

Ewing, J. A. (1984). Detecting alcoholism: The CAGE questionnaire. *Journal of the American Medical Association, 252*, 1905–1907.

Facebook. (2011). Facebook statistics. Retrieved July 13, 2011, from http://www.facebook.com/press/info.php?statistics

Facebook. (2015). Facebook statistics. Retrieved July 13, 2015, from http://www.statisticbrain.com/facebook-statistics/

Falicov, C. J. (2002). Ambiguous loss: Risk and resilience in Latino immigrant families. In M. Suarez Orozco & M. Paez (Eds.), *Latinos: Remaking America* (pp. 274–288). Berkeley: University of California Press.

Falicov, C. J. (2005). Mexican families. In M. McGoldrick, J. Giordano, & N. Garcie-Preto (Eds.), *Ethnicity and family therapy* (3rd ed., pp. 134–163). New York: Guilford Press.

Fals-Stewart, W. (2003). The occurrence of partner physical aggression on days of alcohol consumption: A longitudinal diary study. *Journal of Consulting and Clinical Psychology, 71*, 41–52.

Fals-Stewart, W., & Kenndy, C. (2005). Addressing intimate partner violence in substance-abuse treatment. *Journal of Substance Abuse, 29*, 5–17.

Feree, M. C. (2002). Sexual addiction and co-addiction: Experiences among women of faith. *Sexual Addiction and Recovery, 9*(4), 285–293.

Fineran, K., Laux, J. M., Seymour, J., & Thomas, T. (2010). The Barnum Effect and chaos theory: Exploring college student ACOA traits. *Journal of College Student Psychotherapy, 24*(1), 17–31.

Fingarette, H. (1988). *Heavy drinking: The myth of alcoholism as a disease.* Berkeley: University of California.

Fiorentine, R., & Hillhouse, M. P. (2000). Drug treatment and 12-step program participation: The addictive effects of integrated recovery activities. *Journal of Substance Abuse Treatment, 18*, 65–74.

Fischer, J. L., Pidcock, B. W., Munsch, J., & Forthun, L. (2005). Parental abusive drinking and sibling role difference. *Alcoholism Treatment Quarterly, 23*(1), 79–97.

Fischer, J. L., Spann, L., & Crawford, D. W. (1991). Measuring co-dependency. *Alcoholism Treatment Quarterly, 8*(1), 87–100.

Fisher, G. L. (2011). *Understanding why addicts are not all alike: Recognizing the types and how the differences affect intervention and treatment.* Westport, CT: Praeger.

Fisher, G. L., & Harrison, T. C. (1992). Assessment of alcohol and other drug abuse with referred adolescents. *Psychology in the Schools, 29*, 172–178.

Fisher, G. L., & Harrison, T. C. (1993a). The school counselor's role in relapse prevention. *School Counselor, 41*, 120–125.

Fisher, G. L., & Harrison, T. C. (1993b). *Codependent characteristics of prospective counselors as compared to other graduate students.* Paper presented at American Counseling Association National Conference, Atlanta, GA, March.

Forcehimes, A. A., Venner, K. L., Bogenschutz, M. P., Foley, K., Davis, M. P., Houck, J. M., & Begaye, P. (2011). American Indian methamphetamine and other drug use in the southwestern United States. *Cultural Diversity and Ethnic Minority Psychology, 17*(4), 366–376. doi:10.1037/a0025431

Forsberg, S., & Lock, J. (2015). Family-based treatment of child and adolescent eating disorders. *Child and Adolescent Psychiatric Clinics of North America, 24*(3), 617–629. doi:10.1016/j.chc.2015.02.012

Forward, S. (1986). *Men who hate women and women who love them.* New York: Basic Books.

Foster, B. (1999). The mind-body connection. *Body Positive, 12*(9), 1–5. Retrieved April 4, 2003, from www.thebody.com/bp/sept99/yoga.html

Franklin, A. J. (2004). *From brotherhood to manhood: How Black men rescue their dreams and relationships from the invisibility syndrome.* Hoboken, NJ: Wiley.

Fraser, J. J., McAbee, G. N., & Committee on Medical Liability. (2004). Dealing with the parent whose judgment is impaired by alcohol or drugs: Legal and ethical considerations. *Pediatrics, 114*(3), 869–873.

Fredriksen-Goldsen, K., Kim, H., Emlet, C., Muraco, A., Erosheva, E., Hoy-Ellis, C., & Petry, H. (2011). *The aging and health report: Disparities and resilience among lesbian, gay, bisexual and transgender older adults.* Seattle, WA: Institute for Multigenerational Health.

Fredrickson, G. M. (1971). *The Black image in the White mind: The debate on Afro-American character and destiny, 1817–1914.* New York: Harper & Row.

Freehling, W. W. (1968). *Prelude to civil war: The nullification controversy in South Carolina, 1818–1836.* New York: Harper & Row.

Freemantle, J., Ring, I., Arambula Solomon, T. G., Gachupin, F. C., Smylie, J., Cutler, T. L., & Waldon, J. A. (2015). Indigenous mortality (revealed): The invisible illuminated. *American Journal of Public Health, 105*(4), 644–652. Retrieved from http://search.proquest.com.unr.idm.oclc.org/docview/1667326677/abstract/10C6C45F9EEB419APQ/1?accountid=452

Friedman, M. S., Marshal, M. P., Stall, R., Kidder, D. P., Henny, K. D., & Courtenay-Quirk, C. (2009). Associations between substance use, sexual risk taking and HIV treatment adherence among homeless people living with HIV. *AIDS Care, 21*(6), 692–700.

Friel, J. C. (1984). *Co-dependency and the search for identity: A paradoxical crisis.* Pompano Beach, FL: Health Communications.

Friese, B., Grube, J. W., Seninger, S., Paschall, M. J., & Moore, R. S. (2011). Drinking behavior and sources of alcohol: Differences between Native American and White youths. *Journal of Studies on Alcohol and Drugs, 72*(1), 53–60.

Fukuyama, M., & Inoue-Cox, C. (1992). Cultural perspectives in communicating with Asian/Pacific Islanders. In J. Wittmer (Ed.), *Valuing diversity and similarly: Bridging the gap through interpersonal skills* (pp. 93–112). Minneapolis: Educational Media Corporation.

Fuller, J. A., & Warner, R. M. (2000). Family stressors as predictors of codependency. *Genetic, Social and General Psychology Monographs, 126*(1), 5–23.

Gagnon, M., & Stuart, M. (2009). Manufacturing disability: HIV, women and the construction of difference. *Nursing Philosophy, 10*(1), 42–52.

Gainsbury, S. M., Russell, A., Wood, R., Hing, N., & Blaszczynski, A. (2015). How risky is internet gambling? A comparison of subgroups of Internet gamblers based on problem gambling status. *New Media & Society, 17*(6), 861–879. doi:10.1177/1461444813518185

Gallardo, M. E., & Curry, S. J. (2009). Shifting perspectives: Culturally responsive interventions with Latino substance abusers. *Journal of Ethnicity in Substance Abuse, 8*(3), 314–329.

Gamble, S. A., Talbot, N. L., Cashman-Brown, S. M., He, H., Poleshuck, E. L., Connors, G. J., & Conner, K. R. (2013). A pilot study of interpersonal psychotherapy for alcohol-dependent women with co-occurring major depression. *Substance Abuse, 34*(3), 233–241. doi:10.1080/08897077.2012.746950

Gamblers Anonymous. (2015). *Twenty questions.* Retrieved from http://www.gamblersanonymous.org/ga/content/20-questions

Garcia, F. D., & Thibaut, F. (2010). Sexual addictions. *American Journal of Drug and Alcohol Abuse, 36*, 254–260.

Garcia-Preto, N. (2005). Latino families: An overview. In M. McGoldrick, J. Giordano, & N. Garcia-Preto (Eds.), *Ethnicity and family therapy* (pp. 153–165). New York: Guilford Press.

Garfinkel, P. E., & Kaplan, A. S. (1986). Anorexia nervosa: Diagnostic conceptualizations. In K. D. Brownell & J. P. Foreyt (Eds.), *Handbook of eating disorders* (pp. 266–282). New York: Basic Books.

Garner, D. M. (2005). *Eating Disorder Inventory-3. Professional manual.* Odessa, FL: Psychological Assessment Resources.

Garza, C. F., & Gasquoine, P. G. (2013). Implicit race/ethnic prejudice in Mexican Americans. *Hispanic Journal of Behavioral Sciences, 35*(1), 121–133. doi:10.1177/0739986312462083

Gąsior, K. (2014). Diversifying childhood experiences of adult children of alcoholics. *Alcoholism and Drug Addiction, 27*(4), 289–304. doi:10.1016/S0867-4361(14)70021-5

George, W. H., La Marr, J., Barrett, K., & McKinnon, T. (1999). Alcoholic parentage, self-labeling, and endorsement of ACOA-codependent traits. *Psychology of Addictive Behaviors, 13*(1), 39–48.

Gerstein, D. R. (1997). *Final report: The National Treatment Improvement Evaluation Study.* Rockville, MD: Center for Substance Abuse Treatment. Retrieved February 8, 2016, from http://www.icpsr.umich.edu/files/SAMHDA/NTIES/NTIES-PDF/ntiesfnl.pdf

Gilley, B. J., & Co-Cké, J. H. (2005). Cultural investment: Providing opportunities to reduce risky behavior among gay American Indian males. *Journal of Psychoactive Drugs, 37*(3), 293–298.

Giordano, J., & McGoldrick, M. (2005). Euro-American families. In M. McGoldrick, J. Giordano, & N. Garcia-Preto (Eds.), *Ethnicity and family therapy.* New York: Guilford Press.

Gladding, S. T. (2011). *Family therapy: History, theory, and practice.* Boston: Pearson.

Glazier, R. E., & Kling, R. N. (2013). Recent trends in substance abuse among persons with disabilities compared to that of persons without disabilities. *Disability and Health Journal, 6*(2), 107–115. doi:10.1016/j.dhjo.2013.01.007

Godier, L. R., & Park, R. J. (2014). Compulsivity in anorexia nervosa: A transdiagnostic concept. *Frontiers in Psychology, 5*, 1–18. doi: 10.3389/fpsyg.2014.00778

Gone, J. P., & Looking, P. E. C. (2011). American Indian culture as substance abuse treatment: Pursuing evidence for a local intervention. *Journal of Psychoactive Drugs, 43*(4), 291–296. doi:10.1080/02791072.2011.628915

Goodman, R. W. (1987). Adult children of alcoholics. *Journal of Counseling and Development, 66*, 162–163.

Goracci, A., Casamassima, F., Iovieno, N., di Volo, S., Benbow, J., Bolognesi, S., & Fagiolini, A. (2015). Binge eating disorder: From clinical research to clinical practice. *Journal of Addiction Medicine, 9*(1), 20–24. doi:10.1097/ADM.0000000000000085

Gordon, J. U. (Ed.). (1994). *Managing multiculturalism in substance abuse services.* Thousand Oaks, CA: Sage.

Gorman, D. M. (1998). The irrelevance of evidence in the development of school-based drug prevention policy, 1986–1996. *Evaluation Review, 22*, 118–146.

Gorski, T. T. (1988). *The staying sober workbook: A serious solution for the problem of relapse.* Independence, MO: Independence Press.

Gorski, T. T. (1989). *Passages through recovery: An action plan for preventing relapse.* Center City, MN: Hazelden.

Gorski, T. T. (1990). The Cenaps model of relapse prevention: Basic principles and procedures. *Journal of Psychoactive Drugs, 22*, 125–133.

Gorski, T. T. (1992). Creating a relapse prevention program in your treatment center. *Addiction & Recovery,* July/August, 16–17.

Gorski, T. T. (1993). Relapse prevention: A state of the art overview. *Addiction & Recovery,* March/April, 25–27.

Gorski, T. T., & Miller, M. M. (1986). *Staying sober: Guide to relapse prevention.* Independence, MO: Herald House.

Gowing, L. R., Ali, R. L., Allsop, S., Marsden, J., Turf, E. E., West, R., & Witton, J. (2015). Global statistics on addictive behaviours: 2014 status report. *Addiction, 110*(6), 904–919. doi:10.1111/add.12899

Grafsky, E. L., Letcher, A., Slesnick, N., & Serovich, J. M. (2011). Comparison of treatment response among GLB and non-GLB street-living youth. *Children & Youth Services Review, 33*(5), 569–574.

Granfield, R., & Cloud, W. (2001). Social context and "natural recovery": The role of social capital in the resolution of drug-associated problems. *Substance Use and Misuse, 36*, 1543–1570.

Grant, J. E., Potenza, M. N., Weinstein, A., & Gorelick, D. A. (2010). Introduction to behavioral addictions. *American Journal of Drug and Alcohol Abuse, 36*, 233–241.

Greeff, A. P., & Du Toit, C. (2009). Resilience in remarried families. *American Journal of Family Therapy, 37*(2), 114–126.

Greenbaum, P. E., Wang, W., Henderson, C. E., Kan, L., Hall, K., Dakof, G. A., & Liddle, H. A. (2015). Gender and ethnicity as moderators: Integrative data analysis of multidimensional family therapy randomized clinical trials. *Journal of Family Psychology, 29*(6), 919–930. doi:10.1037/fam0000127

Greenfield, S. F., Brooks, A. J., Gordon, S. M., Green, C. A., Kropp, F., McHugh, R. K., . . . Miele, G. M. (2007). Substance abuse treatment entry, retention, and outcome in women: A review of the literature. *Drug and Alcohol Dependence, 86*(1), 1–21.

Greenfield, S. F., & Grella, C. E. (2009). Alcohol and drug abuse: What is "women-focused" treatment for substance abuse disorders? *Psychiatric Services, 60*, 880–882.

Gresham, S. L. (2009). Negotiating cultural contexts: An exploratory investigation of Black gay male strategy employment. *Journal of GLBT Family Studies, 5*(3), 247–267.

Griffing, S., Fish-Ragin, D., Sage, R. E., Madry, L., Bingham, L. E., & Primm, B. J. (2002). Domestic violence survivors' self-identified reasons for returning to abusive relationships. *Journal of Interpersonal Violence, 17*, 306–319.

Griffin-Shelley, E. (1991). *Sex and love.* New York: Praeger.

Griffith, J. D., Rowan-Szal, G. A., Roark, R. R., & Simpson, D. D. (2000). Contingency management in outpatient methadone treatment: A meta-analysis. *Drug and Alcohol Dependence, 58*, 55–66.

Griffiths, M. D. (2000). Does Internet and computer "addiction" exist? Some case study evidence. *Cyberpsychology and Behavior, 3*, 211–218. doi: 10/.1089/1094931003 100316067

Griffiths, S., Angus, D., Murray, S. B., & Touyz, S. (2014). Unique associations between young adult men's emotional functioning and their body dissatisfaction and disordered eating. *Body Image, 11*(2), 175–178. doi:10.1016/j.bodyim.2013.12.002

Guerrero, E. G. (2009). Managerial capacity and adopton of culturally competent practices in outpatient substance abuse treatment organizations. *Journal of Substance Abuse Treatment, 39*(4), 329–339.

Gutierrez, I. A., Goodwin, L. J., Kirkinis, K., & Mattis, J. S. (2014). Religious socialization in African American families: The relative influence of parents, grandparents, and siblings. *Journal of Family Psychology, 28*(6), 779–789. doi:10.1037/a0035732

Haber, J. R., Grant, J. D., Jacob, T., Koenig, L. B., & Heath, A. (2011). Alcohol milestones, risk factors, and religion/spirituality in young adult women. *Journal of Studies on Alcohol and Drugs, 73*, 34–43. doi: http://dx.doi.org/10.15288/jsad.2012.73.34

Hahm, H. C., & Adkins, C. (2009). A model of Asian and Pacific Islander sexual minority acculturation. *Journal of LGBT Youth, 6*(2), 155–173.

Haley, J. (1973). *Uncommon therapy: The psychiatric techniques of Milton H. Erickson, M.D.* New York: Ballantine Books.

Hall, C. W., & Webster, R. E. (2002). Traumatic symptomatology characteristics of adult children of alcoholics. *Journal of Drug Education, 32*(3), 195–211.

Hall, C. W., Webster, R. E., & Powell, E. J. (2003). Personal alcohol use in adult children of alcoholics. *Alcohol Research, 8*(4), 157–162.

Hall, J. C. (2007). An exploratory study of differences in self-esteem, kinship social support, and coping responses among African American ACOAs and non-ACOAs. *Journal of American College Health, 56*(1), 49–54.

Hall, P. (2014). Sex addiction-An extraordinarily contentious problem. *Sexual and Relationship Therapy, 29*(1), 68–75. doi:10.1080/14681994.2013.861898

Hall, W., & Pacula, R. L. (2010). *Cannabis use and dependence: Public health and public policy reissue edition.* Cambridge, UK: Cambridge University Press.

Hammad, T. A., Laughren, T., & Racoosin, J. (2006). Suicidality in pediatric patients treated with antidepressant drugs. *Archives of General Psychiatry, 63*, 332–339.

Hardee, J. E., Weiland, B. J., Nichols, T. E., Welsh, R. C., Soules, M. E., Steinberg, D. B., Zubieta, J., Zucker, R. A., & Heitzeg, M. M. (2014). Development of impulse control circuitry in children of alcoholics. *Biological Psychiatry, 76*(9), 708–716. doi:10.1016/j.biopsych.2014.03.005

Harkness, D., & Cotrell, G. (1997). The social construction of codependency in the treatment of substance abuse. *Journal of Substance Abuse Treatment, 14*, 473–479.

Harkness, D., Manhire, S., Blanchard, J., & Darling, J. (2011). Codependent attitude and behavior: Moderators of psychological distress in adult offspring of families with alcohol and other drug (AOD) problems. *Alcoholism Treatment Quarterly, 25*(3), 39–52.

Harkness, D., Swenson, M., Madsen-Hampton, K., & Hale, R. (2001). The development, reliability, and validity of a clinical rating scale for codependency. *Journal of Psychoactive Drugs, 33*, 159–171.

Harper, F. D. (Ed.). (1976). *Alcohol abuse and Black America*. Alexandria, VA: Douglass.

Harper, M. (2006). Ethical multiculturalism: An evolutionary concept analysis. *Advances in Nursing Science, 29*(2), 110–124.

Harris, T. (1969). I'm okay, you're okay. *A practical guide to Transactional Analysis*. New York: Galahad Books.

Harrison, T. C. (2004). *Consultation for contemporary helping professionals*. Boston: Allyn & Bacon.

Harrison, T. C., Gentile, T., & Harrison, T. F. (2012). Transforming the managerial class: Binary and dialectical thinking in counseling. In *Ideas and Research You Can Use: VISTAS 2012*. Retrieved from http://www.counseling.org/knowledge-center/vistas

Harrison, T. C., & Harrison, T., F. (2015). Toward a deeper understanding of adoption family structure: Concepts borrowed from social justice, attachment theory, and relational dialectics. In *Ideas and Research You Can Use: VISTAS 2015*. Retrieved from http://www.counseling.org/knowledge-center/vistas

Haverfield, M. C., & Theiss, J. A. (2014). A theme analysis of experiences reported by adult children of alcoholics in online support forums. *Journal of Family Studies, 20*(2), 166–183. doi:10.1080/13229400.2014.11082004

Hawkins, J. D., Catalano, R. E., & Miller, J. Y. (1992). Risk and protective factors for alcohol and other drug problems in adolescence and early adulthood: Implications for substance abuse prevention. *Psychological Bulletin, 112*, 64–105.

Hawkins, J. D., Lishner, D. M., & Catalano, R. E. (1985, April). *Childhood predictors and the prevention of adolescent substance abuse*. Presented at the National Institute on Drug Abuse research analysis and utilization system meeting, etiology of drug abuse: Implications for prevention.

Henderson, C. E., Dakof, G. A., Greenbaum, P. E., & Liddle, H. A. (2010). Effectiveness of multidimensional family therapy with higher severity substance-abusing adolescents: Report from two randomized controlled trials. *Journal of Consulting and Clinical Psychology, 78*(6), 885–897.

Herd, D. (1991). The paradox of temperance: Blacks and the alcohol question in nineteenth-century America. In S. Barrows & R. Room (Eds.), *Drinking: Behavior and belief in modern history* (pp. 354–375). Berkeley: University of California Press.

Hergenrather, K. C., & Rhodes, S. D. (2008). Consumers with HIV/AIDS: Application of theory to explore beliefs impacting employment. *Journal of Rehabilitation, 74*(1), 32–42.

Herzog, D. B., & Eddy, K. T. (2009). Eating disorders: What are the risks? *Journal of the American Academy of Child and Adolescent Psychiatry, 48*(8), 782–783.

Hester, R. K. (2003). Behavioral self-control training. In R. K. Hester & W. R. Miller (Eds.), *Handbook of alcoholism treatment approaches: Effective alternatives* (3rd ed., pp. 152–164). Boston: Allyn & Bacon.

Heyman, B., & Huckle, S. (1995). Sexuality as a perceived hazard in the lives of adults with learning disabilities. *Disability and Society, 10*, 139–155.

Hickey, K., Kerber, C. H., Kim, M., Astroth, K. S., & Schlenker, E. (2014). Gambling and perceived health among adult jail inmates. *Journal of Forensic Nursing, 10*(1), 36–43. doi:10.1097/JFN.0000000000000019

Higgins, S. T., Budney, A. J., Bickel, H. K., Badger, G., Foerg, F., & Ogden, D. (1995). Outpatient behavioral treatment for cocaine dependence: One-year outcome. *Experimental & Clinical Psychopharmacology, 3*, 205–212.

Hines, P. M., & Boyd-Franklin, N. (1982). Black families. In M. McGoldrick, J. Pierce, & J. Giordano (Eds.), *Ethnicity and family therapy* (pp. 84–107). New York: Guilford Press.

Hines, P. M., & Boyd-Franklin, N. (2005). African American families. In McGoldrick, M., Giordano, J., & Garcia-Preto, N. (Eds.), *Ethnicity and family therapy* (3rd ed., pp. 87–100). Guilford Press: New York.

Ho, M. K. (1992). *Minority children and adolescents in therapy*. London: Sage.

Hodge, D. R., & Lietz, C. A. (2014). Using spiritually modified cognitive-behavioral therapy in substance dependence treatment: Therapists' and clients' perceptions of the presumed benefits and limitations. *Health & Social Work, 39*(4), 200–210. doi: 10.1093/hsw/hlu022

Hoenigmann-Lion, N. M., & Whitehead, G. I. (2006). The relationship between codependency and borderline and dependent personality traits. *Alcoholism Treatment Quarterly, 24*(4), 55–77.

Hoerster, K. D., Jakupcak, M., Hanson, R., McFall, M., Reiber, G., Hall, K. S., & Nelson, K. M. (2015). PTSD and depression symptoms are associated with binge eating among US Iraq and Afghanistan veterans. *Eating Behaviors, 17*, 115–118. doi:10.1016/j.eatbeh.2015.01.005

Hogan, J. A., Reed-Gabrielsen, K., Luna, N., & Grothaus, D. (2003). *Substance abuse prevention: The intersection of science and practice*. Boston: Allyn & Bacon.

Hollingsworth, W. G. (2011). Community family therapy with military families experiencing deployment. *Contemporary Family Therapy, 33*, 215–228. doi:10.1007/s10591-011-9144-8

Hong, Y., Fang, Y., Yang, Y., & Phua, D. (2013). Cultural attachment: A new theory and method to understand cross-cultural competence. *Journal of Cross-Cultural Psychology, 44*(6), 1024–1044. Retrieved from http://jcc.sagepub.com.unr.idm.oclc.org/content/44/6/1024

Hook, J. N., Hook, J. P., & Hines, S. (2008). Reach out or act out: Long-term group therapy for sexual addiction. *Sexual Addiction and Compulsivity, 15*(3), 217–232.

Hook, J. N., Reid, R. C., Penberthy, J. K., Davis, D. E., & Jennings, D. J. (2014). Methodological review of treatments for nonparaphilic hypersexual behavior. *Journal of Sex & Marital Therapy, 40*(4), 294–308. doi:10.1080/0092623X.2012.751075

Howard, K. N., Heston, J., Key, C. M., McCrory, E., Serna-McDonald, C., Smith, R. K., & Hendrick, S. S. (2010). Addiction, the sibling, and the self. *Journal of Loss and Trauma, 15*(5), 465–479.

Hser, Y., Grella, C. E., Hubbard, R. L., Hsieh, S. C., Fletcher, B. W., Brown, B. S., & Anglin, M. D. (2001). An evaluation of drug treatment for adolescents in four U.S. cities. *Archives of General Psychiatry, 58*, 689–695.

Hubbard, R. L., & French, M. T. (1991). New perspectives on the benefit-cost and cost-effectiveness of drug abuse treatment. In W. S. Cartwright & J. M. Kaple (Eds.), *Economic costs, cost-effectiveness, financing and community-based drug treatment* (NIDA Research Monograph #113, pp. 94–113). Rockville, MD: National Institute on Drug Abuse.

Hudsen, J., Hiripi, E., Pope, H., & Kessler, R. (2007). The prevalence and correlates of eating disorders in the national comorbidity survey replication. *Biological Psychiatry, 61*, 348–358.

Hughes, T. (2011). Alcohol use and alcohol-related problems among sexual minority women. *Alcoholism Treatment Quarterly, 29*(4), 403–435. doi: 10.1080/07347324.2011.608336

Hughes, T. L., Wilsnack, S. C., Szalacha, L. A., Johnson, T., Bostwick, W. B., Seymour, R., . . . Aranda, F. (2006). Age and racial/ethnic differences in drinking and drinking-related problems in a community sample of lesbians. *Journal of Studies on Alcohol, 67*, 579–590.

Humphreys, J. D., Clopton, J. R., & Reich, D. A. (2007). Disordered eating behavior and obsessive-compulsive symptoms in college students: Cognitive and affective similarities. *Eating Disorders, 15*, 247–259.

Hurcom, C., Copello, A., & Orford, J. (2000). The family and alcohol: Effects of excessive drinking and conceptualizations of spouses over recent decades. *Substance Use & Misuse, 35*, 473–502.

Hussong, B. M., Huang, W., Curran, P. J., Chassin, L., & Zucker, R. A. (2010). Parent alcoholism impacts the severity and timing of children's externalizing symptoms. *Journal of Abnormal Child Psychology, 38*(3), 3677–380.

Immonen, S., Valvanne, J., & Pitkälä, K. H. (2013). The prevalence of potential alcohol-drug interactions in older adults. *Scandinavian Journal of Primary Health Care, 31*(2), 73–78. doi:10.3109/02813432.2013.788272

Indian Health Service. (2015). *Disparities*. Retrieved from http://www.ihs.gov/factsheets/index.cfm?module=dsp_fact_disparities

International Telecommunications Union. (2013). Retrieved on February 22, 2016 from http://www.itu.int/en/ITU-D/Statistics/Pages/default/aspx [MMI]

Internet World Stats. (2013). *Internet world stats: Usage and population statistics*. Retrieved from http://www.internetworldstats.com/

Iron Eye Dudley, J. (1992). *Choteau Creek: A Sioux reminiscence*. Lincoln: University of Nebraska Press.

Irvine, L. (1999). *Codependent forevermore*. Chicago: University of Chicago Press.

Ivey, A. E., Bradford-Ivey, M., & Simek-Morgan, L. (1996). *Counseling and psychotherapy: A multicultural perspective* (4th ed.). Boston, MA: Allyn & Bacon.

Ivey, A. E., D'Andrea, L., Bradford-Ivey, M., & Simek-Morgan, L. (2007). *Counseling and psychotherapy: A multicultural perspective* (6th ed.). Boston: Allyn & Bacon.

Jackson, D. D. (1957). The question of family homeostasis. *Psychiatric Quarterly Supplement, 31*, 79–90.

Jacobs, T., Windle, M., Seilhamer, R. A., & Bost, J. (1999). Adult children of alcoholics: Drinking, psychiatric, and psychosocial status. *Psychology of Addictive Behaviors, 13*(1), 3–21.

Jappe, L. M., Frank, G. K. W., Shott, M. E., Rollin., M. D. H., Pryor, T., Hagman, J. O., Davis, E. (2011). Heightened sensitivity to reward and punishment in anorexia nervosa. *International Journal of Eating Disorders, 44*(4), 317–324.

Jarosz, P. A., Dobal, M. J., Wilson, F. L., & Schram, C. A. (2007). Food cravings and disordered eating among urban obese African American women. *Eating Behaviors, 8*(3), 374–381.

Jay, S., Freisthler, B., & Svare, G. M. (2004). Drinking in young adulthood: Is the stepparent a risk factor? *Journal of Divorce and Remarriage, 41*(2/3), 99–114.

Jellinek, E. M. (1952). Phases of alcohol addiction. *Quarterly Journal of Studies on Alcohol, 13*, 673–684.

Jellinek, E. M. (1960). *The disease concept of alcoholism*. New Haven, CT: Hillhouse Press.

Jemigan, V. B., Peercy, M., Branam, D., Saunkeah, B., Wharton, D., Winkleby, M., & Buchwald, D. (2015). Beyond health equity: Achieving wellness within American Indian and Alaska Native communities. *American Journal of Public Health. 105*(S3), S376–S379. doi:10.2105/AJPH.2014.302447

Jennings, K. M., Kelly-Weeder, S., & Wolfe, B. E. (2015). Binge eating among racial minority groups in the United States: An integrative review. *Journal of the American Psychiatric Nurses Association, 21*(2), 117–125. doi:10.1177/1078390315581923

Johnson, V. E. (1973). *I'll quit tomorrow.* Toronto, Canada: Harper & Row.

Johnston, L. D., O'Malley, P. M., Miech, R. A., Bachman, J. G., & Schulenberg, J. E. (2016). *Monitoring the future: National results on adolescent drug use. Overview of key findings, 2015.* Ann Arbor: Institute for Social Research, the University of Michigan.

Jones, A. C. (1985). Psychological functioning in black Americans: A conceptual guide for use in psychotherapy. *Psychotherapy, 22,* 363–369.

Jones, D. J., Runyan, D. K., Lewis, T., Litrownik, A. J., Black, M. M., Wiley, T. & Nagin, D. S. (2010). Trajectories of childhood sexual abuse and early adolescent HIV/AIDS risk behaviors: The role of other maltreatment, witnessed violence, and child gender. *Journal of Child and Adolescent Psychology, 39*(5), 667–680.

Jones, J. M. (2008). One in six Americans gamble on sports: Gallup Poll, December 6–9, 2007. Retrieved June 20, 2011, from http://www.gallup.com/poll/104086/One%E2%80%90Six%E2%80%90Americans%E2%80%90Gamble%E2%80%90Sports.aspx

Jones, J. W. (1985). *Children of alcoholics screening test.* Chicago: Camelot Unlimited.

Joseph, E. B., & Bhatti, R. S. (2004). Psychosocial problems and coping patterns of HIV seropositive wives of men with HIV/AIDS. Retrieved July 24, 2007, from www.haworthpress.com/web/SWHC

Juarascio, A. S., Manasse, S. M., Espel, H. M., Kerrigan, S. G., & Forman, E. M. (2015). Could training executive function improve treatment outcomes for eating disorders? *Appetite, 90,* 187–193. doi:10.1016/j.appet.2015.03.013

Juliana, P., & Goodman, C. (1997). Children of substance abusing parents. In J. H. Lowinson, P. Ruiz, R. B. Millman, & J. G. Langrod (Eds.), *Substance abuse: A comprehensive textbook* (2nd ed., pp. 808–815). Baltimore: Williams & Wilkins.

Kaminer, W. (1990). Chances are you're codependent too (p. 16). *New York Times Book Review,* February 1.

Kanuha, V. K. (2005). N‾aóhaha: Native Hawaiian families. In M. McGoldrick, J. Giordano, & N. Garcia-Preto (Eds.), *Ethnicity and family therapy* (pp. 64–76). New York: Guilford Press.

Kaplan, L. (2008). *The role of recovery support services in recovery-oriented systems of care.* DHHS Publication No. (SMA) 08-4315. Rockville, MD: Center for Substance Abuse Treatment, Substance Abuse and Mental Health Services Administration.

Karacostas, D. D., & Fisher, G. L. (1993). Chemical dependency in students with and without learning disabilities. *Journal of Learning Disabilities, 26,* 491–495.

Kaskutas, L. E. (2009). Alcoholics Anonymous effectiveness: Faith meets science. *Journal of Addictive Disease, 28,* 145–157.

Kasl, C. D. (2002). *Many roads, one journey: Moving beyond the 12 steps.* New York: HarperCollins.

Kasl, C. S. (2002). Special issues in counseling lesbian women for sexual addiction, compulsivity, and sexual codependency. *Sexual Addiction and Compulsivity, Special Issue: Women and Sexual Addiction, 9*(4), 191–208.

Kass, A., Kolko, R., & Wilfley, R. (2013). Psychological treatments for eating disorders. *Current Opinion in Psychiatry, 26*(6), 549–555.

Kaufman, E., & Kaufman, P. (1992). From psychodynamic to structural to integrated family treatment of chemical dependency. In E. Kaufman & P. Kaufman (Eds.), *Family therapy of drug and alcohol abuse* (2nd ed., pp. 34–45). Boston: Allyn & Bacon.

Kearney, F., Moore, A. R., Donegan, C. F., & Lambert, J. (2010). The ageing of HIV: Implications for geriatric medicine. *Age and Ageing, 39,* 536–541.

Kearns-Bodkin, J. N., & Leonard, K. E. (2008). Relationship functioning among adult children of alcoholics. *Journal of Studies on Addiction and Drugs, 69*(6), 941–950.

Keen, L. I., Whitehead, N. E., Clifford, L., Rose, J., & Latimer, W. (2014). Perceived barriers to treatment in a community-based sample of illicit-drug-using African American men and women. *Journal of Psychoactive Drugs, 46*(5), 444–449. doi:10.1080/02791072.2014.964382

Kelley, M. L., Bravo, A. J., Braitman, A. L., Lawless, A. K., & Lawrence, H. R. (2016). Behavioral couples treatment for substance use disorder: Secondary effects on the reduction of risk for child abuse. *Journal of Substance Abuse Treatment, 62,* 10–19. doi:10.1016/j.jsat.2015.11.008

Kelley, M. L., Cash, T. F., Grant, A. R., Miles, D. L., & Santos, M. T. (2004). Parental alcoholism: Relationships to adult attachment in college women and men. *Addictive Behaviors, 29*(8), 1633–1636.

Kelley, M. L., French, A., Bountress, K., Keefe, H. A., Schroeder, V., Steer, K., & Gumienny, L. (2007). Parentification and family responsibility in the family of origin of adult children of alcoholics. *Addictive Behaviors, 32,* 675–685.

Kelley, M. L., Linden, A. N., Milletich, R. J., Lau-Barraco, C., Kurtz, E. D., D'Lima, G. M., Bodkins, J. A., & Sheehan, B. E. (2014). Self and partner alcohol-related problems among ACOAs and non-ACOAs: Associations with depressive symptoms and motivations for alcohol use. *Addictive Behaviors, 39*(1), 211–218. doi:10.1016/j.addbeh.2013.08.037

Kendler, K. S., Edwards, A., Myers, J., Cho, S. B., Adkins, A., & Dick, D. (2015). The predictive power of family history measures of alcohol and drug problems and internalizing disorders in a college population. *American Journal* of Medical Genetics Part B: Neuropsychiatric Genetics, 168(5), 337–346. doi:10.1002/ajmg.b.32320

Kerker, B. D., Bainbridge, J., Kennedy, J., Bennani, Y. Agerton, T., Marder, D., & Thorpe, L. E. (2011). A population-based assessment of the health of homeless families in New York City, 2001–2003. American Journal of Public Health, 101(3), 546–553.

Keyes, K. M., Liu, X. C., & Cerda, M. (2012). The role of race/ethnicity in alcohol-attributable injury in the united states. Epidemiologic Reviews, 34(1), 89–102. doi:10.1093/epirev/mxr018

Kim, H. J. (2002). Codependency: The impact of Confucian marriage and family structure on women in Korea. Dissertation Abstracts International: Section B: The Sciences and Engineering, 63(5-b), 2569.

Kim, J., Xiang, H., Yang, Y., & Lewis, M. W. (2010). Disparities in alcohol treatment utilization by race and type of insurance. Alcohol Treatment Quarterly, 28(1), 2–16.

King, K. A., Vidourek, R. A., & Merianos, A. L. (2013). Sex and grade level differences in lifetime nonmedical prescription drug use among youth. The Journal of Primary Prevention, 34(4), 237–249. doi:10.1007/s10935-013-0308-1

King, V., Boyd, L. M., & Thorsen, M. L. (2015). Adolescents' perceptions of family belonging in stepfamilies. Journal of Marriage and Family, 77(3), 761–774. Retrieved on March 2, 2016, from http://search.proquest.com.unr.idm.oclc.org/docview/1678728377?accountid=452

Kingree, J. B., & Sullivan, B. F. (2002). Participation in Alcoholics Anonymous among African Americans. Alcoholism Treatment Quarterly, 20(3–4), 175–186.

Kirkpatrick, J. (1990). Turnabout: New help for the woman alcoholic. New York: Bantam Books.

Kitchens, J. A. (1991). Understanding and treating codependence. Upper Saddle River, NJ: Prentice Hall.

Klar, H. (1987). The setting for psychiatric treatment. In A. J. Frances & R. E. Hales (Eds.), American Psychiatric Association Annual Review (Vol. 6, pp. 336–352). Washington, DC: American Psychiatric Association Press.

Kovač, A., Vukadin, I. K., Zoričić, Z., Peco, M., & Vukić, V. A. (2014). Characteristics of female drinking by age. Alcoholism: Journal on Alcoholism and Related Addictions, 50(1), 49–62. Retrieved from http://search.proquest.com/docview/1547883894?pq-origsite=summon

Koven, N. S., & Abry, A. W. (2015). The clinical basis of orthorexia nervosa: Emerging perspectives. Neuropsychiatric Disease and Treatment, 11, 385–394. doi: 10.2147/NDT.S61665

Kreider, R. M., & Ellis, R. (2011). Living arrangements of children: 2009. Household Economic Studies. (70–126). Retrieved on March 2, 2016, from United States Census Bureau website: https://www.census.gov/prod/2011pubs/p70-126.pdf

Kreider, R. M., & Lofquist, D. A. (2014). Adopted children and stepchildren: 2010. Population characteristics. (20–572). Retrieved on February 23, 2016, from http://www.census.gov/prod/2014pubs/p20-572.pdf

Krentzman, A. R., & McClellan, M. L. (2011). Introduction to the special issue: Women and alcohol: Multidisciplinary perspectives. Alcoholism Treatment Quarterly, 29, 325–331. doi:10.1080/07347324.2011.608598

Krestan, J. (2000). Addiction, power, and powerlessness. In J. Krestan (Ed.), Bridges to recovery. Addiction, family therapy, and multicultural treatment (pp. 15–44). New York: Free Press.

Krestan, J., & Bepko, C. (1990). Codependency: The social reconstruction of the female experience. Smith College Studies in Social Work, 60, 216–232. Also reprinted in Babcock and McKay, 1995.

Kubicek, K., Carpineto, J., McDavitt, B., Weiss, G., Iverson, E. F., Au, C., & Kipke, M. D. (2008). Integrating professional and folk models of HIV risk: YMSM's perceptions of high-risk sex. AIDS Education and Prevention, 20(3), 220–238.

Kuhn, C. M. (2011). Alcohol and women: What is the role of biologic factors? Alcoholism Treatment Quarterly, 29(4), 479–504. doi:10.1080/07347324.2011.608340

Kumpfer, K. L., Williams, M. K., & Baxley, G. B. (1997). Drug abuse prevention for at-risk groups. Rockville, MD: National Institute on Drug Abuse.

Kurian, A. (1999). Feminism and the developing world. In S. Gamble (Ed.), Feminism and postfeminism (pp. 66–79). New York: Routledge.

Kwon, S. Y. (2001). Codependence and interdependence: Cross-cultural reappraisal of boundaries and relationality. Pastoral Counseling, 50(1), 39–52.

Kyzer, A., Conners-Burrow, N. A., & McKelvey, L. (2014). Environmental risk factors and custody status in children of substance abusers. Children and Youth Services Review, 36, 150–154. doi:10.1016/j.childyouth.2013.11.020

LaBrie, J. W., Hummer, J., Kenney, S., Lac, A., & Pedersen, E. (2011). Identifying factors that increase the likelihood for alcohol-induced blackouts in the prepartying context. Substance Use & Misuse, 46(8), 992–1002. doi:10.3109/10826084.2010.542229

Landen, M., Roeber, J., Naimi, T., Nielsen, L., & Sewell, M. (2014). Alcohol-attributable mortality among American Indians and Alaska Natives in the United States, 1999–2009. American Journal of Public Health, 104(S3), S343–S349. doi:10.2105/AJPH.2013.301648

Larkin, J. R. (1965). Alcohol and the Negro: Explosive issues. Zebulon, NC: Record.

Lauby, J. L., LaPollo, A. B., Herbst, J. H., Painter, T. M., Batson, H., Pierre, A., & Milnamow, M. (2010). Preventing AIDS through live movement and sound:

Efficacy of a theater-based HIV prevention intervention delivered to high-risk male adolescents in juvenile justice settings. *AIDS Education and Prevention, 22*(5), 402–416.

Laudet, A. B., Harris, K., Kimball, T., Winters, K. C., & Moberg, D. P. (2015). Characteristics of students participating in collegiate recovery programs: A national survey. *Journal of Substance Abuse Treatment, 51*, 38–46. doi:10.1016/j.jsat.2014.11.004

Laudet, A. B., Savage, R., & Mahmood, D. (2002). Pathways to long-term recovery: A preliminary investigation. *Journal of Psychoactive Drugs, 34*, 305–311.

Laudet, A. B., & White, W. (2004). *An exploration of relapse patterns among former poly substance users.* Retrieved February 9, 2016, from https://apha.confex.com/apha/132am/techprogram/paper_75426.htm

LaVeist, T. A., & Wallace, J. M. (2000). Health risk and inequitable distribution of liquor stores in African American neighborhoods. *Social Science & Medicine, 51*(4), 613–617.

Lavner, J. A., Waterman, J., & Peplau, L. A. (2014). Parent adjustment over time in gay, lesbian, and heterosexual parent families adopting from foster care. *American Journal of Orthopsychiatry, 84*(1), 46–53. doi:10.1037/h0098853

Lay, K., King, L. J., & Rangel, J. (2008). Changing characteristics of drug use between two older adult cohorts: Small sample speculations on baby boomer trends to come. *Journal of Social Work Practice in the Addictions, 8*(1), 116–126.

Ledoux, S., Miller, P., Choquet, M., & Plant, M. (2002). Family structure, parent-child relationships, and alcohol and other drug use among teenagers in France and the United Kingdom. *Alcohol and Alcoholism, 37*, 52–60.

Lee, E. B., & Mattson, M. P. (2014). The neuropathology of obesity: Insights from human disease. *Acta Neuropathologica, 127*(1), 3–28. doi:10.1007/s00401-013-1190-x

Lee, E., Esaki, N., & Greene, R. (2009). Collocation: Integrating child welfare and substance abuse services. *Journal of Social Work Practice in the Addictions, 9*, 55–70.

Lee, E., & Mock, M. R. (2005). Asian families: An overview. In M. McGoldrick, J. Giordano, & N. Garcia-Preto (Eds.), *Ethnicity and family therapy* (pp. 269–289). New York: Guilford Press.

Lee, S. E., & Valencia, A. (2013). Counseling Asian and Pacific Islander Americans. In C. C. Lee (Ed.), *Multicultural issues in counseling: New approaches to diversity* (4th ed., pp. 53–65). Alexandria, VA: American Counseling Association

Leehr, E. J., Krohmer, K., Schag, K., Dresler, T., Zipfel, S., & Giel, K. E. (2015). Emotion regulation model in binge eating disorder and obesity—A systematic review. *Neuroscience and Biobehavioral Reviews, 49*, 125–134. doi:10.1016/j.neubiorev.2014.12.008

Legha, R., Raleigh-Cohn, A., Fickenscher, A., & Novins, D. (2014). Challenges to providing perspectives of staff from 18 treatment centers. *BMC Psychiatry, 14*(1), 181–190. doi:10.1186/1471-244X-14-181

Lemert, E. M. (1964). Forms and pathology of drinking in three Polynesian societies. *American Anthropology, 66*, 361–374.

Leshner, A. I. (2000). Treating the brain in drug abuse. *NIDA Notes, 15*, 1.

Lesieur, H. R., & Blume, S. B. (1987). The South Oaks Gambling Screen (SOGS): A new instrument for the identification of pathological gamblers. *American Journal of Psychiatry, 144*, 1184–1188.

Lester, B. M., Andreozzi, L., & Appiah, L. (2004). Substance use during pregnancy: Time for policy to catch up with research. *Harm Reduction Journal, 1*(5), 28–37.

Levine, S. B. (2010). What is sexual addiction? *Journal of Sex and Marital Therapy, 36*, 261–275.

Li, L., & Moore, D. (2001). Disability and illicit drug use: An application of labeling theory. *Deviant Behavior, 22*(1), 1–21.

Liddle, H. A. (2010). Multidimensional family therapy: A science-based treatment system. *Australian & New Zealand Journal of Family Therapy, 31*(2), 133–148.

Lind, K., Kääriäinen, J., & Kuoppamäki, S.-M. (2015). From problem gambling to crime? Findings from the Finnish national police information system. *Journal of Gambling Issues, 30*, 98–123. doi:10.4309/jgi.2015.30.10

Lindblad, F., Lindberg, L., & Hjern, A. (2006). Anorexia nervosa in young men. *International Journal of Eating Disorders, 39*(8), 662–666.

Lindley, N. R., Giordano, P. J., & Hammer, E. D. (1999). Codependency: Predictors and psychometric issues. *Journal of Clinical Psychology, 55*(1), 59–64.

Liu, Q., Fang, X., Yan, N., Zhou, Z., Yuan, X., Lan, J., & Liu, C. (2015). Multi-family group therapy for adolescent Internet addiction: Exploring the underlying mechanisms. *Addictive Behaviors, 42,* 1–8. doi:10.1016/j.addbeh.2014.10.021

Lo, C. C., Cheng, T. C., & Howell, R. J. (2014). The role of immigration status in heavy drinking among Asian Americans. *Substance Use & Misuse, 49*(8), 932–940. doi:10.3109/10826084.2013.852578

Logan, S. M. L. (1992). Overcoming sex and love addiction: An expanded perspective. In E. M. Freeman (Ed.), *The addictive process: Effective social work approaches* (pp. 207–222). White Plains, NY: Longman.

Longabaugh, R. (2001). How does treatment work? *Brown University Digest of Addiction Theory and Application, 20*, 8.

Longest, K. C., & Shanahan, M. J. (2007). Adolescent work intensity and substance use: The mediational and moderational roles of parenting. *Journal of Marriage and Family, 69*(3), 703–720. doi:10.1111/j.1741-3737.2007.00401.x

Lopez, F. (1994). *Confidentiality of patient records for alcohol and other drug treatment* (Technical Assistance

Publication, #13). Rockville, MD: Center for Substance Abuse Treatment.

Lopez, M. H., Morin, R., & Taylor, P. (2010). *Illegal immigration backlash worries, divides Latinos*. Retrieved from Pew Hispanic Center website: http://www.pewhispanic.org/2010/10/28/illegal-immigration-backlash-worries-divides-latinos/

Luk, J. W., Emery, R. L., Karyadi, K. A., Patock-Peckham, J. A., & King, K. M. (2013). Religiosity and substance use among Asian American college students: Moderated effects of race and acculturation. *Drug and Alcohol Dependence, 130*(1–3), 142–149. doi:10.1016/j.drugalcdep.2012.10.023

Lurie, N. O. (1971). The world's oldest on-going protest demonstration: North American Indian drinking patterns. *Pacific Historical Review, 40*, 311–332.

Lussier, J. P., Heil, S. H., Mongeon, J. A., Badger, G. J., & Higgins, S. T. (2006). A meta-analysis of voucher-based reinforcement therapy for substance abuse disorders. *Addiction, 101*, 192–203.

Lydecker, J. A., & Grilo, C. M. (2016). Different yet similar: Examining race and ethnicity in treatment-seeking adults with binge eating disorder. *Journal of Consulting and Clinical Psychology, 84*(1), 88–94. doi:10.1037/ccp0000048

Maart, S., & Jelsma, J. (2010). The sexual behavior of physically disabled adolescents. *Disability and Rehabilitation, 32*(6), 438–443.

Madras, B. K., Compton, W. M, Avula, D., Stegbauer, T., Stein, J. B., & Clark, H. W. (2009). Screening, brief interventions, referral to treatment (SBIRT) for illicit drug and alcohol use at multiple healthcare sites: Comparison at intake and 6 months later. *Drug and Alcohol Dependence, 99*, 280–295.

Mair, J. (2009). Duty of confidentiality and HIV/AIDS: PD v Harvey. *Health Information Management Journal, 38*(2), 49–54.

Maisel, N. C., Blodgett, J. C., Wilbourne, P. L., Humphreys, K., & Finney, J. W. (2013). Meta-analysis of naltrexone and acamprosate for treating alcohol use disorders: When are these medications most helpful? *Addiction, 108*, 275–293.

Malinowska, D., & Tokarz, A. (2014). The structure of workaholism and types of workaholic. *Polish Psychological Bulletin, 45*(2), 211–222. doi:10.2478/ppb-2014-0027

Mandara, J., Rogers, S. Y., & Zinbarg, R. E. (2011). The effects of family structure on African American adolescents' marijuana use. *Journal of Marriage and Family, 73*(3), 557–569. doi:10.1111/j.1741-3737.2011.00832.x

Manley, G., & Feree, M. C. (2002). Special issues in counseling lesbian women for sexual addiction, compulsivity, and sexual codependency. *Sexual Addiction & Compulsivity, 9*(4), 191–209.

Manning, W. D. (2013). *Trends in cohabitation: Over twenty years of change, 1987–2010.* (FP-13-12, National Center for Family & Marriage Research, Bowling Green State University). Retrieved from Bowling Green State University, National Center for Family & Marriage Research website: https://www.bgsu.edu/content/dam/BGSU/college-of-arts-and-sciences/NCFMR/documents/FP/FP-13-12.pdf

Manning, W. D., Brown, S. L., & Payne, K. K. (2014). Two decades of stability and change in age at first union formation. *Journal of Marriage and Family, 76*(2), 247–260. doi:10.1111/jomf.12090

Marlatt, G. A. (1985). Relapse prevention: Theoretical rationale and overview of the model. In G. A. Marlatt & J. R. Gordon (Eds.), *Relapse prevention: Maintenance strategies in the treatment of addictive behaviors* (pp. 3–70). New York: Guilford Press.

Marlatt, G. A., Demming, B., & Reid, J. B. (1973). Loss of control drinking in alcoholics: An experimental analogue. *Journal of Abnormal Psychology, 81*, 223–241.

Marlatt, G. A., & Gordon, J. R. (Eds.). (1985). *Relapse prevention: Maintenance strategies in the treatment of addictive behaviors.* New York: Guilford Press.

Marlatt, G. A., & VandenBos, G. R. (Eds.). (1997). *Addictive behaviors.* Washington, DC: American Psychological Association.

Martsolf, D. S. (2002). Codependency, boundaries, and professionalism. *Orthopaedic Nursing, 21*(6), 61–68.

Matsumoto, D., & Hwang, H. C. (2013). Assessing cross-cultural competence: A review of available tests. *Journal of Cross-Cultural Psychology, 44*, 849–873. Retrieved from http://jcc.sagepub.com.unr.idm.oclc.org/content/44/6/849

Mattis, J. S., & Mattis, J. H. (2011). Religion and spirituality in the lives of African American children. In N. Hill, T. Mann, & H. Fitzgerald (Eds.), *African American children and mental health, Vol. 1* (pp. 125–150). Santa Barbara, CA: ABC-CLIO.

May, P. A., Baete, A., Russo, J., Elliott, A. J., Blankenship, J., Kalberg, W. O., . . . & Hoyme, E. (2014). Prevalence and characteristics of fetal alcohol spectrum disorders. *Pediatrics, 134*(5), 854–866. doi:10.1542/peds.2013-3319

May, P. A., Gossage, J. P., Kalberg, W. O., Robinson, L. K., Buckley, D., Manning, M., & Hoyme, H. E. (2009). Prevalence and epidemiologic characteristics of FASD from various research methods with an emphasis on recent in-school studies. *Developmental Disabilities Research Reviews, 15*(3), 176–192. doi:10.1002/ddrr.68

McCarthy, B. W. (2002). The wife's role in facilitating recovery from male compulsive sexual behavior. *Sexual Addiction and Recovery, 9*(4), 275–285.

McCarty, C. A., Zimmerman, F. J., DiGuiseppe, D. L., & Christakis, D. A. (2005). Parental emotional support and subsequent internalizing and externalizing problems among children. *Journal of Developmental and Behavioral Pediatrics, 26,* 267–275.

McClellan, M. L. (2011). Historical perspectives on alcoholism treatment for women in the United States, 1870–1990. *Alcoholism Treatment Quarterly, 29,* 332–356. doi: 10.1080/07347324.2011.608597

McCormack, A., & Griffiths, M. D. (2013). A scoping study of the structural and situational characteristics of internet gambling. *International Journal of Cyber Behavior, Psychology and Learning, 3*(1), 29–49. doi:10.4018/ijcbpl.2013010104

McCown, W. G., & Chamberlain, L. L. (2000). *Best possible odds: Contemporary treatment strategies for gambling disorders.* New York: Wiley.

McDade, R., King, K. A., & Vidourek, R. A. (2015). Parental influences on African American adolescent marijuana use. *Journal of Substance Use, 20*(4), 268–273. doi:10.3109/14659891.2014.909894

McKay, K., Ross, L. E., & Goldberg, A. E. (2010). Adaptation to parenthood during the post-adoption period: A review of the literature. *Adoption Quarterly, 13*(2), 125–144.

McKinney, C. M., Caetano, R., Rodriguez, L. A., & Okoro, N. (2010). Does alcohol involvement increase the severity of intimate partner violence? *Alcoholism: Clinical & Experimental Research, 34*(4), 655–658.

McLellan, A. T., Lewis, D. C., O'Brien, C. P., & Kleber, H. D. (2000). Drug dependence, a chronic medical illness: Implications for treatment, insurance, and outcome evaluation. *Journal of the American Medical Association, 284,* 1689–1695.

McLellan, A. T., Luborsky, L., O'Brien, C. P., & Woody, G. E. (1980). An improved diagnostic instrument for substance abuse patients: The Addiction Severity Index. *Journal of Nervous and Mental Disorders, 168,* 26–33.

Mellor, D., Hucker, A., Waterhouse, M., binti Mamat, N. H., Xu, X., Cochrane, J., & Ricciardelli, L. (2014). A cross-cultural study investigating body features associated with male adolescents' body dissatisfaction in Australia, China, and Malaysia. *American Journal of Men's Health, 8*(6), 521–531. doi:10.1177/1557988314528370

Mendelson, T., Dariotis, J. K., & Agus, D. (2013). Psychosocial strengths and needs of low-income substance abusers in recovery. *Journal of Comparative Psychology, 41*(1), 19–34. doi:10.1002/jcop.21507

Meness, M. M. (2000). The specificity of disrupted processes in families of adult children of alcoholics. *Alcohol and Alcoholism, 35,* 361–367.

Messina, N., Jeter, K., Marinelli-Casey, P., West, K., & Rawson, R. (2014). Children exposed to methamphetamine use and manufacture. *Child Abuse & Neglect, 38*(11), 1872–1883. doi:10.1016/j.chiabu.2006.06.009

Methikalam, B., Wang, K. T., Slaney, R. B., & Yeung, J. G. (2015). Asian values, personal and family perfectionism, and mental health among Asian Indians in the United States. *Asian American Journal of Psychology, 6*(3), 223.

Metlife Mature Market Institute®2 and The Lesbian and Gay Aging Issues Network of the American Society on Aging. (2010). 'Out and aging: The MetLife study of lesbian and gay baby boomers. *Journal of GLBT Family Studies, 6*(1), 40–57.

Miele, G. M. (2007a). Substance abuse treatment entry, retention, and outcome in women: A review of the literature. *Drug and Alcohol Dependence, 86*(1), 1–21.

Milan, S., & Wortel, S. (2015). Family obligation values as a protective and vulnerability factor among low-income adolescent girls. *Journal of Youth and Adolescence, 44*(6), 1183–1193. doi:10.1007/s10964-014-0206-8

Miller, J. C., Meier, E., & Weatherly, J. N. (2009). Assessing the reliability of the gambling functional assessment. *Journal of Gambling Studies, 25,* 121–129.

Miller, W. R. (2003). Enhancing motivation for change. In R. K. Hester & W. R. Miller (Eds.), *Handbook of alcoholism treatment approaches: Effective alternatives* (3rd ed., pp. 131–151). Boston: Allyn & Bacon.

Miller, W. R. & Arkowitz, H. (2015). Learning, applying, and extending Motivational Interviewing. In, H. Arkowitz, W. R. Miller, & S. Rollnick (Eds.), *Motivational Interviewing in the Treatment of Psychological Problems* (2nd ed., pp. 1–32). New York: The Guilford Press.

Miller, W. R., & Hester, R. K. (2003). Treating alcohol problems: Toward an informed eclecticism. In R. K. Hester & W. R. Miller (Eds.), *Handbook of alcoholism treatment approaches: Effective alternatives* (2nd ed., pp. 1–12). Boston: Allyn & Bacon.

Miller, W. R., & Kurtz, E. (1994). Models of alcoholism used in treatment: Contrasting AA and other perspectives with which it is often confused. *Journal of Studies on Alcohol, 55,* 159–166.

Miller, W. R., & Rollnick, S. (2013). *Motivational interviewing: Preparing people for change* (3rd ed.). New York: Guilford Press.

Miller, W. R., Wilbourne, P. L., & Hettema, J. E. (2003). What works?: A summary of alcohol treatment outcome research. In R. K. Hester & W. R. Miller (Eds.), *Handbook of alcoholism treatment approaches: Effective approaches* (3rd ed., pp. 13–63). Boston: Allyn & Bacon.

Milrad, R. (1999). Coaddictive recovery: Early recovery issues for spouse of sex addicts. *Sexual Addiction and Recovery, 6,* 125–136.

Minuchin, S. (1974). *Families and family therapy.* Cambridge, MA: Harvard University Press.

Mojtabai, R. (2005). Use of specialty substance abuse and mental health services in adults with substance abuse use disorder in the community. *Drug and Alcohol Dependence, 78,* 345–354.

Moos, R. H., Brennan, P. L., Schutte, K. K., & Moos, B. S. (2010). Spouses of older adults with late-life drinking problems: Health, family, and social functioning. *Journal of Studies on Alcohol & Drugs, 71*(4), 506–514.

Mueller, M. D., & Wyman, J. R. (1997). Study sheds new light on the state of drug abuse treatment nationwide. *NIDA Notes, 12*, 1, 4–8.

Murphy, E. M., & Kelley, M. L. (2015). Examining the risk for developing alcohol-related problems among adult children of alcoholics. *Drug and Alcohol Dependence, 146*, e47–e48. doi:10.1016/j.drugalcdep.2014.09.500

Myers, L. (2016). Immigration's growing impact on counseling. *Counseling Today, 58*(8), 23–31.

NA World Services. (2014). NA World Services Annual Report. Retrieved February 16, 2016, from http://www.na.org/admin/include/spaw2/uploads/pdf/reports/ar/2014/AR2014_FD.pdf

Nace, E. P. (1987). *The treatment of alcoholism*. New York: Brunner/Mazel.

Nace, E. P. (2005). Alcoholics Anonymous. In J. H. Lowinson, P. Ruiz, R. B. Millman, & J. G. Langrod (Eds.), *Substance abuse: A comprehensive textbook* (4th ed., pp. 587–599). Baltimore: Williams & Wilkins.

Najavits, L. M., Weiss, R. D., & Shaw, S. R. (1997). The link between substance abuse and posttraumatic stress disorder in women. *American Journal on Addictions, 6*, 273–283.

National Alliance for Drug Endangered Children. (2013). *Drug endangered children guide for law enforcement.* Retrieved from: http://ric-doj.zai-inc.com/Publications/cops-p258-pub.pdf

National Center on Addiction and Substance Abuse at Columbia University. (2009). *Shoveling up II: The impact of substance abuse on federal, state, and local budgets.* Retrieved January 5, 2011, from http://www.casacolumbia.org/articlefiles/380-ShovelingUpII.pdf

National Center on Addiction and Substance Abuse at Columbia University. (2010). *Behind bars II: Substance abuse and America's prison population.* Retrieved January 5, 2011, from http://www.casacolumbia.org/templates/PressReleases.aspx?articleid=556&zoneid=85

National Coalition for the Homeless. (2013). Retrieved on August 29, 2016 from http://nationalhomeless.org/about-homelessness/

National Council on Alcohol and Drug Dependence, Inc. (2015, January 22). *Facts about alcohol.* Retrieved from: https://ncadd.org/about-addiction/alcohol/facts-about-alcohol

National Council on Problem Gambling (NCPG). (1997). *Problem and pathological gambling in America: The national picture.* Washington, DC: The Council.

National Council on Problem Gambling. (2009). *About problem gambling.* Retrieved June 17, 2011, from http://www.ncpgambling.org/i4a/pages/Index.cfm?pageID=3315

National Council on Problem Gambling. (2015). *National council on problem gambling: Help and treatment.* Retrieved from http://www.ncpgambling.org/help-treatment/faq/

National Gambling Impact and Policy Study Commission. (1999). *National Gambling Impact Study Commission's final report, June 18, 1999.* Retrieved March 11, 2003, from http://govinfo.library.unt.edu/ngisc/reports/fullrpt.html

National Institute of Allergy and Infectious Diseases. (2009). *Tuberculosis and HIV infection.* Retrieved June 7, 2011, from http://www.niaid.nih.gov/topics/tuberculosis/understanding/pages/tbhiv.aspx

National Institute of Allergy and Infectious Diseases. (2015). *Research on HIV and co-infections.* Retrieved on March 12, 2016 from http://www.niaid.nih.gov/topics/hivaids/research/therapeutics/Pages/co-infections.aspx

National Institute on Alcohol Abuse and Alcoholism. (2007). *Helping patients who drink too much: A clinician's guide* (updated edition). Retrieved January 28, 2016, from http://pubs.niaaa.nih.gov/publications/Practitioner/CliniciansGuide2005/clinicians_guide.htm

National Institute on Alcohol and Alcoholism, (2016). Alcohol facts and statistics. Retrieved on March 22, 2016, from http://pubs.niaaa.nih.gov/publications/AlcoholFacts&Stats/AlcoholFacts&Stats.htm

National Institute on Drug Abuse. (2003). Prevention principles. In *Preventing drug use among children and adolescents.* Retrieved February 17, 2016, from https://www.drugabuse.gov/publications/preventing-drug-abuse-among-children-adolescents-in-brief/prevention-principles

National Institute on Drug Abuse. (2015). *Trends and statistics.* Retrieved July 22, 2015 from http://www.drugabuse.gov/related-topics/trends-statistics

National Institutes of Health. (2011a). *HIV/AIDS: Turning discovery into health.* Retrieved June 7, 2011, from http://www.nih.gov/about/discovery/infectiousdiseases/hiv.htm

National Institutes of Health. (2011b). *Neonatal abstinence syndrome.* Retrieved June 30, 2011, from www.nlm.nih.gov/medlineplus/ency/article/007313.htm

Neff, J. A. (2008). A new multidimensional measure of spirituality-religiosity for use in diverse substance abuse treatment populations. *Journal for the Scientific Study of Religion, 47*(3), 393–409.

Neger, E. N., & Prinz, R. J. (2015) Interventions to address parenting and parental substance abuse: Conceptual and methodological considerations. *Clinical Psychology Review, 39*, 71–82. doi:10.1016/j.cpr.2015.04.004 Old Dominion University, Norfolk, VA. Available online 16 December 2014

Nie, N. H., & Erbing, L. (2000). *Internet and society: A preliminary report.* Palo Alto, CA: Stanford Institute for Quantitative Study of Society.

Nishimura, S. T., Hishinuma, E. S., & Goebert, D. (2013). Underage drinking among Asian American and Pacific Islander adolescents. *Journal of Ethnicity in Substance Abuse, 12*(3), 259–277. doi:10.1080/15332640.2013.805176

Noone, R., & Reddig, R. (1976). Case studies in the family treatment of drug abuse. *Family Process, 15*, 325–332.

Noordenbos, G., & Seubring, A. (2006). Criteria for recovery from eating disorders according to patients and therapists. *Eating Disorders, 14*, 41–54.

Norwood, R. (1985). *Women who love too much: When you keep wishing and hoping he'll change.* New York: Pocket Books.

Nower, N., & Blaszczynski, A. (2008). Recovery in pathological gambling: An imprecise concept. *Substance Use and Misuse, 43*, 1844–1864.

Oates, W. (1971). *Confessions of a workaholic.* New York: World.

O'Brien, C. P., Oster, M., and Morden, E. (Eds.). (2013). *Substance use disorders in the U.S. armed forces.* Washington, DC: The National Academies Press.

O'Farrell, T. J., & Fals-Stewart, W. (2003). Marital and family therapy. In R. K. Hester & W. R. Miller (Eds.), *Handbook of alcoholism treatment approaches: Effective alternatives* (3rd ed., pp. 188–212). Boston: Allyn & Bacon.

O'Farrell, T. J., & Fals-Stewart, W. (2006). *Behavioral couples therapy for alcoholism and drug abuse.* New York: The Guilford Press.

Office of National Drug Control Policy. (2010). National Drug Control Strategy: FY 2011 budget summary. Retrieved February 16, 2016, from https://www.whitehouse.gov/sites/default/files/ondcp/Fact_Sheets/FY2011-Budget-Summary-March-2010.pdf

Office of National Drug Control Policy. (2014). FY 15 Budget and Performance Summary. Retrieved February 16, 2016, from https://www.whitehouse.gov/sites/default/files/ondcp/about-content/fy2015_summary.pdf

O'Hara, R. E., Boynton, M. H., Scott, D. M., Armeli, S., Tennen, H., Williams, C., & Covault, J. (2014). Drinking to cope among African American college students: An assessment of episode-specific motives. *Psychology of Addictive Behaviors, 28*(3), 671–681. doi:10.1037/a0036303

Ogdon, C. L., Carroll, M. D., Kit, B. K., & Flegal, K. M. (2014). Prevalence for childhood and adult obesity in the United States, 2011–2012. *Journal of the American Medical Association, 311*(8), 806–814. doi:10.10001/jama.2014.732.

Ohlms, D. L. (1995). *The disease concept of alcoholism.* Cahokia, IL: GWC.

O'Neill, T. A., Hambley, L. A., & Bercovich, A. (2014). Prediction of cyberslacking when employees are working away from the office. *Computers in Human Behavior, 34*, 291–298. doi:10.1016/j.chb.2014.02.015

Onder, G., Landi, F., Vedova, C., Atkinson, H., Pedone, C., & Bernabei, R. (2002). Moderate alcohol consumption and adverse drug reactions among older adults. *Pharmacoepidemiology and Drug Safety, 11*(5), 385–392. doi:10.1002/pds.721

Orzack, M. H. (2004). *Computer compulsion services.* Retrieved July 24, 2007, from www.computercompulsion.com

Ostermann, J., Sloan, F. A., & Taylor, D. H. (2005). Heavy alcohol use and marital dissolution in the USA. *Social Sciences and Medicine, 61*(11), 2304–2316.

Otten, R., van der Zwaluw, C. S., van der Vorst, H., & Engels, R. C. M. E. (2008). Partner effects and bidirectional parent-child effects in family alcohol use. *European Addiction Research, 14*(2), 106–112.

Owen, B. (2004). Women and imprisonment in the United States: The gendered consequences of the U.S. imprisonment binge. In B. Price & N. Sokoloff (Eds.), *The criminal justice system and women* (2nd ed., pp. 195–206). New York: McGraw-Hill.

Page, D. (2015). Teachers' personal web use at work. *Behaviour & Information Technology, 34*(5), 443–453. doi:10.1080/0144929X.2014.928744

Paglia, A., & Room, R. (1998). *Preventing substance use problems among youth: A literature review and recommendations.* Paper presented at the Alcohol Policy XI Conference, May 10–13, 1998, Chicago.

Palacios, J., & Brodzinski, D. M. (2010). Adoption research: Trends, topics, and outcomes. *International Journal of Behavioral Development, 34*, 270–284. doi:10.1177/0165025410362837

Paltrow, L. M. (2004). The war on drugs and the war on abortion. In B. Price & N. Sokoloff (Eds.), *The criminal justice system and women* (2nd ed., pp. 165–194). New York: McGraw-Hill.

Pargament, K. I. (2006). The meaning of spiritual transformation. In J. D. Koss-Chioino & P. Hefner (Eds.), *Spiritual transformation and healing: Anthropoligical, theological, neuroscientific, and clinical perspectives* (pp. 10–24). Lanham, MD: AltaMira.

Park, S., Anastas, J., Shibusawa, T., & Nguyen, D. (2014). The impact of acculturation and acculturative stress on alcohol use across Asian immigrant subgroups. *Substance Use & Misuse, 49*(8), 922–931. doi:10.3109/10826084.2013.855232

Park, S., & Schepp, K. G. (2015). A systematic review of research on children of alcoholics: Their inherent resilience and vulnerability. *Journal of Child and Family Studies, 24*(5), 1222–1231. doi:10.1007/s10826-014-9930-7

Parker, F. (1980). Sex-role adjustment in women alcoholics. In C. Eddy & J. Ford (Eds.), *Alcoholism in women* (pp. 6–15). Dubuque, IA: Kendall/Hunt.

Parrino, M. W. (2002). Methadone maintenance and other pharmacotherapeutic interventions in the treatment of opioid dependence. *Drug Court Practitioner Fact Sheet, III*, 3.

Patel, A. S., Bowler, M. C., Bowler, J. L., & Methe, S. A. (2012). A meta-analysis of workaholism. *International Journal of Business and Management, 7*, 2–17.

Patterson, T. L., & Jeste, D. V. (1999). The potential impact of the baby boom generation on substance abuse among elderly persons. *Psychiatric Services, 50*, 1184–1188.

Paul, N. (1967). The use of empathy in the resolution of grief. *Perspectives in Biology and Medicine, 2,* 153–169.

Pearson, C. M., Guller, L., McPherson, L., Lejuez, C. W., & Smith, G. T. (2013). Validation of an existing measure of eating disorder risk for use with early adolescents. *Eating Behaviors, 14*(2), 113–118. doi:10.1016/j.eat-beh.2013.01.006

Pedersen, E. R., Hsu, S. H., Neighbors, C., Lee, C. M., & Larimer, M. E. (2013). The relationship between collective self-esteem, acculturation, and alcohol-related consequences among Asian American young adults. *Journal of Ethnicity in Substance Abuse, 12*(1), 51–67.

Pedersen, P. B. (2002). Ethics, competence, and other professional issues in culture-centered counseling. In P. B. Pedersen, J. Draguns, W. Lonner, & J. Trimble (Eds.), *Counseling across cultures* (5th ed., pp. 3–28). Thousand Oaks, CA: Sage.

Pedersen, P. B., Lonner, W. J., Draguns, J. G., Trimble, J. E., & Scharron-del Rio, M. R. (2016). *Counseling across cultures* (7th ed). Los Angeles, CA: Sage.

Peele, S. (1988). On the diseasing of America. *Utne Reader, 30,* 67.

Penn, P. E., Brooke, D., Mosher, C. M., Gallagher, S., Brooks, A. J., & Richey, R. (2013). LGBTQ persons with co-occurring conditions: Perspectives on treatment. *Alcoholism Treatment Quarterly, 31*(4), 466–483. doi:10.1080/07347324.2013.831637

Pereira, A. (2010). HIV/AIDS and discrimination in the workplace: The cook and the surgeon living with HIV. *European Journal of Health Law, 17,* 139–147.

Peters, E. N., Nordeck, C., Zanetti, G., O'Grady, K. E., Serpelloni, G., Rimondo, C., & Schwartz, R. P. (2015). Relationship of gambling with tobacco, alcohol, and illicit drug use among adolescents in the USA: Review of the literature 2000–2014. *American Journal on Addictions, 24*(3), 206–216. doi:10.1111/ajad.12214

Petry, N. M., & Martin, B. (2002). Low-cost contingency management for treating cocaine- and opioid-abusing methadone patients. *Journal of Consulting and Clinical Psychology, 70,* 398–405.

Phoca, S. (1999). Feminism and gender. In S. Gamble (Ed.), *Feminism and postfeminism, 1999* (pp. 55–65). New York: Routledge.

Pienkowski, D. (2014). Classical adlerian assessment of an adult child of an alcoholic: 'Queen of the derelicts'. *The Journal of Individual Psychology, 70*(4), 379–389. doi:10.1353/jip.2014.0030

Pike, K. M., Hoek, H. W., & Dunne, P. E. (2014). Cultural trends and eating disorders. *Current Opinion in Psychiatry, 27*(6), 436–442. doi:10.1097/YCO.0000000000000100

Piran, N. (2015). New possibilities in the prevention of eating disorders: The introduction of positive body image measures. *Body Image, 14,* 146–157. doi:10.1016/j.bod-yim.2015.03.008

Polich, J. M., Armor, D. M., & Braiker, H. B. (1981). *The course of alcoholism: Four years after treatment.* New York: Wiley.

Pope, M. (2012). Native American and gay: Two spirits in one human being. In S. H. Dworkin & M. Pope (Eds.), *Casebook for counseling lesbian, gay, bisexual, and transgendered persons and their families* (pp. 163–172). Alexandria, VA: American Counseling Association.

Pope, R. C., Wallhagen, M., & Davis, H. (2010). The social determinants of substance abuse in African American baby boomers: Effects of family, media images, and environment. *Journal of Transcultural Nursing, 21*(3), 246–256.

Potenza, M. N. (2014). Non-substance addictive behaviors in the context of the DSM-V. *Addictive Behaviors, 39,* 1–2.

Potter-Efron, R. T., & Potter-Efron, P. S. (1989). Assessment of codependency with individuals from alcoholic and chemically dependent families. *Alcohol Treatment Quarterly, 6,* 37–57.

Prendergast, M., Podus, D., Finney, J., Greenwell, L., & Roll, J. (2006). Contingency management for treatment of substance use disorders: A meta-analysis. *Addiction, 101,* 1546–1560.

Primm, B. J. (1992). Future outlook: Treatment improvement. In J. H. Lowinson, P. Ruiz, R. B. Millman, & J. C. Langrod (Eds.), *Substance abuse: A comprehensive textbook* (2nd ed., pp. 612–627). Baltimore: Williams & Wilkins.

Prochaska, J. O., & DiClemente, C. C. (1982). Transtheoretical therapy: Toward a more integrative model of change. *Psychotherapy: Theory, Research, and Practice, 19,* 276–288.

Proehl, R. A. (2007). Social justice, respect, and meaning-making: Keys to working with the homeless elderly population. *Health & Social Work, 32*(4), 304–307.

Project MATCH Research Group (1997). Matching alcoholism treatments to client heterogeneity: Project MATCH posttreatment drinking outcomes. *Journal of Studies on Alcohol, 58,* 7–29.

Pryor, J. (2014). *Stepfamilies: A global perspective on research, policy, and practice.* New York: Routledge.

Quirk, D. E., Hodgen, C., Springhorn, D., Howell, G. E., & Daus, L. J. (2010). *Gambling patient placement criteria (GPPC): A guide to placing problem gamblers at the optimum level of care.* Reno: Institute for the Study of Gambling & Commercial Gaming, College of Business, University of Nevada, Reno.

Race, K. D. (2003). Revaluation of risk among gay men. *AIDS Education and Prevention, 15*(4), 369–381.

Rawson, R., Shoptaw, S., Obert, J. L., McCann, M., Hasson, A., Marinelli-Casey, P., . . . Brethen, P. R. (1995). An intensive outpatient approach for cocaine abuse: The Matrix Model. *Journal of Substance Abuse Treatment, 12,* 117–127.

Reas, D. L., & Stedal, K. (2015). Eating disorders in men aged midlife and beyond. *Maturitas, 81*(2), 248–255. doi:10.1016/j.maturitas.2015.03.004

Reczek, C., Liu, H., & Spiker, R. A. (2014). A population-based study of alcohol use in same-sex and different-sex unions. *Journal of Marriage and Family, 76*(3), 557–572. doi:10.1111/jomf.12113

Reilly, D. M. (1992). Drug-abusing families: Intrafamilial dynamics and brief triphasic treatment. In E. Kaufman & P. Kaufman (Eds.), *Family theory of drug and alcohol abuse* (pp. 105–119). Boston: Allyn & Bacon.

Reynaud, M., Karila, L., Blecha, L., & Benyamina, A. (2010). Is love passion an addictive disorder? *American Journal of Drug and Alcohol Abuse, 36*(5), 261–267.

Rhodes, T., Bernays, S., & Houmoller, K. (2010). Parents who use drugs: Accounting for damage and its limitation. *Social Science & Medicine, 71*(8), 1489–1497.

Rice, J. (1992). Discursive formation, life stories, and the emergence of codependency: Power/knowledge and the search for identity. *Sociological Quarterly, 33,* 337–364.

Richardson, J. J., Johnson, W. J., & St. Vil, C. (2014). I want him locked up: Social capital, African American parenting strategies, and the juvenile court. *Journal of Contemporary Ethnography, 43*(4), 488–522. doi:10.1177/0891241613520453

Robbins, T. W. & Clark, L. (2015). Behavioral addictions. *Current Opinion in Neurobiology, 30,* 66–72.

Robinson, B. (2000). Chained to the desk. *Family Therapy Networker, 24*(4), 26–33.

Robinson, B. E. (1999). The Work Addiction Risk Test: Development of a tentative measure of workaholism. *Perceptual and Motor Skills, 88,* 199–210.

Robinson, B. E. (2013). *Chained to the desk: A guide book for workaholics, their partners and children, and the clinicians who treat them* (3rd ed.). New York: New York University Press.

Robinson, T. N., & Killen, J. D. (2001). Obesity prevention for children. In J. K. Thompson & L. Smolak (Eds.), *Body image, eating disorders, and obesity in youth* (pp. 237–260). Washington, DC: American Psychological Association.

Rohleder, P. (2010). Educators' ambivalence and managing anxiety in providing sex education for people with learning disabilities. *Psychodynamic Practice, 16*(2), 165–182.

Room, R. (2005). Multicultural contexts and alcohol and drug use as symbolic behavior. *Addiction Research and Theory, 13*(4), 321–331.

Room, R., & Mäkelä, K. (2000). Typologies of the cultural position of drinking. *Journal of Studies on Alcohol, 61,* 475–483.

Roozen, H. G., Boulogne, J. J., van Tulder, M. W., van den Brink, W., De Jong, C. A. J., & Kerkhof, A. J. F. M. (2004). A systematic review of the effectiveness of the community reinforcement approach in alcohol, cocaine and opioid addiction. *Drug and Alcohol Dependence, 74,* 1–13.

Rosenberg, K. P., Carnes, P., & O'Connor, S. (2014). Evaluation and treatment of sex addiction. *Journal of Sex & Marital Therapy, 40*(2), 77–91. doi:10.1080/00926 23X.2012.701268

Rowan, N. L., & Faul, A. C. (2011). Gay, lesbian, bisexual, and transgendered people and chemical dependency: Exploring successful treatment. *Journal of Gay & Lesbian Social Services, 23*(1), 107–130.

Rowe, C. L., La Greca, A. M., & Alexandersson, A. (2010). Family and individual factors associated with substance abuse involvement and PTS symptoms among adolescents in Greater New Orleans after Hurricane Katrina. *Journal of Consulting and Clinical Psychology, 78*(6), 806–817.

Royce, J. E. (1989). *Alcohol problems and alcoholism: A comprehensive survey* (Rev. ed.). New York: Free Press.

Rusnáková, M. (2014). Codependency of the members of a family of an alcohol addict. *Social and Behavioral Sciences, 132,* 647–653. doi:10.1016/j.sbspro.2014.04.367

Rutherford, K., McIntyre, J., Daley, A., & Ross, L. E. (2012). Development of expertise in mental health service provision for lesbian, gay, bisexual and transgender communities. *Medical Education, 46*(9), 903–913. doi:10.1111/j.13652923.2012.04272.x

Ryan, S. M., Jorm, A. F., & Lubman, D. I. (2010). Parenting factors associated with reduced adolescent alcohol use: A systematic review of the longitudinal studies. *Australian and New Zealand Journal of Psychiatry, 44*(9), 774–783.

Sanders, M. (2002). The response of African American communities to alcohol and other drug problems: An opportunity for treatment providers. *Alcoholism Treatment Quarterly, 20*(3–4), 167–173.

Sass, D. A., & Henderson, D. B. (2007). Psychologists' self-reported adoption knowledge and the need for more adoption education. In R. A. Javier, A. L. Baden, F. A. Biafora, & A. Camacho-Gingerich (Eds.), *Handbook of adoption: Implications for researchers, practitioners, and families* (pp. 312–322). Thousand Oaks, CA: Sage Publications.

Satir, V. M. (1964). *Conjoint family therapy: A guide to theory and technique.* Palo Alto, CA: Science and Behavioral Books.

Schaef, A. W. (1987). *When society becomes addict.* San Francisco: Harper & Row.

Schroeder, D. S., Laflin, M. T., & Weis, D. L. (1993). Is there a relationship between self-esteem and drug use? Methodological and statistical limitations of the research. *Journal of Drug Issues, 23,* 645–665.

Schuck, A. M., & Spatz, W. C. (2003). Childhood victimization and alcohol symptoms in women: An examination of protective factors. *Journal of Studies on Alcohol, 64,* 247–257.

Schultz, E. (1994). If you use firm's counselors, remember your secrets could be used against you. *Wall Street Journal,* May 26, C2.

Schwitzer, A. M., & Choate, L. H. (2015). College women eating disorder diagnostic profile and DSM-V. *Journal of*

American College Health, 63(1), 73–78. doi:10.1080/07448481.2014.963110

Sehm, M., & Warschburger, P. (2015). The specificity of psychological factors associated with binge eating in adolescent boys and girls. *Journal of Abnormal Child Psychology, 43*(8), 1563–1571. doi:10.1007/s10802-015-0026-7

Seigel, B., & Davis, B. (2013). Health and mental health needs of children in U. S. military families. *Pediatrics, 131*, 2002–2015. doi:10.1542/peds.2013-0940

Selwyn, P. A. (1992). Medical aspects of human immunodeficiency virus infection and its treatment in injecting drug users. In J. H. Lowinson, P. Ruiz, R. B. Millman, & J. G. Langrod (Eds.), *Substance abuse: A comprehensive textbook* (2nd ed., pp. 744–774). Baltimore: Williams & Wilkins.

Selzer, M. L. (1971). The Michigan Alcohol Screening Test: The quest for a new diagnostic instrument. *American Journal of Psychiatry, 127*, 1653–1658.

Senreich, E. (2009). A comparison of perceptions, reported abstinence, and completion rates of gay, lesbian, and heterosexual clients in substance abuse treatment. *Journal of Gay & Lesbian Mental Health, 13*, 145–169.

Senreich, E. (2010). Are specialized LGBT program components helpful for gay and bisexual men in substance abuse treatment? *Journal of Gay and Lesbian Social Services, 45*, 1077–1096.

Serovich, J. (2001). A test of two disclosure theories. *AIDS Education and Prevention, 13*, 355–364.

Sheppard, S., Malatras, J., & Israel, A. (2010). The impact of deployment on U. S. military families. *American Psychologist, 65*(6), 599–609. doi:10.1037/a0020332

Sher, K. (1991). *Children of alcoholics: A critical appraisal of theory and research.* Chicago: University of Chicago Press.

Shon, S. P., & Ja, D. Y. (1982). Asian families. In M. McGoldrick, J. Pierce, & J. Giordano (Eds.), *Ethnicity and family therapy* (pp. 208–228). New York: Guilford Press.

Sideman, L. M., & Kirschbaum, E. (2002). The road to recovery: A gender-responsive program for convicted DUI females. *Corrections Today, 64*, 84–89.

Sim, L. A., McAlpine, D. W., Grothe, K. B., Himes, S. M., Cockerill, R. G., & Clark, M. M. (2010). Identification and treatment of eating disorders in the primary care setting. *Mayo Clinic Proceedings, 85*(8), 746–751.

Simpson, D. D., Joe, G. W., & Broome, K. M. (2002). A national 5-year follow-up of treatment outcomes for cocaine dependence. *Archives of General Psychiatry, 59*, 538–544.

Skinner, H. A. (1982). The drug abuse screening test. *Addictive Behaviors, 7*, 363–371.

Slomkowski, C., Conger, K. J., Rende, R., Heylen, E., Little, W. M., Shebloski . . . Conger, R. D. (2009). Sibling contagion for drinking in adolescence: A micro process framework. *European Journal of Developmental Science, 3*(2), 161–173.

Small, J., Curran, G. M., & Booth, B. (2010). Barriers and facilitators for alcohol treatment for women: Are there more or less for rural women? *Journal of Substance Abuse Treatment, 39*(1), 1–13.

SMART Recovery. (2016). SMART Recovery: Self-management and recovery training. Retrieved February 16, 2016, from http://www.smartrecovery.org/

Smedema, S. M., & Ebener, D. (2010). Substance abuse and psychosocial adaptation to physical disability: Analysis of the literature and future directions. *Disability and Rehabilitation: An International, Multidisciplinary Journal, 32*(16), 1311–1319. doi:10.3109/09638280903514721

Smith, D. C., Davis, J. P., Ureche, D. J., & Dumas, T. M. (2016). Six month outcomes of a peer-enhanced community reinforcement approach for emerging adults with substance misuse: A preliminary study. *Journal of Substance Abuse Treatment, 61*, 66–73. doi:10.1016/j.jsat.2015.09.002

Smith, W. W., Thomas, J., Liu, J., Li, T., & Moran, T. H. (2014). From fat fruit fly to human obesity. *Physiology & Behavior, 13*, 615–621. doi:10.1016/j.physbeh.2014.01.017

Sobell, L. C., Cunningham, J. A., & Sobell, M. B. (1996). Recovery from alcohol problems with and without treatment: Prevalence in two population surveys. *American Journal of Public Health, 86*, 966–972.

Sobell, L. C., & Sobell, M. B. (1973). A self-feedback technique to monitor drinking behavior in alcoholics. *Behavior Research and Therapy, 11*, 237–238.

Sobell, L. C., Sobell, M. B., & Toneatto, T. (1991). Recovery from alcohol problems without treatment. In N. Heather, W. R., Miller, & J. Greeley (Eds.), *Self-control and addictive behaviors* (pp. 198–242). New York: Pergamon Press.

Sories, F., Maier, C., Beer, A., & Thomas, V. (2015). Addressing the needs of military children through family-based play therapy. *Contemporary Family Therapy: An International Journal, 37*(3), 209–220. doi:10.1007/s10591-015-9342-x

Spada, M. (2014). An overview of problematic internet use. *Addictive Behaviors, 39*(1), 3–6. doi:10.1016/j.addbeh.2013.09.007

Spear, S. E., Crevecoeur-MacPhail, D., Denering, L., Dickerson, D., & Brecht, M. (2013). Determinants of successful treatment outcomes among a sample of urban American Indians/Alaska Natives: The role of social environments. *The Journal of Behavioral Health Services & Research, 40*(3), 330–341. doi:10.1007/s11414-013-9324-4

Spence, J. T., & Robbins, A. (1992). Workaholism: Defintion, measurement, and preliminary results. *Journal of Personality Assessment, 58*(1), 160–179.

Spielmans, G. I., Benish, S. G., Marin, C., Bowman, W. M., Menster, M., & Wheeler, A. J. (2013). Specificity of psychological treatments for bulimia nervosa and binge eating disorder? A meta-analysis of direct comparisons. *Clinical Psychology Review, 33*(3), 460–469.

Springer, C. A., & Lease, S. H. (2000). The impact of multiple-AIDS related bereavement in the gay male population. *Journal of Counseling and Development, 78*(3), 297–305.

Stampp, K. (1956). *The peculiar institution: Slavery in the ante-bellum South.* New York: Knopf.

Stanley, L. R., Harness, S. D., Swaim, R. C., & Beauvais, F. (2014). Rates of substance use of American Indian students in 8th, 10th, and 12th grades living on or near reservations: Update, 2009–2012. *Public Health Reports, 129*(2), 156–163. Retrieved from http://www.ncbi.nlm.nih.gov/pmc/articles/PMC3904895/?tool=pmcentrez

Statistics Brain Research Institute. (2015). Online dating statistics. Retrieved on January 5, 2016, from http://www.statisticbrain.com/onlin-dating-statistics/[MMl]

Sterne, M., & Pittman, D. J. (1972). *Drinking practices in the ghetto.* St. Louis, MO: Washington University, Social Science Institute.

Sterne, M. W. (1967). Drinking patterns and alcoholism among American Negroes. In D. J. Pittman (Ed.), *Alcoholism* (pp. 66–98). New York: Harper & Row.

Stevens, E. P. (1973). Marianismo: The other face of machismo in Latin America. In A. Pescatello (Ed.), *Female and male in Latin America: Essays* (pp. 89–102). Pittsburgh, PA: University of Pittsburgh Press.

Stewart, S. D. (2010). The characteristics and well-being of adopted stepchildren. *Family Relations, 59*(5), 558–571.

Stitzer, M. (2006). Contingency management and the addictions. *Addiction, 101*, 1536–1537.

Stoltzfus, K. M. (2007). Spiritual interventions in substance abuse treatment and prevention: A review of the literature. *Journal of Religion & Spirituality in Social Work, 26*(4), 49–69.

Strauch, M., & Strauch, I. (2010). Using current-day reconstructions in the treatment of eating disorder. *Journal of Individual Psychology, 66*(4), 356–365.

Stuart, G. L., O'Farrell, T. J., & Temple, J. R. (2009). Violence, intimate partner and substance abuse treatment. In G. L. Fisher & N. A. Roget (Eds.), *Encyclopedia of substance abuse prevention, treatment, and recovery* (pp. 990–993). Los Angeles: Sage.

Stukin, S. (2003). Health, hope and HIV. *Yoga Journal.* Retrieved April 4, 2003, from www.yogajournal.com/health/581.cfm

Substance Abuse and Mental Health Services Administration and Department of Veterans Affairs. (2003). *Self-help organizations for alcohol and drug problems: Towards evidence-based practice and policy.* Workgroup on substance abuse self-help organizations. (February 2003 Technical Report).

Substance Abuse and Mental Health Services Administration. (2009). *Guiding principles and elements of recovery-oriented systems of care: What do we know from research?* Retrieved February 3, 2016, from http://www.viahope.org/assets/uploads/SAMHSA_guiding_principles_Whitepaper.pdf

Substance Abuse and Mental Health Services Administration, Center for Behavioral Health Statistics and Quality. (2012). *Treatment episode data set (TEDS): 2000–2010. National admissions to substance abuse treatment services.* (DASIS Series S-61, HHS Publication No. (SMA) 12-4701). Retrieved from Substance Abuse and Mental Health Services Administration website: http://www.samhsa.gov/data/sites/default/files/WebTEDSNational2010/TEDS2010NWeb.pdf

Substance Abuse and Mental Health Services Administration (2013). *Drug Abuse Warning Network, 2011: National Estimates of Drug-Related Emergency Department Visits.* HHS Publication No. (SMA) 13-4760, DAWN Series D-39. Rockville, MD: Substance Abuse and Mental Health Services Administration.

Substance Abuse and Mental Health Services Administration. (2014). *Treatment episode data set (TEDS): 2002–2012. National admissions to substance abuse treatment services.* (BHSIS series S-71, HHS publication no. (SMA) 14-4850). Retrieved from Substance Abuse and Mental Health Services Administration website: http://www.samhsa.gov/data/sites/default/files/TEDS2012N_Web.pdf

Substance Abuse and Mental Health Services Administration (2014a). *Veterans and military families.* Retrieved January 13, 2016 from http://www.samhsa.gov/veterans-military-families

Substance Abuse and Mental Health Services Administration. (2014b). *Treatment episode data set (TEDS) 2002-2012: National admissions to substance abuse treatment services.* Retrieved February 3, 2016, from http://www.samhsa.gov/data/sites/default/files/2002_2012_TEDS_National/2002_2012_Treatment_Episode_Data_Set_National_Tables.htm#Tbl1.1a

Substance Abuse and Mental Health Services Administration. (2014c). *National survey of substance abuse treatment services (N-SSATS): 2013 data on substance abuse treatment facilities.* Retrieved February 3, 2016, from http://www.samhsa.gov/data/sites/default/files/2013_N-SSATS_National_Survey_of_Substance_Abuse_Treatment_Services/2013_N-SSATS_National_Survey_of_Substance_Abuse_Treatment_Services_Tables.html

Substance Abuse and Mental Health Services Administration. (2015a). *Fetal alcohol spectrum disorders among Native Americans.* Retrieved on March 22, 2016, from http://fasdcenter.samhsa.gov/documents/WYNK_Native_American_Teal.pdf

Substance Abuse and Mental Health Services Administration. (2015b). *About FASD.* Retrieved on March 22, 2016, from http://www.fasdcenter.samhsa.gov/aboutUs/aboutFASD.aspx#2

Substance Abuse and Mental Health Services Administration. (2015c). *Results from the 2013 National Survey on Drug*

Use and Health: Detailed Tables. Retrieved July 21, 2015, from http://www.samhsa.gov/data/sites/default/files/NSDUH-DetTabs2013/NSDUH-DetTabs2013.htm

Substance Abuse and Mental Health Services Administration. (2015d). *Behavioral health barometer United States, 2015.* Retrieved February 3, 2016, from http://www.samhsa.gov/data/sites/default/files/2015_National_Barometer.pdf

Substance Abuse and Mental Health Services Administration (2016a). *Co-occurring disorders.* Retrieved September 1, 2016, from http://www.samhsa.gov/disorders/co-occurring.

Substance Abuse and Mental Health Services Administration. (2016b). *NREPP: SAMHSA's national registry of evidence-based programs and practices.* Retrieved February 17, 2016, from http://www.samhsa.gov/nrepp.

Sullivan, B. (2004). *Porn at work problem persists.* Retrieved August 3, 2007, from www.msnbc.msn.com/id/5899345

Sunshine, R. M., & Starks, B. M. (2010). Racial/ethnic differences in religiosity and drug use. *Journal of Drug Issues, 40*(2), 729–753.

Sussman, S., Lisha, N., & Griffiths, M. (2011). Prevalence of the addictions: A problem of the majority or the minority? *Evaluation & the Health Professions, 34*(1), 3–56.

Sussman, S., & Moran, M. B. (2013). Hidden addiction: Television. *Journal of Behavioral Addictions, 2*(3), 125–132.

Sutton, C. T., & Broken Nose, M. A. (2005). American Indian families. In M. McGoldrick, J. Giodano, & N. Garcia-Preto (Eds.), *Ethnicity and family therapy* (pp. 43–54), New York: Guilford Press.

Szalavitz, M. (2015). Genetics: No more addictive personality. *Nature, 522,* S48–S49.

Szapocznik, J., & Kurtines, W. M. (1989). *Breakthroughs in family therapy with drug-abusing and problem youth.* New York: Springer.

Taggart, L., McLaughlin, D., Quinn, B., & McFarlane, C. (2007). Listening to people with intellectual disabilities who misuse alcohol and drugs. *Health and Social Care in the Community, 15*(4), 360–368.

Taleff, M. J., & Babcock, M. (1998). Hidden themes: Dominant discourse in the alcohol and other field. *International Journal of Drug Policy, 9,* 33–41.

Tao, R., Huang, X., Wang, J., Zhang, H., Zhang, Y., & Li, M. (2010). Proposed diagnostic criteria for Internet addiction. *Addiction, 105,* 556–564.

Taylor, O. D. (2010). Barriers to treatment for women with substance abuse disorders. *Journal of Human Behavior in the Social Environment, 20*(3), 393–409.

Teen Challenge. (2016). *Teen Challenge USA.* Retrieved February 4, 2016, from http://www.teenchallengeusa.com/

Thai, N. D., Connell, C. M., & Tebes, J. K. (2010). Substance use among Asian American adolescents: Influence of race, ethnicity, and acculturation in the context of key risk and protective factors. *Asian American Journal of Psychology, 1*(4), 261–274.

Thurang, A., & Tops, A.B. (2013). Living an unstable everyday life while attempting to perform normality-The meaning of living as an alcohol-dependent woman. *Journal of Clinical Nursing, 22*(3–4), 423–432. doi: 10.1111/j.1365-2702.2012.04293.x

Tobler, N. S. (1986). Meta-analysis of 143 adolescent drug prevention programs: Quantitative outcome results of program participants compared to a control or comparison group. *Journal of Drug Issues, 16,* 537–567.

Tobler, N. S. (1992). Drug prevention programs can work: Research findings. *Journal of Addictive Diseases, 11,* 1–28.

Tobler, N. S., & Stratton, H. H. (1997). Effectiveness of school-based drug prevention programs: A meta-analysis of the research. *Journal of Primary Prevention, 18,* 71–128.

Torres, S. (1993). Cultural sensitivity: A must for today's primary care provider. *Advance for Nurse Practitioners, 1,* 16–18.

Toyokawa, N., & Toyokawa, T. (2013). The construct invariance of family values in Asian and Hispanic immigrant adolescents: An exploratory study. *Asian American Journal of Psychology, 4*(2), 116–125. doi:10.1037/a0029170

Tracy, E. M., Min, M. O., Park, H., Jun, M., Brown, S., & Francis, M. W. (2016). Personal network structure and substance use in women by 12 months post treatment intake. *Journal of Substance Abuse Treatment, 62,* 55–61. doi:10.1016/j.jsat.2015.11.002

Trenz, R. C., Dunne, E. M., Zur, J., & Latimer, W. W. (2015). An investigation of school-related variables as risk and protective factors associated with problematic substance use among vulnerable urban adolescents. *Vulnerable Children and Youth Studies, 10*(2), 131–140. doi:10.1080/17450128.2015.1029034

Tripodi, C. (2006). Long term treatment of partners of sex addicts: A multi-phase approach. *Sexual Addiction and Compulsivity, 13*(2/3), 269–288.

Trocki, K. F., Drabble, L. A., & Midanik, L. T. (2009). Tobacco, marijuana, and sensation seeking: Comparisons across gay, lesbian, bisexual, and heterosexual groups. *Psychology of Addictive Behaviors, 23,* 620–631.

Tse, S., Hong, S. I., Wang, C. W., & Cunningham-Williams, R. M. (2012). Gambling behavior and problems among older adults: A systematic review of empirical studies. *The Journals of Gerontology Series B: Psychological Sciences and Social Sciences, 67*(5), 639–652.

Tuchfield, B. S. (1981). Spontaneous remission in alcoholics: Empirical observations and theoretical implications. *Journal of Studies on Alcohol, 42,* 626–640.

Turner, M. (2009). Uncovering and treating sex addiction in couples therapy. *Journal of Family Psychotherapy, 20,* 283–302.

Turner-Bowker, D., & Hamilton, W. L. (2000). *Cigarette advertising expenditures before and after the master settlement agreement: Preliminary findings.* Massachusetts

Department of Public Health and Abt Associates, Inc. Available from Cesar Fax, Volume 9, Issue 26.

Ullman, S. E., Najdowski, C. J., & Adams, E. B. (2012). Women, Alcoholics Anonymous, and related mutual aid groups: Review and recommendations for research. *Alcoholism Treatment Quarterly, 30*(4), 443–486. doi: 10.1080/07347324.2012.718969

UNAIDS, (2012). *Infographic: Every minute, a young woman is newly infected with HIV.* Retrieved on March 12, 2016 from http://www.unaids.org/en/resources/infographics/20 120608gendereveryminute

U.S. Census Bureau. (2010). State and County Quickfacts. Retrieved February 14, 2011, from http://quickfacts.census.gov/qfd/states/00000.html

U.S. Census Bureau (2011). State and Country Quickfacts. Retrieved February 14, 2011, from http://quickfacts.census.gov/qfd/states/00000.html

U.S. Department of Health and Human Services. (2007). Eating away at health. Retrieved on July 5, 2007 from www.nimh.nih.gov/publicat/eatingdisorders.cfm? textSize=L

U.S. Department of Health and Human Services. (2010). National Survey on Drug Use and Health. Retrieved June 7, 2011, from http://www.oas.samhsa.gov/2k10/182/AmericanIndian.htm

U.S. Department of Justice, National Intelligence Center. (2015). National drug threat assessment 2015. Retrieved February 16, 2016, from http://www.dea.gov/docs/2015%20NDTA%20Report.pdf

U.S. Department of Labor, Office of Disability Employment Policy. (2011). Frequently asked questions. Retrieved March 18, 2011, from http://www.dol.gov/odep/faqs/people.htm

USA.gov. (2011). Lottery results. Retrieved June 17, 2011, from http://www.usa.gov/Topics/Lottery_Results.shtml

Vaillant, G. E. (1983). *The natural history of alcoholism.* Cambridge, MA: Harvard University Press.

Van Damme, J., Maes, L., Kuntsche, E., Crutzen, R., De Clercq, B., Van Lippevelde, W., & Hublet, A. (2015). The influence of parental drinking on offspring's drinking motives and drinking: A mediation analysis on 9 year follow-up data. *Drug and Alcohol Dependence, 149,* 63–70. doi:10.1016/j.drugalcdep.2015.01.020

Vandermause, R., & Wood, M. (2009). See my suffering: Women with alcohol use disorders and their primary care experiences. *Issues in Mental Health Nursing, 30*(12), 728–735.

van der Walde, H., Urgensen, F. T., Weltz, S. H., & Hanna, F. J. (2002). Women and alcoholism: A biosocial perspective and treatment approaches. *Journal of Counseling and Development, 80,* 145–153.

Van der Zee, K., & van Oudenhoven, P. (2013). The role of personality as a determinant of intercultural competence. *Journal of Cross-Cultural Psychology, 44*(6), 928-940. doi:10.1177/0022022113493138

Van Rooij, A. J., & Prause, N. (2014). A critical review of "Internet addiction" criteria with suggestions for the future. *Journal of Behavioral Addictions, 3*(4), 203–213. http://doi.org/10.1556/JBA.3.2014.4.1

Vasquez, M. J. T. (2009). Latino/a culture and substance abuse. *Journal of Ethnicity in Substance Abuse, 8*(3), 301–313.

Vaughan, E. L., Gassman, R. A., Jun, M. C., & de Martinez, B. S. (2015). Gender differences in risk and protective factors for alcohol use and substance use problems among Hispanic adolescents. *Journal of Child & Adolescent Substance Abuse, 24*(5), 243–254. doi:10.1080/10678 28X.2013.826609

Vazsonyi, A. T., Trejos-Castillo, E., & Young, M. A. (2008). Rural and non-rural African American youth: Does context matter in the etiology of problem behaviors? *Journal of Youth Adolescence, 37,* 798–811.

Vega, W. A., Canino, G., Cao, Z., & Alegria, M. (2009). Prevalence and correlates of dual diagnoses in U.S. Latinos. *Drug and Alcohol Dependence, 100*(1–2), 32–38.

Vega, W. A., & Sribney, W. (2011). Understanding the Hispanic health paradox through a multi-generation lens: A focus on behaviour disorders. In G. Carlo, L. J. Crockett, & M. A. Carranza (Eds.), *Health disparities in youth and families: Research and applications* (pp. 151–168). New York, NY: Springer.

Velezmoro, R., Lacefield, K., & Roberti, J. W. (2010). Perceived stress, sensation seeking, and college students' abuse of the Internet. *Computers in Human Behavior, 26*(6), 1526–1530.

Vernig, P. M. (2011). Family roles in homes with alcohol-dependent parents: An evidence-based review. *Substance Use and Misuse, 46*(4), 535–542.

Villella, C., Martinotti, G., & Di Nicola, M. (2010). Behavioural addictions in adolescents and young adults: Results from a prevalence study. *Journal of Gambling Studies, 27,* 203–214.

Waldron, H. B., & Turner, C. W. (2008). Evidence-based psychosocial treatments for adolescent substance abuse. *Journal of Clinical Child & Adolescent Psychology, 37,* 238–261.

Waldron, M., Grant, J. D., Bucholz, K. K., Lynskey, M. T., Slutske, W. S., Glowinski, A. L., Henders, A., Statham, D. J., Martin, N. G., & Heath, A. C. (2014b). Parental separation and early substance involvement: Results from children of alcoholic and cannabis dependent twins. *Drug and Alcohol Dependence, 134,* 78–84. doi:10.1016/j.drugalcdep.2013.09.010

Waldron, M., Vaughan, E. L., Bucholz, K. K., Lynskey, M. T., Sartor, C. E., Duncan, A. E., & Heath, A. C. (2014a). Risks for early substance involvement associated with parental alcoholism and parental separation in an adolescent female cohort. *Drug and Alcohol Dependence, 138,* 130–136. doi:10.1016/j.drugalcdep.2014.02.020

Wang, K. T. l, Yuen, M., & Slaney, R. B. (2009). Perfectionism, depression, loneliness, and life satisfaction: A study of high school students in Hong Kong. *The Counseling Psychologist, 37*(2), 248–274.

Wang, Y., & Andrade, L. H. (2013). Epidemiology of alcohol and drug use in the elderly. *Current Opinion in Psychiatry, 26*(4), 343–348. doi:10.1097/YCO. 0b013e328360eafd

Wang, Y. L., Wang, J., P., & Fu, D. D. (2008). Epidemiological investigation on Internet addiction among Internet users in elementary and middle school students. *Chinese Mental Health Journal, 22*, 678–682.

Washington, T., Gleeson, J. P., & Rulison, K. L. (2013). Competence and African American children in informal kinship care: The role of family. *Children and Youth Services Review, 35*(9), 1305–1312. doi:10.1016/ j.childyouth.2013.05.011

Waskul, D. D. (2004). *Net.seXXX: Readings on sex, pornography, and the Internet*. New York: Peter Lang.

Watt, T. T. (2002). Marital cohabiting relationships of adult children of alcoholics. *Journal of Family Issues, 23*(2), 246–265.

Wegscheider, S. (1989). *Another chance: Hope and health for the alcoholic family* (2nd ed.). Palo Alto, CA: Science and Behavior Books.

Weibe, J. M. D., & Cox, B. J. (2005). Problem and probable pathological gambling in older adults assessed by the SOGS-R. *Journal of Gambling Studies, 21*(1), 205–221.

Weichold, K., Wiesner, M. F., & Silbereisen, R. K. (2014). Childhood predictors and mid-adolescent correlates of developmental trajectories of alcohol use among male and female youth. *Journal of Youth and Adolescence, 43*(5), 698–716. doi:10.1007/s10964-013-0014-6

Weinstein, A. (2014). Sexual addiction or hypersexual disorder: Clinical implications for assessment and treatment. *Directions in Psychiatry, 34*(3), 185–195.

Weir, K. N., & Brodzinski, D. M. (2013). Treatment and therapy considerations for adopted children and their families. *Adoption Quarterly, 16*(3–4), 153–155. doi: 10.1080/ 10926755.2013.843926

West, S. L., & Graham, C. W. (2006). Assessing parental alcoholism. *Alcoholism Treatment Quarterly, 24*(3), 93–107.

West, S. L., Graham, C. W., & Cifu, D. X. (2009). Rates of alcohol/other drug treatment denials to persons with physical disabilities: Accessibility concerns. *Alcoholism Treatment Quarterly, 27*(3), 305–316.

Westermeyer, J. (1999). The role of cultural and social factors in the cause of addictive disorders. *Psychiatric Clinics of North America, 22*, 253–271.

Westermeyer, J. O. (1991). Cultural perspectives: Native Americans, Asians and new immigrants. In J. H. Lowinson, P. Ruiz, R. B. Millman, & J. G. Langrod (Eds.), *Substance abuse: A comprehensive textbook* (2nd ed., pp. 890–896). Baltimore: Williams & Wilkins.

Westermeyer, J., & Baker, J. M. (1986). Alcoholism and the American Indian. In N. J. Estes and M. E. Heinemann (Eds.), *Alcoholism: Development, consequences, and interventions* (pp. 273–282). St. Louis, MO: Mosby.

Westermeyer, J., Bennett, L., Thuras, P., & Yoon, G., (2007). Substance use disorder among adoptees: A clinical comparative study. *American Journal of Drug and Alcohol Abuse, 33*, 455–466.

Westermeyer, J., Yargic, I., & Thuras, P. (2004). Michigan Assessment-Screening Test for Alcohol and Drugs (MAST/AD): Evaluation in a clinical sample. *American Journal on Addictions, 13*, 151–162.

Westphal, J. R. (2006). The evidence base supporting the subtyping of gamblers in treatment. *International Journal of Mental Health and Addiction, 5*(2), 127–140.

Whitaker, C. L. (1991). *Co-dependence: Healing the human condition: The new paradigm for helping professionals and people in recovery*. Deerfield Beach, FL: Health Communications.

White Bison Inc. (2002). *The red road to Wellbriety in the Native American way*. Colorado Springs, CO: White Bison Inc.

White Bison, Inc. (Producer). (2007). *Medicine wheel and 12 steps for men, medicine wheel and 12 steps for women* [video sets, workbooks, facilitator's manuals]. Available from www.whitebison.org/wellbriety-training/medicine-wheel-12-steps-program.php

White, W. (2002). *Recovery as a heroic journey*. Retrieved February 9, 2016, from http://www.williamwhitepapers. com/pr/2002RecoveryasaHeroicJourney.pdf

White, W. L. (1998). *Slaying the dragon: The history of addiction treatment and recovery in America*. Section 5: A.A. and the modern alcoholism movement (pp 127–198). Bloomington, IL: Chestnut Health Systems/Lighthouse Institute.

Whiteman, S. D., Bernard, J. M. B., & McHale, S. M. (2010). The nature and correlates of sibling influence in two-parent African American families. *Journal of Marriage and Family, 72*(2), 267–281. Retrieved from http://search.proquest.com. unr.idm.oclc.org/docview/325119488?accountid=452

Whitfield, C. L. (1984). *Alcoholism, other drug problems and spirituality: A transpersonal approach*. Baltimore: Resource Group.

Wiechelt, S. A. & Straussner, S. L. (2015). Introduction to the special issue: Examining the relationship between trauma and addiction. *Journal of Social Work Practice, 15*, 1–5.

Wilens, T. E., Faraone, S. V., Biederman, J., & Gunawardene, S. (2003). Does stimulant therapy of attention-deficit/ hyperactivity disorder beget later substance abuse? A meta-analytic review of the literature. *Pediatrics, 111*, 179–185.

Williams, C. N. (1990). Prevention and treatment approaches for children of alcoholics. In M. Windle & J. S. Searles (Eds.), *Children of alcoholics. Critical perspectives* (pp. 187–216). New York: Guilford Press.

Williams, C. N., & Collins, E. W. (1986). The connection between alcoholism, child maltreatment, and family disruption. In S. H. Lease & B. J. Yanico (1995), Evidence of validity for the children of alcoholics screening test. *Measurement and Evaluation in Counseling and Development, 27*(4), 200–210.

Wilsnack, S. C., Wilsnack, R. W., & Kantor, L. W. (2013). Focus on: Women and the costs of alcohol use. *Alcohol Research: Current Reviews, 35*(2), 219–228. Retrieved from http://search.proquest.com/docview/1512625353?pq-origsite=summon

Wilson, G. T., & Sysko, R. (2009). Frequency of binge eating episodes in bulimia nervosa and binge eating disorder: Diagnostic considerations. *International Journal of Eating Disorders, 42*, 603–610.

Woititz, J. G. (1983). *Adult children of alcoholics.* Pompano Beach, FL: Health Communications.

Womenshealth.gov. (2012). *ePublications: Lesbian and bisexual health fact sheet.* Retrieved on March 12, 2016, from http://womenshealth.gov/publications/our-publications/fact-sheet/lesbian-bisexual-health.html

Wong, P. W. C., Chan, W. S. C., Conwell, Y., Conner, K. R., & Yip, P. S. F. (2010). A psychological autopsy study of pathological gamblers who died by suicide. *Journal of Affective Disorder, 120*(1–3), 213–216.

Wood, R. T., Williams, R. J., and Lawton, P. K. (2007). Why do Internet gamblers prefer online versus land-based venues? *Journal of Gambling Issues.* Retrieved August 5, 2007, from www.camh.net/egambling/issue20/07wood.htm

World Health Organization. (2007). *Women and HIV/AIDS.* Retrieved August 7, 2007, from www.who.int/gender/hiv_aids/en

Wright, P. H., & Wright, K. D. (1991). Codependency: Addictive love, adjusting relating, or both? *Contemporary Family Therapy, 13*, 435–454.

Wu, L., & Blazer, D. G. (2015). Substance use disorders and co-morbidities among Asian Americans and Native Hawaiians/Pacific Islanders. *Psychological Medicine, 45*(3), 481–494. doi:10.1017/S0033291714001330

Yamaguchi, R., Johnston, L. D., & O'Malley, P. M. (2003). The relationship between student illicit drug use and school drug-testing policies. *Journal of School Health, 73*, 159–164.

Yang, C., Davey-Rothwell, M., & Latkin, C. (2013). "Drinking buddies" and alcohol dependence symptoms among African American men and women in Baltimore, MD. *Drug and Alcohol Dependence, 128*(1–2), 123–129. doi:10.1016/j.drugalcdep.2012.08.016

Yau, Y. H. C., Crowley, M. J., Mayes, L. C., & Potenza M. N. (2012). Are internet use and video-game playing addictive behaviors? Biological, clinical and public health implications for youth and adults. *Minerva Psiciaitrica, 53*, 153–170.

Yean, C., Benau, E. M., Dakanalis, A., Hormes, J. M., Perone, J., & Timko, C. A. (2013). The relationship of sex and sexual orientation to self-esteem, body shape satisfaction, and eating disorder symptomatology. *Frontiers in Psychology, 4*, 1–11. doi:10.3389/fpsyg.2013.00887

Yellowlees, P. M., & Marks, S. (2005). Problematic Internet use or Internet addiction? *Computers in Human Behavior, 23*, 1447–1453.

Young, K. (2010). Killer surf issues: Crafting an organizational model to combat employee Internet abuse. *Information Management, 44*(1), 34–38.

Young, K. S. (1996) Psychology of computer use: XL. Addictive use of the Internet: A case that breaks the stereotype. *Psychological Reports, 79*(3), 899–902. doi:10.2466/pr0.1996.79.3.899

Young, K. S. (1998). *Caught in the act: How to recognize the signs of Internet addiction and a winning strategy for recovery.* New York: Wiley.

Young, K. S. (1999). The evaluation and treatment of Internet addiction. In L. VandeCreek & T. Jackson (Eds.), *Innovations in clinical practice: A source book* (pp. 17, 19–31). Sarasota, FL: Professional Resource Press.

Young, K. S. (2004). Internet addiction. *American Behavioral Scientist, 48*(4), 402–415.

Young, K. S. (2008). Internet addiction: Risk factors, stages of development, and treatment. *American Behavioral Scientist, 52*(21), 21–37.

Young, T. J. (1992). Substance abuse among Native American youth. In G. W. Lawson & A. W. Lawson (Eds.), *Adolescent substance abuse: Etiology, treatment and prevention* (pp. 381–390). Gaithersburg, MD: Aspen.

Yu, J., Clark, L. P., Chandra, L., Dias, A., & Lai, T. M. (2009). Reducing cultural barriers to substance abuse treatment among Asian Americans: A case study in New York City. *Journal of Substance Abuse Treatment, 37*(4), 398–406.

Yücel, M., Whittle, S., Youssef, G. J., Kashyap, H., Simmons, J. G., Schwartz, O., & Allen, N. B. (2015). The influence of sex, temperament, risk-taking and mental health on the emergence of gambling: A longitudinal study of young people. *International Gambling Studies, 15*(1), 108–123. doi:10.1080/14459795.2014.1000356

Zanetti, T., Santonastaso, P., Sgaravatti, E., Degortes, D., & Favaro, A. (2013). Clinical and temperamental correlates of body image disturbance in eating disorders. *European Eating Disorders Review, 21*(1), 32–37. doi:10.1002/erv.2190

Zangeneh, M., & Hason, T. (2006). Suicide and gambling. *International Journal of Mental Health and Addiction, 4*(3), 191–193.

Zapolski, T. B., Pedersen, S. L., McCarthy, D. M., & Smith, G. T. (2014). Less drinking, yet more problems: Understanding African American drinking and related problems. *Psychological Bulletin, 140*(1), 188–223. doi:10.1037/a0032113

Zimmerman, M., Chelminski, I., & Young, D. (2006). Prevalence and diagnostic correlates of DSM-IV pathological gambling in psychiatric outpatients. *Journal of Gambling Studies, 22*(2), 255–262.

Zucker, R. A., Donovan, J. E., Masten, A. S., Mattson, M. E., & Moss, H. B. (2009). Developmental process and mechanisms. *Alcohol Research & Health, 32*(1), 16–29.

CREDITS

Chapter 2: Page 14 (Figure 2.1): From *Drugs, brains, and behavior: The science of addiction*. Published by National Institute on Drug Abuse © 2010; Page 15 (Figure 2.2): Science Source; Pages 16–17 (Table 2.1): Fisher, G. L. & Harrison, T. C. (2018). *Effect of drugs on neurotransmitters* (6th ed.).

Chapter 3: Page 40 (Figure 3.1): Fisher, G. L. & Harrison, T. C. (2018). *Effect of drugs on neurotransmitters* (6th ed.); Pages 41–42: National Institute on Drug Abuse; National Institutes of Health; U.S. Department of Health and Human Services; Page 42: From *Twelve steps and twelve traditions*, by William Griffith Wilson. Published by Alcoholics Anonymous World Services © 2009.

Chapter 4: Page 57: From *Ethnicity and family therapy*, by Valli Kalei Kanuha. Published by Guilford Press © 2005; Page 60: From *Drinking: Behavior and belief in modern history*, by Susanna Barrows. Published by University of California Press © 1991; Page 61: From *Drinking: Behavior and belief in modern history*, by Susanna Barrows. Published by University of California Press © 1991; Page 61: From *The Black image in the white mind: The debate on Afro-American character and destiny, 1817–1914*, by George M. Fredrickson. Published by Harper & Row © 1971; Page 61: From *The peculiar institution: Slavery in the ante-bellum South*, by Kenneth Milton Stampp. Published by Knopf © 1956; Page 61: From *The peculiar institution: Slavery in the ante-bellum South*, by Kenneth Milton Stampp. Published by Knopf © 1956; Page 76: From *Ethnicity and family therapy*, by Monica McGoldrick, Joe Giordano, and Nydia Garcia-Preto. Published by Guilford Press © 1982; Page 80: From *LGBTQ persons with co-occurring conditions: Perspectives on treatment*, by Patricia E. Penn, Denali Brooke, Chad M. Mosher, Sandra Gallagher, Audrey J. Brooks, and Rebecca Richey. Published by Taylor & Francis Group © 2013.

Chapter 7: Page 126 (Figure 7.1): From *Helping patients who drink too much: A clinician's guide*. Published by National Institute on Alcohol Abuse and Alcoholism © 2005.

Chapter 8: Page 135: From *Naltrexone and alcoholism treatment (Treatment Improvement Protocol #28)*. Published by Center for Substance Abuse Treatment © 1998; Page 139: From *Naltrexone and alcoholism treatment (Treatment Improvement Protocol #28)*. Published by Center for Substance Abuse Treatment © 1998; Page 141–142: From *Principles of drug addiction treatment: A research-based guide*. Published by National Institute on Drug Abuse © 1999.

Chapter 9: Page 155: From *Integrated treatment for co-occurring disorders evidence-based practices (EBP) toolkit*. Published by Center for Substance Abuse Treatment © 2010; Page 157: From *Addiction and recovery in Native America: Lost history, enduring lessons*, by Don Coyhis and William L. White. Published by Quantum Units Education © 2002.

Chapter 10: Pages 175–176: White, W. L. (2002). Recovery as heroic journey. *Perspectives: A Journal on Addiction Research and Public Policy, 12*(3), 2; Page 176: Kaplan, L. (2008). *The role of recovery support services in recovery-oriented systems of care*. DHHS Publication No. (SMA) 08-4315. Rockville, MD: Center for Substance Abuse Services, Substance Abuse and Mental Health Services Administration.

Chapter 11: Page 180: Permission to reprint AA Grapevine, Inc. copyrighted material (in this publication, organization, or website) does not in any way imply affiliation with or endorsement by either Alcoholics Anonymous or AA Grapevine, Inc.; Page 181: From *Twelve steps and twelve traditions*. Published by Alcoholics Anonymous World Services, Inc. © 1981; Page 182: *Twelve Steps and Twelve Traditions* are reprinted with permission of Alcoholics Anonymous World Services, Inc. (A.A.W.S.). Permission to reprint *Twelve Steps and Twelve Traditions* does not mean that A.A.W.S. has reviewed or approved the contents of this publication, or that A.A. necessarily agrees with the views expressed herein. A.A. is a program of recovery from alcoholism only—use of *Twelve Steps and Twelve Traditions* in connection with programs and activities which are patterned after A.A., but which address other problems, or in any other non-A.A., does not imply otherwise.

Chapter 12: Page 194: From *Family therapy of drug and alcohol abuse*, by Edward Kaufman and Pauline Kaufmann. Published by Gardner Press © 1979; Pages 195, 204, 210: From *Family therapy of drug and alcohol abuse*, by Edward Kaufman and Pauline Kaufmann. Published by Allyn & Bacon © 1992; Page 196: From *Conjoint family therapy: A guide to theory and technique*, by Virginia Satir. Published by Science and Behavior Books © 1964.

Chapter 13: Page 220: From *Children of alcoholics: A critical appraisal of theory and research*, by Kenneth J. Sher. Published by University of Chicago Press © 1991; Page 225: From *When chemicals come to school: The student assistance program model*, by Gary L Anderson. Published by Community Recovery Press © 1987; Page 226: From *Alcoholism, other drug problems & spirituality: A transpersonal approach*, by Charles L. Whitfield. Published by Resource Group © 1984; Page 231: From *Codependent forevermore: The invention of self in a twelve step group*, by Leslie Irvine. Published by University of Chicago Press © 1999.

Chapter 14: Page 240 (Table 14.1): From *HIV among African Americans*. Published by Centers for Disease Control and Prevention © 2016; Page 242 (Figure 14.1): From *CDC fact sheet: HIV testing in the United States*. Published by Centers for Disease Control and Prevention © 2016.

Page 242 (Figure 14.2): From *CDC fact sheet: HIV testing in the United States*. Published by Centers for Disease Control and Prevention © 2016; Page 243 (Figure 14.3): From *CDC fact sheet: Reported STDs in the United States, 2014 National data for chlamydia, gonorrhea, and syphilis*. Published by Centers for Disease Control and Prevention © 2015.

Chapter 15: Page 258: From *Final report*. Published by National Gambling Impact Study Commission © 1999; Page 258: Ciaccio, C. P., Jr. (2010). Internet gambling: Recent developments and state of the law. *Berkeley Technology Law Journal, 25*(Annual Review); Page 260: Gowing, L. R., Ali, R. L., Allsop, S., Marsden, J., Turf, E. E., West, R., & Witton, J.

(2015), Global statistics on addictive behaviours: 2014 status report. *Addiction, 110*, 904–919; Page 262: Dazzi, F. & Di Leone, F. G. (2014). The diagnostic classification of eating disorders: Current situation, possible alternatives and future perspectives. *Eating and Weight Disorders—Studies on Anorexia, Bulimia and Obesity, 19*(1), 11–19; Page 264: From *Handbook of eating disorders: Physiology, psychology, and treatment of obesity, anorexia, and bulimia* (Vol. 236), by Kelly D. Brownell and John Paul Foreyt. Published by Basic Books © 1986; Page 270: From *Confessions of a workaholic: The facts about work addiction*, by Wayne Edward Oates. Published by World Publishing Company © 1971; Page 272: From *Best possible odds: Contemporary treatment strategies for gambling disorders*, by William George McCown and Linda L. Chamberlain. Published by Wiley © 2000; Page 278: Hook, J. N., Hook, J. P., & Hines, S. (2008) Reach out or act out: Long-term group therapy for sexual addiction. *Sexual Addiction & Compulsivity: The Journal of Treatment & Prevention, 15*(3). Published by Taylor & Francis Group © 2008.

Chapter 15: Page 283 (Table 16.1): Fisher, G. L. & Harrison, T. C. (2018). *Effect of drugs on neurotransmitters* (6th ed.).

INDEX

A

ABC analysis, rational emotive therapy, 189
Abry, A. W., 262
abstinence
  in African American community, 60
  in Cenaps model, 165
  disease concept of addiction and, 41
  slips and relapses and, 163–164
  treatment approaches based on, 131–134
abstinence violation effect (AVE), 167–168, 174–175
abuse, defined, 99
acamprosate, AOD abuse therapy and, 134
acculturation model
  dominant group influences in, 214–216
  Latino and Hispanic Americans and, 68
  risk factors for alcohol and other drug abuse and, 57–59
Acquaintance Description Form-C3, 228
Across Ages program, 296
action stage of change, 122–124
Adams, E. B., 210
addiction. *See also* specific types of addictions
  case studies, 34–35
  cultural and ethnic diversity and, 47–82
  defined, 13, 99–100
  models of, 34–46
  neurobiology of, 14–15
Addiction Severity Index (ASI), 109
adolescents
  African Americans, 64–65, 77–78
  co-occurring mental disorders in, 158
  drug marketing to, 284–285
  eating disorders in, 263–265
  educational history and, 105
  family systems and, 206–207
  HIV/AIDS and, 244
  Internet abuse and, 268–269
  for Latino and Hispanic populations, 69–70
  Native Americans, 52–54
  prevalence of AOD use in, 213–214, 282–283
  prevention strategies involving, 290–295

Problem-Oriented Screening Instrument for Teenagers and, 109
  signs of abuse in, 106–107
  social relationships and, 104
  sociocultural model of addiction and, 37–38
  treatment programs for, 135–136
adoptees, AOD abuse and, 73
adoptive families, 204–205
adult children of alcoholics (ACOAs)
  assessment of, 223
  case studies of, 219
  clinical characteristics and empirical research on, 221–222
  criticism of research on, 231–233
  intervention with, indications for, 223–224
  statistics on, 220–221
  treatment for, 223–224
Adult Children of Alcoholics (Woititz), 220
Adult Children of Alcoholics (ACOA) group, 136, 231–233
adverse childhood experiences (ACEs), 195
advertising, AOD prevention and, 285
advice, interventions and, 127
affective disorders, drugs for, 31
affective roles, 196–197
Affordable Care Act
  AOD abuse treatment and, 210
  HIV/AIDS patients and, 243–248
African American community
  adolescents in, 206–207
  alcohol and other drugs in, 59–66
  assessment and treatment of, 77–78
  childhood roles in families of, 196–197
  co-occurring mental disorders in, 156–157
  developmental issues in, 64–65
  family subsystems in, 193–195
  HIV/AIDS in, 244–245
  integrative cross-cultural model in, 213–216
  risk factors for alcohol and other drug abuse in, 64–65
  spirituality in, 212
  statistical overview of, 65–66
  women's AOD use in, 207–210
African American Survivors Organizations, 78

aftercare, treatment of AOD abuse and, 137–138
aggression, confrontation treatment strategy and, 146–147
Akhtar, M., 70
Al-Anon Family Group, 179, 185–186, 191–192, 220
  codependency and, 231–233
Alaska Natives
  addiction among, 48–54
  assessment and treatment for, 76
  history of addiction among, 49–50
  risk factors for alcohol and other drug abuse in, 51–52
  statistical overview of, 53–54
  values of, 50–51
Alateen, 179, 185–186, 191–192
Albdour, M., 64–65
alcohol
  administration routes, 19
  as central nervous system depressant, 18
  as gateway drug, 284–285
  overdose, 19
  prevention of abuse of, 283
alcohol and other drugs (AOD)
  addiction models and, 36–46
  in African American community, 59–66
  in Asian American and Pacific Islanders community, 54–59
  assessment protocols for, 3
  co-occurring disorders and, 151–161
  definitions relating to, 13–14, 98–100
  denial, minimization, projection, and rationalization for use of, 6–7
  elderly, disabled, and sexual minority populations, 71–73
  history of use, 102–103
  Latino and Hispanic Americans and, 66–70
  in military families, 206
  moral model of addiction to, 36–37
  in Native American/Alaska Native community, 48–54
  prevention of abuse, 282–297
  screening, assessment and diagnosis, 98–113